EUROPEAN SOCIETIE

Mapping structure and chan

Steffen Mau and Roland Verwiebe

First published in Great Britain in 2010 by

The Policy Press
University of Bristol
Fourth Floor
Beacon House
Queen's Road
Bristol BS8 1QU
UK

Tel +44 (0)117 331 4054
Fax +44 (0)117 331 4093
e-mail tpp-info@bristol.ac.uk
www.policypress.co.uk

North American office:
The Policy Press
c/o International Specialized Books Services (ISBS)
920 NE 58th Avenue, Suite 300
Portland, OR 97213-3786, USA
Tel +1 503 287 3093
Fax +1 503 280 8832
e-mail info@isbs.com

British Library Cataloguing in Publication Data
A catalogue record for this book is available from the British Library.

Library of Congress Cataloging-in-Publication Data
A catalog record for this book has been requested.

ISBN 978 1 84742 654 3 paperback
ISBN 978 1 84742 655 0 hardcover

Cover design by Robin Hawes
Front cover: image kindly supplied by www.alamy.com
Printed and bound in Great Britain by Hobbs, Southampton
The Policy Press uses environmentally responsible print partners

FSC
Mixed Sources
Product group from well-managed
forests and other controlled sources
Cert no. SA-COC-001530
www.fsc.org
© 1996 Forest Stewardship Council

Contents

List of tables

List of figures

Acknowledgements

Our thanks go to all those who encouraged us and helped in the production of this book. We thank Martin Gross, Holger Lengfeld and Patrick Präg for reading the entire text – their suggestions were very valuable. Critical comments on individual chapters were offered by Sonja Drobnič, Johannes Giesecke, Katja Marjanen and Patrick Sachweh. Steffen Mau is grateful to the Social Science Research Center Berlin (WZB), in particular to Jens Alber and Jutta Allmendinger, for hosting him during the Winter Term 2009/10. Thanks go to Niels Winkler, Djubin Pejouhandeh, Nina-Sophie Fritsch and Laurenz Ennser for their great support in the collection of statistical data, the creation of graphs and figures and in the review of the relevant literature. Chapter 10 was co-authored with Patrick Präg. Parts of Sections 13.1 and 13.2 are taken from joint publications by Steffen Mau and Sebastian Büttner. This book is a fully revised and updated version of our German text *Die Sozialstruktur Europas* (Konstanz: UVK, 2009). For the English-speaking market, we have brought the book up to date and also made substantial changes. Gregory Sims and Benjamin Veghte took on the challenging task of translating the book. Our thanks to them for their proficiency, their impressive abilities and the care they took in rendering our comprehensive, detailed text into English. Finally, we would like to thank Emily Watt and Jo Morton from The Policy Press, who supported the project with great enthusiasm.

Steffen Mau and Roland Verwiebe
Berlin, April 2010

List of EU countries

EU-15

Austria (AT), Belgium (BE), Denmark (DK), Finland (FI), France (FR), Germany (DE), Greece (EL), Ireland (IE), Italy (IT), Luxembourg (LU), Netherlands (NL), Portugal (PO), Spain (ES), Sweden (SE), United Kingdom (UK) (without Northern Ireland: Great Britain/GB)

EU-25

EU-15, Cyprus (CY), Czech Republic (CZ), Estonia (EE), Hungary (HU), Latvia (LV), Lithuania (LT), Malta (MT), Poland (PL), Slovakia (SK), Slovenia (SI)

EU-27

EU-25, Bulgaria (BG), Romania (RO)

Introduction and conceptual considerations

This book is about European societies, their structures and change. The main objectives are to describe contemporary European societies along a broad range of dimensions, highlight commonalities as well as variations, understand processes of integration and characterise the ongoing transformation of the European social space. To talk about European societies in the plural means that we not only focus on European unity or ways to achieve it, as some scholars do, but view European societies as national and European at the same time. However, we emphasise that within the European context, and particularly with the nascent European polity, national societies have been challenged and transformed fundamentally and are no longer independent entities, but closely interwoven and connected.

European or national societies?

Taking the national and European context into consideration poses a true challenge. Most research on patterns of social change, inequality and social stratification focuses on nation-states. Core concepts of research on social stratification, for example, class, profession, income distribution, mobility and education, have been developed within the framework of the nation-state and national society. By the same token, Favell (2007: 122) states that most sociological research is still wedded to national society and that it seems to be 'very difficult to systematically study pan- or transnational social structures, because of the way nation-states have carved up the world and its populations, statistically speaking'. However, as a result of processes of European integration, globalisation and internationalisation, the world of European nation-states has been shaken up. Hitherto focused on national societies, social science is not equipped to do justice to these processes, and this is particularly true for the process of Europeanisation. Sociology as a whole, and research into social stratification and inequality in particular, have therefore been accused of 'methodological nationalism' (Agnew and Corbridge, 1995: 122), since they unquestioningly assume a congruence of territorial, political, cultural, economic and social boundaries:

Methodological nationalism

> The methodological nationalism of the sociology of inequality and research on the welfare state is as obvious as the self-containing relation between these two sociological disciplines. The basic assumption is the nation-state as the basic unit of

> social conflicts and their regulation by the state, generally without giving a singly thought to the presuppositions which guide research.... Thanks to this analytical mindset, this kind of theory and research is blind to Europe. The result is the failure to appreciate that the mixing, blurring and redrawing of boundaries between Member States, and also between Europeans and their others, has far-reaching implications for the pan-European conflict dynamic – for the question of recognition, social inequality and societal redistribution. Likewise the problems and dilemmas resulting from the intersection of these issues are not appreciated. (Beck and Grande, 2007: 174)

In this textbook, we will argue that the European Union is an important frame of reference for analysing European societies. Through European integration, that is, through exchange, integration and the development of new forms of solidarity and conflict, a new space of societal relations is being created, redefining fields of activity that previously fell within the compass of the nation-state (Heidenreich, 2006a). The EU is not just an intergovernmental arrangement for the harmonisation of markets, but also a supranational entity *sui generis*, which has major social consequences for the lives of people in the member countries and their chances of prosperity. As Medrano (2008: 4) puts it:

> The new European Union has a tremendous impact on the lives of Europe's citizens, whether they know it or not. The European Union is a multi-tiered polity, where government competences are distributed or shared by European, national, and subnational institutions. It is thus worth exploring what impact these dramatic institutional transformations have had on Europe's social structures rather than focus exclusively, as political scientists have done so far, on the impact of European social structures on the institutionalization process of the European Union.

A comprehensive sociological description of overall societal interdependency, a description of the social, economic and political effects of the unification process on the development of a European society and its social structure, remains a desideratum of sociological research. Systematic research on the Europeanisation of national societies as well as on Europe as a whole is lacking. What is also needed, moreover, is a sociological approach to the EU and Europe that not only focuses on culture and social theory, but would 'reintroduce social structural questions of class, inequality, networks and mobility, as well as link up with existing approaches to public opinion, mobilization and claims-making in the political sociology of the EU' (Favell and Guiraudon, 2009: 550).

The Europeanisation of societies is something fundamentally different from the globalisation processes affecting national societies. Europe, or more specifically the European Union, appears as a new level of aggregation, which, while not superseding nation-states, produces new forms of vertical and horizontal integration. Populations once isolated from each other now come into frequent contact. Borders are being deinstitutionalised and goods, services, capital and people can circulate freely. Labour markets are being Europeanised and educational institutions standardised. The European Union is also developing regulatory and redistributive forms of intervention. Whereas the globalisation perspective assumes that the scope for government action influencing the distribution of wealth and life chances is shrinking dramatically, research on Europeanisation is focusing on a new structuring formation situated between the nation and global society (Delanty and Rumford, 2005; Bach et al, 2006; Hettlage and Müller, 2006; Beck and Grande, 2007; Fligstein, 2008; Outhwaite, 2008; Eigmüller and Mau, 2010; Immerfall and Therborn, 2010). Every social scientist who examines the case of Europe must ask herself what the appropriate concepts, parameters and indicators are for a survey of European societies. Two alternatives present themselves: either one takes the individual Member States as the appropriate level at which to study social inequality and social structuration and then adopts a comparative perspective, or one refers to Europe as a whole, meaning that Europe is understood as a specific entity to be compared with other macro-societies.

Since the mid-1990s, analyses of social structure in Europe have been predominately comparative (see also Therborn, 1995; Hradil and Immerfall, 1997; Boje et al, 1999; Crouch, 1999; Immerfall and Therborn, 2010). These approaches are united by the attempt to identify the similarities and differences between European societies. In recent decades, comparative researchers and the reporting system of the European Union have compiled a substantial body of data that makes it possible to compare quite different aspects of European societies. Empirical research provided by, for example, the Eurobarometer (EB), the EU–SILC data, the European Social Survey (ESS) or the European Quality of Life Survey (EQLS) has fostered a standardisation of research instruments and thus improved comparability. In addition to these comparative approaches, in the future it will become increasingly important to examine the reciprocal effects and interactions between and across European societies (Kaelble, 1987, 2005; Fligstein, 2008). This is the perspective adopted by transnational approaches to research on Europeanisation. The main thrust of transnational approaches 'is to identify processes and dynamics that occur in several societies and are therefore "transnational" or European. Such processes of Europeanization will in general refer to new state–society relations, especially the interconnected nature of societies' (Delanty

Europeanisation versus globalisation

The comparative perspective

and Rumford, 2005: 8). They deal with the question of the extent to which, through the elimination of borders and supranational integration, a new space of social interaction is being created, so that national social structures can no longer be viewed as isolated and independent units. On the one hand, we understand the Europeanisation of national societies as referring to the process of integration and interaction between national societies; on the other hand, it refers to the process of convergence of European societies, brought about and influenced by the process of European integration.

Inter-connectedness

European integration, therefore, can also be described as a process by which national societies become interconnected and also build a supranational community (Figure 1.1). In the economy and politics, European integration processes are increasingly limiting the freedom of action of nation-states. Yet in the societal realm, nations are growing and interacting more closely at the level of collective actors, social groups and individuals. In addition, the European Union has itself become a political player in the arena of redistribution, managing intra-European social inequality through its regulatory and distributive measures. Finally, frames of reference are also shifting when it comes to evaluating and addressing inequality in the allocation of resources and in social positions. The context of relationships in which people and groups situate themselves is broadening. As a result of European integration, the perceptual barriers that previously obscured inequalities among countries are disappearing and Europe is becoming a frame of reference for the perception and comparison of inequality and social development. The dismantling of borders does not diminish the problem of inequality: 'rather conflict threatens to flare up because the perceptual barriers to comparing different national situations are being removed, so that equal levels of inequality can be assessed equally and corresponding adjustments can be demanded' (Beck and Grande, 2007: 177).

Figure 1.1: The growing interrelatedness of national societies

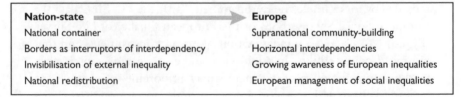

Nation-state ⟶	Europe
National container	Supranational community-building
Borders as interruptors of interdependency	Horizontal interdependencies
Invisibilisation of external inequality	Growing awareness of European inequalities
National redistribution	European management of social inequalities

Against this background, research into societal structures and change clearly must take account of the Europeanisation of European societies, which includes the various forms of interdependence and interactions among national societies, the similarities of traditions and social and cultural resources, as well as the question of new, specifically European, lines of conflict and tension, which can no longer be understood by referring solely to the nation-state (Vobruba, 2005; Beck and Grande, 2007; Fligstein, 2008; Haller, 2008; Outhwaite, 2008; Rumford, 2008, 2009).

This textbook constitutes a first attempt to present the social structure of Europe comparatively, at the same time taking into account the growing interdependence among European societies – of course without claiming to be able to offer a complete picture of a self-contained object of study.

Now with 27 member countries and nearly 500 million people, the majority of the countries and inhabitants of Europe are integrated into the European Union as a form of supranational community. It therefore seems justified to us to delimit our object of enquiry, namely European social structure, primarily on the basis of the current territorial area and membership of the European Union. The systematic inclusion of all member countries of the EU makes it possible to delve more deeply into differences in the East–West comparison than is the case in many publications that focus primarily on Western Europe. Readers will notice that the data in individual subsections are of varying quality. Data gathering in official, administrative circles and in the social sciences seldom deviates from the nation-state as the main object of enquiry, and forays into the analysis of European social structure are still in their infancy.

The book is divided into three main parts. We begin with a historically oriented section, which deals with issues of territorial and social order in Europe. We show how the geographical boundaries of Europe were constituted and how they have changed over time. At the same time, we trace the relationship between territorial expansion and the European population. In this historical process, Europe did not in any way present itself as a uniform and homogeneous macro-order, but rather as a horizontally segmented entity. Of decisive importance in this respect was the nation-state model of integration. This notwithstanding, one finds in Europe a broad range of commonalities and forms of exchange. For instance, one can identify a European model of industrial society, with specific social structures, with typical institutionalised forms of the relationship between the state, market and family, and specific forms of social classes and class compromise. Horizontal interconnections and the emergence of similar social structures provide the basis for seeing Europe as more than a random arrangement of geographically adjacent countries.

In the second part of the book, we adopt a comparative perspective. First, we turn our attention to different institutional arrangements in Europe, examining the organisation and design of institutions of social policy, education and industrial relations. We then compare EU countries in terms of their demographic structure – that is, population and age structure, fertility and mortality rates, and family structures. A further chapter is devoted to the changes in social structures caused

Overview of the book

by migration, and examines patterns and systems of migration. In the chapter on the labour market, we look at economic development, labour-force participation, unemployment, sectoral and occupational changes, as well as mobility in the EU labour market. This is followed by some considerations on inequality in education in Europe, and we then look at the classic parameters of social inequality such as income, gender-specific inequality, wealth and poverty. In the final chapter of Part Two, we present selected aspects of the quality of life in European countries from a comparative perspective.

The third part focuses on recent societal developments in the context of European integration. Although European integration is originally a political project, it strongly affects society, including the living conditions and life chances of individuals, and links together national regimes of inequality. At the beginning of Part Three, we present the institutional and political framework of European integration. In the subsequent chapters we explore new structures of social inequality and conflict that are emerging in the course of Europeanisation. Moreover, we examine the forms and density of horizontal Europeanisation, that is, the ways in which a European space of experience and social interaction is being constituted. In a final chapter on 'Subjective Europeanisation', we discuss the role played by the European Union or Europe in the minds of the people.

Part I
The European social model from a historical perspective

2

Commonalities and intra-European exchange

European integration derives its power and legitimacy from Europe's shared history, geographical unity, common cultural achievements, similarities in society and politics, multiple forms of solidarity and exchange, and shared values. The often-vaunted 'unity in diversity' refers precisely to this common foundation, which is the basis of the integration process. In the following sections, these areas of commonality will be presented and discussed. We begin with the borders of Europe and their different interpretations, which is still among the most delicate issues in the process of European integration. We will also describe the internal and enduring disparities that have developed in the social and economic space of Europe. Next, we describe shared values in Europe, which form the basis for conceptions of integration and amalgamation. In the third section, we examine networks and interconnectedness within Europe from a historical perspective. We will argue that Europe, despite all its turmoils, has always been a space of social communication and exchange.

2.1 Territoriality, borders and internal structuration

Historical border demarcations

Determining the borders of the European continent is no easy task, as 'Europe has been mapped by numerous borders, both internal and external' (Delanty and Rumford, 2005: 31). From a historical perspective, one can differentiate between the geographical-topological determination of borders and the historical-cultural dimension (Haller, 1988). A topological determination refers first of all to a territorial unit, which is separated from adjacent territories by 'borders'. The concept 'continent', derived from Latin, means 'contiguous land'. In today's parlance we use it primarily to describe a mainland continent. The territorial expansion of Europe has been bounded to the west by the Atlantic Ocean, to the north by the North Sea and to the south by the Mediterranean Sea. Only in the east is there no clear morphological boundary. Europe and Asia form a contiguous land mass and can be viewed as a single large continent. Its boundaries stem mainly from political and cultural-religious divisions.

The land border between Europe and Asia has been far from stable over the course of history, with inconsistent and changing attempts to

Europe as a construct

establish it between the Caspian and Black Seas. The Greeks looked upon the Bosporus and the Caucasus as Europe's borders. In the Middle Ages, it was the Bosporus and the River Don. Political and academic debates over these boundaries persisted into modern times. In particular, determining the boundaries of Russia caused controversy among geographers. From 1725, they increasingly began to subdivide the land mass in the Urals into an Asian and a European part, even though the mountains did not even serve as a provincial Russian border. In medieval sea charts, the contours of the European continent were finally made visible to the public. This demarcation from Asia was reflected in the Eurocentrism of early European history, which saw the influence of Asia on Europe's development as rather weak (see Blaut, 1993; Iggers et al, 2008). From this emerged an understanding of the spatial arrangement of the world in which Europe held a distinctive place. Today the border between Europe and Asia is marked by the Ural River and Ural Mountains, the Black Sea, the Bosporus and the Marmara Sea.

Different borders and boundaries

In European cultural and social history there was no firm concept of Europe that was able to lay claim to the same degree of definitional authority for different periods: Europe is therefore a construct with very different historical meanings (Therborn, 1995; Davies, 1996; Balibar, 2004). In antiquity, late antiquity and the Middle Ages, the concept of Europe was defined geographically rather than in terms of substance. In the ancient world, Europe was seen primarily as a cartographic concept and, furthermore, was inconsistently defined. In the Middle Ages, the concept of 'Europe' did not play a significant role; one spoke rather of *christianitas* (Christendom). Much more important than the territorial and geographical determination of commonality were the religious origins. This also applies in the context of a religiously divided continent with a Western Church and a Byzantine East. Belonging to Christianity played a significant role in the idea of a unified Europe, where the Roman Catholic Church with the Pope at its head had an important unifying significance; it remains influential today:

> It is important to note that this European unity was defined by religion and those many aspects of culture which at that point flowed from religion; it was not a political or military unity, nor a social one in those elements of social life that escaped a religious influence. (Crouch, 1999: 9)

The territorial structure of Europe

Core Europe

The emergence of modern Europe took place over an extended historical period and was characterised by numerous conflicts. On the one hand, these were caused by religious and ideological differences, but also by unequal dynamics of development in different regions. Thus, there were sparsely populated peripheral zones in Europe, which over a long period were cut off from central developments, and population-rich core zones. Although trade and the commercialisation of economic activity in the 16th century ensured that more and more areas were integrated into a network of economic interdependence, in the early modern period Europe was not a unified and homogeneous entity. The Holy Roman Empire, Switzerland, the British Isles, France and the Netherlands may be regarded in certain respects as a 'core area' of Europe, because they imparted their cultural, economic and political influence to the rest of the continent. Thanks to developments in the economy, art and culture from the 13th to the 16th century, the Italian city-states also figured among the major centres. Overall, these different European regions influenced each other's development reciprocally. At the same time, disparities in both living conditions and economic and social dynamics occasioned distinct forms of social mobilisation (Martines, 1988; Merriman, 2004).

Many scholars have attempted to divide Europe into macro-regions, by **Central places** identifying areas that exhibit intense social, economic and cultural activity. Walter Christaller (1950), a German geographer, studied the functions of 'central places' and their manifold forms of interconnectedness. He developed a model of the spatial structure of Europe, which included nine subregions with certain structures of habitation, production and communication. Christaller's spatial model is based on Europe's North–South and East–West axes, with Germany and the Benelux countries as its geographical centre, surrounded by a number of sub-centres such as France, Italy, the former Hapsburg monarchy (Austria, Hungary, Bohemia) and Scandinavia. The Iberian peninsula, the north-west of Britain, Ireland, the Balkans, Poland and the Baltic states are seen as peripheral regions. Conceiving of European space in terms of core and peripheral regions is supported theoretically by the international division of labour. In his world-system approach Wallerstein (1974, 1980, 1989), for example, argues that there are core states, which are in a position to exploit the surrounding peripheries and keep them in a condition of dependence.

The availability of coal reserves in the economic centres of north-west **Blue banana** Europe facilitated the development of basic and other energy-dependent industries there, thereby strengthening these economies even further. The resulting intensification of production, commerce and trade led to major social transformations. Especially in England, there were seismic changes in the social structure: a rapid decrease in the agricultural population, urbanisation and the emergence of the industrial classes. This development affected countries like Holland and Belgium, and emerging industrial regions in Germany, but also Northern Europe. Intense economic exchange relationships developed between these regions. A model that depicts this development is that of the 'blue banana', developed by Roger Brunet (1989). It refers to a long corridor of industrial and service regions, which connects the regions of central England (Manchester, Birmingham) with the Greater London area, runs through the Benelux countries, Germany and Switzerland, and ends in the industrial centres around Genoa, Milan and Turin. All the regions of the 'blue banana' are characterised by a high population density, a dense network of infrastructure, high productivity and economic interdependence. Important for the economic development of these regions are the close cooperation among interdependent industries and the connection to European and international transportation networks. Brunet sees the 'blue banana' as a direct result of historical developments, such as the evolution of major trade routes and processes of industrial capital accumulation.[1] An extension of the model is known as the 'Golden Banana' (the European sunbelt), which runs along the Mediterranean coast from Nice to Marseille, Montpellier, Barcelona and Valencia (Figure 2.1).

Centre and periphery

While these models of spatial structure lend themselves to describing economic disparities within Europe, they are not particularly revealing when it comes to related social and political factors (Haller and Höllinger, 1995). The Norwegian political scientist Stein Rokkan (1999) developed a model of the spatial structure of Europe, differentiating between centres and peripheries (see also Bartolini, 2005). According to Rokkan, the Western European city belt, which began to develop from the 13th century, was influential for later developments. The city belt was the locus of dynamic merchant capitalism, a well-developed agricultural economy and a network of highly autonomous cities; there was also a common religion and a corpus of traditional norms derived from Roman law. All attempts to form new centres in this region failed until the 19th century. Rokkan explains the variations of later state- and nation-building on the basis of a West–East axis, with a highly monetarised economy in Western Europe and the dominance of agriculture in the East (Rokkan, 1999). At the same time, there were fundamental differences in political structures. In Western Europe, as a result of the network and strength of autonomous cities, structures developed that were more federative in nature, while Central and Eastern Europe were dominated by empires, which resulted in stronger, more centralised, structures. The North–South axis entails different forms of cultural integration, such as the continuing supra-territorial influence of the Catholic Church in the South, while the North opted for early closure of its borders. The central idea of Rokkan's work is that deep-rooted cleavages in Europe at large as well as domestic political and social structures are grounded in specific historical configurations of economic, cultural and administrative structures (Bartolini, 2005).

Religious divisions

Confessional boundaries also proved to be important, in particular those between Protestantism, Catholicism and the Orthodox religions, as well as the boundary between Christianity and Islam (Chadwick and Evans, 1987; Knippenberg, 2005). Since 1054 there had been no uniform European religion, but rather a split into two main religions, Catholicism and the Orthodox Church (Remond, 1999). Then, after 1517, with the Reformation, the Protestant Church appeared on the map, spreading mainly in Northern Europe. One could add Judaism, but it was geographically far less concentrated. The religions not only offered a particular set of beliefs, but also influenced specific patterns of social

Figure 2.1: European regional structuration

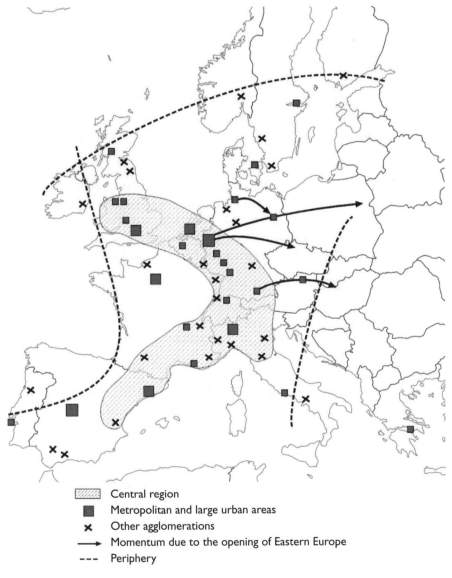

	Central region
	Metropolitan and large urban areas
✗	Other agglomerations
→	Momentum due to the opening of Eastern Europe
---	Periphery

Source: Adapted from Schätzl (1993: 28).

organisation, economic activities and the relationship between Church and state. With the secession of the Orthodox Church from Rome, the East was dominated by a confession that emphasised close ties between secular and spiritual power. The Catholic Church, for its part, retained its centralised and hierarchical character, but came to terms with a separation of Church and state. In the north and north-west of Europe, Protestantism prevailed, and with it came a more rationalist worldview and secular orientation, which allowed the establishment of democratic forms of the rational exercise of power. This was accompanied by various economic and social developments; as examined by Weber (1934) in *The Protestant Ethic*, where he defended the thesis that the modern economic culture of Europe goes back to a specific kind of rationalism in Western culture. His main argument is that the link between the rational ethic of emergent Protestantism and a specific form of economic activity explains why modern capitalism did not spread to the same degree on other continents, but rather originated in Europe. With regard to the role of the state and the concept of the nation we find a difference between 'Eastern' and 'Western' nations too, one more civic-territorial, the other more ethnic:

> The Western model of the nation tended to emphasize the centrality of a national territory or homeland, a common system of laws and the importance of a mass, civic culture binding the citizens together. The Eastern model, by contrast, was much more occupied with ethnic descent and cultural ties. (Smith, 1991: 324)

Religion and the state

Religious boundaries are not congruent with national borders, but overlap with them. In core Europe, there were a large number of mixed-confessional countries in which the Protestant elites were able to fill important social positions, but nevertheless had to involve the Catholic minorities. In many countries in Southern Europe, but also in the Hapsburg Empire and in France after 1685, a close alliance formed between the Catholic Church and the *Ancien Régime*. In Northern Europe, Protestantism was dominant and became the quasi-state Church. As a result, there was also no need for Christian parties in the political spectrum, whereas in Central Europe such parties came to define it. In the mixed-confessional countries, a lasting tension developed between the state with its interest in national unity, often represented by liberal or Protestant elites, and the Church's claim to take part in political decision-making. Out of this tension emerged the Catholic centre parties and other Christian parties, which were able to secure adherence from their respective constituencies. Although the basic map of religions has remained relatively stable since the mid-17th century, the process of secularisation is on the rise throughout Europe, as evidenced by the declining commitment to one's Church and decreasing frequency of church attendance (Lane and Ersson, 1987). One also observes trends towards religious pluralism, which are caused by processes of global communication, migration and mobility, and which are weakening territorially bound national religions (Kippenberg, 2005).

If one looks at the historical–cultural, economic, (former) imperial and religious boundaries that have been crucial in shaping the spatial structure of Europe then, according to Stefan Immerfall (2006: 16ff), the following major borders can be distinguished (Figure 2.2):

Figure 2.2: Historical borders

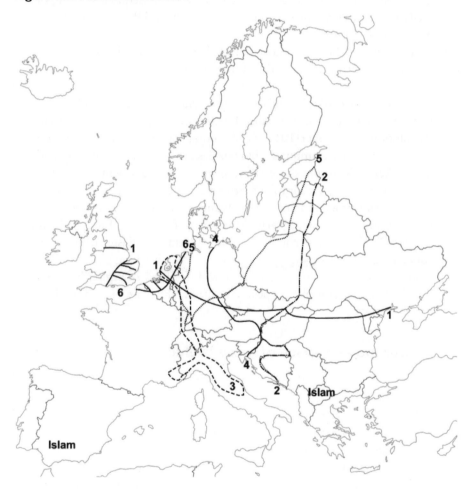

Source: Adapted from Immerfall (1995).

Note: Historical structure of borders: 1. influence of Mediterranean antiquity (476); 2. occidental schism (1054); 3. Central-European city belt; 4. border of different agrarian regimes (1500); 5. religious schism (1517); and 6. Atlantic capitalism.

- the borders of the Roman Empire as an intermediary of Greek and Roman culture (fall of the Roman Empire, 476);
- the division of the Roman/Byzantine Empire in 395, and the splitting of Christianity into the Latin and the Orthodox Church (the Great Schism of 1054);
- the Central European city belt running from the Alps along the Rhine to the largely autonomous northern cities;
- the various developments in rural areas from 1500, with the feudal and large landowners in the East ('the second feudalism'), and less authoritarian and oppressive forms in the West (the class of free farmers);
- the advent of the Reformation in 1517, and the subsequent splitting of the Church into Catholics (mainly in the South) and Protestants (mainly in Northern Europe);
- the beginning of a long period of industrialisation and social modernisation in north-western Europe in the 16th century.

To this map, one could also add the more recent and historically ephemeral line between socialist and capitalist Europe. Beginning with the Russian Revolution in October 1917, the founding of the Soviet Union and the formation of a Communist bloc in Eastern Europe after the Second World War, a deep split arose at the heart of the continent. Even after the collapse of state socialism, the structural differences between Eastern and Western Europe did not simply disappear, so that the East–West axis still constitutes one of the main structuring features of Europe today (cf. Part 2). However, particularly in the Central and Eastern European countries that have joined the EU, harmonisation is taking place in many spheres. At the same time, there are new differences emerging between the Central and Eastern European countries, which are discarding their previous unity.

2.2 Europe as a space of shared values

□ DEFINITION

Social values are supra-individual conceptions of something to which it is considered worth aspiring; norms (such as laws, moral norms, informal rules and prohibitions) are derived from values, and determine everyday behaviour. Generally speaking, values stand in relation to certain socio-cultural entities. One can speak in terms of European values if referring to specific cultural, religious and social traditions of Europe, and if these are widespread in European societies.

This book is centred on the 27 Member States of the EU, which demarcate the space of European integration and of the development of a European community. As already made clear in the previous section, the historical boundaries of Europe are not identical with the geographic area of the EU. This is also reflected in the development of Europe as a space of shared values and as a cultural space. The EU is not the sole bearer of European values, but the member countries of the EU and the EU as a whole are in a special way informed by specific values (Lattes, 2005; Outhwaite, 2008). More importantly, these shared values are often regarded as the basis for the steps to unification (see Chapter 13). When we speak of Europe today, we usually mean more than a mere geographic formation – we also mean a social, ideational and political history, which separates Europe from Asia and binds Europe together from within. Europe owes the dawn of philosophy and science, as well as its commitment to the arts, to the tradition of ancient Greece. The classical culture of the Greeks with Homer, Plato and Aristotle also gave rise to the institutional precursors of democracy and discovered the citizen as the subject of a political community of shared responsibility. To the Roman tradition we owe our legal system and the creation of a unified political order. The Christian origin of European values goes back to the Hebrew Bible, with its predominant image of the relationship between God and Man. Values such as charity and human dignity belong to the basic canon of this tradition. Although the cultural form of Europe can be explained to a large extent on the basis of these roots, Europe is not a 'Christian club' in the sense of a closed religious community. Europe is also so tightly bound up with the Jewish tradition that one can speak in terms of common Judaeo-Christian traditions, and a substantial impetus for the development of Europe also came from Islam. Compared with other regions of the world, Europe has absorbed or developed very different cultural and religious traditions (Delanty, 2009):

Historical roots of European values

> The symbolic pluralism was evident in the multiplicity of traditions out of which its own tradition crystallized – the Judeo-Christian, the Greek, the Roman and various tribal ones; and unlike in the case of Islam, by a greater multiplicity of cultural codes and orientations. (Eisenstadt, 1987: 47)

Furthermore, from the 16th century, Europe increasingly came to the fore as a place of freedom and enlightenment. Essential basic principles such as human equality, the primacy of rationality, the legitimacy of political rule, the recognition of individual rights and the separation of the public and private spheres were assigned their place in the European canon of values (Outhwaite, 2008). There is also a whole range of modern values that are closely linked to the development of Europe – for instance, the

Modern values

concept of human rights, which, while universalist in its claims, marks the rise of a European concept of reciprocity, tolerance and recognition of the Other. Whereas until the beginning of the modern period in Europe hierarchies of social class and social standing still pervaded a worldview of dominance and subordination, subsequently ideas of individualism and egalitarianism began to spread. These ideas involved a new ethical constellation that saw human beings as free, to be viewed only as an end, and never as a means to an end. In its essential features, the concept of human rights also contains the notion that these rights are inalienable and unconditional, the idea of the individual dignity of every human being, protection against injury and against attacks on dignity and on the free development of the individual personality. European thinkers such as John Locke, Immanuel Kant and Jean-Jacques Rousseau made major contributions to the concept of human rights and encouraged its global spread. However, the universalist discourse in Europe can also be viewed critically, because Europe was also the locus of particularistic aspirations and exclusion (Delanty, 1995).

Europe versus the 'New World'   The emergence of civil society in Europe placed a new model of society on the agenda, which still has a leading function today. Instead of a class-based social structure with a low degree of permeability and ascriptive social status, the blueprint for civil society promised greater equality. Here, Europe entered into a dialogue with the 'New World', the United States, which was considered the only civilisation on an equal footing, and was partly even admired – in contrast to Africa, Asia or South America, which were often regarded as backward. In the United States, the concept of freedom was, from the outset, on a par with that of equality, so that there was widespread acceptance of economic inequalities and strong reservations concerning an overly strong and redistributive state (Tocqueville, 2000 [1835/40]). By contrast, the pursuit of equality in Europe was always bound up with a strong fixation on the state, which was viewed as the main entity to turn to for equalisation claims. The rapid progress of industrialisation, such as mass production in the United States, was observed with some fascination from Europe; but there was also no lack of criticism – for instance, of certain excesses of 'consumerism' and of 'philistinism' among the Americans. However, whether there is truly a cultural gulf between Europe and America is subject to debate (Alber and Gilbert, 2010; Baldwin, 2010).

Alexis de Tocqueville's two-volume work, *Democracy in America* (2000 [1835/40]), provides a wealth of observations on culture and society in the US and Europe. It is a comprehensive analysis of democratic structures and the structures of civil society in the US, which Tocqueville saw as a model for European societies, especially France. In *Democracy in America* he saw the value of equality as having been brought to fruition, in spite of unequal wealth and income, since, through the absence of a rigid class structure, participation in public affairs and conflict-free conciliation of interests had been made possible. By contrast, democracy in Europe was still 'shackled' by monarchies and old hierarchies. At the same time, Tocqueville was not uncritical and raised the question whether American democracy would be able to provide equal social conditions for the black population as well.

As one can see from the example of the United States, self-descriptions of Europe often involved a comparison with other continents and regions. To an extent, European civilisation was presented as the model case of the changes that were taking place worldwide (Lattes, 2005). The adoption of universal values, of rationalisation, democratisation and economic modernisation, were postulated as general objectives for development, and also as guiding values for other regions of the world. However, the delineation of the pioneering function of general models of modernisation, referring to 'evolutionary universals' (Parsons, 1964b), such as a market economy, money, bureaucracy, law, a meritocratic system of stratification and distribution, universally valid norms and democratic association, was never completely clear-cut. Here, too, a general development model is assumed, a model that makes its effects felt in other countries, but we are no longer dealing with a European model in the narrow sense, but rather with a Western model of modernisation. **Europe in context**

The connection with Europe was created mainly through the cultural legacy of the Western world, but this legacy has also left its traces in the United States. According to this interpretation, the United States can be seen as an offshoot or even as an intensification of European modernity. The recent debate on 'multiple modernities' shows that there were very different models of social and cultural order, which produced social innovations and successfully disseminated them (Eisenstadt, 2002). Thus, it is inadequate to argue that modernity can only be understood in the context of Europe, or that it emerged exclusively from the potential of European culture. Nevertheless, it is perfectly legitimate to speak in terms of a specifically European interpretation and experience of modernity, which arose from specific historical and ideational contexts (Wagner, 2008b). According to some, Europe and the United States can be seen as two variants of Western modernity, which share a common heritage, but they also differ in terms of their dominant values, understanding of freedom, view of the state, tolerance of inequalities and roles of mobility, status and individual achievement (Martinelli, 2008).

In 2003, at the initiative of Jürgen Habermas, a group of intellectuals launched a discussion on fundamental European values. In an essay, Habermas and Derrida (2003) defined specifically European values, contrasting them with the political theology of Islam and with Christian **Europe's self-understanding and self-reflection** fundamentalism, which is influential in the US. In contrast to an individualistic ethos in which compensation is based on performance measured by market worth, Habermas and Derrida see secularisation, which emanated from painful experience, the domestication of state power, the rule of law and democracy, and the commitment to social justice as central elements of Europe's overall set of values. Though there is no grand narrative or unity of values, Europe's self-understanding is inherently self-problematising (Delanty and Rumford, 2005). Individual freedom, tolerance, inwardness and self-realisation can be considered as typical European values too (Joas and Wiegandt, 2008). International surveys on attitudes towards values show that Europeans are very tolerant, enlightened and aware of social and political problems (Inglehart, 1990). Democracy, human rights and social solidarity elicit agreement throughout Europe. At the same time, however, major differences obtain across European countries in the spheres of family, marriage, work and sexuality (comprehensively documented in the *Atlas of European Values*; see Halman et al, 2005).

Conflict and peace

Only with difficulty, however, can the question of European values be traced back to a single, firm core. Europe has always been characterised by 'unity in diversity', with numerous internal variations, self-images and influences. This diversity alone is often mentioned as one of Europe's characteristics. Moreover, Europe is a place of profound social change, so that change and dynamics can be considered part of Europe's 'special path' (Wagner, 2008a). At the same time, Europe has been the site of painful experiences of war, violence, expulsion and totalitarianism. In modern history, the experience of deep-seated, violent conflict ranges from the Thirty Years' War between secular and religious powers (1618–48), to the Napoleonic Wars (1800–1814/15), to the two World Wars of the last century and the conflicts following the disintegration of the former Yugoslavia after 1990. This heritage also forms the background for all the efforts to create a European order of peace and reconciliation among peoples.

The political concept of Europe as we know it today developed only relatively late, in the context of political unification efforts. It has also always been a counter-concept to excessive nationalism, which resulted in hostility and rivalry among the peoples of Europe. In European history there have been a number of pan-European projects and movements. Starting with the premise of achieving peace and unity among otherwise hostile and conflict-torn regional powers, there have always been intellectuals and statesmen who were enthusiastic about the idea of a united Europe, but had very different personal styles and political motivations. Such projects can be found very early on. They go back, for example, to the 'grand plan' of the Duke of Sully (1560–1641) to curtail the power of the Hapsburgs and establish a Council of Europe, which was meant to deal with problems between European states in the way that a national parliament would. The social utopian Saint-Simon (1760–1825) can also be regarded as a modern, forward-thinking pioneer of the United States of Europe. He was in favour of uniting the peoples of Europe within the framework of a common European constitution, while maintaining their national independence. Similar ideas can be found in Victor Hugo's work, who at the Second International Peace Congress in Paris on 22 August 1849 called for a union of European states (Niess, 2001).

2.3 Europe as a space of social experience and connectivity

In the preceding sections we emphasised that the historical-social space known as Europe can invoke a number of commonalities. Europe is not a random arrangement of neighbouring states, but is characterised instead by a specific territorial order and a common reservoir of cultural and intellectual history. In addition, despite all the conflicts and tendencies towards isolation, Europe has been and continues to be characterised by extensive forms of integration and communication. Although opportunities for mutual exchange were much more restricted in past eras than today (when one thinks of communication technologies and means of transport, for example), Europe was nevertheless endowed with a transnational social space, characterised by dense social relations and overlapping social circles. Geographic conditions and efforts to create mobility and trade routes played a role in this:

Communicative spaces

> One should not underestimate the lengthy process whereby the highways and byways of Europe were opened up to human movement and settlement. On the other hand, there is no comparison between the relative ease of travel in Europe and that in the greater continents. Caravans on the ancient silk route from China needed a year or more to cross the body of Asia. Yet from time immemorial any fit and reasonably enterprising traveller has been able to move across Europe in a matter of weeks, if not days. (Davies, 1996: 51)

With the creation of new transportation routes, for example, through the spread of the railways in the 19th century, but also through the development of waterways, it became even easier to move around within Europe (Hansen, 2001; Vleuten and Kaijser, 2006). Although there were also contacts beyond the borders of Europe, the degree of institutionalisation and concentration remained far below the level within Europe.

Prior to the formation of nation-states and national cultures, Europe was a space of dense networks and interactions. Contributing factors were the spread of Roman law, the inter-ethnic and international organisation of the Catholic Church, the structure of the kingdoms, the networks of independent cities and flourishing trade. In particular, the organisation of the Catholic Church, with its simultaneously centralised and decentralised structure, also ensured that a network of connections was created on European territory (and eventually also outside it) (Thompson, 1998; Bireley, 2009). The religious communities and denominations were geographically widely scattered and had to be organised. Monks travelled on behalf of their various orders, and thousands of people took part in pilgrimages. Thus, the manifold divisions of Europe into different spheres of power and influence did not lead to contacts being disrupted or broken off, but rather to a specific dynamic of difference and interconnectedness.

European nobility

Also noteworthy are the close links between European noble houses who created a pan-European network of transnational families through their calculated choice of spouses. In aristocratic circles, multilingualism and cross-border social experience were the norm. They met on festive occasions, intermarried, visited each other and forged political alliances. Even the lower and geographically marginal nobility sought affiliation with the European aristocratic culture in order to secure their own social status and loosen restrictions on the choice of spouse imposed by the strict rules of marriage (Dewald, 1996; Conze and Wienfort, 2004). Since the time of Peter the Great, Russian nobility was also oriented towards (Western) Europe, and thus integrated into European noble circles. Even after the abolition of the monarchy or its relegation as a result of the onset of liberalism and ultimately democratisation in many major European countries, European royal and noble families remained intertwined.

> ## Europe as a space of experience
>
> Social exchange: mobility, migration, family networks, especially noble family networks.
>
> Economic exchange: trading routes, alliances between cities and regions (for example, the Hanseatic League), specialisation and division of labour, cities as magnets for trade and textiles.
>
> Cultural exchange: student mobility, networks of scholars and scientists, the dissemination of publications, exchange within religious communities.

Student mobility

A large number of key community groups maintained close connections over greater geographical distances. Travel was undertaken for business, educational, religious or political reasons (Steidl et al, 2009). Until the First World War, migration and mobility were far less regulated than they are today, because there were no systems of passports or border control. Students and teacher mobility between different educational institutions and beyond national borders had long been part of the culture of the European university. Even the very first European universities operated in a common space of higher education. As Walter Rüegg (1996: xix) puts it in his standard work on the European University:

> The university is a European institution; indeed, it is the European institution *par excellence*.... It has developed and transmitted scientific and scholarly knowledge and the methods of cultivating that knowledge which has arisen from and formed part of the European intellectual tradition. It has at the same time formed an academic elite, the ethos of which rests on common European values and which transcends all national boundaries.

With the *studia generalia* there was a core curricular component of university education, which served to encourage mobility. Since the number of fields of study offered at universities was not very large and knowledge was concentrated in specific places, a large number of students moved from university to university. There is a tradition of exchanges between scholars and academics, and the educational biographies of the late Middle Ages and the Renaissance appear very cosmopolitan from today's perspective. A man like the humanist Erasmus of Rotterdam, from whom the largest European student exchange scheme (the Erasmus programme) takes its name, lived and worked in Italy, France, the Netherlands and England and eventually died in Basel. Itinerant workers, seafarers and merchants wandered throughout Europe to offer their services. These people were not always welcome, especially 'travelling people' often encountered suspicion and qualms. Although wandering from place to place was also prohibited or regulated for political or economic reasons (when it came to access to markets), these restrictions were not comprehensively developed. In the life of a journeyman there was the ritual phase of moving from place to place, often with standardised cross-border routes. Certain trades and businesses were pursued mainly in individual nations and their representatives were then based in the various regions of Europe. This was typical of tailors, artisans and goldsmiths, for example.

In addition to these more minor travels, there were migrations of large groups, often triggered by material deprivation or social conflicts, as was the case with the early modern religious refugees, such as the Dutch in the 16th century or the Bohemians and the Protestant citizens of Salzburg in the 17th century. Between 1685 and 1705, more than 150,000 Protestants left France in order to escape conversion to Catholicism. They were often welcome on foreign territory, and some

Mass migration

23

of them were recruited by sovereigns of the same religious persuasion. Recruitment was also commonplace for many forms of labour migration. In the 17th century, Frederick William I deliberately brought foreigners (for example, from France and the Netherlands) to Prussia, which had been devastated by the Thirty Years' War. His policy of increasing the population through the settlement of larger groups saw people first and foremost as a resource that increased the power of the state. At the end of the 19th century, thousands of Poles migrated to the Ruhr area, meeting the labour requirements of the coal-mining industry. Similar examples can be cited from other countries, such as England, France, Belgium and the Netherlands. From a historical perspective, these migrations can be viewed as belonging to a series that includes labour migration from the peripheries of Europe to the industrial centres of Europe in the 1950s and 1960s (Bade, 2003).

Multicultural cities? In many places, mobility resulted in an ethnic, cultural and social population mix. Many large cities, ports and trading centres were multicultural (Hohenberg and Lees, 1985; Therborn, 1995), but most immigrants were not integrated with equal rights into the social order and had a restricted status. However, there were groups that were able to wrest some social status for themselves through economic success. Ultimately, there has always been ethnic segregation within the different forms of urban settlement. These ranged from the creation of special quarters to the formation of ghettos, which meant that 'foreign' groups were only allowed to settle in a particular place, and contact with other groups was subject to strict social control. The climate in numerous spa towns of the 18th and 19th centuries was freer: Davos, Carlsbad and Nice had an international flair and were meeting places for the European upper class.

One can assume that only certain social groups were directly involved in the immediate social experience of a European space of mobility and communication. Nonetheless, through written reports, stories and contact with foreigners, images of other places and cultures on the continent were disseminated. This also affected groups that were not mobile and those who, due to poor reading and writing skills, had only limited opportunities for communication via letters. These earlier forms of interconnectedness laid the foundation for later forms of pan-European transnationalisation. However, some of these exchange relationships were subject to reverses due to the formation of nation-states with their emphasis on territoriality and territorial control, the armed conflicts of the 19th and 20th centuries and the East–West division after the Second World War.

Note

[1] There are various explanations for the origin of the name 'blue banana', but all agree that this industry and service belt is shaped like a banana. The colour blue is due either to the flag of the European Union or to the colour of the working clothes worn by ordinary ('blue collar') workers.

3

Socio-structural characteristics of European societies

> **DEFINITION**
>
> A state is a political unit made up of a people living within a defined geographical area with a sovereign authority over its territory, its own citizens and other people within its territory. Nationality is acquired either by birth or naturalisation. With acquisition by birth, there are two different principles: the principle of descent (*jus sanguinis*), where the nationality of the parents is the determining factor; and the territorial principle (*jus soli*), where the determining factor is the national territory on which a person is born. A nation can be described as a group of people characterised by common features such as language, culture, history or ancestry. In general one can make a basic distinction between ethnic conceptions of the nation and conceptions that place stronger emphasis on cultural or political dimensions.

In the previous chapter we examined the spatial structure of Europe, its foundation of shared values, and its forms of interdependence and connectedness. We showed that certain common features and basic social patterns underlie the current integration process. However, Europe is also characterised by great diversity, which is the result of processes that led to the formation of nation-states in the 18th and 19th centuries. The latter had their origins in the establishment of territorial states, which, through the creation of national institutions, were then in a position to establish themselves as nation-states. The process entailed the political-administrative, legal and cultural interpenetration and unification of different social spheres. With this model of society a specific form of social organisation came into being, characterised by demarcation with respect to the outside world and internal integration. Giddens (1990: 14) even makes demarcation a trademark of modern nation-state formations: 'Modern societies [nation-states], in some respects at any rate, have a clearly defined boundedness.... Virtually no pre-modern societies were as clearly bounded as modern nation-states.' This is particularly true for Europe, the birthplace of nations and nation-states.

State-building as horizontal segmentation

According to this argument, the closed boundedness of the nation-state and the implementation of a territorialised form of social integration are important characteristics of the European type of social order. This does not mean, however, that the advent of the nation-state model entails the

Modernisation and industrialisation

annulment of the existing commonalities between European societies. Despite great social and institutional diversity and despite real differences in pace and timing, European societies have an identifiable common core of development, often described as the modernisation process (Flora and Alber, 1981). In sociology, the concept of modernisation describes the transition from traditional societies to modern societies, usually accompanied by a profound change in social organisation. Decisive in this regard were processes of industrialisation that facilitated transformations of the material bases of society, its social organisation and system of value creation, and, in turn, its social structure (Aron, 1961; Goldthorpe, 1971; Crouch, 1999). These industrialisation processes included an increasing division of labour and social differentiation, the imposition of a system of social stratification centred around a hierarchy of professions, the standardisation of the life course, the spatial separation of family and work, and the formalisation of employment relations. Europe is the place where this model of industrial society prevailed with marked success, and it still determines the contours of the social structure today. With industrialisation a capitalist class society also developed, which over the course of time became increasingly differentiated. Lastly, Europe is also the locus of institutionalised class compromise and the emergence of extensive forms of socio-political intervention. In the following sections, we will examine these aspects successively, in order to determine more precisely in what respect it is possible to speak of a European model of society.

3.1 The European model of industrial society

DEFINITIONS

Industrialisation refers to the increase in the share of industrial production in the value creation of a country and to changes in the forms of production, away from individual, small-scale crafts and farming practices, and towards standardised and automated processes. Industrialisation entails a comprehensive transformation of society through processes such as urbanisation, population growth, the emergence of an industrial workforce and changes in the forms of life and family.

Urbanisation refers to the migration of the rural population into urban areas and the emergence of centres of agglomeration. This migration is triggered mainly by an oversupply of labour in rural areas, which can be caused by population growth, for example. In the era of industrialisation, these freed-up workers were absorbed by the newly created production facilities in the cities. New urban residential forms emerged.

The Industrial Revolution

Until the 19th century, Europe was predominantly agrarian and rural in character, but then a very rapid phase of industrialisation and urbanisation began. Industrialisation entailed larger quantities of goods being produced, more efficient chains of production being developed, better use of available energy sources, and a far-reaching transformation of the labour process (Landes, 1969; Cipolla, 1972–76; Hansen, 2001; Kaelble, 2004b). As a result of mechanical and technological innovation, productivity increased significantly. Jean Fourastié (1949) integrated this process of transition from agrarian to industrial production into a historical phase model (three-sector model). As Fourastié presents it, the age of industrialisation, where employment is predominantly in the secondary sector (in industry), constitutes the transitional period between the phase of traditional civilisation, where employment is concentrated in the agricultural sector, and the phase of tertiary civilisation, where employment is concentrated in the service sector. In tertiary civilisation, less labour is needed in the agricultural and manufacturing sectors. Although some of his predictions proved to be untenable – for instance, the assumption concerning the elimination of unemployment – this model maps the long-term structural transformations of many countries fairly well.

Changes in production

The Industrial Revolution ushered in processes of growth in large parts of Europe. In many countries, industrial structures developed with a new organisation of work and production, mass production and fixed channels of sales and distribution. The Industrial Revolution began in England in the second half of the 18th century, and in the 19th century reached the majority of European countries and regions. However, it has to be pointed out that development in Europe was uneven: although industrial centres were to be found in many countries, some remained agrarian until the middle of the 20th century. In countries like Albania, Poland, Romania, Bulgaria, Hungary, Greece, Finland and the Baltic states, at the beginning of the Second World War the majority of the workforce was still engaged in agriculture. By the 1990s, however, Albania was the only country still predominantly agricultural (Therborn, 1995; see also Section 7.4). The socio-structural transformation brought about by industrialisation reshaped societies' socio-spatial order, most notably through the spatial separation of production and reproduction. It also transformed family structures, increased spatial and social mobility, and facilitated the emergence of new notions of individual autonomy and self-determination.

Industrialisation led to urbanisation, which involved changes in residential forms and ways of living as a result of urban growth and density (Lees and Hollen Lees, 2008). Even before this took place,

Industrialisation and urbanisation

European towns and cities were tightly connected with economic, social and political development (Le Galès, 2002). The European tradition of city-states linked autonomy, self-government and legal jurisdiction with engagement in transport, production and trade. The free cities became centres of intellectual life and progress in economics, administration and politics. With industrialisation, towns and cities assumed key functions in the production process – factories were often located near cities and, because of the demand for labour, this led to the creation of new urban residential forms. In England, the pioneer in the Industrial Revolution, fully half the population was urbanised by 1850. Decades later, Germany was the second nation to surpass that mark, followed by most of the countries of north-west Europe by 1930. Today, the majority of the European population – in some cases as much as 80% – lives in towns with 10,000 or more inhabitants (Jordan-Bychkov and Bychkova Jordan, 2003).

Population growth

With the increase in productivity came bursts of population growth (Rothenbacher, 2002). In the year 1000, approximately 40 million people lived in Europe. Then came rapid growth, with a population of 135 million by the mid-18th century, 267 million by the mid-19th century and almost 600 million by the mid-20th century (Figure 3.1). Unlike other world regions, there was a positive correlation between economic growth and population growth. During this phase of industrialisation, the economy grew annually by an average of 2%. Productivity growth thus consistently exceeded population growth, so that Europeans per capita were twice as rich in 1913 as they were in 1850 (Sperber, 2009). In other regions of the world, economic growth came mostly at the cost of deterioration of the social and natural environment, or was exhausted by excessive growth in the demand for food and other goods needed for

Figure 3.1: Economic development and population growth (1500–1998)

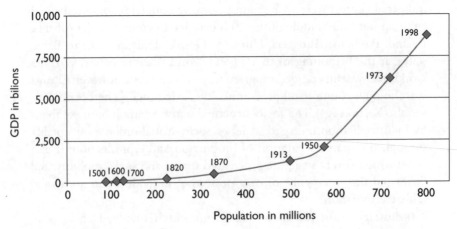

Source: Maddison (2001); own calculations. Data relate to the whole of Europe (not EU-27), GDP in billion USD from 1990 (constant prices).

the sustenance of the population. Although the emergence of industrial centres and the massive influx of the rural population into cities initially led to poverty and deprivation, economic growth nevertheless facilitated sustained improvements in living conditions. Further consequences were demographic changes such as an increasing life expectancy and declines in child mortality and fertility rates, since lower mortality rates meant that large numbers of children were no longer necessary to ensure the continuity of the family (Chesnais, 1992).

However, a considerable part of the growing population was 'exported' to North America, Australia and South America. Between the mid-19th century and 1915, nearly 42 million people emigrated, over half of them to the United States. The causes lay in economic crises, famine and armed conflicts. These emigrations defused social conflicts within Europe and for emigrants opened up access to new territories and resources that were not available in their homelands to the same degree. Emigration, therefore, functioned as a release valve for the immense population growth. This demographic wave also served to establish Europe's social and geostrategic ascendance, since its culture and way of life were thereby able to take root long term elsewhere in the world. This is particularly visible in the cases of colonial occupation of new territories. The waves of emigration differed in time and place of origin: the first emigrants came mainly from the countries in north–western Europe, followed only later by increasing numbers of emigrants from the South and the East.

Emigration

> The relationship between political repression, economic hardship and migration is especially evident in Irish history. From 1800 to 1840, the Irish population almost doubled and Ireland had thereby become the most densely populated country in Europe. According to the census of 1841, there were more than eight million people living in the Emerald Isle. In 1845, the potato blight spread and destroyed the livelihoods of millions of people. During the Great Famine (1846–51), 1.5 million people died and 1.3 million emigrated. The country became impoverished and therefore even in subsequent decades remained a country of emigration, with five million more emigrants by the beginning of the 20th century.

The socio-structural imprint of industrialisation

Typical of European development was the establishment of a society based on industrial employment, which, on the one hand, meant employment in the industrial sector, and, on the other, the classification and organisation of work into a hierarchical, formalised system of collective units of production (Kocka, 2010). In the 19th and 20th centuries, the majority of employees worked in industry and commerce, and most value creation occurred in these sectors. Although modernisation theory assumes that

The changing role of work

all societies go through similar stages of development (moving from agrarian to industrial to service society), in fact only in Europe was there such a pronounced era of industrial society (Kaelble, 1989). In Europe, and especially in Western Europe, within a half-century a massive reorganisation of (gainful) employment occurred (Crouch, 1999). The number of those employed in the agricultural sector fell rapidly while the number of industrial workers rose. At the same time, employment in the service sector was still not widespread. Various reasons can be cited for the historically very late growth of the service sector, such as the emigration of large numbers of the poor, who often became employed in badly paid service jobs in other parts of the world, but also the early export orientation of the European economy, which stimulated the production of goods.

The working class   With the establishment of the system of capitalist industrial society, the position of workers also changed, especially that of the working class. Whereas employment was previously limited to the household domain, and exploitative working conditions perceived as the fate of individuals, with the growth of the factory system exploitation was experienced collectively, which facilitated political consciousness and mobilisation. It became clear that poverty and misery were bound up with the emerging system of work. At the same time, there was growing awareness that this was a situation held in common, characterised, on the one hand, by material deprivation and, on the other, by social and legal weaknesses in the relationship with employers.

White-collar workers   Meanwhile, another type of worker was emerging in the system of industrial relations, namely white-collar workers. Although they, too, were wage-earners and employees, they differed from the working class in that their jobs entailed far less manual labour, they worked in an office rather than on a factory floor, and they had a higher level of formal education (Lockwood, 1958). They also habitually differentiated themselves from (blue-collar) workers by endeavouring to distance themselves from the milieu of work and to orient themselves towards the higher classes (Kocka, 2004). In his study of white-collar workers, Siegfried Kracauer (1998 [1930]) points out that although they had little contact with manual workers and did not take part in the latter's struggles to improve their social lot, they were nevertheless bound into a rationalised system of sub- and superordination. The class of white-collar workers always stood apart from the main socio-structural axis of capital and labour. It was only with the growth of tertiary employment that white-collar workers became numerically predominant. This took place, however, due to the expansion of simple and to some extent unskilled white-collar work, which led to a weakening of the traditional distinction between blue- and white-collar workers.

Industrialisation also served as a boost for the formation of the bourgeoisie. 'Bourgeoisie' refers to a diversely structured social class, ultimately hard to delineate in detail, positioned between farmers and workers on the one hand, and the upper class on the other (Pilbeam, 1990). Some groups were characterised more by their economic power and are hence often referred to as the economic bourgeoisie (industrialists, bankers, wholesale merchants, owners of capital); others were distinguished by their high level of educational capital, mostly professionals (doctors, lawyers, engineers, academics, teachers, public officials). Crucial forces strengthening the bourgeoisie were economic development, the emergence of new careers in the field of management and administration, as well as the valorisation of educational capital (O'Boyle, 1966). Ordinary white-collar workers and small merchants are often counted among the *petite bourgeoisie* (Kocka, 1990). The *petite bourgeoisie* lives in social and spatial proximity to the working class and shares many of the latter's hardships (Crossick and Haupt, 1995). Their cultural values and lifestyles are predicated on education, family values, a certain kind of emotional control, urbanity, self-determination and the importance of individual accomplishment. However, the meaning of the term varies from country to country in Europe: what in England is referred to as the middle class is not identical to the French *bourgeoisie* or the Italian *borghesia* (Kocka, 2004).

Middle class

Population, family, the life course

A further consequence of industrialisation was a change in the model of the family (Rothenbacher, 2002). The concentration of production and the emergence of urban and industrialised centres resulted in spatially dense forms of dwelling. More and more families lived together in relatively small spaces, and this reinforced the tendency to regard the apartment as a closed family space. Accordingly, life was organised between the twin poles of the family home as refuge and the factory as the locus of work. Although gender inequality was also prevalent in agrarian society, with the advent of capitalist industrial production this gender difference was reinforced, mainly through the spatial separation of production and reproduction. The typical industrial worker was male, and women were increasingly relegated to the domestic role. In the traditional male breadwinner model, women were mainly responsible for the domestic reproductive activities (laundry, caring for the children, meal preparation), whereas men earned their income in the market (Julémont, 1993). The separation of domestic and industrial work brought about a devaluation of family-centred activities and an increased valorisation of activities outside the home. This family model was especially pronounced after the Second World War in Western Europe, when female participation in the labour

Family and industrial production

force was very low and the male breadwinner model was widespread (Blossfeld and Hakim, 1997). Eastern European countries, and to some extent the Scandinavian countries, gave sustained encouragement to the employment of women, so that there are significantly higher labour force participation rates for women in these countries.

Social historians have distinguished between two models of family formation: the model of very early marriage, as was common in Asian and African countries and parts of South America, and the European model, where late marriage and high shares of single people are typical (Hajnal, 1965; Wall and Robin, 1983; Laslett, 1988). These different models remained characteristic well into the 20th century. Only later in (Western) Europe did a trend set in towards a higher marriage rate and a younger age at first marriage (Höpflinger, 1987). This trend reached its peak in the 1950s and 1960s, but was followed by a reversal, with a renewed trend towards lower frequency of marriage and a higher age at first marriage. Typical of the European family is that it shielded itself from social influences such as the community or neighbourhoods. In other cultures, however, the family is embedded in wider social networks, whether they are relatives or not, so that the tasks of bringing up and caring for children are assumed by a larger group of people. In Europe, the parent–child relationship was central, and remains so; the frequency of the multi-generation household has also declined. Regarding choice of partner, the idea of marrying for love spread through Europe at an early stage, transferring the responsibility for the choice of partner from the family to the individual (see Section 5.3).

Separation of work and family life
At the same time, the importance of the family for individuals declined because economic opportunities to live independently of the family grew. This was directly connected with the emergence of gainful employment: employment was relocated from the house or immediate local surroundings to factories, and became subject to a standardised organisational structure of work flows, working hours, formal qualifications and paths of advancement (Hareven, 1982). The factory system did not involve 'the whole person', as was previously the case, but rather manpower alone, on the basis of an exchange between job performance and income. A fundamental condition for this system of contractually guaranteed income was the contractualisation of work through employment contracts. Together, these steps led to a gradual separation of the spheres of family and work. This separation, in turn, ushered in one of the core distinctions in bourgeois society – that between private and public (Demos and Boocock, 1978). In conjunction with the emergence of the industrial working class, clear, class-specific differences developed in questions of fertility and familial values, and persist to this day.

A further development was the extensive structuring and standardisation of individual lives, which is often described as the institutionalisation of the life course (Kohli, 1986; Mayer, 2000). From accounts of life in pre-industrial times, we know that the life of an individual was bound to the fate of the family. Starting with industrialisation and lasting into the 1950s and 1960s, a four-part structure of the normal life course developed, with the phases of childhood, youth, adulthood and old age. Firm institutional arrangements were linked to these stages, stipulating status and transitions, and ensured that the course of an individual life was supported by a solid framework.

Modern institutions like the system of schools, training, employment and social security had a structuring effect, regulating and standardising the pathways of life (see Section 4.2). Industrialisation also brought the imposition of compulsory education: enrolments in secondary and post-secondary schools increased, and the proportion of people with vocational training increased. While it is true that efforts to enforce compulsory education go back further in history and were religiously motivated, with the increasing role of education in production there was a growing need to provide qualifications. In addition, the life course was structured in such a way that the chances of earning an income were no longer directly dependent on physical development and health, but instead other criteria for compensation, such as qualifications and seniority, gained in significance. Furthermore, with a defined retirement age came a formal status beyond the labour market, which was no longer immediately linked to physical deterioration (Kohli, 1987).

The model of industrial society is obviously not the end point of societal development. Fourastié's model describes the transition to the post-industrial society, with a growing proportion of employment in the service sector (Bell, 1973; Harvey, 1990). This change has been under way in Western industrialised countries since the 1970s. Through automation and increased productivity, industrial production has become ever cheaper and is carried out with less reliance on labour. At the same time, there has been significant growth in the field of public and private services and in the number of jobs in transport, communications, nursing care, education and leisure (see Section 7.4). This has brought about a quantitative meltdown of the industrial working class and has led to the emergence of new classes. These include new professions with high levels of qualification and a whole class of workers in the service sector, especially the public sector, but also growing groups in low-skilled areas. In addition to changes in the material base, the advent of the service society has also provoked changes in social values and norms, such as the emergence of post-materialist values and processes of individualisation (Inglehart, 1990).

Institutional-isation of the life course

The post-industrial society

3.2 Class structure and social differentiation

> ⌐☐ DEFINITION
>
> Social class describes a large social group that is characterised by a structurally similar
> position in the economic process and/or by common socio-economic characteristics.
> In Marxist theory, a class is characterised by its position in relation to the means of
> production. Often the concept of class includes common interests, a specific feeling
> of belonging together, or class consciousness.

Capital and labour

In the previous section, we pointed out that the development of the European model of industrial society was connected to the emergence of new classes and class relations (i.e. relations of oppression and exploitation). Societies that are structured and dominated primarily by classes are called class societies. In his early works, Karl Marx (1963 [1852], 1964 [1850]), the most significant proponent of class theory, analysed very specific classes and defined them on the basis of common conditions of existence, such as their ways of life and education. It was only later, in his major work, *Capital* (1992 [1867]), that Marx developed an abstract concept of class, which took as its point of departure the position in the production process and ownership – or non-ownership – of the means of production. On this basis, he distinguished between two main classes: that of wage-earners (the working class) and that of capital-owners (the capitalist class). Marx's class analysis identifies exploitation as the central causal process that generates inequality: one group obtains profits by monopolising resources and positions and appropriating the product of the labour of another. In his empirical descriptions, Marx referred to European societies, such as England and France, and from these observations deduced a general model of social change. For him, class conflicts were the engine of social change.

Classes and living conditions

Max Weber (1978 [1922]) oriented his concept of class more towards the actual living conditions and life chances of social groups. According to him, one can assume the existence of classes if, under the conditions of the market, a majority of people have in common specific causal factors that influence their life chances, namely, the economic ownership of goods and the interests involved in earning a living. One speaks in terms of classes when the market is the institution that is ultimately responsible for one's social position and attendant life chances. Weber distinguishes between the commercial (acquisition) classes and property classes, where the former are characterised by differences in the possibilities of making use of one's chances in the market and the latter by property ownership. He uses the concept of social class to describe the totality of class positions between which it is readily feasible to move, in the course of one's own life or within successive generations. This approach allows Weber to produce a far more nuanced model of social stratification. He could see that the radicalisation of the working class predicted by Marx had not fully transpired, and that segments of the working class could no longer be subsumed under the concept of the proletariat.

The emergence of classes

The Marxist interpretation of the process of industrialisation assumed that, with the development of a capitalist industrial society, differences in skills and wages would be blurred to such an extent that unified, homogeneous classes would emerge. The massive changes in production and reproduction that were brought about by industrialisation did indeed contribute to the formation of large new social groups with a common life context and specific interests. Class relations became the dominant axis of conflict in capitalist industrial society, but with major variations across countries (Katznelson and Zolberg, 1986). After 1850, in England, Germany and France there was a large increase in the working class and, concomitantly, new forms of protest and resistance developed. Between 1900 and 1914, hardly a year went by in France with fewer than 500 industrial disputes; in 1912, more than one million German workers took part in industrial action; in Britain, there were also numerous trouble spots in industrial centres like Manchester and Liverpool.

Classes as social movements

Working-class formation as a political movement occurred in many Western countries. This included the establishment of independent labour parties, the organisation of trade unions and the formation of associations and organisations located in the workers' milieus (Geary, 2004). Although the mobilisation of workers in trade unions and through new forms of protest such as strikes became a new structural feature of capitalist society, organisation across class lines was not comprehensive. At the beginning of the 20th century, the percentage of workers in the manufacturing industry involved in trade union organisations varied across Europe from between 30% and 40% in Britain, to between 25% and 30% in Germany and only 15% in France (Kriegel and Becker, 1964). In some countries, such as Italy and England, the working class remained fragmented and divided. One reason for these differences lay in the heterogeneity of religion and language, but also in that of the socio–political structures of individual countries (Lane and Ersson, 1987; Bartolini, 2000).

Trade unions

While in Eastern Europe the working class was involved in a series of profound conflicts, it never was able to attain the position it had achieved in Western Europe. In the second half of the 19th century, many countries in Eastern Europe were influenced by the capitalist development that began in Western Europe. The transfer of modern economic forms to countries that were still predominantly agricultural involved a wealth of social and political problems, which were exacerbated by the weak development – or outright absence – of constitutional bodies that would have made it possible to reconcile these antagonisms. At the time of the October Revolution of 1917, 80% of the Russian people still lived in agrarian conditions, which meant there was no possibility of a comprehensive labour movement emerging. Therefore, it was a relatively small group of workers' and soldiers' councils in the major cities that ultimately made it possible for the Bolsheviks to come to power.

Although the formation of a working class was perfectly evident, to conceive it as a large, single and unified group is to overstate the case. Thus, the distinction between the skilled and the unskilled workforce became clear at an early stage, and extended beyond the narrow confines of work into the domains of popular culture and ways of life. The *Lumpenproletariat* and the aristocracy of labour were worlds apart (Ritter and Tenfelde, 1992). It also became apparent that one cannot derive forms of political consciousness or political movements from abstract class relations; nor do the latter automatically lead to unified class positions.

The working class and the political system

The political organisation of the working class

There were major differences between countries with regard to the involvement of the working class in the political system. Significant socialist or social-democratic parties capable of securing the adherence of the working class did not develop in all countries (Geary, 1999; Mikkelsen, 2005). Despite these major differences across Europe, the connection between working-class formation and social democracy is regarded as a thoroughly European phenomenon. Werner Sombart's famous essay, *Why is There No Socialism in the United States?* (1976 [1906]) took up the question of why, unlike in Europe, socialist movements were not able to gain a foothold in the United States. He observed that the political culture of the United States is substantially different from its European equivalent. Thus, in the US there was no division of political parties along the lines of social class, as was customary in Europe. He also saw American mobility, that is, the permeability of class boundaries, as responsible for the fact that a workers' movement was not able to develop. Instead of battling collectively as a class for more rights and better living conditions, Americans pursued individual goals of advancement. This contrast between Europe and America has been subsequently widely discussed in social science research, with some researchers finding that the differences in mobility levelled out as industrialisation proceeded, but at the same time pointing to differences in the late 19th and early 20th centuries (Lipset and Bendix, 1959; Kaelble, 1983; Erikson and Goldthorpe, 1992). In addition to actual mobility opportunities, different values and cultures were advanced as key explanations for the differences: in this view, the US presents itself as a particularly liberal and individualistic country, while in Europe hierarchical relations of superordination and subordination prevail (Lipset, 1996). This liberalism was also combined with an egalitarianism that, at that time, was still foreign to European societies (Tocqueville, 2000 [1835/40]).

A very important issue for the discussion on Europeanisation is the internationalisation of the workers' movement, which occurred quite early but remained incomplete. In the context of his endeavours for the First International (International Workingmen's Association) in 1864, Karl Marx himself had called for an international alliance of the working class. To combat the international nature of capitalism, he argued, an international workers' movement was needed, able to overcome national barriers. It soon became clear that there was not enough cohesion to establish an International Workers' Party. The willingness to display international solidarity also remained limited, and only quite belatedly did important issues such as dealing with the colonies find a place on the agenda (Stjernø, 2004). Despite various attempts at international (or European) amalgamation, the concepts that were associated with the workers' movement ultimately remained national.

International solidarity?

Differentiating social structure

In research on social stratification, there has been an intense debate over the extent to which traditional concepts of class are capable of adequately describing social-structural differentiation. For in advanced industrial societies, it is less the ownership of the means of production that determines one's position in the social structure than one's position in the occupational hierarchy, which has a decisive impact on income, social prestige, power and influence, and on access to beneficial social relationships. Functionalist theories highlight that stratification is universal and necessary and that the layering and ranking of individuals and groups in society takes place according to the resources or human capital they possess, such as skills and education (Davis and Moore, 1945). However, beyond the major classes such as capital and labour, one finds new social groups such as the middle class, and a differentiation between blue-collar and white-collar workers, which all make class distinctions less clear-cut. At the same time, technological progress is altering work processes and conditions so that greater diversity in skills and compensation is emerging. Finally, other dimensions of social inequality are coming into view, such as regional inequalities or religious affiliation.

The end of class?

Theodor Geiger (1972 [1932]) argued already in the 1930s that society can be divided into many different groups, and that diverse factors such as occupation, education, social origin and religion all play a role in this division. At the same time, one's objective situation and subjective awareness do not stand in a fixed and deterministic relationship to each other. Moreover, social stratification becomes ever more diverse, and new groups emerge (for example, white-collar workers and public officials). The spread of prosperity, the expansion of social policies, equal opportunity, mobility and the increasing role of consumption and leisure can also further reduce the importance of traditional class structures. Instead of class polarisation, this can lead to a strengthening of the social middle and a tendency towards the de-stratification of society. Thus, data in all Western societies show that the middle class has grown significantly, and approximately 50% of the population can be included in it, with upward and downward deviations (Sylos-Labini, 1975; Allum, 1995). Going even further are theses concerning the dissolution of classes and social strata, and social destructuration (Beck, 1992).

Against this view, it has been argued that it underestimates the ongoing presence of important vertical distributions of inequality in terms of ownership, income and mentalities. Newer approaches to class theory continue to assign a central role to the work process in shaping social structure, but they also increasingly refer to power and decision-making hierarchies in the economic process, to qualifications, job-requirement profiles and income sources (Wright, 1985). Goldthorpe's theory of class (Goldthorpe, 1987; Erikson and Goldthorpe, 1992) assumes that in modern Western societies, with their bureaucratic work organisation, the service class occupies a dominant position. Thus, higher-level professionals, such as engineers, senior managers, managers and big-business people, are subsumed into the upper and mid-level service class. Bourdieu extends the concept of class by distinguishing social, cultural and economic capital, and also incorporates lifestyle (Bourdieu, 1984).

Classes in Eastern Europe under socialism

Eastern Europe after the Second World War, and up until 1989, presented a different picture. These political systems described themselves as workers' and farmers' states, ascribing social and political pre-eminence to these groups. Their social structures were regarded as essentially reduced to one level. However, certain groups enjoyed special privileges that were politically based. The party bureaucracy and technocratic intelligentsia had a key role in the exercise of social power and in the control of the economy and public sphere (Konrad and Szelényi, 1974). The promise of equality was therefore only partially kept. The establishment of the socialist order resulted in a decrease in socio-structural mobility, as can be shown by the example of East Germany. An intergenerational comparison revealed an increase in the risk of moving down into the working class, while the odds of advancement into the socialist service class declined over time (Huinink and Solga, 1994; Solga, 1995). With the collapse of socialism, this political interference in the social structure was eliminated, and the countries of Eastern Europe moved towards Western, market-mediated forms of socio-structural differentiation, while also drawing on the stock of their own traditions. In a relatively short time, inequalities were exacerbated and new (technocratic) elites were able to gain in influence (Eyal et al, 1998).

3.3 The European social model

> ⌐□ DEFINITION
>
> The welfare state includes all forms of governmental intervention whose purpose is to afford protection against the risks of life and to compensate for inequalities produced by the market. These are institutions that provide safeguards against risks such as illness, unemployment, old age and poverty, as well as government programmes in areas such as housing, education, social services and care. ■

European societies are considered to be sites not just of class conflict, but also of institutionalised class compromise. Contrary to Marx's predictions, no impoverishment of the proletariat occurred in the wake of capitalist development, but rather an expansion of state intervention in favour of enhanced social participation and protection against risk, thus arriving at an institutionalised class compromise. With the welfare state came a new social arrangement, whose purpose was to afford protection against the risks of life and to compensate for inequalities generated by the market (Esping-Andersen, 1990; Leibfried and Mau, 2008). Also important for the balance of interests are forms of workers' participation, social partnership relations between trade unions and employers' organisations, regulations of wage structures and of employment, and protection against dismissal (see Sections 4.1 and 4.3).

Collectivisation of risk

Citizenship rights and social classes

With the development of the welfare state in Europe, far-reaching changes in the organisation of social inequality converged. In his famous lecture *Citizenship and Social Class*, Thomas H. Marshall (1950) described Western development as a three-stage process involving the establishment of civil, political and social rights. Marshall classifies these different rights on the basis of their historical sequence, and takes the developments in England as a generalisable model (see Figure 3.2). The first to develop, in the 18th century, were civil rights, which were linked to the emergence of independent legal jurisdictions, and which guarantee freedom and personal rights. The 19th century saw the development of rights of political participation through the extension of universal suffrage, the creation of new forms of representation and the parliamentarisation and democratisation of political decision-making. These new opportunities

Rights and inclusion

for access to political power, which gave the working class a great deal of political weight, did not, however, mitigate class relations. The workers did not use the newly acquired rights to overthrow the system in a fundamental way, but rather channelled their demands within the existing economic and political system. The third element, the establishment of social rights, which grants a minimum level of economic welfare, social security and material chances of participation in society, is directly predicated on political rights. Only through political mobilisation and the expansion of universal suffrage were social needs able to be effectively articulated (Flora and Alber, 1981). One consequence of this was the emergence of the welfare state and the state assumption of responsibility for key risks in life.

Figure 3.2: Dimensions of citizenship

Historical phase	Type of rights	Contents	Institution
18th century	Civil rights	Freedom of speech, thought and belief Freedom of property and contract Right to take court proceedings Legal equality	Courts
19th century	Political rights	Citizens' right to seek to influence and participate in the public affairs of the society Political participation, active and passive suffrage Freedom of association	Parliaments
20th century	Social rights	Public education, health, social security entitlements/welfare	Welfare-state/social security institutions

Rights and status

With the expansion and enhancement of these rights, the status of individuals within a state system is fundamentally altered. In the wake of the institutionalisation of citizenship rights, a new relationship emerges among individuals on the one hand, and between individuals, the state and the law on the other (Marshall, 1950). In feudal society, rights were closely linked to socio-economic and political status. In modern societies, this connection is abolished. Marshall sees clearly that the transition from a society based on standing and rank to an organisation of society shaped purely by the market, namely capitalism, brings with it major inequities and distortions, but through the connection between citizenship and capitalism a new state system develops that makes all citizens, formally speaking, equals, regardless of class affiliation. As Marshall understands it, it is not a matter of abolishing inequality in general, but rather of eliminating inequality in terms of status and rights. Through civic equality, which finds its limits in the domain of economic necessity, market inequalities are legitimised. Marshall thus develops a counter-perspective to the Marxian notion of a radical restructuring of the system, and shows how the relationship between political democracy and a capitalist market economy can be regulated.

The emergence of the welfare state

The main point of departure for the extension of state responsibility and regulation was, however, not the pursuit of social justice, but rather the search for an answer to the 'social question' raised by the industrialisation process – that is, the newly created social risks and the social 'dynamite' associated with them. Bismarck's social reforms in the late 19th century can be understood, for example, as a 'defensive modernisation', where the aim was to defuse social problems and increase the ties of working people to the state (Zapf, 1986). Initially it was less a question of 'welfare for all', but rather a question of social protection for workers in the core productive sectors. As a group, industrial workers were particularly economically and socially exposed to the risks of modern industrial development. At the same time, it was clear that many of the risks involved in using machines were not attributable to individual failure, but were instead collective risks, and that ultimately only a collective approach could succeed in dealing with them (Ewald, 1986; Baldwin, 1990). It is thus not surprising that in many countries accident insurance was the first measure to be introduced, since it was important to find an effective way of countering the hazards to life and health created by industrial production. This was done in parallel with other regulatory measures introduced by the state, such as occupational safety and inspection procedures. Only later were other forms of social security added, such as health, disability and old-age insurance. While the first two measures were still directly linked to the risks of the production process, old-age insurance went further by helping workers to plan for the future. It was not until relatively late that unemployment insurance was introduced, its purpose being to counter the risks associated with fluctuations in the economy, which for workers meant the danger of finding themselves unemployed. This sequence of the introduction of social insurance was replicated in almost all (West) European countries, albeit at different times (Flora, 1986–87). Although initially only certain professions and groups of workers were covered by social insurance, it gradually expanded to cover other segments of the population, in certain instances even the entire population. In some systems, however, for instance in Germany, there remained an enduring, constitutive separation between employment-based social policy and anti-poverty policy. Other systems, with a stronger tradition of caring for the poor, did not draw such a strong dividing line between social security and the securing of a subsistence level by the state.

Social insurance

State—nation solidarity

The development of the European welfare state was closely connected to the emergence of nation-states (Rokkan, 1974; Bartolini, 2005). Transcending differences between classes and groups, national solidarity arrangements emerged. This entailed new conceptions of reciprocal responsibility among citizens (Ewald, 1986). Starting from the idea of a national collectivity, the state created institutions that served the collective interest and thus re-regulated the relationship between individuals and the collective. In this sense, the conception of a nation bound together by history, language and identity, institutionalised by the state, made it possible to expect citizens of that state to make redistributive sacrifices to the benefit of their fellow citizens.

What drives welfare state development?

The emergence of the welfare state is often regarded as an aspect of a comprehensive modernisation process: functionalism conceives the welfare state as a response to the growing socio-economic pressure caused by urbanisation, population growth and socioeconomic development, to which all modernising societies were subjected (Wilensky, 1975). The politicised variant of this thesis points out that modernisation is a multidimensional social process, with economic growth, social and political mobilisation and democratisation, and bureaucratisation of the state all occurring simultaneously. A further consequence of this transformation of social order is increasing socio-political intervention and regulation (Flora and Heidenheimer, 1981). Adherents of the power-resources approach are critical of the foregoing theories and underscore the role of class conflict as the motor for the development of the welfare state (Korpi, 1983). They see the growing political influence of leftist parties and trade unions as a driving force behind the expansion of welfare states. The significant differences in the extent of social welfare are explained by the strength of the various working-class organisations (social democratic parties, trade unions). It is interesting that, although there was an 'elective affinity' between mass democracies and the welfare state, authoritarian and fascist systems also enacted social policy programmes. Countries under state socialism also used social policy in order to win the adherence of their populations. In this case acting paternalistically, the state assumed responsibility for a comprehensive range of social policy functions, far beyond the field of social security proper, in areas such as family policy or housing.

Stages of development

Historical research shows that Western Europe can be regarded as having led the way in the development of the welfare state (Flora and Alber, 1981; Alber, 1982). In close temporal proximity, large and also numerous smaller countries acted as pioneers of social policy development. This had a long history, beginning with the anti-poverty policies of the municipalities, guilds, churches and philanthropic organisations. The first state health insurance systems and pension schemes were introduced in Germany and in the British Isles in the late 19th century. Later, many continental European countries followed suit, then Scandinavia. In the course of development of the welfare state, large state bureaucracies were created, which were specifically developed for the administration and control of these measures. At the same time, the welfare state created new professions such as social workers and social service providers, and new groups of transfer payment recipients, whose social situation and income were largely determined by government benefits (de Swaan, 1988). Developments in Eastern European countries approximated to the Western European model, especially in the interwar period, and by the beginning of the 1950s the most important forms of social insurance had been established (Tomka, 2004). Typical of the socialist phase were state-operated insurance programmes, the securing of a subsistence level, workplace-based provision of social services (for example, child care facilities) and social policy interventions through price subsidies for basic foodstuffs, rents and public transport. Unemployment insurance did not exist, because in general it was mandatory to work, an obligation that was enforced through employment in state-owned enterprises.

Nowadays, when we speak of a European social model, we mean not just that the welfare state is a European invention but also that in Europe it has taken on a specific form (see Figure 3.3). Despite major differences in forms of state insurance and protection (see Section 4.1), there are basic similarities among the various European welfare state types. Specifically, they are all characterised by public and community services, the institution of compulsory insurance for a range of key risks in life, the inclusion of all citizens, financing from public funds, the institutionalisation of social relations, as well as ideas of compensatory justice and solidarity (Kaelble, 1990; Crouch, 1999). These characteristics stand in contrast to, for example, the US and many other countries outside Europe, in which there is still no universal, state-funded health insurance and the middle classes are much less involved in the system of welfare services generally. Social spending in Europe – except for some smaller and poorer countries – is also comparatively high in a global context. Unlike philanthropic or discretionary forms of public welfare, the European welfare state grants its citizens legal rights to social services, rights that are broadly anchored in the national legal systems. In many regions of the world, this is not necessarily the case (Kaelble, 2004a). However, the idea of a single, unified model that characterises all European societies is an overstatement of the situation (see Chapter 4). One can also point to the problematic side of the European social model, such as problems of structural unemployment (Gallie and Paugam, 2000; Alber and Gilbert, 2010). Welfare states with relatively generous coverage and low levels of income inequality are in danger of producing less employment and a less dynamic economy (Iversen and Wren, 1998; Iversen, 2005). Especially in low-paid service-sector jobs, there is a lower level of employment

The European social model

in Europe than, for example, in the US. However, the Scandinavian countries have managed to combine high growth with successful social policy, and have been able to minimise the problems of continuing high unemployment, especially by expanding public services.

Figure 3.3: Characteristics of the European social model

State responsibility	Provision of public goods, extensive risk prevention
Redistribution	Taxation and welfare measures to decrease income inequalities and to correct market outcomes
Covered risks	Important sectors of risk protection: age, health, disability, unemployment
Labour relations	Extensive codified employment law, strong lobby groups Regulated negotiation procedures for reconciliation of social conflicts
Coverage/inclusion	Inclusion of all citizens, extensive concept of minimum care for every citizen with legal claim to public benefits
Financing	Collective financing from tax revenues or contributions to social insurance institutions
Role of different welfare providers	Governmental institutions primary, non-governmental forms of social security (neighbourhood, region, family, religious communities) subordinated or supplemental

Overall, the European welfare state has proved to be one of the most important social innovations of the last century. In a broad sense, it has contributed to a transformation of the social order, in that it rejected the pure market model and developed a secondary distribution system that is able to provide comprehensive social services. The welfare state thus served not just as an insurance institution, but also structured people's lives and circumstances in a more encompassing fashion (Esping-Andersen, 1990). In particular, the tremendous growth the welfare state experienced after the Second World War, coupled with prolonged periods of full employment and an economic boom, led to an increase in what was expected of the state. These expectations were supported by a broad social consensus and resulted in the situation whereby societal problems and conflicts led to an intensification of the demands made on the state. At least since the 1970s it has become clear, however, that, as successful as it is, this model cannot be made permanent. European welfare states are currently facing challenges such as the labour market crisis, the exhaustion of fiscal resources and the ageing of society, as well as processes of internationalisation and globalisation (Scharpf and Schmidt, 2000; Bermeo, 2001; Esping-Andersen et al, 2002; Goul Andersen et al, 2002).

Part 2
European societies compared

4

Political-economic models and institutional arrangements

The European social model described in the previous sections crystallised out of the various national models of social organisation in its nation-states. Despite enduring differences in their concrete institutional arrangements, these national models share key fundamental principles like the institutionalisation of relations between social partners, the correction of market outcomes, the collective financing of social security systems and notions of securing social peace through justice and solidarity. Central elements of these national models of social organisation are characteristically European welfare, educational and industrial relations systems.

National models of social order

From the perspective of modernisation theory, national models of social organisation can be expected to converge in their development (Marshall, 1950; Parsons, 1964b; Wilensky, 1975). This is already evident in the institutionalisation of educational programmes at primary, secondary and tertiary levels or in the introduction of social insurance schemes to protect against life risks (old age, illness and unemployment). However, for quite some time now scholars have pointed out that although European states have developed similar fundamental institutions, they continue to differ at the level of their specific institutional arrangements. These differences are due not to varying degrees of modernisation and hence to disparities between 'pioneers' and 'laggards', but rather to distinct institutional profiles. This means that there are marked differences across Europe in terms of the construction of models of societal organisation; these are the products of specific social and political compromises, cultural traditions and values. These distinct national historical trajectories are characterised by path dependency, meaning that institutional forms – once introduced – prove strikingly resilient and difficult to change (see North, 1990; Ebbinghaus, 2009; Beyer, 2010).

Path dependency

4.1 Welfare state regimes

NOTE ON METHODOLOGY ▬▬▬▬▬▬▬▬▬▬

Social expenditures are denoted as a percentage of the country's Gross Domestic Product on the basis of Eurostat data.[1] They encompass all public cash or in-kind transfers intended to relieve households and individuals of the burden of a defined set of risks or needs, as well as the costs incurred in the administration and management of these social protection systems.

Standard deviation (SD) is a measure of dispersion, which provides information about the heterogeneity of values in a data set. Standard deviation measures the variation in data around its arithmetic mean and has the same units as the data measured. Mathematically speaking, standard deviation is the square root of deviational values squared and divided by the total number in the sample:

$$s = \sqrt{\frac{1}{n} \sum_{i=1}^{n} (x_i - \bar{x})^2}$$

Welfare state models

One of the most influential classifications of welfare state policies was proposed by Richard M. Titmuss (1958, 1974) with his three models of social policy: residual, industrial achievement-performance and institutional-redistributive models of social policy. Each of these three models is characterised by a different scope of social protection. The residual welfare model sees the market and the family as the core institutions responsible for satisfying social and material needs. The industrial achievement-performance model conceives welfare state benefits in close relationship to citizens' position in the employment sphere. Finally, the institutional-redistributive model provides universal benefits based on material needs and egalitarian principles. Titmuss interprets these three welfare state models as historical models of development. Which countries belong to which ideal type can thus vary over time.

Richard M. Titmuss

Otto von Bismarck

An alternative to Titmuss's classification scheme is the distinction between the Bismarck and Beveridge models of social protection (Ferrera, 1993; Bonoli, 1997). The Bismarck–Beveridge distinction hinges in particular on the historical comparison of the institutionalisation of welfare states and their historically predominant guiding principles in various European countries (see Section 3.3). In Germany, Otto von Bismarck's authoritarian approach to social policy focused on social insurance. It provided social protection above all for wage-earners and was institutionalised around employment (Leibfried and Mau, 2008: 6). Britain's Sir William Beveridge, on the other hand, proposed a model

Sir William Beveridge

of state provision that was oriented towards the entire population and was organised as a flat-rate system (Hills et al., 1994). Each system has distinct consequences for stratification. While the Bismarck model promises those who are already well positioned in the labour market a high degree of social security, the Beveridge model does not provide more than a minimum level of state provision. In the Beveridge model, therefore, citizens are dependent on supplementary benefits from private insurance if they wish to preserve their achieved level of social status over the long term (Hills et al, 1994).

Building on Titmuss, the work of Esping-Andersen (1990, 1999) represents the most ambitious attempt to formulate a typology of Western welfare states. Esping-Andersen proceeds from the assumption that although these societies are all characterised by market economies, democracy and state intervention, they differ in their institutional arrangements, welfare objectives and the extent of their public support measures. He terms these distinct welfare state types 'welfare state regimes' (Esping-Andersen, 1990: 29ff). The crystallisation of a welfare state system is influenced by a country's constellation of political actors and the social policy tenets that guide them. Esping-Andersen's study of mostly Western European welfare states is predicated on the assumption that institutional arrangements, societal organisation and social structure are closely interconnected. Different welfare state regimes are based on distinct social and political structures, he maintains, and hence constellations of classes and actors play an important role in the formation and programmatic design of specific welfare state policies. On the other hand, he emphasises that the form the welfare state takes, in turn, shapes the patterns of social stratification in society (Esping-Andersen, 1990: 23ff). Taken together, a far-reaching complementarity and reciprocal influence thus exists between institutional and social structures.

Welfare state regimes

Esping-Andersen views the provision of social security as the shared responsibility of state programmes, collective non-state schemes (e.g. through employers) and private provision. He thus builds a bridge to classical political economy, which focuses on the relationship between the economy and politics, the market and the state, capitalism and democracy. Esping-Andersen ultimately asks how specific value conceptions and institutionalised forms of political economy give rise to distinct forms of social policy. He demonstrates that the institutional design of social protection schemes is the product of distributional conflicts in which different (class) interests are expressed. As a result, the capacity to mobilise power resources and the respective national balance among political groups are decisive for the organisation of the welfare state. This means, too, that state social policy varies with changes in political power relations, and that existing social security systems are the product of past socio-political priorities (Esping-Andersen, 1990: 16ff, 29ff).

Decommodi-fication

Stratification through welfare state intervention

Relationship of state, market and family

Esping-Andersen distinguishes three worlds of welfare capitalism: the liberal, social-democratic and conservative types. He classifies them in terms of three dimensions: (1) decommodification, that is, the extent to which systems of social security contribute to a reduction in the market dependency of individuals; (2) the consequences of social policy for social stratification; and (3) the relationship between the state, market and family (Esping-Andersen, 1990: 21ff). The central concept of decommodification expresses the extent to which recourse to state benefits enables an individual to secure a livelihood independent of the (labour) market. It is operationalised in terms of eligibility rules for benefit access, income replacement rates and the scope of social rights (Esping-Andersen, 1990: 47). With regard to stratification, Esping-Andersen is concerned with the structuring of inequality by different types of welfare states, measured, for example, in terms of the inequality of income distribution or in terms of the redistributive effects of state transfers. He addresses political-ideological traditions above all via an examination of the relationship between the state, market and family, that is, the responsibility attributed to each for the welfare of citizens:

> Regimes can be compared with respect to which essential human needs are relegated to private versus public responsibility. The division of social protection between private and public provides the structural context of de-commodification ... and the stratificational nexus of welfare-state regimes. (Esping-Andersen, 1990: 80)

Several years later, Esping-Andersen (1999: 74) defined this dimension even more clearly: 'The private–public axis was the principal analytical axis that underpinned the "three worlds" typology; the key defining dimensions were degree of de-commodification and modes of stratification.'

Liberal welfare state regimes

Examples of the liberal type are the US, Canada, the UK and Australia. In this type of welfare state regime, the responsibility of the state is limited. The social security systems are based primarily on a combination of the market-based insurance principle and tax financing (e.g. for social assistance). A relatively large share of benefits is means-tested. Access to such support payments is often stigmatising and their level is low, for it is assumed that generous welfare state benefit levels serve as a disincentive to work and foster dependency. This preference for minimalistic state engagement is in the tradition of liberalism, for it is assumed that the market is the best solution for the societal distribution of goods. In the liberal welfare state, the commodity character of labour is unmistakable, and decommodification is weak: the barriers to dismissing workers are lower, the costs of hiring new workers less formidable and the labour market is subject to little state regulation. In this analysis of the European variants of welfare state capitalism, the UK[2] represents the liberal type (Esping–Andersen, 1990, 1999).

The social-democratic welfare state, which has developed primarily in Northern Europe (the prime example is Sweden), aspires to the maxims of 'equality', 'the common good' and 'solidarity'. Social policy functions as an economic and social investment that does not necessarily have to contradict the logic of the market. The system of social security is characterised by a mixture of citizenship rights and comprehensive social insurance and has a universal character. Overall, benefit levels are very high. Together with the tax system, the welfare state has strong egalitarian effects, and decommodification is high. Further salient characteristics are the high value placed on active labour-market policy and the prominent role of the state as employer (especially of women). Hence in social-democratic welfare states, employment is also supported by a political consensus for policies fostering equality of opportunity such as egalitarian educational policies, as well as by employment protection policies (OECD, 2002: 91f; Green-Pedersen and Klitgaard, 2009: 138ff; Hort, 2009: 431ff). In other words, social-democratic welfare states do not assume equality of opportunity, as liberal welfare state regimes arguably do to justify the fairness of market outcomes, but instead go to great lengths to foster it. Moreover, people experience social protection less through individual occupational schemes insuring against employment-based risks, than through universalistic participation as citizens.

The conservative welfare state type prevails in countries such as Germany, France, Austria, Belgium and Italy. This conservative welfare model intervenes in market distributional processes more than the liberal one does. Yet its social security schemes largely reproduce market inequalities. This occurs particularly through the social insurance schemes. These operate according to the principle of vested benefits with an equivalence between contributions and benefit entitlements. As a result, one's degree of social security is closely linked to one's level of achieved labour-market status. The system is limited in its redistributive scope, for it is oriented far more towards redistribution across the life course than to redistribution across groups. The corporatist organisation of this welfare state type yields a plethora of different insurers organised by occupation, and self-administered by various collective actors such as unions and employer organisations, within a statutory framework. Conservative welfare states evince an intermediate level of decommodification. The labour market tends to be relatively stable, employment trajectories are characterised by relatively few job changes, and mobility within a class is more prevalent than upward or downward mobility (Allmendinger and Hinz, 2009: 245ff). Countries with a conservative welfare state share an emphasis on the centrality of the family in meeting material needs and

Social-democratic welfare state regimes

Conservative welfare state regimes

support institutionally the gendered division of paid and domestic labour. This familialism is most pronounced in countries like Italy, Spain and Greece (Esping–Andersen, 1999). It is based, on the one hand, on the male breadwinner model, that is, the conditioning of many social benefits on employment, and, on the other, on the responsibility of the family to produce welfare. The more 'familialist' the regime, the less support families receive from the state. As a consequence, the career prospects of women are compromised and lone parents are often marginalised (Esping–Andersen, 1999: 83).

Figure 4.1: Classification of welfare state regimes

Model	Liberal	Social-democratic	Conservative	Post-socialist
Type of protection	Residual; self-provision	Universal provision	Contribution- and status-oriented	Contribution- and status-oriented
Basis of eligibility	Need	Citizenship	Employment	Employment and indigence
Goal	Fighting poverty	Mitigation of inequality	Status preservation	Rudimentary protection
Decommodification	Low	High	Medium	Very low
Primary locus of welfare provision	Market	State	Family	Family
Social stratification	High	Low	Medium	Very high
Level of redistribution	Low	High	Low	Very low
Share of private expenditures on old age and health	High	Low	Low	Medium
Role of the state in structural change	Market activator	Employer	Compensator	Reformer, market activator
Example	United Kingdom	Sweden	Germany	Czech Republic

Comment: Redistributive capacity: tax progressivity, benefit equality.

Critique of the concept of welfare state regimes

Critique of Esping-Andersen's welfare state typology has centred on inconsistencies between the three ideal types and empirical reality (Lewis, 1992; Boje, 1996; Goodin et al., 2000; Arts and Gelissen, 2002). Scholars have argued, for example, that the Mediterranean welfare states (e.g. Spain, Italy, Greece and Portugal) constitute a distinct form of the conservative type – one that Esping-Andersen failed to sufficiently portray (Ferrera, 1996). While these countries also have social insurance schemes along the lines of the continental European model, they evince considerable gaps in protection. The level of state aid provided when insured risks do occur is often inadequate, making it necessary for those affected to access supplementary familial support networks (Natali, 2009; Papatheodorou, 2009; Pereirinha et al, 2009; Villota and Vázquez, 2009). The result is a characteristic gendered division of labour: women assume the domestic tasks of care and support, as these are neither provided by the state nor available on the market. Familialism is highly pronounced in Mediterranean welfare states. One component of this subsidiary familialist model is various formal and informal arrangements in civil society, such as by charities or the Church. Further, perhaps the most serious critique is that it is problematic to equate Esping-Andersen's ideal types with specific welfare states, for some are mixtures of more than one type, such as Finland (high decommodification, moderate stratification) and there are many countries in which the typology's classification dimensions are not very pronounced (Ireland, Switzerland). Moreover, since the publication of Esping-Andersen's typology, additional salient dimensions have been proposed to characterise welfare states, such as family or gender structures (Lewis, 1992; Ostner and Lewis, 1995; Ostner and Knijn, 2002). A final group of critics notes that although Esping-Andersen rightly proceeds from the assumption that a central goal of the welfare state is to secure individuals' and families' welfare independent of the market, welfare state interventions are not necessarily directed against the market. The literature on the varieties of capitalism is predicated on the assumption that the market and the welfare state can be understood as complementary institutions (Crouch and Streeck, 1997; Soskice, 1999; Ebbinghaus and Manow, 2001), for the welfare state exists above all because it functions in areas where private markets would be inefficient or would not exist at all (Barr, 2004).

Mediterranean welfare state regimes

Esping-Andersen's classification of three worlds of welfare capitalism was largely accurate until well into the 1990s. It runs into great difficulty, however, when applied to the structures of state social policy that have emerged in the post-socialist societies of Central and Eastern Europe in the course of their transformation. Nonetheless, as Fuchs and Offe (2009: 421) have observed, many scholars have attempted to classify these 'new' Eastern European welfare states as belonging to Esping-Andersen's liberal type. In our view it makes more sense to describe what has developed in the Eastern European EU accession countries as a novel 'mixed' welfare state type (Manning, 2004; Aidukaite, 2006; Cerami, 2006; Rajevska, 2009; Tausz, 2009; Trumm and Ainsaar, 2009), which in most cases embodies elements of the conservative and liberal types, as well as faint residues of a paternalistic one:[3]

Welfare state regimes in Eastern Europe

> [W]hat we are witnessing in Central and Eastern Europe is ... a rather complex mechanism of institutional creation, in which an on-going process of structuring, de-structuring and restructuring

of existing welfare institutions is resulting in the emergence of a new ... Eastern European welfare regime. (Cerami, 2006: 225)

The conservative element in these Eastern European welfare states came via the introduction of a system of social insurance against employment-based risks, which was modelled on the German system (Cerami, 2006). In most of these countries, it is financed – as in Germany – by employer and employee contributions; in Latvia and Poland the system is partially financed by tax revenues (Fuchs and Offe, 2009). Additionally, 'familialism' is very strong, meaning that family and primary social networks are pivotal in the securing of individual welfare. The liberal element in these post-socialist welfare states is evident above all in their low level of decommodification, in their means-tested, minimal public benefits, and in the resulting prevalence of poverty and pronounced social stratification. Female labour-market participation is lower here than the EU-15 average (see Section 7.2). Much as in liberal welfare states, in Central and Eastern European accession countries the costs of hiring and the barriers to firing are low. As a result, occupational trajectories are unstable and characterised by multiple job changes. Decommodification is very low.

Social expenditures in Europe

Level and structure of social expenditures

In social-scientific research, empirical analysis of welfare state regimes has been (among other things) strongly based on the level and structures of social expenditures in European societies. According to this literature (e.g. Baldock et al, 2009; Evans and Williams, 2009; Bahle et al, 2010), social expenditures are the result of explicit government provisions that require the payment of taxes and social contributions to meet the costs of adverse circumstances that affect individuals and/or households. It is a fact that social expenditure involves a sometimes substantial degree of redistribution from the less needy to the more needy (Baldock, 2009: 10). In evaluating expenditures in the realm of social policy, one must consider which social groups benefit from such expenditures, and based on which criteria. The level of social expenditure in a country is strongly influenced by economic and demographic factors (level of national prosperity, ageing of the population); the structure of social expenditures is shaped primarily by political decisions and power relations (Esping-Andersen, 1990: 137). Empirically, the average level of social expenditures in the European Union is very high. Among the EU-15 in 2007, nearly 26% (EU-27: 25%) of the Gross Domestic Product (GDP) was used for social transfers. That is much higher than in the US, where in 2006 social expenditures constituted roughly 18% of GDP (OECD, 2009l: 97). Social spending as a share of GDP is markedly higher than in other developed capitalist states as well, such as New Zealand, Australia and Japan, where in 2006 between 21% and 23% of GDP was spent on social programmes (OECD, 2009l: 97).

Table 4.1: Social expenditures

	Social spending as % of GDP			Social spending levels in PPS (euros) per capita
	1995	**2000**	**2007**	**2007**
EU-15	27.6	26.8	25.9	7,186
Belgium	27.4	26.5	28.0	8,235
Denmark	31.9	28.9	28.1	8,399
Germany	28.3	29.3	26.7	7,642
Ireland	18.8	13.9	17.6	6,543
Greece	19.9	23.5	23.8	5,576
Spain	21.6	20.3	20.5	5,392
France	30.3	29.5	29.0	7,868
Italy	24.2	24.7	25.5	6,464
Luxembourg	20.7	19.6	19.0	12,992
Netherlands	30.6	26.4	26.8	8,766
Austria	28.8	28.4	27.1	8,375
Portugal	21.0	21.7	23.4	4,442
Finland	31.5	25.1	24.6	7,094
Sweden	33.6	30.1	29.0	8,842
United Kingdom	27.7	26.4	24.8	7,316
Bulgaria	–	–	14.6	1,358
Czech Republic	17.4	19.5	18.0	3,596
Estonia	–	14.0	12.3	2,130
Cyprus	–	14.8	18.1	4,099
Latvia	15.3*	15.3	10.7	1,537
Lithuania	–	15.8	13.9	2,077
Hungary	–	19.3	21.9	3,412
Malta	16.1	16.9	17.9	3,461
Poland	–	19.7	17.8	2,380
Romania	–	13.2	12.6	1,333
Slovenia	23.8#	24.2	20.8	4,639
Slovakia	18.5	19.4	15.4	2,570
EU-27	–	26.4	25.2	6,283

Source: Eurostat (2010b); #1996, *1997.

Social expenditures vary considerably across Europe. The highest level of social expenditure we find in countries with a social-democratic or conservative welfare state. Examples are Sweden, France, Denmark, the Netherlands and Belgium; in 2007 these countries spent between 27% and 29% of their GDP funding their social security systems. The

Low social spending in post-socialist welfare states

lowest social expenditures occurred in the post-socialist welfare states (Romania, Bulgaria, the Baltic countries). Between these two poles lie the conservative Mediterranean welfare states (Spain, Greece, Portugal) as well as the Czech Republic, Hungary, Poland, Slovenia and the liberal Ireland; these countries spent between 18% and 25% of their GDP on social benefits. A nearly identical group of countries emerges when one examines social expenditures per capita: in 2007 Sweden and the Netherlands, for example, devoted EUR 8,800 (in purchasing power standards – PPS) to social benefits. As in most other social-structural parameters, Luxembourg is a special case within Europe (EUR 13,000 in PPS). Those in need of social benefits in Romania, Bulgaria, Latvia, Lithuania or Estonia can hope to receive only a small portion of this sum. In these countries citizens receive (after accounting for differences in purchasing power) between EUR 1,300 and EUR 2,100-worth of social support on average. A simple calculation renders the degree of polarisation in welfare state programmes within Europe clear: Sweden and the Netherlands expend 700% more on social programmes per capita than do Romania or Bulgaria. Analogous to Esping-Andersen's assumptions, these differences in social spending levels correspond to a large extent to the differences between these two sets of countries in terms of economic prosperity, political priorities and demographic make-up.

Polarisation of welfare state generosity in Europe

The development of social expenditures between 1995 and 2007 points to a consistently high level of spending on average. This is remarkable, for since the 1970s there has been discussion of a crisis of European welfare states and of the need to downsize social programmes (for a synopsis of this discussion see Korpi, 2003). The OECD (2006g: 40) attributes this trend in social spending, which has continued more or less steadily since the 1980s, to increasing prosperity in Europe and to the ageing of European societies (resulting in greater demand for retirement income security and health care provision). This development can also be explained, however, as an example of the path dependency of established institutional forms (North, 1990; Ebbinghaus, 2009; Beyer, 2010) and of the unbroken acceptance of solidarity and justice as the societal foundation of the European social model (cf. Chapter 3, as well as Mau, 2003; Mau and Veghte, 2007).

A closer look reveals a decrease in social spending in the Scandinavian welfare states, and an even more marked decline in the Slovak Republic and Baltic states; the latter already have a very low level of social spending compared to European standards. For Denmark, Sweden and Finland, this development can be explained with reference to a comparatively favourable demographic development (limited ageing), a strong increase in female labour-market participation as well as a reduction of welfare benefits in recent years (Green-Pedersen and Klitgaard, 2009; Hort, 2009). In the Baltic states and in the Slovak Republic, the decline in social expenditures is primarily due to privatisations in various realms of social policy. In these countries, the state is receding increasingly from the fields of health care, retirement income security and even education (Aidukaite, 2006, 2009; Rajevska, 2009; Trumm and Ainsaar, 2009; Wientzek and Meyer, 2009). The decline in social spending is exacerbated by an unfavourable demographic trend: in the Baltic countries in recent years, the population has been ageing at an above-average pace (see Section 5.1); this increases the circle of persons needing social protection from the pension and health-care systems. Together, the consequence of these demographic and social policy developments is an increase in poverty, as the analyses in Section 8.2 reveal.

An increase in social spending can be observed in the Mediterranean welfare states (e.g. Portugal, Greece) as well as in Hungary. In Portugal, this is due to increases in the social and minimum pensions and in the number of pension beneficiaries, but also in the level of support payments in case of unemployment (Pereirinha et al, 2009); in Greece, this is primarily due to a nominal increase in pension benefits combined with a growing number of pension beneficiaries (Papatheodorou, 2009). In Italy as well, social spending has risen in recent years. In these cases the cause is not an institutional expansion of the welfare state, but a rapid ageing of the society and above-EU-average unemployment (see Sections 5.1 and 7.3). As a result, the circle of those eligible to claim health, pension and unemployment insurance benefits has expanded (Natali, 2009).

In discussions of social spending levels in Europe a perennial question is whether these are converging. In particular, in the course of the aforementioned developments, have spending levels converged or have divergent levels of welfare state activity persisted? Calculations of the standard deviations (SDs) of social spending for the EU-27 countries show that between 1995 and 2007 variation in these levels has increased slightly (1995: SD of 5.80; 2007: SD of 6.60). If, like Kaelble (2007: 352), one considers a broader temporal frame of reference, however, one indeed finds evidence of convergence, especially for the period from the early 1970s to the early 1990s.

Currently no convergence of social spending levels

A more detailed examination of the structure of social expenditures (Table 4.2) reveals a series of significant commonalities among social policies across Europe. Nearly everywhere, retirement income security is the most important welfare state domain. On average in the European Union in 2007, 40% of all social expenditures were in this realm. In Italy and Poland, more than one out of every two euros spent in social policy were for retirement benefits. Strikingly, many Eastern European accession states spend a larger percentage of their social budgets on retirement income security than do the principal Member States in the West. The least amount was spent on public pensions in Ireland and Luxembourg, where between 23% and 27% of social expenditures fell into this realm.

Retirement security the leading social policy domain in Europe

Table 4.2: Social expenditures by policy domain

	1995						2000						2007					
	Health	Disability	Pensions	Families	Unemployment	Housing	Health	Disability	Pensions	Families	Unemployment	Housing	Health	Disability	Pensions	Families	Unemployment	Housing
EU-15	27.2	8.3	37.6	8.0	8.3	2.2	27.5	7.8	40.2	8.3	6.2	2.2	29.3	8.0	39.4	7.9	5.2	2.3
Belgium	23.6	8.8	32.1	8.8	13.0	–	24.2	9.3	33.6	8.8	11.8	0.1	26.5	6.6	35.3	7.1	11.7	0.5
Denmark	17.8	10.6	37.6	12.4	14.8	2.4	20.2	12.0	38.0	13.1	10.5	2.4	23.0	15.0	38.1	13.1	5.6	2.5
Germany	30.9	7.4	33.1	8.2	8.8	1.0	29.5	6.5	34.8	11.3	7.9	1.1	29.8	7.7	35.4	10.6	5.8	2.3
Ireland	36.2	4.8	20.3	12.0	15.3	3.3	41.4	5.3	19.5	13.7	9.6	2.4	41.1	5.5	22.8	14.7	7.7	1.6
Greece	26.0	4.8	49.6	8.8	4.5	2.6	26.5	4.8	46.4	7.4	6.2	3.1	28.1	4.9	43.6	6.2	4.5	2.0
Spain	28.6	7.4	39.6	2.0	16.5	1.1	29.4	7.9	41.6	4.9	11.6	0.8	31.2	7.6	31.9	6.0	11.7	0.9
France	28.3	5.9	37.3	10.0	7.9	3.2	28.8	5.9	38.4	9.1	7.2	3.2	29.9	6.1	38.7	8.5	6.1	2.6
Italy	23.2	7.1	52.5	3.2	3.0	0.0	25.1	6.1	52.5	3.8	1.7	0.0	26.1	6.0	51.4	4.7	1.8	0.1
Luxembourg	24.9	12.7	41.2	13.1	3.1	0.1	25.4	13.4	36.8	16.6	3.2	0.6	26.0	12.3	27.4	16.6	4.9	0.8
Netherlands	28.5	12.6	32.4	4.6	9.9	1.4	29.3	11.8	37.0	4.6	5.1	1.5	32.5	9.1	35.0	6.0	4.3	1.4
Austria	25.6	9.7	37.2	11.3	5.8	0.3	25.6	9.7	39.7	10.8	4.9	0.3	26.0	8.0	41.7	10.2	5.3	0.4
Portugal	36.2	11.8	34.3	5.2	5.3	0.0	32.0	12.7	37.6	5.4	3.7	0.0	28.3	10.0	42.9	5.3	5.1	0.0
Finland	20.9	15.0	28.9	13.4	14.4	1.5	23.8	13.9	31.8	12.5	10.5	1.5	26.3	12.6	35.0	11.6	7.8	1.0
Sweden	21.8	11.9	35.4	11.4	10.9	3.3	27.0	13.0	37.2	9.0	7.1	2.1	26.1	15.3	39.0	10.2	3.8	1.7
United Kingdom	24.0	10.9	39.3	8.9	5.6	6.9	25.5	9.4	44.4	6.9	3.0	5.7	30.6	9.8	41.8	6.0	2.1	5.8

continued

Table 4.2 (continued)

	1995						2000						2007					
	Health	Disability	Pensions	Families	Unemployment	Housing	Health	Disability	Pensions	Families	Unemployment	Housing	Health	Disability	Pensions	Families	Unemployment	Housing
Bulgaria	–	–	–	–	–	–	–	–	–	–	–	–	27.1	8.3	46.8	8.6	2.0	0.0
Czech Republic	37.2	7.5	35.0	11.9	2.3	0.0	33.6	7.7	38.9	8.4	3.5	0.7	33.9	8.1	39.7	9.2	3.5	0.3
Estonia	–	–	–	–	–	–	32.1	6.6	43.4	11.9	1.3	0.7	33.4	9.3	43.0	11.6	1.2	0.2
Cyprus	–	–	–	–	–	–	27.2	3.4	41.8	6.3	7.2	3.1	25.2	3.7	40.6	10.8	4.8	3.5
Latvia	18.0#	8.7#	55.6#	10.2#	2.7#	1.0#	16.7	7.9	56.9	10.2	3.8	0.7	29.7	7.0	44.9	11.0	3.3	1.2
Lithuania	30.3*	9.2*	44.2*	7.0*	2.0*	–	29.8	8.4	44.0	8.8	1.8	0.0	30.7	10.4	43.3	8.7	1.9	0.0
Hungary	–	–	–	–	–	–	27.9	9.6	39.9	13.2	4.0	2.9	25.5	9.6	37.8	12.8	3.4	4.1
Malta	27.6	4.7	48.1	12.8	2.3	2.0	29.3	5.9	48.6	9.4	2.6	1.1	29.2	6.3	42.3	5.9	2.8	1.3
Poland	–	–	–	–	–	–	19.6	14.0	44.5	5.0	4.6	0.9	22.1	9.6	49.1	4.5	2.2	0.5
Romania	–	–	–	–	–	–	25.6	7.9	47.5	10.0	7.7	–	23.8	10.0	43.2	13.2	2.2	–
Slovenia	30.8*	8.5*	44.1*	8.5*	4.3*	0.0*	30.7	9.0	43.2	9.2	4.3	–	32.1	7.8	39.3	8.7	2.3	0.1
Slovakia	33.0	6.8	36.9	14.0	3.5	0.0	34.9	7.6	36.3	9.0	4.8	0.3	30.8	8.5	38.3	10.0	3.6	–
EU-27	–	–	–	–	–	–	–	–	–	–	–	–	29.1	8.1	39.6	8.0	5.1	2.3

Source: Eurostat (2010b), *1996, #1997, +1998, –2004, figures are percentages.

In the case of Ireland this is due to private pensions playing a large and growing role in providing incomes in old age. More than 40% of overall retirement income stems from market-based pension schemes (OECD, 2009k: 28ff).

Health care

The second most important realm is health care, consuming 29% of social expenditures. The largest share of social spending on health care can be found in Romania, the Czech Republic and Ireland. In these countries, between 34% and 41% of all social expenditures is for health care. Moreover, Ireland is exceptional in this regard, for it is the only European country in which health care exceeded pension spending in 2007. After health care, the next three welfare state realms, of roughly equal magnitude, are family policy (EU-27: 8.0%), measures to mitigate the impact of disabilities (EU-27: 8.1%), and unemployment benefits and policies (EU-27: 5.1%). In the field of family policy, spending levels across Europe vary far more than they do in disability or unemployment policy. Countries like Denmark, Finland, Ireland, Hungary and Luxembourg devote a share of their social expenditures to family policy several times greater (between 12% and 17%) than that spent by Poland, Italy or Portugal (between 4% and 5%). In the case of Denmark, the generosity of family-related policies is reflected, for example, in the high coverage rates of the child-care system (Green-Pedersen and Klitgaard, 2009: 147). About 90% of all one- to five-year-olds were cared for by this public system, which means that child care in Denmark (just as Denmark's pension spending) is the most generous among the social democratic welfare states (Green-Pedersen and Klitgaard, 2009: 147). A similar story can be told for the Irish Republic and Finland. In both countries programmes that support families with children play a crucial role in social policy, mostly via child allowances (Kangas and Saari, 2009: 198; McCashin and O'Shea, 2009: 265). Housing policy is the social policy field to which all EU countries devote the smallest percentage of their social budgets. By far the leader in housing spending is the UK (for a detailed analysis of housing and social policy in the UK, see Pickvance, 2009), followed by Hungary, Cyprus and France.

Causes of social spending priorities

The causes of the differences in the structure of social expenditures across Europe are, first, distinct political power constellations and hence policy priorities. Second, in many countries it is considered to be a self-evident necessity for the state to take action in certain policy realms. For example, in the United Kingdom and Ireland, housing – in particular the construction of single-family homes – has always been a social policy concern, for it represents a form of investment and savings (Bazant and Schubert, 2009). Italy, Greece and Poland are states that as a result of the demographic shift have to devote considerable shares of their social budgets to retirement income security. States with a high level of unemployment spend as a rule a disproportionate share of their social expenditures in this area; examples are Spain and France. There are also countries, however, in which spending priorities do not match objective needs. The Slovak Republic, for example, which has had one of the highest unemployment rates in Europe since the early 1990s (see Section 7.3, Table 7.3), devotes only a below-average share of its social budget to this policy realm. Overall, though, while these findings suggest that socio-economic and demographic conditions are important for the distribution of expenditures, politically chosen priorities appear to shape specific national profiles of social spending most of all (Bazant and Schubert, 2009: 530).

Tracing in detail the changes in the spending patterns of the individual countries would go beyond the scope of this book. For the European Union as a whole, we can observe, however, that expenditures for retirement income security and health increased between 1995 and 2007, while those for unemployment benefits declined. This can be interpreted as a consequence of decreasing unemployment and population ageing. In other realms of social policy, spending patterns have changed little over this period. With regard to convergence processes among EU states, calculations of the standard deviations for social policy areas discussed here reveal a decrease in variance: the structure of social spending within the EU is thus converging.

Rise in expenditures on retirement and health

4.2 Educational institutions

DEFINITIONS

Educational systems can be distinguished according to their degree of stratification and standardisation. The stratification of an educational system can be measured by the degree of selectivity in transitions to higher educational levels, that is, how many pupils from a cohort reach the highest level of formal education. The standardisation of an educational system can be measured in terms of the institutional uniformity of the training components and curricula. Stratification and standardisation of educational systems have a direct influence on individual labour-market prospects and occupational trajectories (Allmendinger, 1989; Allmendinger and Hinz, 2009).

Across European states, largely comparable educational institutions exist at the primary, secondary and tertiary levels. At the same time, considerable institutional diversity prevails (e.g. in school systems and in vocational education), and these diverse institutions have converged only to a limited extent over the past 50 years (Green et al, 1999; Hörner and Döbert, 2007; Müller and Kogan, 2010)[4]:

Institutional diversity

These systems did not emerge along some rational plan. They rather are the result of historically specific cultural orientations, socio-economic conditions and power relations among interest groups and political parties in the long periods in which the educational systems were gradually built up and further developed: in the process of alphabetisation from the 18th century onwards; in the second part of the 19th century, when compulsory elementary education for the general populations was first introduced; in the early part of the 20th century especially following WWI when various forms of vocational and general secondary education slowly expanded; and in the second part of the 20th century, when secondary education became more or less universal and also tertiary education strongly expanded and changed from elite to mass institutions. (Müller and Kogan, 2010: 219)

Not until the last few years has there been a reduction in this institutional diversity, especially in the tertiary educational sector. A decisive cause of this convergence has been exerted by the 'Bologna process' to harmonise European higher education systems by 2010 (Reinalda and Kulesza, 2005; Keeling, 2006; Neave and Maassen, 2007; Cardoso et al, 2008). This has led most European universities to implement BA/MA programmes – degrees that are expected to be more useful on the European labour market.

School-based, vocational and tertiary educational institutions

In analysing the systemic features of European educational systems, it is first necessary to distinguish school-based training at the primary and secondary levels from vocational training and tertiary education. The Scandinavian, Southern European and Eastern European states have comprehensive school systems (Hörner et al, 2007; Eurydice, 2009). In the German-speaking countries, the Benelux states and the UK, school-based educational systems vary by region, and in some cases private schools play a prominent role. Vocational training systems vary greatly across Europe. The spectrum ranges from the dual system of Germany to exclusively firm-based vocational training systems, such as those prevalent in the United Kingdom. At the tertiary level, a system of polytechnics and universities exists that is organised either in parallel fashion (German-speaking countries) or sequentially (France) (Brauns et al, 1997; Müller, 2001; Duru-Bellat et al, 2008; Müller and Kogan, 2010). Among the most important criteria for distinguishing European educational institutions (Hörner et al, 2007; Eurydice, 2009; Müller and Kogan, 2010) are:

- the degree of centralisation of state control;
- the division between the public and private sectors in sponsorship and funding;

- the degree of stratification of school-based education; and
- the degree of standardisation of vocational training.

School-based educational institutions – primary and secondary level

In countries like Germany, Austria, Luxembourg, Malta and Belgium, the school system is organised in multiple tracks. At the beginning of the 20th century in these countries, distinct types of schools were institutionalised: elementary schools and various forms of secondary schools (mid-level, grammar and specialised grammar schools with, for example, a technical or artistic focus). Transitions between the levels of the school system are selective, and early tracking is the rule. Compared to other European countries, in Austria and Germany only a small share of pupils reach university, generally after graduating from a grammar school. This selectivity of the educational system in the German-speaking realm is a contentious topic among scholars (Eder et al, 2007; Lörz and Schindler, 2009; Mayer et al, 2009; Reimer and Pollak, 2009), for it serves as a measure of the extent of equality of opportunity in the educational system. However, another segment of the secondary school population in German-speaking countries qualifies for university admission by attending specialised grammar schools or vocational upper secondary schools (OECD, 2009b). Overall, then, between 40% and 50% of pupils graduate from secondary school with qualifications that allow them to enrol at university (Figure 4.2). Private educational institutions play a role in school-based education above all in Belgium and Austria (Brusselmann-Dehairs and Valcke, 2007; Eder et al, 2007). In all EU countries except Germany, educational policy is controlled centrally in the national education ministry. In Europe, only Germany and (outside the EU) Switzerland leave control of education to the states (*Länder*).

Multi-track school systems, selective, early tracking

In the Scandinavian and Eastern European countries as well as Spain, Portugal, the Netherlands and Cyprus, a comprehensive type of school system exists in which all pupils of a given age cohort spend eight or nine years together in the same institution, and tracking occurs late (Hörner et al, 2007), much as in the US school system. In Scandinavia and the Eastern European accession countries, private schools play no or only a marginal role. In countries such as Belgium, Austria, Italy, Greece, Spain, Cyprus and the Netherlands, private schools are more relevant. In countries with a comprehensive school system, educational policy is coordinated on a national level. Educational institutions sometimes have the authority to fashion their own curricula. The share of pupils in the Scandinavian, Eastern European and Southern European countries who reach university is very high. In Finland over 95% of students achieve the high school diploma. In countries like Estonia, Sweden and Poland, in some cases considerably more than three quarters of all pupils qualify for

Comprehensive school systems, late tracking

university admission. Laggards in this group are Slovenia and Spain, where 34% and 45% of all pupils acheived the high school diploma, respectively. Between these two poles are grouped countries with comprehensive school systems in which roughly 60% of students qualify for university admission.

Figure 4.2: Secondary school graduates with access to tertiary education

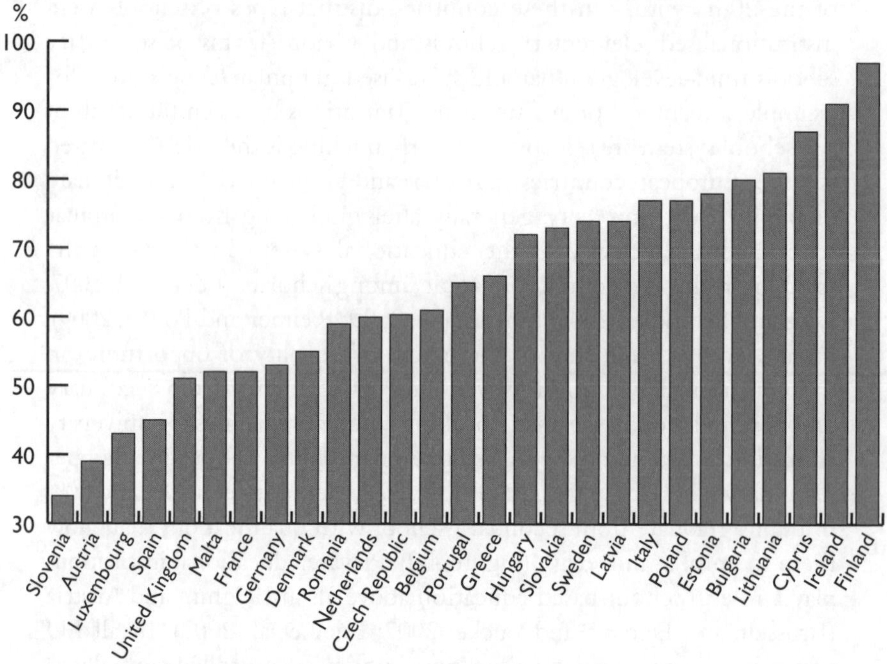

Source: UNESCO (2006, 2009), OECD (2009b), data for 2005–07.

Comprehensive, multi-tracked schools systems

A comprehensive, multi-tracked school system in which the institutionally distinct Secondary Level I is open to all pupils (only in Italy is there a final exam at the end of the primary school, see Brinkmann and Hörner, 2007) can be found in the UK, France, Italy, Greece and Ireland. Elementary schooling in these countries takes five to six years. Thereafter, most pupils continue their education in a comprehensive secondary school, such as the grammar schools in Greece, the *collèges* in France, the *scuole medie* in Italy or the comprehensive schools in the United Kingdom and Ireland (Müller and Kogan, 2010: 223). Private schools play a role above all in the UK and Ireland. An essential feature of the educational systems of countries with a comprehensive, multi-tracked school system is, further, a high degree of coordination of national educational policy. Thus in the United Kingdom and France there is a mandatory, uniform national curriculum, and in Greece the national educational administration supervises the activities of local actors (Green et al, 1999: 79ff; Eurydice,

2009: 53, 73, 77ff). In states with such a school system (France, the UK), at least 50% of pupils achieve the highest school qualification. At the head of this class is Ireland. Here, about 90% of pupils in a given cohort qualify for university admission.

Vocational educational institutions

Vocational training institutions vary across Europe more than do their school-based counterparts (Green et al, 1999: 24; Shavit and Müller, 2000: 34):

> What is counted as vocational education in different countries is quite diverse. Sometimes it is hard to see what the 'vocational'element is. For example, what Italy counts as vocational education has much less practical, workplace based training than Germany's vocational education. There is probably more diversity between countries in the character of vocational education than in any other kind of secondary education. (Müller and Kogan, 2010: 228)

Thus, a schematisation cannot capture all aspects of vocational educational institutions across Europe. What they share, however, is a relationship both to the general school system and to the employment system. To classify these institutions, scholars typically distinguish between dual systems of education and training, school-based vocational education and purely company-based training (Shavit and Müller, 2000; Müller, 2001; Iannelli and Raffe, 2007; Cedefop, 2009; Müller and Kogan, 2010).

In Germany and Denmark, a multi-tracked school system is followed by a standardised system of vocational education and training (a 'dual system'). In France, the Czech Republic, Slovenia, Hungary, Austria, the Netherlands and Portugal, vocational training is structured by institutional arrangements similar to the dual systems of Germany and Denmark (Müller and Kogan, 2010: 229). Other vocational training forms exist in these countries as well, however, such as full-time vocational schools or purely company-based training (Eurydice, 2009: 41ff). The dual system of vocational education and training is closely intertwined with the labour market. The system prepares its graduates to work not in a specific firm, but in an occupational field. This facilitates cross-firm mobility, but makes it more difficult to ascend to higher-skilled positions within a given company.[5]

Dual system of education and training

In Sweden, Finland and France, but also in the Southern and Eastern European states, vocational training takes place primarily within programmes organised within the traditional school setting. Expert opinions diverge on the quality of these programmes. Allmendinger and

School-based training

Hinz (1998, 2009) expect from such a system at most the transmission of basic skills, and criticise the limited degree of standardisation of curricular components. Other scholars (Green et al, 1999: 196f; da Costa et al., 2009: 155ff; Gendron, 2009: 6ff; Masson, 2009: 91f) point to the certification of vocational training degrees. They too see a downside of these programmes vis-à-vis the dual system, though, in that they fail to provide sufficient linkage between praxis-related training in firms and broadly framed knowledge transfer in vocational schools. The coupling of secondary vocational educational systems with the labour market is not well developed. This leads to relatively frequent changes in occupation, especially early in employment careers, for the utility of these degrees is sometimes unclear. Firms thus often employ comprehensive assessment tests or hire new employees only after extended internships.

On-the-job training
The United Kingdom and Ireland constitute examples of a system of on-the-job training. Vocational training here is not organised by an industrial sector via trans-firm cooperation, as in the German dual system, but rather predominantly within a specific company. Some of those who seek vocational secondary educational degrees pursue them in programmes organised within the traditional school setting (eg vocational schools in Ireland) or in youth-training programmes (UK). These systemic features lead to uncertain occupational trajectories due to limited professionalism and the lack of standardisation in training. Moreover, this form of organisation of vocational training renders young people highly bound to one company, and any change in employer entails high adjustment costs – for both the employer and the employee (Allmendinger and Hinz, 1998, 2009; Hillmert, 2002; Breen, 2004; McGinnity and Hillmert, 2004).

Classification of school-based and company-based educational institutions in Europe

Stratification
Allmendinger (1989) proposes a means to systematically distinguish school-based from company-based educational systems. To do so she uses two analytic dimensions: the degree of stratification and the degree of standardisation of educational systems. With regard to the distribution of individual life chances, stratification is of particular importance for school-based education and standardisation is key to company-based training. If the school-based education preceding company-based training is highly selective, then youth of a given birth cohort are not availed of equal training and hence occupational opportunities. Vocational education can be judged by the degree to which it transmits universal skills independent of specific companies (Figure 4.3).

Standardisation

In a country with a highly stratified school system, educational certificates earned in the vocational training system are extremely valuable

Figure 4.3: Classification of educational systems

	Standardised vocational education system	**Unstandardised vocational education system**
Highly stratified school system	e.g. Germany, Austria, Eastern Europe until 1990	e.g. United Kingdom
Less stratified school system	e.g. Denmark, Portugal, Czech Republic, Netherlands	e.g. Sweden, Finland, Spain, Italy, Poland, Hungary, Slovakia, Estonia, Latvia, Lithuania, Slovenia

Source: Based on Verwiebe (2004: 89).

in the labour market. Employers tend to rely on the selection process carried out by the educational system. The system of education and training is closely meshed with the employment sphere. Graduates seldom change occupations and little (intragenerational) mobility is perceptible, for early placement on a specific level of the occupational hierarchy allows for little class mobility later in the life course (Allmendinger and Hinz, 1998, 2009). The best examples of a close coupling of a hierarchically organised labour market and a highly stratified educational system are Austria and Germany.

In countries with unstratified educational systems and hierarchically organised labour markets – for example, the Scandinavian and post-socialist welfare states, Portugal and Spain – the labour market position of individuals is determined less by their level of success in school and vocational training, and more by the employment and hiring policies of employers. The link between education and employment is fairly loose, and job change is common (early in one's career). Mobility beyond class boundaries is not atypical in these countries.

Standardisation of school-based and company-based education has consequences for individual employment trajectories. In standardised systems, vocational educational certificates are extremely valuable; there is a comparatively close fit between open positions and jobseekers, and acquired educational capital (independent of any specific company's processes) tends to be highly useful in the job market. In countries with unstandardised vocational educational systems – for example, the UK, Italy and Poland – educational certificates are less relevant to hiring decisions, and employers have to accept longer on-the-job training periods.

Tertiary educational institutions

Modern tertiary educational institutions in Europe share the educational ideals developed by thinkers like Rousseau and Humboldt at the end of the 18th and beginning of the 19th centuries. Among other things, these consist of academic freedom for faculty and students, the unity of research and teaching, the goal of enlightenment and the primacy of

Educational ideals

pure scholarship (Pritchard, 2004; Nyborn, 2007). On this basis, in most (Western) European countries a dualism has emerged in the tertiary educational sector: on the one hand are universities and other higher educational institutions with a scientifically ambitious orientation and longer periods of study, and on the other hand are polytechnics and comparable institutions (well-known cases are the *Hogschoolen* in the Netherlands, or the *Fachhochschulen* in Austria and Germany), which have a distinctly applied orientation and typically shorter periods of study (Müller, 2001: 232; Müller and Kogan, 2010). This dichotomy of the tertiary educational sector is traditionally common in countries like the United Kingdom, Belgium, the Netherlands, Germany, Austria, Spain and Italy, as well as in most Central and Eastern European accession countries. Exceptions are the Scandinavian countries, which rely more on a comprehensive higher educational system with minimal access barriers. In other countries classical European universities predominate, offering a broad range of disciplines in the natural and human sciences. The educational systems in France and the UK are unique in the European higher educational landscape: in France university education is centrally organised and highly stratified. At the peak of the higher educational system are elite state universities such as the *Ecole Normale Supérieure* in Paris. In the United Kingdom, too, the higher educational system is highly stratified. In contrast to France, however, the elite universities are private. The best-known examples of such institutions are the universities of Oxford and Cambridge.

The Bologna process and the Lisbon strategy have played a major role in the standardisation of universities and polytechnics based on European educational norms (Keeling, 2006; Gornitzka, 2007; Neave and Maassen, 2007). Participation in the Bologna process has been voluntary and open to all signatories of the European Cultural Convention. Building on this process, the European Union launched the more binding Lisbon strategy (Keeling, 2006: 205f.; Allmendinger et al, 2010: 315ff). The goals of its institutional reforms of the tertiary European educational sector are, among others, the creation of a system of comparable degrees, the introduction of a credit point system along the lines of the European Credit Transfer System (ECTS), and the institutionalisation of a two-level system of degrees (undergraduate and graduate) in the university system. The architects of this reform process envision it contributing to the creation of a European Research and Higher Education Area (Keeling, 2006: 214). The latter, reformers hoped, would preserve the competitiveness of European universities in the globalised educational market (Reinalda and Kulesza, 2005: 99; Lefrere, 2007: 202f):

> At the national level, the perception of an emerging international higher education market was increasing towards the turn of the

Dualism of tertiary educational sector

Bologna and Lisbon processes

century, and – anticipating a knowledge society – concerns were growing in many countries of Europe that they could lose in the competition with America's higher education and the brain drain resulting from its attractiveness to many talented young people. (Müller and Kogan, 2010: 237)

In all likelihood, the changes that emerged in the European educational system during the Bologna process will lead to a convergence of higher educational systems across the European Union. Over the medium term, resolutions passed by the European Council in Lisbon in March 2000 can be expected to lead to a restructuring of higher educational systems in Europe as well as to enhanced compatibility among these national systems (Keeling, 2006; Witte, 2006; Neave and Maassen, 2007; Cardoso et al, 2008). It can be expected that the institutional diversity described by Müller (2001: 288, 296ff) in the early 2000s will lessen in the wake of these reforms. However, the Bologna process is a result of many circumstances, forces and actors. And because the process encompasses many countries outside the EU and is influenced by international developments and agencies beyond the EU, its international origins probably lie in globalisation as well as Europeanisation. Future research will show whether the educational systems of the EU Member States indeed become more similar and, if so, in which respects (Müller and Kogan, 2010: 241).

Convergence of higher education

Despite the many good ideas and intentions behind the Bologna reforms, however, both they and their sometimes misguided implementation are viewed critically by many scholars: 'Europe would benefit from reform in the direction of the Anglo-Saxon system of higher education with much more choice, differentiation and competition, but should not throw out the baby with the bathwater' (Jacobs and Ploeg, 2006: 585). Despite – or in part because of – the Bologna reforms, the tertiary educational sector is currently in crisis: 'European higher education seems to be hijacked by inert politicians with visionless and mistaken egalitarian policies, which impose a straightjacket for students and institutions. Central planning and control deny possibilities to reform in response to changing societies' (Jacobs and Ploeg, 2006: 581). In other words, implementation of these reforms would be more successful if done with greater flexibility, that is, by giving greater discretion to those closer to conditions on the ground.

The features of European educational systems sketched earlier, together with the welfare state traditions prevailing in the individual Member States, yield specific forms of financing university education (Figure 4.4). These structure the opportunities for access to tertiary education in the context of students' resources. Two dimensions are important here. The first one depicts the scope and mode of distribution of state support. In

Financing, access to higher education

Europe, one can distinguish between universal funding of all students and targeted support typically for students of lower socio-economic status. The second dimension is the degree of students' financial and legal independence from their parents. At one pole here are countries in which students are completely independent and parents receive no financial support or tax breaks whatsoever. At the other pole are countries in which students are financially and legally dependent on their parents and the latter are completely responsible for the funding of a university education. As a rule, they receive financial assistance from the state (child benefit in Austria, for example, as long as the child is attending university) or tax relief (e.g. in Belgium, France, Portugal and Slovenia).

Figure 4.4: Financing of tertiary education

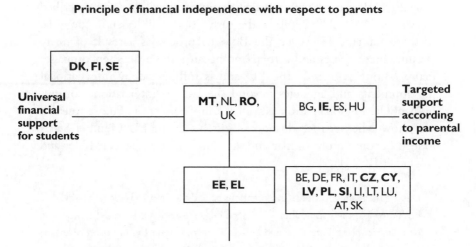

Principle of financial independence with respect to parents

Principle of financial dependence with respect to parents

Source: Eurydice (2007: 17); countries printed in bold have no tuition fees.

Scandinavia: universal state support, low access barriers

Cross-national patterns in the financing and societal regulation of higher educational access coincide empirically with the welfare state regimes described in Section 4.1. In social-democratic welfare states, university students are financially and legally independent of their parents' resources. In these countries, every student receives state support unless they personally receive such a high income that this support is unnecessary. Moreover, up to now at least, there is no university tuition in Scandinavian welfare states (European Commission, 2007b: 17) due to their core principle of unimpeded access to higher education. It can be assumed that such an educational and welfare state policy improves the educational opportunities of young people from educationally and socio-economically disadvantaged families.

In most conservative and post-socialist welfare states (e.g. France, Germany, Austria, Italy, the Slovak Republic, Poland, the Czech Republic, Slovenia), students are typically highly dependent on the financial resources of their parents, while targeted programmes funding students from poor families exist as well (European Commission, 2007b: 16). Corresponding to the systemic logic of conservative and post-socialist welfare states, the parents of students in higher education are supported by direct state aid or tax abatement. Under this model, family allowance is extended and/or tax relief awarded. These provisions generally benefit all parents (see Figure 4.4). In these countries a tuition fee is common, although its level varies. As a rule, grant and loan programmes exist as well, administered either by state authorities or by banks (e.g. Student Loans Company in the UK, BAföG in Germany). Different forms of financing and hence of regulating access to higher education have consequences for the social composition of the student body. Children from lower socio-economic strata must surmount more formidable access barriers (see Chapter 8). Moreover, students from such strata are found to have worse odds of finishing their degree in conservative and post-socialist welfare states than in Scandinavian social-democratic ones (OECD, 2007a: 87).

Access barriers for students from lower socio-economic strata

Between these two poles are countries like the United Kingdom, Malta and the Netherlands. They have universal systems of student loans for which all students are eligible, largely independent of their parents' income. Universities do charge for tuition (European Commission, 2007b: 16). In the UK, this has been the case since the late 1990s, while in the Netherlands, fees were introduced in 1986.

4.3 Systems of industrial relations

DEFINITIONS

Industrial relations encompass the entirety of relations between capital and labour at the firm, sectoral and macroeconomic levels. At these various regulatory levels, distinct actors exist. Within a system of institutions, they negotiate agreements and contracts. The state as mediating and regulatory authority is the third central actor in the system of industrial relations.

The most important instrument for shaping industrial labour relations is the collective bargaining agreement. It determines compensation, working conditions, working hours and procedures for resolution of employer–employee conflicts. The collective bargaining agreement encompasses measures agreed upon by the contractual parties that go beyond standard wage rates, such as no-strike clauses obtaining for the duration of the collective bargaining agreement, guarantees of apprenticeship and employment positions, and regulations governing early retirement and illness. Collective bargaining agreements in Europe are generally negotiated voluntarily by representatives of capital and labour at the firm or branch level (Dell'Aringa and Pagani, 2007; Traxler, 2003a, 2003b).

NOTE ON METHODOLOGY

In this section, we use various indicators to characterise industrial relations in Europe. The scope of collective bargaining agreements is a parameter that depicts the share of workers whose compensation is subject to collective agreements. Strike frequency is given in terms of the number of strike days per thousand employees. Union density measures the number of union members as a share of all employees. The analysis is based on Eurostat data as well as on publications by Carley et al (2007), Visser (2006, 2009) and Ebbinghaus and Visser (1997).

Institutionalised relations between capital and labour

The system of industrial labour relations in Europe is based on institutionalised and statutorily framed relations between capital and labour. This institutionalised interaction can also be understood as a conflictual relationship between societal actors, one characterised by political battles over power and control (Ebbinghaus and Kittel, 2005; Streeck, 2005). At the firm level, they can manifest themselves in opportunities for participation by labour representatives and are thus an expression of the institutionalisation and pacification of class conflicts (see Sections 3.3 and 3.4). Factors impacting on industrial relations are union density and employer association density, the role of the state, the level of intensity of labour conflicts, and forms of conflict resolution in the system of labour relations.

Four levels of industrial relations

Firm level

The divergent interests of employers and employees are reflected at the firm level above all in conflicts over working conditions, working hours, overtime, hiring and firing. To address these conflicts of interest, Austria, Germany and the Netherlands have a system of employees' interest representation: the works council. It gives the employees of an organisation far-reaching rights of co-determination in shaping operational processes. France, Spain, Italy, the UK, Ireland, Finland and Denmark also have works councils or shop stewards, but these typically possess 'only' informational or consultative authority, not far-reaching operational co-determination. In some of these countries (the UK, Ireland, France, Spain), negotiations over compensation also occur at the firm level (Visser, 2005, 2009;

Carley et al, 2007; Dell'Aringa and Pagani, 2007). In the early 1990s, some Central and Eastern European accession countries (Hungary, Slovenia, the Czech Republic, the Slovak Republic, Lithuania, Latvia) institutionalised systems of employee interest representation modelled in part on the German/Austrian model (Kohl and Platzer, 2004; Meardi, 2007). As a rule, these employee representatives possess informational and consultative authority. In Slovenia and Hungary, they also dispose of some co-determination authority – albeit weaker than in Germany – in such matters as occupational safety, working hours and the administration of social services (Neumann, 2002; Feldmann, 2006; Visser, 2009).

Employers' and employees' representatives negotiate with each other above the firm level in order to thrash out agreements covering a given industrial sector concerning compensation, working hours and working conditions. The central instrument for this is the industry-wide collective bargaining agreement or simply the collective agreement (Dell'Aringa and Pagani, 2007). At this societal, national level, the opposing interests of capital and labour articulate their positions in conflicts over political and economic power. This phenomenon is evident, for example, in open alliances between political parties and unions or in candidate endorsements by unions, as are common in France, Italy or Spain due to the traditionally close relationship between parts of the union movement and political parties (van der Meer, 2000; Visser, 2000a, 2000b). In countries like the United Kingdom and Germany, such coalitions are not part of the political culture (Hyman, 2001). In most countries throughout the European Union, the media are used strategically by both camps to pursue their interests (on taxes, wages and working hours). **Sectoral and national level**

A new, fourth level of regulation of negotiation processes between capital and labour has arisen through the process of Europeanisation. The European Works Councils Directive of 1994 made it possible for the first time for workers to organise works councils in firms operating throughout Europe (Council of Europe, 1994; Arrowsmith and Marginson, 2006). The law applies to companies with 1,000 or more employees, of which at least 150 have to be employed in two different EU Member States (Council of Europe, 1994: §3). From every Member State in which the firm employs workers, at least one worker representative is delegated (Council of Europe, 1994: §10). The responsibilities of the firms vis-à-vis these European works councils consist primarily in listening to and informing them (Council of Europe, 1994: §1); there is no mandate for co-determination. **European level, convergence**

Four ideal types of European industrial relations

Within Western Europe, Crouch (1993) identifies multiple ideal types of labour relations between employers and workers. These are historically evolved configurations and evince a 'strong degree of resilience, for they reflect societal cleavages' (Ebbinghaus and Visser, 1997: 338, authors' translation). In the real world, of course, a range of concrete forms of industrial relations exist, which are not fully captured by any one ideal type. We have added to Crouch's classification a fourth, Eastern European, type.

Corporatist/ social-partnership type

In the corporatist/social-partnership ideal type – for Crouch (1993) these are two different types, but for our purposes they are combined – collective bargaining is carried out by well-organised employer organisations and unions. This type is found in Sweden, Finland, Denmark, Austria, Germany, Belgium, the Netherlands and Luxembourg (Ebbinghaus, 2000a, 2000b, 2000c; Kjellberg, 2000). Of the Eastern European reform states, Slovenia and (with some qualifications) the Slovak Republic can be assigned to this type. Negotiations between employer associations and unions are characterised by the search for consensus and are pursued within a framework of social-partnership institutions. As a result, wage demands and firm or sectoral interests are linked to macroeconomic considerations. The state supports this approach in part via the pervasive statutory regulation and institutionalisation of social partnership[6] at the firm and sectoral levels. According to findings from the Employment Protection study of the OECD (Venn, 2009: 8ff), job security in countries of this type ranges from medium (e.g. the Netherlands, Austria, Finland) to very good (Germany, Slovenia). With the exception of Finland, strikes occur in these countries very rarely (see Table 4.3), and collective agreements cover the vast majority of employees (Carley et al, 2007). In the corporatist/social-partnership type, the branch of industry is the most important negotiating arena. In recent years, however, there has been an unmistakable trend towards weakening[7] collective bargaining agreements, while firm-based negotiations have become more common. This development notwithstanding, the corporatist/social-partnership type is generally characterised by strong coordination among the three levels of the firm, sector and macroeconomy.

Conflict- oriented type

In the conflict-oriented ideal type, the relationship between labour and capital is polarised and largely unregulated on the firm level. For this reason, labour often resorts to work stoppages during political showdowns, and state intervention is often necessary to resolve conflicts. This pattern prevails above all in France, Italy, Portugal, Greece and Spain (Naumann and Stoleroff, 2000; van der Meer, 2000; Visser, 2000a, 2000b). The typical cultural and political multiplicity of Latin countries is reflected in the fragmentation of the labour movements there in multiple unions. In the basic conflict-oriented type, there is greater emphasis on firm-level agreements. Occasionally there are also supra–firm, sectoral negotiations between capital and labour. Although union density in this type is comparatively low, strikes are employed in industrial disputes more often than in other European states, which points to the high mobilisation capacity and fighting power of unions there. Corresponding to this is the fact that despite comparatively low union density (see Table 4.3) in countries of the conflict-oriented type, job security there is the highest in Europe (Venn, 2009: 8ff). The scope of collective bargaining agreements (see Figure 4.6) is also very extensive (Carley et al, 2007).

Examples of the pluralistic type are the UK and Ireland (Crouch, 1993; Edwards et al, 1998; Roche, 2000). There, the opposing interests of capital and labour are only partially institutionalised and regulated. Unions and employer associations are fragmented. The various interest groups tend thus to primarily pursue their own particular interests. In the basic pluralistic type, the state stays out of negotiation processes as a rule and relies on voluntary agreements by capital and labour. There the traditional strength of firm-level agreements is still evident (Ebbinghaus and Visser, 1997). On the whole, industrial relations in this type are subject to only minimal state regulation. Strikes are more common there than in most countries of the corporatist/social-partnership type of industrial relations, but less common than in the conflict-oriented type. Job security is tenuous in countries with pluralistic industrial relations (Venn, 2009: 8ff).

Pluralistic type

Figure 4.5: Classification of industrial relations systems

Model	Corporatist, based on partnership	Conflict-oriented	Pluralistic	Post-socialist (liberal)
Dominant regulatory level	Sectors	Mainly businesses, also sectors	Businesses	Mainly businesses, also sectors
Importance of collective agreements	High to very high, branch level	High	Medium	Low to very low
Role of the state	Major	Major	Minor	Relatively major
Job security	Medium to high	High	Low	Very low
Union density	Medium to high	Low	Medium	Very low
Strike frequency	Low	High	Medium	Very low
Examples	Sweden, Denmark, German-speaking countries, Benelux countries, Hungary, Slovakia	France, Italy, Portugal, Greece, Spain	United Kingdom, Ireland	Poland, Estonia, Lithuania, Latvia

**Industrial
relations in
Eastern Europe**

The industrial relations institutions of Central and Eastern Europe are captured only partially by Crouch's (1993) ideal types. It is thus appropriate to assign these countries to a new, post-socialist type conceived for the relationship between capital and labour prevalent there. Ideal-typical representatives of this type are Poland and Estonia; and in a somewhat attenuated form, Latvia, Lithuania and the Czech Republic (Kohl and Platzer, 2004; Meardi, 2007). The post-socialist type differs from all West European societies most significantly in that unions are very weak at all (firm, sectoral and national) levels. This corresponds with much lower union density there. In Poland, Bulgaria or the Baltic states, union density is around 15–20%, and only in Slovenia does it reach a significantly higher level (Visser, 2006, 2009; Carley et al, 2007). Since employer associations are also of marginal significance in this type (Mailand and Due, 2004), only two to three out of ten workers are covered by a collective agreement (Carley et al, 2007). The state, by contrast, plays a comparatively important role (Kohl and Platzer, 2007: 617), similar to the function of the state in the French system of industrial relations. Further features of the post-socialist type of industrial relations are the absence of strikes (see Table 4.3) and very tenuous job security (OECD, 2004; Kohl and Platzer, 2007: 633).

The collective bargaining agreement

The most important instrument for shaping industrial labour relations is the collective bargaining agreement (Traxler, 2003a, 2003b; Dell'Aringa and Pagani, 2007; Traxler and Brandl, 2009). Collective agreements determine directly or indirectly the formal and material employment conditions of two thirds of all Western European workers (Traxler, 2003a, 2003b; Visser, 2006). In the Eastern European accession countries, the share of workers whose working conditions and compensation are governed by collective agreements is markedly lower (with the exceptions of Slovenia and the Slovak Republic) (Kohl and Platzer, 2004; Mailand and Due, 2004; Carley et al, 2007). Collective agreements can apply beyond the individual firm to entire branches of industry. They can also apply just to one company, as is typical in those states that do not have the corporatist/social-partnership type of industrial relations.

**Collective
bargaining
agreement**

As a rule, collective agreements are binding for companies that belong to an employers' association. The vast majority of employees (over 80%) are covered by such agreements in Austria, Belgium, the Netherlands, France, Portugal, Spain, Slovenia and in Scandinavia (Figure 4.6). In the UK and Ireland, on the other hand, only 35% and 45% of workers, respectively, have their compensation, working conditions and hours regulated in this way. In Germany, it is mostly in the old (western) *Länder* that employees' working conditions and compensation are determined by collective agreements. Seventy per cent of workers there are covered by such agreements.

Figure 4.6: Collective bargaining coverage

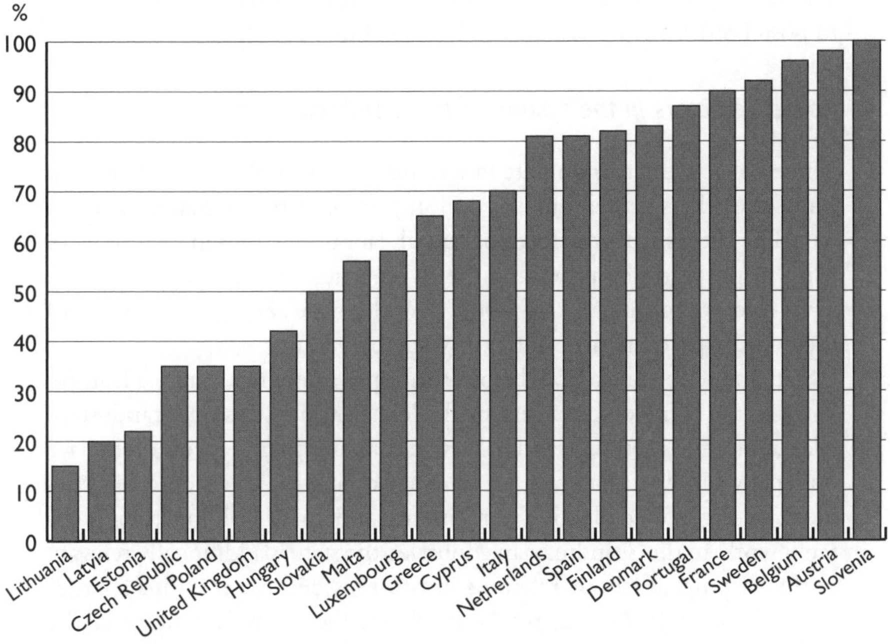

Source: Carley et al (2007); only EU-25 data available (2000 to 2004).

The substance of collective agreements is, as a rule, negotiated voluntarily between the representatives of capital and labour. At times, large differences in interests and power collide. Empirically, since the middle of the 1980s, there has been a tendency throughout Europe to weaken collective bargaining agreements (Katz, 2002: 30; Ebbinghaus and Visser, 1997: 369). Traxler and Brandl (2009: 180f) describe this phenomenon as the '*Americanization* of collective regulation'.[8] Scenarios like these are justified by employers in terms of the need to render these agreements more flexible in response to Europe's high labour costs and resulting competitive disadvantage in global markets (Traxler, 2003b: 207). Employers argue that working conditions should be regulated at the lowest level possible, and that machine run times should be increased and working hours made more flexible. On the company level, employers are increasingly negotiating exit and escape clauses to ensure the requisite flexibility to deal with economic problems, the need to restructure, and so on. This shift in the locus of negotiations between capital and labour towards the firm level (Traxler, 2003a, 2003b; Visser, 2005) points ultimately to a problem constellation, which unions can deny or evade

Downward shift toward firm-level negotiations

only with great difficulty. Collective and industry-wide bargaining agreements presume a similarly high level of prosperity and profitability among all firms in individual branches. With the turn towards a system of flexible accumulation, however, this is less true than it was in the 1960s and 1970s (for a detailed discussion of the transformation from Fordist to post-Fordist flexible accumulation, see Lutz, 1990).

Collective actors in the system of industrial relations

Three collective actors operate in systems of industrial labour relations in Europe: workers' representatives (unions), employers' associations and the state. The latter shapes the form of capital–labour relations in various ways. Most importantly, by providing the two parties with a legal framework in its role as promulgator of labour law, the state serves as guarantor of the conflict partners' autonomy in wage bargaining.

State State influence on capital–labour relations varies greatly across Europe. The United Kingdom is exceptional. Here, the state stays out of industrial relations for the most part, and collective bargaining agreements often have no legally binding character. In all other countries, the state intervenes more strongly in collective agreements and in upholding their legal framework. In the Scandinavian countries, the state is additionally relevant in the shaping of labour relations institutions because it is also a large-scale employer. In Austria, the Netherlands, Germany and Slovenia, the state is also the guarantor of the representation of workers' interests at the firm level. Here, industrial relations laws (or works councils acts) regulate worker participation in co-determination of management decisions. This can assume far-reaching forms and affect issues such as short-time work, overtime work, rationalisation and investment decisions. Additionally, in labour disputes, the state functions as the arbiter of last resort.

Employer Great institutional diversity obtains with regard to the organisation of employer associations across Europe. In the corporatist/social-partnership type of industrial relations, the employer side has an umbrella organisation charged with wage bargaining, lobby associations responsible for economic policy and regional Chambers of Commerce representing the interests of firms in specific geographic areas. Ebbinghaus and Visser (1997: 369) speak here of a functional differentiation and division of labour. In countries of the conflict-oriented, pluralist and post-socialist types, employer associations are active both in wage policy and on a macro-societal level with regard to economic policy issues (Kohl and Platzer, 2004, 2007; Mailand and Due, 2004). In Southern European countries, lines of conflict run between large firms on the one hand, and small and medium-sized enterprises on the other, and these are reflected in the specific organisational forms of employer associations. Moreover, here the regional anchoring of associations is particularly pronounced

(Ebbinghaus and Visser, 1997: 369). In countries like Belgium and the Netherlands, religious affiliation – in part even into the 21st century – structures the institutional landscape of employer representation.

In the system of industrial relations, employers' associations are not only in a conflictual relationship with unions, but also – as one of their core functions – serve to protect their employees via collective bargaining agreements:

Degree of organisation

> Many employees benefit from the protections of collective agreements not because they are members of a union, but because their firm as a member of an employers' association is obligated to abide by the collective agreement. (Ebbinghaus and Visser, 1997: 350, authors' translation)

This pattern is found in Austria, Belgium, the Netherlands, Germany, France and Spain, where a relatively high degree of employer organisation is juxtaposed with moderate-to-weak union density. In Scandinavia, employers and employees are equally well-organised. In countries of the pluralistic type and in the post-socialist countries of Estonia, Latvia and Lithuania (Mailand and Due, 2004: 182) as well as in some countries of the conflict-oriented type (Portugal, Italy), the degree of organisation among employers is fairly weak. This is due, on the one hand, to the fact that large corporations often opt not to be members of employers' associations in order to minimise external influence on their wage and benefits decisions. On the other hand, small- and medium-sized enterprises abound here and, given their often paternalistic ownership and organisational structures, are seldom members of employer associations (Ebbinghaus and Visser, 1997: 369).

Unions as representatives of workers' interests are the third central actor in the system of industrial relations institutions. Unions are particularly influential, traditionally, in manufacturing and public administration (cf. Ebbinghaus and Visser, 2000). In the private service sector they are far less relevant. In the corporatist/social-partnership model, trade union associations are especially important. In the conflict-oriented model – for example, in France, Spain or Greece – unions are traditionally fragmented along confessional and political lines (Ebbinghaus and Visser, 1997; van der Meer, 2000; Visser, 2000a).

Unions

Important parameters of the influence and strength of unions are their density and the size of their membership. Throughout Europe, union density has been declining since the 1970s (Table 4.3). In 2007 in Europe, a little more than one third of workers were organised in unions, on average, compared to nearly 40% union density in the 1970s and 1980s. In countries like Sweden, Denmark and Finland, union density (70%) is very high by European standards and in 2007 was even greater than it had been in the 1970s. Yet here, too, union density declined slightly during the 1990s. These countries are followed by a group of countries in which over 50% of workers are organised in unions (Belgium, Malta and Cyprus) (Visser, 2009).

Table 4.3: Union density and days on strike

	Union membership as percentage of workforce				Average number of days on strike per 1,000 workers				
	1970	1980	1995	2007	1974	1980	1995	2000	2007
EU-15	38	40	30	36	–	–	90	56	39
Belgium	42	54	55	54	187	34	32	8	35
Denmark	60	77	77	68	68	142	81	49	34
Germany	32	35	29	20	41	22	7	0	12
Ireland	53	57	46	35	585	248	128	70	3
Greece	–	39	34	23+	–	–	32	–	–
Spain	–	13	16	15*	809	371	121	233	58
France	22	18	9	8	160	50	291	111	116
Italy	37	50	38	33	998	1564	57	52	47
Luxembourg	47#	52	42§	40*	–	–	60	5	–
Netherlands	37	35	26	21	19	12	122	1	4
Austria	63	57	41	32	1	2	0	1	0
Portugal	–	60	23^	18*	–	–	291	111	116
Finland	51	69	80	71	334	326	547	110	43
Sweden	68	78	83	74	24	164	162	0	3
United Kingdom	45	51	33	29	470	268	18	20	38
Bulgaria	–	–	32§	21*	–	–	–	–	–
Czech Republic	–	–	60	21*	–	–	–	–	–
Estonia	–	–	37$	13	–	–	0	0	0
Cyprus	–	–	71	62	–	–	–	5	110
Latvia	–	–	30	16*	–	–	–	0	0
Lithuania	–	–	40	14*	–	–	–	10	8
Hungary	–	–	45°	18+	–	–	94	55	10
Malta	–	45~	53	57*	–	–	38	32	5
Poland	–	85#	56°	14*	–	–	6	8	19
Romania	–	–	46µ	34*	–	–	34	122	75
Slovenia	–	–	43µ	41	–	–	–	–	–
Slovakia	–	–	55	35*	–	–	0	0	0
EU-27	–	–	–	33	–	–	–	52	36

Source: Strikes: Ebbinghaus and Visser (1997) for 1974 and 1980, Eurostat (2010b) for 1995 to 2007, EU-15 and EU-27 unweighted means for 2007; Union membership: Visser (2009); ^1979, #1981, ~1983, °1993, $1994, §1997, µ1998, *2006, +2005.

An intermediate level of union density can be found today in Ireland, the UK, Austria, Italy and the Slovak Republic. This rate has declined continuously, however, since the 1970s. Especially marked has been the decline within this group in the Netherlands and Austria, where unions have lost roughly half their members. The lowest share of unionised workers is found in post-socialist societies (the Baltic countries, Poland, Hungary) and in countries such as France, Portugal and Spain, where one in twelve and one in six workers, respectively, is organised in a union. A particularly rapid drop in membership has occurred in the Central and Eastern European countries since 1989. Before the fall of the Iron Curtain, the vast majority of the workforce here was union-organised, albeit not always by choice. Union membership has declined unabated in Eastern Europe since then, especially since the mid-1990s (e.g. in Poland and Hungary as well as in the Baltic states).

Five factors have contributed to this decline in membership:

1 The shrinkage of economic sectors such as manufacturing which were traditionally union strongholds has depleted union membership over the past few decades above all in Western Europe. This development has been most salient in large economies such as the United Kingdom, France and Germany (Ebbinghaus and Visser, 1997: 369; McIlroy, 2009: 36).

2 Unions have lost influence in Eastern European states in the course of the post-socialist transformation. In reality, they did not exist as independent representatives of workers' interests prior to 1989.

3 Demographic change (juvenescence) of the workforce has also negatively affected union density, for younger workers are rarely union members.

4 The lifeworld change and establishment of new lifestyles have attenuated the societal cleavages between capital and labour that had been relatively stable over decades. For many workers, having interest representation through unions appears to be decreasingly relevant.

5 A growing discrepancy between the interests of workers on the shop floor and those articulated by trade union associations has further contributed to the workforce turning away from unions.

Decline in membership

The decline in union membership has had less of an impact on the system of industrial relations than one might have expected, however. The assumption that the coverage of collective agreements is directly proportional to union density is only partially true for the system of industrial relations in Europe. In Scandinavia, the UK, Ireland and the post-socialist countries, this relationship does indeed hold. In the Continental European countries, though, the coverage of collective agreements is several times greater than union density (11 times greater in France, five times greater in Portugal and Spain, three times greater in Germany, for example).

Strikes   The second major indicator used to measure union strength is the capacity to mobilise workers for strikes. Work stoppages are the most effective means of pursuing worker interests. The frequency of strikes has developed over time in Europe as follows: between the end of the 1960s and the middle of the 1970s, strikes were widespread in Western Europe (see Table 4.3, columns 6–10). These strikes occurred above all in countries with conflict-oriented or pluralistic industrial relations systems (Spain, Italy, the UK, Ireland). Since the beginning of the 1980s, strikes have become less common. An exception early in this period was the case of Italy, which in 1980 had 1,564 strike days per 1,000 employees. Starting in the 1990s strikes became ever less frequent in Europe, numbering only 39 strike days per 1,000 employees in the EU-15 in 2007. Over the long term, this indicator evinces a clear tendency towards pacification of industrial relations.. When strikes do occur, it is most often in industry. In recent years, though, strikes have increased in the realm of public administration as well. In countries like Ireland, the UK, Spain, France, Italy, Portugal, Hungary and Finland, strikes peaked in the years 1999 to 2001 (Eurostat, 2010b). With regard to the four ideal types of industrial relations, a characteristic North–South divide has emerged in recent years (with the exception of Finland). A decreasing but still comparatively high strike frequency in the Latin countries of the conflict-oriented type is juxtaposed with an intermediate or low strike frequency in the countries of the three other ideal types. In countries like the Slovak Republic, Latvia, Estonia, Sweden, the Netherlands, Austria and Ireland, work stoppages did not lead to lost work days to any appreciable extent in 2007. Denmark, Belgium and the United Kingdom are positioned between these two poles with an intermediate strike frequency

Pacification of conflicts between capital and labour

Decline in strike frequency, convergence   Over the course of the changes sketched here, variation in strike frequency across Europe has declined drastically (1974: SD of 337; 2007: SD of 39). In our view, this can be interpreted as an indicator of the convergence of industrial relations across the European Union, for during this period variation in the indicator 'union membership' has increased only slightly.

Notes

[1] The Gross Domestic Product (GDP) corresponds to the total value of all goods and services produced in a national economy within a year. It can be expressed either as nominal GDP in prices of the year of production, or as real GDP in prices of a base year (adjusted for inflation).

[2] In the case of the UK, however, the welfare state, in contrast to that of the United States, also contains decommodifying elements. The public health care system is responsible for this; despite many deficiencies (poor care, long waiting periods even for life-saving operations), it provides all citizens with free health care.

[3] Examples of this are the pension system in Slovenia and the health insurance system in Bulgaria, which remain universal and redistributive (Cerami, 2006: 108; Fuchs and Offe, 2009: 433).

[4] Due to both the increasing educational participation and resulting expansion of the tertiary educational sector during the last three decades of the 20th century, and the diverse educational policy responses of European governments to the labour-market crisis of the 1980s and 1990s, Müller (2001) comes to the conclusion that the structure of education and training systems in Europe at the outset of the 21st century is more diverse than it was immediately after the Second World War.

[5] Changes in Eastern Europe since 1990 are interesting in this context. Until then, vocational schools comparable to those of the dual system predominated in these countries. In recent years, however, privatisation of the system has allowed a variety of educational institutions to emerge.

[6] Examples of such statutory regulation are, for example, the provisions of the Industrial Relations Law in the Netherlands (*Wet op de ondernemingsraden – WOR*) and in Austria (*Arbeitsverfassungsgeset*).

[7] For years now in Germany employers have been pushing back against collective bargaining agreements, but have succeeded thus far only in the new (Eastern) *Länder*, where only 25% of the workforce is paid based on collective bargaining agreements (Upchurch, 2007). Thus, firm-level bargaining is especially important, whereby employee representatives sometimes take very different positions from those espoused by trade union umbrella associations. In Sweden – the prime example of solidaristic and consensual wage policy – employers quit collective negotiations back in 1991 and called on their members to reach firm-level agreements.

[8] The system of labour relations would dramatically change if the *Americanisation* of collective regulation succeeds. In the US, wage setting is highly decentralised, unions are weak, there is very little coordination and collective agreements set wages for only a small portion of the labour force (Freeman, 2002: 284; Traxler and Brandl, 2009: 181).

5

Population and family

Demographic structures and change is an important field of research on European societies. Key parameters include population development, age distribution, fertility statistics, life expectancy, mortality, the ethnic structure of the population, as well as family forms. Sociological studies of population structures are integral to demographic research, to sociological analyses of the family, as well as to the sociology of ageing. Such studies are of major social relevance, since they raise questions such as those relating to an ageing society, the increase in life expectancy, the fall in the birth rate, changes in the forms of family life and the challenges associated with immigration.

Like political or social structures, the demographic structures of modern societies are the result of human actions. Therborn (2004: 5ff) suggests that there is a connection between processes of social action (ways of life, preferences, lifestyles), social change and demographic parameters. For example, growth and industrialisation tend to accelerate population growth, while war and economic crises tend to thwart it. Changing approaches to marriage, reproduction, death and dying also impact on demographic patterns. Most theories of population development explore this relationship. These theories have their origins in classical political economics, which argued that population development is a function of supply and demand in the labour market. At the turn of the 18th century, drawing on this line of thought, Thomas Malthus (1999 [1798]) published his enduringly influential writings on the theory of populations, in which he argued that unbridled population growth is part of the formation and development of modern industrial societies.

Malthus's theory of population is the classic in the literature. According to him, high birth rates lead to overpopulation, with which agricultural and industrial development cannot keep up. The consequences are famines, crises, wars and epidemics. According to Malthus, such 'checks on population' of unbridled population growth are unavoidable; he based his views on the laws of nature. Social policy interventions designed to counter such crises are ill advised, since the implementation of a welfare state only promotes the tendency to overpopulation (Malthus, 1999 [1798]). In the second half of the 20th century, however, it became clear that key aspects of Malthus's conception were empirically untenable: social policy actually has the opposite effect on population development to that assumed by Malthus; the gainful employment of women or improved rights for women do not lead to a higher birth rate, but instead to lower birth rates; and higher education leads to fewer births, because people plan with more foresight.

Demographic approaches

Currently, the most influential approach to explaining population development is the theory of demographic transition (e.g. Caldwell and Schindlmayr, 2003; Caldwell, 2006). At its core is a multi-phase model of the development of birth and mortality rates, which postulates at a second stage a fall in both rates with the establishment of industrial society. As industrialisation proceeds, population growth falls to a low rate and then levels off, with the birth rate exceeding the mortality rate. According to van de Kaa (1987: 5ff) or Rothenbacher (2005: 20ff), European societies exhibit a remarkable degree of congruence in this phase of demographic transition.

Birth rates fall below mortality rates

As a society moves from the industrial to the post-industrial phase, its birth and mortality rates change. Factors such as increasing affluence, better medical care and shorter working lives have led in the second half of the 20th century to a marked increase in life expectancy in Western societies. At the same time, longer phases of training and (higher) education, changing behaviour patterns in couples' relationships, as well as myriad processes of individualisation have led to a decline in birth rates. In post-industrial society, the birth rate ultimately reaches a point where it falls below the mortality rate (Figure 5.1, phase V). This is known as the second demographic transition (Caldwell and Schindlmayr, 2003; van de Kaa, 1987), and leads to population decline. This explanatory model forms

Figure 5.1: Demographic transition

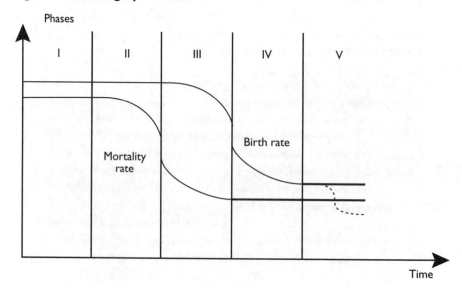

the foundation for contemporary theories of change in demographic structures, which seek to explain this change through economic/ technological progress, rationalisation, urbanisation and suburbanisation, increasing affluence and the expansion of education.

Approaches that are more sociologically oriented take their lead from the idea that generative behaviour (fertility patterns of couples, having children, raising children, etc) is dependent on social context and conditions, such as norms concerning the ideal number of children in a family, the socially legitimated planning of parenthood and the absence of social crises (unemployment, revolutions, upheavals, wars), but is also dependent on personal attitudes and preferences, affiliation with specific social milieus, and one's material situation (Cohen, 2004: 183ff; Cheal, 2008: 5ff).[1] In economic population theories, on the other hand (for a useful overview, see Carlin, 1999; Mason, 2005), individual behaviour in the areas of marriage and reproduction are conceptualised from the perspective of rational choice theory: decisions for or against marriage/ couple formation, or for or against having a child, are understood as the rational weighing of alternatives by social agents seeking to maximise their utility. If the costs associated with birth of a child (loss of the mother's income, less leisure time, financial obligations, making do with less sleep and other problems) outweigh the benefits (feelings of personal happiness, children as a form of old-age insurance, or as future members of the workforce), then the potential desire to have a child will be deferred or simply rejected.

Sociological approaches

Economic approaches

5.1 Structure and age distribution of the population

NOTE ON METHODOLOGY

The population forecasts discussed in this section (figures given are in millions of inhabitants) are based on data from Eurostat on ageing, mortality rates, fertility rates and migration (for an overview of the various methods of forecasting population, see Swanson and Siegel, 2004; Alwin et al, 2006).

In order to illustrate the ageing of the population, we use a ratio between the total number of people over the age of 65 and the number of people aged between 15 and 64, who are generally speaking economically active. The data come from Eurostat.

As of 1 January 2009,. there were 500 million people living in the European Union, 397 million in the EU-15 states, and 103 million in the accession states that joined the EU in 2004 and 2007. With half a billion inhabitants, the European Union has a population that is two thirds larger

500 million people living in the EU in 2009

than that of the US (307 million) and almost 40% of the world's largest population, China (1,340 million inhabitants). The relative weight of the EU-27's population is 7.5% of the world total (1960: 13%). The most populous country in the EU is Germany, with 82 million inhabitants, followed by France, the UK and Italy, each with around 60 million people. Malta, Luxembourg, Cyprus, Estonia and Slovenia have the smallest populations, ranging from 400,000 to two million inhabitants. The average population of an EU Member State is 18.4 million.

Population growth

In the years between 1995 and 2009, the population of the EU increased considerably by 22 million inhabitants, but not all Member States contributed in equal measure to this growth. Most of it has taken place within the EU-15 states, whereas in the states that have only recently joined the EU, the population has stagnated, and in some cases dwindled considerably. The increase in population is especially noticeable in Ireland, Spain, France and the Netherlands. This development can be attributed in the first place to an increase in the birth rate and the growing life expectancy in these countries (see Section 5.2), but also to an increase in immigration (see Section 6.1). The latter is responsible for a marked increase in population in the last 10 years in Ireland and Spain, in particular (Barrett et al, 2006; Fernández and Ortega, 2006; OECD, 2008b). Currently, none of the principal Member States is experiencing a decline in population. Even in Italy, which has an unfavourable age distribution and a low birth rate, the population has increased between 1995 and 2009 by 3.3 million.

Population decline in Eastern Europe

Particularly in the Baltic states, in Romania and in Bulgaria, however, there has been a notable decline in population: between 1995 and 2009, these countries lost between 5% and 10% of their inhabitants. Three factors have led to this development (Cockerham, 1999; Cornia and Paniccia, 2000; Meslé, 2004; Billari, 2005a; Bradatan and Firebaugh, 2007; Kruger and Nesse, 2007): first, the birth rates in these countries are very low; second, they have experienced hardly any immigration but a comparatively high rate of emigration to Western Europe; and third, the mortality rate in these countries, especially among males, increased in the 1990s, which also had a negative effect on population development.

Population growth until 2050

Given these findings, it is interesting to look at projected population development in Europe. Table 5.1 shows the projected population for the period 1995 up to 2050, indicating a decline in population in some countries and an increase in others. Altogether, the population is set to rise by around 15 million by the end of the period in question (EU-27). These increases in the population will only affect Western European societies. There will be an increase in population over this period, in the vicinity of 28 million people, which corresponds to the combined populations of Belgium and the Netherlands. The most marked population growth will occur in France, Belgium, Sweden, Spain, the UK, Ireland and Cyprus.

In recent years, the statistics for these countries have shown an above-average birth rate (see Table 5.2), in some instances a strong increase in immigration numbers (Ireland, the UK, Spain, Cyprus – see Chapter 6), as well as an age distribution with a large proportion of young people and a low proportion of middle-aged people (European Commission, 2007d: 50ff.).

Table 5.1: Population development and forecast

	1995	2005	2009	2020	2030	2040	2050
EU-15	371.9	387.5	396.5	412.0	421.0	425.2	424.6
Belgium	10.1	10.4	10.8	11.3	11.7	12.0	12.2
Denmark	5.2	5.4	5.5	5.7	5.8	5.9	5.9
Germany	81.5	82.5	82.1	81.5	80.2	77.8	74.5
Ireland	3.6	4.1	4.5	5.4	5.9	6.2	6.5
Greece	10.6	11.1	11.3	11.6	11.6	11.6	11.4
Spain	39.3	43.0	45.8	51.1	52.7	53.3	53.2
France	59.3	62.6	64.4	65.6	68.0	69.9	71.0
Italy	56.8	58.5	60.1	61.4	61.9	62.0	61.2
Luxembourg	0.4	0.5	0.5	0.6	0.6	0.7	0.7
Netherlands	15.4	16.3	16.5	16.9	17.2	17.2	16.9
Austria	7.9	8.2	8.4	8.7	9.0	9.1	9.1
Portugal	10.0	10.5	10.6	11.1	11.3	11.5	11.4
Finland	5.1	5.2	5.3	5.5	5.6	5.5	5.4
Sweden	8.8	9.0	9.3	9.9	10.3	10.5	10.7
United Kingdom	57.9	60.1	61.6	65.7	69.2	72.0	74.5
Bulgaria	8.4	7.8	7.6	7.2	6.8	6.3	5.9
Czech Republic	10.3	10.2	10.5	10.5	10.4	10.2	9.9
Estonia	1.4	1.3	1.3	1.3	1.3	1.2	1.2
Cyprus	0.6	0.7	0.8	1.0	1.1	1.2	1.3
Latvia	2.5	2.3	2.3	2.2	2.0	1.9	1.8
Lithuania	3.6	3.4	3.3	3.2	3.1	2.9	2.7
Hungary	10.3	10.1	10.0	9.9	9.7	9.4	9.1
Malta	0.4	0.4	0.4	0.4	0.4	0.4	0.4
Poland	38.6	38.2	38.1	38.0	37.0	35.2	33.3
Romania	22.7	21.7	21.5	20.8	20.0	19.2	18.1
Slovenia	2.0	2.0	2.0	2.1	2.0	2.0	1.9
Slovakia	5.4	5.4	5.4	5.4	5.3	5.1	4.9
EU-27	478.1	491.0	499.8	513.8	519.9	520.1	515.3

Source: Eurostat (2010a), figures represent millions of inhabitants.

However, a decline in population will affect all new Member States in Central and Eastern Europe. According to the most recent predictions of the European Union, Bulgaria, Latvia, Lithuania and Romania will experience dramatic declines, with their respective populations expected to be around 20% smaller in 2050 than in 2009. The population will also continue to fall in the rest of the new Member States in Eastern Europe. As a result of negative birth rates, high mortality rates and emigration, these states will lose some 13 million inhabitants altogether, which is equivalent to the current combined populations of Bulgaria and all three Baltic states. Among Western European societies, only Germany will see its population decline, with eight million fewer inhabitants by 2050.[2]

The ageing of society

A growing number of sociologists (e.g. Bond et al, 1993; Bonoli and Shinkawa, 2005; Baars et al, 2006; Binstock et al, 2006; Johnson et al, 2006; Kohli et al, 2009; Malmberg et al, 2010) are researching the many facets of the ageing of modern societies. Their research shows that the ageing of the population is characterised by, among other things, retirement lived out as a prolonged phase of life, a reduction in the relative significance of the work phase of life, an increasing incidence of people living alone, increasing social inequality in old age and a change in generative relationships (for an excellent overview of the many concepts and theories of ageing, see Bengtson et al, 2009b). Three factors are at the heart of Europe's ageing society (Walker and Maltby, 1997; Bengtson et al, 2006a; Sánchez-Barricarte and Fernández-Carro, 2007): first, in the second half of the 20th century, life expectancy increased significantly; second, in the decades since the baby boom of the 1950s and 1960s, birth rates have fallen noticeably; and, third, the baby boomers are now in the final years of their working lives and will soon leave the workforce. Together with other factors, such as unemployment and changes in the span of the average working life, the age structure of society impacts on the numerical balance between persons not working compared with those in work.

One can sum up the most important elements of the ageing of modern societies in the following manner (Uhlenberg, 2005; Dittmann-Kohli, 2006; Hendricks and Hatch, 2006; Moen and Spencer, 2006; Settersten, 2006):

1   As a result of shorter working lives, retirees are becoming younger and at the same time leading a more active life, also thanks to an – on average – distinctly improved material situation for older people.
2   The majority of older people do not pursue an occupation during their retirement and old age, which, historically speaking, is a new phenomenon in developed societies.
3   Living alone: with increasing age, the number of those who find themselves living alone also increases, which brings with it a number of social problems (isolation and poverty).

This phenomenon can also be described as an individualisation of old age, whereby older people manifest a pronounced desire for social independence.

4 Feminisation of old age: as a rule, women live a healthier life than men, and therefore have a higher life expectancy. In addition, women often marry older men. As a result, the lifestyles of men and women in their old age are quite different. The majority of very old men (80 and older) live as part of a couple, which is not the case with the majority of women in the same age group.

5 Trend towards extreme old age: only a third of those who were born at the end of the 19th century lived long enough to celebrate their 70th birthday, whereas 50% of those born in 1930 lived to the age of 70 or more, and half of those born in 1940 will live until they are 80 or older. In spite of this trend, the reality is that many very old people are faced with health problems and social isolation.

Consequences of the ageing of society

The ageing of the population can be expected to have an effect on many social institutions and areas of society – for example, the health care system (with an increasing number of elderly people in poor health and in need of care), the pension system (a change in the relationship between contributors and pension recipients), the labour market (a shortage of skilled workers) and the housing market (shrinking towns and cities, as well as a change in demand in relation to apartment size, fixtures and overall design). The system encompassing the representation of social interests and the regulative capacities of governments will also change. In 20 years' time, policies unfavourable to the elderly will be barely conceivable (Kohli, 2006b), which raises manifold problems of (intergenerational) social justice (Kohli, 2006a). In addition, ageing societies are faced with the task of adapting numerous aspects of urban infrastructure (streets, sidewalks, public transport). Educational institutions, hospitals and health-care facilities (such as nursing homes) will face new tasks and have to provide new services. Lastly, changes in consumer behaviour will have an impact on what firms can produce and place on the market (Szmigin and Carrigan, 2001: 24ff.). On the level of social stratification, the ageing of society will be accompanied by increasing social and material inequality among the elderly. While it is true that in most (Western) European countries the economic situation of pensioners in the early 21st century is far better than it was even as recently as the 1960s and 1970s, and that it is no longer possible to equate old age with poverty, the proportion of elderly people with low incomes has nevertheless increased.

Measuring the ageing process

In order to quantify the ageing of society empirically, various so-called 'old-age ratios' are employed in the literature, which illustrate the ratio of people of retirement age (65 and older) to those who are of working age. In order to measure the ageing of the population, the European Union uses the relation between the total number of older people, who are generally speaking economically inactive (over 65 years old), and the number of people between the ages of 15 and 64 (Figure 5.2). In 2007, within the core Member States of the EU, this old-age ratio was just on 26, and in the EU as a whole slightly lower. Italy and Germany had the highest proportion of elderly people, with just one third of the population over 65, while Ireland, Romania, Luxemburg, Slovakia and Cyprus had the lowest proportions. All other Western and Eastern European countries lie somewhere in between.

Figure 5.2: Share of population above the age of 65

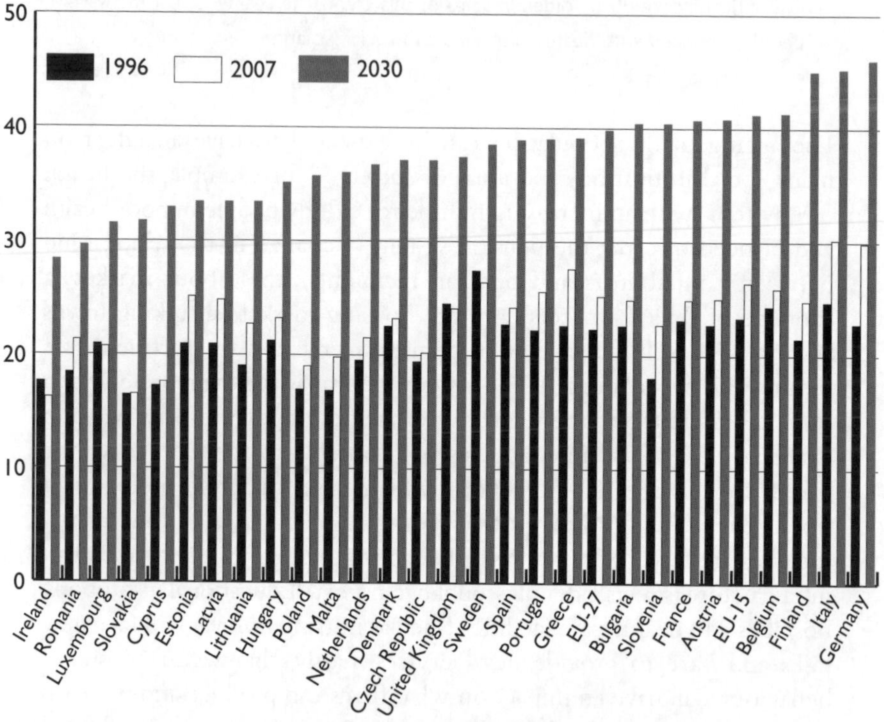

High pace of
ageing process
in Germany,
Slovenia,
Italy, Estonia,
Greece,
Lithuania

European states differ greatly not just with respect to the magnitude of the ageing of society, but also with respect to its pace. If one looks at developments over a period of 11 years (1996–2007), the old-age ratio in the core European states increased by an average of 13% (which corresponds to 3.1 points on the scale in Figure 5.2). During this period, the most pronounced increase in the proportion of those over 65 took place in Germany, Slovenia, Italy, Greece, Estonia and Lithuania, where the old-age ratio rose by between 20% and 31%. Italy can serve to illustrate the quantitative dimensions that underlie these dramatic changes, which, from a demographic perspective, have occurred in a very short period.

An old-age ratio of 24.7 for the year 1996 corresponds to 14.0 million people over the age of 65. By 2007, the number of people over 65 living in Italy had increased to 17.9 million (an old-age ratio of 30.2). In absolute figures – 3.8 million – this increase in the proportion of older people matches the total population of the capital city, Rome.

The situation in Ireland, Sweden, the UK, Luxemburg, Slovakia, Cyprus, Denmark and the Czech Republic looks quite different: these are countries in which one finds a much smaller proportion of people over the age of 65, compared to the numbers of those between 15 and 64. Interestingly, these countries registered either a smaller increase or even a fall in the old-age ratio during the period in question. Between the two groups sit countries like France, the Netherlands, Austria or Hungary, where the proportion of the population over 65 compared to those between 16 and 64 climbed by roughly 10%, and by 15% in the case of Finland, for example.

If one looks at predictions on the ageing of European societies between now and 2030 (Figure 5.2), it is obvious that all EU countries will experience a significant increase in their old-age ratios (the EU-15 countries will climb from 25.9 to 41.2). Europe will at that point exhibit a more adverse age distribution than the US, Canada, Japan or China (European Commission, 2007d: 169). In 2030, the countries most affected within the EU will be the same as in 2007: Germany and Italy will have the highest proportion (old-age ratio above 45), and Ireland the lowest proportion, of economically inactive older people in relation to those of working age.[3] Between these countries, which will retain their current positions in the list, the situation in some nations will worsen, while in others it will improve: Finland, Austria, France and Slovenia, for example, will have a larger proportion of economically inactive inhabitants in 2030 than in 2007. Apart from Ireland, a lower proportion of elderly people (an old-age ratio below 33) is predicted for Romania, Slovakia, Cyprus, Estonia and Lithuania. All in all, Western European countries will exhibit a less favourable age distribution than those of Central and Eastern Europe. As a result of these developments, social security systems – especially in Italy, Finland, Germany and Austria – will be confronted with financing problems even more serious than those they currently face (Walker and Maltby, 1997; Bonoli and Shinkawa, 2005; Schludi, 2005; Arza and Kohli, 2008). In addition, the pronounced ageing of European society is likely to have a negative effect on economic capacity (European Commission, 2007d: 66f): it is by no means unrealistic to expect the Gross National Product of some EU-27 states to stagnate or even decline as a result of the dramatic ageing of the population.

Significant ageing processes in all European countries until 2030

Western Europe: less favourable age structure than Eastern Europe in 2030

5.2 Development of birth and mortality rates

NOTE ON METHODOLOGY ▆▆▆▆▆▆▆▆▆

In this section, the birth rate is presented as the average number of live births per female, using data from Eurostat. It can be assumed that to maintain steady population numbers a birth rate of 2.1 children per female is required. In order to determine the annual birth rates, age-specific fertility figures for females between the ages of 15 and 49 in a given calendar year are considered. Life expectancy at birth is given as the average number of years that a newborn child is predicted to live if the prevailing conditions (at the time of birth) affecting death and dying were to remain in effect for the child's entire life. Life expectancy for a 60-year-old is given as the average number of years that a person of this age can be expected to live if the prevailing conditions affecting death and dying were to remain in effect. Both indicators are based on Eurostat data.

Low fertility in Europe

The birth rate in the Member States of the European Union is very low (see Table 5.2). For around 30 years, it has been below the replacement rate of 2.1 births per female, and during recent years the rate was hovering around 1.5 live births per female (Eurostat, 2010a). By comparison, the birth rate in the US was 2.05, in India 2.72, in China and Australia 1.79 and in Canada 1.58 (CIA, 2009). Unless there is a significant increase in the birth rate in the medium term, then Europe's population can only be stabilised through immigration. Birth rates are markedly higher in Western Europe than in Eastern Europe. In 2008, the highest numbers of births were registered in Ireland, France, the UK, Denmark, Finland and Sweden, with birth rates between 1.84 and 2.1. In Scandinavia and France, the comparatively high birth rates are the result of welfare state policies (above all, providing sufficient numbers of places in childcare facilities), which are designed to promote the compatibility of career and family (Bahle, 2008; Esping–Andersen, 1999). In the liberal welfare states, social norms and attitudes regarding couples with large numbers of children are also responsible for higher birth rates (Esping–Andersen, 1999; Bahle, 2008).

Birth rates are lowest in Eastern Europe

The lowest birth rates were to be found in Slovakia, Poland, Romania and Hungary, where the average number of live births per female was between 1.32 and 1.39, meaning that the birth rates in these Eastern European countries have fallen to 60% of 1990 levels (Eurostat, 2010a). Such a fall in the birth rate cannot be found in any other region of Europe during the same period, and historically and socially there are scarcely any other examples. One can see the causes in political, economic and social upheavals, the emergence of anomie and the often pessimistic outlook of the population (Billari, 2005a, 2005b; Bradatan and Firebaugh, 2007).

In Greece, Spain, Italy, Portugal, Austria and Germany – all countries that can be categorised as conservative welfare states – the birth rates in 2008 were also well below the European average, with rates of between 1.37 and 1.51 live births per female. The reasons for the low birth rates in these countries are to be found in three interrelated spheres. First, the number of women in employment – especially in the Southern European states – has increased significantly in recent years (see Section 7.2); second, there is a shortage of widely affordable childcare facilities (Billari, 2005b: 81ff; Bahle, 2008: 114); and, third, the younger cohorts in the labour market are subject to particularly high risks (a higher

Table 5.2: Fertility rates

	1960	1980	1995	2000	2008
EU-15	2.67	1.72	1.50	–	–
Belgium	2.54	1.68	1.55	1.61	1.72⁻
Denmark	2.57	1.44	1.80	1.77	1.89
Germany	2.37	1.56	1.25	1.38	1.38
Ireland	3.91	3.24	1.84	1.90	2.10
Greece	2.22	2.23	1.32	1.27	1.51
Spain	2.86	2.20	1.18	1.27	1.46
France	2.83	1.88	1.71	1.89	2.00
Italy	2.50	1.64	1.18	1.26	1.37⁻
Luxembourg	2.33	1.49	1.69	1.78	1.61
Netherlands	3.17	1.60	1.53	1.72	1.77
Austria	2.78	1.65	1.42	1.36	1.41
Portugal	3.16	2.25	1.41	1.55	1.37
Finland	2.76	1.63	1.81	1.73	1.85
Sweden	2.25	1.68	1.73	1.55	1.91
United Kingdom	2.86	1.90	1.71	1.64	1.84⁺
Bulgaria	2.31	2.05	1.24	1.27	1.48
Czech Republic	2.11	2.10	1.28	1.14	1.50
Estonia	2.25	2.02	1.32	1.39	1.65
Cyprus	3.47	2.46	2.13	1.64	1.46
Latvia	1.94	2.01	1.26	1.24	1.44
Lithuania	2.57	1.99	1.55	1.39	1.47
Hungary	2.02	1.91	1.58	1.33	1.35
Malta	3.16	1.98	1.83	1.67	1.44
Poland	2.76	2.33	1.61	1.37	1.39
Romania	2.10	2.44	1.34	1.31	1.35
Slovenia	2.25	1.91	1.29	1.26	1.53
Slovakia	2.93	2.31	1.52	1.30	1.32
EU-25	2.23	1.79	1.56	–	1.57

Source: Eurostat (2010a), European Commission (2007d); *2005, ⁺2006; ⁻2007; unweighted means for EU-27 in 2008.

proportion of limited-term contracts or half-time positions, poor pay), which also has negative effects on the behaviour of couples and attitudes towards starting a family (Bernardi and Nazio, 2005: 376f; Kurz et al, 2005: 64ff; Mills et al, 2005: 443ff; Noguera et al, 2005: 401ff). Ultimately, the conservative welfare state runs up against its own, built-in limitations: it is hardly possible to reconcile the principle of familialism (the family is central to welfare and also to child care) with the requirements of modern, service-based societies (the demand for qualified male and female workers) and women's desires to have a career. In that context, a growing number of women, especially in Italy and Germany, decide on principle against having children, which is effecting a profound cultural transformation in those countries.

Convergence of birth rates prior to 1990

The changes in the birth rates in the last five decades are the expression of a definite demographic transformation in Europe (Kiernan, 2004; Council of Europe, 2006; Lutz et al, 2006), which all-in-all amply confirm the assumptions of theoretical models of demographic transition (van de Kaa, 1987; Caldwell and Schindlmayr, 2003). As recently as the 1960s, the fertility rate in the EU-15 countries was roughly 75% above the current rate. In some countries – for example, Austria, Ireland, Spain, Poland, Malta, Portugal, Cyprus and Slovakia – the birth rate in 1960 was actually twice as high as it was in 2008. More recent trends from the period between 1995 and 2008, however, do indicate a slight increase in births in most Western European as well as some Eastern European countries. At the same time, though, there has been no equalisation or alignment of the fertility rates: the standard deviation in the birth rates was equally high in 1995, 2000 and 2008. If one opens the window of observation somewhat wider, however, one discerns a convergence in birth rates – specifically, a decline, which took place in the period between 1960 and 1990, before the fall of the Iron Curtain.

The age at which women have children

Women have children at later age

In Europe, the average age at which women have children is considerably higher than, for example, in the US, Russia or most Asian countries (Casterline, 2001: 21ff; Kohler et al, 2002: 645; Billari, 2005a: 73). At the same time, women do not display a uniform approach to reproductive behaviour. On the contrary: the time of life at which women decide to start a family or have a child varies, depending on social class, educational level, lifestyle, employment status, religion, place of residence or the pertinence of a prolonged adolescence (Giddens, 2009: 337ff).

Differences between East and West

This indicator also reveals major empirical differences between the populations of Western European and Eastern European countries (Figure 5.3). In 2008, the age at which women in Bulgaria, Romania, Lithuania and Latvia had children was comparatively low (between 26 and 28), while in Sweden, Italy, the Netherlands and Ireland the age was quite high (around 31). Situated between these two poles are countries such as the Czech Republic, Belgium and Austria.

Between 1995 and 2008, the age at which women in Europe had children rose by an average of 1.5 years. Here one observes the phenomenon of childbirth being deferred to later stages of life, which, according to the assumptions concerning the second demographic transition, is typical of developed societies (Reher, 2007; Sánchez-Barricarte and Fernández-Carro, 2007). This phenomenon is especially marked in some Central and Eastern European countries, for example in Hungary and Lithuania, where an above-average fall in the birth rate is combined with a pronounced increase in the age at which women have children. In Ireland, the UK, the Netherlands and Finland, one finds only minor increases. As this development proceeds, an equalisation is emerging within the European Union, as is revealed by the standard deviation calculation of this indicator.

Age at which women have children is rising

Figure 5.3: Age of women at child's birth

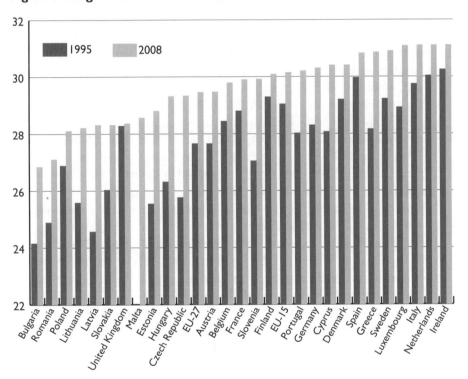

Source: Eurostat (2010a); figures represent years; data from 2008, UK; 2006, Belgium, Sweden and the Netherlands; 2007, EU-15 and EU-27 as unweighted mean value.

Life expectancy

Explanatory
models

Theoretical models of life expectancy and mortality in modern societies can be differentiated according to whether they take a biological, medical, psychological, socio-economic or socio-cultural approach to explaining the data; quite often a multidisciplinary approach is used as well (Bengtson et al, 2006b, 2009a). The early years of population studies were dominated by biological explanations, but since then social-scientific models have come to the fore (Coleman, 2005; Hoffmann, 2008). A central concern of theories of mortality is to make assumptions on the differing life expectancies of men and women, principally using economic, cultural and social arguments (Luy, 2003; Riley, 2005). In this view, for example, shorter working hours, more health-conscious behaviour (less alcohol, fewer cigarettes, more frequent visits to the doctor) and better social integration are seen as the factors that help women to live longer (Bird and Rieker, 2008: 183ff).

High life
expectancy in
Europe

The empirical data show that life expectancy in Europe is very high in comparison to other continents. The average for EU-15 countries for someone born in 2008 was 82.2 years for women and 76.6 years for men.[4] Figures for the US show a somewhat lower life expectancy of 80.6 years for women, and 75.6 for men. In China and India, the two most populous countries on Earth, people have a significantly lower life expectancy at birth: in China, 71.6 for men and 75.5 for women; in India, 67.5 for men and 72.6 for women (CIA, 2009). The gap between Europe and Africa is especially wide, with Africans having a life expectancy that is 30 years lower than that of Europeans (European Commission, 2007d: 54).

Women have
higher life
expectancy
than men

Men in the EU-15 countries have a life expectancy at birth that is, on average, 5.6 years shorter than for women, and in the EU-27 countries it is 6.1 years lower. The sex-specific differences in life expectancy are more pronounced in Eastern Europe than in Western Europe. This is especially so in the Baltic countries, where women have a life expectancy that is more than 10 years longer than that of men. In the mid-1990s, these differences were even greater than they were in 2008. The reasons for the comparatively low life expectancy of men in Eastern Europe lie in their distinctly unhealthy lifestyles (alcohol abuse, smoking – see Section 10.3), a mounting suicide rate, an increase in the number of work-related injuries and traffic accidents, as well as a rise in work-related stress levels and pressure (Cornia and Paniccia, 2000; Meslé, 2004; Kruger and Nesse, 2007).

Convergence of
life expectancies
since mid-1990s

The figures in Table 5.3 also make it clear that the life expectancy of European men and women has risen significantly in recent decades. As recently as the early 1960s, life expectancy for both men and women in the core EU countries was 10 years lower at birth than it is at present. Between 1960 and 2008, the increase in life expectancy in the EU-15 countries was more marked than in the Eastern European accession states, which is an indication of the overall higher standard of living in Western Europe. Between 1995 and 2008, the increase in life expectancy picked up momentum, with the gain for men more rapid than that for women. In the course of this process, life expectancy in Eastern Europe is slowly catching up with Western Europe, as indicated by the gradually diminishing standard deviations (women, 1996: SD of 2.6; 2008: SD of 2.3; men, 1996: SD of 4.2; 2008: SD of 4.0). At the same time, however, it is also clear that between the 1960s and 1980s, life expectancy for men in Europe varied less noticeably than it did in the 1990s. This was caused by the decrease in life expectancy in the early 1990s as a result of the major transformations that were taking place in a number of Eastern European states.

Table 5.3: Life expectancy at birth

	Women					Men				
	1960	1980	1996	2000	2008	1960	1980	1996	2000	2008
EU-15	73.2	77.7	80.6[+]	81.4	82.2*	67.6	71.0	74.2[+]	75.4	76.6*
Belgium	73.5	76.5	80.7	81.0	82.6[#]	67.7	69.9	73.9	74.6	77.1[#]
Denmark	74.4	77.2	78.4	79.2	81.0	70.4	71.2	73.1	74.5	76.5
Germany	72.4	76.1	80.1	81.2	82.7	66.9	69.6	73.6	75.1	77.6
Ireland	71.9	75.6	78.7	79.2	82.3	68.1	70.1	73.1	74.0	77.5
Greece	72.4	76.6	80.2	80.6	82.4	67.3	72.2	75.1	75.5	77.7
Spain	72.2	78.2	82.0	82.9	84.3	67.4	72.2	74.5	75.8	78.0
France	73.6	78.3	79.8[+]	83.0	84.9[#]	66.9	70.2	73.9[+]	75.3	77.8[#]
Italy	72.3	77.2	81.8	82.8	84.2[#]	67.2	70.6	75.4	76.9	78.7[#]
Luxembourg	72.2	75.4	80.2	81.3	83.1	66.5	70.3	73.3	74.6	78.1
Netherlands	75.3	79.1	80.5	80.7	82.5	71.5	72.5	74.7	75.6	78.4
Austria	72.7	76.0	80.2	81.2	83.3	66.2	69.0	73.7	75.2	77.8
Portugal	66.8	74.9	79.0	80.2	82.4	61.2	68.0	71.6	73.2	76.2
Finland	72.5	77.8	80.7	81.2	83.3	65.5	69.3	73.1	74.2	76.5
Sweden	75.4	78.8	81.7	82.0	83.3	71.5	72.8	76.6	77.4	79.2
United Kingdom	73.7	76.9	79.5	80.3	81.8[#]	67.9	70.8	74.3	75.5	77.7[#]
Bulgaria	72.2	73.8	74.5	75.0	77.0	68.5	68.4	67.4	68.4	69.8
Czech Republic	73.4	73.9	77.5	78.5	80.5	67.5	66.8	70.4	71.7	74.1
Estonia	71.6	74.1	75.6	76.2	79.5	64.3	64.1	64.2	65.2	68.7
Cyprus	–	77.0	80.0	80.1	83.1	–	72.3	75.3	75.4	78.5
Latvia	73.1	73.9	73.1[+]	76.2	77.8	66.1	63.6	60.3[+]	64.9	67.0
Lithuania	77.1	75.4	75.9	77.5	77.6	66.6	65.4	64.6	66.8	66.3
Hungary	70.8	72.7	75.0	76.2	78.3	66.4	65.5	66.3	67.6	70.0
Malta	70.7	72.7	79.6	80.3	82.3	67.1	68.5	74.8	76.2	77.1
Poland	71.0	74.4	76.6	78.0	80.0	65.1	66.0	68.1	69.6	71.3
Romania	69.1	71.8	72.8	74.8	77.2	65.1	66.6	65.1	67.7	69.7
Slovenia	72.0	75.2	79.0	80.0	82.6	65.6	67.3	71.1	72.2	75.5
Slovakia	73.0	74.3	77.0	77.5	79.0	68.4	66.8	68.9	69.2	70.9
EU-27	73.0	77.2	79.7[+]	80.8	82.2[#]	67.3	70.3	72.8[+]	74.4	76.1[#]

Source: Eurostat (2010a), [#]2007, *2006, [+]1995.

As a result of developments in prosperity and the modernisation of European societies, the life expectancy of older people has also risen considerably in recent decades. More so than with middle-aged or younger cohorts, the major factor in this instance is the medical and technological progress made in combating heart disease and cancer (Land and Yang, 2006: 43). Data from 2008 show in the first instance that 60-year-old women have longer to live than men of the same age (Figure 5.4). Statistically speaking, women in Bulgaria, Romania, Latvia, Slovakia and Hungary had the lowest remaining life expectancy (between 20.5 and 22.0 years), whereas women in Austria, Finland, Italy, Spain and France had the highest (25.5 to 27.5 years). For 60-year-old men, the outlook was worst in the Baltic countries, with an average of about 16 years of life remaining. In Spain, Sweden, Cyprus, Italy and France, 60-year-old men could expect to live a further 22 years. Positioned between these two groups one finds, for example, the Netherlands, the UK and Germany. The greatest sex-specific differences for this indicator are to be found in Poland, Hungary, Latvia, Slovenia, Lithuania and Estonia, where a 60-year-old woman can expect to live five to seven years longer than a man of the same age. In Sweden, Denmark, the UK, Cyprus and Greece, the differences in life expectancy for men and women at 60 are the lowest (two to three years).

Figure 5.4: Life expectancy at age 60

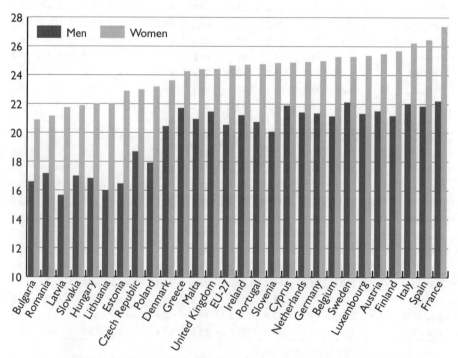

Source: Eurostat (2010a); data for EU-27 from 2006, data for France, Italy, UK, Belgium from 2007, other data from 2008.

Against the background of the findings sketched out in this section, and given the limits of our current knowledge, it is difficult to give a clear-cut answer to the question of to what extent life expectancy in Europe will continue to climb. Increasing environmental pollution, mounting stress in many areas of life, the rising intensity of work and the growing insistence on flexibility all tend to suggest that life expectancy is unlikely to go on climbing. On the other hand, improved medical care and a more health-conscious lifestyle (a healthy diet) among, for example, the European middle classes do point to a further increase in life expectancy. In addition, the increase in life expectancy has tended in the past to be underestimated rather than overestimated. For example, Murray and Lopez's (1997: 1499) forecasts for life expectancy in the year 2020 were already exceeded in 2008 for both men and women in the EU-15 countries.

5.3 Family structures

NOTE ON METHODOLOGY

In this section, the marriage rate will be employed in a twofold fashion. On the one hand, using data from the European Council, it will be given as the index of the frequency of first marriages among single women under 50, per 100 women. The index will be established from the sum of marriage rates typical of a given age group per calendar year. A value of more than 1.0 indicates a shift towards first marriages at a young age (an above-average number of very young people get married) or a concentration of marriages in a specific year. Very low values indicate deferral of first marriages. On the other hand, using Eurostat data, the marriage rate will be given as the so-called 'crude marriage rate', in other words as the ratio of the number of marriages to the average population (per 1,000 people) in a calendar year. The age at which people marry will be operationalised using the average age of women at the time of their first marriage.

Divorce rates within the EU will be given as a total divorce rate, meaning the proportion of the number of marriages celebrated in year *n* that end in divorce over the total number of marriages celebrated in year *n* (Council of Europe, 2006).

The number of children born outside of marriage will be given as the percentage of such births per 100 live births. The number of one-person households is measured as the proportion of the total population living in such households. These indicators are based on data from the Council of Europe (2006) or from Eurostat.

Families are the locus of the biological and social reproduction of our society. They are an integral part of the social structure, and shape the lives of individuals in manifold ways. Sociological research on families has as its object the economic, political, social and cultural factors that

Families as the locus of reproduction

influence whether, and at what stage of their lives, individuals start a family, how they configure their family life, and what effects all these factors have on their life courses (Giddens, 2009: 338; Schaefer, 2008: 199). These processes, which ultimately are centred around extremely different forms of establishing, fostering and dissolving parent–child relationships, have manifold social-structural consequences: the ways in which they are emotionally, socially, culturally and materially embedded in family structures shape children for life. Thus, families also reflect and reproduce structures of social inequality in many ways (Cohen, 2004: 182ff).

Theories on family can be categorised into four different groups (compare Bernardes, 1997: 37ff; Schaefer, 2007: 299ff; 2008: 203ff; Giddens, 2009: 369ff). Functionalist approaches emphasise that the family satisfies the needs of its members (e.g. companionship, love, protection) and contributes to societal stability via its reproduction and socialisation function (Parsons and Bales, 1956). Conflict theories, mostly but not always stemming from a Marxist tradition (Engels, 1962 [1884]), see the family as a quasi-economic system in which typical, hierarchical forms of production, consumption and distribution of resources can be found. Family is viewed as reflecting the inequality of means and power that is found within the larger society. The unequal status of women in society is the starting point for feminist theories on the family. They identify family-based households as an important locus of the reproduction of gender roles and male domination in society. Interactionist approaches focus on the many forms of social exchange and relationships between family members.

Familial processes impact social structures

Access to educational and employment market opportunities is predetermined within the family. In addition, in European families, resources are increasingly passed on through inheritance, which leads to a further accentuation of inequalities. Lastly, the number of children in a household has substantial consequences for the financial and material prosperity of the family. In Western Europe at present one has to spend approximately '150,000 Euros to bring a child to the age of maturity. On top of that there are the costs of vocational training or university studies, as well as lower income from employment, which especially affects mothers, since the child-care situation leaves them with less time for paid employment. Starting a family increases the risk of poverty' (Szydlik, 2007: 78, authors' translation). Clearly, women's chances in the employment market are worsened by childbirth and raising children (Coltrane, 2000).

Transformation of family structures

Since the 1970s, social and economic developments, in conjunction with changes in social values, have brought about a significant transformation of family structures (for historical background on these changes, see Section 3.2). Worthy of mention are, among other developments, lengthier apprenticeships and traineeships, a stronger career orientation among women, an intensification of demands in the world of work, urbanisation and suburbanisation. As a result, the traditional (Christian) middle-class family model, which stipulated a clear interlocking of romantic love, sexuality, cohabitation and having children within the framework of a specific way of life, namely marriage (Coltrane, 1998: 44ff; Turner, 2004: 296), was joined by a whole array of new forms of family life. The spectrum ranges from a growing number of single parents, unmarried couples with children, same-sex couples (with and without a marriage certificate), to patchwork families and so-called DINKS[5] (Coltrane, 2000; Therborn, 2004). Thus, the pessimistic predictions regarding the crisis and even demise of the family, which have been issued for decades now, appear to be unfounded. It is more plausible, according to Giddens (2009: 360ff) or Beck and Beck-Gernsheim (2004: 504ff), to talk in terms of a transformation of family structures, of an adaptation to societies that are in the process of modernising themselves. Given the increased economic pressure, it is amazing just how capable and resourceful family structures and resources have remained.

A number of these transformations in family forms are common to all European states, but there are also certain ongoing differences, depending, for example, on the degree of modernisation, the extent of processes of social transformation or the persistence of cultural and religious norms (Kiernan, 2004; Haavio-Mannila and Rotkirch, 2010). As empirical indicators of these commonalities and differences, researchers refer to the (growing) proportion of single-person households, single parents and patchwork families, the (shrinking) size of families, prolonged adolescence in metropolitan milieus, the deferral of marriage and having children, the (rising) number of divorces, the (increasing) number of births outside marriage, the return of multi-generation households, or the 'new' rejection of pre-marital cohabitation on the part of young people. In what follows, we illustrate some of these changes in family structures, using the available data. Against the background of the population as a whole, we also specifically discuss the situation of marriage, births outside marriage, and divorce rates as well as the proportion of single-person households, unmarried couples and families with three or more children.

Marriages and the proportion of births outside marriage

The number of marriages in relation to the total population in the EU-27 countries is currently 4.9 (EU-15: 4.6) per 1,000 inhabitants (Table 5.4, middle column). People in Romania, Cyprus, Denmark, Lithuania and Poland are most likely to marry, with a rate of about seven marriages per 1,000 in 2008. Comparatively few marriages (a rate between 3.2 and 4.1) were registered in Slovenia, Bulgaria, Portugal and Italy.

Combined marriage rate

Low first marriage rates in Eastern Europe

If one goes beyond this relatively crude indicator, the rate of first marriages allows one to account for the divergent marriage rates of different age groups and the age distribution of a given society[6] (Table 5.4, columns 2–5). First of all, one sees that in Europe the probability of a first marriage for women has declined in recent decades. In principle, as recently as 1960, the first marriage rate for women was at 100%. In 2004, this only applied to some 60% of women. In Eastern European countries such as Slovenia, Hungary, Estonia or Latvia, the rate of first marriages is low (between 41% and 46%) – far lower than Sweden (56%), which used to lead the way in Europe with ways of life that do not involve marriage. According to Höpflinger and Fux (2007: 60), the low rates of first marriages in Eastern Europe are not primarily the result of an increasing share of unmarried couples living together, but rather the result of deferring first marriages until later in life, a phenomenon linked with social and economic upheavals. In the case of Latvia, Estonia or the Czech Republic, the comparatively high crude marriage rates tend to support this conclusion. In Slovenia, however, this explanation is less plausible, since in this case one finds a very low first marriage rate as well as a very low crude marriage rate – which may indicate a deinstitutionalisation of marriage (Ule, 2004).

High first marriage rates in Southern Europe, Finland, Denmark

High first marriage rates of 60% and more are to be found in Catholic or Orthodox countries, as well as in Denmark and Finland. In Romania, Lithuania, Cyprus,[7] Malta, Greece, Denmark and Finland, the high likelihood of a first marriage also corresponds with a – by European standards – high overall marriage rate (per 1,000 inhabitants). In these countries, the classical model of marriage remains very popular, and other ways of life (cohabiting as an unmarried couple) outside the traditional model of the family are less prevalent (cf. Figure 5.6). Denmark and Finland are somewhat special cases, however: as early as the 1970s and 1980s (in common with Sweden), cohabiting as an unmarried couple was more popular there than in other European countries (Höpflinger and Fux, 2007: 58). An explanation for the current high marriage rates could be the high frequency of divorce (see Table 5.5) and the high incidence of second marriages, since, at the beginning of the 21st century, single-person households and ways of life not involving marriage are also generally very widespread.

Marriages on the decline

The developments displayed in Table 5.4 make it clear that, since the beginning of the 1980s, the number of first marriages has been declining. Only in Denmark, Sweden and Finland has the number of women marrying for the first time increased. In all other countries, the rate of first marriages has fallen; in the Baltic states, the Czech Republic and Slovakia it has even fallen by some 50%. This decline in the percentage of first marriages, above all in Eastern Europe, lends credence to the assumption that the deferral of marriage is conditioned by socio-political transformation and upheaval. Furthermore, if one leaves aside the special case of Cyprus, an alignment or equalisation of first marriage rates can be discerned within the EU–27 states (1980: SD of 13.3; 1990: SD of 10.6; 2004: SD of 10.0).

Table 5.4: Marriage rates and women's age at first marriage

	Rate of first marriages per 100 unmarried women				Rate per 1000 persons	Women's age at first marriage			
	1960	1980	1995	2004	2008	1960	1980	1995	2004
EU-15	0.99	0.72	0.59	0.58	4.6⁺	24.2	23.6	26.7	28.4
Belgium	1.05	0.77	0.57	0.46	4.4	22.8	22.2	25.4	27.1
Denmark	1.01	0.53	0.65	0.75	6.8	22.8	24.6	29.0	30.4
Germany	1.06	0.69	0.56	0.55	4.6	23.5	22.9	26.4	28.4
Ireland	0.98	0.83	0.59	–	5.2*	26.9	24.6	27.9	–
Greece	0.79	0.87	0.75	0.68	4.6	24.6	23.3	25.7	27.5
Spain	1.00	0.76	0.60	0.58	4.5*	26.0	23.4	26.8	28.6
France	1.03	0.71	0.50	0.53	4.3	23.0	23.0	26.9	28.5
Italy	0.98	0.78	0.63	0.60	4.1	24.8	23.8	26.6	28.0
Luxembourg	–	0.66	0.56	0.50	3.9	–	23.0	26.6	28.1
Netherlands	1.05	0.68	0.53	0.51	4.6	24.2	23.2	27.1	28.7
Austria	1.03	0.68	0.57	0.59	4.2	24.0	23.2	26.1	27.9
Portugal	0.94	0.89	0.78	0.57	4.1	24.8	23.2	24.7	26.3
Finland	0.96	0.67	0.57	0.68	5.8	23.8	24.3	27.0	29.0
Sweden	0.95	0.53	0.44	0.56	5.5	24.0	26.0	28.7	30.7
United Kingdom	1.04	0.76	0.54	0.55	4.4*	23.3	23.0	26.2	28.1
Bulgaria	1.05	0.97	0.55	0.68	3.6	21.3	21.3	22.6	25.6
Czech Republic	1.04	0.90	0.50	0.48	5.0	22.0	21.5	22.7	26.0
Estonia	0.96	0.67	0.45	0.44	4.6	–	22.6	23.5	25.7
Cyprus	–	0.78	1.21	1.58	7.5*	–	23.3	25.2	27.5
Latvia	–	0.97	0.47	0.46	5.7	–	22.8	22.9	25.1
Lithuania	–	0.94	0.70	0.62	7.2	–	23.0	22.3	24.7
Hungary	0.99	0.89	0.56	0.45	4.0	22.0	21.2	22.9	26.2
Malta	–	–	0.89	0.76	6.0	–	24.7	25.4	26.5
Poland	–	0.90	0.67	0.57	6.8	–	22.7	23.1	24.9
Romania	1.15	1.02	0.73	0.74	7.0	22.1	21.5	22.7	24.1
Slovenia	–	0.79	0.51	0.41	3.1	–	22.5	25.1	27.8
Slovakia	1.03	0.87	0.58	0.56	5.2	22.1	21.9	22.6	25.0
EU-27	1.00	0.79	0.62	0.61	4.9*	23.6	23.1	25.6	27.2

Source: Eurostat (2010a), Council of Europe (2006); data from 2008; ⁺2006; *2007.

If one looks at the age at which women first marry (Table 5.4, right-hand side), clear differences between Eastern and Western Europe can be discerned. Women in Eastern Europe marry at a considerably younger age than their counterparts in the West. In 2004, women in Romania,

Average age at marriage high in Western Europe

Lithuania and Poland, for example, married on average between the ages of 24 and 25, whereas in Sweden and Denmark, most women did not marry until they were over 30. In addition, in all European states in recent decades there has been an increase in the age at which people first marry, which provides additional support for the thesis of a structural change in family relationships in Europe (Kiernan, 2004; Therborn, 2004). A particularly clear increase in the age at which people marry is to be found in some of the Eastern European accession states. The smallest increase in the age at which women first marry is found in Ireland, Germany and Italy. Calculating the standard deviation of the age at which people marry indicates, moreover, that the differences within Europe have become larger, although with a slight downward trend in the 1990s (1980: SD of 1.12; 1995: SD of 2.02; 2004: SD of 1.75).

Increase of births outside marriage in Eastern Europe

In accordance with our findings hitherto, the proportion of children born outside marriage is also climbing (Figure 5.5). The largest increases are to be found in Eastern and Southern European countries, where in the period from the 1960s to the 1980s the proportion of births outside marriage was still very low (e.g. 1980: 7% in Hungary; 3.9% in Spain). Along with Hungary and Spain, other examples include Bulgaria, Lithuania, Cyprus and Romania: here the proportion of all live births that

Figure 5.5: Births outside marriage

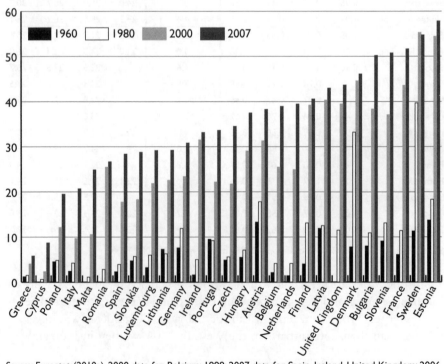

Source: Eurostat (2010a), 2000 data for Belgium: 1999; 2007 data for Spain, Ireland, United Kingdom: 2006.

occur outside of marriage has increased by a factor of between four and ten. Below-average increases are found in countries such as Sweden and Denmark, where the proportion of births outside marriage is very high anyway. In Sweden in 2007, for example, 55% of all births were registered as births outside marriage. In the early 1980s, this proportion already stood at around 40%. Over the course of these changes, however, there are no discernible converging tendencies (1980: SD of 9.1; 1995: SD of 14.0; 2007: SD of 13.0). On the contrary: there is no sign of a lessening in the differences (which have existed for decades) between Southern European and Eastern European Catholic countries on the one hand, and Northern and Continental European countries on the other hand; the latter group having a very high proportion of births outside marriage, ranging from 44% in the UK to 55% in Sweden in 2007. Cyprus, Greece, Italy and Poland are typical of the first group of countries, where only a small number of children are born outside marriage at the beginning of the 21st century.[8]

North–South and East–West differences remain

Divorce

High divorce rates

The divorce rate in Europe is also high, and can be seen as a further indication of the structural change in family relations: the figures show that, in the EU-27 countries in 2008, the total divorce rate is at 42 (Table 5.5), displaying the proportion of marriages ending in divorce over the total number of marriages celebrated in that year (Council of Europe, 2006). It is also the case that the frequency of divorce within Europe varies considerably, as Wagner and Weiß (2006) have shown in their comprehensive analyses, which sum up a whole series of studies. There is, however, no clear-cut line of separation on this front between the core Member States of the EU and the Central and Eastern European accession states. One does find, though, a difference between, on the one hand, Catholic and Orthodox countries mostly in Southern and Eastern Europe (Italy, Greece, Spain, Romania, Poland, Ireland) and Northern and Central European states on the other hand (for example, Belgium, Estonia, Hungary, the Czech Republic, Austria, Sweden, France, the UK). In the former group, one finds a comparatively low total divorce rate per 100 marriages (between 15% and 25% in 2008), with marriage as a way of life continuing to occupy a central place. In the latter group, more than half of all marriages end in divorce, and in the majority of these countries divorce is often followed by a second marriage (Höpflinger and Fux, 2007: 70). In addition, in Sweden, France and Austria, substantial welfare assistance is provided by the state for single parents, as a safeguard against the risk of poverty, which also serves to make divorce an easier option. And lastly, cultural factors are important: in those countries in which it is prevalent, divorce is much more socially acceptable than it is in Catholic and Orthodox countries in Southern and Eastern Europe (Höpflinger and Fux, 2007: 70; Huinink and Konietzka, 2007: 82).

Transformation
of partnership
model

In addition, one notices that the frequency of divorce has increased quite dramatically over the course of time. Huinink and Konietzka (2007: 81ff) conjecture that this need not lead directly to the conclusion that the institution of marriage is losing importance, since many divorces

Table 5.5: Divorce rates

	Divorces per 100 marriages				
	1960	1980	1990	2000	2008
EU-15	10	27	29	37	44
Austria	14	29	36	50	57*
Belgium	7	22	31	60	78
Germany	11	28	30	46	51*
Denmark	19	51	44	37	39
Spain	–	–	11	17	–
Finland	11	32	53	53	43
France	10	22	–	38	51#
Greece	4	11	10	23	21*
Ireland	–	–	–	14	15*
Italy	–	4	9	13	21
Luxembourg	7	27	33	48	51
Netherlands	6	29	30	39	42
Portugal	1	8	13	30	–
Sweden	18	53	48	54	53
United Kingdom	–	35	41	51	53*
Bulgaria	10¯	19	19	30	51
Cyprus	–	4	6	12	28*
Czech Republic	17	35	35	54	60
Estonia	21	50	49	77	50
Hungary	19	35	37	50	–
Lithuania	8	38	35	64	43
Latvia	22	51	46	67	48
Malta	–	–	–	–	–
Poland	6	13	17	20	25
Romania	19	19	17	23	24
Slovenia	11	19	22	30	34
Slovakia	7	17	22	36	45
EU-27	–	22	26	35	42+

Source: Eurostat (2010a), own calculations; *2007; #2006; +2005, ¯based on Council of Europe (2006: 75); means for EU-15 not adjusted for size of population; divorces are not legal in Malta, they became legal in Italy in 1970, in Spain in 1981 and in Ireland in 1997.

are followed by a further marriage, and the subjective significance of marriage and divorce cannot be assessed on the basis of these data alone. We believe, however, that the presented findings indicate an overall deinstitutionalisation of marriage as a lifelong bond and as a dominant mode of family life: when one compares a 10% total divorce rate in 1960 to a rate of 51% in 2008, as is the case for France, then we consider it legitimate to view this as a profound social and cultural change. This change in the model of marriage and the family in Europe, however, does not mean that relationships between couples in general are in jeopardy. In place of an institutionalised model of marriage and the family, one finds a partnership model. To the extent that mutual love and understanding can be considered as forming the basis of the modern relationship between couples, the disappearance of this emotional-affective basis implies the fundamental possibility of ending the relationship (Höpflinger and Fux, 2007: 69).

If one looks at the changes that took place over the course of the first sustained data-gathering between 1980 and 2008, the increase in the number of divorces in the Catholic countries of Central and Southern Europe (for example, France, Italy, Portugal and Cyprus) stands out clearly. Against the general trend, there are also some European states in which the divorce rate has risen only slightly or has even decreased in recent decades – the Baltic states, for instance, which, interestingly, displayed consistently high divorce rates over the period in question (cf. Eglite, 2004; Haavio-Mannila and Rotkirch, 2010). However, if one calculates the standard deviation in divorce rates, one notices no or only very slight tendencies in the direction of equalisation for this indicator in Europe between 1980 and 2008 even though the divorce patterns in Catholic countries changed as much as they did during the last 30 years.

Increase in divorces in Catholic countries

Forms of the family

One consequence of the decrease in the number of marriages and the increase in divorces is a larger number of people living in single-person households: the European average is one out of every seven inhabitants. There are clear differences in this regard between Northern and Central European countries on the one hand, and the Central and Eastern European accession states, as well as countries such as Spain and Portugal, on the other (Figure 5.6). In Sweden, Germany, Finland, the Netherlands and France, an especially high proportion of the population lives alone. By contrast, in Southern European countries, such as Portugal or Spain, as well as the accession states of Cyprus, Malta and Slovakia, only one out of every 17 people lives in a single-person household. In countries such as Italy or the Czech Republic, the number of people living alone lies between these two poles.

Single households and cohabiting couples

Figure 5.6: Single households, cohabiting persons, households with three or more children

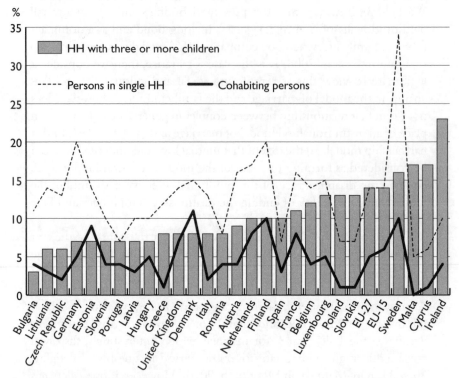

Source: Eurostat (2007b, 2008, 2010a).

There are also clear differences between countries with respect to the prevalence of couples cohabiting outside of marriage: one finds a very high proportion of such couples in Scandinavia, Estonia, the Netherlands and France, and a very low proportion in Eastern and Southern Europe, examples here being Catholic or Orthodox countries, such as Malta, Cyprus, Poland, Slovakia, Spain, Greece and Italy, where between 1% and 3% of the population have opted for this particular way of life. Between these two poles lie states such as Hungary and Germany, where unmarried couples make up 5% of the population.

Families with three or more children

In Europe, the increasing incidence of single-person households and unmarried couples living together correlates negatively with the occurrence of families with three or more children. Ireland, Malta, Cyprus, Slovakia and Poland are countries with a comparatively small number of single-person households and unmarried couples living together, and at the same time numerous families with three or more children. At the other end of the spectrum are the Scandinavian countries, France and the Netherlands, where a high incidence of single-person households and unmarried couples living together coincides with a moderate number of families with three or more children. Between these two poles lies a group of countries with a lower incidence of unmarried couples living together, a moderate number of families with three or more children and a moderate proportion of the population living in single-person households (e.g. Slovenia, Hungary).

When one takes all the findings of this section (5.3) into account, it is apparent that the structural change in the family in Europe is reflected in a decline in the number of first marriages, an increased divorce rate, an uninterrupted rise in the incidence of births outside of marriage, as well as a rise in the numbers of unmarried couples living together and an increased attractiveness of living alone. A comparison of all EU states also shows that, despite several indications of tendencies towards alignment, the traditional North–South distinctions have remained in place (Kiernan, 2004; Therborn, 2004; Oinonen, 2008). Superimposed on the latter distinctions is a division between Eastern European Catholic countries such as Poland and Romania, and the Baltic states in Eastern Europe, where family structures now show some similarities with the Scandinavian family type.

Notes

[1] Recently, in sociology, demographic behaviour is also conceptualised based on theories of the life course (Gershuny, 2004; Mabry et al., 2004). According to this approach, a person's life is divided into specific phases, and every person is concurrently integrated into different spheres of activity (work, family, leisure, charity work). Demographic behaviour thus faces the challenge of having to be coordinated with the requirements of other spheres of activity.

[2] This population decline will further exacerbate the problems of the social security systems in Germany. The combination of fewer inhabitants, the attendant decrease in the numbers of those in employment and the ageing of the population leads to a double constellation of problems: the number of those paying into the system falls, while the number of those drawing on it climbs. This negative development could be attenuated by an increase in the birth rate (which would require an improved family policy: for example, a sufficient number of places in child-care facilities, eliminating career disadvantages for women with children, providing affordable housing for families with children), by an increase in immigration, or by restricting unemployment benefits, health insurance benefits, as well as old-age pensions.

[3] However, the relative gap between these countries will lessen. In 2007, the old-age ratio in Italy and Germany was twice as high as that of Ireland.

[4] Life expectancy in Western Europe is markedly higher than in Eastern Europe. Italians, the French, Swedes and Spaniards can expect to have the longest lives, while people in the Baltic countries, Romania, Bulgaria and Hungary currently have the lowest life expectancy.

[5] So-called 'DINKS' (double income, no kids) are households with two incomes and no children, often with good jobs and incomes frequently several times higher than the income of families with children. The life model of DINKS corresponds to the ideal image of a market actor: totally flexible on the work front, willing and able to accept a heavy workload, and as free-spending consumers. Patchwork families come into existence when children from a previous relationship are brought into a new relationship. In these constellations, children are often confronted with new (step-)siblings and simultaneously integrated into the respective patchwork families of their separated, biological parents. Sociologists describe this form of living together as a 'multi-nuclear family'.

[6] Lithuania, for example, is a country with a high proportion of young men and women and a correspondingly high marriage rate per 1,000 inhabitants.

[7] The rate of first marriages in Cyprus points to a tendency to marry earlier. In the 1980s and 1990s, the rate was significantly lower (Council of Europe, 2006). Moreover, increasing numbers of foreigners are getting married in Cyprus, which overall makes it a special case (Sardon, 2004: 276).

[8] In 1990, Estonia, Latvia and Slovenia already had an above-average proportion of births outside marriage, Poland and Slovakia a below-average proportion. These patterns remain constant, in spite of the transformation phase in Eastern Europe; this can be understood as an indicator of path dependence.

6

Migration

In the social sciences, a variety of theoretical concepts are used to explain the causes, process and consequences of migration. One can distinguish between macro- and micro-oriented approaches, concepts illuminating the integration of migrants, and transnational migration theories (an overview of the concepts and the history of migration is provided by Bade, 1987; Fassmann and Münz, 1994; Portes and DeWind, 2007; Brettell and Hollifield, 2008; Castles and Miller, 2009; and Bade et al, 2011).

A model that is particularly important in research on migration is the 'push-pull model'. Adopting a macro-theoretical perspective, this concept explains the causes of migration in terms of the interplay between factors of repulsion (away from the country of origin) and factors of attraction (towards the destination country), and places income differentials at the centre of the model of explanation (Lee, 1966). In classical research on migration, it is assumed that migrants behave in accordance with the principle of economic rationalism, meaning that they are intent on improving their income and standard of living by migrating (Lee, 1966; Rist, 1978; Hoffmann-Nowotny, 1981; Stark, 1984; Castles, 1986; Feithen, 1986). In this view, the causes of migration lie above all in disparities in economic and demographic conditions (the labour market, wage levels, population development) in the origin and target regions. The central push factor as well as the main pull factor, it is argued, resides in the labour market, namely wage differentials. This argument stems from concepts developed in economics endeavouring to explain labour market mobility (Stark, 1984, 1993; Stark and Bloom, 1985; Chiswick, 2008).

Since the 1980s, migration researchers have argued that the push-pull concept is no longer adequate as an explanation of the causes of migration and decisions to migrate. Economic motives alone do not lead to migration: a complex set of motives serves as the basis for the decision to migrate. The critique of the previously dominant push-pull paradigm was accompanied by the establishment of micro-theoretical approaches that explain migration as a social process, in which aspects of the micro-level (human behaviour) and aspects of the macro-level (social structures) work together (Esser, 1982; Portes and Rumbaut, 1990). A whole bundle of motives are at work in the process of forming and reaching the decision to migrate (cf. Scott, 2006; Fourage and Ester, 2007; Lundholm, 2007; Verwiebe, 2010): personal disposition, family constellation, income situation, embeddedness in social networks,[1] cultural interests and language abilities, the transferability of qualifications,

Push-pull concept

availability of financial resources to cover an initial period without employment, entry regulations in the destination country, and political conditions in the country of origin as well as the destination country.

Integration and assimilation

A second important line of research in the sociology of migration is concerned with the integration of migrants (Alba and Nee, 1997; Özcan and Seifert, 2000; Kalter and Granato, 2002; Portes et al, 2005; Amuedo-Dorantes and Rica, 2007; Kristen and Granato, 2007; Alba, 2008; Greenman and Xie, 2008). In this research, up until the 1950s and 1960s, and especially in the US, the concept of assimilation was central (Eisenstadt, 1953; Taft, 1953; Gordon, 1964). According to this concept, over the course of time the spatial, linguistic and cultural segregation of migrants dissipates, so that by the third generation, at the latest, migrants are fully assimilated into their adopted society. Following on from this concept, researchers began to examine the integration of migrants using not just the normative concept of conformity to the adopted society, but also the perspective of discrimination and inequality of opportunity (Becker, 1971; Heckman and Payner, 1989; Massey and Denton, 1993; Turner and Ross, 2005; Aguirre and Turner, 2007; Pager and Shepherd, 2008). Thus, greater emphasis was placed on the question of how the target society reacts to migrants and what concepts and programmes are made available in order to facilitate integration. In current migration research, the concept of partial assimilation is used in order to argue that migrants will ultimately only partly, and not fully, adapt to the social, cultural and political structures of their adopted society (see e.g. Alba and Nee, 1997; Brubaker, 2001).

Transnational migration

Recently, a growing number of researchers have been examining transnational migration (Goldring, 1997; Faist, 2000; Peixoto, 2001; Pries, 2001b, 2004b; Levitt et al, 2003; Portes, 2003). The point of departure for this work is the idea that the old distinction between temporary and permanent migration no longer applies to many migrants, since they shuttle back and forth between their new and old home countries. The lifeworld of these transmigrants spans a variety of domiciles and a variety of social and geographic spaces. The central argument here is that mobility across national borders is closely connected with a far-reaching process of economic, cultural, political and social globalisation (Pries, 2001b). Thus, in this view, globally active enterprises, the new communications technology, the internet and the global consumption of mass media culture all weave a network of globalised transactions of information, goods and people, which leads to new transnational spaces beyond customary societies and social systems. In transnational migration research, a growing number of authors (Salt and Findlay, 1989; Salt, 1992; Koser and Salt, 1997; Peixoto, 2001; Amit, 2002; Martin and Lowell, 2002; Beaverstock, 2005) have been studying the migration of highly qualified persons.[2] Some of those authors put highly qualified migration in the context of the Europeanisation process. Favell (2008), for example, has focused in his recent work on highly skilled European migrants (mainly in services, IT, banking and media) in 'Eurocities' such as Brussels, Amsterdam, Paris and London, which benefit from specific European structures of opportunity. King argues in a similar way: 'The movement of skilled persons lies at the heart of the attempts to integrate Europe through the free movement of people, goods, services and capital within the EU' (King, 2002: 98). These types of migration are to be found especially among younger age groups and student populations. The phenomenon of student migration, for example, is described by Findlay et al (2006: 291f) in the following manner: 'Given its link with ... European integration, it is not surprising that international student migration has increased rapidly in most parts of Europe.'

A number of these issues will be examined in the following three sections. We will discuss the causes and motivations for migration, as well as the patterns and dynamics of integration, in the course of presenting: (a) an overview of migration in Europe, (b) the development of the proportion of the population with a migration background, and (c) the systems of migration in the EU that have crystallised out of these processes.

6.1 Migration patterns and dynamics

NOTE ON METHODOLOGY ▬▬▬▬▬▬▬▬▬

The difference between the numbers of immigrants and emigrants in a specific region in the course of a year is described as the net migration balance. Since in most countries there are no precise figures on immigration and emigration, we use calculations from Eurostat, where net migration balances are estimated on the basis of the difference between actual population growth and natural population growth (referring to developments in the birth and mortality rates). Figure 6.1 shows the cumulative net migration for the years 1997 to 2008 proportionate to the average population size in these years.

After natural fluctuations in population size due to changes in birth and mortality rates (cf. Sections 5.1 and 5.2), migration – that is, the relationship between immigration and emigration – is the second decisive factor that determines the composition of the population in European states. In the second half of the 20th century, with the prolonged economic boom phase, many countries in Western Europe became countries of immigration. Immediately after the Second World War, in the wake of the altered political map of Europe, migration took the form of resettlement. Well into the 1950s, Europe was an important source of

Migration in second half of the 20th century

emigrants departing for North America and Australia. The mid- and late 1950s, however, brought an increase in the number of immigrants due to labour migration and post-colonial migration. During this same period, intra-European labour migration began, with migrants moving from Southern Europe to the industrial centres of France, Belgium, Germany and the Netherlands (Castles, 1986, 2006; Feithen, 1986; Fassmann and Münz, 1994).[3] Later, politically motivated migration (refugees and asylum-seekers) became significant, as did the migration of those coming to join family members already in Europe. Since the late 1990s, however, the number of official asylum-seekers has fallen dramatically (Eurostat, 2010a) due to the more restrictive asylum policy of EU Member States. Most asylum-seekers in the 1990s came from the Balkan states, the former Soviet states and North Africa (OECD, 2009e). As far as migration within the EU is concerned (see Section 13.3 for more detail), since the mid-1990s important factors have been resolutions in the Maastricht Treaty, such as the stipulation on freedom of movement, the recognition of foreign qualifications, the Erasmus/Socrates programme, as well as the creation of a network of European employment offices (Gordon, 2001; King and Ruiz-Gelices, 2003; Bracht et al, 2006; Findlay et al, 2006; Verwiebe et al, 2010).

Population gain through migration in EU-15

For the European states being examined here, there is very little reliable data covering the period since the end of the Second World War. In what follows, we shall therefore be focusing on recent migrational movements, between 1997 and 2008. Figure 6.1 shows the cumulative net result for migration during this period – specifically, immigration and emigration in relation to overall population size. One can deduce from the percentage figures that, as a result of immigration, the population of the EU-27 states increased by 14.5 million between 1997 and 2008. Given that during this period the Central and Eastern European accession states lost roughly two million inhabitants as a result of emigration, the gain in population through immigration is primarily concentrated in the core EU states and the Mediterranean states of Malta and Cyprus. In relative figures, the core states of the EU have experienced a growth in population of around 4%.

In recent years, Greece, Portugal, Italy, Malta, Luxembourg, Ireland, Spain and Cyprus have all seen strong increases in immigration, with population growth ranging from 4.5% to 12.1%, which corresponds to an overall increase of one million inhabitants through immigration. This is a noteworthy development in the history of European migration, since, well into the second half of the 20th century, Greece, Portugal, Italy, Ireland and Spain were among the most important countries for emigration (Castles, 1986, 2006; Feithen, 1986; Fassmann and Münz, 1994). The rise in immigrant numbers in Ireland is the result of labour migration from Eastern and Western Europe, and from English-speaking countries (Burnham, 2003; OECD, 2009j). In the Mediterranean states, the increase is due to the admittance of immigrants looking for work and of refugees from Eastern Europe, Latin America and Africa, but also to growing numbers of retirees from within the EU (Williams et al, 1997; Cavounidis, 2006; Fernández and Ortega, 2006; OECD, 2009e; Recchi and Favell, 2009; Bertagna and Maccari-Clayton, 2011).

Figure 6.1: Cumulative net migration

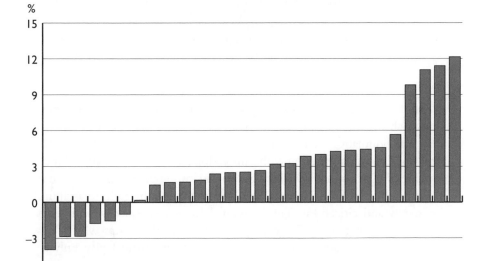

Source: Eurostat (2010a); net migration from 1997 to 2008, as percentage of 2008 population.

In the period under consideration, the Baltic states, Romania, Bulgaria and Poland, have experienced dramatic emigration, with people leaving for Western Europe and the US. The opening of the British, Irish and Swedish labour markets to citizens from the new Member States of the EU in 2004 led to a major increase in immigration from Eastern Europe, as did the opening of the labour markets in most of the other EU-15 states in 2006 (Borzeda, 2002; Nowak-Lewandowska, 2006; OECD, 2009e). In the case of Estonia and Latvia, significant numbers of emigrants have left for Russia, Belarus and the Ukraine (Eurostat, 2010a), the overall loss amounting to roughly two million people, which corresponds to between 4% and 6% of their respective populations. There has been a moderate increase in population through immigration in countries such as the UK, Sweden, Belgium and Austria. These immigrants have come mainly from the new EU Member States, the former Yugoslavia, Germany,

Population decline through emigration in Eastern Europe

the French-speaking African countries (to Belgium), war zones in Africa and Asia (to Sweden), and the Commonwealth states of India, Pakistan, Australia or South Africa (to the United Kingdom) (Eurostat, 2010a).

6.2 Population with a migration background

NOTE ON METHODOLOGY

The population with a migration background is presented using two indicators: first, the proportion of the population with foreign citizenship; and, second, the proportion of the population born abroad. The data come from Eurostat and the OECD.

Within the European Union there are differing conceptions of the way in which the national population is to be distinguished from the non-national population, that is, how to categorise a person as a migrant, foreigner, immigrant, citizen with a migration background or national (i.e. 'native' of the country). The laws governing immigration vary across the Member States of the EU, as do the laws governing the right to asylum, residency and citizenship. The individual EU states also have different traditions of migration. For example, certain ethnic groups which for historical reasons are significant in France (North Africa) play only a subordinate role in other nations. The following discussion concerning the portion of the population with foreign citizenship and persons born abroad can therefore be considered as one possible way of looking at issues of migration from a comparative perspective.

In all European countries, a basic distinction is drawn between foreigners and those who have state citizenship, but this distinction obscures the fact that a number of migrants acquire citizenship in their adopted country. Certain migrants have privileged access to citizenship, such as, in the case of Germany, so-called 'late resettlers' (*Spätaussiedler* – immigrants of German ethnic origin from formerly German-speaking regions of Eastern Europe), and, in the case of the UK, France and the Netherlands, citizens from former colonies (the Commonwealth countries, North Africa, Surinam, Indonesia). Policies regarding citizenship for children born of foreigners also vary from one EU state to another: in some cases, when such children are born in the EU state in question, they are automatically entitled to citizenship (*jus solis*), whereas in other cases it is dependent on the citizenship of the parents (*jus sanguinis*). Those who do not have citizenship of the country in which they are living are subject to special regulations concerning their right to stay and other associated rights. The number of foreigners in a country does not reveal how many migrants have actually come there, due partly to the naturalisation of migrants, but also to processes of return migration and onward migration (to a third destination). Therefore, only a part of the whole migration movement to Europe appears in the census statistics. Empirically, in the countries of Western Europe (EU-15), one sees a clear increase in the number of foreigners in the second half of the 20th century: in the 1950s, there were only around four million foreigners altogether living in these countries, in the early 1970s there were 11 million, in 1982 15 million, and 19.5 million in 2000. By 2007, the number of foreigners had reached 26 million (Fassmann and Münz, 1994; Eurostat, 2010a).

Using current EU and OECD data, if one looks at the proportion of the population that has foreign citizenship, one notices major differences within the EU. At one end of the spectrum one finds Eastern European countries such as Romania, Bulgaria, Slovakia and Lithuania, where 1% or less of the population are foreigners; at the other end of the spectrum are Central European industrial countries such as Austria, Belgium and Germany, which, since the late 1950s, have been the preferred destinations for labour migrants and refugees (Krane, 1979; Castles, 1986, 2006; Feithen, 1986; Bade, 1987; Fassmann and Münz, 1994; Castles and Miller, 2009). In 2008, between 8% and 10% of the population in these countries had foreign citizenship. This proportion of foreigners is currently exceeded only in Spain, Cyprus, Estonia, Latvia and Luxembourg. Being in the Mediterranean region, Spain and Cyprus have been an increasingly favoured choice for migrants in recent years, whereas in the first decades following the Second World War, the number of emigrants from these countries exceeded the number of immigrants. Those who have settled there in recent years are mostly either Western European retirees or labour migrants from Asia (for example, from the Philippines, Sri Lanka, India and China), from Latin America (Bolivia, Argentina, Peru, Brazil, among others), North Africa (Morocco) and Eastern Europe (Romania, Bulgaria, Russia and the Ukraine) (Williams et al, 1997; OECD, 2009e; Statistical Service of Cyprus, 2009).

Population with foreign citizenship

Latvia and Estonia also assume a special place: one fifth of their populations have foreign citizenship, the majority being of Russian origin, although their numbers have fallen as a result of naturalisation and emigration between 2000 and 2007. Leading the way, however, is Luxembourg, the second least-populous Member State of the EU, with 42% of the population having foreign citizenship. This is due to the fact that Luxembourg is home to a number of major European institutions. Countries such as the United Kingdom, the Netherlands, Denmark, France, Italy and Sweden occupy the statistical middle ground, with the proportion of foreigners ranging from 4% to 7%. Between 2001 and 2008, the most marked growth in the proportion of the population with foreign citizenship occurred in the UK, Portugal, Malta, Cyprus,[4] Italy,

Ireland and Spain. We have already mentioned the special situation of states in the Mediterranean region. In the case of the UK and Ireland, the increases in recent years are the result of intra-European labour migration and immigrants arriving from other English-speaking countries (the US and the Commonwealth) (OECD, 2009e; Lunn, 2011; Smyth, 2011).

Figure 6.2: Foreign and foreign-born residents

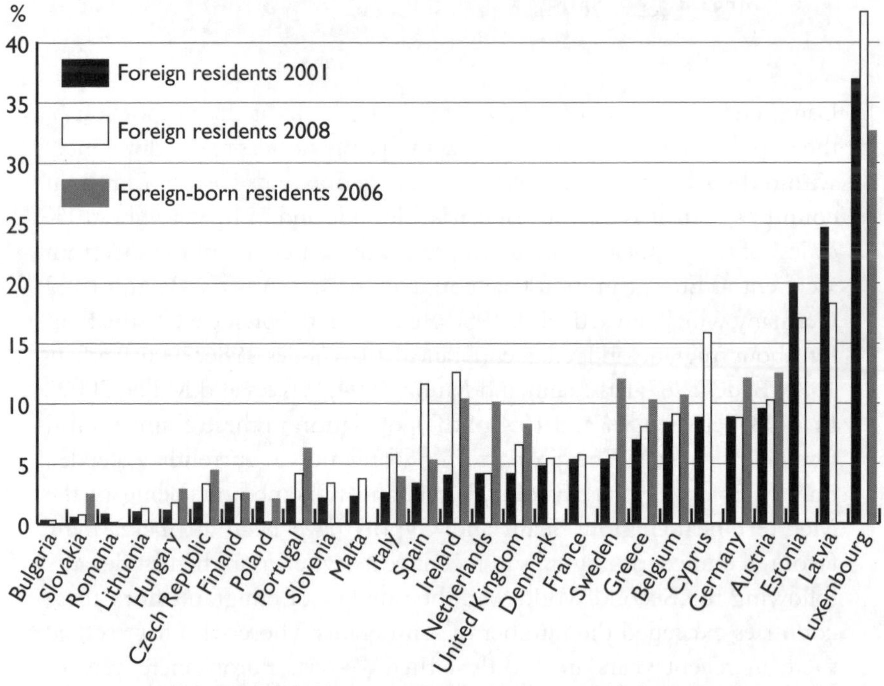

Source: Eurostat (2010a); OECD (2009f), own calculations. No data available for foreign-born residents in Bulgaria, Romania, Lithuania, Slovenia, Malta, Cyprus, Estonia, Latvia.

Naturalisation We mentioned earlier that these figures provide only an incomplete picture of actual migration movements, since a certain proportion of migrants take on citizenship in their guest country. Naturalisation procedures vary greatly from country to country: in countries where it is difficult for migrants to get citizenship, there is often a higher number of officially registered foreigners than in countries where access to citizenship is relatively straightforward. Examples here are Estonia and Latvia: in Latvia there were approximately 75,000 naturalisations between 2002 and 2006, and in Estonia 25,000 (Eurostat, 2010a). This corresponds to a naturalisation rate of around 10% of the foreigners living in these two countries in 2000.[5] By contrast, in France and the United Kingdom, the moderate proportion of foreigners indicates that it is easier for migrants (especially so-called second-generation migrants) to be naturalised: between 2002 and 2006, approximately 150,000 people per year were granted citizenship (Eurostat, 2010a). Extrapolating, one can conclude that this amounts to around one quarter of the foreigners living in France and the UK in the year 2000 being granted citizenship over the period of four years.

These indicators can be usefully supplemented by OECD data on the proportion of people born abroad (white bars in Figure 6.2). Here the numbers are, in some cases, significantly higher: in countries such as Sweden, France, the Netherlands, the Czech Republic, Portugal and the UK, the proportion of those born abroad is at least twice as high as the proportion of foreigners. Slovenia and Lithuania should be mentioned separately, since in both cases the proportion of inhabitants born abroad is several times higher than the proportion of inhabitants without citizenship. In Lithuania, the people in question are mostly citizens of the former USSR, and in the case of Slovenia, they are mostly citizens from other parts of the former Yugoslavia. In the United Kingdom, many of those who have a British passport belong to ethnic minorities who migrated to the country and then acquired citizenship. In Greece, Italy and Finland, there are only slight differences between the proportion of foreigners and the proportion of inhabitants born abroad, which at least indirectly suggests low naturalisation rates. The drawback of the indicator for 'persons born abroad' is that it only covers migration movements 'within one generation'. Foreigners who are born in the country and who have not acquired citizenship – which applies, for example, to many Turks and Kurds born in Austria – are not covered in the statistics. At the same time, neither this indicator nor that for the overall proportion of foreigners shows how large the group of people with a migration background actually is. If one applies a broader definition of 'persons with a migration background', including (a) all those who do not have citizenship, (b) those who are naturalised (with or without personal experience of migration), and (c) citizens who have at least one naturalised parent or a parent who is a foreigner, then the proportion of people with a migration background increases dramatically, exceeding both the proportion of foreigners in the population and the proportion of the population born abroad. There are, however, no reliable comparative data for this form of measurement. For Germany, for example, one can use information from a new survey of the Federal Statistical Office, according to which in 2007 15.4 million Germans (18.7% of all inhabitants) have a migration background (Federal Statistical Office, 2009). This number is significantly higher than the figures given for the proportion of foreigners (9%) or the proportion of the population born abroad (12.5%).

People born abroad

People with a migration background

6.3 Migration systems

> ☐ DEFINITION
>
> Migration systems are the result of institutionalised and relatively stable interactions between the regions of origin and the target regions of migrations. They are characterised by various factors, such as the legal regulation of migration, the scope and origin of migrant flows, the integration of migrants into the labour market, the ethnic composition of migrant groups, and policies regarding the naturalisation of migrants.

Differentiation of migration systems

In Europe, a number of different systems of migration can be distinguished. However, systems that for many years had remained relatively stable underwent major changes as a result of the transformation processes in Eastern Europe, which led to extensive migration movements from East to West. On the one hand, this has given rise to a differentiation of migration systems in Europe in comparison with the 1980s and 1990s; on the other hand, researchers refer to an increasing convergence of the integration processes for immigrants in the various target countries (Meyers, 2002), whereby the different migration systems are becoming increasingly similar. The explanation for this convergence lies in the coordination of migration policies within the EU and liberal approaches to intra-European migration.

Scandinavian migration system

The Scandinavian migration system (shown in Figure 6.3, second column from left) is comprised of Sweden and Denmark. Here one finds a moderate proportion of the population with foreign citizenship (around 5%) and a somewhat higher proportion of those born abroad. From the 1990s through to the early 21st century, the Scandinavian migration system registered a positive net result, due to the admission of refugees from crisis- and war-affected regions (for example, from Somalia, Ethiopia, Iraq, Iran, Sri Lanka, Bosnia), which is traditionally more characteristic of Scandinavia than of many other European states. In addition, migration within Scandinavia is an important component of the migration system – the large Finnish population in Sweden, for instance, among other examples. The integration of migrants is oriented towards assimilation, with newly arriving migrants being dispersed across the entire country in order to prevent the development of ethnic enclaves. For decades, foreigners have had the right to vote in local (communal) elections, and integration into the educational system and labour market is actively promoted. The Scandinavian system does, however, also have problems with social integration and integration into the labour market (Rosholm et al, 2006; Blume et al, 2007). Moreover, starting in the 1990s, Scandinavian immigration policy changed: by the early 21st century, for example, Danish immigration policy contained elements of strict barriers to further immigration and an exclusion of foreigners (Kjeldstadli, 2011). This development (which is not limited to Scandinavia) can be attributed to the politicisation of immigration as a topic, to the rise of political parties explicitly hostile to foreigners, fears of losing one's job and social status, or to cultural and religious conflicts between immigrants and the local population (O'Rourke and Sinnott, 2006). In the future, however, migration to Scandinavia appears set to increase rather than decrease (Kjeldstadli, 2011). The reasons for this lie in immigrants coming to join family members already in the country, regulations concerning residency rights for refugees, as well as the labour requirements of the Scandinavian economy.

A second European migration system can be found in the UK, Ireland, France, the Netherlands and Belgium, countries where the proportion of the population with foreign citizenship lies between 4% and 7%, with between 9% and 12% of the population born abroad. A comparison of the two percentages indicates a high proportion of migrants with target country citizenship. Approximately 15% of the workforce in these countries is comprised of people born abroad (Figure 6.3, row 5), which is the highest percentage in Europe. In the UK, France and the Benelux states, post-colonial migration has a special significance. Before they actually arrive in their destination country, many immigrants have already undergone a social and cultural orientation with respect to the former colonial power, and existing immigrant networks also facilitate the integration of new arrivals. At the same time, immigrants from former colonies are given preferential treatment when it comes to residency permits, which makes it relatively easy for people from Ireland, Pakistan, Bangladesh, India or South Africa to migrate to the United Kingdom (Lunn, 2011). For immigrants from the Maghreb states (Morocco, Algeria, Tunisia) moving to France (Moch, 2011) or immigrants from Surinam or the Antilles moving to the Netherlands, similar conditions apply (Lucassen and Lucassen, 2011). Despite having a good command of the language of their destination countries, and despite having to some extent the same rights as citizens, these large migrant groups have not been integrated wholly successfully, as is demonstrated by myriad social and political conflicts in recent years (Meurs et al, 2008; Lucassen and Lucassen, 2011; Lunn, 2011; Moch, 2011).[6] In metropolises such as London, Amsterdam and Paris, large ethnic enclaves have formed – often located in quarters with many social problems – and have completely altered the image of entire areas of the cities in question. The situation of specific migrant groups is less problematic, such as the Irish in the UK or the Portuguese in France[7] (Moch, 2011), who respectively comprise a not inconsiderable fifth of all foreigners. The United Kingdom and Ireland have recently experienced migration from the new Eastern European Member States, having opened up their labour markets to workers from these countries at

Migration system: North-west and central

Figure 6.3: Subsystems in the European migration space

	Scandinavia	Central/North-west	Central	Mediterranean	Central/East	East/South-east	Baltics
Dynamics, extent of migration	Stable, medium level	Stable, medium to high level	Stable, high level	Increasing, currently high level	Stable, low level	Very low	Low
Migration balance	Positive	Positive	Positive	Strongly positive	Weakly positive	Negative	Negative
Foreign citizenship	5%	3–8%	9–10%	5–9%	0–3%	below 1%	Latvia, Estonia ca. 20%
Foreign-born residents	7–12%	8–10%	12%	5–10%	2–4%	0–2%	see notes
Share of foreign born in workforce	6–13%	ca. 15%	10–12%	9–13%	2%, n/a for Slovenia	below 1%	n/a
Largest groups of migrants	Second-generation migrants from Turkey, Balkans, Lebanon, Iran Scandinavia New: migrants from Asia (China, Thailand), Eastern Europe	Second-generation migrants from former colonies and Turkey New: strong migration from Eastern Europe and Western Europe (especially from Germany)	Second-generation migrants from Turkey, the Balkans and Southern Europe New: strong migration from Eastern Europe, migration of Germans to Austria	Second-generation migrants mostly from Africa, the Balkans and South America New: European retiree migration, strong migration from Eastern Europe	Migrants from Romania, Ukraine, Belarus, and the Balkans	Only small groups of migrants, strong ethnic minorities (Turks, Hungarians, Sinti and Romanies) New: strong emigration to Western Europe	Only small groups of migrants, large groups of Russian origin New: emigration to Western Europe, US, GUS-countries
Examples	Sweden, Denmark	United Kingdom, Ireland, France, Netherlands, Belgium	Germany, Austria	Spain, Greece, Cyprus	Hungary, Czech Republic, Slovenia, Poland	Romania, Bulgaria, Slovakia	Latvia, Estonia, (Lithuania)

Source: OECD (2007c: Ch 8; 2009d: 14ff, 71ff; 2009f), European Commission (2008: Ch 5).

Note: A large number of non-natives in the Baltic states were born in the former Soviet Union, mostly within the present-day borders of Latvia, Estonia and Lithuania, or had already been living there before the foundation of these states in 1991.

a relatively early stage (Meardi, 2009; OECD, 2009e; Lunn, 2011; Smyth, 2011). In recent times, migration of Germans to the Netherlands, the UK and Ireland has also played an increasing role (OECD, 2009e: 17f).

The German-speaking countries of Europe constitute a further subsystem of European immigration. By European standards, the proportion of foreigners and of inhabitants born abroad in the total population is high. Immigration occurs at a consistently high level. In recent years, in relation to population size, Austria has experienced a higher level of immigration than Germany (OECD, 2009f; Eurostat, 2010a). If one considers absolute figures, with over 15 million inhabitants with a migration background, Germany is by far the most important migration country in Europe. The main causes of immigration in German-speaking countries are the labour migrations of the 1960s and 1970s, which brought numerous immigrants to Germany and Austria from Turkey, Yugoslavia, Spain, Portugal, Greece and Italy. Although these migrations were originally envisaged as temporary rotations of the workforce, many migrants ended up staying, and, despite incentives, could not be persuaded to return to their home countries. The stream of migrants continued even once the recruitment programme was stopped, as a result of large numbers of migrants coming to join family members already settled in the target country (Bade and Oltmer, 2011; Hahn, 2011). It was not until the 1990s that return migration began to occur, for example pensioners retiring to Turkey (Dustmann et al, 1996; Dustmann, 2003; Krumme, 2004; Razum et al, 2005). As a result of the specific histories of immigration in Germany and Austria in the second half of the 20th century, ethnic minorities have developed. Not infrequently, these groups are only partly integrated into society and are confronted with manifold disadvantages. Even in the second and third generations, in the labour market and the education system, one encounters forms of ethnic segmentation and entrenched structural inequalities between the local ('native') population and immigrant groups (Bender and Seifert, 1998; Riphahn, 2003; Kogan, 2004; Kogan and Kalter, 2006; Kristen and Granato, 2007; OECD, 2007b; Kristen, 2008; Hahn, 2011). A further numerically significant group of migrants – especially in Germany – consists of so-called 'late resettlers' (*Spätaussiedler*) from former German-speaking regions of Eastern Europe, most of whom come from the Commonwealth of Independent States and Poland, with a smaller number from Romania (Bade and Oltmer, 2011). These groups have privileged access to citizenship rights, as compared to the great majority of migrants from Southern Europe and Turkey.

Migration system in German-speaking countries

EU Mediterranean states such as Spain, Greece and Cyprus (and, to a lesser extent, Italy and Portugal)[8] have only recently become migration countries, and constitute a distinct, Southern European migration system. The proportion of the population with foreign citizenship lies between 8% and 13%, with around one in ten inhabitants born abroad. The level

Southern European migration system

of immigration has risen markedly in recent years, much more rapidly than in the rest of Europe. Due to the demand for labour, the integration of migrants into the labour market is proceeding more successfully than in many other European states, although most of the jobs are in the low-wage sectors. In Greece, unemployment among migrants is lower than it is among the local population, and in Spain and Portugal, unemployment is only slightly higher among migrants than among Spaniards and Portuguese (OECD, 2007b: 86ff). The Southern European migration system is also interesting in the European context because for most of the 20th century, the Mediterranean states were themselves emigration countries, being the source of a significant number of the labour migrants who moved to Northern Europe (Feithen, 1986; Fassmann and Münz, 1994; Bertagna and Maccari-Clayton, 2011; Pietschmann, 2011). As a result of their EU membership and growing prosperity, these countries have also become in recent years target countries for migration movements, above all from Eastern Europe and North Africa, as well as Central and South America (Cavounidis, 2006: 640; OECD, 2009e: 101). More so than other European countries, Southern European countries are confronted with illegal immigration (Fasani, 2009; González-Enríquez, 2009; Pietschmann, 2011; Bertagna and Maccari-Clayton, 2011) and the problems associated with it, such as clandestine employment, human trafficking and criminality. As participants in the Schengen Agreement,[9] they are required to protect the outer borders of the EU, and they find themselves exposed to increased pressure from migration. Various movements in favour of legalisation have made it clear in recent years that it is necessary to acknowledge the growing numbers of people who live and work in these countries without any legal standing, and to grant them a secure status (European Commission, 2008). In the medium to long term, the number of immigrants in the EU Mediterranean states will stabilise at a high level or even increase (Bertagna and Maccari-Clayton, 2011; Pietschmann, 2011), which, it seems, will make it necessary to introduce a more active policy of integration and a more positive social climate for migrants than have been in evidence hitherto.

In recent decades, the countries of Eastern Europe have emerged predominantly as sources of migration, and to a lesser extent as target countries for larger migration flows. However, the slight increase in the proportion of foreigners in recent years (for example, in the Czech Republic, Hungary and Slovenia), but also the very large proportion of the population with foreign citizenship (the Baltic states) and the associated models of integration and naturalisation of migrants, together necessitate a differentiated examination of these countries. They also form the eastern and south-eastern outer borders of the EU and are therefore confronted, in the medium term, with immigration flows that will be different from those of the past 15 years (Wallace and Vincent, 2009).

Against this background, one can reasonably distinguish three different migration systems in the Eastern European accession states.

The first Eastern European migration system consists of the Central-Eastern states, which include the Czech Republic, Hungary, Slovenia and, to a lesser extent, Poland. In these countries, one finds a very low proportion of foreigners by European standards (between 2% and 3%), which is comparable with Finland. In recent years, this proportion has risen slightly. The current net result for immigration shows a slight increase, except in Poland. Most of the immigrants have come from the former Soviet states, China, India and Vietnam (especially family members coming to join Vietnamese contract workers), some of them entering illegally. Also important is fixed-term labour migration from Belarus, Russia and the Ukraine, which is meant to fill the demand for labour – for example in Poland, where young, well-qualified employees have been leaving for Western Europe, creating a major labour shortage in some sectors, such as construction and health (Kaczmarczyk, 2006; Praszalowicz, 2011). The return of political refugees and labour migrants who left prior to 1989 is also contributing to a positive net result in the Central-Eastern European migration system (Praszalowicz, 2011; Zeitlhofer, 2011). In all these countries, especially in Slovenia and the Czech Republic, the proportion of those born abroad is markedly higher than the proportion of foreigners. A small number of them are highly qualified migrants, an international elite who have come to Eastern Europe in order to assist in the expansion of multinational corporations (Rudolph and Hillmann, 1998; Inzelt, 2007; Zeitlhofer, 2011). In the case of Slovenia and the Czech Republic, the majority of those born abroad are people from the former Yugoslavia and the former Czechoslovakia (Eurostat, 2010a), who possess a special status as a result of regulations that followed the partition of these states. Finally, in this group of countries, residency visas and rights to citizenship are typically awarded only after a waiting period of some years – in the Czech Republic, for instance, it has recently been reduced from 15 to 10 years (OECD, 2007b: 240; Zeitlhofer, 2011).

Romania, Bulgaria and Slovakia constitute an additional migration system, located in the south-east of the European Union. In these countries, there are hardly any people with foreign citizenship (less than 1% of the population). In the case of Romania, for instance, the largest groups were Moldavians, Turks and Chinese, and in the case of Slovakia, they were Czechs, Ukrainians and Poles (Eurostat, 2010a). The proportion of inhabitants born abroad is somewhat higher – in Slovakia, for example, it is 2.5% of the population. A further characteristic of this migration system is the dramatic decline in population as a result of emigration to Southern and Western Europe, with Romania losing 735,000 people and Bulgaria 250,000 between 1996 and 2007, which corresponds to a fall of some 3% in each case (Eurostat, 2010a). The policy on migrants

Migration system in Central and Eastern Europe

Migration system in South-eastern Europe

(asylum, residency, naturalisation) is restrictive. In Slovakia, for instance, of 11,500 asylum–seekers in 2004, only 15 people were granted permanent residency. In 2006 and 2007, 10 out of 3,000 asylum–seekers were being granted permanent residency (Statistical Office of the Slovak Republic, 2008). Moreover, in South–eastern Europe, ethnic minorities play a relatively important role in the population structures and structures of migration.

> In Slovakia, 10% of the population belong to the Hungarian minority and 2% to the Sinti and Romanies. In Romania, approximately 7% of the population belong to the Hungarian minority and some 3% to the Sinti and Romanies. In Bulgaria, 10% of the population belong to the Turkish minority and 5% to the Sinti and Romanies. Economic and social discrimination against the Sinti and Romanies (labour market, health, housing, political representation) is particularly severe. In Slovakia, these ethnic groups comprise well over 100,000 people, the great majority of whom live in economically under-developed rural areas. According to recent census figures, in Romania and Bulgaria there are in each case approximately half a million Sinti and Romanies (National Statistical Institute of Bulgaria, 2008; Romanian National Institute of Statistics, 2008; Statistical Office of the Slovak Republic, 2008). It is widely suspected that these groups are actually considerably larger, since the official statistics systematically underestimate their real numbers. According to estimates, there are several hundred thousand Sinti and Romanies living in Slovakia, 600,000 in Bulgaria and 1.5 million in Romania (Friedrich-Ebert-Stiftung, 2002: 9; Zeitlhofer, 2011). While nowadays Sinti and Romanies have manifold local ties, they still display a relatively high level of transnational mobility.

Baltic migration system

In the Baltic countries one finds one final European migration system, with Estonia and Latvia being most representative, and Lithuania to a lesser extent. In Estonia and Latvia, one finds a proportion of foreigners that is much higher than the EU average: approximately one fifth of the population does not have local citizenship (Eurostat, 2010a). Most of these people are of Russian origin, who have been living in the Baltic region for up to four generations. Those who were not born in the Baltic countries mostly settled there before 1990, during the Soviet period, for work reasons. In 1989, Russians made up 10% of the population in Lithuania, 34% in Latvia and 30% in Estonia (Garleff, 2011). In all three countries, minority rights, rights to citizenship and naturalisation, as well as language issues, constitute sources of conflict that can verge on being explosive. Lithuania has done a better job of getting these problems under control than Estonia and Latvia, by ensuring cultural autonomy for the Russian, Polish and White Russian minorities, and by enacting relatively liberal naturalisation laws (Garleff, 2011). While Estonia and

Latvia are in fact much more multicultural countries than Lithuania, this is not acknowledged by the social majority, a denial that is expressed in restrictive contact with the ethnic minorities. The naturalisation process here is sluggish, and is based on citizenship and language tests. As a result, in 2005 there were still 400,000 stateless persons living in Latvia, and 130,000 in Estonia, because the old Soviet passports are no longer valid, and their holders have not received a new passport. Also characteristic of the Baltic states is a high level of emigration to Northern and Western Europe (the UK, Ireland, Germany), to the US, as well as to the Commonwealth of Independent States (Eurostat, 2010a). Between 1996 and 2007, the resulting decline in population amounted to 150,000 for Lithuania, 50,000 for Latvia and 30,000 for Estonia, corresponding to a loss of 2% to 4% of the population (Eurostat, 2010a).

It remains to be seen how lasting the developments that we have sketched out here will prove to be. Migration systems are not necessarily stable, and their characteristic features can change with time, as is shown by the strong increase in immigration in the Mediterranean countries of the EU in the 1990s. Whether in the future the various migration systems in Europe will become increasingly alike, as Kaelble (2007: 261ff) predicts, is an open question. According to Kaelble, factors that speak in favour of convergence include the growing similarities of immigration (flows and composition) within the core states of the EU, mainly caused by the high level of immigration in the Mediterranean countries, as well as Ireland. Harmonisation of policies on integration and asylum is also leading to greater congruity between migration models. Moreover, the socio-structural composition of migrant groups has become increasingly similar: men and women emigrate on the same scale to and within Europe, and among them one finds many more qualified and highly qualified people than was the case even as recently as the 1970s (see Section 13.3). In many countries, the forms of migration have also become more differentiated: along with labour migrants, who change their country of residence permanently, one also finds migration where no permanent change of residence is involved, such as among retired people who spend part of their lives abroad, (temporary) migrants who are pursuing their education (students and school pupils), or transnational migrants (for example, commuters who live in border regions). A final point that speaks in favour of convergence is the tentative opening of Eastern Europe for immigrants. Although the level of immigration to Eastern Europe is currently still very low, the example of the Central-Eastern European states shows that Western, Northern and Southern European countries are no longer the only ones that are attractive for migrants.

Convergence in the European migration space?

Notes

[1] In his critically acclaimed book, Faist (2000), for example, emphasises the high relevance of social networks for migration processes. Based on an elaborated action theory, he argues that 'social relations, viz. ties in collectives and networks, constitute distinct sets of intermediate structures on the meso level. It is via these relations that actors relate their resources to opportunity structures' (Faist, 2000: 100). He concludes that, in the case of international migration, new (and also old) ties and corresponding capital often crystallise in migrant networks. The uneven distribution of resources mobilised through these social networks helps to account for different rates of migration out of various regions and differences within migration communities (Faist, 2000: 123).

[2] Important causes of the increase in migration of the highly skilled have been the boost in foreign direct investment and the growth of multinational corporations. Such individuals are crucial to the flows of knowledge and capital movements of these corporations.

[3] From the 1950s to the 1970s, many states induced streams of migration through targeted recruitment based on bi-national programmes designed to expand their labour force with migrants from Southern Europe, who were, in the case of Germany for example, 'carrying out work that Germans would typically no longer do' (Blotevogel et al, 1993: 85). In the 1980s, most European countries changed their policies in order to curb migration flows again (Entzinger, 2000; Castles, 2004; Faist and Ette, 2007). Since the early 1990s, the EU has been strongly promoting intra-European migration through institutional and cultural programmes (i.e. Socrates, Erasmus). A turning point for intra-European migration was the implementation of the Maastricht Treaty, according to which all Member State citizens became entitled to unrestricted mobility within the EU.

[4] Prior to its EU accession, Cyprus offered the right of domicile to citizens from Russia, Bulgaria and Romania, which led to an increased influx of highly skilled and wealthy migrants from these countries. In addition, labour migration from the Turkish north of the island is rising because of the higher wage level in the south (Mehmet et al, 2007; Statistical Service of Cyprus, 2009).

[5] The naturalisation rate is relatively low in Estonia and Latvia if one considers the high numbers of foreign citizens living there. A different angle can be taken if one takes into account that both countries have a small population (Estonia, 1.3 million inhabitants; Latvia, 2.3 million inhabitants in 2009), for which the naturalisation of 25,000 and 75,000 people, respectively, is quite a challenge.

[6] Because of immigration during the second half of the 20th century, the UK moved towards a more multicultural society. At the same time the societal tensions stemming from a long history of migration are still prevalent at the beginning of the 21st century and amplify the problems of migration and integration in Britain's contemporary society that is in parts defensive and socially fragmented (Lunn, 2011).

[7] Indication of the successful integration of about one million Portuguese into French society is given by the educational success of young Portuguese, a high electoral turnout and marital behaviour: more than 50% of the second generation marry French partners (Moch, 2011).

[8] Hillmann (2007: 73ff) considers Italy and Portugal as belonging to this group. However, the low level of immigration during the 1990s and the modest share of foreign citizens and foreign-born residents cast doubt on such a classification.

[9] For more on the Schengen Agreement see Section 11.1.

7

Labour market and employment

The labour market is pivotal for economic and social actors because of its material and social functions. Its distributional outcomes strongly shape social structures by determining individual welfare as well as generating social contacts and integration. The most important actors in the capitalist labour market are labour, capital and the state.

Labour market theories

Most economic theories of the labour market are predicated on the assumptions of neo-classical models. According to these, the point of departure of any economic activity is a *Homo Oeconomicus* who chooses and exchanges freely and behaves rationally (Cahuc and Zylberberg, 2004: 6). In neo-classical theory, the labour market is a market like any other, and the same laws apply to labour as to any other commodity. Perfect competition obtains, that is, there are neither barriers to labour market entry nor constraints on competition, and all suppliers of labour are equally productive and substitutable. No discrimination of suppliers of labour occurs. In neo-classical theory, the labour market is viewed through the standard model of the exchange of goods: wages are interpreted as the price of a unit of labour and are determined by supply and demand (Cahuc and Zylberberg, 2004: 249; Samuelson and Nordhaus, 2005: 249). An imbalance in the labour market in the form of unemployment or a labour shortage triggers an adjustment mechanism. This means that when labour market conditions change, suppliers of labour are amenable to spatial mobility and also accept the adjustment of wages to market conditions. Theoretically, such adjustment mechanisms continue to occur until full-employment equilibrium is reached (for a more in-depth treatment, see Cahuc and Zylberberg, 2004; Samuelson and Nordhaus, 2005; Benjamin et al., 2007).

Neo-classical theory

The most important advancement of the standard economic model was made in the 1960s by Gary S. Becker (1964), Jacob Mincer (1974) and others in the field of human capital theory. They transformed the idea of the homogeneity of labour, assumed in the neo-classical model, into a one-dimensionally conceived heterogeneity of the volume of human capital. The extent of an individual's human capital allows inferences about their productive capacity and corresponds with their level of income (Becker, 1964: 29ff, 59ff). Labour becomes a capital good, and investments in labour enhance productivity. These investments consist of the sum of

Human capital theory

the costs of one's education and training plus one's opportunity costs – in the form of forgone wages and diminished leisure time – incurred while pursuing these (Mincer, 1974). In the wake of human capital theory's endogenisation of training in the calculus of economic optimisation, wage levels must now accord with the value of output and training costs.[1]

Social-scientific labour market theory

The main criticism levelled by social scientists at economic labour market theories is the discrepancy between their assumption that labour markets tend towards equilibrium and the reality that labour markets are not markets like other organised commodity markets (e.g. wheat or stock markets) because volume and price adjustments occur due to structural constraints (state regulation, the market-influencing power of unions and large firms, employer transaction costs). Prices are thus not infinitely flexible. Moreover, the microeconomic view of the labour market does not take into consideration the macroeconomic interdependence of the markets for goods, commodities and labour. A drop in wages, for example, drives down the demand for goods, which can further depress wages, as prices on consumer markets and prices on factor markets are strongly interrelated (Samuelson and Nordhaus, 2005: 29). In light of this critique, segmentation theories in particular have gained resonance within social-scientific labour market research. Underlying all segmentation theories is the notion that the labour market is divided into partial markets in which training programmes, compensation patterns and employment dynamics are subject to institutional regulation. Whereas economic theory argues deductively, that is, from the general theory of equilibrium down to the specific problems of labour markets, segmentation approaches proceed inductively and juxtapose an analysis of the demand side (of firms and their structures) with an equivalent analysis of the supply side (Doeringer and Piore, 1971; Blossfeld and Mayer, 1988).

Regulation of labour markets

Contemporary economic theory does not deny the existence of partial labour markets. Yet its decisive assumption is that such sub-markets operate according to identical principles, that they are separated only by pervious boundaries and that mobility across these is a result of wage discrepancies. According to labour market theories in social science, however, the labour force is not an undifferentiated mass wherein each worker can be substituted by another and all compete against all. Rather, it is composed of distinct, distinguishable segments, among which mobility occurs only to a limited extent. Theories of segmentation ultimately argue that the wage mechanism is not the only allocation rule. Labour market institutions and existing social and legal norms hinder full wage flexibility (Doeringer and Piore, 1971).

Despite these differences between economic and social-scientific labour market theories, commonalities exist across both schools of thought as well. Both approaches view the labour market – the central institution of modern societies – as a locus of permanent change. These change processes concern among other things the temporally and spatially varying demand for labour, measurable via labour market participation and unemployment (Sections 7.2 and 7.3), the sectoral and occupational structure of the labour market (Section 7.4) and mobility across the labour market (Section 7.5). Before discussing the state of these indicators in European labour markets, we will begin with a discussion of the latter's economic performance.

7.1 Economic performance and living standards

NOTE ON METHODOLOGY

Gross Domestic Product (GDP) is a general indicator of a country's economic condition and material wealth. It represents the total market value of goods and services produced in a calendar year net of the value of goods and services used as intermediate inputs. Using Eurostat data, this indicator is expressed here in terms of purchasing power standards (PPS) so as to control for differences in price levels across countries. Calculations on a per capita basis allow comparison of economies of varying sizes.

The GDP growth rate derives from Eurostat data on Gross Domestic Product per capita in constant prices (base year 1995). The data are inflation adjusted.

A society's levels of economic productivity and achieved prosperity decisively shape its social structure:

> Prosperity is the foundation not only of an individual's standard of living, but also of a society's ability to avail its members of public goods such as education, health care, transportation and communications infrastructure. (Hradil, 2006: 188, authors' translation)

Even a society's lifestyles and mentalities are influenced by its levels of productivity and prosperity. These indicators are also crucial for government policies and for debates on the future of European societies.

The differences in the value of the goods and services produced in Eastern versus Western Europe are considerable. With regard to levels of socio-economic development, one can distinguish three groups within the European Union. In the middle group – and there alone – one can find both principal Member States and new accession countries. In the strongest group one finds only principal Member States, and in the weakest group only countries that acceded to the Union during the last two rounds of expansion. Luxembourg boasts the largest per capita

Productivity and living standards vary across Europe

Gross Domestic Product (GDP) in purchasing power standards (PPS), namely 68,000 euro. Its per capita GDP is roughly 170% higher than the average of the EU–27 (Table 7.1, second column from the right). Ireland, the Netherlands, Austria, Sweden and Denmark also enjoy very high GDP figures ranging 30,000 to 34,000 euro (in PPS). By comparison, Switzerland's GDP is about 35,000 euro (in PPS) per inhabitant (Eurostat, 2010b). Germany's and France's GDPs are around the EU–15 average.

In accession countries GDP is 60% of EU-15 average

The total value of the goods and services produced per capita in the accession countries, and thus their living standards, is considerably lower than in the principal Member States. It amounts on average to about 58% of the level of the latter, which is an expression of the continuing gap in economic development (OECD, 2006b, 2006d, 2007d, 2007e). Indeed, the GDP in countries like Bulgaria, Romania, Latvia and Poland amounts to 50% or less of the EU–15 average. In the middle of the 1990s, the GDP in Eastern European countries was only 40% of that of the principal Member States. To put this in context, one should also recall that the latter are some of the most productive economies in the world. A catch–up process is thus occurring.

The lowest per capita GDPs in the EU in 2008 were to be found in Bulgaria (€10,400) and Romania (€12,000). The residents there enjoy only a fraction of the living standards of the EU–15 average. The highest per capita GDPs in the Eastern European accession countries are those of Slovenia (€22,800) and the Czech Republic (€20,200), which have almost reached the prosperity level of Greece. Both countries have already passed Portugal and Malta. The reasons for this economic success in the Czech Republic and Slovenia are successful industrial location policies, comparatively high volumes of foreign direct investment, strong export sectors, low to moderate inflation and large supplies of highly skilled and (by Western standards) inexpensive labour (Bank of Slovenia, 2009: 13ff; Czech National Bank, 2009: 18ff). For the Czech Republic, high growth rates in the tourism sector play an additional role.

High GDP growth in Eastern Europe

Over the course of time, European economies have developed at different paces (see Table 7.1, right column). Relative to the principal Member States, the accession countries (with the exception of Malta) are growing at above-average rates. The Baltic states, for example, have been able to more than double their GDP between 1995 and 2008 (inflation-adjusted based on constant prices from 2000). In the Slovak Republic, Poland and Slovenia, too, GDP has grown markedly in recent years. Even in the Czech Republic, the country with the lowest growth rates in Eastern Europe, GDP increased by about 50% during the observed period. These figures point to the aforementioned catch-up process in Eastern Europe. The prosperity gap between Western and Eastern Europe has grown smaller.

Table 7.1: Gross Domestic Product

	1995 (in PPS)	2000 (in PPS)	2008 (in PPS)	2008 (EU-27 = 100)	Real growth 1995–2008 in %
EU-15	17,000	22,000	27,800	110.8	25.4
Belgium	18,900	24,000	28,900	115.1	26.0
Denmark	19,300	25,100	30,100	119.9	21.7
Germany	18,900	22,600	29,000	115.5	21.1
Ireland	15,000	24,900	33,900	135.1	82.4
Greece	12,300	16,000	23,600	94.0	52.6
Spain	13,400	18,500	25,700	102.4	34.9
France	17,000	22,000	27,100	108.0	21.3
Italy	17,700	22,300	25,600	102.0	11.9
Luxembourg	32,600	46,400	69,300	276.1	51.0
Netherlands	18,100	25,600	33,600	133.9	33.7
Austria	19,700	25,000	30,900	123.1	30.7
Portugal	11,000	14,900	19,000	75.7	24.5
Finland	15,800	22,300	29,400	117.1	52.1
Sweden	18,400	24,100	30,100	119.9	36.5
United Kingdom	16,600	22,700	29,200	116.3	34.2
Bulgaria	4,700	5,300	10,400	41.4	63.8
Czech Republic	10,800	13,000	20,200	80.5	48.8
Estonia	5,300	8,600	16,900	67.3	146.5
Cyprus	13,000	16,900	24,000	95.6	31.4
Latvia	4,600	7,000	14,400	57.4	148.7
Lithuania	5,200	7,500	15,500	61.8	137.9
Hungary	7,600	10,500	16,100	64.1	62.1
Malta	12,700	15,900	19,100	76.1	15.8
Poland	6,300	9,200	14,100	56.2	82.7
Romania	–	5,000	12,000	47.8	–
Slovenia	10,900	15,200	22,800	90.8	70.8
Slovakia	7,000	9,500	18,100	72.1	89.6
EU-27	14,700	19,100	25,100	100.0	29.1

Source: Eurostat (2010b), figures are purchasing power standards in euros; real growth rate: own calculations based on GDP in constant prices (base 2000).

Among the principal Member States, the highest growth rates are found in Ireland (+80%), Luxembourg, Greece, Finland and Sweden (all about +50%). Luxembourg has thus been able to put even more distance between itself and the rest of the pack, boasting an absolute increase in its per capita GDP of 37,000 euro. Economic growth in Ireland, Greece and Spain has also been impressive, especially when one recalls that in the 1970s and 1980s these countries – in contrast to Finland or Sweden (economies with traditionally good or excellent growth rates) – were among the least developed in Europe.

Low GDP growth in Italy, Germany, France

Below-average economic growth occurred between 1995 and 2008 in Italy, Germany and France (+16% to +22%). In the case of Germany, this was due to specific problems stemming from unification, high wage and non-wage labour costs and weak domestic demand (OECD, 2006c: 21ff; 2008a: 11ff). Italy's economy developed even more anaemically during this period. In 1995 the country was still ranked seventh in terms of its economic output and standard of living. By 2007 it had fallen to fourteenth. Failure to enact structural political reforms, daunting national debt and inflation, inefficient public administration, and low industrial competitiveness were the causes of this development (OECD, 2005c: 19ff, 32ff, 42ff; 2009i: 11ff). In France, similar factors led to below-par economic growth, such as the failure to enact reforms in the public administrative sector, substantial national debt and high wage and non-wage labour costs (OECD, 2005b: 21ff, 95ff; 2009h: 9ff). Faring better than Italy, Germany and France were a group of countries whose growth rates of about 30% hovered slightly above the EU-15 average – Austria, the Netherlands, the United Kingdom.

Eastern catch-up yet continuing EU disparities

On the whole, EU Member States have seen positive economic growth in recent years. Particularly salient has been the ability of the Eastern European states to narrow the gap with their Western counterparts. Despite this catch-up process in the East, though, inequalities in economic output and living standards have not diminished within the expanded European Union, for at the same time some Western European economies have declined relative to the EU-27 average. Variation in GDP increased from 1995 to 2008, which is, however, partially due to the mathematical logic of the standard deviation (it increases automatically with increasing mean).

> The global economic and financial crisis that began with the collapse of large American investment banks and insurance companies in 2008 also had profound effects on economic production in Europe. At the time of production of this textbook, no official statistical data is yet available on the impact of this crisis on GDP growth within the European Union. Foreseeable trends can be estimated for 2009, though, using OECD prognoses (compare OECD, 2009a). According to these projections, countries like Ireland, Finland, Hungary, the Slovak Republic and the UK will see a decline in GDP of between 6% and 9% by the end of 2009 compared to the end of 2008. Smaller losses can be expected in France, Belgium, the Netherlands and Austria (–4%). Between these two poles are countries like Sweden, Denmark, Germany and Italy, which suffered a decline in GDP during 2009 of roughly 5%.

7.2 Labour market participation

NOTE ON METHODOLOGY

Labour market participation is calculated as the number of employed persons between the ages of 15 and 64 divided by the total population within this age group. The Eurostat indicator used covers those living in private households, but excludes those living in institutional arrangements such as retirement homes, student dormitories, prisons or hospitals.

In labour market research the term 'labour market participation' is used to characterise broadly all forms of integration in the labour market. This concept is also central to social-structural processes, for a person's income, social contacts, scope for action, sense of self-esteem and personal identity all depend on his or her labour market integration (Giddens, 2009: 923f). Participation in the labour market thus has a dual significance in socialisation processes, namely both in the securing of a livelihood and in terms of social integration. Already in the classics of Marx, Weber or Durkheim, employment was considered to be a central institution of socialisation (see Box below; cf. Section 3.1), as the great majority of the population at this time participated in production processes. In the 1980s, after gainful employment had ceded some of its structuring power for society, a lively debate flourished, particularly in Europe, about the end of the work society (for the contours of the debate, see, for example, Dahrendorf, 1980; Offe, 1985; Sabel and Zeitlin, 1985; Zuboff, 1989). But this thesis turned out to be premature, and the employment sphere continues to play a central role in the structuring of society in the 21st century. Economists view labour market participation as a key indicator of the demand for human capital. From this perspective it is common to analyse comparatively the labour market participation of various population groups based on class, gender or age (e.g. Erikson and Goldthorpe, 1992; Bernhardt et al, 1995; Hardy, 2006; Bertola et al, 2007; Weeden et al, 2007).

Labour force participation

Historically, the centrality of gainful employment can be traced back to the industrialisation process of the 19th century (see Chapter 3). For the sociological classics, which were penned in this era, the work sphere is considered to be 'the' socialising institution. For Marx the analysis of the employment sphere is central because through it the conditions and relations of production as well as conflicts between social groups become visible. Durkheim sees labour and the division of labour as a source of solidarity and social integration. For Weber, on the other hand, the ways in which labour is organised in industrial societies (key concepts: rationalisation, bureaucracy, the work ethic) are of primary concern, for these function as structuring principles for the entire society. In the 1980s many scholars discussed the thesis of the end of the work society (e.g. Dahrendorf, 1980; Offe, 1985; Sabel and Zeitlin, 1985; Zuboff, 1989; Appelbaum and Schettkat, 1994). According to this thesis, the structuring power of the work world had declined in significance as a result of the decreasing duration of the typical working life and the increase in leisure. Current research focuses on a change in the significance of employment and its transformation (McManus, 1999; Wilthagen and Tros, 2004; Blossfeld and Hofmeister, 2006a; Blossfeld et al, 2006; Pettinger et al, 2006; Perrucci and Perrucci, 2007; Rogerson, 2008). Themes include the change from an industrial to a service society; the end of the male breadwinner model; the increasing labour market participation of women; the individualisation of work; the dovetailing of work processes across economic sectors through computerisation, the internet and multimedia; the rationalisation and enrichment of work in high-wage areas; the outsourcing of work to low-wage areas; the increasing flexibility of work as a result of the breakdown of inflexible work-time norms; and the spread of temporary and part-time work.

Labour market participation across the European Union varies greatly. Among the principal Member States it is much higher than in the accession countries. In Sweden, Denmark, the UK and the Netherlands, 72–77% of the entire working-age population was actively pursuing employment in 2008. Even though these countries have high wage and non-wage labour costs, firms' demand for labour is great. The demand in accession countries like Poland, Malta, Bulgaria, Hungary and Romania, as well as Italy, is relatively low: there, only 54–59% of the population participates in the labour market. Countries like Germany, Slovenia or Portugal evince roughly average labour-market participation rates: 67–68% of working-age persons were integrated in the labour market in 2008.

Labor market participation higher among men than women

More men than women are active in the European labour market. Particularly high rates of male labour market participation could be found in 2008 in Denmark, the Netherlands, Cyprus, the UK and Austria (77–82%); particularly low rates in Poland, Hungary and Romania. The leading countries in terms of female labour market participation are the social-democratic welfare states (Denmark, Sweden, Finland), the Netherlands and the liberal economies (the UK and Estonia) (employment rates of 66–74%). The reasons for these high rates of female labour market participation vary (Sainsbury, 1999; van der Lippe and van Dijk, 2002; Pettit and Hook, 2005; Mandel and Semyonov, 2006): in the Scandinavian states and in the Netherlands they stem from a considerable share of part-time work, in part state-subsidised. Welfare state expansion also plays a role here, for it has created many public sector jobs in administration, health care and education, a large share of which have been filled by women. In liberal economies, the generally high market pressure (low decommodification), greater human capital among women (on average) and strong employer demand lead to a high rate of female labour market participation. In some Southern European countries (Malta, Italy, Greece) and in Hungary this rate is rather low: here, currently between 37% and 50% of women are working. Thus cross-national variation in labour market participation is greater among women than men. Nearly 40 percentage points distinguish Denmark at the high end from Malta at the low end.

Table 7.2: Labour force participation

	Women				Men				Total			
	1993	1998	2003	2008	1993	1998	2003	2008	1993	1998	2003	2008
EU-15	49.2	51.6	56.2	60.4	71.0	71.2	72.7	74.2	60.1	61.4	64.5	67.3
Austria	–	58.8	61.6	65.8	–	77.0	76.4	78.5	–	67.9	68.9	72.1
Belgium	44.5	47.6	51.8	56.2	67.0	67.1	67.3	68.6	55.8	57.4	59.6	62.4
Germany	55.1	55.8	58.9	65.4	74.9	71.9	70.9	75.9	65.1	63.9	65.0	70.7
Denmark	68.2	70.2	70.5	74.3	75.8	79.9	79.6	81.9	72.1	75.1	75.1	78.1
Spain	30.7	35.8	46.3	54.9	63.0	66.8	73.2	73.5	46.6	51.3	59.8	64.3
Finland	59.5	61.2	65.7	69.0	62.5	67.8	69.7	73.1	61.0	64.6	67.7	71.1
France	51.5	53.1	58.2	60.7	67.3	67.4	69.9	69.8	59.3	60.2	64.0	65.2
Greece	36.6	40.5	44.3	48.7	72.1	71.7	73.4	75.0	53.7	56.0	58.7	61.9
Ireland	38.5	49.0	55.7	60.2	64.8	72.1	75.2	74.9	51.7	60.6	65.5	67.6
Italy	35.8	37.3	42.7	47.2	69.3	66.8	69.6	70.3	52.3	51.9	56.1	58.7
Luxembourg	44.8	46.2	50.9	55.1	76.4	74.5	73.3	71.5	60.8	60.5	62.2	63.4
Netherlands	52.2	60.1	66.0	71.1	74.6	80.2	81.1	83.2	63.6	70.2	73.6	77.2
Portugal	55.0	58.2	61.4	62.5	75.8	75.9	75.0	74.0	65.1	66.8	68.1	68.2
Sweden	69.7	67.9	71.5	71.8	73.0	72.8	74.2	76.7	71.3	70.3	72.9	74.3
United Kingdom	60.8	63.6	65.3	65.8	73.9	77.3	77.8	77.3	67.4	70.5	71.5	71.5
Bulgaria	–	–	49.0	59.5	–	–	56.0	68.5	–	–	52.5	64.0
Cyprus	–	–	60.4	62.9	–	–	78.8	79.2	–	–	69.2	70.9
Czech Republic	–	58.7	56.3	57.6	–	76.0	73.1	75.4	–	67.3	64.7	66.6
Estonia	–	60.3	59.0	66.3	–	69.6	67.2	73.6	–	64.6	62.9	69.8
Hungary	–	47.2	50.9	50.6	–	60.5	63.5	63.0	–	53.7	57.0	56.7
Lithuania	–	58.6	58.4	61.8	–	66.2	64.0	67.1	–	62.3	61.1	64.3
Latvia	–	55.1	57.9	65.4	–	65.1	66.1	72.1	–	59.9	61.8	68.6
Malta	–	–	33.6	37.4	–	–	74.5	72.5	–	–	54.2	55.2
Poland	–	51.7	46.0	52.4	–	66.5	56.5	66.3	–	59.0	51.2	59.2
Romania	–	58.2	51.5	52.5	–	70.4	63.8	65.7	–	64.2	57.6	59.0
Slovenia	–	58.6	57.6	64.2	–	67.2	67.4	72.7	–	62.9	62.6	68.6
Slovakia	–	53.5	52.2	54.6	–	67.8	63.3	70.0	–	60.6	57.7	62.3
EU-27	–	52.0	54.9	59.1	–	70.3	70.3	72.8	–	61.2	62.6	65.9

Source: Eurostat (2010b); figures are percentages of 15–64 year olds.

Labour market
participation
rising

Between 1993 and 2008, the period before the economic crises, demand for labour by firms in Europe rose (Table 7.2). In the principal Member States in 2008, 67.3% of 15–64 year olds participated in the labour market versus 60.1% in 1993. Labour market participation rose particularly strongly in Spain, Ireland, the Netherlands and Finland (+10% to +18%). Portugal and Sweden evince the smallest growth among the principal Member States. In the accession countries one finds a similar pattern as in Western Europe, with a few exceptions. Here, however, one can often only observe the changes that took place between 1998 and 2008. Within this relatively short time span, labour market participation rose above all in Slovenia, Estonia and Lithuania. Herewith the employment outlook in Europe as a whole recovered somewhat. Romania is a special case within Europe. There labour market participation has declined significantly (compare Vlad, 2004; Glass and Kawachi, 2005; OECD, 2006d). As a result of the broad overall trend, variation in labour market participation rates across Europe has lessened over time (1993: SD of 7.6; 2008: SD of 6.0).

Labour market
participation
has risen
more among
women than men

.For women and men this development has not proceeded uniformly, as within the European Union female labour market integration has increased more rapidly. As a result, the gender gap has shrunk over time. On average within the principal Member States, female labour market participation increased from 49.2% to 60.4% from 1993 to 2008, while that of men rose by barely 3% to reach 74.2%. Among men, the rise in employment rates is particularly evident in Spain, Finland and Ireland. Above all in Romania, but also in Poland, the Czech Republic, Portugal and Luxembourg, labour market participation rates of men have declined. The greatest increases in female labour market participation are found in the principal Member States of Spain, Ireland, Italy, the Netherlands and Greece (compare Jaumotte, 2003; Kaiser, 2006). In the accession countries a similar pattern obtains. Among both women and men, labour market participation has increased in most countries. Apart from a few exceptions (Slovenia, the Slovak Republic), here too it has risen more among women than men. As a result of this development, patterns of labour market integration for men and women – and the associated opportunities for income and prosperity – have converged, above all in the principal Member States.

Convergence of
labour market
partcipation

7.3 Unemployment

NOTE ON METHODOLOGY

This section is based on Eurostat data. The unemployment rate is the share of unemployed persons in the labour force. The labour force is the sum of employed and unemployed persons. Eurostat defines the unemployed as all persons of 15–74 years of age who at the time of the survey were not employed.

In most European countries, unemployment is associated with a high risk of poverty, restricted opportunities for consumption and direct dependence on state and private support. The unemployed are thus largely excluded from the socialisation processes that go hand-in-hand with labour market integration. The risk of losing one's job is not distributed equally across modern societies, but shaped by the given social structure. High risks are borne by new entrants to the labour market, older workers, migrants and women (Layard et al, 2005).

For many decades, discussions of unemployment were predicated on the assumptions that it affects primarily those of low socio-economic status, and that unemployment leads to enduring social exclusion for those who fall victim to it. Following the introduction of biographical and longitudinal methods in unemployment research, however, scholars increasingly began to understand unemployment as a transitory phenomenon and as a quasi-normal part of occupational trajectories – even, and increasingly, among the middle classes (Newman, 1999). Research interest became focused less on the loss of employment and more on the challenge of (re-)entry, that is, how various groups of persons in a state of unemployment find re-entry into the employment system (Bernardi et al, 2000; Konietzka, 2003; McArdle et al, 2007; Promberger et al, 2008). In the process, the notion gained ground that unemployment no longer leads necessarily to impoverishment, social deprivation, apathy and resignation, as classic unemployment research had portrayed (Jahoda et al, 2002 [1933]). Studies conducted as early as the mid-1990s (Bernardi et al, 2000; McArdle et al, 2007) showed that during phases of non-employment, at least a smaller fraction of the unemployed are able to cultivate and utilise individual tools and strategies.

Against that background, and turning to the empirical side of the phenomenon, in 2008 the unemployment rate was 7%, meaning that every 14th worker in the EU was unemployed (Table 7.3). The lowest rates could be found in the Netherlands, Denmark, Cyprus, Austria, the Czech Republic and Slovenia. With rates below 5%, these countries experienced near-full employment. The highest rates of unemployment in 2008 were in Spain, the Slovak Republic, Hungary and France.

Unemployment in Europe is lower on average among men than women. Women lack gainful employment particularly often in Southern European countries like Greece, Spain and Italy. In some of these countries, female unemployment is twice that of men. One reason is that women are employed predominantly in the service sector and in smaller businesses. Another is that the public sector, in which women have traditionally had good employment opportunities, is less well developed than in Scandinavia or Germany (see Section 7.4). As a result, women – despite constituting a lower share of high-school dropouts and a higher share of university graduates – work disproportionately in unstable jobs

Full employment

Consequences of unemployment

Unemployment in Europe lower among men than women

and are exposed far more directly to market risks than are men (Cousins, 1999; Flaquer, 2000; Blossfeld and Hofmeister, 2006b; Noguera, 2006; Pisati and Schizzerotto, 2006; Zambarloukou, 2007). Moreover, among recent immigrants a disproportionate share are female; this has sharpened competition in traditionally 'female' labour market segments of the tertiary sector (personal services, nursing, tourism) (Ayres and Barber, 2006: 29).[2] In some Eastern European accession countries (the Czech Republic, the Slovak Republic), too, the unemployment risks of women are markedly higher than those of men. In the relevant literature, this is seen as a negative consequence of transformation and modernisation processes (Lauerová and Terrell, 2002; Cazes and Nesporova, 2007). Over the medium term, the disadvantages of women in the labour market can be expected to improve, for here too women are now better educated than men (Eurostat, 2010b). In Romania, Ireland, the UK and the Baltic countries, on the other hand, women have a lesser risk of unemployment than men. This is because women there tend to be equipped with more human capital (a smaller share of women who are low-skilled or high-school dropouts, and a larger share who are university graduates) (Evans, 1998; Eamets and Ukrainski, 2000; Feldmann, 2005; Azmat et al, 2006; European Commission, 2007b; Eurostat, 2010b).[3]

Unemployment has declined more among women than men

Between the beginning of the 1990s and 2008 unemployment declined in Europe by about one third. The growing integrative capacity of the European labour market can be interpreted as an expression of its economies' increasing economic prosperity and competitiveness in world markets. In addition, structural labour market reforms (promotion of part-time work, programmes for decreasing long-term unemployment, tax incentives for job creation), eased transitions into retirement, growth in the high-skilled workforce and also increasing immigration into certain Member States have together combined to improve the labour market situation (Blanchard, 2006; OECD, 2007f; Biagi and Lucifora, 2008). A particularly noticeable decline in unemployment could be observed in recent years in the Netherlands and Denmark, where, respectively, the unemployment rate sank in 2008 to one fourth and one third of 1993 levels. This is further evidence of the economic progress these countries have made in recent years. Portugal is one of the few countries whose labour market problems – contrary to the general trend from 1993 to 2008 – have intensified. This is due above all to rising unemployment among men, while that among women has declined.

Change in employment structures

The data show a clear pattern: in most European states unemployment among women has sunk more markedly than among men. As a result, the labour market evinces a far less severe gender gap than ever before. The structuring power of this labour market dynamic for broader societal processes cannot be underestimated (e.g. decline in the birth rate and increase in the age of first marriage – see Chapter 5). In the course of

Table 7.3: Unemployment

	Women					Men					Total				
	1993	1998	2003	2008	2009	1993	1998	2003	2008	2009	1993	1998	2003	2008	2009
EU-15	11.2	10.7	8.7	7.6	9.0	9.1	8.2	7.3	6.7	9.1	10	9.3	7.9	7.1	9.0
Austria	5.1	5.4	4.7	4.1	4.7	3.1	3.8	4.0	3.6	5.2	4.0	4.5	4.3	3.8	5.0
Belgium	11.5	11.6	8.9	7.6	8.2	6.7	7.7	7.7	6.5	7.7	8.6	9.3	8.2	7.0	7.9
Germany	9.0	9.4	8.7	7.2	6.9	6.6	8.8	9.8	7.4	8.0	7.6	9.1	9.3	7.3	7.5
Denmark	9.9	6.0	6.1	3.7	5.4	9.3	3.9	4.8	3.0	6.5	9.6	4.9	5.4	3.3	6.0
Spain	23.6	21.1	15.3	13.0	18.4	15.5	11.2	8.2	10.1	17.7	18.4	15.0	11.1	11.3	18.0
Finland	14.4	12.0	8.9	6.7	7.6	18.1	10.9	9.2	6.1	8.9	16.3	11.4	9.0	6.4	8.2
France	12.9	12.8	9.9	8.4	9.8	9.5	9.4	8.1	7.3	9.1	11.0	11.0	9.0	7.8	9.4
Greece	–	16.8	15.0	11.4	–	–	7.0	6.2	5.1	–	–	10.8	9.7	7.7	–
Ireland	16.0	7.3	4.4	4.6	8.0	15.4	7.7	5.0	7.1	14.8	15.6	7.5	4.8	6.0	11.8
Italy	13.9	15.4	11.4	8.5	–	7.4	8.8	6.5	5.5	–	9.8	11.4	8.5	6.8	–
Luxembourg	3.3	4.0	4.9	5.9	6.2	2.2	1.9	3.0	4.1	5.3	2.6	2.7	3.8	4.9	5.7
Netherlands	7.5	5.0	3.9	3.0	3.5	5.4	3.0	3.5	2.5	3.4	6.2	3.8	3.7	2.8	3.4
Portugal	6.6	6.2	7.3	9.0	10.3	4.6	4.0	5.6	6.6	9.0	5.5	5.0	6.4	7.7	9.6
Sweden	7.3	8.0	5.2	6.5	8.0	10.7	8.4	6.0	5.9	8.6	9.1	8.2	5.6	6.2	8.3
United Kingdom	7.8	5.3	4.3	5.1	6.4	12.1	6.8	5.5	6.1	8.6	10.2	6.1	5.0	5.6	7.6

continued

147

Table 7.3 (continued)

	Women					Men					Total				
	1993	1998	2003	2008	2009	1993	1998	2003	2008	2009	1993	1998	2003	2008	2009
Bulgaria	–	–	13.2	5.8	6.6	–	–	14.1	5.5	6.9	–	–	13.7	5.6	6.7
Cyprus	–	–	4.8	4.3	5.5	–	–	3.6	3.2	5.1	–	–	4.1	3.7	5.3
Czech Republic	–	8.1	9.9	5.6	7.8	–	5.0	6.2	3.5	6.0	–	6.4	7.8	4.4	6.8
Estonia	–	8.3	9.9	5.3	10.6	–	9.9	10.2	5.8	16.9	–	9.2	10.0	5.5	13.8
Hungary	–	7.8	5.6	8.1	9.7	–	9.0	6.1	7.6	10.3	–	8.4	5.9	7.8	10.0
Lithuania	–	11.7	12.2	5.6	10.5	–	14.6	12.7	6.1	17.4	–	13.2	12.5	5.8	14.0
Latvia	–	13.6	10.4	6.9	14.4	–	15.1	10.6	8.0	20.6	–	14.3	10.5	7.5	17.6
Malta	–	–	9.1	6.6	7.7	–	–	6.9	5.6	6.6	–	–	7.6	6.0	7.0
Poland	–	12.2	20.5	8.0	8.7	–	8.5	19.0	6.4	7.8	–	10.2	19.7	7.1	8.2
Romania	–	–	6.4	4.7	–	–	–	7.6	6.7	–	–	–	7.0	5.8	–
Slovenia	–	7.5	7.1	4.8	5.9	–	7.3	6.3	4.0	6.1	–	7.4	6.7	4.4	6.0
Slovakia	–	13.1	17.8	10.9	12.6	–	12.2	17.4	8.4	11.2	–	12.6	17.6	9.5	11.9
EU-27	–	–	9.7	7.5	8.8	–	–	8.4	6.6	9.0	–	–	9.0	7.0	8.9

Source: Eurostat (2010b); numbers for 2009 are projections by Eurostat.

these changes, cross–national differences among European women (as shown by the standard deviations of unemployment) have decreased, while they have increased for men. In light of these findings, one can speak of a transformation and feminisation of gainful employment in Europe.

For the increase in unemployment resulting from the global economic and financial crisis, harmonised, internationally comparable data for 2009 are not yet available, but rather merely estimates (compare Table 7.3). According to these, the European Union can expect unemployment to have risen by the end of 2009, returning to 2003 levels. Particularly marked increases in unemployment are to be expected in Spain and the Baltic countries. In Spain at the height of the economic and financial crisis, nearly every fifth worker was unemployed, and in Latvia nearly 15% of the labour force was unemployed. In Scandinavia and in several Continental European countries (the Netherlands, Germany, Austria, Belgium) we observed only low to moderate increases in unemployment in the wake of this crisis. Quite possibly, the employment figures in Europe could normalise over the medium term. Robust prognoses are not yet available, however.

7.4 Transformation of the sectoral and occupational structure

NOTE ON METHODOLOGY

Changes in the sectoral structure of the labour market were calculated in terms of the percentage of workers in the primary (agriculture, forestry, mining, fishing), secondary (industry and construction) and tertiary (private and public services) sectors. The basis for these observations is the Eurostat Labour Force Survey.

The share of workers in the public sector was determined using the Eurostat Labour Force Survey. Proceeding from the European Union's NACE scheme for classifying economic sectors,[4] we combined the fields that are dominated by public employment: NACE groups L (public administration, defence, social insurance), M (education) and N (health and social work).

To capture change in the occupational structure in Europe, the shares of various occupational groups in the population as a whole were depicted using the Eurostat Labour Force Survey. Specifically, we distinguished: high-skilled service activities; skilled and routine service activities; skilled activities in agriculture, industry and construction; and unskilled activities.

Theories of the post-industrial society

In the preceding sections some of the most important characteristics of European labour markets were discussed. A further, central feature is the sectoral and occupational structure of the labour market and changes therein. Changes in the sectoral and occupational structure are discussed in the literature with reference to theories of the post–industrial society. If one accepts the 'classical' theories of the service society by Fourastié (1949), Baumol (1967), Bell (1973), Castells (1996) and Harvey (1990), then, over the long term, capitalist societies are undergoing a transformation from industrial to service societies (see also Section 7.3). In this view, the expansion of management and planning functions in firms, the spread of information technologies and the expansion of consumption-oriented services, marketing and advertising are leading to massive restructuring. Industrial society, according to Fourastié, was merely a transition society. In tertiary society, he predicts, 80% of the labour force will work in the service sector and only 20% in industry and agriculture. The tertiarisation of modern society is bringing about a transformation of the employment system towards higher-skilled and physically less demanding (service) work. As a result, the employment system becomes dominated by a class of professionally and technically

The role of knowledge

skilled occupations. Knowledge – the 'axial principle' of post-industrial society, according to Bell – becomes the foundation of technical, political and social innovation. In the process, information technology assumes a new position alongside machine technology (Bell, 1973: 189ff).

> Bell (1973: 19f, 112ff) argued that knowledge was gradually displacing property and the control of capital as the primary source of power in society. In post-industrial society the class of scientists, technicians and political technocrats dominates. In this theoretical approach, scientific analysis becomes the privileged means of interpreting the world and technical problem-solving becomes the paradigm of social planning. Value orientations, social fault lines and power structures thus shift in post-industrial society, and private property no longer constitutes the axial principle in this new societal form.

Three-sector hypothesis

The so-called three-sector hypothesis marks the beginning of discussion of the service society. In the primary sector, according to Fourastié (1949), moderate productivity growth is possible, while in the secondary sector relatively high rates of productivity growth can be achieved on an enduring basis. The tertiary sector harbours the lowest potential for rationalisation and productivity growth, for there are limits to the application of modern technology here.[5] The combination of the redundancy of industrial labour, the limited potential for rationalisation in the service sector and changes in individual demand have caused the 'less productive' tertiary sector to be able to absorb a vast number of workers. According to Fourastié (1949: 63ff, 179ff), the rise of the service society thus has dual origins: in the differential developmental potential of technology and productivity across economic sectors, and in a shift in the structure of demand from meeting the exigencies of physical subsistence to the satisfaction of leisure and consumption needs.

Scharpf (1986) has suggested that to estimate the labour market effects of tertiarisation, it is helpful to differentiate between production- and consumption-related services.[6] These realms yield distinct employment opportunities, which Scharpf attributes to their divergent potential for rationalisation as well as to the institutional structure of modern societies.[7] The employment potential of consumption-oriented services is generally greater. The most important precondition for this is that the lower labour productivity in this realm also be reflected in wages, otherwise there is a danger that the 'cost disease' described by Baumol (1967) will cause the supply of services to disappear from the market.[8]

Production-versus consumption-related services

The reason labour productivity in consumption-oriented and personal services is low, and rises only to a limited extent, lies in the *uno-actu* relationship between service production and consumption. In many consumption-related services, provision of the service requires the presence or active collaboration of the client. From this and from the temporally fluctuating claiming of these services, it follows that surplus capacities are required on the supply side. These stand in the way of a thoroughgoing rationalisation of service production (Scharpf, 1986: 29ff). Due to low value creation in consumption-oriented services, the demand for labour in this realm is mostly limited to low-wage occupations. In the public sector, the state can utilise subsidies to maintain supply (e.g. in child care). Employment potential in the production-related service realm is more modest (Feinstein, 1999: 43f, 49). This is mainly because the *uno-actu* principle does not apply here. To the contrary, at most during the placing of an order and possibly during delivery after its completion does a temporally and spatially synchronised meeting of the two contracting parties occur. In today's world, given the potential of modern communication technologies, even these personal encounters are no longer certain. At the same time, modern information and communication technologies are indispensable preconditions for the production of services. As a result, greater rationalisation potential can be found here than in consumption-related services. For this reason, in the future as well, employment growth in production-related services will in all likelihood not exceed the increase in demand.

Uno-actu principle

Theories postulating strong sectoral changes in the structure of European labour markets in recent decades are indeed supported by empirical evidence. While a significant portion of the labour force is still employed in industry, the service realm has now become the most important

Service industry as dominant economic sector

economic sector (Table 7.4). As late as the 1970s, several times as many persons worked in agriculture as do now (Feinstein, 1999). At that time, in some countries (e.g. Spain, Italy, Greece, Germany) a roughly equal share of employees was engaged in the industrial and service sectors respectively. In most other (Western) European states, however, already by the early 1970s the tertiary labour market segment had become dominant, a trend that continued throughout the 1980s.

In the 1990s, the tertiary structural transformation picked up speed across the whole of Europe. From 1998 to 2008, job losses in agriculture continued, as roughly three million more persons lost employment in this sector. Most severe was shrinkage of the agricultural labour market in accession countries like the Slovak Republic, Hungary and the Baltic states, as well as in Spain, Ireland and Greece. In addition, approximately half a million industrial jobs were lost in Europe. During this same decade, more than 26 million jobs were created in service industries (Labour Force Survey, 2009, own calculations). This notable shift in the sectoral structure of the European labour market accords in most respects with the theory of the post-industrial society (Fourastié, 1949; Bell, 1973; Scharpf, 1986).

Strong trend towards tertiarisation

In 2008 between two thirds and four fifths of all employees in the principal Member States worked in the service economy. This amounts to a 35% increase vis-à-vis the 1970s. Only one in four Western European workers can still be found in industry. Tertiarisation is particularly advanced in Denmark, Sweden, Belgium, the Netherlands, France, the UK and Luxembourg; in these countries 75–81% of the workforce is employed in the service sector. In the US, by comparison, the share was 76% in 2002 (UNDATA, 2008). In Eastern Europe, tertiarisation has been less marked than in Western European states or the US. The smallest proportions of workers in the service sector are to be found in Romania, Poland and Slovenia. The service sector labour market shares of Central and Southern European countries lie in the middle of the EU levels (around two thirds).

The East–West and North–South gaps in tertiarisation are matched by stronger agricultural sectors in Eastern and Southern European states (Slovenia, Latvia, Portugal, Greece and Lithuania). Poland and above all Romania are particularly worthy of mention in this regard, for these countries boasted agricultural labour market shares that in 2008 were, respectively, three and six times the EU-15 average. In Hungary, Estonia, Bulgaria, Slovenia, Slovakia and the Czech Republic, industrial firms continue to exert strong labour market demand in the early 21st century. In these countries 32–38% of the workforce is still engaged in industry or construction, although many industrial jobs were lost at the end of the 20th century. Exposed to world markets in the early 1990s, these (previously state-owned) industrial enterprises initiated massive layoffs over the following half-decade in order to ensure their survival

Table 7.4: Employment by sector

	Primary sector				Secondary sector				Tertiary sector			
	1970	1991	1998	2008	1970	1991	1998	2008	1970	1991	1998	2008
EU-15	16.2	7.6	4.5	3.4	37.4	28.6	26.6	23.2	54.0	73.0	68.9	73.5
Austria	14.0	7.0	8.4	6.4	42.0	37.0	26.6	23.6	56.0	56.0	65.0	70.1
Belgium	5.0	2.0	2.5	1.8	42.0	25.0	23.3	19.9	53.0	73.0	74.2	78.3
Germany	8.0	3.4	2.5	2.1	48.0	35.0	30.4	25.3	44.0	62.0	67.1	72.5
Denmark	11.0	5.6	3.8	2.9	36.0	28.0	23.7	20.8	53.0	66.0	72.6	76.3
Spain	25.0	10.0	7.1	4.3	37.0	31.0	29.2	27.3	38.0	59.0	63.7	68.5
Finland	20.0	8.0	6.3	4.8	34.0	29.0	27.8	25.6	46.0	63.0	65.9	69.6
France	15.0	5.7	4.3	3.3	37.0	26.0	22.5	20.1	48.0	69.0	73.2	76.6^
Greece	41.0	22.0	–	11.4	27.0	27.0	–	19.5	32.0	51.0	–	69.1
Ireland	25.0	13.0	9.0	5.8	31.0	24.0	28.6	25.6	56.0	73.0	62.4	68.6
Italy	16.0	8.9	5.3	3.9	42.0	29.0	30.3	28.2	42.0	63.0	64.5	67.9
Luxembourg	9.4	3.1	1.7	1.4	44.3	29.7	25.3	21.8	46.3	67.1	73.0	76.7
Netherlands	6.0	4.0	3.6	3.0	36.0	24.0	19.9	16.7	58.0	72.0	76.5	80.3
Portugal	30.0	11.0	13.2	11.6	30.0	33.0	33.0	27.9	40.0	56.0	53.8	60.5
Sweden	8.0	4.0	3.1	2.2	39.0	28.0	25.1	22.7	53.0	68.0	71.8	75.1
United Kingdom	3.0	2.1	1.9	1.5	42.0	25.0	–	17.7	55.0	73.0	75.3	80.7

continued

Table 7.4 (continued)

	Primary sector				Secondary sector				Tertiary sector			
	1970	1991	1998	2008	1970	1991	1998	2008	1970	1991	1998	2008
Bulgaria	–	–	24.7	19.3	–	–	29.6	28.3	–	–	45.8	52.5
Cyprus	–	–	6.3	4.2	–	–	22.5	20.3	–	–	71.3	75.5
Czech Republic	13.5#	10.0	5.6	3.5	49.4#	45.9	41.4	38.0	37.0#	44	53.0	58.6
Estonia	–	18.0+	8.8	3.9	–	36.0+	33.0	34.7	–	46+	58.2	61.4
Hungary	–	11.4+	7.6	7.5	–	35.6+	34.4	31.7	–	53+	58.0	60.8
Lithuania	–	19.6+	19.1	7.9	–	38.0+	28.6	30.4	–	42.4+	52.2	61.7
Latvia	–	20.0+	18.7	7.9	–	31.9+	25.5	28.0	–	48.1+	55.9	64.1
Malta	–	–	2.0	2.6	–	–	36.0	22.4	–	–	62.0	75.0
Poland	–	25.0	26.8	14.0	–	31.5	28.6	31.4	–	43.5	44.6	54.6
Romania	–	–	45.3^	30.3^	–	–	–	30.7^	–	–	–	38.7^
Slovenia	–	–	13.0	8.6	–	–	38.1	34.6	–	–	48.9	56.8
Slovakia	–	10.2~	7.0	3.6	–	39.7~	36.6	34.4	–	50.1~	56.3	62.0
EU-27	–	–	7.7	5.7	–	–	27.9	24.9	–	–	64.4	69.4

Source: Eurostat (2010b) for 1998, 2008; Haller (1997) for 1970, 1991; #1975, +1992, –1994, *1999, ^2006; figures are percentages.

and competitiveness (Stark and Bruszt, 1998). In the meantime, industrial employment in Eastern Europe has stabilised, and initial positive effects of outsourcing of industrial production from higher-wage countries such as Sweden, Belgium or Germany are evident (Hunya, 2004).

A glance at the share of the workforce in the public sector shows that the service society has developed in different ways across Europe. Figure 7.1 shows, on the basis of data from the Labour Force Survey, the proportion of workers in economic sectors in which public employment predominates (public administration and defence, compulsory social security, education, and health and social work).[9]

Public employment

In Ireland, Spain and to a certain extent Italy, the transformation from an agricultural to a service society has been accompanied by a moderate expansion of public services, as is also evident from a comparison with the sectoral transformation depicted in Table 7.4. More striking, however, has been the growth in the share of the labour force in the private service sector (personal and consumption-related services, trade and tourism) in those countries. In Scandinavia, Belgium and France, tertiarisation over the last three decades has gone hand-in-hand with employment growth in the areas of public administration, education, health and social work and with a simultaneous decline in industrial employment. Currently, the share of the total labour force that works in the public sector in these countries ranges from 29% to 32%, and thus four to five out of every 10 service sector employees are in the public sector.

In the Eastern European accession countries, different patterns can be observed. In most of these states the share of employees in agriculture and industry is still considerably higher than in all other European countries under study. The share of the workforce in the public sector is considerably lower than in Western European states, in large part due to the scaling back of public sector employment and the privatisation of public enterprises during the 1990s (Åslund, 2002: 255ff; Gabrisch and Hölscher, 2007: 60ff). The Czech Republic, Slovakia and the Baltic states are examples of economies with a low-to-moderate share of workers in the tertiary sector (see Table 7.4). In contrast to the aforementioned Western European countries, there employment in public services is relatively low, far outweighed by the private service sector.

Expansion of public employment, decline in industrial employment

Complete data series on employment in the public sector since the early 1970s are unfortunately unavailable for the European Union. An assessment of these countries over this entire period is therefore difficult, but data on the last 15 years do exist. Broadly speaking, one can see that despite privatisation and liberalisation across Europe, no decline in public sector employment has occurred between the mid-1990s and 2008. However, in some countries (Italy, Slovakia, Bulgaria, Finland, Estonia, Latvia), employment has been modestly scaled back over this period in the fields of public administration, defence, education, health and compulsory social insurance.

Dovetailing of labour market structures

In light of these findings, it seems that as service displaces industrial society, sectoral labour market structures are dovetailing within the European economic and social space, despite ongoing national differences. This observation is statistically supported: the standard deviation of employment shares in the primary, secondary and tertiary labour market sectors has declined in recent years.

Figure 7.1: Public sector employment

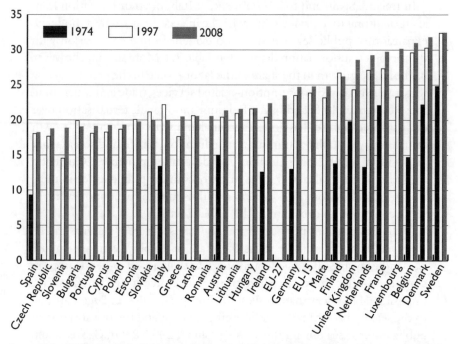

Source: Haller (1997) for 1974; all other numbers are based on the Eurostat Labour Force Survey (2009), own calculations; figures for 1997: data for Bulgaria, Poland, Malta and Cyprus from 2000; data for Slovakia, Lithuania and Latvia from 1998; figures for 2008: data for Slovenia, Bulgaria, Poland, EU-27, EU-15 and Sweden from 2007; data for Romania from 2006.

Transformation of the occupational structure of the labour market

Greater demand for high-skilled labour

Tertiary structural change has consequences for employment conditions and occupational structure. Research in recent years has repeatedly described how tertiarisation processes give rise to a restructuration and polarisation of employment relations, compensation and working conditions. Particularly in consumption-related services, poorly paid and precarious jobs are the norm. In production-related services, on the other hand, occupations for people with advanced training predominate, and these jobs are more secure and better paid. This development is buoyed in developed Western societies above all by marked increases in labour market demand for high-skilled service workers and decreases in labour market demand for skilled and unskilled workers in the industrial sector (Katz and Autor, 1999; Acemoglu, 2002; Card and DiNardo, 2002).

In the tertiary sector, it is assumed that increasing demand for high individual productivity and work enrichment go hand-in-hand with greater expectations of flexibility and social and process-oriented skills. This development is part and parcel of the displacement or weakening of so-called normal by atypical employment relations (Offe, 1985; Breen, 1997; Grip et al, 1997; Standing, 1997; Kalleberg, 2000). The consequence is a destandardisation of work processes, work hours and working conditions, as well as a shift in firm and sectoral compensation structures. The lion's share of jobs in consumption-related services are poorly paid due to the low rates of value creation therein. Similarly, the use of fixed-term employment contracts and a rise in project-specific hires – which have become widespread in many realms of the service sector (internet, advertising, media, film, marketing) – have had negative consequences for compensation and other benefits. Exempted from these are high-skilled workers, as Giesecke and Groß (2003) demonstrate. At the same time, the number of very well-paid jobs in production-related services has increased. DiPrete et al (2002) show that value creation now occurs far more than hitherto across organisational and firm boundaries. For enterprises, the group of analysts, strategists, problem-solvers and managers is becoming ever more important. In the course of this development, rewards based on job tenure or seniority have lessened, and firms pay more based on skills and occupational experience. High-skilled workers (e.g. analysts) have benefited from this structural transformation while low-skilled service providers and manual labourers have been forced to accept income losses.

In Western European industrialised countries at the beginning of the 1960s, the share of the workforce employed in high-skilled service professions ranged from 10% to 15% (Haller, 1997: 398). At this time, demand for skilled workers in industry, construction and agriculture predominated, as it was typical for the Fordist regime of accumulation (see Bell, 1973: 117; Toniolo, 1998: 259). The share of skilled workers in the total workforce ranged from 35% to 43% across Western Europe. By contrast, unskilled activities constituted only a small segment of the labour market. Skilled and routine service activities were already in relatively strong demand, as reflected in an employment share of 28%–38% (Haller, 1997: 398). At the dawn of the 21st century, Europe's occupational structure looks much different than it did in the 1960s and 1970s (see Table 7.5). The share of high-skilled service occupations has increased, while that of skilled activities in the primary and secondary sectors has shrunk. In 2008, the largest proportions of high-skilled service

1960s and 1970s: strong demand for skilled workers

Increase in high-skilled jobs

Table 7.5: Transformation of the occupational structure

	High-skilled services			Skilled routine services			Skilled manual jobs			Unskilled jobs			Part-time workers		
	1992	1998	2008	1992	1998	2008	1992	1998	2008	1992	1998	2008	1995	1998	2008
EU-15	–	18.5	19.9	–	44.9	46.9	–	26.5	22.0	–	9.8	11.2	15.8	17.7	21.0
Belgium	–	25.2	28.7	–	40.3	41.6	–	23.8	19.4	–	10.3	10.3	14.0	18.9	22.6
Denmark	17.1	17.2	20.1	47.1	49.0	51.8	21.2	20.2	17.0	12.8	13.5	11.1	21.8	21.3	24.6
Germany	13.1	15.3	17.3	42.8	47.4	49.3	30.4	28.8	24.2	8.1	8.1	9.2	16.3	19.4	25.9
Ireland	26.7	25.5	28.7	39.5	38.6	42.1	23.0	24.8	19.4	9.4	11.0	9.9	11.6	16.4	18.6
Greece	18.5	18.2	19.4	37.7	42.1	46.0	33.6	29.8	24.7	9.0	9.6	9.9	4.8	4.5	5.6
Spain	12.9	15.3	15.9	33.5	37.2	40.9	33.2	30.2	26.3	19.5	17.2	16.9	7.5	7.9	12.0
France	14.1	14.7	19.4	46.4	49.1	47.6	29.4	26.8	22.1	8.7	9.1	10.9	15.8	16.7	16.9
Italy	11.6	12.4	11.3	41.7	44.9	50.4	32.8	31.3	27.0	12.6	10.7	11.3	6.3	8.4	14.3
Luxembourg	21.9	17.6	28.5	35.3	46.3	42.9	42.6	24.4	16.9	–	11.6	11.8	8.5	10.4	18.0
Netherlands	23.8	25.1	26.8	43.8	45.9	47.4	21.3	20.1	15.8	7.2	8.0	10.0	37.4	41.5	47.3
Austria	–	14.8	14.5	–	44.9	51.1	–	30.0	22.0	–	10.3	12.4	13.6	16.3	23.3
Portugal	9.3	9.0	12.4	44.1	36.4	39.6	34.9	39.7	32.7	10.1	14.8	15.3	7.9	10.9	11.9
Finland	–	23.7	26.8	–	41.8	41.8	–	25.3	22.6	–	8.8	8.9	11.6	12.3	13.3
Sweden	–	19.4	24.0	–	51.3	49.6	–	23.5	19.9	–	5.7	6.5	20.5	19.5	26.6
United Kingdom	27.5	29.4	29.1	41.1	42.7	45.9	21.1	19.4	13.8	9.2	8.4	11.1	24.1	25.1	25.3

continued

Table 7.5 (continued)

	High-skilled services			Skilled routine services			Skilled manual jobs			Unskilled jobs			Part-time workers		
	1992	1998	2008	1992	1998	2008	1992	1998	2008	1992	1998	2008	1995	1998	2008
Bulgaria	–	17.3#	16.9	–	35.4#	35.1	–	34.2#	34.0	–	11.5#	14.1	–	–	2.3
Czech Republic	–	13.2	15.7	–	40.1	43.1	–	36.8	35.0	–	9.9	6.2	–	5.3	4.9
Estonia	–	23.7	24.8	–	30.6	32.0	–	33.6	32.9	–	12.1	10.3	–	8.1	7.2
Cyprus	–	14.7*	19.5	–	45.1*	45.5	–	23.4*	18.1	–	15.5	16.9	–	8.4	7.8
Latvia	–	20.7	22.1	–	33.1	36.1	–	31.6	27.9	–	14.7	13.8	–	11.3	6.3
Lithuania	–	24.5	29.2	–	25.9	29.1	–	36.3	31.6	–	13.2	10.1	–	10.2	6.7
Hungary	–	17.3	20.2	–	36.3	38.2	–	36.4	32.6	–	10.0	9.1	–	3.5	4.6
Malta	–	19.6#	21.2	–	41.3#	45.1	–	–	19.5	–	11.8#	14.1	–	6.8	11.5
Poland	–	17.6	22.9	–	35.8	34.7	–	35.7	32.6	–	11.0	9.8	–	10.5	8.5
Romania	–	12.2	17.1	–	31.7	34.6	–	47.7	38.7	–	8.5	9.6	–	16.5	9.9
Slovenia	–	15.2	22.5	–	42.8	41.9	–	36.5	28.6	–	5.5	7.0	–	6.5	9.0
Slovakia	–	13.3	14.0	–	38.1	41.4	–	37.4	35.1	–	11.2	9.5	–	2.1	2.7
EU-27	–	18.4#	19.9	–	43.3#	44.9	–	27.2#	24.2	–	10.0#	10.9	–	16.2	18.2

Source: Labour Force Survey (2009), own calculations; *1999, #2000; High-skilled services: ISCO main groups 1 + 2 ; Skilled, routine services: ISCO main groups 3 + 4 + 5; Skilled manual jobs: ISCO main groups 6 + 7 + 8; Unskilled jobs: ISCO main group 9. Part-time workers: Eurostat (2010b). jobs in agriculture, industry, construction: ISCO main groups 6 + 7 + 8; Unskilled

activities were found in the UK, Ireland and the Benelux countries. In these countries, nearly three out of 10 workers are engaged in such work. A moderate share of high-skilled service jobs can be found in Sweden, Denmark, France and Slovenia, for example. The smallest labour market share of such jobs is found in Italy, Portugal, the Slovak Republic and Austria (11–14%).

Growth in routine service jobs

In the realms of skilled and routine services, too, major shifts have occurred over the last few decades. On average, these occupations now constitute 47% of the workforce in the principal Member States versus just over 30% in the early 1960s (Haller, 1997: 398). In countries like Denmark, Sweden, Germany, the UK, Austria and Italy, this segment of the occupational structure witnessed double-digit growth rates between 1970 and 2008. In Southern European countries like Spain and Portugal, but also in the majority of the Eastern European accession countries, one finds a lower percentage of skilled and routine service jobs. The labour market segment consisting of skilled employment in agriculture, industry and construction is larger there than elsewhere in Europe.

Decline in skilled jobs in agriculture, industry and construction

Employment has been scaled back in skilled agricultural and industrial occupations in recent decades. Between the early 1960s and 2008 the share of these jobs in the workforce shrank by half. On average in the principal Member States, however, every fourth worker still works in such jobs. In this labour market segment, too, there is variation across Europe. In the Eastern European accession countries the proportion of these activities in the labour force (38%–52%) is much higher than in Western Europe. In the United Kingdom and the Netherlands only one in six workers is employed in skilled agricultural and industrial occupations. The opposite trend can be observed in unskilled occupations. While at the beginning of the 1960s in the principal Member States 1%–5% of the workforce was engaged in unskilled occupations (Haller, 1997: 398), now over 10% are. This trend is particularly marked in Sweden, Finland and Austria, where at the beginning of the 1960s only about 1% of workers was employed in

Increase in unskilled jobs

unskilled occupations (Haller, 1997: 398). However, the share of unskilled workers in the labour force in these countries is still much lower in 2008 than in Mediterranean countries like Spain, Portugal, Malta and Cyprus (14%–17%), where sectors like farming, construction and tourism offer employment opportunities for unskilled workers.

A glance at the far right column in Table 7.5 further confirms the thesis of a transformation of the occupational structure of Europe. It is obvious that above all in Western European states the number of part-time jobs has increased dramatically in recent years. Today, more than one in five employees in the EU-15 is engaged in part-time work. The job boom of the past decade (26 million additional positions in the service sector) is thus primarily a boom in part-time work. The European leader by far in this domain is the Netherlands, with a part-time share of 47% in 2008, followed by the UK, Sweden, Denmark, Austria and Germany (about 25%). In Southern Europe and especially Eastern Europe, by contrast, the share of part-time jobs in the labour force is much lower. The smallest shares of part-time work are in Bulgaria and the Slovak Republic.

This section has shown that Europe is undergoing a tertiary transformation process that is reorganising both the sectoral composition of national economies and their occupational structures. The expansion of the service sector brings employment growth above all in consumption-oriented and personal services, for the temporal linkage of production and consumption of these services stands in the way of their thoroughgoing rationalisation and thus makes substantial personnel investments necessary (Scharpf, 1986). Although the available data do not permit a distinction between personal/consumption-oriented and production-related services, the official statistics do clearly show that the tertiarisation process in Europe has created an abundance of new jobs in the service sector (more than 26 million positions in the 1990s alone). A transformation of the occupational structure is thus occurring. On the one hand, high-skilled and skilled employment in the service sector is on the rise, but, on the other hand, skilled jobs in industry and agriculture are on the decline, while the share of jobs for unskilled workers and part-time jobs is growing. This development has consequences for the social structures of European states. Individual opportunities to participate in the labour market are distributed less equally at the beginning of the 21st century than in the 1970s, 1980s or 1990s.

7.5 Social mobility

DEFINITIONS

When a person moves from one position in the social structure to another (usually measured in terms of occupational position), this is considered to be upward mobility if the person achieves greater income, influence or prestige. Conversely, downward mobility is when a person changes to a position endowed with less income, influence or prestige. Both forms of vertical social mobility are considered to be indicators of the permeability of modern societies.

Intergenerational mobility characterises a shift in social position from one generation to the next, traditionally measured by a comparison of the occupational positions of fathers and sons. Analyses of intragenerational mobility compare upward and downward mobility chances within a generation (birth cohorts or age groups).

The permeability of modern societies can be measured by the degree of social mobility in the labour market. Research on social mobility builds on the work of Pitrim Sorokin, who in the mid-1920s laid the groundwork for modern mobility research. He developed the lion's share of the conceptual apparatus used in mobility research. Sorokin defines social mobility as every vertical or horizontal shift of an individual from one social position to another in the social structure. He terms horizontal social mobility the transition from one social group to another social group on the same level. Vertical social mobility is the transition of an individual from one social stratum to another. Upward and downward movements can be differentiated into economic, occupational and political spheres (Sorokin, 1927: 133). Conceptually, Sorokin distinguishes between intragenerational and intergenerational mobility (Sorokin, 1927: 394ff, 463ff). The most important mobility concepts today are vacancy-competition theory and life course research. Sørensen's (1983, 2000) vacancy-competition theory argues more in terms of the labour market than do life course or classic mobility theories. Building on Max Weber's (1978 [1922]) theory of open and closed relations, Sørensen defines labour markets and/or partial labour markets as arenas in which dependent workers exchange their labour for wages and status, but also as entities framed by various structural factors (e.g. the training of workers, the firm's internal labour market, union co-determination). On this basis, vacancy-competition theorists distinguish between two ideal types of labour market: closed and open. Life course researchers study the temporal structure of mobility trajectories using longitudinal data. Compared to the rest of the sociological research on mobility, life course research focuses more strongly on intragenerational mobility and encompasses life realms such as one's family, living situation or social-structural background (Mayer and Tuma, 1990; Blossfeld and Huinink, 2006; Elder, 2009; Mayer, 2009).

Intra- and intergenerational mobility

Vacancy-competition theory, life course research

In vacancy-competition theory it is argued that in closed labour market systems, management control over access to positions and the distribution of rewards is constrained by institutional and organisational factors (labour market regulations, certification regimes, collective bargaining agreements, etc). The distribution of rewards is linked more closely to positions and less to the performance of the individuals in these positions. Mobility occurs through the creation of new posts and the fluctuation of position holders. In an open labour market system, control over positions and rewards lies almost entirely in the hands of management. Competition for positions is weaker than for rewards. Mobility in open labour markets is higher than in closed systems most of all because employees can be substituted out at any time based on market conditions. Life course research has a different focus. According to that school, individuals act on the basis of cumulative experiences and resources, and the life course is understood as a self-referential process. Subsequent events can be explained with reference to conditions, decisions and experiences of preceding life stages (Mayer, 2009: 423f).

The lifetime of individuals is seen as a constraint on agency. There are pivotal phases in the life course such as, for example, the transition from school to work. Life course structures are formed at the nexus between macro-societal institutions and individual action. These structures are partially overlaid with welfare state interventions.

Analyses of labour market mobility and hence of the relative permeability of modern societies are essential to social stratification research (for an excellent overview of the research of the last three decades, see Hout and DiPrete, 2006). Despite the significance of this subject matter,[10] data on labour market mobility are missing from European population statistics. Comparative EU analyses that include the Eastern European states are also lacking. For this reason, this section is based on a summary of existing research (Breen, 2004; Saar et al, 2008). It will allow us to show the degree of inter- and intragenerational mobility for a range of important European countries.

Lack of census data

Intergenerational mobility

If one observes the degree of intergenerational and intragenerational mobility in Europe with the aid of the analyses of Breen and Luijkx (2004), a series of interesting findings emerge concerning men's and women's chances of upward mobility (see Table 7.6). For their calculations of upward, downward and non-vertical mobility (lateral mobility without a change in status), we use data from nine developed industrial countries that all belong to the European Union. The basis of their analyses are positions within the seven-category class schema of the mobility study of Erikson and Goldthorpe (1992). Breen and Luijkx operationalise intergenerational mobility as a comparison of the occupational class positions of men and women vis-à-vis those of their fathers (at the time of the respondents' first employment). They thus focus on mobility processes mediated by the labour market.

Comparison of class positions of men and women with their fathers'

Looking first at the findings for men in Western Germany, France, Italy, Ireland, the UK, Sweden, Poland, Hungary and the Netherlands, one sees that the percentage of intergenerationally mobile men is relatively stable over time (Table 7.6, top half). On average, roughly two thirds of men in these countries assume a class position that does not accord with that of their fathers. Both upward and downward mobility are prevalent. Vertical mobility (whether upwards or downwards) occurs more often than lateral mobility (a change across occupational classes within the same status level).[11] Particularly high rates of intergenerational mobility occurred during the period from the 1970s to the 1990s in Italy, Sweden and Hungary. The lowest rates were found in Germany and the

More vertical than horizontal mobility

UK. Over this period Europe saw a slight increase in mobility overall, most strongly in Ireland and Poland. The Irish case can be explained with reference to the expansion of the service sector and an increase in educational opportunities (Layte and Whelan, 2004). For Poland, Mach (2004) explains the marked increase in rates of absolute mobility there during the 1990s vis-à-vis earlier periods in terms of the economic and social transformations after the fall of the Iron Curtain. By contrast, an intergenerational decline in rates of absolute mobility occurred between the 1970s and 1990s above all among men in Hungary.[12]

Upward intergenerational mobility

Upward mobility among men in Europe is far more common than downward mobility. Particularly salient in recent decades has been the upward intergenerational mobility achieved in Sweden and the Netherlands. This has been due in large part to the expansion of educational opportunities, the growth of the tertiary sector and, in the case of Sweden, the welfare state policy of supporting children from lower socio-economic strata (Jonsson, 2004; Luijkx et al, 2006). In Poland and France, on the other hand, a far more modest level of intergenerational upward mobility is evident. Mach (2004) attributes the Polish figures to an ossification of its society in the 1970s and 1980s. Whereas in the 1950s and 1960s Polish men achieved a high degree of intergenerational mobility due to the post-war modernisation and industrialisation surge, during the 1970s and 1980s such upward mobility among men did not continue (see Table 7.6). Instead, one sees 'very strong inheritance effects in the case of the service class and owners outside agriculture' (Mach, 2004: 270) – a pattern of reproduction of status positions that, according to the analyses of Diewald et al (2002) or Völker and Flap (1999), occurred in a similar fashion in East Germany before the fall of the Iron Curtain. For France there are grounds to assume that relatively rigid class boundaries led to a comparatively low level of upward mobility across generations (Vallet, 2004).

Downward intergenerational mobility

Downward mobility from one generation to the next occurs roughly half as often as upward mobility (1990s: 16.1%). In the 1990s a high level of downward mobility occurred among men in the United Kingdom and Poland, which, in the case of the UK, was due to increasing labour market flexibility and to a worsening market position of men vis-à-vis women (women's increasing labour market participation, decreasing unemployment and higher skill levels) (Golsch, 2006). A glance at the data from the 1970s and 1980s shows a high rate of intergenerational decline among Hungarian men, which can be explained by the economic stagnation during this period (Robert and Bukodi, 2004). In Germany and Italy one finds very few cases of male decline vis-à-vis the occupational positions of their fathers. In both cases the explanation is similar. For Italy, Pisati and Schizzerotto (2004: 154) speak of a 'massive upgrading of the occupational structure ... testifying to the constant movements of sons of farmers, agricultural workers, and blue-collar workers into the ever growing white-collar positions'. As a result, cases of upward mobility clearly outnumber those of downward mobility. This explanation accurately describes the development of the labour market in Germany as well, and one can add to it the argument, echoed by Kurz et al (2006: 107), that typical male careers in Germany are institutionally strongly protected.

The data in Table 7.6 show that not just in Germany and Italy, but in Europe as a whole, upward mobility has increased over time, while downward mobility has become more rare. This is a clear indication that the permeability of European societies has increased. The most dramatic increases in upward mobility over time have occurred in Ireland and Hungary (about +10 percentage points each). For men in the UK, intergenerational upward mobility decreased from the 1970s to the 1990s. An important finding of the analyses of Breen and Luijkx (2004) is the increasing dovetailing during the 1990s of mobility rates across Europe. Both for the overall rate and for upward and downward mobility, the standard deviations suggest a clear convergence of the patterns of intergenerational mobility in Europe.

Convergence of patterns of intergenerational mobility

The findings for women are similar to those for men. Comparing male and female mobility patterns is constrained, however, by the fact that female labour market behaviour – especially in the 1970s and 1980s – differed markedly from that of men (lower participation rates, fewer working hours, more frequent transitions from employment to non-employment).

Empirically, women evince a greater degree of intergenerational mobility than men. Between 71.9% (1970s) and 74.6% (1990s) of all women assume a different class position than their fathers. In the 1990s, women in Hungary, Poland and France achieved above-average mobility. In the two decades before, it was women in the UK, Hungary and Germany who very often reached a different class position than their fathers. Like men, women achieve vertical more often than horizontal intergenerational mobility. In contrast to men, among women the differences between upward and downward mobility are not so marked. While more women experience upward than downward intergenerational mobility, these differences did not fully emerge until the 1990s. On average in the European countries observed here, there was twice as much upward (34.7%) as downward (16.9%) mobility. In the 1970s women moved upward at an above-average rate in France and the Netherlands; in the 1990s, and above all in Hungary and Italy. Downward moves among women were widespread especially in Sweden and Hungary. In the 1990s they occurred comparatively often in the United Kingdom and Sweden.

In the course of these changes, female mobility patterns became far more similar to those of men in most countries under study (Jonsson,

Convergence of female mobility rates

Table 7.6: Intergenerational mobility

	Total mobility			Vertical mobility			Upward			Downward		
	1970s	1980s	1990s	1970s	1980s	1990s	1970s	1980s	1990s	1970s	1980s	1990s
Men												
Germany	61.6	62.1	60.3	44.1	45.8	46.3	31.7	33.6	33.3	12.4	12.2	13.0
France	66.6	67.5	67.0	43.8	45.9	46.3	25.9	29.1	29.9	17.9	16.8	16.4
Italy	–	69.5	72.1	–	40.8	46.3	–	29.0	35.9	–	11.8	10.4
Ireland	56.7	61.3	66.1	39.9	42.6	45.5	21.6	27.9	31.4	18.4	14.7	14.1
United Kingdom	63.0	61.8	60.8	50.7	50.8	50.7	32.8	33.1	31.7	17.9	17.7	19.0
Sweden	70.8	71.4	71.0	54.0	54.7	55.2	35.1	35.3	36.6	19.0	19.4	18.6
Poland	59.4	61.0	67.4	40.9	42.9	45.9	22.1	24.8	26.3	18.8	18.0	19.6
Hungary	77.5	74.9	71.6	53.0	55.8	53.7	26.9	34.7	35.9	26.2	21.1	17.8
Netherlands	66.3	67.7	65.7	50.6	54.1	54.0	36.1	38.9	37.7	14.5	15.2	16.3
Mean	65.2	66.4	66.9	47.1	48.2	49.3	29.0	31.8	33.2	18.1	16.3	16.1
SD	6.6	5.1	4.3	5.6	5.8	4.0	5.7	4.4	3.7	4.0	3.1	3.1
Women												
Germany	74.0	75.6	72.6	48.6	48.8	47.3	25.8	29.6	32.3	22.8	19.2	15.2
France	71.4	77.6	77.2	41.7	45.7	46.0	27.8	32.9	33.2	13.9	12.8	12.8
Italy	–	74.3	75.0	–	51.0	47.9	–	38.5	36.7	–	12.5	11.3
Ireland	–	–	–	–	–	–	–	–	–	–	–	–
United Kingdom	78.8	76.3	73.9	52.1	52.6	53.2	27.5	29.0	30.6	24.6	23.7	22.5
Sweden	73.1	73.6	73.2	55.4	56.4	57.9	23.9	27.5	33.5	31.5	28.9	24.4
Poland	50.8	66.3	76.2	34.0	48.5	50.3	19.5	31.7	34.1	14.4	16.8	16.2
Hungary	81.0	79.5	76.5	54.1	58.2	55.7	23.3	38.8	42.0	30.8	19.4	13.7
Netherlands	74.0	73.9	72.3	51.4	51.4	53.6	30.9	33.6	34.8	20.5	17.8	18.8
Mean	71.9	74.6	74.6	48.2	51.6	51.5	25.5	32.7	34.7	22.6	18.9	16.9
SD	9.9	3.9	1.9	7.7	4.1	4.3	3.7	4.2	3.5	7.0	5.4	4.7

Source: Compiled according to Breen and Luijx (2004: 48, 66); figures are percentages; unweighted means.

2004; Layte and Whelan, 2004; Mach, 2004; Pisati and Schizzerotto, 2004; Robert and Bukodi, 2004; Vallet, 2004). Internally among women, too, a convergence of mobility patterns occurred. In the 1970s, variance of mobility rates among European women was markedly higher than among men. Breen and Luijkx (2004: 49) adduce adaptation processes in the economies under study to explain this convergence. Of particular importance, they argue, were the growth of these countries' service sectors and the contraction of the agricultural sector in Poland, Hungary and France, among others. Another plausible cause of the lessening of differences in female mobility patterns is the increasing labour market participation and decreasing unemployment, as well as the decline in the variation in labour market participation and unemployment, among women (see Sections 7.3 and 7.4).

Intragenerational mobility

As in the case of intergenerational mobility, data are lacking for intragenerational mobility. Homogenised national statistics such as the European Commission offers for many of the other social-structural dimensions discussed in this volume are not available. Moreover, there are only a handful of publications that allow a systematic comparison of most Western and Eastern European countries (examples include Blossfeld et al, 2005, 2006; Blossfeld and Hofmeister, 2006a; Saar et al, 2008). Because Saar et al (2008) examine by far the most countries (22 of the EU-27 states), we will use their study as the basis for the final section of this chapter.

To characterise mobility processes in Eastern and Western Europe at the beginning of the 21st century, we utilise the following information (see Table 7.7): first, a general, aggregate mobility rate (transition rate) of labour market entrants between the ages of 15 and 35 within the first year of employment. This can be a transition into another job or into unemployment. This mobility measure captures a critical phase in the life course, namely the transition from school/training to work (Mayer, 2001, 2009). One can assume that this life course phase is influenced by welfare state and labour market institutions (e.g. regulations on the time-limitation of employment contracts and on dismissal protection). Second, the relative risks of downward mobility for labour market entrants; here, the mean value of occupational prestige is compared between the group of labour market entrants and all other labour market participants. If this score is high, the downward mobility risk for labour market entrants is low vis-à-vis labour market participants of the same skill level with occupational experience (Saar et al, 2008: 53); in that case, there would be no difference in the two groups' occupational standing in the labour market.

Aggregate mobility rate

Table 7.7: Intragenerational mobility and the risks of downward mobility

	Mobility rate in %	Risk of downward mobility
EU-22	42.3	0.85
Belgium	42.0	0.82
Denmark	51.2	0.90
Germany	37.1	0.92
Ireland	–	0.84
Greece	37.6	0.79
Spain	53.1	0.81
France	–	0.77
Italy	40.4	0.73
Netherlands	–	0.88
Austria	40.4	0.91
Portugal	39.1	0.79
Finland	47.2	0.89
Sweden	44.9	0.83
United Kingdom	50.6	0.94
Czech Republic	41.2	0.80
Estonia	40.2	0.87
Latvia	43.4	0.90
Lithuania	38.1	0.86
Hungary	37.9	0.85
Poland	33.3	0.85
Slovenia	48.6	0.80
Slovakia	37.1	0.83

Source: Saar et al (2008: 46, 54); data for 2004; EU-22: unweighted mean.

Downward mobility
The figures in Table 7.7 show marked variation across Europe in the mobility rates and relative risks of downward mobility for labour market entrants. The highest overall mobility rates are found among labour market entrants in Spain, Denmark, the UK, Slovenia, Finland and Sweden. In these countries, between 45% and 53% of workers change jobs within their first year of employment (2003/04). For a liberal labour market like the UK's this is no surprise. It is also well known that in Scandinavian countries labour market entrants are engaged in the most flexible segments of the labour market (Bygren et al, 2005; Saar et al, 2008). The findings for Slovenia are interesting: although its labour market has strong institutional similarities with the German one, its labour market for occupational entrants is very flexible (Saar et al, 2008: 49). At the other end of the mobility spectrum are labour market entrants in Poland, the Slovak Republic, Germany and Greece, of whom slightly more than one third either changed jobs or transitioned from employment to unemployment between 2003 and 2004. This finding was expected for Germany, for its labour market is considered to be comparatively inflexible (Müller and

Pollack, 2004; Streeck and Trampusch, 2005; Kurz et al, 2006). In the case of the Eastern European accession countries, the findings of Saar et al (2008) seem astounding at first glance, for recent findings suggest growing labour market pressure as a result of increasing flexibility of the labour market for younger cohorts in Eastern Europe (Mills et al, 2005). Saar et al (2008: 49) interpret this result as a sign of the emergence of an insider–outsider labour market in which labour market entrants are disadvantaged, for in these countries moderate downward mobility risks (when a job is taken), high unemployment risks and long unemployment episodes are simultaneously typical. This pattern strongly resembles the situation of labour market entrants in Greece (Saar et al, 2008: 49). Near the middle of the mobility spectrum of European labour market entrants are countries like Portugal, Italy, Austria, the Czech Republic, Latvia and Belgium, in which occupational entrants evince intermediate rates of intragenerational mobility.

Looking at the second indicator, labour market entrants in the UK, Germany, Austria and Denmark experience the lowest risks of relative downward mobility. The operationalisation of this indicator is worth recalling: it deals with 'occupational prestige distance' between different labour market groups of the same skill level, not with actual downward mobility. The low downward mobility risks for Germany and Austria confirm previous analyses of these countries. It has long been hypothesised, for example, that in Germany's highly hierarchical labour market, educational degrees and training diplomas would be particularly significant and that downward mobility would be rare by comparison with other societies (Allmendinger and Hinz, 2009). Surprising, on the other hand, is the United Kingdom's low risk of downward mobility, for previous research had shown that mobility in many cases transcends boundaries of class and educational attainment, and that academic degrees played a lesser role in occupational standing than in Germany (Allmendinger and Hinz, 2009: 239, 243ff). In the Danish case, high mobility rates and low downward mobility risks are a result of labour market flexibility. In contrast to the UK, however, Denmark has an active labour market policy and its educational system and labour market are tightly meshed. As a result, workers amenable to mobility both receive support in their job search (Gangl et al, 2003; Saar et al, 2008) and – based on the evidence available – can expect to find a position that correlates with their skill level. The data suggest that Italy, Greece and Portugal might constitute a distinct Southern European type of labour market mobility (Gangl et al, 2003; Saar et al, 2008). Moderate to below-average overall mobility rates there coincide with high downward mobility risks and relatively high unemployment. Sweden and most of the Eastern European countries form an intermediate group in which moderate risks of downward mobility coincide with mid-range general mobility rates.

Notes

[1] Even though human capital theory overcomes deficits in the neo-classical economic model, it has its own limitations. Discrimination theory reveals that even at equal levels of educational investment and resulting productive outputs, gender, age and ethnicity lead to wage differences. Human capital theory cannot explain these (England, 1982). Similarly, it cannot explain the emergence of unemployment, for just like neo-classical theory it assumes that at all times the flexibility of wages can lead to labour market equilibrium. At most it can explain the structure of unemployment in terms of differential investments in human capital (Layard et al, 2005).

[2] In addition, Ferrera (1996) and Cousins (1999) cite political and cultural causes of high female unemployment rates in Southern Europe. Blossfeld and Hofmeister (2006b: 439) argue in a similar way: a traditional male-oriented workplace culture denies women promotion opportunities, while the rise in education for women makes them better qualified, adding to the frustration of the situation.

[3] In the case of the Baltic states this could be a residue of the 'female-friendly' labour market policy of the Soviet period and the high educational level of the female labour force (Eamets et al, 2008: 126). Other authors have argued that this development is a result of the retreat of a large group of women from the labour market. Feldmann (2005: 72) and Eamets and Ukrainski (2000: 469) claim that this has occurred voluntarily in some cases because women want to devote themselves more to their families and children. To some extent this retreat from the employment sphere is involuntary, however, in that there simply are not enough jobs available, the costs of pre-school are too high and government policies support an exit from the labour force. In many cases these are low-skilled women; hence their exit from the labour force has improved the skill profile of the remaining female workforce vis-à-vis male workers. Above all in the UK, but also in Ireland, women have long evinced lower unemployment rates than men (Evans, 1998; OECD, 2006e). This is due to the greater human capital of female workers (Azmat et al, 2006; European Commission, 2007b; Eurostat, 2010b). Even more decisive, according to Evans (1998), are improvements in the support and legal protection of young women who seek to return to work after a period of work interruption stemming from familial caregiving responsibilities. These social policy measures have greatly reduced unemployment among women in the United Kingdom.

[4] The 'Nomenclature générale des activités économiques dans les Communautés Européennes' (NACE) is a system for classifying economic activities. It was developed by the European Union in 2001 on the basis of the UN's 'International Standard Industrial Classification of all Economic Activities' (ISIC).

[5] This can be demonstrated, for example, by examining the differences in productivity between employees in the health and automobile sectors. In Germany, the latter group has increased its productivity over the last 30 years roughly eightfold. Health sector employees

today are also more productive than ever, but lag far behind the productivity increases that have been common in industry.

[6] Production-related services arise in the course of the rationalisation of industrial production. Research, development, market research, advertising, finance, transportation, management, organisation and accounting have become ever more important vis-à-vis the actual production of goods. Personal and consumption-related services include services in the realms of health, care provision, education, entertainment, leisure, nutrition and tourism (Scharpf, 1986; Greenhalgh and Gregory, 2001).

[7] Tertiarisation does not per se yield positive labour market effects. According to Scharpf (1986), employment growth in service society depends on: (1) income distribution; (2) the level of the tax burden, which directly influences the price of services; and (3) the scope of publicly funded services. Where high income inequality and a low tax burden obtain, as in the US, private services can survive in the market despite low productivity. Conversely, in countries with low levels of economic inequality and a high tax burden, unproductive services can expand when – as in the Scandinavian welfare regime – they are state-subsidised.

[8] The theory of cost disease maintains that the service sector will not expand when wages therein are not tied to productivity growth. If the service sector has the same wage levels and similar rates of wage growth as the production sector, then the supply of services will disappear from the market or must be artificially sustained by state subsidies.

[9] This approach leads to a slight overestimation of the share of employees in the public sector in countries, for example, where pre-school child care is also offered by non-state institutions (the UK, Ireland, the Netherlands and Belgium). Alternatively, one could look only at the realms of public administration, defence and social insurance. This would lead to a considerable underestimation of the proportion of the labour force in the public sector, for in many European states the vast majority of employees in the areas of education, health and compulsory social insurance work in public enterprises. Moreover, working conditions, compensation, organisational size and job security in non-state institutions in, for example, the educational or health sectors resemble those in state institutions in the same sectors far more than they do those in industry, construction or personal services.

[10] A list of relevant works would include, among others: Blau and Duncan (1967), Featherman and Hauser (1978), Mayer (2009), Erikson and Goldthorpe (1992), Breen (2004), Blossfeld et al (2006), Morgan et al (2006) and Blossfeld and Hofmeister (2006a).

[11] Breen and Luijkx (2004: 47) define upward or downward mobility as a change between two of three distinct categories of positions: (1) higher and lower grade professionals; (3) semi- and unskilled manual workers, and agricultural workers; and (2) routine, non-manual employees in administration, commerce, service and sales, and skilled manual workers, lumped together into one category in between.

[12] Robert and Bukodi (2004) also attribute this to the societal changes after 1989. They emphasise that the decline in rates of absolute mobility primarily represent a decline in horizontal mobility, which during the 1970s occurred with unusual frequency. The shrinking industrial sector led to increasing unemployment but also to clinging to jobs already held. Mobility without perceptible advancement became too risky (Bukodi and Robert, 2006). Nonetheless, upward mobility chances increased during this period. This suggests an opening of Hungarian society, despite the decline in rates of absolute mobility. Interestingly, men profited less than women from these opportunities for upward mobility (Robert and Bukodi, 2004).

8

Education

The elements of and changes in the social structure are linked to developments in the educational system in myriad ways. For this reason, it is unsurprising that one of the central themes of research and debate on inequality and social stratification is the unequal distribution of education in modern societies. The sociological debates on education 'are debates about the direction of society itself' (Giddens, 2009: 834).

Current discussion in educational sociology can be divided into two schools of research. The first tradition, inspired by functionalism (Parsons, 1952; Durkheim, 1961 [1925]), focuses on the role played by the educational system in modern society. Its functions can be expressed ideal-typically as: (a) transmission of basic knowledge in primary education according to authoritative standards; (b) specialisation in vocational secondary education corresponding to the division of labour in modern economies; and (c) identification of talent and training of this talent at the university level. This conceptualisation of the relationship between the educational system and social structure stems from the US sociologists Kingsley Davis and Wilbert E. Moore, whose functionalist stratification theory of the 1940s and 1950s greatly advanced research on inequality and social structure (Davis and Moore, 1945).[1]

Arguably the most important functions of the educational system in the functionalist logic are the selection of suitable individuals for higher education and their subsequent assignment to positions important to modern society, which are in turn well compensated. Education and the skills acquired and certified therein are considered in our society to constitute innovation potential and are a central precondition for economic success and societal prosperity (Collins, 1971). Closely linked to this is the idea of meritocracy: individual effort and investments in education should be rewarded (Giddens, 2009: 835). Another argument for the functional significance of education would include the idea that in modern, 'post-industrial societies' technical, societal and political relations become ever more complex. They demand ever more knowledge from the individual. No longer are machines the motor of economic development, but human knowledge and skills. Hence these societies are characterised as 'knowledge societies' or 'information societies'. However, in today's research the functionalist model has lost much of the influence it had in the post-war period (Moore, 2004: 49).

A second tradition of sociological research approaches education with a concern for inequalities produced and reproduced in the system.

Selection function of the educational system

Inequality perspective

This school focuses on the relative equality of opportunity of access to coveted educational institutions and of attainment of higher educational degrees (Gregg, 2004; Goldthorpe, 2007; Jackson et al, 2007; Duru-Bellat et al, 2008; Ballarino et al, 2009; Blanden and Breen et al, 2009). Other studies examine the problem of educational poverty (Allmendinger and Leibfried, 2003) and the connection between inequalities in educational and labour market opportunities (Shavit and Müller, 1997; Solga, 2002; Breen and Jonsson, 2005; Heinrich and Hildebrand, 2005; Müller, 2005). Further, some scholars analyse societal processes that structure the unequal distribution of educational capital, as well as the role of the educational system in the reproduction of inequalities (Bourdieu and Passeron, 1970; Bourdieu, 1984). Despite their different foci, all these studies come to the consistent finding that equality of educational opportunity does not obtain in modern societies.

Against the background of these theoretical perspectives, let us now shift to an empirical analysis of the development of educational opportunities in Europe over the past few decades. In the 1950s and 1960s, children from working-class households, girls and children in rural regions with poor educational infrastructure had lesser educational opportunities. Thus in France or Germany, for example, one spoke of the Catholic working-class girl from the countryside as the ideal-typical icon of the underprivileged child (Geißler, 2005: 71). This image has changed. In modern societies, the educational discrimination of young women has become largely a relic of the past (Jacobs, 1996). Discrepancies in educational opportunities along religious or urban–rural lines have declined in significance as well. These changes can be seen as a product of the educational expansion of the 1960s and 1970s in Western European countries, the goal of which was to broaden access to secondary and tertiary education for broader strata of the population (Schofer and Meyer, 2005; Müller and Kogan, 2010). Despite these reforms, however, social background remains relevant to the allocation of educational opportunities. The opportunities for children of working-class households to attain a high-school diploma or even a university degree have not changed significantly (Reimer and Pollak, 2009: 12; Müller and Kogan, 2010: 253). The educational expansion has benefited above all children from middle-class households headed by white-collar workers, civil-servants and the self-employed. It improved the educational opportunities of all strata, yet without eliminating stratum-typical inequalities. The principal losers have been working-class children; despite improved opportunities, their distance from all other strata has increased considerably. In most (Western) European countries, the educational opportunities of children from migration backgrounds are particularly poor (e.g. Ours and Veenman, 2003; Valverde and Vila, 2003; Marks, 2005). The children of workers who migrated to Europe in the 1960s and 1970s can thus be seen as the real losers of the educational

Migrant children: poor educational opportunities

expansion. Geißler captures the changes in these structural inequalities in the pithy formula: 'the metamorphosis of the worker's daughter into a migrant's son' (Geißler, 2005: 71).

European educational systems have evolved, according to Müller et al (1997: 178), in three stages: (1) from 1870 to 1914 national educational systems developed under state control, often against the resistance of the Church; (2) between 1914 and 1939 the parallel structure of elementary schools (grades 1–8) for the masses and grammar schools (grades 5–13) for the college-bound was dissolved and different educational levels were institutionally integrated; (3) after 1945 secondary and tertiary education were opened to broader social strata. Higher education lost its exclusivity in Europe as mass universities came into being. To explain this educational expansion, scholars have employed both economic and sociological theories (for a recent account of the many facets of the educational expansion in Europe and the US, see the different chapters in Hadjar and Becker, 2009).

Economic explanations have employed human capital theory (Becker, 1964), suggesting that demand for (higher) education is driven by anticipation of the ensuing returns (increased income). According to this account, the expansion of the educational sector in Europe was a result of increased demand by individual actors for educational degrees, which they could later 'cash in' on the labour market. Alternatively, one could conceive of education as a consumption, lifestyle or status good that individuals acquire through the market for intrinsic satisfaction. If educational costs remain constant, educational expansion would then be expected to occur over the long term in modern societies. Structuralist labour market theory (Thurow, 1975) would argue that educational institutions perform selection and ranking functions that yield feedback effects on the labour market. If some labour market actors increase their educational investments, others have to do so as well in order to not suffer a competitive disadvantage. In this view, competition for education developed in the post-war period, and the result was an educational expansion. The most important sociological explanation for educational expansion stems from modernisation theory (Flora and Alber, 1981). It argues that the educational expansion was part of a broader modernisation process and a side effect of the industrialisation, urbanisation and bureaucratisation of European societies. Formal, comparable educational degrees were a precondition to and integral part of these modernisation processes. They play a pivotal role in the normative and political integration of society and are an essential medium of socialisation. Conflict theory (Collins, 1971) would conceive of the educational expansion as a product of a conflict among social classes for power, prestige, income and welfare. Since educational degrees are crucial for access to beneficial status and professional groups, the expansion of

Educational expansion

the educational sector in the second half of the 20th century can also be seen as an expression of political conflict.

8.1 Educational expenditures

The following sections will assess the performance and selectivity of national educational systems in Europe. A good starting point is overall public expenditures on education in the European Union's Member States between 1995 and 2006.

High public expenditures on education in Scandinavia

Government educational expenditures vary strongly across the EU (see Table 8.1). As a percentage of their total budgets, the countries with the highest educational expenditures spend roughly twice that which the lowest-spending country, Romania, does. The leaders in educational spending in 2006 were the Scandinavian welfare states and Cyprus. In these states, between 6.1% and 8% of Gross Domestic Product was devoted to education. This accords with these countries' political-cultural tenet that education is a collective good (e.g. Telhaug et al, 2004), which leads them to generously fund the predominantly public educational sector. Educational spending in 2006 was also above the EU-27 average in Belgium, France and Slovenia. Here, roughly 6% of Gross Domestic Product was invested by the public sector in education.

By contrast, Luxembourg, Spain, Greece, Italy, Germany and several accession countries such as the Slovak Republic, the Czech Republic, Bulgaria and Romania spend less of their Gross Domestic Product than the EU-27 average on public education. In the case of the Southern European states, one explanation for this is the high number of private schools (see Section 4.2), which reduces public educational expenditures. Sub-par investment in education was found in Germany and Luxembourg, too, which helps explain why these countries have fared poorly in international educational comparisons (Baumert et al, 2001; Stanat and Christensen, 2006). These low educational expenditures are particularly noteworthy in light of the fact that the private educational sector, at least in the case of Germany, is negligible.[2] If one observes development

Convergence of educational expenditures

over the period from 1995 to 2006, the following changes are evident in public educational expenditures: a clear rise in relation to Gross Domestic Product in the Netherlands, the United Kingdom, Romania, Bulgaria, Greece and Cyprus; and a percentage decline in educational expenditures in the Slovak Republic, Latvia, Estonia and Luxembourg. This was particularly drastic in the latter three, Eastern European states, and can be explained in part by their government budget crises but also by their privatisation of public educational institutions in recent years (Aidukaite, 2009; Rajevska, 2009; Trumm and Ainsaar, 2009). In the context of these changes, educational expenditures across Europe have converged slightly over the past decade (1995: SD of 1.10; 2006: SD of 1.05).

Table 8.1: Public expenditure on education

	1995	2000	2006
EU-15	–	4.9	4.9[+]
Belgium	–	6.0*	6.0
Denmark	7.7	8.3	8.0
Germany	4.6	4.5	4.4
Ireland	5.0	4.3	4.9
Greece	2.9	3.4	4.0
Spain	4.7	4.3	4.3
France	6.0	6.0	5.6
Italy	4.9	4.6	4.7
Luxembourg	4.3	3.7*	3.4
Netherlands	5.1	5.0	5.5
Austria	6.0	5.7	5.4
Portugal	5.4	5.4	5.3
Finland	6.9	5.9	6.1
Sweden	7.2	7.2	6.9
United Kingdom	5.0	4.5	5.5
Bulgaria	3.4	4.0	4.2
Czech Republic	4.7[#]	4.0	4.6
Estonia	5.9	6.1	4.8
Cyprus	4.6	5.4	7.0
Latvia	6.2	5.6	5.1
Lithuania	5.1	5.9	4.8
Hungary	5.4	4.4	5.4
Malta	–	4.5	4.8[+]
Poland	5.1	4.9	5.3
Romania	–	2.9	3.5
Slovenia	–	5.9*	5.7
Slovakia	5.0	3.9	3.8
EU-27	–	4.9	5.1

Source: Eurostat (2010a); *2001; [+]2005. [#]1996; figures are percentages of GDP.

8.2 Distribution of educational opportunities

NOTE ON METHODOLOGY ▮▮▮▮▮▮▮▮▮▮▮▮▮▮

The first indicator in this section is the share of early school leavers (dropouts), presented using Eurostat data. This is the percentage of 18- to 24-year-olds who do not take part in any training or continuing education and who at most have a lower secondary (i.e. middle) school degree (equivalent to ISCED Level 2). The second indicator is pupils' reading and maths proficiencies as measured by PISA data, and the third the number of 20- to 24-year-olds who attend higher educational institutions as a share of the total population aged 20–24 years.

Differences in the level of funding of public educational budgets, like diverse political and welfare state traditions, yield divergent performance levels of national educational systems as well as distinct patterns of distribution of educational opportunities. The distribution of educational opportunities can be explained by means of economic or sociological explanatory approaches. Among the former, human capital theory is central (Becker, 1964). Educational attainment is modelled here as a consequence of individual investment decisions. The costs of an educational investment are weighed against the costs of forgone wages, tuition fees and lost leisure time. Children from families with low socio-economic status often forgo tertiary education or even leave secondary school prematurely because school fees together with the loss of the child's contribution to the family's income are too burdensome. Sociological theories, on the other hand, focus on the unequal distribution of resources across society and on the functional logic of institutions. Bourdieu's (Bourdieu and Passeron, 1970; Bourdieu, 1984) and Coleman's (Coleman, 1990) theories of capital, and Boudon's (1974) and Esser's (1982, 2000) reference to distinct conditions of socialisation and hence educational opportunities (e.g. access to universities) are prominent examples (see Box below).

Bourdieu embeds his reflections on educational inequality in a socio-cultural theory of class and inequality, which hinges on the relationship between class position, educational participation and lifestyle. Possession of capital – including cultural capital in the form of educational degrees, attitudes, behaviours, language proficiencies and intellectual competencies – serves to reproduce class structures. Furthermore, Bourdieu has thoroughly examined the role of educational institutions and national educational policy in the reproduction of societal (educational) inequalities (Bourdieu and Passeron, 1970). James Coleman articulates a theory of capital with a different focus. Here, possession of social capital is pivotal to educational success: above all social networks and the support measures that family members and other network partners provide are decisive for educational success (McDill and Coleman, 1965). An intermediate position is taken by Boudon (1974) and Esser (1982, 2000). They are inspired, on the one hand, by the model assumptions of the theory of rational choice, according to which educational inequalities in modern societies are a result of the decisions of individual actors guided by cost–benefit calculations; on the other hand, Boudon, for example, points out that children's concrete conditions of socialisation (their parents' socio-economic status and cultural resources) have a considerable impact on their educational success. Esser, by contrast, emphasises the selectivity of access to higher education and the divergent prospects of success in the realm of primary and secondary education as well as the social consequences of these: 'The greater objective restrictions, the lower estimation of the necessity of education, the virtual lack of role models of success, the higher estimation of the subjective risks' (Esser, 2000: 223, authors' translation) all simultaneously influence those in lower socio-economic strata.

Inequalities in educational systems, and the educational policy concepts that give rise to these, are evident not only in terms of access to higher education, but also in the distribution of opportunities and risks in primary education, as well as, for example, with the problem of school dropouts among 18- to 24-year-olds (Figure 8.1). In Scandinavia and Austria – countries with high public educational expenditures – one finds few persons whose highest educational attainment is a lower secondary (i.e. middle) school degree (equivalent to ISCED Level 2). In several Eastern European accession countries, such as the Czech Republic, Poland, the Slovak Republic and Slovenia, too, the share of early school leavers is very low, hovering between 5% and 7%. At least in the cases of Poland and Slovenia, this low proportion of school dropouts corresponds with above-average educational expenditures. Moreover, one can adduce the traditionally high value placed on education in these countries (Daun and Sapatoru, 2001), as well as the low level of stratification in the educational systems of post-socialist societies (see Section 4.2). Both arguments are supported by the fact that in 2008 only one Eastern European accession country (Romania) experienced a school dropout rate that was near the EU–15 average.

In the conservative welfare states of Southern Europe (Portugal, Spain, Italy), as well as in Malta, the share of early school leavers among 18- to 24-year-olds is very high. In 2008, 20–40% of this age group possessed only a lower secondary degree. This high rate of early school leavers has a history in Southern Europe, since many activities in agriculture and manufacturing do not require any particular training and hence labour market entry for low-skilled persons is relatively easy (Mills et al, 2005: 426; OECD, 2006f: 67f). However, the data here suggest that the share of early school leavers between 1995 and 2008 in these countries has declined, in some cases markedly. This could be a reflection of the increasingly precarious fate of low-skilled youth in the labour market (Mills et al., 2005). Countries like France, Germany, Estonia and Latvia evince shares that are in the middle of the European pack. Also worthy of note is the fact that in all Member States of the European Union, the

High rate of early school leavers in Southern Europe

proportion of young adults with low educational attainment declined from 1995 to 2008. This is a result above all of changed labour market demand in post-industrial society. At the same time, intra-European differences in this parameter have lessened (1995: SD of 11.0; 2008: SD of 8.5).

Figure 8.1: Early school leavers

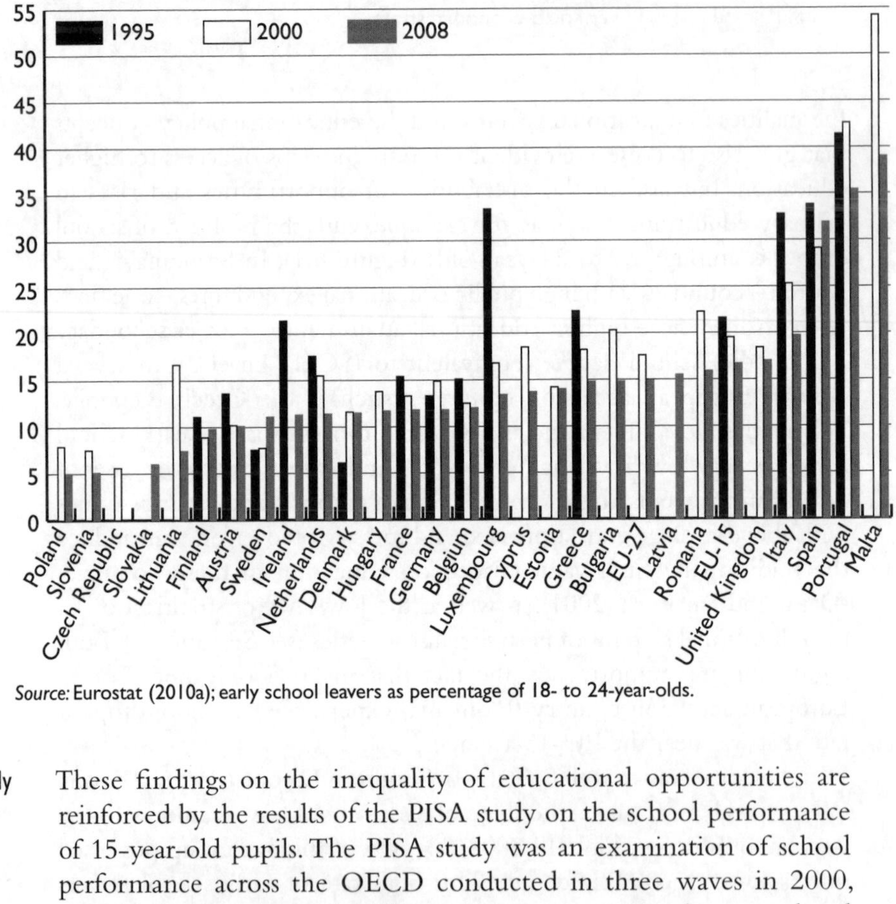

Source: Eurostat (2010a); early school leavers as percentage of 18- to 24-year-olds.

PISA study   These findings on the inequality of educational opportunities are reinforced by the results of the PISA study on the school performance of 15-year-old pupils. The PISA study was an examination of school performance across the OECD conducted in three waves in 2000, 2003 and 2006. The goal of the study was to measure the general and occupationally relevant knowledge of 15-year-old pupils in three areas: reading, mathematics and natural science.[3] For reasons of space, we will treat only the first two here. The main focus of the PISA studies lies in the mastery of processes, the understanding of concepts and the ability to deal with different situations within a field (OECD, 2003). The findings of the PISA studies conducted thus far have unleashed a political debate in many European countries about structural deficits in the educational sector (dearth of teachers, underfunding, educational problems of children of migrants), for these studies have revealed both considerable intra-European disparities and clear performance gaps within individual EU Member States.

Table 8.2: Students' proficiency in reading and mathematics

	Reading proficiency		Mathematics proficiency	
	2000	**2006**	**2000**	**2006**
EU-15	498	492	494	498
Belgium	507	501	520	520
Denmark	497	494	514	513
Germany	484	495	490	504
Ireland	527	517	503	501
Greece	474	460	447	459
Spain	493	461	476	480
France	505	488	517	496
Italy	487	469	457	462
Luxembourg	441	479	446	490
Netherlands	–	507	–	531
Austria	507	490	515	505
Portugal	470	472	454	466
Finland	546	547	536	548
Sweden	516	507	510	502
United Kingdom	523	495	529	495
Bulgaria	–	402	–	413
Czech Republic	492	483	498	510
Estonia	–	501	–	515
Cyprus	–	–	–	–
Latvia	458	479	463	486
Lithuania	–	470	–	486
Hungary	480	482	488	491
Malta	–	–	–	–
Poland	479	508	470	495
Romania	–	396	–	318
Slovenia	–	494	–	504
Slovak Republic	–	466	–	492

Source: OECD (2001, 2007g); EU-15-mean unweighted, no data for EU-27.

Finland boasted the highest average reading proficiency scores of all pupils in Europe in 2006 (Table 8.2). Ireland, Poland, the Netherlands, Sweden and Belgium were also placed in the upper quarter of the countries under study. In the middle of the pack were France, the UK, Germany, Denmark and Austria. In maths skills, too, Finland's comprehensive school system produced the best results, followed by the Netherlands, Belgium,

Finland: best results of PISA study

Estonia, Denmark and the Czech Republic. Teenagers fared particularly poorly in Romania and Bulgaria, as well as Greece, Spain and Italy. These are countries in Europe that devote a below-average share of their Gross Domestic Product to educational expenditures (see Table 8.1).

For several of these countries, these 2006 reading and maths scores constitute an improvement over their results in the first PISA study of 2000. Then, German, Polish and Latvian students scored well below average. Only 35% of pupils in Germany, for example, reached the average level of those in the top-scoring countries like Finland or Belgium (OECD, 2001: 253ff).[4] There has been a catch-up process in these countries in recent years. By contrast, school performance has deteriorated considerably between 2000 and 2006 in the UK, France and Austria.

Group differences
To judge the performance of educational systems, it is often most instructive to examine how the best and weakest students fare (not depicted in Table 8.2). In the 2006 PISA study, Greece, Spain, Italy, the Slovak Republic and the Czech Republic evinced an above-average share of pupils (roughly 10%) who were unable to attain even the lowest reading proficiency level (Level 1: basic information recognition). Students from these countries were also over-represented among those who managed to attain only Proficiency Level 1 (OECD, 2007g). In mathematical literacy, too, the proportion of pupils in these countries whose skills do not extend beyond elementary school arithmetic is very high. A disproportionate share of the best maths and reading students, on the other hand, can be found in Finland and Belgium (OECD, 2007g).

The degree of intra-country variation in reading and maths skills varies greatly across Europe. The variation around the mean reading and maths test scores was lowest in Finland and greatest in Germany, Bulgaria, the Czech Republic and Belgium. This is an indication that greater inequality of opportunity obtains in these countries' educational systems than in those of most other European states. The PISA findings strongly suggest that these inequalities are related to social background, ethnicity, school type and place of residence (state/province) (Allmendinger and Leibfried, 2003; Entorf and Minoiu, 2005; Marks, 2005; Baldi et al, 2007; Brozo et al, 2007; Fuchs and Wößmann, 2007; Schnepf, 2007; Levels and Dronkers, 2008).

The discussion thus far demonstrates that young students in Europe are availed of unequal opportunities for knowledge acquisition. The following indicator (share of students in the total population aged 20–24) reveals further intra-European inequality of opportunity – this time in higher education (Figure 8.2). The numbers show that the selectivity of secondary educational systems in EU states has considerable consequences for higher educational opportunities. In Malta, Cyprus, Germany, the Unitd Kingdom and Austria in 2007 the smallest shares of young people in all of Europe (16–24%) had an opportunity to go to college. Of this group, Austria, Germany and Malta have selective transitions between the various levels of the educational system. Still, a relatively low share of pupils in these systems (see Section 4.1) are granted access to the higher educational system at the end of their secondary school career (OECD, 2007a).

Figure 8.2: Share of students (ISCED 5+6) among 20- to 24-year-olds

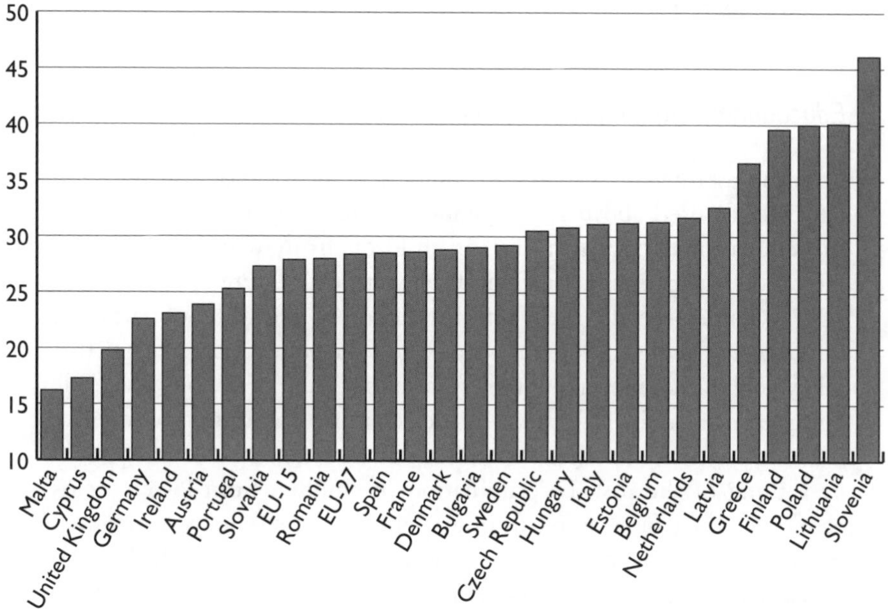

Source: Eurostat (2010a); data for 2007; no data available for Luxembourg.

Access to higher education is greatest in Slovenia, Poland, Finland, Greece and the Baltic countries. The share of polytechnic and university students in the 20–24 age group in these countries in 2007 ranged from 31% to over 45%. These are countries with comprehensive school systems, in which all pupils of a given age cohort spend eight or nine years together in one institution (Hörner et al, 2007). The proportion of pupils who achieve university admission is typically high. At least three quarters of all pupils acquire a high school degree. The case of Slovenia is particularly interesting: its high school graduation rate is almost as low as that of Germany or Austria, yet access to higher education there is greater. Between these two groups of countries, France, Spain and Denmark evince intermediate shares of students in the 20–24 age group who attend a higher educational institution.

Differences in the share of students in European countries

8.3 Educational inequality among EU Member States

NOTE ON METHODOLOGY ▓▓▓▓▓▓▓▓▓▓▓▓▓▓▓▓▓▓▓▓▓

In this section, we present the PISA study results in terms of social and ethnic background. Thereafter, on the basis of data from the OECD and from the European Commission, we will break down higher education graduates in terms of gender and social background.

Educational inequality among EU Member States in the school system

Over the last three decades, research interest in the sociology of education has been focused above all on gender-based inequalities as well as on the educational opportunities of children from working-class and migration backgrounds (Breen and Jonsson, 2005; DiPrete, 2007; Jaeger, 2007). Gender-specific inequalities were considered to be of particular importance (Jacobs, 1996), for as a target of the educational reforms that followed the 1968 movement they were at the centre of not only scientific but also social-reform debates. In the scientific community, consensus has long prevailed that the educational discrimination of women should be a thing of the past. Discrimination of children from lower socio-economic strata, for example from working-class households, is, however, still a problem in many European societies. Additionally, over the last two decades it has become clear that ethnic heritage plays a major role in the allocation of educational opportunities.

Reading proficiency

Against this backdrop, we will portray in this section the disparate performance of European educational systems and the selectivity of their distribution of educational opportunities, differentiated based on social and ethnic background, looking first at reading proficiency scores from the PISA test.

Differences in performance across social strata

In all countries under study, social disparities are evident in the acquisition of reading proficiency. These disparities are greatest in Bulgaria, Luxembourg, France, Belgium, Hungary and Germany. In these countries, the degree to which teenagers from higher social classes are better able to analyse texts than those from lower social classes is most striking. Even the United States, which is often cited as an example of significant social disparities in educational opportunities, evinces smaller socio-economically based performance gaps (Marks, 2005: 491). More promising is the focus on school systems. Marks suggests (2005: 492) that countries with highly tracked educational systems, such as Luxembourg, Belgium and Germany, show a higher level of educational inequalities. The maths portion of the study (not depicted in the figure) further confirms the poor showing of children from households with low educational attainment in those countries. They are far worse off than students from low social strata in other countries participating in the PISA study.

Figure 8.3: Reading proficiency by social background

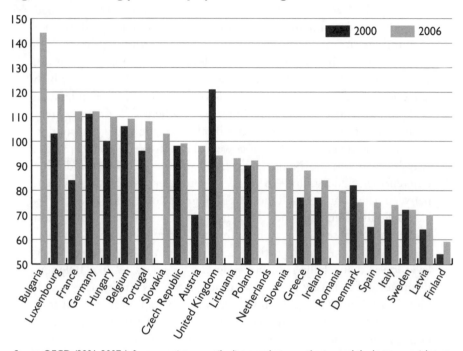

Source: OECD (2001, 2007g); figures are interquartile distances between the top and the bottom social strata.

The European country in which social background has the least impact on educational success in achieving reading proficiency is Finland, followed at some distance by Denmark, Spain, Italy, Latvia and Sweden. The example of Finland is notable for two reasons. First, it is the country with the best test scores in all of Europe. Second, the disparities in social status among its pupils' families are not less marked than those in other countries. One could hardly find a more convincing demonstration of an educational system's overall high performance level and striking equality of opportunity for teenagers of diverse social backgrounds than Finland's:'It is evident that the decoupling of social origin and proficiency attainment need not be achieved at the expense of educational standards' (Baumert and Schümer, 2001: 389, authors' translation).

If one examines country performance over time, a series of interesting developments emerge. In the first wave of the study in 2000, Finland already evinced the smallest differentials in student proficiency levels across social strata. Further, the scores in Figure 8.3 show that in most EU states the performance disparities between students from the highest and lowest quartiles of social strata have increased in recent years. Austria and France are examples of clearly worsening performance of students from households with low educational attainment. Sweden and the United Kingdom are the only countries in which proficiency differences based on socio-economic background have lessened. Meanwhile, Sweden, Germany, the Czech Republic and Poland have witnessed little change.

Performance disparities across ethnic groups

Building on these findings, we will now compare the school performance of pupils with and without a migration background (Figure 8.4), considering only those countries where at least 2.5% of families are migrant. In 2006, the greatest disparities in reading proficiency (102 points, which amounts to roughly 1.5 proficiency levels) between children from migration backgrounds and children from households where at least one parent speaks the native language as his/her mother tongue could be found in Belgium. The next greatest disparities were in Denmark, Germany, Portugal, Italy, Sweden and the Netherlands. In all these countries, considerable differences in skill level (66–78 points = 1 proficiency level) were evident between native students and those from migrant households. In countries like Belgium, Denmark and Germany, even children with a migration background whose parents were both born in those countries (yet who speak the mother – not the native – tongue at home) test one proficiency level lower than children of non-migrants in countries like Belgium, Denmark and Germany. In maths and natural science competencies as well (not depicted in Figure 8.4), in Germany and Belgium the performance of teenagers from migration backgrounds diverged far more from that of non-migrants than in the other countries under study (Entorf and Minoiu, 2005: 356). Within Europe, the narrowest achievement gaps between migrant and native children were found in Ireland, Greece and the United Kingdom. In Ireland and the UK many immigrants speak English as a second language, so that disadvantages caused by lack of fluency are far less severe and hence have less of an impact on their children's educational performance than they do elsewhere. These countries are case studies for successful integration policy in the educational sphere – despite an increased influx of both European and non-European migrants during the 1990s (see Chapter 6). Finally, one can note that between the first and third PISA studies, the differences in performance between children from migrant and native backgrounds have lessened in some countries. In others they have increased considerably. Among the former group are Denmark, Austria, Germany and the Netherlands; among the latter are the United Kingdom, Sweden and, above all, Portugal.

Explanation for low performance of immigrant children

Baumert and Schümer (2001: 394) offer an explanation for these results: the greatest disparities across ethnic groups exist in those states that can be considered destination countries for more recent European labour immigration and countries receptive to political and civil-war refugees. Schnepf (2007: 543f) argues, based on a comprehensive study that includes data from PISA, TIMSS and PIRLS, that immigration countries can be divided into two groups: English-speaking countries with generally low immigrant disadvantage and Continental European countries with relatively high immigrant disadvantage in educational achievement. Similarly, Entorf and Minoiu (2005) draw a distinction between traditional countries of immigration (e.g. Australia, Canada, the US), with often highly qualified migrants, and countries like Sweden, the Netherlands and Germany, which are concerned with labour migration. In Canada, Australia, the UK and the US, immigrant pupils quite often have better language skills than immigrant students in Sweden, the Netherlands and Germany. Entorf and Minoiu (2005: 372) show that the language spoken at home is absolutely crucial in this regard. Reading proficiency scores of migrant students improved significantly when the language spoken at home is the national language as opposed to a foreign language. In addition, the position of countries in terms of the native–immigrant gap in educational achievements could be explained by differences in socio-economic composition between natives and immigrants. Hence, some countries, predominantly those with firm immigration controls, have easier preconditions to integrate immigrants (Levels et al, 2008: 848) than others (for example, former guest-worker countries), given that their immigrants do not differ greatly in terms of composition and characteristics from the native population.

Figure 8.4: Reading proficiency by ethnic background

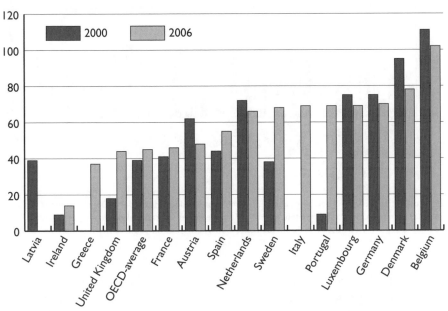

Source: OECD (2001, 2007g); figures are differentials between students with and without a migration background.

Educational inequality among the EU Member States in higher education

In light of discrimination against women in the 19th and 20th centuries, gender-specific educational opportunities form an important topic in discussions of educational inequality within developed Western societies. The data suggest, however, that educational discrimination against women in European societies has now largely been relegated to the past. In fact, a greater share of women than men attend higher educational institutions in all EU Member States (Figure 8.5), they are conspicuously under-represented among school dropouts (Eurostat, 2010a), and they achieve better test scores in some sections of the PISA studies (OECD, 2007g, 2009c).

Figure 8.5: Number of female students and female higher educational graduates

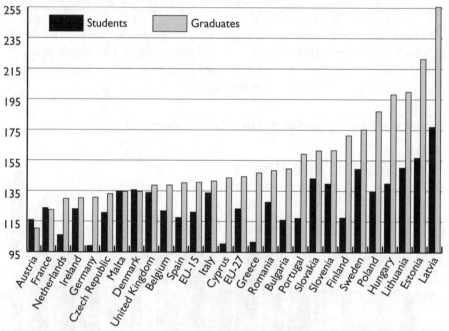

Source: Eurostat (2010a); black bars represent number of female students per 100 male students in tertiary education; grey bars represent number of female higher educational graduates per 100 male higher educational graduates: no data available for Luxembourg; EU-15 as unweighted mean value; data for 2007.

A particularly large share of women attend tertiary educational institutions in the Baltic states, Hungary, Sweden, Poland, the Slovak Republic, Slovenia and Finland. In these countries, for every 100 men who graduate from college, 160–255 women do. Small gender differences in educational success are observed in countries such as Austria, Germany, France and the Netherlands. The UK, Belgium, Spain and Italy are among the countries occupying an intermediate position; here, 40% more women graduated from a higher educational institution than men. In all European states, the disparity between the relative shares of female students (black bars in Figure 8.5) and the relative shares of female higher educational graduates (grey bars in Figure 8.5) points to the remarkable educational aspirations of women in Europe in the 21st century.

Female students are no longer gravitating towards the 'classically feminine' disciplines (social work, teacher training, pedagogy, social science). To the contrary, recent data demonstrate clearly that increasingly women are pursuing degrees in the natural and engineering sciences (European Commission, 2007b; OECD, 2009b; Eurostat, 2010a). The generally improved educational opportunities of European women (EU-27 average: 45% more female graduates) in tertiary educational institutions is unsurprising to the extent that in all European states (with the exception of Malta) more women than men graduate from college. According to Eurostat (2010a), the share of girls in the European Union who attain a high school diploma that qualifies them for university admission is 25% higher than that of boys. That in some countries (e.g. Ireland, the UK, the Baltic states) this development also manifests itself in better labour market opportunities has already been discussed in Chapter 7.

High participation of women in tertiary education

Figure 8.6 shows how unequal access to tertiary education is across social groups in some EU Member States. Germany, Austria, France and Portugal are examples of countries with high barriers to higher education for children from working-class families. Between 16% and 29% of students come from such households. The proportion of working-class men among the general population is roughly twice this high. Compared to other European countries, in the Netherlands a strikingly low proportion of children from working-class families can be found in higher educational institutions (about 5% of all students). This share, however, is not much lower than the share of workers in the population cohorts of their fathers between the ages of 40 and 60. In contrast to the former group of countries, discrimination against children from working-class households with regard to access to tertiary education is less marked in Spain, Finland and particularly Ireland.

Germany, Austria, France, Portugal: discriminaton of working-class children

Children whose father has a higher educational degree have much better odds of going to college in the countries under study than do other children (see right half of Figure 8.6). The highest share of students from such households can be found in the United Kingdom. In Germany, France and Austria, teenagers from households with high levels of educational capital have roughly twice as good a chance of going to college as do others. Portuguese youth with a similar background have even better educational opportunities, for here 29 out of 100 students come from households in which the father has a higher educational degree (for an analysis of the selectivity of the Portuguese education system, see e.g. Cabrito, 2001). The share of this group in the population cohort of 40- to 60-year-old men in 2005 was only 9%. Ireland and to a lesser extent Spain and the Netherlands are examples of societies in which children from households with greater educational capital are privileged in terms of access to higher education to a lesser extent.

Figure 8.6: Social background of students in higher education

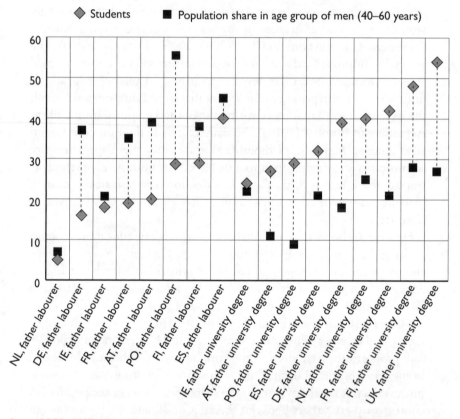

Source: OECD (2007a: 116, 119); data for 2005; data for UK only England and Wales; depicted are: (a) the share of students from working-class households; (b) the share of workers in the population cohort of 40- to 60-year-old men; (c) the share of students from households in which the father has a higher educational degree; (d) the share of higher educational graduates in the population cohort of 40- to 60-year-old men.

| Educational inequalities in the 21st century | When considering all the findings from this chapter, it becomes clear that the best educational outcomes (low shares of school dropouts and high proportions of secondary school graduates and higher educational graduates) in Europe are achieved in Scandinavia and several Eastern European accession countries, and that the outcomes in Southern |

Europe are considerably worse. Between these two poles are countries like the UK, France, the Benelux countries and Germany. Educational opportunities at the beginning of the 21st century are less unequal than they were in the 1950s, when one considers the changes in access to higher education for women or the decline in school dropout rates. Nevertheless, one can claim, based on the tremendous disparities observed here among and within nation-states based on ethnic and social background – evident in access to tertiary education and in the PISA scores in most European countries – 'that educational inequalities will remain the social question of the 21st century' (Becker and Lauterbach, 2007: 9, authors' translation) and hence continue to be at the centre of public and scientific discussions. These educational inequalities based on social and ethnic background are most salient in France, Germany, Portugal, Hungary and Bulgaria. In Finland and Ireland they are least evident.

Notes

[1] Modern societies, according to Davis and Moore (1945), must allocate their members to social positions and bring them to fulfil their duties. Suitability for a position stems from innate talent and/or training. Given that (1) talent is scarce, (2) no one will aspire to difficult tasks without a realistic expectation of appropriate reward, and (3) social positions are attained via open competition, important positions must be better compensated if these tasks are to be carried out effectively. Training requires sacrifice (investment of time, opportunity cost), which must be compensated for via higher income. This argument from Davis and Moore later became central to human capital theory. The endowment of positions with varying levels of compensation has far-reaching consequences for social stratification. In Davis and Moore's view, it is central to the functioning of modern societies. The resulting social inequality is 'an unconsciously evolved device by which societies ensure that the most important positions are conscientiously filled by the most qualified persons' (Davis and Moore, 1945: 243).

[2] Müller and Kogan (2010: 218) suggest that two crucial factors can explain differences in educational expenditures among countries: first, differences in the general economic, technological and cultural development of countries (advanced countries require higher levels of education and thus spend more on it), and, second, differences in the institutional design of the educational system (e.g. the rules that govern the provision of and access to education, as well as the costs that are imposed on those who participate in education). The specific level of development and institutional arrangements constitute the setting within which the general mechanisms of investing in education come into play and then can lead – because conditions vary – to different outcomes.

[3] To measure the reading proficiency of 15-year-olds, a five-point scale was used, ranging from a 1 for recognition of basic information to a 5 for demonstration of the ability to completely understand and critically assess the text (OECD, 2003). To measure mathematical competency, a five-point scale was used here as well. To attain Level 1 on this

scale pupils must be able to perform elementary-level arithmetic; for Level 5 they must demonstrate a capacity for fairly complex modelling and mathematical argumentation.

[4] Portugal, Germany, Latvia and Luxembourg were the countries in the first (2000) wave of the PISA study in which in the reading proficiency section an above-average share of pupils (over 10%) did not master the skills required to attain Proficiency Level 1. Students from Germany, Greece, Bulgaria, Hungary and Luxembourg were also over-represented among those who managed to attain only Proficiency Level 1 or 2. In the maths section, in the 2000 test the share of pupils whose abilities did not extend beyond elementary school arithmetic was much higher in Germany, Hungary, Greece and Portugal than in the other countries in the OECD.

9

Social inequality

DEFINITION

The unequal distribution of resources like income, wealth, prestige and power is termed social inequality. These unequally distributed resources yield further advantages or disadvantages and accrue to individuals as a result of their position in the social structure and in social networks. Thus, when one speaks of social inequality, one speaks of societally anchored forms of privileging some over others. Across modern societies, social inequality exists to different degrees and in myriad forms. It is institutionalised in classes, strata and milieus, which as a structured ranking of entire groups of individuals can be termed the system of social stratification.

Scientific discussion about the causes of social inequality date from the writings of Karl Marx (1963 [1852]; Marx and Engels, 1952 [1848]) and Max Weber (1978 [1922]) (see also Section 3.2).[1] Both authors traced the unequal distribution of resources and life chances back to structures and processes in the economy. Even more clearly than Weber, Marx espoused in this regard a vertical conception of social inequality, according to which individuals – based on their specific economic situation – can be assigned to distinct social groupings, namely social classes. Both authors founded within the nascent discipline of sociology a tradition of analysing vertical inequalities. This tradition inspired modern theories of class (Dahrendorf, 1959; Giddens, 1973; Featherman and Hauser, 1978; Giddens and Mackenzie, 1982; Erikson and Goldthorpe, 1992; Wright, 1997),[2] of social strata (Davis and Moore, 1945; Lenski, 1966; Dahrendorf, 1967; Geiger, 1969) and of social milieus or social capital (Bourdieu, 1984; DiMaggio and Zukin, 1990; DiMaggio, 1997). In these theories, central dimensions of inequalities are power, prestige, education, income and property. In the 1980s, the focus of inequality research switched to non-vertical, horizontal disparities. Age- and gender-specific inequalities became more important, as did inequalities across regions, among household and family forms, or ethnicity. At the same time, realms of inequality beyond labour market-related realms (e.g. poverty and discrimination) came into focus. This development manifested itself in a differentiation of a plethora of theoretical concepts, whereby, for example, analyses of lifestyles gained in importance (e.g. Miles, 2000; Bögenhold, 2001; Trepper and Rouse, 2002; Blyton et al, 2010).

Vertical social inequality

Horizontal social inequality

Levelling thesis

In this context, the current debate on the future development of inequality in modern capitalism is framed by two camps. The 'optimistic' camp – shaped by the writings of Kuznets (1955), Bell (1973) and Beck (1999, 2007) – sees class inequalities declining in significance over the medium term. Vertical inequality will be levelled, those in this camp argue, by the enhancement of skill profiles, greater teamwork and flattening of hierarchies in manufacturing; by the fostering of equality of opportunity through the expansion of the educational system and the intervention of welfare state programmes; by the spread of individualisation and horizontal differentiation; and by the burgeoning of lifestyles and the destandardisation of life courses. The notion of a vertical structure of classes and strata defined primarily by occupational position, as well as that of a close relationship between objective inequalities and individual opportunities, is, according to this view, becoming less plausible (Bradley, 1996).

Polarisation thesis

Such positions are contradicted by a series of authors (Baumol, 1967; Esping-Andersen, 1993, 2007; Braverman, 1998 [1974]; Alderson and Nielsen, 2002; Autor et al, 2006; Beynon and Nichols, 2006; Hout et al, 2006) who point to growing income and wage inequality, mass unemployment and poverty as salient features of the post-industrial social structure. They also observe the proletarianisation and feminisation of service sector work, and persistently high educational inequality. These dynamics of inequality are reinforced by the dismantling of the welfare state, an increase in social and ethnic segregation in big cities, and an accentuation of vertical inequalities. As a result of these developments, the polarisation of the social structure is one of the central structural features of modern society. In this reading, the post-industrial social structure is divided – to put it pointedly – between a group of high-skilled, white-collar workers on the one hand, and an underprivileged service and industrial proletariat on the other (Scharpf, 1986; Gorz, 1989; Erikson and Goldthorpe, 1992; Braverman, 1998 [1974]).

Differences between nation-states

Yet no clear-cut empirical findings have yet been produced to support that either levelling or polarisation of the social structure is occurring. Undermining the levelling thesis is the fact that hardly any data indicate that social inequalities are receding. At the same time, evidence of polarisation is scarce. Moreover, institutional arrangements (the welfare state, the educational system) that shape inequality structures in very specific ways differ across Europe. In countries with a social-democratic welfare state, social inequality is limited; in liberal and post-socialist societies, resources are distributed highly unequally. Between these two poles are societies with conservative welfare states, in which inequality among various social groups is moderately pronounced. If one compares Europe with the US, or with countries such as India or Russia, then it appears to have comparatively modest social inequalities (Firebaugh, 2003; Lee et al, 2007).

Most attempts to examine social inequality empirically study the distribution of those goods considered to be valuable in a society, and which formatively shape the living conditions and action horizons of individuals (Schaefer, 2007: 182; Giddens, 2009: 432). Disposition of income and property constitutes an important component of the macro-societal distribution of goods, for monetary resources are easy to convert and as a rule go hand-in-hand with real opportunities to realise one's life chances. The pattern of distribution of income and wealth across social groups makes clear whether life chances in a society are markedly unequal, as well as whether the vertical distribution of resources is becoming more or less equal over time. The following sections on income inequality (market income, minimum wages, gender-specific wage differentials and household incomes, Section 9.1) and wealth inequality (Section 9.2) are devoted to this central theme of inequality research. Thereafter, we report the shares of the population in or at risk of poverty both within and across Member States of the European Union (Section 9.3).

9.1 Income inequality

NOTE ON METHODOLOGY

For labour market income we use Eurostat data on the gross annual income of full-time employed persons in the industrial and service sectors in companies with at least 10 employees. These data are adjusted for differences in Purchasing Power Standards (PPS) across the EU.

A minimum wage is a statutorily set minimum gross income (on an hourly or monthly basis) for a legally employed worker. In this section, minimum wages are empirically depicted with the help of Eurostat data: (a) in terms of the share of minimum-wage recipients among all full-time employed persons in the respective Member States of the EU; and (b) as monthly gross wages, that is, wages prior to withholding of income taxes and social insurance contributions, expressed in euros (PPS).

To observe income inequality at the household level we use an indicator created on the basis of Eurostat data, namely the ratio of total income received by the 20% of the population with the highest income (top quintile) to that received by the 20% of the population with the lowest income (lowest quintile), or Q5/Q1. Income is understood as equivalised disposable income – after deduction of income taxes, property taxes and social insurance contributions, and taking into account transfers between households. Additionally we note the Gini-Index for household incomes. The Gini-Index is a widely used measure of income inequality. It can take values ranging from

0 to 1, where 0 represents completely equal distribution and 1 represents maximum inequality of distribution.

The Gender Pay Gap (GPG) represents the difference between the average gross hourly earnings of male and female employees as a percentage of the average gross hourly earnings of male employees. The population consists of all employees in firms with 10 or more employees. Only those members of the labour force between the ages of 16 and 64 who work at least 15 hours per week are considered. Agricultural workers and civil servants are not included. The analysis is based on Eurostat data.

Income inequality is one of the central themes of research on social stratification (Atkinson, 2003). Income inequality is of interest to sociologists above all when specific groups evince markedly higher or lower incomes than others. When these inequalities coincide with other social differences such as those based on ethnicity or gender, multiple disadvantages result, and these can be a source of political conflict as well. Income distributions are predominantly structurally determined, that is, by the level of productivity, a society's institutional structure (educational institutions, welfare state) and the manifest structures of the labour market (e.g. workforce skill levels, share of large firms, employment rate, female labour market participation rate).

Wages, household income   In research on income inequality, studies of individual wages (DiPrete and McManus, 1996; Smeeding, 1997; Acemoglu, 2002; Mouw and Kalleberg, 2007; Weeden et al, 2007; Gottschalk and Machin, 2008; Giesecke and Verwiebe, 2009) can be distinguished from analyses of household income inequality (Townsend, 1979; Burkhauser and Poupore, 1997; Kenworthy, 2007; Western et al, 2008; Whelan and Maitre, 2008). The former discussion is limited to inequalities generated in the labour market. One speaks here of market income and of the primary income inequality stemming from it. It obscures, however, the structure of inequality at the household level. This is typically shaped not only by earned income levels but also by welfare state benefits and the number of persons living in households. What is decisive for individual welfare is, according to Klein (2005: 338), ultimately the opportunities for an individual to access all income resources of a household.

Income inequality among EU Member States

If we first consider individual earned (market) income, we see at the beginning of the 21st century considerable inequality among Member States of the European Union (see Figure 9.1). The core Member States of the EU are on one end of the income distribution, and the Eastern European accession countries are on the other. In Denmark, average gross annual earnings in the industrial and service sectors in 2007 amounted to about 53,200 euro (2001: 41,700 euro). If one controls for differences in purchasing power, as we have done here, then the earnings of the Danish workers exceeded even those of their counterparts in Switzerland and Norway, who have traditionally been the earnings leaders in Europe (Eurostat, 2010b). In the United Kingdom, Luxembourg, the Netherlands, Ireland and Germany, similarly high incomes are reported, ranging from 40,000 to 46,000 euro (2001: 35,000 to 39,000 euro). With incomes just above 15,000 euro, Portugal and Greece lie just below the EU-15 average. Among the group of new, Eastern European EU countries, workers in Hungary, the Slovak Republic and the Czech Republic achieve the highest levels of market income. By far the lowest levels of gross annual earnings in the industrial and service sectors in 2007 were those of workers in Bulgaria (2,600 euro) and Romania (4,800 euro).

Figure 9.1: Gross earnings in industry and services

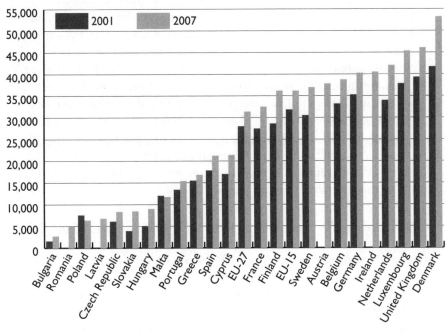

Source: Eurostat (2010b); 2007 data for the Czech Republic, Malta, Spain, Cyprus, EU-27 and EU-15 from 2006, for Poland and Ireland from 2005, Greece from 2003; 2001 data for the Czech Republic from 2002; the table displays income in PPS.

If one considers these figures in relation to average earnings in the expanded European Union (EU-27, 2007: 31,302 euro), the contours of income inequality across Europe become clear. In Bulgaria, workers earn one eighth of that which the average EU-27 worker earns. Bulgarians earn

Social cleavage in Europe

only one twentieth of the average Danish worker's income, indicating the tremendous differences in value creation and productivity between these two countries (OECD, 2007c: 29, 138). Even workers in Hungary, the Eastern European accession country with the highest market incomes, earn incomes that are less than 30% of the EU-27 average. Overall, these income data suggest that there is a substantial social cleavage in Europe. The very high level of social inequality across Europe is especially remarkable given that we controlled for differences in price levels and living costs. If these differences in purchasing power had not been accounted for, we would have found an even more dramatic degree of inequality in market wages across the Union.[3]

Catch-up process in Eastern Europe

The numbers presented in Figure 9.1 are also useful in describing changes in market wage inequality over time. One can use the ratio of the highest and lowest income as a measure of the overall level of inequality within the EU-27. It evinces a slight decline in wage inequality from 2001 to 2007 within the European Union. Market incomes in the industrial and service sectors in Bulgaria were at 3.5% of those in Denmark in 2001 versus 4.9% in 2007. Bulgaria has also narrowed the gap somewhat vis-à-vis EU-27 mean income (5.5% in 2001, 8.4% in 2007). A similar economic catch-up process can be observed in countries such as the Czech Republic, Hungary and the Slovak Republic. Despite the decline in earnings inequality among Member States of the European Union, variation in earnings in Europe as a whole around their arithmetic mean is increasing (2001: SD of 13,493 euro; 2007: SD of 16,301 euro), which is partially due to the mathematical logic of the standard deviation (it increases automatically with increasing mean). However, in light of these findings, convergence of market incomes across the EU is imaginable only in the very distant future, if at all.

Differences in the minimum wage among Member States of the EU

In the 20 states of the European Union, a statutory minimum wage is one of the fundamental instruments of labour market regulation. Only Germany, Austria, Italy, Cyprus and the Scandinavian countries lack a comprehensive, legally binding minimum wage. This is mitigated in many cases by wage agreements between employers and employees, though. Thus, extensive collective bargaining agreements in Scandinavia (Ebbinghaus, 2000a, 2000b; Kjellberg, 2000; Carley et al, 2007) protect at least four fifths of workers there from low wages (Schulten and Watt, 2007: 3). In Austria and Germany, too, it is up to the social partners whether to establish the levels of wages. In Austria, unions and employer associations established a minimum wage, which took effect in 2009. In Germany, minimum wages have been agreed upon in construction, postal services, the electrician trade, mining, nursing and commercial cleaning. In both countries, minimum wages apply only to employees of companies that pay according to collectively negotiated pay scales (on the coverage rates of collective agreements see Section 4.3).

There is no consensus in scientific circles concerning the labour market effects of the introduction of minimum wages. In economics, the dominant view has traditionally been that minimum wages have negative employment effects (above all for younger workers) and exert upward pressure on wages (e.g. Brown et al, 1982). Over the past two decades, however, research has shown that whether negative or even positive labour market and compensation effects follow upon the introduction of a minimum wage depends on a series of specific factors (general economic prosperity, level of the minimum wage(s), share of potential recipients of the minimum wage among all workers) (Card and Krüger, 1995; Dolado et al, 1996; Freeman, 1996; OECD, 1998; Ragacs, 2002; Metcalf, 2007; Schulten and Watt, 2007; McLaughlin, 2009). The view of classical economics on the phenomenon of minimum wages thus has no claim to universal validity. For our purposes it makes sense to take a step back from this debate and to focus instead on the implications of the concrete design of minimum wage provisions on inequality structures within and across European societies (Figure 9.2).

Labour market effects of minimum wages

The data on minimum wages – presented here as the share of minimum wage recipients among all workers as well as the level of the wage in PPS (euros) – reveal a social cleavage in Europe between prosperous Western European states on the one hand, and less prosperous Eastern and Southern European states on the other. In some Western European economies (the Netherlands, the UK, Ireland), minimum wage workers are scarce, making up only 2–3% of all full-time employees. At the same time, average wages in these countries are comparatively high. In Germany and Austria one finds a much larger segment of employees who earn wages in the realm of the minimum wage (9–10%).[4] These workers' earnings levels (about 1,100 euro) are similar to those of minimum wage workers in the UK. In countries such as the Slovak Republic, Poland, the Czech Republic, Slovenia, Spain and Portugal, minimum wage work is present only to a limited to moderate extent, typically at low to very low wage levels (about 300 to 700 euro in PPS). Interestingly, the US – with its minimum wage of about 850 euro and its limited share of minimum wage work – lies between the first and third group (Eurostat, 2010b). Finally, there is another group of countries (Romania, Latvia, Lithuania, Hungary) in which a comparatively large share of the workforce earns the minimum wage, and this wage is very low (150–270 euro in PPS).

Europe divided with regard to minimum wages

This dichotomy of European states in the design of minimum wages is supplemented by two special cases: France and Bulgaria. They indeed evince a similarly high share of workers in low-paid activities (about one sixth of all full-time employees), but they differ significantly with regard to the degree of socio-economic protection of these workers. In Bulgaria, the statutory minimum wage in PPS is 120 euro; in France it is 1,320 euro. All in all, the data indicate a U-shaped relationship between the level and prevalence of the minimum wage. Low and very low as well as very high minimum wages (Latvia, Bulgaria, Luxembourg, France) correlate with a high share of minimum wage recipients. Moderate minimum wage levels are associated with low-to-moderate shares of such workers (Portugal, Spain, Slovenia).

Figure 9.2: Minimum wages

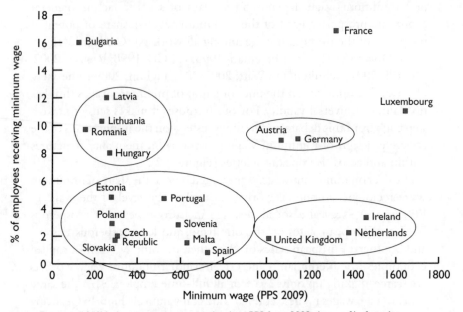

Source: Eurostat (2010b); data on minimum wage levels in PPS from 2009, data on % of employees receiving a minimum wage are the latest available (2005–07); minimum wages in PPS in Belgium: 1,387 euro (2009); in Greece: 681 euro (2008); in Belgium and Greece no data available on % of employees receiving a minimum wage.

Gender-specific income differences in EU Member States

For most of the 20th century, researchers proceeded from the assumption that structures of inequality in industrial societies were primarily caused by the different life chances conferred on individuals by their occupational status. Social-scientific analyses focused on the income levels and/or occupational positions of men in standard employment relationships, and the class concept dominated social stratification research (Blau and Duncan, 1967; Featherman and Hauser, 1978; Goldthorpe, 1987). In post-industrial service societies, Giddens (2009: 448) argues, the socio-economic situations of individuals have become more diversified due to rapid and complex economic transformations, and are now shaped more by gender since women's economic roles in Western societies changed fundamentally in the last two decades.

Geißler (2006) also considers gender to be relevant to social inequality in myriad ways. In his view, gender-based inequalities are constitutive elements of the social stratification of modern societies:

> Characteristic differences exist in the socio-economic situation and societal role expectations of women and men, and through gender-specific socialisation processes these manifest themselves in personality development, attitudes, motivation and behavioural patterns. Of particular interest for the analysis of inequality are those gender-specific differences which can be interpreted hierarchically, i.e. as patterns that structurally disadvantage women. (Geißler, 2006: 301, authors' translation)

Admittedly, in most developed capitalist societies such gender-specific inequalities have diminished since the middle of the 20th century (see also Section 8.3). At the same time, a consciousness has spread that those inequalities between the genders that remain are illegitimate. Geißler speaks here of a variation on the Tocqueville paradox, according to which the 'dismantling of social inequalities simultaneously raises sensitivity concerning those inequalities which remain' (Geißler, 2006: 301, authors' translation).[5]

Table 9.1 shows data on gender-specific income inequality in Europe. Women in the European Union in 2008 earned wages 5% to 30% lower than those of men. These gender-specific wage differences are less pronounced in Southern and Eastern Europe than in the more developed countries of Central and Northern Europe. It is important to remember that this social-structural indicator largely controls for differences between men and women in working hours by using hourly wages.

With incomes at least 25% less than men, women in Austria, the Netherlands, the Czech Republic and Estonia are the most disadvantaged in the labour market. Research in this field has tended to attribute income differences between men and women to, among other factors, the low representation of women in executive positions and in higher-wage labour market segments, attribution of 'soft skills' to women and 'hard skills' to men, and labour market discrimination against women (Bernhardt et al, 1995; Petersen and Morgan, 1995; Tomaskovic-Devey and Skaggs, 2002; Blau and Kahn, 2003; Johansson et al, 2005; Van der Meer, 2008; Magnusson, 2009; Breen and Salazar, 2010). Comparatively small differences between the earnings of women and men can be found in Italy, Malta, Poland, Slovenia, Portugal and Belgium (5% to 10%). An intermediate-sized income gender gap exists, for example, in Sweden and Denmark.

Table 9.1: Gender wage gap

	1995	2000	2008
EU-15	17	16	18⁻
Belgium	12	13	9
Denmark	15	15	17
Germany	21	21	23
Ireland	20	19	17⁻
Greece	17	15	22
Spain	13	15	17
France	13	13	19
Italy	8	6	5
Luxembourg	19	15	12
Netherlands	23	21	24⁻
Austria	22	20	26
Portugal	5	8	9
Finland	17*	17	20
Sweden	15	18	17
United Kingdom	26	21	21
Bulgaria	–	22⁺	14
Czech Republic	21*	22	26
Estonia	27	25	30⁻
Cyprus	29	26	22
Latvia	–	20	13
Lithuania	27	16	22
Hungary	22	21	17
Malta	–	11	9
Poland	–	12⁺	10
Romania	21	17	13⁻
Slovenia	14	12	9
Slovakia	–	22	21
EU-27	–	17	18

Source: Eurostat (2010a); *1996, ⁺2001, ⁻2007; figures are pay differentials in percentages.

Stable gender pay gap on average

Between 1995 and 2008, gender-specific wage differences remained roughly constant on average within the European Union; in some countries they decreased, in others they increased over time. In Italy, Belgium, Ireland and the UK, for example, the gender wage gap has declined in recent years. This can be attributed to the increase in the labour market experience and educational capital of women (see Section 8.3) as well as to the decrease in the gender-specific segmentation of the labour market (OECD, 2004: 142ff). In Ireland, declining gender-specific wage differences are also a consequence of the economic boom of the past two decades, from which women have profited more than men in the form of increasing labour market participation and decreasing unemployment. In most accession countries as well (with the exception of the Slovak Republic, Estonia and the Czech Republic), gender-specific wage inequality has declined markedly. Women in Eastern Europe seem to have taken advantage of the change in the economic system introduced in 1989 (Plantenga and Remery, 2006: 14). The positive development is most striking in Bulgaria, Romania and Slovenia (compare Heyns, 2005; Plantenga and Remery, 2006; Andrén and Andrén, 2007; Kovac et al, 2009).[6]

In some Western European countries between 1995 and 2008, gender-specific wage inequalities have increased. Examples are Sweden, Denmark, Finland, Portugal, Spain, France and Austria. For Portugal, this appears to be one of the downsides of the country's modernisation (Budria, 2007). Plantenga and Remery (2006: 20) argue that occupational differences account for much of the pay gap between men and women. According to them, differences in experience and tenure could be the driving force behind the increasing gender wage gap. With regard to Denmark, Gupta et al (2005) explain the growth in gender-specific wage differences by pointing to the increase in the supply of female labour and to institutional changes in the labour market (decreasing returns on education for the highly skilled). At the same time, however, family-friendly policies have not only enhanced women's opportunities to achieve and maintain access to the labour market (via paid parental leave, flexitime, family leave, part-time positions), but have also depressed wages. With regard to Sweden, Johansson et al (2005) argue that the growing gender wage gap is the result of an overall increase in earnings differentiation. Moreover, the distribution of typically male (well-paid) and typically female (low-paid) jobs has not been favourable. With regard to Austria, Plantenga and Remery (2006: 20) argue that only a smaller fraction (about 30%) of the increasing gender pay gap can be explained in terms of individual and job characteristics, whereas discrimination makes up the largest part. Unequal pay can largely be traced back to the unequal valuation of 'men's work' and 'women's work'. A greater share of part-time work and career breaks among women as well as the vertical and horizontal segregation of the labour market play important roles as well. In closing, we can observe that between 1995 and 2008, variation in the size of gender wage gaps across Europe slightly increased (1995: SD of 6.25; 2008: SD of 6.4), while across countries gender gaps did not converge.

No decline or convergence of gender wage gap in Europe

Inequality of household incomes within EU Member States

Let us now shift our focus from market incomes and their distribution to inequalities at the household level. We will use an indicator based on equivalised disposable household income. Because this takes into account whether the members of a household are living off one or multiple incomes, it is a better gauge of family living standards. To calculate equivalised income, Eurostat employs the widely used modified OECD equivalence scale. This weights the first household member with a factor of 1.0, every additional member aged 14 and over with 0.5 and those under the age of 14 with 0.3.[7]

The data on the inequality of household incomes (Table 9.2) underscore our findings thus far concerning the intra-European divide: post-socialist and Southern European countries evince a comparatively high degree – and Scandinavia a limited degree – of social inequality. More concretely, Table 9.2 shows that on average in EU countries in 2008 the upper 20% of household incomes were five times the size of those in the bottom 20%. The average Q5/Q1 ratio in 2008 was slightly higher among the EU-27 than among the EU-15 countries; in other words, household income inequality is greater in Eastern than in Western Europe. It is least pronounced in Scandinavia, where in 2008 the total income of the population segment with the greatest earnings was a little more than three times the size of that of the bottom group. This comparatively modest degree of inequality in household incomes can be seen as evidence of the effectiveness of social-democratic welfare state policies (Esping-Andersen, 1990, 1999). Countries like Ireland and Germany evince quintile income ratios that are around the average for the European Union.

Inequality low in Scandinavia, high in Southern and Eastern Europe

The distribution of household incomes is highly polarised in Southern European states like Greece, Italy and Portugal (even from a global standpoint, Portugal has a very high inequality of household income, see e.g. Budria, 2007), and also in the accession countries of Lithuania, Latvia, Romania and Bulgaria. In these countries in 2008, the income of the population segment with the highest earnings was six to seven times the size of that of the bottom quintile. This finding concerning Southern European countries is remarkable, for scholars typically assign them to the conservative welfare state type, which is generally characterised by an intermediate level of social inequality. Ultimately, the high degree of social inequality in these states may suggest a rather different interventionist role of the welfare state (Ferrera, 1996).

Increase in inequality in Eastern Europe

Over time, income inequality has developed differently in Eastern and Western Europe: in most Western European states, inequality in household incomes has declined, while in most Eastern European states it has risen (very markedly in Latvia, Romania and Bulgaria). A change in the Q5/Q1 relation in, for example, Bulgaria from 3.7 to 6.5 can be interpreted as follows: the total income of the top quintile was 270% in 2000 and 550% in 2008 higher than the size of the total income of the bottom quintile. Above all in Portugal, France, Belgium, Greece and Spain, income inequality declined significantly. Among Western European states, Denmark, Finland and Sweden are the only countries in which the distribution of household incomes has increased in recent years, albeit from levels that were among the lowest in the world. Very possibly this is due in large part to the scaling back of the welfare state in these countries, as evident in the decline in social spending there since the mid-1990s (see Section 4.1). Further, the comparatively high labour market participation of women in Scandinavia (see Section 7.2) and the resulting increase in the share of two-earner households with high incomes could help explain this development.

Table 9.2: Inequality of household incomes

	1995 (Q5/Q1)	2000 (Q5/Q1)	2008 (Q5/Q1)	2008 Gini
EU-15	5.1	4.5	4.9	0.30
Belgium	4.5	4.3	4.1	0.28
Denmark	2.9	3.0	3.6	0.25
Germany	4.6	3.5	4.8	0.30
Ireland	5.1	4.7	4.5	0.31
Greece	6.5	5.8	5.9	0.33
Spain	5.9	5.4	5.4	0.31
France	4.5	4.2	4.2	0.28
Italy	5.9	4.8	5.1	0.31
Luxembourg	4.3	3.7	4.1	0.28
Netherlands	4.2	4.1	4.0	0.28
Austria	4.0	3.4	3.7	0.26
Portugal	7.4	6.4	6.1	0.36
Finland	3.0*	3.3	3.8	0.26
Sweden	3.0+	3.4~	3.5	0.24
United Kingdom	5.2	5.2	5.6	0.34
Bulgaria	–	3.7	6.5	0.36
Czech Republic	–	3.4	3.4	0.25
Estonia	–	6.3	5.0	0.31
Cyprus	–	4.1~	4.1	0.28
Latvia	–	5.5	7.3	0.38
Lithuania	–	5.0	5.9	0.34
Hungary	–	3.3	3.6	0.25
Malta	–	4.6	4.0	0.27
Poland	–	4.7	5.1	0.32
Romania	–	4.5	7.0	0.36
Slovenia	–	3.2	3.4	0.23
Slovakia	–	–	3.4	0.24
EU-27	–	4.5 (EU-25)	5.0	0.31

Source: Eurostat (2010a); *1996, +1997, ~2001, ~2001; #2007.

The mitigation of household income inequality across most of Western Europe is surprising in light of the fact that between the early 1980s and the early 21st century, inequality in market incomes increased – in some cases dramatically – in most European countries as well as in the United States (Katz and Autor, 1999: 1503; Atkinson, 2000: 8; European Commission, 2005b: 165; Burkhauser and Couch, 2010: 283). This opposing development in the inequality of market and household incomes, for example in Italy, France or Germany, could be explained by reference to a very high level in social expenditures and the ageing of the population in recent years (see Sections 4.1 and 5.1). When the share of retired civil servants and other retirees rises, income inequality at the household level can decline, for this group earns intermediate level incomes, and within this group income differentials are less pronounced than among the labour force.

Convergence of household income inequality

All in all, this observed decline in household income inequality confirms a trend identified by Beckfield (2009) for the EU-15 countries in the second half of the 1990s. Whether this constitutes evidence of convergence of EU Member States, as Beckfield (2009: 501f) postulates, will have to be tested by future analysis. Our data suggest in this regard that during the last decade, the distribution of household incomes in the EU-27 has indeed converged (1995: SD of 1.30; 2008: SD of 1.15). This development is due mostly to a more unequal distribution of household incomes in Scandinavia and a less unequal distribution of household incomes in Southern Europe.

9.2 Wealth inequality

NOTE ON METHODOLOGY

Wealth statistics evince greater distortions than do income statistics, for the wealthiest are often not captured, and many among the wealthy are not interested in rendering their assets transparent. Substantively, we can distinguish between business assets, real-estate assets and financial assets.

Sociological research on wealth inequality is much less extensive than that on income inequality. This is striking given that the former is far more pronounced than the latter, and indeed formative of the social structure of modern societies.

Data on wealth inequality

There are two reasons why analyses of wealth inequality have been comparatively rare hitherto. The first reason lies in the history of sociological theory. Sociology as a whole, like many of its sub-disciplines, treats primarily phenomena that have their origins in the employment sphere (see Chapter 3). This is especially true of research on inequality, which traditionally has explained the social stratification of society using theories based on the inequality of work incomes, on status differences in the occupational hierarchy or on the distribution of occupational prestige. The second reason is the comparative scarcity of wealth data (Sierminska et al, 2006: 3) together with the methodological challenges in adequately surveying it (Brandolini et al, 2004: 10)[8]:

> It should be stressed that estimates of personal wealth inequality are very sensitive to the choice of data source, definition of wealth, accounting conventions, unit of analysis, and the sampling frame, particularly the degrees of stratification on high income families or persons. (Wolff, 1996: 433)

In many modern societies, studies of wealth inequality are hard to carry out because wealth is highly concentrated. Surveys of special subgroups of the population are required, and tend to yield low unit response rates and high item non-response rates.

Despite these methodological problems in the study of wealth inequality, there are a growing number of studies dedicated to this phenomenon (Atkinson and Harrison, 1978; Huster, 1995; Wolff, 1996, 2006; Brandolini et al, 2004; Klevmarken, 2006; Sierminska et al, 2006; Davies et al, 2008; Statistics Sweden, 2010). One can summarise the results of these studies in the following manner:

Central findings

1 In European states, but also in the US, Canada, Australia, New Zealand and Japan, wealth inequality is far more pronounced than income inequality.
2 Wealth inequality in countries like the US, Argentina, Mexico, Brazil and Russia is greater than in European – and especially Western European – societies.
3 The majority of all asset values consist of real-estate holdings, while the significance of financial assets has increased over the past two decades.
4 The development of wealth inequality correlates with the dynamism of international capital and equity markets.
5 In modern societies, the distribution of wealth is socially structured. Women possess fewer assets than men. Persons with a migration background have significantly fewer assets than those without one. Across skill levels and occupational groups, the differences are considerable. Households in which the earners possess low or no skilled training have a greater risk of having negative wealth (i.e. debt). Marital status also influences wealth accumulation. Marriage yields positive, and divorce negative, effects. Further, great differences in wealth can distinguish different regions of a country (on regional inequality in Europe, see also Section 12.2), for example, Southern from Northern Italy, Central from Southern Portugal or Eastern from Western Germany.

Wealth inequality socially structured

6 Finally, in many European societies wealth transference via inheritance is likely to exacerbate wealth inequality in the future.

Figure 9.3: Inequality of wealth

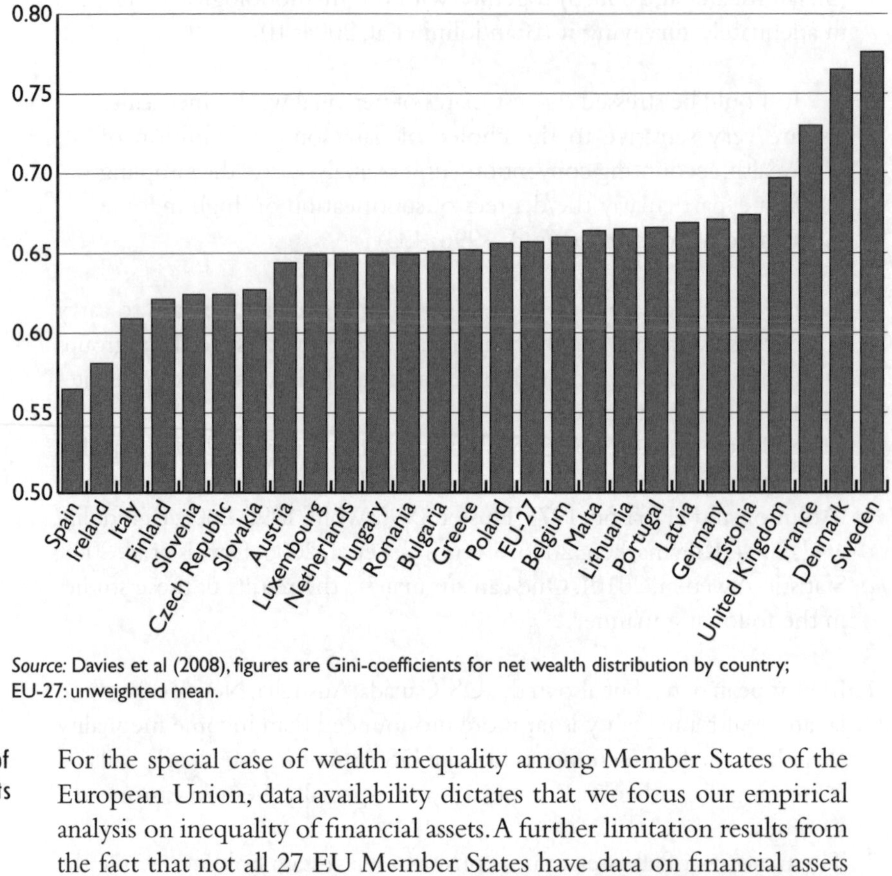

Source: Davies et al (2008), figures are Gini-coefficients for net wealth distribution by country; EU-27: unweighted mean.

Inequality of financial assets

For the special case of wealth inequality among Member States of the European Union, data availability dictates that we focus our empirical analysis on inequality of financial assets. A further limitation results from the fact that not all 27 EU Member States have data on financial assets (Figure 9.3). Empirically, the data show that within the EU, wealth inequality is greater than income inequality. While average household incomes across the EU-27 evince a Gini-coefficient of 0.31 (see Table 9.2), financial assets yield significantly higher Gini values. On average across the EU states observed here, financial asset inequality is twice that of household incomes. After controlling for purchasing power disparities, financial asset inequality is greatest in Italy and Bulgaria, and lowest in Greece.

Moreover, the Gini values of the observed countries differ with regard to wealth (Figure 9.3) and household (Table 9.2) inequality: countries with comparatively low levels of household income inequality, like Denmark or Sweden, evince comparatively high levels of wealth inequality (Sierminska et al, 2006). Conversely, countries in which household incomes are highly unequal, such as Greece, Portugal, Bulgaria and Romania, reveal moderate levels of wealth inequality, as Cardoso and Cunha (2005) have elaborated. In the context of the European societies discussed here, relatively low levels of inequality of financial assets can be found in countries like Ireland, Spain and Italy.

Wealth is distributed highly unequally in many European countries. In Spain, for example, wealth is highly unequally divided across household types and regions. Here, as in most other European countries, wealth grew more rapidly than income. Average wealth was 4.15 times as high in 2005 as in 1982, while average income was only 2.6 times as high in 2005 as in 1982. Real estate constitutes an extremely large fraction – about 80% – of total wealth. Only the very rich hold a substantial share of their wealth in the form of stock holdings. The top 1% of the population owned 25% of the entire financial wealth in 2005 (Alvaredo et al, 2009: 1156f).

In Germany, too, to take another example, wealth is strongly unequally distributed. In 2003 eastern German households held on average only 40% (60,000 euro) of the assets available to western German households (about 150,000 euro). The greatest wealth in Germany is found among the self-employed (310,000 euro) and retired civil servants (250,000 euro) in the western German states, and the least wealth among other retirees (50,000 euro) and the unemployed (30,000 euro) in the eastern German states. If one breaks these data down by deciles, one sees that the wealthiest 10% of households was able to increase its wealth on average from 475,000 euro in assets in 1993 to 625,000 euro in 2003, while the bottom 10% of households possessed no assets whatsoever, but instead saw its debts rise from 2,100 euro to 7,900 euro between 1993 and 2003 (BMAS, 2005).

Some detailed data are also available for the UK. This reveals that the wealthiest 1% of households in the UK were able to increase their share of total wealth from 17% in 1988 to 23% in 2002 (Dorling et al, 2007: 4). At the other end of the socio-economic spectrum, the share of the bottom 50% dropped from 10% in 1986 to 6% in 2002. Dorling et al (2007: 43) emphasise in their report the spatial concentration of exclusive, wealthy households (those living above a higher wealth line that is so high that people are able to exclude themselves from participating in the norms of society if they so wish) in an area spreading from the Cotswolds to west London and including much of the Home Counties. There are also two small clusters of high rates in rural Worcestershire and Cheshire. Low rates are clustered, for example, in an arc spreading around from the valleys of South Wales, West and North Wales, Liverpool, Manchester, South and West Yorkshire, Humberside, Lincolnshire and north Norfolk. Approximately 15% of the British population in higher social class positions, or 5% of the population as a whole, belong to the group of exclusive, wealthy households (Dorling et al, 2007: 100f).

Wealth in Sweden is also very unevenly distributed (see Statistics Sweden, 2010). The 10% of the population with the largest financial assets accounted for 71% of these assets in 2007. The richest 1% owned 32% of these assets. Financial savings were relatively evenly distributed among women and men up to about age 65. But for ages above 65, men's assets grow substantially for those up to age 90, while women's generally become smaller with increasing age. Among 80- and 90-year-olds, men's median value for financial assets was between 21,200 euro and 31,800 euro (women of that age group averaged 16,000 euro). Despite the gender difference at higher age, the younger population's savings are considerably less. Those aged 30–40 had a median value of around 3,000 euro. Persons under age 30 had 2,000 euro or less. On average, Swedish households possessed financial assets of about 133,500 euro in 2007. The lowest 10% of the population had negative assets, that is, debt, of about 44,802 euro on average in 2007. For the richest 10%, the mean asset value was 750,000 euro and the mean value for households at the median level (the fifth percentile level) was 290,000 euro in 2007. The richest municipalities in terms of inhabitants' financial assets are found in the Stockholm counties.

9.3 Poverty

NOTE ON METHODOLOGY

Poverty will be discussed in this section on the basis of three Eurostat indicators:

1 At-risk-of-poverty rate before social transfers: the share of persons with a disposable equivalence income below 60% of median national disposable equivalence income.[9] Civil-service pensions and other retirement benefits are counted as income before social transfers.
2 At-risk-of-poverty rate after social transfers: the share of persons with a disposable equivalence income below the at-risk-of-poverty level, which is defined as 60% of median national disposable equivalence income.
3 At-risk-of-poverty rate after social transfers differentiated by household type, gender, age, occupational status and education.

Poverty prevention as minimum standard of civilised societies

In research on poverty, scholars often take the position that prevention of misery and poverty should be a minimum standard of civilised societies. At the same time, poverty is a gauge of the social condition of a society (Leisering and Leibfried, 1999: 5). There is also a growing concern that poverty may have negative macro-level effects on total economic output, on the political and social legitimacy of the welfare state, and on ethnic unrest, as Grusky and Kanbur argue (2006a: 1). However, in research on inequality, scholars have traditionally focused on the economically active population. One could argue that this focus, which illuminates social groups defined through their relationship to the employment sphere such as blue-collar workers, white-collar workers, the self-employed and managers, has hindered our ability to perceive and analyse the condition of the poorest among us (Leibfried et al, 1995: 14).

Poverty research was thus long the exclusive domain of research on marginal groups. Not until the last two decades has poverty become a central topic also of research on the social structure and inequality, as evidenced by a plethora of publications (e.g. Nolan and Whelan, 1996; Atkinson, 1998; Bradbury et al, 2001; Fodor, 2002; Grusky and Kanbur, 2006b; Fahey, 2007; Jenkins and Micklewright, 2007; Whelan and Maitre, 2008).

A high risk of poverty is borne in European societies by the **Risk groups** unemployed, persons with a migration background, individuals with low levels of education, the elderly, the homeless, lone mothers and large families. The fact that even in affluent societies like the United Kingdom, the Netherlands, France and Germany children are heavily affected by poverty is particularly worthy of mention and can be considered to be a grave societal failure (see chapters in Bradbury et al, 2001; Bradshaw, 2006). Contemporary analyses, for example, of the Netherlands reconfirm the quantitative dimensions of this problem: over 330,000 children, that is, roughly 9% of all children below the age of 14, lived in a household that had to get by on an income below the low-income threshold in 2008 (Statistics Netherlands, 2009).

Researchers vary in their determinations of what constitutes poverty. Myriad poverty concepts and contexts exist (e.g. extreme poverty, absolute poverty, relative poverty, traditional versus new poverty, the working poor, the underclass). The most important definitional distinction is that between absolute and relative poverty (O'Boyle, 1999: 282f):

- One speaks of absolute poverty when persons do not possess the goods **Absolute** (i.e. nourishment, clothes, housing) necessary to enable them to physically **poverty** subsist. This form of poverty still predominates in many developing countries, but has been largely relegated to the past in most Western societies.
- Relative poverty is measured in terms of the prevailing living standards **Relative** of a concrete reference society. The concept of relative poverty, however, **poverty** goes beyond the monetary perspective on the measurement of poverty. In this understanding, poverty exists when persons fall below the socio-cultural minimum income of a society.

Since the early 1980s, the European Union also uses a relative poverty measure:

> The poor shall be taken to mean persons, families and groups of persons whose resources (material, cultural and social) are so limited as to exclude them from the minimum acceptable way of life in the Member State in which they live. (European Commission, 1984)

In the literature using a relative definition of poverty, two different approaches can be found.

Resource approach
The resource approach focuses on the income of persons or households. Scholars in this tradition use various threshold values to determine poor populations. Poverty is defined as lacking sufficient income to purchase the goods and services required to attain a socio-cultural minimum income. Typically, a threshold value of 50% of the average national or median income (often weighted by household size) is used. Extreme poverty is defined at a threshold value of 40%. A threshold value of 60% is used to define those at risk of poverty. Applying the resource approach is, according to Bäcker and his colleagues, very difficult, for the scope of action of a household is determined not only by its income, but also by further resources available to it such as assets, educational and skill attainment, human capital, social capital and disposition over time (Bäcker et al, 2008: 357).

Multidimensional deprivation approach
In European poverty research, a multidimensional deprivation approach has gained currency mostly due to the work of Townsend (1979, 1985) and scholars like Atkinson, Jenkins, Leibfried, Nolan, Whelan and many others (see chapters in Nolan and Whelan, 1996; Leisering and Leibfried, 1999; Jenkins and Micklewright, 2007):

> A strong case can be made for the notion that poverty and social exclusion are inherently multidimensional concepts ... even if income were the key determinant of poverty and exclusion and sufficed to identify the poor. The factors affecting income at the household level and its distribution at the societal level are extremely complex, encompassing most obviously the way the labour market, education and tax and transfer systems are structured. Poverty in the highly complex societies of the industrialised world ... can only be understood by taking a variety of causal factors and channels into account. (Nolan and Whelan, 2007: 147f)

Thus, the multidimensional approach explores poverty not only by means of an analysis of disposable income, but also with a view to the endowment of individuals or households with health, clothing, nourishment, living space and income. In such an approach the task remains determining poverty thresholds, and due to the multiple dimensions this has become even more complicated than in the resource approach.

All proposed thresholds in poverty research have in common that they are dependent upon value judgements: every poverty definition is thus ultimately political–normative in nature which reflects the values of those who use it (O'Boyle, 1999: 294). As a result, scientific and political discussion of the existence and extent of poverty in modern societies will always be controversial:

> Depending on the definition of poverty and the determination of poverty thresholds, the circle of the poor population can be drawn smaller or larger. A conscious limitation of the circle relativises the poverty problem and can serve to mask real societal conditions, while a consciously broad definition of the circle can cause us to lose focus on those truly affected. (Bäcker et al, 2008: 359, authors' translation)

The development of poverty research from a subfield of research on marginal groups to a core domain of research on social stratification and inequality has also led to methodological advancements. Using cross-sectional analyses, poverty research of the 1970s and 1980s generally understood poverty as an enduring condition (Klanberg, 1987; Strang, 1970; Wedderburn, 1974). Empirically, relatively stable poverty rates were observed (Atkinson, 1998). More recent poverty research employs longitudinal studies and has reached the consensus that poverty is often an episode in the life course that is successfully overcome by a large share of those afflicted by it. At the same time, poverty as a (temporary) life condition and latent risk reaches deep into the middle classes and is thus no longer limited exclusively to traditional marginal groups (Frank, 2007). Poverty is thus temporalised, individualised and to a considerable extent freed from its traditional social boundaries. Episodes of poverty have a beginning, a duration, a certain trajectory and in most cases also an end (Leisering and Leibfried, 1999: 9). This is not a cause for complacency, note Leisering and Leibfried, for the social policy challenge of fighting poverty has not become less relevant. Rather, because poverty is temporalised and affects the middle classes as well, more people are touched by poverty than the studies of the 1980s had shown.

Methodological development

Poverty differences across the Member States of the European Union

Against the background of these conceptual understandings, let us now compare shares of the population living in or at risk of poverty in the

Member States of the European Union. We will make use of indicators based on the resource approach to poverty research; data surveyed using the living conditions approach are not available as national statistics. We will first analyse the share of the population in or at risk of poverty (threshold: 60% of median equivalence income) before and after welfare state transfers.

Risk of poverty in Europe polarised

On average in the core EU countries the at-risk-of-poverty rate is high (Table 9.3): roughly one fourth of the population has an income (before welfare state transfers) that is less than 60% of the median of equivalence income. In Ireland, the UK, Hungary, Romania and Latvia in 2008, the at-risk-of-poverty rate was highest. In the Czech Republic, the Slovak Republic and the Netherlands, it was lowest. The incomes of persons earning less than 60% of the median equivalence income vary across countries considerably. While a one-person household in Ireland or the UK disposes of over 11,000 euro annual income in purchasing power parities, in Romania and Latvia this income can be roughly 4,000 euro (Eurostat, 2010a). An intermediate at-risk-of-poverty rate prior to welfare state transfers can be found in Germany, Spain, Portugal, Italy and France.

Risk of poverty before social transfers

Between 1995 and 2008, the share of the population living in or at risk of poverty did not change in most Western European countries, except for Germany, Finland and Sweden. In many Eastern European states the share increased – in some cases markedly. With regard to Eastern Europe, this can be understood as the flip side of the processes of societal transformation and modernisation (Heyns, 2005; Pickles, 2008; Whelan and Maitre, 2008). The finding for Germany confirms a long-term trend of growth in the segments of the population living in or at risk of poverty. Time series data analysed by Geißler (2006: 203ff) reveal a continual rise in the share of those living in or at risk of poverty since the mid-1970s. In the case of Sweden, growth in the share of the population living in or at risk of poverty has resulted from the macroeconomic shock of the early 1990s. It has affected primarily migrants, younger labour market cohorts, lone parents and the unemployed (Blume et al, 2007: 381ff; European Commission, 2007g: 391f).

Marked poverty reduction by Scandinavian welfare states

When one examines at-risk-of-poverty rates after welfare state transfers, two groups of countries emerge. On the one hand are countries in which only a small share of the population has an income below the at-risk-of-poverty threshold after such transfers: France, Austria, Germany, the Netherlands, the Czech Republic, the Slovak Republic, Slovenia, Hungary and the Scandinavian countries. These are countries whose social policies significantly reduce poverty (European Commission, 2007g: 25f; BMAS, 2008: 21f). The percentage reduction in the at-risk-of-poverty rate in some cases greatly exceeds 50% (Table 9.3, right column). The greatest impact of such policies is evident in the Scandinavian welfare states, the Netherlands and Hungary. On the other hand are countries in which even after welfare state transfers, about one fifth of the population is living in or at risk of poverty. These countries have liberal, post-socialist or Mediterranean welfare systems (e.g. the UK, Bulgaria, Romania, the Baltic states, Spain, Italy and Greece). The reduction in the share of the population living in or on the brink of poverty achieved by these welfare states averages more than 20%. The weakest impact of social policies on poverty can be observed in the Mediterranean welfare states.

The time series data in Table 9.3 show that post-transfer at-risk-of-poverty rates in EU Member States have developed differently over time. In most core EU countries, these poverty rates declined slightly between 1995 and 2008. In Denmark, Sweden and Finland this was

Table 9.3: Poverty before and after social transfers

	Before transfers			After transfers			Reduction in %		
	1995	2000	2008	1995	2000	2008	1995	2000	2008
EU-15	26	23	25	17	15	16	35	35	38
Belgium	27	23	27	16	13	15	41	44	51
Denmark	–	29+	28	10	10+	12	–	66	61
Germany	22	20	24	15	10	15	32	50	41
Ireland	34	31	34	19	20	16	44	36	50
Greece	23	22	23	22	20	20	4	9	14
Spain	27	22	24	19	18	20	30	18	18
France	26	24	23	15	16	13	42	33	55
Italy	23	21	23	20	18	19	13	14	18
Luxembourg	25	23	24	12	12	13	52	48	50
Netherlands	24	22	20	11	11	11	54	50	58
Austria	24	22	24	13	12	12	46	46	55
Portugal	27	27	25	23	21	18	15	22	31
Finland	23*	19	27	8*	11	14	65	42	55
Sweden	–	17+	28	–	9+	12	–	47	64
United Kingdom	32	29	29	20	19	19	38	35	40
Bulgaria	–	18	27	–	14	21	–	22	17
Czech Republic	–	18+	20	–	8+	9	–	56	55
Estonia	–	26	25	–	18	19	–	31	26
Cyprus	–	–	22	–	–	16	–	–	30
Latvia	–	22	30	–	16	26	–	27	15
Lithuania	–	23	27	–	17	20	–	26	29
Hungary	–	17	30	–	11	12	–	35	66
Malta	–	19	23	–	15	15	–	21	38
Poland	–	30	25	–	16	17	–	47	35
Romania	–	21	31	–	17	23	–	19	28
Slovenia	–	18	23	–	11	12	–	39	53
Slovakia	–	–	18	–	–	11	–	–	43
EU-27	–	23	26	–	16	17	–	30	38

Source: Eurostat (2010a); figures are percentages; *1996, +2001.

not the case. Here, the share of the population with an income below the at-risk-of-poverty threshold after welfare state transfers increased, perhaps due in part to the decline in social expenditures (see Section 4.1) and dismantling of the welfare state programmes (Vis et al, 2008; Green-Pedersen and Klitgaard, 2009; Hort, 2009; Oorschot, 2009). In most accession countries as well, the share of those with an income below the poverty risk threshold even after welfare state transfers increased. In Bulgaria, Romania and Latvia, the increase in the post-transfer poverty rate was particularly marked. In the case of Latvia this is largely a result of sizeable cuts in social programmes (Rajevska, 2009). The increase in poverty in these countries is reflected in the growing inequality of household incomes (see Section 9.1).

Poverty rising in Eastern Europe

Convergence of post-transfer poverty rates

Finally, the question remains whether the at-risk-of-poverty rates have been converging across Europe over time. If we consider poverty rates independent of welfare state interventions, variation across the EU-27 has remained constant (1995: SD of 3.6; 2008: SD of 3.5). If we examine poverty rates after welfare state transfers, however, convergence tendencies are evident. Variation in these rates has lessened markedly over time (1995: SD of 4.7; 2008: SD of 4.3). We see this as an indication of the effectiveness of social programmes in fighting poverty and mitigating cross-national cleavages within Europe.

Differences in poverty across EU Member States

The data in Table 9.4 depict for various social groups – for example, lone parents, large families, the unemployed, retired civil servants and other retirees – the share of those living in or on the brink of poverty. These at-risk-of-poverty rates are also presented in relation to educational attainment. Unfortunately, Eurostat data are insufficient to portray the poverty rates of migrants, one of the most vulnerable groups. The data are also insufficient to represent the differential poverty rates of various regions within countries. Thus, existing differences between, for example, Northern and Southern Italy, Central and Southern Portugal, Wales and West London, or Eastern and Western Germany are not depicted.

Lone parents' poverty rate

If we look first at lone parents, in the EU-15 they evince a poverty rate twice the population average (Table 9.4). In the Baltic countries, Romania, the Czech Republic, Malta and Luxembourg in particular, as well as in the liberal welfare states of Ireland and the United Kingdom, lone parents are disproportionately living in or on the brink of poverty, with at-risk-of-poverty rates ranging from 39% to 57%. These values are especially high given that they already take into account welfare state transfers. In some of these countries this poverty rate among lone parents is more than three times the population average.

Lone parents fare much better in Scandinavia. 'Only' 16–26% of them were living in or on the brink of poverty in 2008. Further, Eurostat data show that for Europe as a whole during the period between 1995 and 2008 the at-risk-of-poverty rate for lone parents declined on average, particularly in Western Europe. The greatest decline in poverty for lone parents took place in Austria, Ireland, the UK and Germany. In Austria and Germany this positive development is presumably due primarily to the manifold increase in child benefit in these countries since the mid-1990s. A similar story can be told for the UK and Ireland. The UK child benefit package has been much improved since 1999 as a result of child tax credits and increases in Income Support scales for children. In Ireland, child benefit increased by a factor of seven between 1992 and 2009. Employment rates have also improved in both countries and were in 2006 and 2007 at the highest levels they have been for over 30 years. This will have had an impact on the poverty rates of lone parents (Bradshaw, 2006: 12). The development in Eastern Europe has been in the opposite direction (strong increases in the poverty rate particularly in Romania and Lithuania) and in the Scandinavian countries. The latter are a special case, however, for despite this development they still boast the lowest share of lone parents living in or on the brink of poverty in the entire EU.

Families with three or more children are also exposed to disproportionately high rates of impoverishment. On average in the EU-15, 24% of such families (EU-27: 26%) were living in or on the brink of poverty in 2008 even after welfare state transfers. Particularly large shares of this population group are living in or at risk of poverty in countries with a conservative/Mediterranean or post-socialist welfare state: in Spain, Italy, Greece, Portugal, Lithuania, Latvia, Romania and Bulgaria four to seven out of 10 large families are living in or on the brink of poverty. In Scandinavia and Germany the situation is comparatively favourable, where between 12% and 15% of large families are living in or at risk of poverty (see Table 9.4). Between 1995 and 2008 the share of large families living in or on the brink of poverty declined in Europe on average. The development differed across countries, however: in Germany, Ireland and Austria this poverty rate declined to an above-average extent, yet it rose markedly in Lithuania, Latvia, Greece and Romania.

Poverty rates of large families

If one considers both of the last two poverty indicators together, these point to an infantilisation of poverty in Europe (see Bradbury et al, 2001; Bradshaw 2006). Children and teenagers are particularly affected by poverty. This problem is most pronounced in the United Kingdom, Spain, Latvia, Lithuania, Greece, Portugal, Italy, Bulgaria and Romania, where in 2008 after welfare state transfers between one fourth and one third of all children and teenagers under 16 years of age lived in poverty (Eurostat, 2010a). The countries with the least number of young people

Infantilisation of poverty in Europe

living in or on the brink of poverty were the Scandinavian countries and Slovenia, with at-risk-of-poverty rates of only 9% and 12%, respectively. Intermediate shares of young people living in or at risk of poverty were found in France, the Netherlands, Germany and the Czech Republic.

Increasing poverty risks for elderly in Eastern Europe

Disproportionate shares of retirees were also living in or at risk of poverty in Europe. In 2008, every sixth member of this population group lived off of an equivalence income of less than 60% of the national median income. The social condition of seniors is particularly problematic in the UK, Bulgaria and Lithuania (at-risk-of-poverty rates around 32%). It is much worse in Cyprus, Latvia and Estonia where approximately half of the retirees are living in or on the brink of poverty. Seniors are doing much better in the Netherlands, Luxembourg, Hungary, the Czech Republic and Poland (at-risk-of-poverty rates of 5–8%). In these states (in some cases far) smaller shares of retirees are living in or at risk of poverty than the population on average. In the case of the Netherlands, this is due to the greater labour market participation of seniors and to the prevalence of occupational pensions (Lefèbvre, 2007: 4). The low at-risk-of-poverty rate among the elderly (i.e. the share of elderly earning less than 60% of median income) in Hungary, the Czech Republic and Poland could be a reflection of the comparatively low wages and relatively high unemployment of the working-age population there (which lowers the median income level) (Zaidi, 2006: 2).[10]

Between 1995 and 2008, the share of the population living in or on the brink of poverty declined in many European states. One reason for this could be the introduction of minimum wages or the bolstering of pensions and minimum incomes in some Western European countries (European Commission, 2007g: 21). However, old-age poverty has drastically increased in many countries. In the Baltic states and Bulgaria this is most striking (Zaidi et al, 2006; Offe and Fuchs, 2007). In Latvia, for example, the share of retired civil servants and other retirees who are living in or on the brink of poverty increased sixfold within a period of six years (Table 9.4).

Unemployed most disproportionately living in poverty

The unemployed form the social group under study which is most disproportionately represented among those living in or on the brink of poverty. On average across the core EU countries, four of every 10 unemployed persons has an income less than the at-risk-of-poverty threshold. Particularly grave is the situation of the unemployed in the UK, Germany, Bulgaria and the Baltic countries (rates between 51% and 61%). The share of those living below this threshold is roughly three times the population average. In the case of Bulgaria and the Baltic countries, welfare state support for the unemployed is very meagre, for political elites in these countries subscribe to the classical liberal notion (Esping-Andersen, 1990, 1999; Bazant and Schubert, 2009) that generous benefit levels discourage work and foster dependency (see Chapter 4.1).

Table 9.4: Groups especially prone to risk of poverty

	Single parents			Families with three or more children			Retired			Unemployed			Level of education (ISCED, 2008)			Youth below 16 years
	1995	2000	2007	1995	2000	2008	1995	2000	2008	1995	2000	2008	0–2	3–4	5–6	2008
EU-15	37	32	35	26	27	24	19	16	16	47	48*	44	22	13	7	19
Belgium	31	25	39	13	7	16	21	18	18	38	49	35	23	11	6	17
Denmark	–	12	16	–	13	12	–	–	17	–	–	34	15	12	8	9
Germany	48	36	36	23	21	15	18	11	15	44	46*	56	23	13	8	15
Ireland	46	42	42	32	37	13	17	35	19	63	55	28	23	12	5	18
Greece	23	37	27	22	26	27	34	29	20	51	48	37	27	16	7	23
Spain	29	42	39	31	34	44	13	16	22	53	46	38	24	13	8	24
France	30	29	27	23	20	23	17	17	10	42	42*	39	17	11	6	17
Italy	28	23	36	31	37	38	16	11	15	58	56	42	23	12	6	25
Luxembourg	25	35	44	20	23	26	12	9	5	68	58	52	17	9	6	20
Netherlands	40	38	29	17	22	17	6	5	8	28	28*	36	11	11	6	13
Austria	28	23	26	24	23	21	15	15	13	36	34	41	24	9	6	15
Portugal	44	39	39	46	49	32	34	28	20	45	49	35	19	8	3	23
Finland	7	17	25	7	12	12	10~	17	22	26	36*	42	22	15	5	12
Sweden	–	13	26	–	8	13	–	–	16	–	–	39	18	11	8	12
United Kingdom	55	43	44	36	28	31	30	23	32	55	65*	54	34	17	8	23

continued

Table 9.4 (continued)

	Single parents			Families with three or more children			Retired			Unemployed			Level of education (ISCED, 2008)			Youth below 16 years
	1995	2000	2008	1995	2000	2008	1995	2000	2008	1995	2000	2008	0–2	3–4	5–6	2008
Bulgaria	–	32	38	–	54	74	–	13	32	–	–	56	39	11	5	26
Czech Republic	–	26	40	–	18	19	–	–	8	–	–	48	19	7	3	12
Estonia	–	29	39	–	21	21	–	18	43	–	–	61	36	20	9	17
Cyprus	41	–	31	16	–	20	–	–	50	–	–	30	32	11	5	13
Latvia	–	31*	42	–	26*	38	–	9	55	–	–	53	43	23	13	24
Lithuania	–	26	48	–	26	46	–	15	31	–	–	51	35	18	7	23
Hungary	–	17	33	–	23	29	–	9	7	–	–	49	18	9	2	19
Malta	–	59*	57	–	31*	27	–	18	22	–	–	30	17	6	3	21
Poland	–	22	30	–	33	34	–	9	8	–	–	39	24	16	4	22
Romania	–	26	40	–	35	57	–	13	19	–	–	43	36	14	1	32
Slovenia	–	20	29	–	8	11	–	15	18	–	–	38	25	10	3	11
Slovakia	–	–	21	–	–	33	–	–	10	–	–	43	20	9	4	16
EU-27	–	–	35	–	–	26	–	–	17	–	–	44	24	13	6	20

Source: Eurostat (2010a); figures are percentages, risk of poverty is 60% of median equivalised income after social transfers; retired and unemployed: at risk of poverty by most frequent activity in the previous year (16 years and older); *2000, +2001, ˜1996.

In relation to the extent of unemployment in these countries, welfare state transfers for the unemployed are very low (see Section 7.3). In the social-democratic welfare states of Sweden and Denmark, the share of the unemployed living below the 60% median income threshold in 2008 was much lower, namely, under 40%. Germany and Austria, along with Finland, are the European countries in which the share of the unemployed living near the poverty threshold has increased most.

With regard to the shares of population subgroups with varying levels of educational attainment living in or at risk of poverty, the figures in Table 9.4 confirm findings from research on the social structure, according to which there is a close relationship between educational capital and socio-economic conditions (Goldthorpe, 1996; Allmendinger and Leibfried, 2003; Bracht et al, 2006; Jaeger, 2007; Mayer et al, 2009; Reimer and Pollak, 2009). Europeans with higher educational degrees (ISCED 5–6) were dramatically under-represented among those living in or at risk of poverty in 2008, with an average rate of only 7% in the EU-15. Among those with mid-level educational attainment (ISCED 3–4) we found a greater percentage living in or at risk of poverty, yet this figure is still below the average rates for the respective national populations. Within Europe, the share of those with mid-level educational attainment living in or on the brink of poverty is particularly high in the United Kingdom, Poland and the Baltic states. The thesis that 'new poverty' extends deep into the middle classes (Frank, 2007) is rendered plausible by this group of countries. Above-average shares of those with low levels of training or no formal educational qualifications (ISCED 0–2) were found to be living in or on the brink of poverty; this is particularly true in the liberal welfare states, in Bulgaria and Romania and in the Baltic states. In social-democratic welfare states, France and the Netherlands, the share of those with low educational attainment living in or on the brink of poverty is much lower. In Denmark and the Netherlands the share of this population group living below the threshold is no greater than the population average.

Finally, data on at-risk-of-poverty rates after welfare state transfers show that cross-national variation is much greater for certain population subgroups than for countries' rates on average. This is particularly true of two groups: large families, and civil servant and other retirees. Moreover, among all these population subgroups, variation in at-risk-of-poverty rates has decreased only for lone parents; for all others it has remained constant or increased. Apparently, each country has its own distinct, relatively static welfare state priorities. These favour or disadvantage different vulnerable groups in each country.

Disproportionate share of low-skilled in poverty

Notes

[1] In the history of social theory, discussion of social inequality goes back even further. The point of departure for modern discussions of this subject is Jean-Jacques Rousseau's 'Discourse on the Origin and Basis of Inequality Among Men' from 1754. Therein, Rousseau distinguishes inequalities rooted in nature from those produced by society.

[2] Crompton's (2008) text on class and stratification provides a good overview of classical and more recent class theories.

[3] The greatest percentage wage increases over time were achieved in Bulgaria, Hungary and the Slovak Republic (at least 70%), while workers in Malta and Poland experienced negative wage growth.

[4] The values for Austria and Germany are based on our own calculations of the share of full-time employees with gross wages under 1,200 euro (data: EU-SILC; GSOEP). This is the threshold in the political discussions on minimum wages. For the sake of an intra-European comparison, these thresholds were converted into PPS (Austria: 1,067 euro in PPS; Germany: 1,145 euro in PPS). However, one has to note that in both countries a nationwide minimum wage has not yet been implemented. The governments, unions and employer associations are still negotiating the conditions of a minimum wage law. As of spring 2010, only employees in companies/branches where wages are covered by collective bargaining agreements receive a minimum wage, which is in some branches even higher than the 'political' mean value used here.

[5] Discussion of the theoretical importance of gender-specific inequalities has yet to be resolved (for a useful introduction to a gender sociology of inequality see Connell, 2009). Still, over the last two decades a multitude of studies have emerged on a diverse range of gender-specific inequalities. Thematically, these treat educational inequality, labour market issues, poverty risks, the relevance of welfare-state protections for women with children, the biographies of migrants, access to attractive jobs and income inequality (Lewis, 1992; Duncan, 1995; Ridgeway, 1997; Fodor et al, 2002; Donato et al, 2006).

[6] Bulgaria's and Romania's preparations in light of their accession to the European Union in January 2007 spurred the adoption of gender equality legislation. Both countries benefited from EU policies towards women's rights and female labour market participation, and this has contributed to the promotion of a number of measures aimed at increasing the participation of women in the labour market and reducing pay gaps. The case of Slovenia is different. Here, the historical effects of declarative equality have resulted in a higher rate of female employees in the industrial sector, which has also resulted in a smaller gender pay gap than in many other European countries.

[7] Equivalence incomes are used to render comparable the income of persons living in households of different sizes. Such weighting makes sense given that larger households enjoy economies of scale (e.g. via the shared use of living space, cars or appliances).

Equivalence incomes are calculated by summing the incomes of all members of the household and then dividing this total income by the household weight. Each member of the household is assigned the same resulting value, that is, the equivalence income.

[8] International comparative analyses of wealth inequality are particularly beset by these problems.

[9] The median is a measure of central tendency. It halves a series of data points ordered by magnitude and thus represents the middle value of the dataset. It can be sensibly applied to ordinal level data or higher. Compared to the mean, it has the advantage of reacting less sensitively to outliers (for an explanation of equivalence incomes, see note 7 above).

[10] Another critical difference between some of the Eastern European accession countries and the EU–15 states is that those aged 65+ made up a much smaller share of the population in the former coutnries. However, the Eastern European countries spend more of their social expenditures on pensions than the countries of the EU–15. The result is a pension level that supports protection against poverty at least in countries like Hungary, Slovakia, the Czech Republic and Poland.

10

Quality of life

Steffen Mau and Roland Verwiebe, with Patrick Präg

☐ DEFINITION

In the social sciences, quality of life is a concept that goes beyond people's mere material standard of living. It treats their standard of living as one indicator alongside other, non-economic ones, such as health, housing, environmental quality and leisure time. Empirically, quality of life is measured in terms of not only objective conditions, but also subjective assessments.

Quality of life has become a popular concept not only in sociology, but also in disciplines like philosophy, the health sciences, psychology and economics (Sirgy et al, 2006). The concept of quality of life encompasses a broad range of concrete living conditions that differ not only across the countries of Europe, but also among social groups within countries. Thus, quality of life is crucial for the stratification of European societies. In particular in studies of Europe, quality of life is a common focus of research (Delhey et al, 2002; Noll, 2002; Alber et al, 2008b; Grasso and Canova, 2008; Böhnke and Kohler, 2010; Drobnič et al, 2010; Präg et al, 2010). This is in part due to the fact that the European Commission funds research in this area (Noll, 2004). As a complement to economic and political integration, the Commission has begun to focus additionally on improving the living conditions of European citizens, and monitors progress herein via social reporting (Alber et al, 2008a).

Research on quality of life has its origins in the social indicators research of the 1960s and 1970s (Noll, 2004). In the economically prosperous Western societies of this period, the quality of life of broad segments of the population had been improved dramatically over the preceding decades. In the wake of this, and in the context of a change in the structures and value systems of European societies (emergence of post-industrial society, rise of post-materialism), scepticism arose as to whether 'more' was always 'better'. People began to question whether economic growth was the sole indicator of social progress (Inglehart, 1990). In addition to its scientific import, quality of life always had a political dimension as well. During this period, the state staked a far stronger claim than it does today on being capable of steering social processes (Rapley, 2003; Noll, 2004).

Social indicators research

Level of living approach

Since the 1960s, many definitions and operationalisations have been developed to better conceive of and empirically measure quality of life. The so-called 'level of living' approach stems from Swedish welfare research (Erikson, 1974, 1993). According to this approach, quality of life entails the disposition of individual resources, which, alongside income and property, encompass education, mental and physical energy, social relations, and security (Allardt, 1993). Additionally, the approach focuses on what could be the determinants of quality of life, such as living conditions, which individuals cannot control – that is, working conditions, the housing market or environmental conditions. Scholars in the 'level of living' tradition view these resources as preconditions for individuals being able to actively manage their life situation and thereby realise their own quality of life. To measure the latter, these researchers exclusively utilise objective descriptions of living conditions. They consider individual value judgements of these conditions to be irrelevant, for these would merely express the degree to which individuals have conformed to their situation (Erikson, 1993).

Subjective well-being approach

A concept that emerged in the United States in the 1970s is the so-called 'quality of life' or 'subjective well-being' approach (Campbell et al, 1976; Diener, 2009). From this perspective, individual resources are not as central. The needs of the individual are central here. Welfare and living conditions are subjectively perceived and experienced. Quality of life thus consists in *positive individual assessment* of one's own living conditions, regardless of how a third party might assess them. To measure quality of life, scholars use measurement scales of satisfaction, happiness and well-being that refer to life in general and to various life spheres (family, work, income). The 'subjective well-being' approach is more prevalent in psychology than in sociology.

Having, loving, being

In light of the fact that neither of these two sources of information could be easily dismissed, concepts soon emerged that attempted to integrate both subjective and objective indicators and thus find a middle ground between these two poles (Allardt, 1976; Zapf, 1984). Allardt sought a synthesis of both perspectives with his 'having, loving, being' approach (Allardt, 1976, 1993). He further developed the resource concept of Scandinavian welfare state research, which had been criticised for being too narrow, and placed US satisfaction research on an intersubjective, societal foundation. Allardt focused not on resources, but on a model of human needs, which he broke down into three groups:

- *Having* encompasses material living conditions that are essential for survival, such as income and property, housing conditions, employment, health, education, but also the condition of the natural environment.

- *Loving* stands for the need for social contacts and belonging, that is, friendships, neighbourhood contacts, nuclear and extended family relationships, membership in organisations and work contacts.
- *Being* characterises the need for personal growth, namely opportunities, participation and self-realisation, that is, control over one's own life, civic participation via participation in political decision-making processes, meaningful work or a good work–life balance. Allardt (1993: 91) characterises the non-fulfilment of this basic need as alienation.

In Allardt's approach it is essential that all three categories be assessed using both objective and subjective indicators, that is, researchers should not just document people's living conditions, but also ask how they experience these. In recent years, the distinction between subjective and objective measures of quality of life has come under scrutiny (Veenhoven, 2000): both types of measurement aim at the same qualities, and the terminology is misleading. 'Objective' measures are not irrefutable, and 'subjective' measures cannot be taken as mere matters of taste. Furthermore, empirical evidence suggests that objective and subjective measures of well-being are highly interrelated (Oswald and Wu, 2010).

An example of an understanding of quality of life that is not directed solely at Western society is the capability approach of the Indian Nobel Prize-winner Amartya Sen (1985, 1993). Functional capabilities determine, according to Sen, the substantive freedom of a human being to live their life. They represent a person's capability to be something (e.g. well nourished, healthy, socially integrated) or to do something (e.g. to read or go to church). Functional capabilities are the freedom to be able to achieve certain functionings. Quality of life is measured in the ability to achieve certain functionings in accordance with one's own preferences. The greater the amount of one's capabilities, the greater one's quality of life.

In this section, we will touch upon the quality of several important life domains. The discussion will be limited to housing, environmental conditions, health and time use. Indicators such as Gross Domestic Product, employment, life expectancy, poverty and education have already been considered in Chapters 5 and 9 and will not be discussed again here. In the presentation of selected domains of the quality of life, we will go beyond using aggregate data to depict differences among EU states, for as Allardt (1993: 89) has demonstrated, mere aggregate and mean values are insufficient to assess countries' quality of life. If the living situation of a large portion of the population is unsatisfactory, its quality of life cannot be characterised as sufficient, even if on average it is comparatively high. Thus we will place emphasis on inequalities in the quality of life.

10.1 Housing

NOTE ON METHODOLOGY

This section will be based on Eurostat data and data from the European Quality of Life Survey (EQLS) of 2007. The empirical assessment focuses on four parameters. Shortage of space: average available living space (m²) per resident; internet access: proportion of households with internet access; tenure status: share of citizens owning their accommodation (either outright or with a mortgage or loan); and maintenance deficiencies: share of citizens reporting rot in windows, doors or floors, and/or damp or leaks in walls or the roof.

Housing inequality

Housing is a complex sociological phenomenon that is shaped by economic, cultural, social and political conditions, as well as processes of social change. Housing and access to living space are basic human needs, which have a decisive impact on the quality of life of individuals (Grzeskowiak et al, 2006). The way in which housing impacts on quality of life varies considerably depending on a household's economic resources. Moreover, tenure status is a key aspect of housing, and home ownership is the most important form of family wealth. Housing is thus a crucial (albeit often overlooked) topic for research on social stratification. Historically, housing was a central feature (see Section 3.1) of the 'social question' of industrialising Western European societies. Housing patterns are structured by societal dynamics, and the industrialisation process gave rise to specific housing forms for different social classes (blue-collar workers, white-collar workers and civil servants, managers). Depending on their role in the mode of production, these classes lived in distinct neighbourhoods or districts. These residential districts differed in terms of the size of the apartments or houses, their tenure status, and the quality of the proximate environment (whether amenities or hazards) (Hamnett, 2001). The segregation of residents into distinct urban spaces can thus be seen as a phenomenon with a specifically European historical pedigree.

Segregation describes the social-spatial structuration of a city, that is, the projection of social structures onto space. It is a product of social inequality, that is, the inequality of opportunity across social groups in finding living space that accords with their preferences through the housing market. Segregation expresses itself in the concentration of population groups in specific parts of town. In describing it, it is important to differentiate between voluntary and forced segregation and to specify which groups are segregated and the type and causal origins of the segregation – that is, to distinguish socio-economically (structurally) rooted from ethnic-cultural (functional) segregation (Massey and Denton, 1993; Hamnett, 1999).

Housing and tangible living conditions are not only decisive for the well-being of residents, but are also resources that can shape life chances. Housing conditions impact on the well-being of individuals and families both directly and indirectly through their effects on various life domains such as health, security, privacy, social relations and access to employment, recreation and services (Sampson et al, 2002; Shaw, 2004). Inequality of housing conditions is addressed in the literature primarily in a national or regional context (Hamnett, 1999; Mulder and Smits, 1999; Kurz, 2004; Norris and Redmond, 2005). On the one hand, scholars analyse differences in tenure patterns. On the other hand, they study amenities (car, dishwasher, TV, cell phone, computer, internet access), quality (heating, indoor plumbing, air-conditioning), square footage and exposure to environmental and noise pollution. International comparative studies of housing inequality are less common (e.g. Kurz and Blossfeld, 2004; Norris and Shiels, 2007; Domanski, 2008).

Disparities in housing quality among EU Member States

In the wake of the industrialisation and urbanisation of Continental European cities in the late 19th and early 20th centuries, housing conditions had become dangerously overcrowded with deficient sanitary and heating facilities and resulting threats to public health. In addition, working-class housing in particular was frequently exposed to environmental hazards as a result of the characteristic failure to separate industrial from residential areas. This was part-and-parcel of the broader, endemic social-structural polarisation of cities during this era. In the 1880s, about half of Milan's population was living in one- or two-room apartments, whereas the number of tenement houses in Roubaix rose from 156 in 1891 to 1,524 by 1912, at which point these housed 157,000 persons in squalid conditions (Clark, 2009: 293). According to Häußermann und Siebel (2000: 65), at the beginning of the 20th century in Hamburg and Munich the average residential living space per person ranged between 10m² and 15m². At the same time, however, due to the highly unequal distribution of living space, one can estimate that roughly half of the population of Germany's big cities lived in slum conditions (Häußermann and Siebel, 2000: 66).

Living space per capita

> Häußermann and Siebel elaborate further on the case of Berlin (2000: 67, authors' translation):
>
> in 1900 there were 27,729 apartments with at most one heatable room and six or more inhabitants.... 7,759 people shared 4,086 apartments that consisted of only a kitchen; 7,412 persons shared 2,419 apartments that

consisted of only one, non-heatable room; 59,746 people shared 32,812 apartments that had only one heatable room; and 726,723 persons lived in 197,394 apartments that consisted of merely a kitchen plus one room. If one adds to these 900,000 persons the 381,118 essentially homeless people who rented a space which they could inhabit only to sleep at night ... these numbers describe the living conditions of roughly half of Berlin's renters.

Under these conditions, it was virtually impossible to have any privacy, to pursue child-rearing in such a way as to cultivate personality development, or to sufficiently recuperate from a day's work. Anyone who could escape such apartments did so, and fled to public spaces. For women, this type of apartment was the place where they spent most of their time – where they prepared the meals and cared for the children, and in many cases had to perform 'outwork' to supplement the household's income. That, under these conditions, it was a fairly hopeless endeavour to try to maintain a normal family life in these overcrowded, poorly equipped apartments is obvious.

Housing conditions have improved dramatically in Europe since the 1920s. This was the result of modernisation of the regulatory and social policy apparatus due to the emergence of urban planning, zoning and building codes, as well of vibrant public and non-profit housing sectors. This modernisation led to a marked increase in the quality of residential life for most Europeans. For example, living space per capita has now reached 38.9m² and 1.7 rooms in the EU-27 (Figure 10.1), which, although precise comparative data are lacking, certainly amounts to a massive increase compared to the beginning of the 20th century. This was achieved despite the marked increase in population growth in European urban regions above all in the first half of the 20th century (Clark, 2009; Therborn, 1995).

Living space varies across Europe

A second glance at Figure 10.1 reveals an obvious East–West divide. At the top of the European hierarchy stands, on the one hand – as before with regard to Gross Domestic Product (see Section 7.1) – Luxembourg with over 60m² (1.8 rooms) per person and Belgium with 2.2 rooms (33.7m²) per person. It is clear that both selected indicators diverge significantly at the high end of the scales: a high square-metre figure does not necessarily coincide with a high number of rooms per person. At the low end of the European hierarchy, the difference between the indicators is much smaller, however. In countries like Romania, Latvia and Bulgaria, where people have only 14m² to 16m² of living space on average, the number of rooms per person is also very low. In Eastern Europe, living space traditionally has been scarce (Hegedüs and Teller, 2005; Domanski, 2008) and this remains so in the post-socialist countries (OECD, 2005a). Several scholars have observed, however, that this problem has been mitigated somewhat by the shrinkage of the population during the 1990s (see Section 5.1) (Lux, 2003). Domanski (2008) attributes the lack of adequate living space in the Eastern European reform states to their comparatively low Gross Domestic Products. Hegedüs and Teller (2005) argue that because of its heavily subsidised rents, state-socialist housing policy was never able to make a sufficient amount of housing available. The cutting of these subsidies after the transition to capitalism and the rapidly ensuing privatisation of housing – ownership was sometimes transferred free-of-charge to renters – could not solve this problem. To the contrary, the new owners were not in a position to maintain their property in good condition (Norris and Shiels, 2007).

Figure 10.1: Living space per person

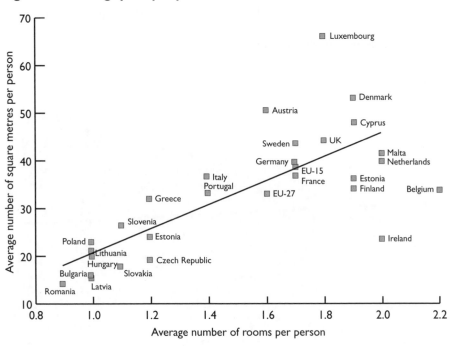

Source: For average number of square meters per person: Eurostat (2010b), Ireland and Cyprus: Norris and Shiels (2007); no values available for Portugal, for United Kingdom only England; data are for 2001 (Ireland 2002, Romania, Latvia, Poland, Estonia, Greece, Spain, Sweden, Austria, Denmark, and Luxembourg 2004); EU-15 unweighted mean. Source for average number of rooms per person: Eurostat (2010a), values for 2008.

With regard to the extent of amenities within homes – that is, bathrooms, indoor plumbing, central heating or colour television – there has been a harmonisation of standards across Europe in recent years. Today, a majority of homes, especially in Western Europe, have these features (Domanski, 2008). Between 94% and 100% of homes in Western Europe have a bathroom (Anderson et al, 2009: 42), and 96% have a TV (The World

Harmonisation of housing amenities

Bank, 2009: 312). In terms of these indicators, then, a catch–up process has already occurred within Europe.

Internet access

One indicator for housing quality that has become increasingly important over the past decade is the share of households with internet access (Figure 10.2). Modern information and communications technologies like the internet are among the most critical foundations of globalisation (Castells, 1996). Internet access represents not only the degree of technical modernisation and the state of economic development of EU countries, but also increasingly the opportunity to fully partake in communal life (in the sense of access to communication and information) and in social and economic development (DiMaggio et al, 2001; Guillén and Suárez, 2005; Korupp and Szydlik, 2005; OECD, 2006a; Räsänen, 2006; Notten et al, 2009). Domestic internet access is thus becoming an ever more significant precondition for the realisation of quality of life.

Figure 10.2: Households with internet access

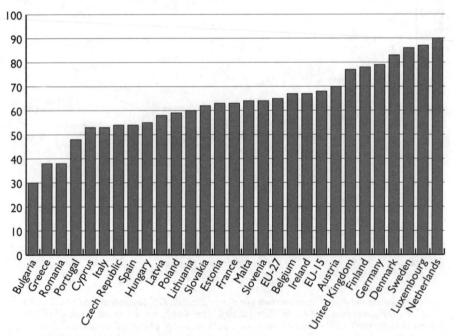

Source: Eurostat (2010b), data for 2009.

Figure 10.2 shows that in 2009, 65% of EU–27 households had internet access. Considerable differences exist across the EU, however. In economically strong Western European countries like the Netherlands, Sweden, Denmark and Luxembourg, 79% to 90% of households have internet access. The smallest proportions of households with internet access are to be found in the two most recently acceded EU Member States, Bulgaria and Romania, as well as in Greece.

Per capita income is an important predictor of the spread of internet connections in modern societies (Beilock and Dimitrova, 2003). For this reason, it is unsurprising that access to this critical information medium is better in the Western European EU states than in their Southern or Eastern European counterparts. Nevertheless, there are interesting findings regarding the latter. For example, Slovenia is only slightly below the EU-15 average with a 64% access rate. Greece's 38% rate puts it in the company of the poorest EU states, Bulgaria and Romania. States like Portugal, Spain and Italy trail Latvia and Estonia, for while the Southern and Western European states had to make costly investments in outdated communications networks, Eastern European countries could catch up by investing directly in modern wireless networks (Howard, 2007).

Inequality of housing conditions across EU Member States

Owning your own home is extremely important to people in modern Western societies. Becoming and being a home-owner has positive effects on individuals' well-being (Dietz and Haurin, 2003; Diaz-Serrano, 2009), serving as a symbol for individual freedom, independence and security. Home ownership affects a household's standard of living, social standing and wealth – albeit not always positively, as the massive devaluation during the 2008 housing crisis has shown.

Value placed on home ownership

Empirically, home ownership is particularly widespread in the post-socialist states of Hungary, Slovenia, Bulgaria, the Slovak Republic and Lithuania (around 90%), and in Finland, Spain, and Italy (around 80%). The average rate of home ownership is about 71% of households (small rectangles in Figure 10.3). The lowest rates are in Germany, Latvia and Austria (51%–56% of households). These are followed by states like Portugal, the UK, Denmark, France and the Netherlands, where about 65%–70% of residents are home-owners. The high home ownership rates in Eastern Europe are not – as mentioned earlier – due to the purchasing power of the populations there, but to the privatisation policies after the end of state socialism.

In Western European states, too, housing policy has impacted on ownership rates. Whereas, for example, in Austria and Germany the majority of the residential rental market is regulated and there is a substantial share of public housing units, in Ireland and the United Kingdom the housing market is largely unregulated, and public (council) housing is made available only for the poor. As a result, in Austria and Germany rents are relatively affordable, whereas in unregulated markets like the UK's it is more attractive to purchase housing (usually with a mortgage) (Kurz and Blossfeld, 2004; Norris, 2008). Moreover, in countries with considerable income inequality, residential property also serves as a sort of safety net (Watson and Webb, 2009). Another explanation for the differences across EU Member States is the high level of urbanisation in countries like the Netherlands, and the large share of rural populations, for example, Greece or Italy, for as a general rule, the highest home ownership rates are in rural areas and the lowest in big cities.

Figure 10.3: Share of home-owners by household income

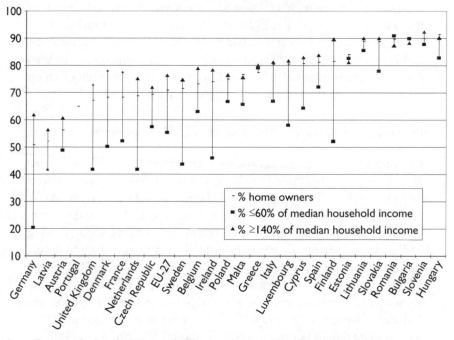

Source: European Quality of Life Survey (2007), own calculations. Question: 'Which of the following best describes your accommodation?' Response options 'Own without mortgage (i.e. without any loans)' and 'Own with mortgage' added up. Income: household equivalence income (old OECD scale).

Unequal distribution of home ownership

A second glance at the available data shows that a correlation exists cross-nationally between a country having a high home ownership rate and that ownership being equally distributed across the income spectrum. Equality of home ownership distribution is greatest in Eastern Europe, Greece, Spain and Italy. By contrast, the most unequal distribution of home ownership – measured in terms of differences in ownership rates among low- and high-earning households – is found in Germany, the Netherlands, the UK, Finland, Sweden and Ireland, countries in which home ownership rates are low.

A second indicator of quality of life with regard to housing is the distribution of housing problems (Grzeskowiak et al, 2006) within the EU (Figure 10.4). The worst housing conditions are found in Latvia, where over 40% of all homes have serious deficiencies. In Hungary, Cyprus,

Lithuania and Estonia over 30% of households complain of problems with the condition of their accommodation. The best maintenance conditions are found in Sweden, Austria, Germany and Ireland, where less than 10% of housing units evince grave deficiencies. It is striking to see that here, again, two Southern European states, Greece and Portugal, rank near the level of the new Member States. Norris (2008) points in this context to the low quality of the public housing stock in Southern European countries.

Figure 10.4: Housing deficiencies by household income

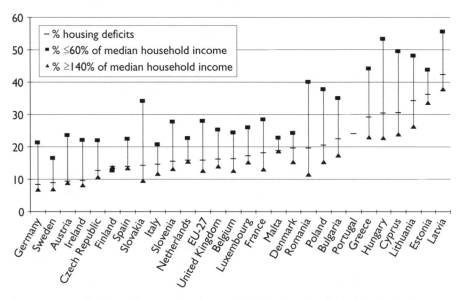

Source: European Quality of Life Survey (2007), own calculations. Question: 'Do you have any of the following problems with your accommodation? Rot in windows, doors, or floors; Damp or leaks in walls or roof'. Income: household equivalence income (old OECD scale).

Within most EU states, the distribution of housing deficiencies correlates clearly with income. In Slovakia, Romania, Germany, Ireland and Austria, households with less than 60% of average household income report far more problems than do those with more than 140%. Considerable equality in the distribution of maintenance problems can be found, by contrast, in Finland, Malta and Estonia.

Housing deficiencies correlate with income

Overall, the findings show that the four indicators cited in this chapter (crowdedness, internet access, home ownership rates and maintenance deficiencies) are related. In all cases there is a marked East–West divide. With regard to living space, maintenance deficiencies and internet access, the quality of life is better in most Western European countries than in Eastern Europe. At the same time, the home ownership rate in Eastern

Europe is higher than in Western Europe. This coincidence of more home ownership, smaller living quarters and greater dissatisfaction in Eastern Europe has been viewed as a paradox (Domanski and Alber, 2006). This reveals the difficulties inherent in choosing quality of life indicators. Whereas in Western Europe the acquisition of residential property is seen as desirable and as yielding improved quality of life, quality of life in Eastern Europe is not tied to home ownership. In addition to this East–West divide, there is a North–South divide within the EU. There are often only minor differences between the Southern and Eastern European states with regard to quality of life. With regard to internet access, for example, it is clear that Eastern European states have already surpassed several of their Southern European counterparts. Independent of these East–West and North–South patterns, within EU states housing conditions often correlate with income. This is particularly evident with regard to home ownership in those countries with low ownership rates and regulated housing markets (e.g. Sweden or Denmark).

10.2 The environment

NOTE ON METHODOLOGY

The urban population's exposure to air pollution by particulate matter is calculated as the population-weighted annual mean concentration of particulate matter (in $\mu g/m^3$). The analysis is based on Eurostat data. Airborne particulates and particulate matter can have deleterious health consequences above all among children and older adults (allergy symptoms, respiratory and lung disorders, cardiovascular disease). The extent of health risks depends not only on the toxicity (lead or mercury content) but most of all on the size of the dust particles. The smaller they are, the more dangerous they are. PM10 is formed from industrial exhaust emissions as well as from emissions from street traffic, private households (heating systems), heat and power plants, the construction industry, and agriculture. The EU's threshold for the yearly average value of particulate matter emission was $40\mu g/m^3$ in 2005. From 2010 on it will be $20\mu g/m^3$.

The urban population's exposure to air pollution by ozone is calculated as the population-weighted yearly sum of maximum daily eight-hour mean ozone concentrations above a threshold ($70\mu g$ of ozone per m^3 per day). The analysis is based on Eurostat data. Higher ozone concentrations can lead to respiratory and lung disorders, headaches and circulatory disorders. The World Health Organisation stipulates an hourly value of $120\mu g/m^3$ as a threshold above which health dangers exist. The EU uses a graduated scale of thresholds: acute health risks exist at an hourly mean value of $360\mu g/m^3$; at $180\mu g/m^3$ the government is obliged to inform the population. By 2010 the Union seeks to limit damage to the ozone layer even further. From then on the higher mean hourly value will be $240\mu g/m^3$ and the eight-hour mean value will be

120µg/m³. The formation of low-level ozone is fostered by industrial exhaust emissions, street traffic, agricultural activities and biogenic emissions (e.g. from forest areas).

A healthy state of the natural environment is seen by Allardt (1993: 90) and Erikson (1974: 278) as a necessary resource for human survival and thus a dimension of the quality of life. Even though the condition of the environment is often overlooked in quality of life research, attempts have recently been made to link discourse on quality of life with that on sustainable development (Noll, 2004; Schäfer et al, 2004). The fundamental idea here is that for human beings, quality of life can be secured over the long term only if the natural foundations of life are used only to such an extent that they can still regenerate themselves.

Researchers operationalise good environmental conditions in different ways. While, for example, Grasso and Canova (2008) take the revenues from environmental legislation, the share of renewable energy in total electricity consumption and the number of pieces of environmental legislation as indicators, Hagerty et al (2001) report operationalisations that are based on subjective evaluations. Other studies focus more on the relationship between the environment and social inequality (cf. Julian, 2004). Such approaches are inspired by Ulrich Beck's *Risk Society* treatise (1992) and are deeply rooted in contemporary political sociology. The guiding idea for this line of research is the notion that global risk constellations can transcend social and territorial borders: 'The worldwide equalization of risk positions must not deceive us about new social inequalities within the affliction by risk. These arise especially where risk positions and class positions overlap' (Beck, 1992: 41). In Beck's view, such overlapping is no coincidence, for he perceives a systematic connection between poverty and environmental risks. The socially disadvantaged tend to be confronted with more pollution.

The environment and quality of life

Environmental sociology is a comparatively recent subfield within the discipline of sociology. Initial forays into environmental-sociological analysis were ventured already in the 1920s and 1930s, namely in the reflections on human ecology by the Chicago School (Park, 1936). More recent prominent theoretical contributions include Luhmann (1989) and Eder (1996). Current research efforts are concentrated in the fields of technology assessment (Goncalves, 2006; Bechmann et al, 2007), environmental awareness (Diekmann and Preisendörfer, 2003; Jones et al, 2009; Franzen and Meyer, 2010), environmental and technology policy (Kuhlmann and Edler, 2003; Cruz-Castro and Sanz-Menendez, 2005) and in analyses of the environmental movement as a social movement (Müller-Rommel, 2002; Rootes, 2003). In addition, several volumes have provided systematic overviews of developments in environmental sociology (White, 2004; Hannigan, 2006; Redclift and Woodgate, 2010).

Inequality of environmental pollution across EU Member States

Pollution from particulate matter

When one considers the environmental pollution to which urban populations are exposed, the image portrayed thus far of an unequal distribution of quality of life across the European Union is further reinforced. Pollution caused by hazardous particulate matter (Table 10.1) is particularly heavy in Bulgarian, Romanian, Greek, Spanish, Czech and Polish cities, whose annual mean values in 2007 approached the EU threshold. Spain, Italy and Greece are well known for their environmental problems, which can be attributed to the late, rapid modernisation of their societies and to their governments' limited regulatory powers (Pridham, 1994). In many Eastern European countries, too, the condition of the environment is problematic. State-socialist economic policy focused on the development of heavy industry and on energy production via brown coal (Bobak and Feachem, 1995; Horak, 2001), while its housing sector used shoddy building materials and poor insulation (see Fenger, 1999, and the previous section); together, these policies had serious hazardous effects on the environment. However, in recent years pollution from particulate matter has receded in some Eastern European countries (Kahn, 2003; Eurostat, 2007a), in part due to the closure of a large number of heavy-industrial factories (Fenger, 1999). By contrast, residents in Scandinavia, the Baltic countries, Ireland, the UK and Germany are faced with comparatively modest environmental risks, especially from particulate matter. In several of these countries, environmental policies and movements are very strong, for example, in the Scandinavian countries and Germany (Paastela, 2002; Jamison and Ring, 2003; Rucht and Roose, 2003). This might help explain the comparative lack of environmental hazards there.

Pollution from ozone

An East–West divide is evident in the distribution of environmental pollution due to hazardous ozone, and it is overlaid by a North–South divide. Ozone pollution was especially severe in 2007 in Greece, Italy, Austria and in the Eastern European accession countries of Hungary, the Slovak Republic, Slovenia and the Czech Republic. Greece was $9,006\mu g/m^3$ over the annual threshold value, and Italy and Hungary were $7,356\mu g/m^3$ and $7,622\mu g/m^3$ over, respectively. A closer look at the ozone pollution with the help of the EEA study, for example in Italy, shows that the threshold value of $180\mu g/m^3$ (not displayed in Table 10.1) was exceeded during the summer of 2008 on 167 days (EEA, 2009). In Southern Europe, alongside deficient environmental and traffic policies (Fenger, 1999), geography plays an important role. Additional sunny days translate into more environmental pollution from low-level ozone. The comparatively strong agrarian sector in these countries (see Section 7.4) can also be adduced as an explanatory factor.

By comparison, the ozone pollution in countries like the UK, Lithuania, the Netherlands and Finland is much less severe. It ranges between 938μg/m³ and 1,758μg/m³. The reasons for this lie in these countries'

Table 10.1: Pollution of the urban environment by ozone and particulate matter

	Ozone		Particulate matter
	2000	**2007**	**2007**
EU-15	–	–	–
Belgium	1,987	2,371	25.1
Denmark	2,574*	2,376	21.0
Germany	2,832	3,142	22.5
Ireland	–	–	12.6
Greece	6,994	9,006	32.3
Spain	3,563	4,108	32.9
France	3,003	3,434	27.3
Italy	6,636	7,356	36.6
Luxembourg	–	–	–
Netherlands	1,275	1,157	29.6
Austria	6,896	6,043	23.8
Portugal	2,211	3,969	30.4
Finland	1,345	1,136	16.8
Sweden	1,612	1,728	17.5
United Kingdom	781	938	23.9
Bulgaria	–	–	59.0
Czech Republic	4,880	4,870	32.0
Estonia	4,255⁻	2,308	18.6
Cyprus	–	–	–
Latvia	3,801*	1,758⁻	–
Lithuania	2,909⁺	1,995	20.2
Hungary	2,895⁺	7,622	–
Malta	–	–	29.3
Poland	3,712	3,610	34.0
Romania	–	–	43.1
Slovenia	6,861	6,514	32.4
Slovak Republic	6,694	5,734	–
EU-27	3,300	3,909	28.1

Source: Eurostat (2010b); *1999, ⁻2001, ⁺2003, ⁻2006. Ozone: population-weighted annual sum of maximum daily eight-hour mean ozone concentrations above the threshold of 70 micrograms of ozone per m³ per day. Particulate matter (PM$_{10}$): population-weighted annual mean concentration of particulate matter (in μg/m³).

favourable geographic locations (few sunny days) and strict environmental standards. Over the course of time, ozone pollution has increased in most European countries. On average in the EU–27, it increased by 18% between 2000 and 2007. Above-average increases in ozone pollution have occurred in Hungary, Portugal and Greece, while marked declines in such pollution have been observed in a few countries, particularly the Baltic states.

East–West
divide of
environmental
risks

All in all, the empirical distribution of environmental risks in the European Union underscores the theme already highlighted repeatedly thus far, namely that of an East–West divide in quality of life. It is overlaid here by a North–South divide in the level of environmental hazards to the population. In terms of the social inequality of environmental risks, our findings support Beck's (1992) thesis that low levels of prosperity correlate with high levels of environmental risk: regarding the distribution of environmental risks across Member States of the European Union, it is primarily those countries with below-EU-average Gross Domestic Product (see Section 7.1) that are strongly polluted by ozone and particulate matter. At the other end of the spectrum are countries with low levels of environmental hazards and above-EU-average prosperity (e.g. Finland, Sweden, Denmark and the United Kingdom).

10.3 Health

NOTE ON METHODOLOGY

The share of smokers in the population is defined as the share of daily tobacco smokers in the population. The data come from national health surveys (1996–2003), harmonised by Eurostat. The share of overweight persons encompasses both overweight and obese persons. Persons with a body mass index (BMI) greater than 25 are considered overweight. Persons with a BMI over 30 are considered obese, that is, seriously overweight. BMI is a measure of the percentage of body fat of adults, calculated as the ratio of one's weight in kilograms to the square of one's height in metres. The data were surveyed by Eurostat between 1996 and 2003. Alcohol consumption is given in terms of the annual average consumption of pure alcohol (in litres) per resident aged 15 or older, on the basis of Eurostat data. The figures were collected between 2003 and 2005. To measure Europeans' subjective health, we used data from the European Quality of Life Survey (EQLS) 2007 on respondents' satisfaction with their own health condition.

Health as a
valuable good

According to the broadly accepted definition of the World Health Organisation, health can be understood as comprehensive physical, psychological and social well-being. This implies that 'an individual or group must be able to identify and to realize aspirations, to satisfy needs, and to change or cope with the environment.... Health is a positive concept emphasizing social and personal resources, as well as physical capacities' (WHO, 1986). Allardt (1993: 89) views health as an essential, fundamental human need. For Erikson, too, health is an important resource for the realisation of quality of life (1974: 276). Health is not only a precondition for securing material existence, but also a critical foundation for social activities, self-realisation, satisfaction and well-being (Rapley, 2003; Marmot and Wilkinson, 2006). Accordingly, the prevailing societal understanding of health is driven not only by medical criteria, but also by a multitude of social and cultural norms. Furthermore, an individual's health behaviour is influenced by his or her concrete living and working conditions, education, social milieu(s) and class, as well as by his or her subjective perception of health impairments (Marmot and Wilkinson, 2006). From a social-structural perspective, health can be viewed as a socially and structurally conditioned opportunity to live a healthy life.

Medical, social, cultural criteria

The field of health sociology studies the social, economic and cultural influences on health and illness as well as the ways in which society deals with health, that is, policies concerning health maintenance and restoration. Multiple research fields can be distinguished within the sociology of health. First, social-structural and cultural influences on health are central (Mirowsky and Ross, 2003; Marmot and Wilkinson, 2006; Siegrist and Marmot, 2006; Huijts et al, 2010). Second, a growing number of studies (Layte and Whelan, 2009; Drieskens et al, 2010; Ljungvall and Gerdtham, 2010) highlight the relationship between social behaviour and health. Moreover, analyses of the health-care system and of health policy are relevant (Blank and Burau, 2007; Fritzell and Lundberg, 2007; Wendt et al, 2010). Finally, research is focusing increasingly on the relationship between health condition and subjective well-being (Michalos et al, 2000; Rapley, 2003). With the increased ability of health care to extend life, the question of the quality of (extended) life has gained importance (Sirgy et al, 2006: 399ff). This line of research explores above all the effects of illness or disability on quality of life (Sanders et al, 1998; Michalos, 2004).

Empirically, health is surveyed in social-scientific studies via the self-disclosure of respondents. Such surveys focus on objective, but occasionally also subjective, health paramaters (such as satisfaction with one's health). In studies using objective indicators, the frequency of doctor visits, duration of hospital stays, medical history, duration of illnesses, weight and eating habits, but also health risk factors such as smoking, alcohol consumption and obesity, are surveyed. Such objective indicators harbour measurement problems, for respondents can often make only imprecise statements about their health problems and illnesses, especially when these lie in the past.

Subjective versus objective health

For this reason, some scholars prefer subjective estimations of health to investigate people's actual health behaviour, which varies with health status (Robine et al, 2003).

Health in the Member States of the EU

We will analyse health inequality in terms of three objective health indicators in the following paragraphs. First, alcohol consumption in EU states is underscored as a significant risk factor for cardiovascular illnesses. Then, we present the share of the population suffering from obesity, which is also a risk factor for cardiovascular illnesses (Lang and Rayner, 2005). Third, the proportion of smokers in the population is reported. Consumption of tobacco is the biggest preventable cause of illness and death in the world today. Smokers have greater risk of cardiovascular illnesses, chronic bronchitis, lung cancer and other maladies (Husten et al, 2000). As a final health indicator in this section, we will discuss differences across Europe with regard to citizens' subjective health.

Alcohol
Excessive alcohol consumption is an important indicator for objective individual health risks. The available data presented in Table 10.2 refer to differences across European countries in this regard. The residents of the Czech Republic, Estonia and Ireland[1] consume a formidable amount of alcohol. By contrast, those in Bulgaria, Malta, Sweden, Poland and Romania drink relatively little, namely less than 9 litres per year per person. Nonetheless, alcohol consumption in most EU states is extremely high compared to the average in the rest of the world, which in 2000 was 5.8 litres (Rehm et al, 2006). A clear East–West divide is not evident with regard to the indicator 'amount of alcohol consumed'; still, the traditional cultural patterns of alcohol consumption in most Eastern European states are considered riskier (binge drinking, preference for hard liquor) than those in Western European states (Rehm et al, 2006; Popova et al, 2007).

Overweight
The problems of being overweight and obesity are present above all in the UK, Germany and Greece, where considerably more than half of the population aged 15 and older is overweight. France and Denmark are the states in Europe with the lowest rates of persons with a BMI of 25 or higher. There is no clear pattern here dividing Eastern from Western European states; both regions are similarly affected. Even in countries such as France, where the share of overweight persons is relatively low, it has been increasing of late (Knai et al, 2007). In research and policy, obesity is viewed as a growing problem, for its long-term costs to the health-care system continue to rise (James et al, 2001; Lang and Rayner, 2005; Fry and Finley, 2007).

Tobacco consumption
In the consumption of tobacco, the East–West divide in European quality of life highlighted earlier is clear again. On average in the EU-15, one out of four adults smokes – more in Eastern Europe. A high

proportion of smokers is found in Latvia, Estonia, Denmark, Slovenia and Austria, where, according to Eurostat data, roughly one third smoke on a daily basis. In Slovenia and Austria, roughly another 10% smoke occasionally, thereby also subjecting themselves to health risks (Eurostat, 2010a). By contrast, only half as many people smoke in Sweden, Finland and Portugal. Countries like Germany, the UK and France evince average population shares subject to health risks from habitual smoking.

Table 10.2: Alcohol consumption, overweight persons, smokers

	Alcohol consumption (in litres)	Overweight individuals (as % of population)	Smokers (as % of population)
EU-15	11.2	47.3	27.9
Belgium	10.9	41.8	24.1
Denmark	12.1	41.7	34.1
Germany	12.7	59.7	26.3
Ireland	13.5	46.2	21.9
Greece	9.0	54.0	27.6
Spain	11.7	49.0	28.1
France	12.3	37.1	26.1
Italy	10.5	39.8	24.5
Luxembourg	18.0	52.7	27.0
Netherlands	9.6	42.3	28.2
Austria	12.6	43.5	36.3
Portugal	11.1	51.5	16.4
Finland	12.7	51.3	18.1
Sweden	6.7	43.8	17.5
United Kingdom	11.4	61.0	26.7
Bulgaria	5.9	46.0	32.3
Czech Republic	16.2	50.8	24.9
Estonia	16.0	44.2	33.3
Cyprus	11.4	46.1	23.9
Latvia	9.9	45.3	32.7
Lithuania	10.4	49.0	27.3
Hungary	11.6	52.7	30.5
Malta	6.7	57.5	23.4
Poland	8.2	43.2	29.9
Romania	8.9	41.8	20.8
Slovenia	10.3	48.5	34.6
Slovak Republic	11.6	46.7	19.2
EU-27	9.9	47.5	28.3

Source: Alcohol consumption: WHO (2007), data for 2003–05; Overweight: Eurostat (2008), data for 1999–2003; EU-15 and EU-25 data on smokers: WHO (2007), for overweight persons, unweighted mean values; data on overweight persons and smokers for Luxembourg: IASO/IOTF (2007) and WHO (2007).

Researchers explain the spread of smoking with a diffusion model (Rogers and Shoemaker, 1971; Graham, 1996; Pampel, 2001). This model postulates that innovations (here: smoking) are accepted in successive phases by different social groups, distinguished as innovators, early adopters, early majority, late majority and latecomers. By means of such a model, one can explain gender and educational differences in tobacco consumption (see the following section). According to the diffusion model, Northern European states (Sweden, Finland) have pioneered efforts to reduce smoking and after a long phase of widespread smoking in the 1970s, rates have now reached a very low level (Graham, 1996). Southern European countries, however, lag behind and will not reach Northern European levels for several years. In Eastern Europe, smoking has become much more popular since the fall of the Iron Curtain, which is attributed to the newly won influence of the tobacco industry on Eastern European governments as well as to the introduction of tobacco advertising (Franceschi and Naett, 1995). The prevalence rates in Eastern Europe are somewhat higher than in the EU-15 states. Moreover, the cigarettes sold in Eastern Europe as a rule contain more tar and nicotine than do those produced for Western Europe, which further increases the health risk from smoking in Eastern Europe (Franceschi and Naett, 1995).

Subjective health

Another key indicator used in health sociology and quality of life research is subjective health. Just as with objective health indicators, however, the surveying and assessment of subjective indicators entail methodological challenges. In making statements about their perceived state of health, respondents use different reference systems. These vary based on age, social status, partnership situation and according to the influence of cultural and societal norms (Olsen and Dahl, 2007). Nonetheless, research has shown that single-item summary self-reports of health status have a remarkable level of reliability and validity, even in longitudinal studies. These were able to predict crucial outcomes such as subsequent mortality and hospital admissions (McDowell, 2006).

East–West differences

On the whole, citizens of the European Union are moderately to highly satisfied with their own health condition. In the EU-27, their degree of satisfaction averages 7.4 on a 10-point scale (on which 10 is the highest level of satisfaction). This indicator points again to a fairly clear East–West divide with regard to subjective health in Europe. In Bulgaria, Hungary, the Slovak Republic and the Baltic states, satisfaction with one's health situation is markedly weaker than in Finland, Cyprus, Malta and Denmark. The gap between Latvia on the low end and Denmark on the high end is nearly 2.0 scale points. Between these two poles are countries like the United Kingdom, France and Germany, where people evince a degree of satisfaction with their health condition on a par with the European average. Social scientists explain this East–West gap with reference to differing levels of socio-economic development (Carlson, 1998; Olsen and Dahl, 2007).

Figure 10.5: Health satisfaction

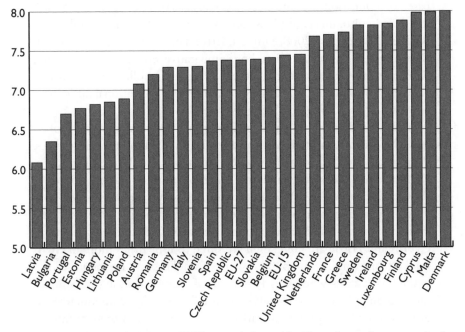

Source: European Quality of Life Survey (2007), own calculations: 'Could you please tell me on a scale of 1 to 10 how satisfied you are with your health?'.

Two general findings can be derived from these data. First, at least with regard to the health risk factors discussed here, objective and subjective health indicators in Europe correspond only partially. Cyprus (high subjective health, low prevalence of risk factors) and Lithuania (low subjective health, strong risk factors) are examples of correspondence; Germany and the UK (moderate subjective health, strong presence of risk factors), by contrast, are examples of a discrepancy between subjective and objective health indicators. On the other hand, the selection of indicators here is necessarily incomplete. Additional factors that impact on health such as working conditions (Danna and Griffin, 1999; Heymann, 2003) or the quality of the health-care system (Kohl and Wendt, 2004; Wendt et al., 2010) have not been considered. The second finding is that, compared to other dimensions of the quality of life (e.g. income), intra-European inequality in citizens' health condition is markedly lower. With regard to risk behaviours in particular, the oft-observed East–West divide does not obtain.

Health inequality across EU Member States

The health risks faced by various social groups are an increasingly important topic in health research today. These risks are found to differ based on education, income, occupational class position, gender, age and social and cultural capital (Ahlström et al, 2001; Olsen and Dahl, 2007; Richter and Lampert, 2008; Lampert, 2010). This degree of differentiation is common in national studies. For comparative European studies, such data have rarely been available hitherto. Hence the following discussion, based on Eurostat data, is restricted to gender and educational differences in relation to smoking and being overweight.

Gender and smoking

Table 10.3 depicts the share of the population that smokes, broken down by educational attainment and gender. In nearly all European states, many more men smoke than women. In Austria, the United Kingdom, Denmark and the Netherlands, the share of smokers among women is above average (25%–32%). In these countries, only a slightly smaller share of women smoke than men. The greatest gender-specific differences are found in Southern and Eastern European states (Greece, the Baltic states, Cyprus and Portugal). Here, men are three to four times more likely to smoke than women. The highest share of smokers among men is found in the Baltic states, where nearly one out of every two adult men smokes tobacco on a daily basis. This hazardous behaviour has consequences, as evidenced by the high rate of early mortality of men in these countries (see Section 5.2).

The diffusion model mentioned earlier suggests that men – particularly those with a high level of education – have functioned as innovators and early adopters of tobacco consumption. In Western Europe, it took 10–20 years before women followed men in this behaviour; women did not begin to smoke in large numbers until a majority of men had been doing so for quite some time, and the prevalence rates among women did not reach their zenith until those for men had already begun to fall (Graham, 1996; Cavelaars et al, 2000; Pampel, 2001; Giskes et al, 2005). Thus, in countries like Ireland and the UK, where smoking was widespread already in the 1950s, today only a negligible difference exists between the genders. In Southern European countries, by contrast, where smoking did not become widespread until much later, large gender differences are still evident. If the Western European trajectory repeats itself in Eastern Europe, women there can expect to see their prevalence rates and attendant health problems increase considerably.

Education and smoking

In a discussion of the spread of smoking, educational attainment is also relevant. The diffusion model claims that high educational attainment makes it likely that an individual both starts and quits smoking at comparatively young ages. This explains why in countries such as the UK, the Netherlands or Sweden, the share of smokers among educated

Table 10.3: Smokers by gender and educational attainment

	Men					Women				
	Total	ISCED 0–1	ISCED 2	ISCED 3	ISCED 4–6	Total	ISCED 0–1	ISCED 2	ISCED 3	ISCED 4–6
EU-15	30.2	30.5	34.4	32.2	23.8	21.0	17.9	24.5	25.0	19.0
Belgium	28.3	28.5	34.7	29.8	21.9	20.1	15.7	23.5	22.6	17.4
Denmark	36.3	–	47.3	41.5	29.2	31.9	–	36.3	37.4	27.5
Germany	30.9	39.4	32.9	30.0	20.3	22.0	28.4	22.7	19.8	17.3
Ireland	23.9	23.2	29.3	18.4	–	20.5	20.2	23.7	17.1	–
Greece	40.8	37.0	48.0	45.0	36.2	15.6	7.8	21.5	24.7	22.4
Spain	34.2	34.0	40.0	35.9	27.9	22.4	13.3	31.6	34.7	25.1
France	31.6	25.1	38.1	32.3	25.4	21.2	11.3	24.7	25.9	21.7
Italy	31.9	25.5	36.4	33.2	25.5	17.6	9.4	21.5	22.1	19.4
Luxembourg	–	–	–	–	–	–	–	–	–	–
Netherlands	31.6	40.5	29.1	32.0	21.5	24.9	29.7	26.1	23.6	16.9
Austria	40.7	40.9	–	43.2	33.9	32.2	28.9	–	35.1	32.5
Portugal	27.1	15.2	36.2	35.3	25.2	6.8	0.9	13.7	22.0	5.4
Finland	21.6	–	22.6	26.3	14.4	15.1	–	16.1	17.7	10.7
Sweden	16.5	19.1	22.1	18.5	10.4	18.5	14.3	26.4	23.1	12.2
United Kingdom	27.0	37.2	30.6	29.3	18.1	25.4	34.3	30.2	23.5	18.1

continued

Table 10.3 (continued)

	Men					Women				
	Total	ISCED 0–1	ISCED 2	ISCED 3	ISCED 4–6	Total	ISCED 0–1	ISCED 2	ISCED 3	ISCED 4–6
Bulgaria	42.6	33.3	38.6	49.0	37.7	22.7	8.8	12.4	32.9	31.1
Czech Republic	32.0	35.0	41.1	22.0	14.4	19.2	16.7	24.6	18.8	9.9
Estonia	49.8	38.0	54.2	53.8	33.2	18.6	4.4	15.3	22.2	17.9
Cyprus	38.1	38.1	34.8	42.5	32.2	10.5	3.4	6.9	14.1	17.2
Latvia	50.6	37.0	54.3	55.0	32.4	17.0	9.4	16.2	19.6	12.4
Lithuania	44.0	–	64.4	51.3	37.8	13.3	–	5.9	13.9	14.1
Hungary	37.0	43.3	44.2	33.1	20.0	24.7	22.0	36.8	25.1	17.7
Malta	29.9	29.8	35.8	24.6	16.5	17.6	10.2	25.0	18.3	12.8
Poland	41.3	36.7	–	46.2	25.6	19.5	12.6	–	25.6	19.4
Romania	32.3	23.7	24.8	37.6	32.5	10.1	3.2	5.6	14.1	17.9
Slovenia	47.1	51.8	48.8	44.1	41.3	23.8	16.1	38.0	26.0	19.1
Slovak Republic	27.8	27.8	35.2	26.4	17.3	11.7	12.9	21.4	10.6	6.6
EU-27	34.4	33.0	38.5	36.0	26.0	19.3	14.5	21.9	22.7	17.7

Source: Eurostat (2010b), data refer to the period 1999–2003 and are the latest available. EU-15 and EU-27 values unweighted.

men (ISCED 4–6 = higher educational qualifications) is now smaller than among less educated men (ISCED 0–1 = no formal educational qualifications). In Eastern and Southern European countries such as Portugal or Latvia, by contrast, one still finds a high rate of smoking among better educated men. The relationship between education and smoking is even more clear among women in countries like Bulgaria, Cyprus and Romania, where smoking is more widespread among better educated women than among those less educated. The model predicts that in the future, smoking in all countries will be widespread above all in the less educated strata (as is already the case today in the UK). The reasons why smoking correlates so strongly with education (and also income) are disputed (Cavelaars et al, 2000; Huisman et al, 2005). On the one hand, some data suggest that the ability to grasp the health consequences of smoking expectations, and hence the degree of success when attempting to quit smoking, are related to educational level; on the other hand, there is some evidence that smoking is a reaction to experiences of material deprivation (Layte and Whelan, 2009).

With regard to being overweight and obesity (Table 10.4), just as with tobacco consumption, the health risks of men and women in Europe are not equally distributed. In nearly all countries, the share of overweight and obese people is about 15 percentage points higher among men than women.[2] Only in Estonia and Latvia is the prevalence of weight problems slightly greater among women (45.4% and 46.3%) than men (42.7% and 44.0%); men in these countries evince the smallest share of weight problems in the entire EU. If one analyses weight problems by degree of educational attainment, marked differences are evident between genders. For women, in nearly all countries a negative relationship exists between education and weight problems; for men, however, this relationship is far less clear. In most EU-15 states, this relationship exists to some extent among men, but in Eastern Europe far less so. While in Estonia, Slovenia and the Slovak Republic overweight men are to be found disproportionately often among both higher educational graduates (ISCED 4–6) and those with low or no educational qualifications (ISCED 0–2), in Bulgaria, Latvia and Lithuania they are found disproportionately in the group with the highest level of educational attainment (ISCED 4–6). The gender difference in the relationship between education and weight problems described here is, moreover, corroborated by other studies as well (Sobal and Stunkard, 1989; Wardle et al, 2002).

More men than women overweight

Table 10.4: Overweight individuals by gender and educational attainment

	Men					Women				
	Total	ISCED 0–1	ISCED 2	ISCED 3	ISCED 4–6	Total	ISCED 0–1	ISCED 2	ISCED 3	ISCED 4–6
EU-15	55.3	61.1	53.6	50.4	51.9	40.7	53.2	41.3	31.7	28.4
Belgium	47.7	56.5	55.4	44.3	40.7	36.2	55.0	45.1	31.0	20.6
Denmark	49.6	–	59.4	53.1	44.9	33.9	–	47.5	34.6	28.8
Germany	66.8	64.5	71.0	49.5	60.4	53.0	45.6	58.1	35.4	29.5
Ireland	57.3	61.0	60.5	50.3	–	38.5	53.4	43.2	28.3	–
Greece	61.4	67.9	55.7	53.9	63.3	47.3	63.4	41.5	28.1	26.7
Spain	56.5	64.2	52.7	48.9	51.2	41.0	59.0	32.7	24.0	20.8
France	44.5	61.7	46.4	33.2	37.0	30.4	49.4	33.1	22.3	18.3
Italy	48.9	62.4	46.5	43.6	42.5	31.4	52.2	26.9	17.8	14.3
Luxembourg	60.9	–	–	–	–	44.6	–	–	–	–
Netherlands	47.3	55.7	30.5	46.8	44.6	37.2	50.7	31.0	31.4	25.9
Austria	59.4	55.4	–	62.0	57.5	28.9	36.3	–	25.6	17.4
Portugal	55.2	54.1	47.8	46.1	60.3	48.3	56.1	34.5	22.8	52.2
Finland	57.5	–	59.9	55.1	56.5	45.8	–	51.6	46.1	36.1
Sweden	50.7	57.7	40.3	54.0	47.4	36.9	49.6	31.1	40.3	29.4
United Kingdom	66.2	71.8	71.2	65.4	68.5	56.6	67.9	61.2	55.6	49.4

continued

Table 10.4 (continued)

	Men					Women				
	Total	ISCED 0–1	ISCED 2	ISCED 3	ISCED 4–6	Total	ISCED 0–1	ISCED 2	ISCED 3	ISCED 4–6
Bulgaria	50.1	39.7	50.0	50.1	57.8	42.3	45.5	52.0	37.3	36.3
Czech Republic	55.5	35.4	62.4	55.5	59.0	46.7	55.6	51.8	35.1	37.8
Estonia	42.7	53.7	40.1	40.2	49.9	45.4	68.6	57.3	40.2	36.8
Cyprus	53.9	65.5	38.2	49.1	59.0	38.7	63.0	29.5	30.1	22.0
Latvia	44.0	32.7	35.6	47.0	54.2	46.3	48.3	42.0	48.6	44.7
Lithuania	57.4	–	48.1	51.9	60.7	42.2	–	54.9	42.7	40.5
Hungary	58.4	59.6	59.3	54.3	62.5	47.7	57.7	51.2	40.2	37.2
Malta	65.6	74.7	64.8	59.3	56.8	50.3	68.5	42.9	36.4	32.2
Poland	47.9	39.8	–	51.2	57.9	38.9	45.8	–	35.4	27.7
Romania	45.8	43.2	44.6	44.5	55.2	38.1	42.4	46.5	32.8	33.7
Slovenia	55.9	57.5	61.1	47.7	58.8	41.7	58.1	46.7	28.5	–
Slovak Republic	57.8	35.4	61.9	55.5	70.3	37.4	41.8	47.7	35.8	30.2
EU-27	54.3	54.3	55.2	52.6	50.5	55.1	41.7	53.6	44.2	34.1

Source: Eurostat (2010b), data refer to the period 1999–2003 and are the latest available. EU-15 and EU-27 values unweighted. Luxembourg from IASO/IOTF (2007).

10.4 Time use

NOTE ON METHODOLOGY ▆▆▆▆▆▆▆▆▆▆▆▆▆▆▆▆

'Paid work time' in Table 10.5 refers to the average number of hours per week actually worked in one's main occupation, reported on the basis of Eurostat data. 'Time pressure' to which employed persons are subjected is measured using data from the European Working Conditions Surveys (EWCS) from the years 1990 to 2005. The table presents the percentage of workers whose work involves time pressure at least three quarters of the time.

Table 10.6 uses data from national time-budget studies conducted by the statistical offices of 18 EU Member States between 1998 and 2004. The table depicts the average amount of time (hours and minutes per day) spent on various activities over the course of a year (Aliaga and Winqvist, 2003). These average amounts of time are of course hypothetical, as days are usually either workdays or weekends. The figures allow for broad comparisons across countries (Gershuny, 2000), but impede more nuanced analyses (Jacobs and Gerson, 2004: 120–3). Data on working hours refer to individuals' day and possible evening jobs as well as to the job search. 'Household work' refers to unpaid domestic activities such as meal preparation, cleaning, caring for children and/or adults, home maintenance and repairs, shopping and errands. 'Travel time' refers to commuting to and from one's place of work or education/training, travel to take care of the family and to maintain the household, as well as travel to and from vacation destinations. 'Leisure time' refers to voluntary work, helping other households, social interaction and entertainment, sports and outdoor activities, hobbies and games, reading, TV, rest, and idleness. The indicator 'sleeping/eating' encompasses not only the time spent sleeping and eating each day, but also time spent on personal hygiene.

Time and inequality

From a social-structural perspective, time has paradoxical qualities. At first glance it is a resource distributed completely equally – independent of stratum and class, everyone has 24 hours per day at their disposal. Yet time is also an expression and source of societal inequalities.[3] People sell their time on the labour market and acquire the working time of others in the form of goods and services. Individuals' position in this market is determined to a large extent by their past use of time – how much time they have invested in work, education, child care or leisure determines the price that they can garner for their time on the labour market today. In this sense, disposition over time constitutes a strategic resource that enhances an individual's opportunities and scope for action.

Time as structuring moment of society

Work time lies at the heart of the temporal institutional make-up of modern societies. It varies across historical time and cultures. In its pure form, it is a product of industrialisation. Work time constitutes the central clock of social life in modern societies. In it are anchored logics of action that shape broad segments of social life. The development of work time since the beginnings of industrialisation resulted in the establishment of work–time institutions. Work time and the complementary temporal institutions of leisure time and household work time provide the framework for the temporal structure of societies on the macro-level. They are characterised in turn by their own respective logics of time use.

Free disposition over one's own time can be understood as a further dimension of quality of life (Gershuny and Halpin, 1996; Goodin et al, 2008; Verbakel and DiPrete, 2008). Increasingly in many European societies, time pressure is viewed as a social problem. Its causes are seen to lie in the intensification of labour or the expansion of work time as a consequence of enhanced competition in the wake of globalisation (Green, 2006; Sennett, 2006; McGovern et al, 2007), in the growing rate of female labour market participation in Western Europe and the erosion in many countries of the traditional breadwinner–homemaker model with the woman as an unpaid caretaker of the children and the household (Drobnič and Blossfeld, 2001; van der Lippe and Peters, 2007), and in a general acceleration of social life due to technical progress and cultural developments (Tomlinson, 2007; Rosa and Scheuerman, 2009).

Measuring time as a dimension of quality of life is a challenge. One possibility is to let respondents estimate the amount of time they spend each day on certain activities (e.g. Brines, 1994). These estimates are prone, however, to systematic over- and underestimation (Lee and Waite, 2005; Otterbach and Sousa-Poza, 2010). Better are diary approaches, whereby a representative sample of individuals keeps a diary for one day during the week and one day at the weekend, capturing activities down to the minute (Michelson, 2005; Chenu and Lesnard, 2006). Even though a considerable number of such studies now exist (Gershuny, 2000; Sullivan and Katz-Gerro, 2007; Lesnard, 2008; Anttila et al, 2009; Carriero et al, 2009; Kraaykamp et al, 2009), it is not yet possible to depict time use in all EU–27 states.

Measurement of time

These procedures say nothing about the quality of the time measured, however. When one considers the problem of unemployment, for example, it is clear that disposition over one's own time is by no means a sufficient indicator of quality of life (Jahoda et al, 2002 [1933]); other indicators have to be examined as well. Possible indicators of the qualitative value of time would be, for example, patterns of time allocation. These could be measured in terms of the degree of balance among paid work, leisure and household work time; the degree of stress and time pressure one's time allocation patterns yield; or the extent to which blocks of leisure time are available for regeneration (i.e. sleeping, eating, sports activities and personal hygiene).

In this context, some authors speak of 'temporal autonomy', expressed in *discretionary time* (Goodin et al, 2008). Goodin et al (2008: 34–5) define discretionary time as that time whose use is not determined by the economic, social or biological necessities of life. Gainful employment is considered to be an economic necessity to the extent that it is necessary to keep one from sliding below the poverty level. Household work is viewed as a social necessity to the extent that it is necessary to keep one's household running. And personal hygiene, eating and sleeping are deemed biological necessities. The emphasis here lies on the aspect of necessity. The concept of discretionary time can also be applied to the employment sphere: if someone voluntarily works 12 hours per day in her profession, even though she could secure her basic needs with five hours of paid work per day, this person may have scarce leisure time, but abundant discretionary time.

Empirical contours of time structures in Europe

A glance at Table 10.5 shows, first, that Western European countries evince a lower amount of average paid work time than do their Eastern European counterparts. The Dutch, for example, averaged 31 hours per week of gainful work in 2008, as a result of an exceptionally high share of part-time workers, not only among women (Visser, 2002; Bosch et al. 2010), but also increasingly among men (OECD, 2009g: 242), while virtually all Eastern European countries evinced average working weeks of 40 hours or more. Countries like Finland, France and Italy are situated around the European average with a weekly work time of 38 hours. Since 1990, weekly work time in most European states has been on the decline. This pattern is robust even with controls for increases in female labour market participation and in part-time work over this period. In some countries like Denmark, Greece, Poland and Spain, weekly work time has remained fairly constant. Only in Bulgaria, Cyprus, Sweden, Finland, Greece and Romania has it increased slightly. Overall, the number of working hours in the EU–15 states shrank by an hour between 1995 and 2008, and in some countries, like Ireland or Portugal, by several hours. This represents the continuation of a long-standing historical trend (Huberman and Minns, 2007).

Time pressure   However, if one observes the share of employed persons in Europe who are subjected to time pressure at work (Table 10.5, right side), a different picture emerges. In comparing countries it becomes clear that in 2005, time pressure was considerable, especially in the Czech Republic, Malta, Cyprus, Greece and Slovenia. Here, between 45% and 48% of workers reported that they have to perform their work under strong time pressure. Workers in Latvia, Portugal, the Slovak Republic and Lithuania, by contrast, seldom experience time pressure. It is evident, further, that in most EU states over time the share of workers subjected to considerable time pressure at work has been increasing almost constantly. In countries like Italy and Portugal, the proportion nearly doubled between 1990 and 2005. In Luxembourg, Denmark and France, too, increases are evident.

On the other hand, in some EU accession countries like Bulgaria, Cyprus and Romania, the share of those subjected to time pressure at work has declined somewhat during the period of observation. Thus, the time problems faced by the bulk of society cannot be explained by the expansion of paid work time; rather, working conditions and/or the content of work itself must be the factors that create time pressure and compromise quality of life (Geist, 2005; Green, 2006; van der Lippe, 2007; Sayer, 2010). In the course of these changes, a dovetailing of both indicators is evident over time. The variance in work time across European countries is declining (1995: SD of 2.7; 2008: SD of 2.5), as is the variance in the time pressure burdening workers (1995: SD of 8.4; 2005: SD of 7.7). One can thus conclude that time structures in Europe seem to be converging.

Convergence of temporal structures

Table 10.5: Paid work time and time pressure

	Paid work time in hours					Time pressure as %			
	1990	1995	2000	2005	2008	1990	1995	2000	2005
EU-15	–	38.1	37.6	36.9	37.1	–	35.1	37.3	37.4
Belgium	40.0	37.8	36.6	36.7	36.8	18.4	22.7	29.5	32.7
Denmark	35.0	34.2	34.1	35.1	35.2	32.0	32.2	29.7	41.8
Germany	39.0	38.6	38.0	36.8	35.6	36.2	36.3	38.4	40.8
Ireland	43.4	39.9	38.7	37.3	36.1	25.7	37.0	42.0	32.6
Greece	41.5	42.2	42.1	41.9	42.4	30.4	29.3	32.9	45.1
Spain	38.9	38.3	38.4	38.6	39.1	19.5	23.4	22.8	33.2
France	39.9	39.7	38.4	36.8	38.1	26.9	31.7	36.9	36.5
Italy	39.6	39.3	39.1	38.1	38.2	14.2	20.8	29.9	29.7
Luxembourg	40.0	39.7	39.2	37.9	36.7	21.4	25.8	29.0	33.6
Netherlands	34.6	30.5	31.5	31.6	30.8	23.4	31.8	33.3	31.5
Austria	–	39.8	39.4	38.7	38.5	–	61.5	40.9	41.2
Portugal	42.8	41.5	38.7	38.4	39.0	11.5	20.8	16.6	27.3
Finland	–	36.8	36.8	37.0	37.6	–	42.6	39.8	42.8
Sweden	–	33.8	36.5	35.6	36.4	–	33.7	39.2	37.4
United Kingdom	36.8	36.7	35.9	35.7	36.9	38.7	50.2	51.7	42.2
Bulgaria	–	–	40.6	40.6	41.6	–	–	36.5	29.1
Czech Republic	–	–	43.0	41.7	41.7	–	–	43.9	48.5
Estonia	–	–	40.5	39.9	39.5	–	–	25.5	32.2
Cyprus	–	–	39.3	39.1	40.2	–	–	50.4	46.2
Latvia	–	–	42.4	41.4	40.1	–	–	24.1	20.6
Lithuania	–	–	39.3	38.1	39.1	–	–	15.0	23.2
Hungary	–	41.1*	40.9	40.3	40.1	–	–	35.4	41.3
Malta	–	–	41.4	39.1	39.0	–	–	46.7	48.5
Poland	–	–	40.6	40.3	41.0	–	–	24.3	30.3
Romania	–	–	39.4	40.1	40.5	–	–	44.4	40.6
Slovenia	–	–	41.6	41.0	40.4	–	–	26.5	44.0
Slovak Republic	–	42.1*	41.0	40.2	41.0	–	–	26.7	25.5
EU-27	–	–	39.0	38.4	37.8	–	–	33.8	36.2

Source: Weekly work time: Eurostat (2010a), *Values for 1996; Time pressure: European Working Conditions Surveys (1990–2005), own calculations; EU-27 values unweighted.

Drawing on time use data, in the following section we will discuss paid work time, household work time, leisure time, travel time and regenerative time. Each will be broken down by gender (Table 10.6). The data show that in most of the European countries under study, paid work time

Paid work
dominates the temporal structure of the day; it takes up more of the day than either leisure or household work time. In Lithuania and Latvia, work time plays a more central role for both women and men than in any other European country. The average daily work time is slightly more than 6:30 hours for men and over 5:45 hours for women. This includes full- and part-time employment, and primary and secondary employment. In countries like the Netherlands or Belgium, work time takes up far less of the day. On average over the course of a year, men in these countries work only five hours, and women three to four hours, per calendar day. This corresponds for women to a weekly work time of 22 to 27 hours, and for men 35 hours. Moreover, empirically, in all EU states under study, characteristic gender differences are evident. First, men work nearly 10 hours more per week than women. Second, the variation in work time among European women is greater than among men. This can be explained in part by more women working part time, and women taking parental leave much more often and for longer than men (Aliaga, 2006: 7).

Leisure is an artefact of modern industrial societies. As an institution, it distinguishes itself from the non-work time of pre-industrial societies in that it gives the pre-eminent value of modernity – the self-realisation of the individual – a legitimate space to unfold. Until the 1980s, in sociological treatises leisure constituted the opposing concept to employment. Leisure was viewed as the time remaining after the normal work period. In more recent research, leisure is often seen as an independent structuring element of society (Gershuny, 2000). The institution of leisure can be broken down into three functional realms: regenerative, suspensive and compensatory functions. Regenerative behaviour serves to physically and psychologically reproduce labour power. Suspensive behaviour in leisure time is oriented towards self-determination and can have a work character; it is antithetical, however, to the abstractness and heteronomy that can characterise paid work time. Examples of suspensive behaviour are volunteer work, political engagement and working in the garden. Compensatory behaviour is activity carried out in direct opposition to occupational work; it serves to balance out the stresses and strains of work through sport or cultural consumption (Best, 2010).

Table 10.6: Time use of employed persons

	Men					Women				
	Paid work	Household work	Travel/ commuting	Leisure	Sleeping/ eating	Paid work	Household work	Travel/ commuting	Leisure	Sleeping/ eating
EU-10	05:29	01:52	01:26	04:26	10:42	04:08	03:30	01:21	03:57	10:56
Belgium	05:00	02:15	01:43	04:08	10:48	03:52	03:46	01:32	03:43	11:01
Denmark	05:24	02:14	01:17	04:31	10:27	04:29	03:13	01:18	04:10	10:46
Germany	05:05	01:52	01:31	05:11	10:21	03:52	03:11	01:27	04:48	10:42
Spain	06:11	01:20	01:23	04:20	10:46	04:57	03:29	01:22	03:33	10:39
France	05:42	01:53	01:10	03:37	11:35	04:30	03:40	01:05	02:56	11:46
Italy	06:13	01:10	01:40	04:07	10:50	04:39	03:51	01:28	03:18	10:44
Netherlands	05:06	01:51	01:12	04:42	11:15	03:10	03:32	01:07	04:36	11:15
Finland	05:24	01:59	01:17	04:45	10:26	04:07	03:21	01:16	04:19	10:48
Sweden	05:09	02:22	01:32	04:36	10:16	03:55	03:32	01:28	04:13	10:48
United Kingdom	05:38	01:53	01:36	04:24	10:21	03:57	03:27	01:33	04:01	10:53
Estonia	04:55	02:16	01:16	04:34	10:54	04:09	04:01	01:11	03:50	10:44
Latvia	06:41	01:26	01:31	03:58	10:24	05:46	03:08	01:26	03:13	10:27
Lithuania	06:31	01:39	01:17	04:02	10:31	05:55	03:24	01:07	03:05	10:29
Hungary	05:19	02:09	01:09	04:24	10:53	04:35	03:53	01:02	03:33	10:51
Poland	06:10	01:59	01:15	04:29	10:13	04:46	03:58	01:10	03:43	10:22
Romania	04:46	02:06	01:06	04:48	11:06	03:23	04:52	00:48	03:52	10:56
Slovenia	05:28	02:12	01:18	04:42	10:20	04:39	04:10	01:14	03:42	10:13
EU-18	05:34	01:55	01:22	04:26	10:40	04:24	03:40	01:16	03:48	10:47

Source: Aliaga (2006) and European Communities (2003); data refer to the period 1999–2003 and are the latest available; data are not available for Ireland, Greece, Luxembourg, Austria, Portugal, Bulgaria, Czech Republic, Cyprus, Malta and the Slovak Republic; data for EU-10 and EU-18 are unweighted.

Leisure time   Corresponding to these cross-national differences in work time are strong differences in available leisure time. Men and women in Germany enjoy the most leisure time (around five hours per day). Both men and women there have on average more leisure than work time. With roughly three hours of leisure time per day, the French, Lithuanians and Latvians (ranked last) have only 60% as much leisure time as the Germans. Moreover, two findings from Table 10.6 are notable. First, women in all European countries have less leisure time than men, although these gender-specific differences are much greater in Eastern than in Western Europe. Second, variation in the volume of leisure time is much greater among women than among men (women: SD of 31 minutes; men: SD of 22 minutes).

Travel time   Travel time encompasses on average between 1:00 and 1:45 hours in the daily time budgets of workers. The Belgians, Italians and British experience the longest travel times, while the Romanians and Hungarians have the shortest ones. Mobility behaviour thus varies by country and gender. In Belgium, Germany, Italy, Finland, Sweden and the United Kingdom, roughly half of travel time is spent in cars. Pedestrian travel is most common in Latvia, Poland and Lithuania. In Hungary and Estonia public transport is the most commonly used means of travel. Men travel more often by car than women, especially in Estonia, Latvia, Lithuania, Hungary and Poland. Overall, women walk more often than men (Aliaga, 2006: 6).

> Household work time is to be distinguished from leisure and paid work time as a temporal institution (Shelton and John, 1996; Coltrane, 2000; Treas and Drobnič, 2010). Because the institution of the family is predicated on different temporal principles, and because social policy as well as family policy regulations occur separately from regulations of the labour market, working couples with children face particular challenges. Women are burdened typically much more than men in this regard, for they perform more household work and care provision – even when both partners are employed (Mattingly and Bianchi, 2003; Drobnič and Blossfeld, 2004). Welfare regimes differ with regard to the gender-specific division of labour among paid work time, leisure and household work time. The most important theories explaining the breakdown of household and paid work time are the household production approach of Becker (1981) and the doing-gender approach of authors like Hochschild and Machung (1990) and West and Zimmerman (1987).

Gender differences in household work   In household work, as in all temporal indicators discussed thus far, clear gender differences can be seen. By far the least amount of time performing housework (1:10 to 1:25 hours daily) is expended by men in the conservative welfare states of Southern Europe (Italy and Spain), as well as in Latvia. Men in Sweden, by contrast, work nearly twice as long in the household. Women in Europe spend an average of 3:40 hours per day caring for children, doing garden work, home maintenance and repairs and grocery shopping. The average time spent by men doing such work amounts to little more than half of this (1:55 hours). Women in the Eastern European accession countries of Poland, Estonia, Slovenia and Romania perform even more household labour (four to five hours daily) than the European female average. Comparatively less time is invested in such work by women in Germany, Denmark and Finland (about 3:15 hours per day); in these countries, the differences between men and women are much smaller than in most Eastern European countries.

The total amount of time spent on work (gainful and household activities together) is greatest among women in the Baltic countries, Slovenia and Poland (8:45 hours or more). With this indicator we see yet again an East–West divide: in Western Europe on average, women work only slightly longer than men – between four and seven minutes in Denmark, Sweden, Finland, Germany and the UK. In countries like Estonia, Hungary, Italy, Slovenia, Lithuania and Romania, women work at least an hour per day longer than men.

In light of these findings, it can be concluded that characteristic differences exist across the Member States of the European Union with regard to quality of life in the realm of discretionary, qualitatively valuable time. The greatest quality of life in the sense of 'discretionary time' can be found among working men and women in the Netherlands and Germany, for the relationship between discretionary leisure time and time spent on gainful and household work is the most favourable here (only two hours' difference daily). In Lithuania and Latvia, discretionary time is more scarce. On average across Europe, men spend four hours longer each day on household and gainful work than on leisure activities. For women this relationship is even less favourable: they spend five to six hours more each day on work than in leisure. Gender differences in discretionary leisure time exist throughout Europe. They are smallest in the Netherlands, the United Kingdom, Sweden, Denmark and Germany, and greatest in Slovenia, Lithuania, Hungary and Romania.

Notes

[1] Luxembourg also evinces a high figure for alcohol consumption, but this is generally attributed to the low taxes on alcohol there, which attract consumers from neighbouring countries.

[2] If one differentiates between being overweight (BMI 25–29.9) and obese (BMI > 30), the share of obese women in most countries is greater than that of obese men.

[3] Such a conception of inequality and time is relatively new. Not until the rise of biographical and life-course research in the mid-1980s did the temporalisation of inequality

become increasingly prominent in social-scientific research (Bertaux and Kohli, 1984; Blossfeld, 1986; Mayer and Tuma, 1990).

Part 3
European integration and European society in the making

11

Institutional and political aspects of Europeanisation

Previous chapters were devoted to the comparison of different societies. In what follows, we want to shift our focus to European integration. We proceed from the premise that EU integration has triggered a fundamental transformation of European societies with greater cross-border interactions and a growing interconnectedness of different national societies. Of course, we concede that European integration is a politically initiated process. Those who initiated and are implementing the process are not ordinary citizens, but rather elites, governments and the heads of national authorities and administrations. However, through their decisions, they set in motion processes of Europeanisation and change the national frameworks of social and political integration. This process of integration involves the transfer of political powers to the European level, which is often referred to as supranationalisation. At the same time, membership of the European Union means that the various national systems have to be changed by the adoption of EU rules.

Integration takes place not just on the political, legal and economic levels, but also on the social level. In the preamble of the Treaty on European Union, integration is referred to as 'an ever-closer union among the peoples of Europe' and thus points far beyond the political dimension of the unification process. In tandem with the efforts towards political and economic integration, the relationship of Europeans to each other and to their national societies is changing (Rumford, 2002; Delanty and Rumford, 2005). Thus, it is essential to explore how 'institutional Europe' affects national societies, their defining features, structures and institutional arrangements. We begin by presenting in summary form the institutional and policy steps of Europeanisation, in order to show the background of the current socio-structural processes of change, and what factors are influencing them.

11.1 History of European integration

DEFINITIONS

Political integration is a process in which political actors in different national contexts direct their loyalties, expectations and political activities towards a new centre. In

> the context of Europeanisation, the integration process involves the creation of supranational institutions and a legal framework (vertical Europeanisation). As a result, a new political community is created that influences the Member States and is superimposed on them (cf. Haas, 1968).
>
> Economic integration refers to the creation of a free trade zone and a common market by eliminating trade barriers, establishing a customs union and granting freedom of mobility for capital, goods, services and employees. In a further step, a supranational economic and financial policy is established, with independent institutions for the implementation of selected goals, such as price stability, economic growth and employment.

The beginning of European integration

The European Coal and Steel Community

The founding of the European Coal and Steel Community (ECSC) in 1951 can be considered a first step towards European integration. The ECSC originated with the so-called Schuman Plan, put forward by the French foreign minister, Robert Schuman, who in 1950 proposed setting up a joint coordination and control authority for German and French coal and steel production. The aim was to pool the national coal and steel markets into a strong common market and to improve conditions for industry, consumers and workers. The foreign policy goal was to replace Allied control of the German industrial Ruhr with a wholly West European institution, including the Federal Republic of Germany. The founding members were France, Belgium, Netherlands, Luxembourg, the Federal Republic of Germany and Italy.

The European Economic Community

The establishment of the European Economic Community through the signing of the Treaty of Rome on 25 March 1957 launched the next stage of European integration. Besides incorporating agricultural policy into the ambit of a European regime, the six founding Member States also set up a customs union, establishing outer customs borders and dismantling internal trade barriers. Thus a new player emerged on the international stage, ensuring the external economic representation of the Member States in their dealings with third parties. Also enshrined in the Treaty of Rome was the aim of creating a common market with free movement of persons, services and capital. Subsequently, intra-Community trade and industrial production experienced strong growth. In 1965, the merger agreement was signed, providing for the establishment of a single Council and a Single Commission of the European Communities (which came into force in 1967). Through this treaty, the institutions of the ECSC, the European Economic Community (EEC) and the European Atomic

Energy Community (Euratom) were merged and then pursued under the concept of the European Community (EC).

The process of European integration is characterised by two trends: the territorial expansion of 'Europe', and the extension of the power of the European Community's institutions (Dinan, 2004; Hooghe and Marks, 2001; Lepsius, 2001; Wallace and Wallace, 2000). In early 1972, the contracts were signed for the northern expansion of the European Community. Subsequently, after a number of controversial disputes, Britain, Denmark and Ireland joined the EC. After the northern expansion, the development of the European Community's institutions came to a standstill. The Commission increasingly shied away from confrontation with the Council of Ministers, a body in which national interests took priority. The freedoms enshrined in the Treaty of Rome had still not been fully implemented, especially because of obstacles to the free pursuit of a trade or profession, the continued existence of tariff barriers and various indirect tax rates.

Northern expansion

At the same time, as a result of the oil crisis, from the mid-1970s economic stagnation in Europe worsened. Only with the first direct elections for the European Parliament in June 1979 was the standstill in the European integration process partially overcome. In 1979 the European Monetary System (EMS) came into force, facilitating stable exchange rates between the currencies of Member States. The next stage of European unification was achieved with the southern expansion. Although within the European Union there was initially fairly significant resistance to the southern expansion, the accession of Greece in 1981 and then of Spain and Portugal on 1 January 1986 was hailed as a success of European integration.

Southern expansion

Consolidation of integration

An important step in extending the authority of the EU was the signing of the Single European Act (SEA) in February 1986 (and which came into force in 1987). The SEA was intended to solve the problem of the structural and institutional stagnation of the EU (referred to as 'Euro-sclerosis'), as well as the economic problems of the member countries. The most important element of the SEA was the creation of a single market, which was supposed to improve the competitiveness of European economies, and which led to expectations of welfare gains for member countries. Finally, in keeping with the logic of market integration, in February 1992 the Treaty establishing the European Union in Maastricht was signed, thereby concluding the reform of the Treaty of Rome. The Community evolved from a mainly economic and political association into a fully fledged European Union. The Economic and Monetary Union and hence the intervention in the currency, monetary and budget policies of member countries of the EU was the most important element of the Maastricht Treaty. The Treaty also led to the inclusion of the areas of defence, justice and internal affairs in the existing Community system.

Four freedoms

The removal and alteration of boundaries between Member States is one of the fundamental elements of EU integration policy (Ferrera, 2005). Thus, in the context of market integration, important steps have been taken to implement the so-called 'four freedoms', namely the free movement of goods, capital, services and persons. The right to free movement within the EU was originally envisaged only for persons in employment, since a single market could not be achieved as long as the mobility of workers was subject to restrictions. But in the wake of political integration, freedom of movement was extended to all population groups, including the self-employed, students and people who are no longer gainfully employed. The Member States now have (almost) no authority to restrict entry and exit. Furthermore, every EU citizen has the right to take on employment in any European member country, thus eliminating all restrictions regarding legal residency and work.[1] This is a great achievement as this grants rights to free mobility and residency to citizens of EU Member States within the whole EU territory.

Non-discrimination

Borders can function as actual physical barriers and restrict mobility, but they can also function as a form of social exclusion, with the help of which members of core groups try to monopolise opportunities. Even in a geographic area without physical hindrances to mobility, it can be difficult to be mobile, because there are forms of discrimination or unequal treatment that hamper access. The simple recognition or non-recognition of professional qualifications gained in another country can have a significant effect on labour market prospects. Within the European Union it became clear at an early stage that the creation of a common market and the deinstitutionalisation of physical borders are not sufficient to reduce social demarcation. Therefore, through the anti-discrimination law and directives, the European Union created a legal framework that provides equality for EU citizens in the area of labour market mobility.

EU citizenship as new membership status

EU citizenship

The Maastricht Treaty also saw the introduction of European citizenship as a new form of membership status in a supranational structure (Wiener, 1998; Eder and Giesen, 2001). EU citizenship does not, however, replace national citizenship; it is more a question of the coexistence of national and supranational citizenship (Maas, 2007). One becomes a citizen of the EU simply by possessing national citizenship in any of the member countries of the European Union. With EU citizenship, the idea of the EU citizen as a pure citizen of the market – thus, as a consumer, worker and so on – changed, and a new understanding of membership rights and membership roles was established (Meehan, 1993). These rights include freedom of movement, thus guaranteeing the right to move to and settle in other EU Member States, political rights, such as the right to vote and to stand for election in local and European elections, and the right to diplomatic and consular assistance. Non-EU citizens who are visiting or residing in the EU are far more limited when it comes to choosing their place of residence or employment.

> The Union has also drafted a Charter of Fundamental Rights, which combines in a single text all the civil, political, economic and social rights of European citizens and all those living within the sovereign territory of the Union. These fundamental rights are based mainly on the rights and fundamental freedoms recognised in the European Convention on Human Rights, on the constitutional traditions of member countries, on the European Social Charter and the Community Charter of Fundamental Social Rights of Workers, as well as on other international conventions signed by the European Union or its member countries. These rights are divided into six major chapters: human dignity, freedoms, equality, solidarity, citizens' rights and legal rights.

Furthermore, the Schengen Agreement can be considered an important step in the elimination of borders. Based on this agreement, all border controls were abolished between the signatory countries, making it possible to travel between them without passport checks. At airports and ports within the Schengen area, a distinction is made between citizens of the Schengen countries and those of other countries. In 1985, Germany, France, Belgium, Luxemburg and the Netherlands signed the agreement, which came into force in 1995. Spain, Portugal, Italy, Greece and Austria also joined the Schengen Agreement. Denmark, Sweden, Finland and two non-EU countries, Norway and Iceland, signed the agreement in December 1996. Today, all EU countries except the United Kingdom and Ireland are Schengen signatories, while the agreement is scheduled to take effect at a later date in Bulgaria, Romania and Cyprus. Switzerland, too, as a non-EU member, has abolished its border controls as part of its Schengen accession.

Schengen Agreement

In a further step, on 1 January 1999, national exchange rates were set, the euro was introduced as the reference currency and, in January 2002, it became the sole currency in the majority of EU countries. For the first time, European integration in everyday practice was conveyed to the public via the crucial exchange medium of money (Parsons, 1964a). This can be considered as a form of 'monetary communitisation' (Nollmann, 2002). In general, the European Union is, more than ever, part of everyday life for its citizens.

The euro

European
Parliament

The Maastricht Treaty (1992) and the follow-up Treaties of Amsterdam (1997) and Nice (2001) also resulted in significantly expanded powers for the European Parliament. Since then, the EU Commission has had to be endorsed by the Parliament, which was also given co-decision powers on matters concerning the internal market, consumer protection, the environment and transport networks. Furthermore, a common foreign and security policy is meant to make the European Union an effective representative of European interests at the international level. Through the Maastricht resolutions, which led to the member countries transferring a significant number of their powers to the EU, the latter became an institutionalised regime with wide-ranging powers and efficacy. A new supranational order was thus created over and above the individual nation-states (Marks et al, 1996).

The territorial expansion of the EU

Enlargement
process

As can already be seen from the northern and southern expansion, the geographical and political space of the European Union is not yet finalised, but is still changing (Beck and Grande, 2007). One can describe the evolution of the European Union as an expansion in the form of concentric circles (Vobruba, 2003), whereby countries in proximity to the periphery are integrated into the EU. While this does indeed lead to a modernisation of the new member countries, allowing them to catch up with the others, new and relatively stable core–periphery relations are nonetheless created between the old and new Member States. The new members become the new peripheral states, and they have to bear the costs of being on the fringes largely alone. They thus have a vested interest in the continued expansion of the EU, in order to draw in 'closer' to the centre. This process leads to the establishment of an order of sliding integration, which turns 'core Europe' (the subject of heated political debates) into social reality.

Eastern
enlargement

This is also the logic of the eastward expansion of the European Union (Beichelt, 2004) (Figure 11.1). Following the 2004 expansion, Poland, Hungary, Slovakia, the Czech Republic, Latvia, Lithuania, Estonia, Slovenia, Malta and Cyprus joined the EU, with Bulgaria and Romania joining in 2007. The European Union thus has 27 Member States, a population of 500 million people and covers a territory from Gibraltar to the Baltic states, and from Greece to the Scottish islands. The eastward expansion involves, on the one hand, massive changes in the accession countries (Schimmelfennig and Sedelmeier, 2005). On the other hand, the European Union itself is facing major challenges, for the diversity of interests to be accommodated in agricultural, financial, asylum and foreign policy continues to grow. Some authors view this process critically, because, given the increasing problems of governance, it is unclear whether

Figure 11.1: Enlargement of the European Union

Founding members (1958)	First northern enlarge- ment (1973)	Southern enlarge- ment (1981/86)	Second northern enlarge- ment (1995)	Eastern enlarge- ment (2004/07)	Remaining European territorial states
Belgium (West) Germany (East Germany joined in 1990 with unification) France Italy Luxembourg The Netherlands	Denmark UK Ireland	**1981** Greece **1986** Portugal Spain	Finland Austria Sweden	**2004** Czech Republic Estonia Latvia Lithuania Malta Poland Slovakia Slovenia Hungary Cyprus **2007** Bulgaria Romania	Iceland[1] Norway Switzerland, ———— Albania[2] Bosnia and Herzegovina[2] Croatia[1] Kosovo[2] (under UN Security Council Resolution 1244) Macedonia[1] Montenegro[2] Serbia[2] Turkey[1] ———— Belarus Moldova Russia Ukraine

Notes: [1] Candidate countries; [2] Potential candidates.

the existing institutional architecture of the EU will be able to deal with future challenges (Zielonka, 2006).

Prior to the expansion, reforms in the decision-making process in the EU were carried out. Thus, majority decision-making in the Council of Ministers was broadened and more rights were transferred to the Parliament. The Treaty of Amsterdam (1997) places the Parliament on an equal footing with the Council of Ministers and extends the Parliament's powers of co-decision. In addition, flexibility clauses were introduced (possibilities of enhanced cooperation, suspension of EU membership). On this basis, the differentiation of integration will be a basis of action for the future of the expanded Union (Lepsius, 2001). With the Treaty of Nice (2001) came further institutional reforms related to the growing number of members, such as the composition of the Commission, the distribution of votes in the European Council and the enforcement of a qualified majority in Council decisions (except in certain areas, such as foreign and security policy, immigration and asylum policy, and tax policy).

A European constitution?   Great expectations surrounded the results of the European Constitutional Convention, which in June 2003 submitted a draft of the European Constitution. The latter was aimed at improving the quality of institutional and legal relationships among European nations. The Constitution is intended to serve as a sort of democratic supplement to an economically united Europe, by setting out civil and social rights. The task of the Convention was to submit proposals for a reordering of existing treaties to a European intergovernmental conference, including a clear delimitation of powers and a new architecture of the distribution of power between the different levels of decision-making within the Union. The difficulties associated with working out a European Constitution in the increasingly complex power and regulatory structures of the EU are demonstrated by the failure of the IGC (Intergovernmental Conference) in December 2003, but also by the rejection of the Draft Constitution by France and by the Netherlands in 2005. Also, problems in the ratification of the Treaty of Lisbon (2007), through which the EU is supposed to be modernised and democratised, show that it is becoming increasingly difficult to organise the EU politically and to structure it effectively. On 1 December 2009, the Treaty of Lisbon entered into force, thus ending several years of negotiation on institutional issues. It strengthened the role of the European Parliament and simplified the working procedures and voting rules of the EU. It also explicitly recognises for the first time the possibility for a Member State to withdraw from the Union.

Widening versus deepening   Over the last few decades, the process of European integration has reached a level of development whereby the social systems of the Member States can be considered as largely Europeanised. In economic, political and legal terms, Europeanisation means a continuous decrease in the influence of national governments, with the nation-states increasingly subjected to restrictions due to the impact of the EU. Issues of employment, social integration and the structure of social conflicts are increasingly determined by the Europeanisation process. The final form of the EU is not fixed, either in terms of its institutional architecture or its geographic expansion. Future development will depend greatly on whether, with a large (and growing) number of Member States, one manages to maintain and enhance the EU's capacity to act, its efficiency and the acceptance of its political system. Different scenarios are being discussed in this context, for example, a 'multi-speed' Europe, with a core Europe and Member States that are less integrated than others. Even with regard to expansion, there are major controversies over the EU's capacity to absorb new members and over the proper balance between consolidation and further expansion, but there are also questions concerning the social, cultural and institutional suitability of other candidates for accession (Klingemann et al, 2006; Gerhards, 2007).

Steps in EU integration

- 1950: Schuman declaration: plan for joint authority for coal and steel production in France and Germany, proposed by the French foreign minister, Robert Schuman.
- 1951: European Coal and Steel Community (ECSC).
- 1958: Establishment of the European Economic Community by Germany, France, Belgium, the Netherlands, Luxembourg and Italy; 1957 the Treaty of Rome.
- 1962: Introduction of a Common Agricultural Policy (CAP).
- 1967: Merger of the European Communities into the European Community; Merger Agreement.
- 1973: Northern expansion: Denmark, the United Kingdom and Ireland join the EC.
- 1979: Establishment of the European Monetary System (EMS).
- 1979: European Parliament elections: the first direct elections to the European Parliament take place.
- 1981: First southern expansion: Greece joins the EC.
- 1986: Second southern expansion: Spain and Portugal become members.
- 1987: Single European Act (SEA), consolidation of the Treaties of Rome, gradual completion of the common market.
- 1990: German reunification, expansion of EU to include the five new German federal states.
- 1992: Treaty on European Union (Maastricht Treaty) establishing the European Economic and Monetary Union; since 1993: 'EU' instead of 'EC'.
- 1995: Accession of Sweden, Austria and Finland.
- 1995: Implementation of the Schengen Agreement on the abolition of border controls (signed in 1985).
- 1997: Treaty of Amsterdam for the common foreign and security policy and domestic policy and judicial cooperation; the introduction of a Social Charter.
- 1998: Establishment of the European Central Bank (ECB).
- 1999: Treaty of Amsterdam came into force: after the Single European Act and the Maastricht Treaty, the basic principles of the Union undergo further fundamental changes.
- 2001: Signing of the Treaty of Nice (came into force 2003). The EU prepares for expansion in four key areas: size and composition of the Commission, weighting of votes in the Council, extension of qualified majority voting and strengthening of cooperation.
- 2002: Introduction of the euro (for cashless transactions in 1999).
- 2004: Accession of 10 new member countries (Eastern and Central European countries, Cyprus and Malta).
- 2007: Expansion of the EU-25 to EU-27, including Romania and Bulgaria. Agreement on the Reform Treaty of Lisbon, which was intended to make the Union more democratic, more efficient and more transparent.
- 2009: Treaty of Lisbon entered into force.
- 2010: Euro crisis; launch of comprehensive rescue package.

11.2 Institutional integration mode of the EU

From
economic
to political
integration

For a long period, the European project was first and foremost an economic alliance, which was legitimised by political elites primarily based on criteria of economic efficiency (Moravcsik, 1998; Scharpf, 1999; Dinan, 2004). The process of European integration has therefore been characterised predominantly by 'negative integration' through the creation and institutional furtherance of the internal free market, rather than by 'positive integration' by creating a framework for enhancing the scope of political intervention (Scharpf, 1999; Münch, 2010). In the context of negative integration, while the Member States have forgone a range of control mechanisms, no comparable mechanisms have been created at the EU level that make it possible to intervene in and regulate the market. Although one finds common policies in a range of relevant policy areas, the effects of deregulation and market liberalisation caused by the development of the market exceed the regulatory and redistributive powers of the EU.

Nevertheless, institution building at the European level is well advanced. The EU has long since become a relevant plane of reference for numerous political and social actors, and the model of national self-determination and autonomy is being significantly altered by the establishment and further development of the EU's powers to act (Stone Sweet et al, 2001). As a result of the high degree of political and administrative integration between supranational and national levels, the legal systems, bureaucracies and, increasingly, other social systems of the Member States are now part of a European regime. In addition, in many political regulatory areas, competing powers have been established, with the result that regulations at the national level have been weakened, European administrative networks have been set up, along with networks of experts, and parallel channels for the allocation of monies have also been created. Taken as a whole, the foundations of political control and democratic governance in Europe have undergone profound change (Bach, 2000; Hix, 2005; Münch, 2010). The key structural features of the European Union include: (a) the overriding importance of the law, (b) bureaucratic decision-making, and (c) the lack of opportunities for citizens to participate democratically in the decision-making process.

Decision-making and integration through the law

Integration
through law

Europeanisation is undoubtedly most advanced in the areas in which European law takes precedence over national law. Directives and regulations of the European Union have to be applied by national authorities; where a national law conflicts with a European law, the European law is given supremacy. Many constitutional lawyers now view the national legal systems as reduced to being a subordinate part of the superordinate European legal system. The central importance of the law finds expression in the fact that the European Union was constituted on the basis of contracts freely concluded between the sovereign member countries, enacted through legislation. In addition, the EU's legitimacy and capacity to enforce its decisions are based on the binding force of European law. This is reflected in the de facto acceptance of a wide range of European legislation in the nation-states, ranging from uniform environmental standards to legally anchored competition checks by the Commission. Then there is the European Court of Justice, whose rulings can hardly be overestimated in their integrative significance. The European Court is often referred to as the 'engine of integration' because through its rulings it has intervened in and actively shaped the integration process.

Bureaucratic decision-making is another key feature of the mode of European integration (Joerges and Everson, 2000). The government actors mainly responsible for shaping European policy move and act in an institutional space that is largely cut off from the will of the public and the Parliament. Together with the Commission (an authority with little democratic legitimacy), interconnected networks of national and supranational experts and administrative staffs determine the objectives and instruments of European policy. Although the influence of the European Commission is to a large degree bound to the mechanisms of legal decisions and regulation setting, as custodian of the Treaties it can set its own political agenda (Hooghe and Marks, 2001; Schmidt, 2001). The Commission's role is often deemed to be problematic because its sole right of initiative is not compatible with national customs, where elected bodies (parliaments and/or local authorities) often possess the right of initiative.

Informal compromise culture

On closer inspection, the bureaucratic-administrative decision-making process weakens the role of democratic structures and procedures: decisions are often reached through informal processes of negotiation, and the public and Parliament cannot effectively monitor these policy processes. 'Comitology' is the name given to this opaque structure of committees that has been set up around the various EU bodies. In addition, a separation of powers has only been partially realised, and in the chain of relationships between the legislature, the executive and the bureaucracy, there is no scope for political openness or the effect of competition between parliamentary parties. Contradictions and conflicts of interest between the participating governments and institutions are mostly resolved within a complex substructure of boards, committees and networks, among the members of the EU 'functions cartel'.

Comitology

The EU as a democracy?

It is no accident that the EU has been diagnosed as suffering from a deficit of democracy: in the European Union, control over political power and the degree of democratic legitimacy stand in an asymmetrical relationship to each other. While it is true that citizens can influence European politics through various channels, such as national elections and European Parliament elections, elections at the national level are generally dominated by domestic and non-European policy issues (Schmitt and Thomassen, 1999). The European Parliament does have an influence on devising concrete policies, but less so when it comes to questions of transferring specific powers from the national to the European level or the path taken by the Europeanisation process itself. In the European Union, however, it is not Parliament that has legislative power, but rather the Council of Ministers, which draws its legitimacy from its nationally elected government representatives. From the standpoint of democracy, this is problematic, especially when through a majority vote of the Council of Ministers direct sovereign acts are enforced in member countries, even though these acts have been rejected by their elected representatives. As the executive arm of the European Union, the EU Commission has considerable power, but a weak basis of legitimacy, since its membership is determined by national governments using an elaborate system of proportional representation.

There are different responses to this problem. Thus, there are proposals to improve democratic processes within the EU through direct election of the President of the Commission, or by abandoning the intergovernmental decision-making process in favour of participatory processes that allow relevant social groups to become more involved in EU decisions (Erikson and Fossum, 2004; Neyer, 2005). Other authors do not consider democratisation and the creation of more forms of participation as a solution, because they cast doubt on the EU's intrinsic 'democratic capacity' (Weiler et al., 1995). If one takes the normative demand for democratic governance seriously, then it is not a question of formal participation rights, but rather a question of the equal participation of all citizens in the processes of decision-making. The further development of democratic participation, so say the critical voices, is not a promising path to follow, because Europe lacks the basic social infrastructure of democracy, meaning a political community based on history, language, experience or culture, a community characterised by a certain degree of homogeneity, cohesion and identity. Furthermore, the will to build up democracy lacks a public sphere in Europe, a public sphere able to serve as a forum for public debate. The decisive factors here are the absence of European media, the fragmentation of Europe into its various national public spheres, issues regarding the continuous exchange of information and opinions, and, finally, linguistic diversity in Europe (for a discussion, see Fossum and Schlesinger, 2007). Finally, there would have to be a certain degree of socio-economic equality, because major inequalities mean unequal material and cognitive capacities for individuals, which stand in the way of equal opportunities for participation.

11.3 The social dimension of European integration

DEFINITION

In the EU context, the term 'cohesion' refers primarily to territorial solidarity within the framework of EU cohesion policy. The EU's cohesion policy has the long-term task of reducing the regional disparities and the socio-economic backwardness of the least-developed regions (convergence) and thus sustainably strengthening economic and social cohesion within Europe.

NOTE ON METHODOLOGY

Eurostat collects specially customised regional statistics on Europe and the European Union, using the so-called NUTS classification (Nomenclature des unités territoriales statistiques [Nomenclature of Territorial Units Statistics]). The NUTS classification subdivides the territory of Europe and the Member States according to population size or by using existing administrative structures in three hierarchical levels of analysis. The NUTS-1 level is the highest level of aggregation and represents areas of larger EU member countries with three to seven million inhabitants. The next level, NUTS-2, consists as a rule of subunits of the NUTS-1 level with up to three million inhabitants. Finally, there is NUTS-3, the level of cities, districts and boroughs. The territorial units play a major role in the context of EU regional policy.

Jacques Delors is credited with the claim that people do not love a single market. Thus, in order to win public support for integration (so went Delors' plea), Europe needs to strengthen its social dimension. By 'social dimension' is generally meant regulatory and redistributive policies in favour of social equality and security. Some academic observers also consider that it is almost inconceivable to develop a political community without reducing the huge regional disparities in life chances of the population and without developing common citizenship rights (Flora, 1993). In particular, increased competition and deregulation pressures have led to a situation where there is greater need for security and social equality, which can no longer be adequately provided by the nation–state system (Taylor-Gooby, 2004). At the same time, the uniform economic and fiscal policy within the European Union ensures that individual Member States have less and less scope for redistributive measures. To address this deficiency, and to achieve the main goal of European integration, namely balanced and sustainable development, the European Union has committed itself to developing Europe's social dimension.

The role of the market

Central to the EU's policy approach is the promotion of employment, growth and innovation (Kleinman, 2001). Numerous social policy initiatives, such as the elimination of discrimination and the creation of uniform standards in the areas of occupational health and safety, are the result of the ambition to create a unified labour market, including worker mobility. This is supposed to eliminate isolated labour markets at the nation-state level. The centrality of economic integration within the European integration process has meant that social policy has virtually become an appendage of economic policy. A hallmark of the first phase of integration was that regulations were implemented that especially related to employees (e.g. concerning wages, working conditions and social security). Only gradually were they extended to EU citizens more generally. Through a series of laws, the Council ensured equal access to social security and improved the cross-border transferability of acquired entitlements (Leibfried and Pierson, 1995; Falkner, 1998; Geyer, 2000). This has happened mainly in areas in which national social policy conflicted with the four basic freedoms of the market. Social policy

Figure 11.2: National and European forms of social security

	National social and employment policies	European social and employment policies
Equality standards	Equality of outcome	Equality of opportunity
Solidarity	Comprehensive (mechanical solidarity)	Limited (organic solidarity)
Relation between economy and society	Extensive political competencies; realised through congruency of regulatory power and regulatory demand	Market-oriented solutions to social problems (for instance through anti-discrimination policies)
Central political level	The sovereign nation-state with the ability to comprehensively shape social and employment policies	State in between regional and European levels of regulation and global interdependencies Coordination of national arrangements
Major political strategy to deal with inequalities	Redistributive measures, welfare policies	Improvement of competitiveness, investment in human capital, employability and regional and national innovation systems

Source: Adapted from Heidenreich (2006b: 44).

initiatives of the EU continue to focus on the area of employment policy and put emphasis on the issue of employability. The employment strategy specifically includes the transition from passive to active measures, qualifications and the integration of older workers, women and young people into the labour market (Figure 11.2).

Despite these steps, there is no sign of the EU acquiring powers in the area of designing a comprehensive welfare policy. The principle of subsidiarity was enshrined in the Maastricht Treaty, meaning that social policy is primarily a matter for Member States. Only when Member States are not able to meet their social responsibilities can the Community step in. Moreover, the rules governing decision-making in the field of social policy are designed in such a way that the diversity of national solutions is broadly protected and recognised. Consequently, Europe has so far not developed welfare policies modelled on those of the individual states, which provide a secure financial buffer against, and compensation for, life's risks. In other words, there is a major difference between the size and scope of national social policy and the modest role of (traditional) social programmes in the process of European integration (Majone, 1996). There are certainly efforts towards greater coordination of the policies of individual Member States, but the most important transfer systems providing safeguards against standard risks are still borne and organised by the individual nation-states. The European Union's efforts are also not aimed at standardising the national systems – the institutional differences between the Member States are simply too great, and there is no political will to bring them into alignment. Rather, emphasis is placed on forms of coordination that are meant to help provide effective solutions to problems that arise at the level of market integration. Accordingly, it is often emphasised that Europe has to limit itself to a social-regulative, rather than redistributive, approach, which is supposed to get by with a negligible budget.

Principle of subsidiarity

Some authors assume, however, that the social dimension will gain significance as a result of enhanced economic integration. It is likely that, in particular, the creation of a European labour market will place further pressure on the social agenda of the EU (Leibfried and Pierson, 1995). At the same time, others have pointed out that in the process of Europeanisation the sovereignty of national welfare states is being weakened, because it is becoming increasingly difficult to limit welfare services exclusively to a nation-state's own citizens, to decide benefit eligibility solely at the national level and to prevent foreign suppliers from providing the services in question. The free movement of workers and the freedom to provide services mean that it is no longer possible to exclude or discriminate against foreigners from other EU Member States (Leibfried and Pierson, 1995; Ferrera, 2003; Threlfall, 2003). Since the development of the market and social policy are unavoidably interwoven

Loss of sovereignty?

and interdependent, there is growing pressure on Europe to intervene more on the social front.

Membership spaces

Ferrera (2003, 2005) has examined the resulting, distinctly new entanglement of membership and territoriality (see Figure 11.3). He distinguishes different territorial spaces for the collectivisation of risks: the subnational space, the national space, the EU as a whole and the area outside the EU. On the level of individual Member States, he distinguishes between systems of social protection such as social welfare, statutory social insurance, supplementary and voluntary insurance, and private insurance. Ferrera shows that there are various pathways that lead between these different spaces. Unlike the self-contained nation-state, in which social services are restricted to its own citizens and where there is little chance of mobility, there is now a fundamental openness to other EU Member States. This is especially true in the area of insurance benefits (A, B and C). The dotted lines show that the upper pillars of the social security systems are relatively easy to access for other EU citizens.

Figure 11.3: The new configuration of boundaries of social sharing

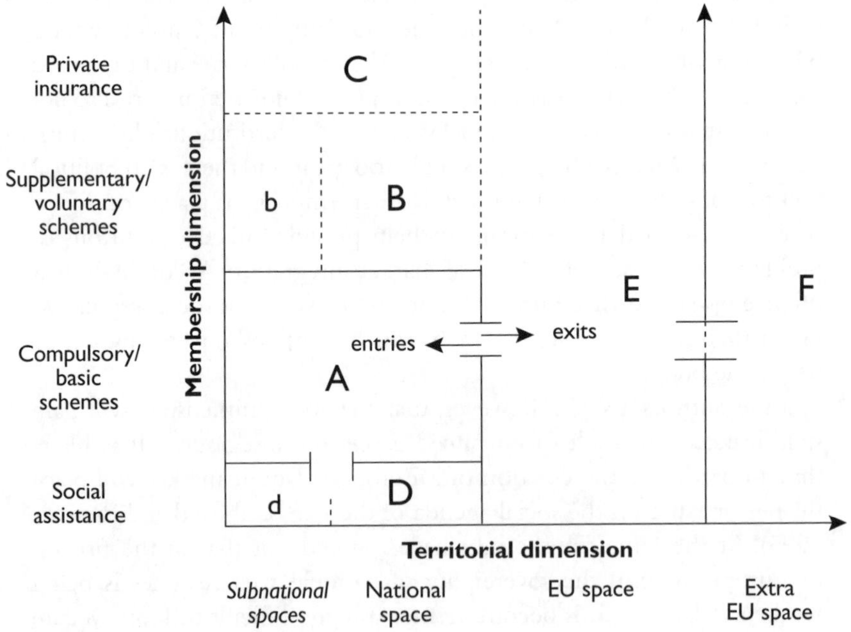

Source: Ferrera (2003: 641).

However, there is no direct access to non–contributory social assistance benefits (D). Since social assistance is usually financed by taxes and not by contributions to social insurance, there are, accordingly, qualms about removing restrictions on access. Especially in this area, there is a perceived risk of 'welfare tourism'. For benefits such as social assistance, however, access is possible, subject to certain minimum periods of residency in the respective country.

Open Method of Coordination and regional policy

Since the meeting of the European Council in Lisbon in 2000, the European Union has committed itself to a new approach to policy coordination, known as the Open Method of Coordination, which is also taking effect in the area of social policy (Büchs, 2007). On the one hand, this is in keeping with the basic principle of subsidiarity; on the other hand, it constitutes a means of aligning different welfare systems. The Open Method of Coordination envisages a situation whereby individual nation–states exercise mutual influence and adapt to each other, accomplishing this through recommendations, the exchange of information and expertise. This is not a centralised approach to social policy, but rather one that respects the autonomy of different national units, with policy-making remaining largely on the national level. However, at the initiative of the member countries or the Commission, agreement is supposed to be reached on identifying and achieving common objectives in certain areas. The Council and Commission agree on common guidelines and goals, as well as timetables to achieve the objectives, on the basis of which each Member State prepares a national action plan. A comparison of national strategies is facilitated by monitoring progress on the basis of EU-wide indicators. The method makes it possible to set common objectives at the European level, but acknowledges that their implementation will take place at the national and regional levels. Through a comprehensive reporting system and the exchange of expertise and information, it should be possible for the Member States to learn from, and employ, 'best practices'. Open Coordination strives to promote greater coherence of social policy through the voluntary adoption of proven practices.

Open Method of Coordination

Not all the policy programmes of the EU rely solely on regulation. Thus, as early as 1974, a fund was set up to provide targeted support for the national regional policy of member countries, the European Regional Development Fund (ERDF). With the passage of time, this fund was supplemented by additional funds for specific political–economic and regional initiatives (Leonardi, 1995). In 1989, the European 'cohesion policy' (as joint efforts in the areas of structural and regional initiatives in the EU are usually called) was finally officially introduced (Hooghe, 1996). The EU's cohesion policy has the long-term task of reducing regional disparities and the socio–economic backwardness of the least-developed regions, thereby strengthening economic and social cohesion within Europe in a sustainable fashion.

Regional policy

The cohesion policy constitutes a discrete redistributive instrument, which, although the extent and use of funds is quite remote from national redistribution policies, can mean significant socio-economic betterment for the recipient countries and regions. Aid provided under the aegis of the Structural Funds and the Cohesion Fund is meant to produce greater convergence within the EU and to counteract the massive imbalances in economic growth, employment and income between member countries and regions. The funds can be used, for example, for investment in infrastructure and for the promotion of human capital. Funding from the Structural Funds is designed to reduce disparities in the level of social and economic development though investment in infrastructure. The European Commission allocates funds in order to redress imbalances among regions in order to mitigate the social costs of integration, since one of the effects of integration can be that depressed areas are exposed to greater pressure and, consequently, fall into a downward social spiral.

Over time, the EU's cohesion policy has been continually expanded. From 1988 to 1999, the proportion of Structural Funds increased significantly, from 20% to over 35% of total EU spending. Whereas during the period 1993–99 a total of about 170 billion euro was spent on structural–political measures (including the Cohesion Fund), the corresponding budget for the period 2000–06 amounted to over 210 billion euro (both figures in 1999 prices). Approximately 308 billion euro have been set aside for the financial period 2007–13 (estimated, see Figure 11.4). Of this amount, 81.5% is for the 'convergence' objective, 16.0% for 'regional competitiveness and employment', and 2.5% for 'European territorial cooperation'. Two thirds of the expenditure from the Structural Funds is allocated to regions with a per capita GDP of less than 75% of the EU average. In the third cohesion report of the European Commission from 2004, the cohesion policy, along with the single market project and monetary union, was highlighted as one of the three central pillars of a unified political and economic space in Europe. With the start of the fourth programming period from 2007 to 2013, the cohesion policy has been further strengthened and broadened: first, because as a result of the eastward expansion of the EU, the number of countries and regions with levels of development below the EU average has increased significantly, and, second, because according to the Lisbon strategy, the cohesion policy is meant to play a central role in the development of knowledge-based economies and in promoting growth and employment in Europe (European Commission, 2005a).

Support for those lagging behind The Cohesion Fund is distributed exclusively to the poorest Member States. Since the eastern enlargement, these are comprised primarily of the new member countries in Central and Eastern Europe; apart from Greece and Portugal, currently no other member of the former EU-15 belongs to the group of cohesion countries. Targeted support from the Structural

Funds is allocated to regions (NUTS-2) whose GDP is lower than 75% of the EU average. For all other NUTS-2 regions over the period 2007–13, financial support from the Structural Funds is also envisaged in order to promote competitiveness and employment, within the framework of the Lisbon Agenda. Furthermore, the majority of border regions at NUTS-3 level receive funding to encourage cross-border cooperation – and on both sides of the border in question, thus beyond the actual territory of the European Union. In this way, all countries and regions of the European Union receive some form of financial support from the Structural and Cohesion Funds. In the coming years, however, the bulk of the funding – more than three quarters of the total – will go to the poorest countries and regions of the EU (cf. European Commission, 2007a).

Figure 11.4: Allocation of funds in the EU cohesion policy (2007–13)

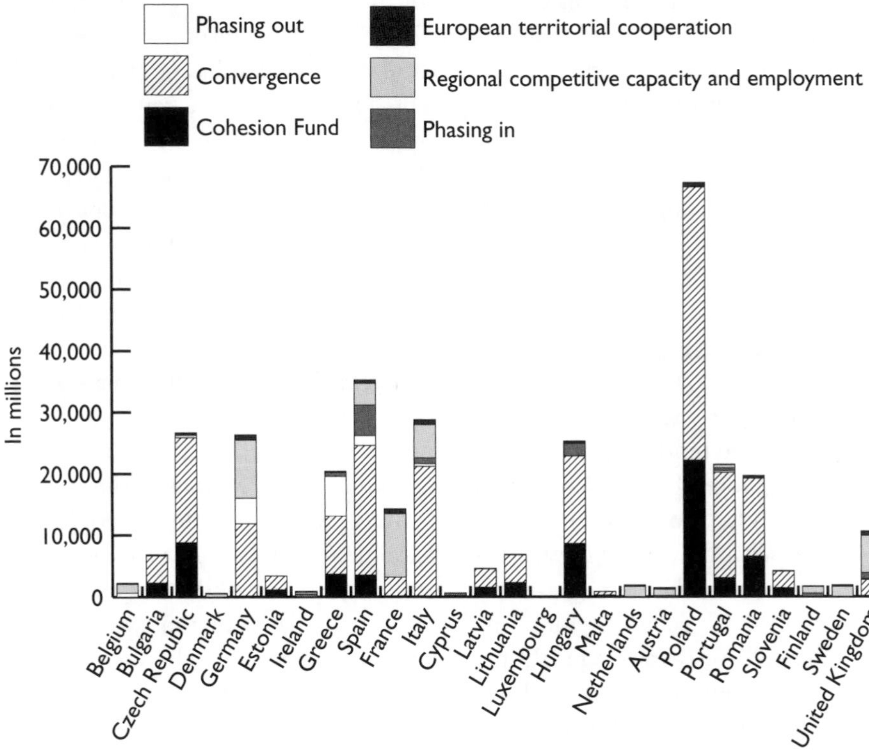

Source: European Commission (2007a); own illustration.

In this context it is important to note that the European cohesion policy is based on a certain degree of solidarity among EU member countries, for without the willingness of the member countries to work together, there would be little or no territorial redistribution. The Structural and

Territorial solidarity

Cohesion Funds make the richer European countries net contributors and the poorer countries net recipients. These tasks are financed through member contributions to the EU budget, which are calculated as a percentage of the national GNP. Thus, the economically strongest EU countries bear the greatest burden of financing these collective responsibilities. But unlike the national framework, in which territorial and interpersonal redistribution measures can count on a kind of internal solidarity that comes from belonging to a specific national community, the legitimation of redistribution across nations is more difficult. Although for understandable political reasons the EU has widened its structural and regional policy, the use of redistributive instruments in the European territorial structure is in need of justification. This was particularly noticeable in the course of the eastward expansion, during the negotiation of the new EU financial framework.

Policy outcomes

The jury is still out on the effects of the cohesion policy thus far. It should be stressed, first of all, that it is difficult to determine precisely to what extent over the past two decades the policy has contributed to reducing disparities in development. There are only a few studies that attempt to filter out the effect of the cohesion policy as opposed to other factors and developments (Armstrong, 1995; Sala-i-Martin, 1996; Armstrong and Taylor, 2000; Leonardi, 2005). In its own reports on cohesion, even the European Commission remains cautious in its assessment of development. On the one hand, the Commission emphasises the great successes of the cohesion policy and progress even beyond the convergence objective, but at the same time points out the challenges that are still to be met, and which have increased exponentially as a result of the expansions (European Commission, 2004, 2007f). Leonardi (2005, 2006), who tends to give a generally positive assessment of the cohesion policy, shows that convergence among countries and regions in the EU has thus far proved to be rather weak and slow. What he does consider especially noteworthy, however, is development in the poorest regions of the EU since the introduction of the cohesion policy: of the original 59 so-called Objective 1 regions in the year 1988, that is, regions with less than 75% of the average EU per capita GDP, approximately one third have surmounted this threshold. Outstanding examples are countries such as Ireland and Spain, but also some areas in Scotland and Greece. By contrast, the situation remains strained in the Italian Mezzogiorno, in many areas of eastern Germany and in the overseas territories of France, despite EU support. With regard to the new EU member countries in Central and Eastern Europe, it will be interesting in the coming years to observe what effect the EU structural and regional policies will have on socio-economic and territorial development as a whole.

Long-term perspectives

The long-term role of the EU as an agent of social policy intervention is controversial. On the one hand, it is true that developing Europe's social dimension can cushion the processes of economic liberalisation and ensure greater legitimacy of political decisions and institutions. Looking back on the pathways taken in the development of nation-states, it is evident that social rights improve the stability and legitimacy of the respective political systems (Leibfried, 1996). On the other hand, the success of institutionalised solidarity at the level of nation-states can be viewed as an obstacle to extending solidarity commitments (Scharpf, 1999; Offe, 2003). National governments and their respective populations may be inclined to leave responsibility in the hands of the national welfare state, and be unwilling to give up the latter's protective function against the vagaries of the market in favour of European solutions. Also, concerning the 'demand side' of solidarity and support, there are fundamental problems: a Europe that assumes too much redistributive power is in danger of overextending itself, since it could find itself faced with dramatic increases in claims to which it could not adequately respond (Lepsius, 2001). It seems that the EU is particularly active in those areas where national regulations do not apply or are no longer sufficient. At the same time, we observe greater significance being accorded to a territorially oriented policy, which responds to the specific dynamics of regional disparities. From a socio-structural perspective, this has as a consequence an accentuation of the territorial-horizontal dimension of social inequality, with an increasing incidence of conflicts between the regions concerning allocations.

Note

[1] There are restrictions on free movement for citizens from Eastern European Member States that have joined the EU since 2004. The Member States of longer standing decide individually when to lift the restrictions, but all restrictions must be lifted by early 2014, at the latest. There are no restrictions on freedom of movement for self-employed people.

12

The dynamics of inequality in Europe

In the previous chapter, we showed how the project of European integration has developed in recent decades. In the social sciences, this process has mainly been analysed from the perspective of vertical Europeanisation, which refers to the shifting of political decision-making competence upwards (Beck and Grande, 2007). However, the European regulatory framework also affects the societies of Member States and brings about new forms of social stratification. We have already highlighted the fact that during the establishment of nation-states, a specific form of social segmentation developed, namely the model of the congruence of social and political integration, a model predicated on territorial and social closure. As a result of Europeanisation, this model has undergone fundamental changes because the societies of individual nation-states are caught up in the process of supranationalisation, and their economic and social structures are coming increasingly under the influence of Europe. It can therefore be assumed that the process of Europeanisation is triggering a new dynamic of inequality – with new groups of winners and losers, new lines of distributional conflict, as well as new normative conceptions of social inequality. At the same time, some of the old cleavages that have characterised Europe already for a long historical period (see Part 1) continue to play a role, although these social and geographical divisions are continually transformed.

12.1 New groups: winners and losers

In research on Europe, it is assumed that in the medium term the European Union is constituting itself not just as a political and economic space, but also as a social space (Rumford, 2002; Heidenreich, 2006a; Beck and Grande, 2007; Fligstein, 2008). This implies that Europeanisation also impacts on social stratification, for example, with regard to the emergence of new social groups and the formation of specific interests and living conditions. In Figure 12.1, some of these new forms of social stratification are summarised. On the one hand, one sees the emergence of a European class of experts, a Europeanised milieu of groups operating transnationally, and recipients of European transfer payments; on the other hand, Europeanisation puts pressure on the regulatory and redistributive powers of nation-states, promotes the marketisation of individual living conditions and alters the structural patterns of inequality within individual nation-states. In the first case, new groups are being formed with a direct relationship to Europe; in the second case, we are witnessing the direct and indirect consequences of Europeanisation, with respect to social circumstances and life chances.

Figure 12.1: Stratification through Europeanisation

Emergence of new groups	Examples
EU elites and Europeanised milieus	EU bureaucracy, lobby and interest groups, Erasmus students
Transnational elites, transmigrants	Mobile groups with high levels of human capital and a transnational habitus; European labour migrants (commuter migration and circular migration, among other forms), migration of retirees
European transfer groups	Economically underdeveloped regions, agricultural enterprises and fisheries as beneficiaries of EU transfers
Effects on social conditions and living conditions	
Marketisation of social conditions	Pressure on older industries, on uncompetitive branches of industry and regions, and on weaker market participants (e.g. those with low qualifications)
Spatialisation of social inequality	Regional disparities and new centre–periphery structures
Diffuse effects	Freedom of movement, common currency, consumption unconstrained by national borders

The Europe of the elites

In numerous works on the sociology of Europe, researchers highlight the fact that Europe is giving rise to a polarisation between the elites and the ordinary citizens (Kauppi, 2005; Haller, 2008). This diagnosis goes back to the observation that, from the very beginning, Europe was a project of elites, championed by idealists and political and economic decision-makers. With the establishment of the EU institutions and decision-making bodies, the EU has also encouraged the formation of new administrative and bureaucratic elites. As seats of the European Commission and of the European Parliament respectively, Brussels and Strasbourg are today the home and workplace of a growing number of people who are employed by European or 'Europeanised' bureaucracies. Studies have shown how the bureaucratisation of Europe occurs and how a self-contained administrative apparatus with its concomitant personnel has developed (Bach, 1999; Stevens and Stevens, 2001). While there are only 25,000 EU civil servants as such, there is a much larger group operating within the ambit of EU authorities, pursuing activities that are directly connected with Europe. As the EU has grown, an array of EU agencies has also been created, based in the individual Member

States, and which concern themselves with special issues such as air traffic safety, drug addiction or gender equality.

Along with the European elite of functionaries, a multitude of new political interest groups and lobby groups have established themselves in Brussels, in conjunction with the creation of various European institutions (Bouwen, 2002; Lahusen, 2005; Michalowitz, 2007). These groups endeavour to influence European policy, and they include representatives of economic associations from areas such as telecommunications, the automobile industry or the tobacco industry, and representatives of trade union interests, such as the European Trade Union Confederation (ETUC), which represents 60 million employees from 36 countries and 81 individual trade unions. While it remains extremely difficult to impart a common European orientation on all these different national interests, there are now major efforts being made on this front towards coordination and even amalgamation.

European interest organisations

However, Europe also provides opportunity structures for new social actors, for example, new social movements, which are afforded possibilities in the European arena that they do not have on the national level (Imig and Tarrow, 2000). Since the formal structures of democratic participation have not yet been fully developed on the European level, new forms of access to political decisions and to the processes of opinion-making have arisen. For new social movements that come into existence outside the parameters of established political structures and which, due to their specific, unconventional repertoire of activities, call for broader forms of participation, Brussels is interesting in that EU policy is generally worked out within the various commissions, which facilitates the involvement of social and political actors who do not have a formal mandate. Interestingly, at EU level, there are relatively few unconventional forms of social protest, whereas intensive lobbying is widespread. There are about 15,000 lobbyists in Brussels who seek to influence the European decision-making process. This suggests that European institutions offer ample opportunities for participation, and that there is no great pressure to resort to unconventional forms of protest in order to gain influence (Marks and McAdam, 1999).

New social movements

Europeanised groups and milieus

Beyond the group of those directly involved in the EU integration process, there now exists a growing milieu with Europe-centred career paths and life plans (Favell, 2008) (cf. Figure 12.1, row 3). This group of people consists of the political and administrative elite, business people, scientists, highly qualified employees in science and private enterprise, and those working in high-skilled fields and in the new service economies. Students who gain new experiences through the Erasmus programme,

An emerging European milieu?

and who are thus 'Europeanised', can also be added to the list. On the one hand, it is the work itself that requires more in the way of transnational activities; on the other hand, these groups also bring with them certain 'transnational competencies' (Koehn and Rosenau, 2002). These include cultural, social and cognitive competencies, as well as foreign language abilities, which make it easy for these people to transcend the borders of the nation-state. One group seen as having special competence when it comes to transcending local borders is that of the highly educated, thanks to their typically greater openness towards other cultures, their knowledge of other languages and their broader horizons (Hannerz, 1996; Fligstein, 2008; Mau, 2010). We are dealing here with a phenomenon that can yield new forms of social inequality, namely when the social horizon of some groups is already largely transnational and Europeanised, while other groups remain trapped in their local and national spheres. This can create new internal social conflicts, which pivot on the tension between opening and closing a nation's social space (Kriesi et al, 2008).

Standardisation of education

Efforts to standardise educational qualifications at the international or European level, a standardisation actively promoted by the Bologna Process, also affect social stratification. The objective goal is to introduce an internationally standardised 'educational currency', which is meant to be universally recognised. The European Union has set out to create a common educational space, characterised by openness and mobility (Keeling, 2006; Neave and Maassen, 2007; Nóvoa and Lawn, 2008). It is also continuing to support a coordination of training requirements, which facilitates an automatic recognition of professional qualifications and school and university diplomas. The latter are thus losing their national specificity. At the same time, at the level of institutions of higher education, national reputation hierarchies are being undermined (for example, through European rankings), which is leading to a reordering of the European higher-educational landscape. The relationship between education and Europeanisation is, of course, even clearer in the case of educational institutions with a direct link to Europe, such as the College of Europe in Bruges (Belgium), or the European University Institute in Florence (Italy).

Transnational habitus

As already mentioned, those who benefit particularly from these efforts are the groups who, along with formal qualifications, also possess cultural and social competencies. In their case, one observes increased opportunities to utilise (on a European or global level) their educational capital. Abundant interactive connections across national borders, organisational involvement in pan-European exchanges, the ability to understand foreign languages, as well as certain cognitive abilities all contribute to the development of an international or transnational habitus (Mau, 2010; Mau and Büttner, 2010). With respect to the recruiting and composition of national economic elites, this feature applies only to a limited extent (Hartmann, 2006, 2010). In the UK, with its Commonwealth tradition, and in smaller countries, one finds an internationalisation of top management, whereas in countries such as Germany, Italy or France, most top-level positions still tend to be filled locally. Although there are distinct types of elite recruitment across Europe with very specific national traditions and institutional pathways, the 'increasing strengthening of central EU institutions and the increasing number of great mergers within European economy may be supposed, however, to result in gradual convergence, so that on the long run there will probably be a much more integrated European model' (Hartmann, 2010: 319).

Groups receiving transfer payments

Europeanisation not only produces Europeanised milieus and elites, however, but also has a direct influence on the living conditions of an increasing number of people and social groups in the average population. European 'transfer groups' (eg welfare recipients, subsidised farmers) can be identified by analogy with Lepsius's (1979) definition of 'transfer classes', as social classes whose chances in life are not primarily determined by the market, but rather through income from state-funded transfer payments (cf. Figure 12.1, row 4). There are a whole series of groups whose livelihoods are directly dependent on European funds: European agriculture, for example, benefits directly from high EU subsidies, which is why the latter are characterised as political welfare support for the rural population (Rieger, 1995). Through the transfer payments from Brussels, prices for agricultural products are massively subsidised. Along with the goals of ensuring supply, stabilising markets and increasing agricultural productivity, a central concern of the Common Agricultural Policy (CAP) is to increase the per capita income of those working in agriculture, and thus ensure an appropriate standard of living. The employees of many fisheries also benefit from EU payments, and are thus able to improve their income and market position.

We have already discussed the structural and regional funds of the EU, which are reallocated among countries and regions (see Section 11.3). *Regional transfers* These political instruments address the needs of the losers in the common market (Andersen, 1995), who are thereby given to understand that European integration will not leave them in a permanently disadvantaged position. The recipients of transfer payments are primarily regions located in the EU accession states, but also peripheral regions in Italy and the UK. The problem is that not all regions are able to make use of the new possibilities for regional development to the same degree. Because the implementation of the new guidelines for the regional and structural policy of the EU requires a clear orientation towards the goals of the 'Lisbon Strategy' (cf. European Commission, 2005a), it is already foreseeable that larger agglomerations will find it easier to implement measures designed to strongly encourage knowledge-based sectors of the economy than will poorer, sparsely populated, agricultural regions. Regions will have to subordinate the encouragement of 'landmark' projects to the goal of balanced regional development, which in all likelihood will further intensify the differences between urban and rural areas.

> In December 2006, the EU earmarked 500 million euro for the European Globalisation Fund, a new instrument that was intended to help 'victims of globalisation' in the Member States. Funding is provided for measures specifically designed to facilitate reintegration in cases where more than a thousand employees have been laid off within a short period of time. The fund was set up in order to demonstrate that the EU not only promotes economic integration, but also shows solidarity by helping to alleviate the perceptibly negative consequences of globalisation. The most recent debt crisis in some European countries (particularly in Greece) has triggered unprecedented measures to ensure financial stability across Europe. In May 2010 the European Finance Ministers agreed on a comprehensive rescue package of about a trillion dollars.

The marketisation of living conditions

Of particular significance are the processes of market-building and liberalisation, which produce specific groups of winners and losers (Rieger, 1995; Vobruba, 2005). These processes are partly the result of a general trend towards globalisation and partly due to economic integration measures of the EU. With the dismantling of constraints on competition, European liberalisation and the creation of a common market, the economic dynamic has become more intense, though institutional differences produce distinct national responses (Menz, 2005). This has put pressure on weaker market participants and on places with obsolete industries, in particular. In contrast, the intensification of the division of labour within Europe is strengthening the position of transnational businesses in the industrial and financial sectors. An integrated and liberalised finance market, for example, means the international actors in the market – investment banks, insurance companies, larger institutional investment funds and pension funds – gain in importance (Harmes, 1998). Unlike the period from the 1950s to the 1980s, when national education and training systems, welfare institutions and employment regulations guaranteed a relatively high level of stability and standardisation, we are now seeing a greater marketisation of living conditions. Arrangements that obtain within individual nation-states no longer provide the same kind of effective buffer against the unpredictability of the market as they once did. One of the consequences is a growing gap between those who, as a result of their abilities and qualifications, are able to stand their ground, and those who, due to their lack of competitive endowments, become socio-economic losers (Walwei, 1999; Münch and Büttner, 2006). It has also been shown that regional integration in the EU increases income inequality as it drives welfare state retrenchment and pushes the adoption of market-oriented policies as well as fiscal austerity. Evidence suggests that regional integration in the EU context explains half of the increase in income inequality in Western European countries. However, it seems that regional integration is associated with economic convergence among the Member States, but also with increased income inequality within national societies (Beckfield, 2006, 2009).

Market opportunities and new risks

This differentiation is especially evident in the division between insiders and outsiders in the labour market: in particular, those with low-level qualifications, employees whose qualifications are outdated and older people clearly have major difficulties finding a permanent position in the labour market. In most European countries, they also constitute the majority of the long-term unemployed, for whom the path to re-employment remains blocked. In their study, Blossfeld et al (2005) discovered, however, that it is not only older people who are finding themselves disproportionately confronted with these problems, but also increasingly the younger generation, those just entering the world of work. This is especially evident in comparison with employees in the middle phase of life, who have mostly established themselves career-wise and are protected by secure labour contracts. For those in the privileged and established social strata, there are better possibilities to make use of the advantages offered by the EU – for instance, through new opportunities for mobility or through market integration (Alvarez, 2002).

The role of human capital

In the context of the development of the market in Europe and around the globe, individual states are becoming increasingly specialised. Advanced industrial countries are specialising in human capital-intensive products, which is leading to an increase in unemployment among low-skilled workers. In many Western European countries, an increase in foreign trade means additional pressure on workers with low-level qualifications. Thanks to their membership of the EU, the accession states in Central and Eastern Europe have undoubtedly been able to improve their access to the market, upgrade infrastructure and boost development in some regions (Hardy and Smith, 2004). They also have access to investment capital and, in the framework of the cohesion policy, to transfer payments from the EU, all under favourable conditions. At the same time, however, they are faced with losses in the production factor of labour as a result of emigration, especially of qualified workers. Eastern European businesses also have difficulty competing with the much more productive industries of Western Europe and their high–quality products. This pressure has brought about a structural transformation whereby old, uncompetitive industries are being dismantled. Foreign investors are interested above all in profiting from access to the EU internal market and from low local costs, meaning that rapidly rising incomes can turn into a brake on investment. In the new Member States, the winners are above all young people with a university degree and those in the upper echelons of public administration, while ethnic minorities and older people can be seen as the losers from Europeanisation (Tang, 2005). Since the global downturn of 2008/09 all European countries face difficulties that affect the living conditions of the population, in particular Ireland, the southern members of the EU and the Central Eastern European accession countries. However, we also can expect the scale and severity of the crisis to differ tremendously (Blaszczynski, 2009). For example, in Central and Eastern Europe, Poland, the Czech Republic and Slovakia seem to be less affected than the Baltic states and Hungary, or the long-term EU member Greece.

Structural change of employment

We are continuing to witness a major change in the structure of employment in Europe, which reflects the transition from an industrial to a service society. While it is true that the overall level of employment in the EU has risen considerably in recent years, this growth has been accompanied by a decline in employment in agriculture and industry, and by an increase in employment in the service sector (see Section 7.4). Between 1998 and 2008, 26 million jobs were created in the service sector, which is absorbing some of the workers who are no longer needed in other sectors. However, especially in the service sector, there are also many poorly paid and insecure jobs. This development is due partly to the liberalisation and privatisation of public services, encouraged by the European Commission, in important areas such as the energy, transport and telecommunications sectors, and postal services, as well as air travel and electricity and gas supply. The Commission assumes that creating markets and allowing competition in the provision of public services will lead to increases in efficiency and to cost reductions (European Commission, 2003). One result of this economic Europeanisation, however, is the dismantling of relatively secure employment relationships and additional pressures exerted on labour costs and wages (Atzmüller and Hermann, 2004; Raza and Wedl, 2003).

Of course, the changes that are accompanying Europeanisation affect not only the labour market and the bureaucracies, but also the lives of many people outside the work sphere (see Chapter 13 on horizontal Europeanisation). For example, improved opportunities arise for consumption, tourism and mobility. It is to be expected that most of these opportunities will not remain restricted to just a few groups. Their advantages and disadvantages are widely dispersed, and they are unlikely to generate new social groups or structures as such.

The advantages and disadvantages of membership

The citizens of Europe also have the impression that the advantages and disadvantages of Europeanisation are unequally distributed. In a Eurobarometer Survey carried out in 2000, the respondents were presented with a list of 23 social groups, and in each case they were supposed to indicate whether, overall, the group was experiencing more advantages or disadvantages as a result of European integration. At the very top of the list of those considered to be winners were politicians, followed by groups with foreign language skills and large corporations. Old people and unskilled workers were seen as the losers. With respect to the various professions, those with high levels of human capital (doctors, architects, managers, civil servants and public officials, lawyers) were generally seen as winners in the process of integration, while farmers, the unemployed, workers and craftspersons were viewed as losers (European Commission, 2000). Europeans were also asked whether they thought membership of the European Union was advantageous or disadvantageous for the average citizen. Forty-five per cent saw things as evenly balanced, 28% said the advantages outweighed the disadvantages, while a minority of 13% saw the disadvantages as dominant.

A similar distribution of opinions results when individuals are asked whether they personally have benefited or suffered as a result of EU membership (Figure 12.2). In 2002 in the EU-15 states, 46% of those surveyed thought the advantages and disadvantages were, all in all, evenly balanced; somewhat more than a quarter (27%) saw themselves as winners, 15% as losers and 12% chose the response: 'I don't know'. This indicates that, despite the considerable significance that European integration has for life in the Member States, it is apparently very difficult to evaluate its impact on the circumstances of one's own life. Across the individual Member States, however, one finds major differences of opinion: 60% of Irish people indicated that they have personally benefited from their country's membership of the EU, while only 20% of the EU-sceptic British felt the same way. It is interesting that in countries that have for many years been net recipients of EU monies, such as Ireland, Spain, Greece and Portugal, noticeably more people present a positive rather than a negative assessment. These countries did indeed experience growth either in the lead-up to, or in the context of, their membership in the EU (Delhey, 2001), which appears not to have gone unnoticed by the respective populations. High percentages of positive evaluations are also found in Luxembourg and in the Netherlands, although these countries belong to the net contributors. Despite the fact that Brussels is the 'capital'

Personal balance

of the EU and many EU institutions are located there, the proportion of positive evaluations in Belgium lies below the EU average. The same is true of Italy, Finland and France.

Figure 12.2: EU membership: personal advantages or disadvantages

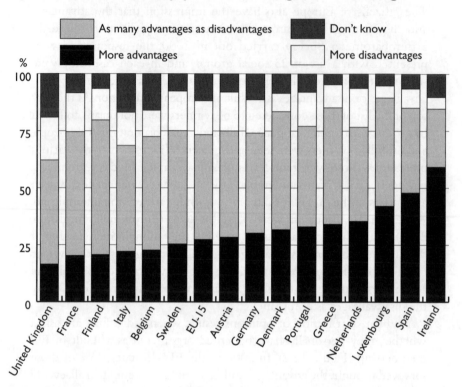

Source: Eurobarometer 58.1 (2002), own calculations, country-specific weighting. Survey question: 'Do you think that [OUR COUNTRY] being a member of the European Union has brought you personally...?' Original answering categories were subsumed as follows: 'more advantages' is composed of 'many more advantages' and 'more advantages', just as 'more disadvantages' is composed of 'many more disadvantages' and 'more disadvantages'. The other categories remain unchanged.

12.2 Intra-European welfare gaps and roles of the regions

NOTE ON METHODOLOGY

Data from Eurostat publications serve as the empirical basis for the discussion of regional inequality. These data make it possible to demonstrate the polarisation between European regions: the 15 regions with the highest and the lowest Gross National Product are juxtaposed, and, at the individual country level, regional differences and the inequalities between urban and rural areas are shown.

As Europeanisation proceeds, cross-border processes are gaining in importance, because the degree of interdependence and the intensity of interactions between Member States are increasing. Cross-border processes with negative consequences (e.g. waves of migrants, pressure on wages) are especially likely where there is a major welfare divide between countries. Welfare gaps emerge between socially and geographically adjacent spaces when there is a significant difference in income between them. Large welfare divides are economically disadvantageous because they can exacerbate polarisations and hamper a unified economic and monetary policy. Politically, inequalities can lead to a reinforcement of divergent interests, hindering efforts to achieve further integration. On the social level, welfare gaps can trigger large migration movements, with tax systems, systems of transfer payments and rates of pay exposed to increased pressure. If one focuses on the welfare gaps within the European Union, one can identify two overlapping processes, namely convergence and expansion (Vobruba, 2003).

The inward-directed process of convergence (see Section 11.3) can be ascribed to (among other factors) the positive overall economic effects of EU membership (Piazolo, 2002; Bornschier et al, 2004). It is indeed the case that, as a result of membership, socio-economically weaker countries have been able to improve their relative affluence (cf. Section 7.1), and economic analyses support the thesis of a slow, intra-European convergence (Barro and Sala-i-Martin, 1992). Over the course of time, the gap between the cohesion countries and the other member countries of the EU has diminished; to some extent, the new Member States have even overtaken the other EU states (for example, Ireland). In its reports on cohesion, the European Union has also pointed to the processes of convergence that are taking place, and, along with growth effects, has called attention to the positive effects of its regional policy instruments (European Commission, 2004). Thus, in numerous countries, the percentage of those employed in the agricultural sector has fallen considerably, the infant mortality rate has declined, in most countries the social security network has been built up and the proportion of women in employment has increased. In addition to these indicators, the Southern European cohesion countries and Ireland exhibit development gains (also in terms of the assumptions of modernisation theory) that, in some areas, even place them at the forefront of the EU (see Part 2).

Convergence as a catch-up process

The successive expansions of the European Union have meant an enlargement of its territory and of the number of Member States. Concomitantly, most of the expansions have led to a massive amplification of disparities and a reduction in the average per capita GDP. With a few exceptions, Europe has become poorer on average as a result of admitting new member countries, and the intra-European welfare divide has grown. The eastward expansion has resulted in a hitherto unique intensification

Enlargement

of economic disparities. Compared to the 15-member EU, the gap between the 10% of the population in the most affluent regions of the EU-27 and the 10% in the poorest regions has more than doubled in size (using per capita GDP as the gauge). In addition, the main weight of the disparities is shifting in the direction of an East–West gulf: six out of 10 inhabitants of the European Union who live in regions with a per capita GDP of less than 75% of the EU average, live in the accession states. Prior to the eastward expansion, the GDP of the richest country, Luxembourg, exceeded that of the poorest country, Portugal, by a factor of 3.5. After the admittance of Bulgaria and Romania in 2007, this factor was at 7.4, with Bulgaria as the poorest country (see Section 7.1). Thus, the expansion has resulted in an East–West divide being superimposed on the previously dominant North–South divide.

Regionalisation of social inequality

Nation-states and regional disparities

Inequalities across the Member States are not the only important factors shaping development in the EU: an intensification of inequalities between regions is also taking place. In a historical perspective, one of the major accomplishments of nation-states was that they were able to even out social differences not just between classes and social groups, but also between regions. As Martin Heidenreich (2003: 318–19) writes:

> It is mainly in the context of a national state, disparities are considered and treated as inequalities. A national state, characterized by a territorially bound monopoly of legitimate physical force, has an essential interest in avoiding, reducing or redefining regional inequalities because if they crystallize into regional, potentially separatist ideologies and identities these inequalities may threaten the territorial integrity and sovereignty of a state.... The EU is increasingly confronted with similar challenges.

In order to achieve this goal, in a number of other EU Member States there are regional development chapters as well as systems of financial redistribution and equalisation. Within the framework of the Europeanisation process, however, changes also arose on this front: on the one hand, Europe limits the autonomy and sovereignty of its nation-states, while, on the other hand, processes of federalisation, regionalisation and decentralisation strengthen the role of the regions as political actors. Thus, questions of territorial structuring in Europe are becoming ever more important for the analysis of social inequality (Rodríguez-Pose, 2002).

Regional polarisation

At the regional level, a major polarisation is apparent: in the richest region of Europe, Inner London, the per capita GDP is 336% of the

European average, while in the north-east region of Romania, the figure is only 25% (see Table 12.1). The regions with the highest per capita incomes are located in Western Europe (with the exception of Prague), and the 15 poorest regions are located, without exception, in the accession states of Romania, Bulgaria and Poland. Figure 12.3 shows that there are also significant differences in per capita GDP inside the individual Member States. Especially in the UK and Belgium, but also in France, Germany, Austria, the Czech Republic and Slovakia, there are major differences between the richest and the poorest regions. Regional inequalities are lowest in the Eastern European accession states of Poland, Slovenia and Bulgaria. The European Union continues to be confronted with pronounced regional differences when it comes to employment and unemployment: in some regions of the EU, the unemployment rate is around 2.5%, while other regions have a rate of over 20%. As far as the levels of employment are concerned, between 2000 and 2005 some convergence occurred: during this period, the difference between the 10% of regions with the highest employment rate and the 10% of regions with the lowest employment rate fell from 30 to 20 percentage points (European Commission, 2007f).

Table 12.1: Regional GDP

15 regions with highest GDP		15 regions with lowest GDP	
Inner London (GB)	335.9	Nord-Est (RO)	24.7
Luxembourg (LU)	267.1	Severozapaden (BG)	25.4
Bruxelles-Capital (BE)	233.3	Severen tsentralen (BG)	26.9
Hamburg (DE)	199.7	Yuzhen tsentralen (BG)	27.8
Groningen (NL)	173.7	Sud-Vest Oltenia (RO)	30.4
Île de France (FR)	169.7	Yugoiztochen (BG)	31.5
Upper Bavaria (DE)	167.9	Severoiztochen (BG)	31.8
Vienna (AT)	165.9	Sud-Muntenia (RO)	32.1
Stockholm (SE)	165.8	Sud-Est (RO)	32.5
Berkshire, Buckinghamshire and Oxfordshire (GB)	164.0	Lubelskie (PL)	35.3
Southern and Eastern (IE)	163.4	Podkarpackie (PL)	35.8
Prague (CZ)	162.3	Nord-Vest (RO)	35.9
Darmstadt (DE)	158.3	Centru (RO)	38.3
Bremen (DE)	156.9	Podlaskie (PL)	38.4
Utrecht (NL)	156.1	Warminsko-Mazurskie (PL)	39.5

Source: Eurostat (2009b). Figures for 2006 in PPS of EU-27 average, regions at NUTS-2 level.

If one looks at Europe as a whole and compares the regional disparities with those of other countries such as the US, China, India or Japan, then it becomes apparent that the differences in income between European regions are extremely large:

Regional disparities in GDP per head are far more extreme in the EU-27 than in the US or Japan, especially after the two recent enlargements. In the EU, GDP per head in the region where this is highest is 8 times greater than in the region where it is lowest. In the US, the difference is only 2.5 times and in Japan just two times.... In China, GDP per head, again in PPS terms, is only one-fifth of the EU average, while in India, it is one-eighth. In Romania and Bulgaria, which have the lowest GDP per head in the EU, the level is still over twice as high as in India and 50% higher than in China.... Despite the vast difference in GDP per head, the size of regional disparities in India and China are similar to that in the EU. The region with the highest GDP per head in both China and India has a level seven times greater than in the lowest regions against eight times in the EU. (European Commission, 2007f: 5)

Inequalities within and between countries

In this context, one has to distinguish between two different aspects of regional inequality: the first concerns to what extent regional inequality reflects the socio-economic disparities among the Member States, and can thus be viewed as an expression of the inequalities across states that have already been discussed. The second aspect concerns inequalities within individual states, which also contribute to the overall regional inequality in Europe. Duro (2001) has been able to show that there are different developmental trends with respect to regional inequality within the Member States and to inequality across states. According to this analysis, in the early 1980s the inequalities among the Member States constituted roughly half of all regional inequalities, whereas the other half consisted of regional inequalities within individual Member States.

Up until the mid-1990s, this feature was moving towards an accentuation of regional inequalities within individual countries, so that one can speak in terms of a regionalisation of social inequality. In a comparison of the development of inequalities across and within EU Member States from the mid-1990s to 2003, Heidenreich (2006b; Heidenreich and Wunder, 2008) shows that inequality across Member States has decreased considerably, by 45% (on the NUTS-3 level), whereas regional inequalities within Member States have increased by 15%. This means that more than two thirds of regional inequalities can be attributed to disparities within individual Member States; on the NUTS-2 level, the proportion is even higher, namely 84%. Thus, if one looks at the regional level, then it is apparent that, on this level, the general trend towards convergence for the Member States proves to be fractured or at least weakened. Uniform living conditions are thus conspicuous by their absence; instead, one finds an increasing convergence between countries but at the same time a regional polarisation within individual countries.

Figure 12.3: Regional income differences

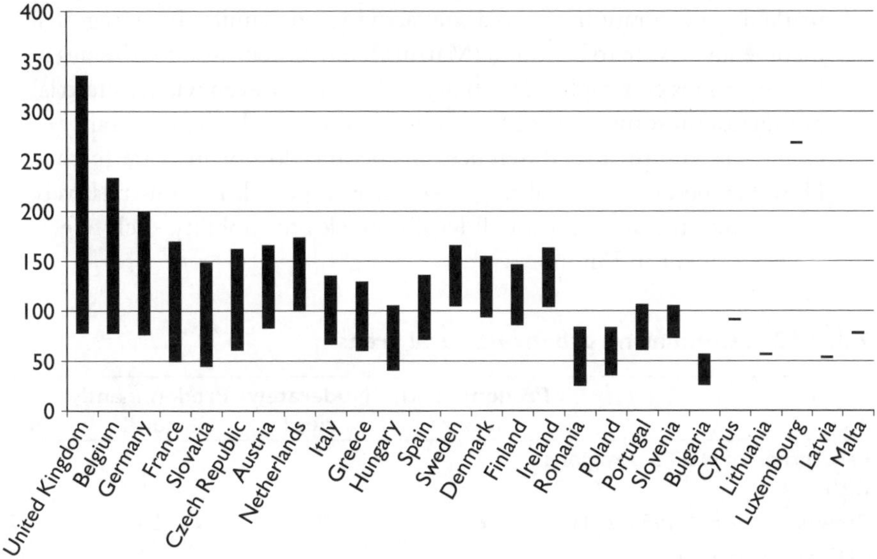

Source: Eurostat (2009b), own calculations. Regional GDP per capita as PPS (2006 data) on NUTS-2 level, EU-27 = 100 (only one region for Cyprus, Lithuania, Luxembourg, Latvia, Malta).

Differing patterns of development are also to be found when comparing rural and urban regions (Table 12.2). The great majority of urban areas have a per capita income that lies above the EU average. The capital city regions throughout Europe are among the most important centres of growth, serving as magnets for employees and investors: in all capitals except Berlin, economic performance currently lies well above the national average; in 14 capital cities, it even lies between 40% and 100% above average for the country. European capital city regions are also characterised by tertiary sectors of above-average significance. Regions on the urban outskirts, however, often have low per capita income and above-average unemployment. While there is a general trend towards suburbanisation of large European cities, this is often accompanied by increasing economic activity, partly due to the fact that many people commute to work in the cities. By contrast, rural regions are confronted with high unemployment, shrinking populations and weaker economic growth.

Rural and urban regions

As far as the causes of this process are concerned, empirical studies have shown that the spatial concentration of economic activities within the European Union leads to inter-regional income differences (Hudson, 1999). The creation of a common market can lead to a concentration of production: companies thus tend to concentrate on a small number of production locations in the vicinity of attractive markets, even when this entails higher wage costs. That this link is not inevitable can be

Inequality and mobility

demonstrated by a comparison with the US, where despite an even more marked concentration of economic activities, no similar inter-regional income divides are to be found (Martin, 2003). One reason for this lies in the enormous geographical mobility of Americans: even when industrial production in some parts of the country thins out, the high mobility of employees ensures that differences in income do not increase further. However, because internal migration in Europe still remains relatively low, despite the abolition of all legal obstacles to mobility, such effects are less evident in Europe.

Table 12.2: Comparing urban and rural areas

	Predominantly urban	Moderately rural	Predominantly rural	Total
Percentage of NUTS-3 regions with				
Growing population, 1995–2004	61	70	54	62
GDP per capita above EU average (PPS 2004)	71	34	23	43
Number of regions	407	441	361	1,209
Total population (millions)	202	173	82	457
Proportion of EU-27 population	44.3	37.8	17.9	100

Source: European Commission (2007f)

Furthermore, it can be shown that regions being unequally endowed with human capital can be construed as a possible cause of the persistence or even the intensification of regional disparities. 'Winner regions' generally have a better-educated and better-qualified population, whereas 'loser regions' prove to be much more poorly endowed with human capital (Rodriguez-Pose, 1998). Similarly to the disparities in per capita GDP, the inequalities in the area of human capital are greater across regions than across countries. Backward regions have a considerably lower proportion of people with tertiary qualifications – on average, around 10% lower – than other regions (European Commission, 2007e).

Overall, it seems clear that the regional level is gaining in importance. This is not only true for matters of inequality, but also for conflicts related to regional disparities. The regionalisation of social inequality could lead to 'place-based inter-class coalitions of political, economic and social actors devoted to the economic development in a specific location' (Keating, 1997: 32). Fabbrini (2004: 185) stresses that this could have serious repercussions for the conflict patterns to which we are accustomed:

[I]n Europe, as an effect of both the structural transformation of economies and cultures and institutional displacement of the decision making resources from the national to the continental arena, traditional class and religious cleavages tended to wane as driving forces of the structure of the party system. On the contrary, sectional and geographical cleavages, concerning both the legitimacy of the EU as a decision-making body and the distributor of the resources it controls, are becoming the sources of the birth and development of new partisan actors and of the structuring of new divisions within the party system.

Regions could thus become contexts of political mobilisation within the national and European political arenas. One can expect that regional movements will grow stronger over time, in particular if identity politics converge with the socio-economic positioning of a region either in defence of a privileged position or because backward regions seek compensation for their disadvantaged status.

13

Horizontal Europeanisation

DEFINITION

By 'horizontal Europeanisation' we mean contacts, interactions and social relationships between different European countries, as well as various forms of pan-European mobility (exchanges and interaction between Member States).

In this chapter, we examine Europe from the perspective of horizontal Europeanisation, which involves cross-border interactions and transactions between the individual countries and their inhabitants (Beck and Grande, 2007). This is an important point of departure for the sociology of Europeanisation, because it allows one to determine whether political and economic integration is being accompanied by more cross-border social intermingling between members of European societies. Karl W. Deutsch's transactionalism approach (1957, 1968; see also Fligstein, 2008) emphasises that economic and political transactions between countries also bring about more close-knit exchanges between individuals. In turn, according to this theory, through the intensification of cross-border exchange, more and more people become aware of the advantages of this exchange and also participate in transnational interaction; as a result, social distance can be overcome and prejudices dispelled. Certain aspects of these processes of bottom-up Europeanisation, however, cannot be deduced from the political process of integration, since social lifeworlds have a character of their own. In addition, it is an open question as to whether horizontal Europeanisation necessarily serves to promote European integration. Favell (2005: 1115), for example, argues that:

Horizontal exchange and interaction

> Political scientists think of voting and 'revealed preferences', of course, but 'being European' nowadays is as much likely to be about this, as it is about shopping across borders, buying property abroad, handling a common currency, looking for work in a foreign city, taking holidays in new countries, buying cheap airline tickets, planning international rail travel, joining cross-national associations – and a thousand other actions facilitated by the European free movement accords. These ways of being European (that can all be counted, or interrogated for meaning), are notably also enjoyed by many who overtly profess themselves to be Eurosceptic or to have no European

identity at all. Thought of this way, we may indeed discover 'social identities' that are genuinely transnational, if they turn out to be rooted behaviourally in new forms of cross-national action and interaction.

In the following sections, we will describe the different forms of horizontal cross-border activities within Europe in order to determine the extent of transnationality and interconnectedness among the citizens of Europe. The frequency and density of connections in everyday life are at the centre of our considerations. We begin with the infrastructure of transnationalisation, meaning the objective and technical conditions for mobility and communication across borders. Then we turn our attention to transnational experiences in the context of travel, sojourns abroad, town twinning and transnational social networks. A final section is devoted to intra-European migration.

13.1 The infrastructure of horizontal Europeanisation

Transport and communication

An important basis for transnational interactions is furnished by the infrastructure of transport and communication. If one understands social structure as a relatively stable system of social relationships, then a crucial consideration is whether and under what conditions social relationships can be established. Europe is considered all in all to be a very highly developed area when it comes to transport and the technology of communication. Compared to continents such as Africa or Asia, where only few people have access to good infrastructure, Europe is endowed with roads, railways and an extensive system of communication and public transport (Jordan-Bychkov and Bychkova Jordan, 2003). The endeavours devoted to political integration have been accompanied by further improvements in the infrastructural conditions of exchange and communication within Europe. A glance at the highways and rail networks alone shows that the most important transport routes extend well beyond national borders (cf. Espon Project, 2004, 2006a).

In the past two decades, numerous transport projects have been carried out with the goal of providing better connections between various regions in Europe. The railway companies of individual neighbouring countries are intensifying their cooperation, creating ever more rapid connections between the urban agglomerations of Europe. Neighbouring countries and regions are joining forces in their efforts to increase the number of border crossings and to simplify regular cross-border traffic. Apart from the individual national regions, the European Commission has also come out strongly in favour of unrestricted European mobility and building up European transport networks. The EU Commission has forecast a doubling of cross-border traffic among EU Member States by 2020, and as a result has allocated substantial funds to promoting the further development of European transport networks.

> An outstanding example of a cross-border infrastructural project is the 31-mile-long Eurotunnel, which connects Dover (Great Britain) with Calais (France). This project had been envisaged as far back as the early 19th century, but it had to be repeatedly deferred due to differences of opinion between the two governments concerned. In the course of growing numbers of cross-border cooperations and ongoing European integration, France and Great Britain decided to go ahead with the project. The tunnel was officially opened in 1994, and today is used by some seven million people per year.

Air traffic

An important role in the development of cross-border transport infrastructure in Europe is played by the liberalisation of air traffic, which is also being encouraged by the European Commission. Private airlines now have full access to the market and are free to determine their own pricing policies. One direct consequence of this reform is an enormous increase in the numbers of European airlines and interconnecting flight destinations. At present, there are more than 130 airlines, servicing a network of over 450 airports. In addition, the rise of newer, so-called 'low-cost airlines' has revolutionised the travel and transport market in recent years, and has considerably increased travel opportunities within Europe.

Traffic networks

In conjunction with the emergence of low-cost airlines, the number of passengers within the European Union has also risen significantly: there was a tripling of air travel in the EU between 1980 and 2000, and a further doubling is expected by 2020. In 2007 over 790 million passengers were carried to or from EU airports, 520 million travelled within the EU. The number of intra-EU routes increased between 1992 and 2008 by 120%. In recent years, moreover, there has been a huge increase in the numbers of same-day return flights (Figure 13.1). A look at the daily flight connections shows that Europe's largest urban centres are already tightly interconnected (cf. Espon Project, 2006a). This is especially the case for Paris, Brussels, Frankfurt am Main and London; to a lesser extent also for other cities, such as Copenhagen, Amsterdam, Hamburg, Berlin, Cologne, Munich, Zurich, Prague, Vienna and Rome.

> The busiest routes within Europe are between Great Britain and Spain (with 33.4 million passengers in 2004) and between Germany and Spain (19.3 million passengers). Other highly travelled routes are France–Great Britain (11.1 million), Ireland–Great Britain (10.6 million), as well as Germany–Great

Britain (10.1 million). The most important routes between the old (EU-15) and the new Member States are between Great Britain and Cyprus (2.8 million passengers) and Great Britain and the Czech Republic (2.1 million) (De La Fuente Layos, 2006; Eurostat, 2006).

Figure 13.1: Daily accessibility of European urban agglomerations

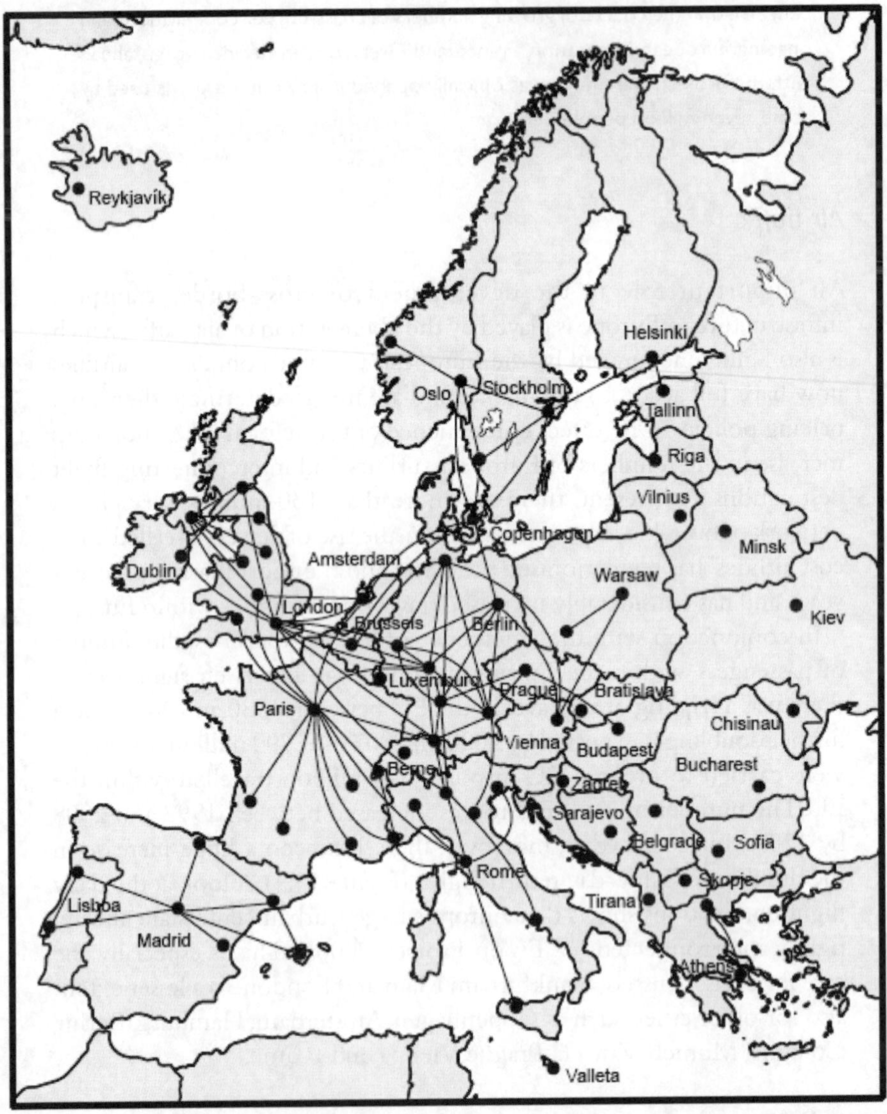

Source: Espon (2006a: 39); own illustration; international air connections providing daily returns (2003, EU-25).

Despite the enormous density and frequency of traffic within Europe, the trans-European traffic and transport network is in no sense uniformly distributed over the territory of the European Union. As far as connectedness to the network and accessibility are concerned, there are, in fact, clear East–West and North–South divides (cf. Espon Project, 2004, 2006b). The Central European countries with the highest population densities, namely Germany, Austria, Belgium, the Netherlands and France, are endowed with good interconnections thanks to numerous daily airline flights, cross-border highways and railway routes (Strelow, 2006). There is also a high level of connectedness between these countries and the British Isles, as well as Italy. By comparison, the highways and railway routes between West European countries and their Eastern neighbours have so far remained in a rudimentary state of development. The places that are easiest to reach in the new EU Member States are the capital cities and some regional centres. The situation is similar in a range of countries in Northern and Southern Europe. Although these countries have very good internal transport routes, only a few of the urban centres serve as hubs for international passenger traffic and the transportation of goods. This applies, for instance, to cities such as Oslo, Stockholm, Athens, Istanbul, Madrid, Barcelona and Lisbon, and to mass tourism destinations like Palma de Mallorca, Malaga, Nikosia and Thessaloniki. All other cities and regions in Northern, Eastern and Southern Europe are better connected through internal rather than cross-border networks.

Inequality of access

Communicative interconnectedness

While the new transport routes open up additional possibilities for mobility and direct contact between people in different European countries, communication technologies enable contact over greater geographical distances. A considerable proportion of everyday transnational interactions now take place via telecommunications and other forms of electronic or digital media. Cross-border communication has never before been so fast, so simple and so affordable. The rapid spread of the new means of communication allows people to maintain relationships with friends or relatives at great distances. The digitalisation of data transmission, as well as the de-monopolisation and privatisation of the telecommunications sector (analogous to that of the airline industry) in the EU Member States have led to a substantial increase in the use and pervasiveness of these technologies. As a result of the dismantling of state monopolies in 1998, the prices for long-distance telephone calls have fallen dramatically within just a few years. The spread of modern communications technology is obviously not a specifically European phenomenon. Nevertheless, the 'digital revolution' and the creation of a European telecommunications market have brought Europeans, too, closer together. With respect to the

Technologies of communication

development of communications infrastructure, Europe constitutes one of the most advanced regions in the world, with numerous possibilities on offer for communication over long distances. More than 90% of all European businesses and more than half (54% in 2007) of all private households in the EU already have access to the internet, and use it regularly (see also Section 10.1). However, there is a discernible North–South divide with respect to internet use. Whereas in countries such as the Netherlands, Sweden, Denmark and Luxembourg, private use of the internet is over the 70% mark, in Southern European countries and in the new EU Member States of Romania and Bulgaria, internet access is considerably less widespread. However, in all Member States the share of households with internet access is increasing over time and some countries like Slovakia are catching up (Eurostat, 2009a: 501).

13.2 Transnational experiences and encounters

NOTE ON METHODOLOGY

The presentation of transnational experiences in this section is based on figures from Eurostat publications (tourism), UNESCO data (student mobility) and Eurobarometer.

A European social space?

A central aspect of horizontal Europeanisation is the increase in transnational experiences for Europeans, which means more encounters and social interaction beyond national borders. The process of Europeanisation and the aforementioned changes in transport and communication are catalysing these developments. While it is true that many transnational connections – for instance, academic networks or the migration of populations (cf. Section 2.3) – are not new, for the great majority of Europeans transnational experiences are not part of everyday life. It was only after the Second World War and in the course of European reconciliation that cross-national contacts and first-hand experiences of Europe were normalised and became more widespread. Today's Europeans are involved in a multifaceted network of social exchange and intercultural contacts. These include, for example, various forms of student mobility, youth exchanges, town twinning, cross-border social relationships and networks, as well as touristic experiences, which make for an increasingly dense communicational and social space in Europe. The broadened possibilities for travelling and working in the EU are viewed positively by the majority of EU citizens, and are more appreciated than, for example, the common currency or the EU as a framework for lasting peace (Krieger, 2008). There are, to be sure, considerably varying degrees of involvement in the processes of horizontal Europeanisation. For instance, we know that Brussels has already developed its own political and administrative elite (see Section 12.1), whereas the daily lives of other social groups and classes – in rural and peripheral regions, for example – involve far fewer European exchanges (Fligstein, 2008).

The spread of tourism in Europe

On the list of answers to the question of in which social contexts 'transnational European experience' is most widespread, tourism occupies first place. Whereas previously only a minority of national populations regularly travelled abroad, tourism has now become a central form of access to other nations and cultures. In recent decades, more and more tourist destinations have opened up. Although there is a certain scepticism concerning the depth and social consequences of touristic experiences, tourism undoubtedly opens up new horizons and spaces of social experience. Therefore, it can be considered an important dimension of crossing not just physical but also cultural borders. In addition, learning and using foreign languages occurs in most cases in the context of going on holiday (TNS Opinion & Social, 2006).

Tourism and transnational experiences

With respect to ease of access and the cost of travel, many domestic tourist destinations are now barely distinguishable from foreign destinations. In fact, one result of the development of modern mass tourism is that destinations abroad are sometimes even easier and cheaper to reach than destinations that are closer (Opaschowski, 2006). Thus, the proportion of people who spend their holidays abroad has risen dramatically. According to the World Tourism Organization (UNWTO), tourism worldwide – as measured by international arrivals – since the 1950s has experienced an almost 40-fold increase, from approximately 25 million in 1950 to more than 900 million in 2008. Hence, in many countries, tourism has become one of the most important industries and sources of income (UNWTO, 2006). It is expected that the number of tourists will continue to increase in the long term, despite problems of environmental degradation and economic crisis, which are slowing development.

Europe is the most important tourist destination worldwide. In the top 10 of the most important tourist countries, there are six member countries of the EU, namely Spain, France, Italy, Britain, Germany and Austria. Due to their relative prosperity and increased leisure time, Europeans today take more vacations than in the 1950s and 1960s, and lead by far the inhabitants of other continents in this respect. In the EU-25 in 2004, a total of 400 million holiday trips lasting more than four days were registered, but with only some of these involving Europeans going abroad, the rest holidaying in their respective home countries (Bovagnet, 2006a). However, nearly 200 million Europeans in the EU-25 took longer trips abroad. Two thirds of all trips abroad are to destinations within the

EU, the most popular destinations for EU-25 countries being Spain, Italy and France. Other popular destinations are Austria, Britain, Germany, the Netherlands, Portugal and Ireland. These countries together account for 90% of international tourism in the European Union (European Commission, 2007e).

Figure 13.2: Most important target countries for European tourism

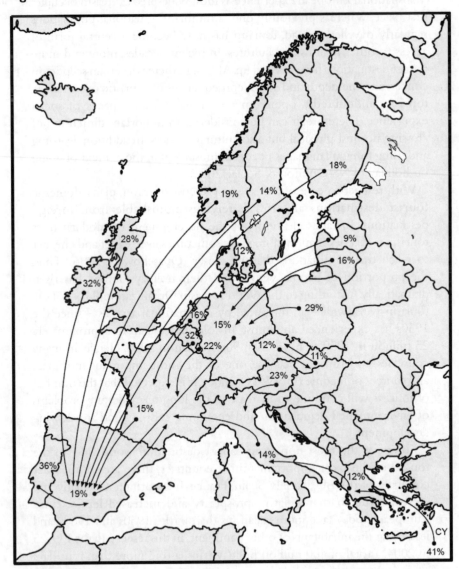

Source: Bovagnet (2006b: 5); own illustration. Arrows show the most important destinations of intra-European tourism by country of origin (EU-25); percentages show the particular share out of all travels abroad for that destination.

Figure 13.2 presents the main currents of European tourism by country of origin and country of destination, showing the most important destination for the respective country of origin as well as the proportion travelling to that destination out of all tourists from the respective country who travel abroad. Spain is by far the most popular holiday destination for all Northern European countries and most of the core countries of the EU. Travel between the UK and Spain is particularly intense. Of all those taking longer trips abroad, 32% of travellers from Ireland and 28% of those from the UK travel to Spain. France is the preferred holiday destination for travellers from Belgium, the Netherlands, Luxembourg and Italy, while people from the Baltic states prefer Poland and Germany.

Table 13.1 shows that with respect to the increase in trips abroad, there are major differences between individual European countries. The citizens of Luxembourg, Belgium, Ireland, Denmark and Germany travel abroad much more frequently than the citizens of France, Spain or Italy. The latter countries are also the most attractive destinations for holiday makers. However, for shorter trips, such as visiting specific towns and cities, traditionally less popular destinations in the north of the continent are becoming increasingly popular. Larger differences can also be seen between the old and the new member countries: the percentage of the population spending holidays domestically is much greater in countries such as Hungary or Poland than the percentage of those who holiday abroad. Where data are available, they show that a very high percentage of holidays take place within the EU rather than outside, with the exception of countries such as Slovenia, Latvia and Lithuania, all situated at the external borders of the EU.

Tourism within Europe

Table 13.1 only shows trips lasting four or more nights. Finnish, Swedish and Spanish tourists show a preference for short trips (70% and higher). In Denmark, Germany, Spain, France, Italy and Luxembourg, the increase in short trips is greater than for longer trips. The majority of these trips are holidays, with business trips representing only a fraction of the total. Overall, these data show that holiday travel and short trips to other European countries have become more and more part of normal life for Europeans. This development is closely related to the structural changes already mentioned in Europe in the last 10 years. The new airlines not only create new opportunities for travel, but also open up cross-border tourism to entirely new population groups.

The Eurobarometer survey in 2006 (EB 65.1) asked EU citizens in member countries whether they had visited another EU country in the previous 12 months (Table 13.2). The results give more precise information on the proportion of those who actually take advantage of travel opportunities in order to experience Europe. Just under 40% in the EU-15 and in the EU-27 indicate that they had visited another EU country at least once during the period in question. Again, the distribution is similar to that for people who travel abroad for their holidays. In countries such as Greece, Spain, Lithuania, Latvia and Poland, the proportion is around 20%. Countries such as Germany, Ireland, Finland and Slovenia accounted for almost half of those who travel abroad within Europe. In Denmark, Belgium, Luxembourg, the Netherlands, Austria and Sweden, significantly more than half the population visited another European country once during the year in question, sometimes even more often.

Table 13.1: Destinations of holiday trips with at least four overnight stays

	Holiday trips by destination (%)			Domestic trips
	Trips abroad			
	Total	Within EU-25	Beyond EU-25	Total
EU-15	44.3	66.6	33.4	55.7
Belgium	78.8	77.1	22.9	21.2
Denmark	69.1	72.3	27.7	30.9
Germany	64.0	67.8	32.2	36.0
Ireland	72.6	78.0	22.0	27.4
Greece	9.8	46.9	53.1	90.2
Spain	11.9	59.1	40.9	88.1
France	17.1	47.6	52.4	82.9
Italy	24.9	54.1	45.9	75.1
Luxembourg	99.3	82.1	17.9	0.7
Netherlands	62.3	76.0	24.0	37.7
Austria	64.7	59.2	40.8	35.3
Portugal	22.6	67.1	32.9	77.4
Finland	30.5	58.9	41.1	69.5
Sweden	47.5	65.6	34.4	52.5
United Kingdom	58.6	72.1	27.9	41.4
Czech Republic	42.1	55.6	44.4	57.9
Estonia	49.3	–	–	50.7
Cyprus	–	68.7	31.3	–
Latvia	51.5	41.0	59.0	41.8
Lithuania	61.1	43.2	56.8	38.9
Hungary	27.2	–	–	72.8
Malta	–	–	–	–
Poland[2]	18.2	71.9	28.1	81.8
Slovenia	73.0	14.1	85.9	27.0
Slovakia	43.4	53.8	46.2	56.6
EU-25[1]	43.1	65.9	34.1	56.9

Source: Bovagnet (2006a: 2); proportion of holiday travellers by percentage of population taking at least one holiday trip including four nights' stay. [1] EU-25 countries with missing values excluded; [2] estimated value.

Table 13.2: Visits to other EU countries

	In the last 12 months have you visited another EU country? (%)		
	On several occasions	**Once or twice**	**No**
EU-15	13.6	25.2	61.2
Belgium	28.7	32.7	38.6
Denmark	40.1	28.3	31.5
Germany	19.1	29.3	51.6
Ireland	12.1	37.3	50.7
Greece	2.6	7.8	89.5
Spain	4.0	13.2	82.8
France	10.7	19.4	69.9
Italy	4.5	23.2	72.4
Luxembourg	60.9	23.9	15.2
The Netherlands	38.7	36.1	25.2
Austria	35.0	33.4	31.6
Portugal	6.5	14.8	78.7
Finland	13.7	38.0	48.3
Sweden	16.9	39.3	43.8
United Kingdom	12.6	31.3	56.1
Czech Republic	19.3	28.5	52.3
Estonia	12.0	18.3	69.7
Cyprus	2.7	35.7	61.6
Latvia	4.5	16.3	79.2
Lithuania	6.3	12.7	81.0
Hungary	10.9	13.4	75.7
Malta	5.9	18.0	76.1
Poland	7.0	14.6	78.4
Slovenia	27.1	25.5	47.4
Slovakia	16.7	25.6	57.7
EU-25	13.1	24.0	63.0

Source: Eurobarometer 65.1 (2006), own calculations.

Student mobility

Another important component of horizontal Europeanisation is student mobility. Studying abroad is often a first important turning point in the lives of young people and sometimes even the beginning of an international career. The special features here are mainly the acquisition of so-called 'intercultural competencies' such as learning foreign languages, making contact with people from other countries and solving everyday problems in an unfamiliar environment. In an international comparison of student mobility, one finds major differences. Globally, the mobility flows

Student exchanges

go from less developed countries to more advanced countries, such as the United States. A large number of mobile students come from Asia or Latin America. If one compares only the most developed countries, then European countries show a high level of mobility. In relation to student numbers, Europe accepts many foreign students, and, in the course of their studies, European students quite often go abroad. The main countries sending and accepting students are Germany, France and Spain.

Erasmus programme

Especially important for European student exchange are the mobility programmes set up and funded by the EU. The Erasmus programme, introduced in 1987, has become the most important catalyst of this mobility. It supports study abroad and enables students from participating universities to study abroad free of charge. In addition, it provides funds for the additional costs of studying abroad and ensures mutual recognition of academic performance. Since its inception, 1.4 million students have been abroad with the support of this programme. The programme had relatively modest beginnings in the winter semester of 1987/88, with around 3,000 participants, while today it has nearly 150,000 participants per semester, involving a total of 22,000 higher educational institutions in 31 countries.

If one considers the mobility of students to Europe and within Europe as a whole, then country-specific patterns emerge. The pattern of student mobility is connected with certain historical relations, and factors such as the geographical proximity of the respective nations. Table 13.3 shows the movements of students in selected EU countries with the respective countries of origin and destination countries: first, the five most attractive countries for students from EU countries, followed by several other selected EU countries (UNESCO, 2006). Students in the various target regions come from widely different countries, with each country of origin having its own set of interconnections. While the majority of foreign students in the UK come from North America, Western Europe, East Asia and the Pacific, students from Central and Eastern Europe make up the majority in Germany. In France, however, students from Western Europe and North America account for only 16% of all foreign students, while more than half of all foreign students come from Arab countries and Africa. Other European countries are very popular among European students.

For all countries shown, there are at least three European countries among the top five destination countries, in most cases there are even four. A new dynamic has emerged thanks to the relatively mobile students from the new EU Member States in Central and Eastern Europe. The number of students leaving these countries far exceeds the number of students travelling to them, the ratio of immigrant to emigrant students being one to four in Poland, and about one to two in Latvia and Romania. There is thus a clear trend of students migrating from Eastern to Western Europe,

Table 13.3: International student mobility in selected EU Member States*

Country	Number of incoming students	Top three shares of incoming students by regions of origin			Number of outgoing students	Top five destinations of outgoing students	Incoming–outgoing ratio
Top five EU destinations:							
United Kingdom	300,056	North America Western Europe 39%	East Asia and the Pacific 31%	South and West Asia 8%	23,542	1. United States (36%) 2. France (11%) 3. Germany (9%) 4. Ireland (9%) 5. Australia (7%)	13:1
Germany	260,314	Central and Eastern Europe 40%	North America Western Europe 21%	East Asia and the Pacific 16%	56,410	1. United Kingdom (21%) 2. United States (16%) 3. France (12%) 4. Switzerland (10%) 5. Austria (10%)	5:1
France	237,587	Arab States 32%	Sub-Saharan Africa 17%	North America Western Europe 16%	53,350	1. Belgium (23%) 2. United Kingdom (21%) 3. United States (13%) 4. Germany (13%) 5. Unknown (12%)	5:1
Italy	40,641	Central and Eastern Europe 39%	North America Western Europe 36%	Latin American and Caribbean 8%	38,544	1. Germany (21%) 2. Austria (16%) 3. United Kingdom (14%) 4. France (12%) 5. Holy See (11%)	1:1
Belgium	37,103	North America Western Europe 60%	Sub-Saharan Africa 12%	Arab States 9%	10,729	1. France (26%) 2. United Kingdom (23%) 3. Netherlands (19%) 4. Germany (10%) 5. United States (8%)	4:1

continued

Table 13.3: continued

Country	Number of incoming students	Top three shares of incoming students by regions of origin			Number of outgoing students	Top five destinations of outgoing students	Incoming–outgoing ratio
Selected cases (according to geographical location):							
Sweden	32,469	North America Western Europe 50%	Unspecified 22%	Central and Eastern Europe 12%	13,392	1. United Kingdom (25%) 2. United States (23%) 3. Norway (8%) 4. Australia (8%) 5. Germany (6%)	2:1
Portugal	15,483	Sub-Saharan Africa 57%	North America Western Europe 21%	Latin American and Caribbean 16%	11,213	1. France (24%) 2. United Kingdom (24%) 3. Germany (17%) 4. Spain (12%) 5. United States (8%)	1:1
Greece	12,456	North America Western Europe 82%	Central and Eastern Europe 11%	Arab States 3%	49,631	1. United Kingdom (46%) 2. Germany (15%) 3. Italy (14%) 4. France (5%) 5. United States (4%)	1:4
Ireland	10,201	North America Western Europe 62%	East Asia and the Pacific 15%	South and West Asia 6%	17,570	1. United Kingdom (84%) 2. United States (6%) 3. France (3%) 4. Germany (3%) 5. Australia (1%)	1:2
Romania	9,730	Central and Eastern Europe 60%	North America Western Europe 22%	Arab States 10%	20,680	1. France (22%) 2. Germany (20%) 3. United States (16%) 4. Hungary (15%) 5. Italy (6%)	1:2
Poland	7,608	Central and Eastern Europe 63%	North America Western Europe 18%	Central Asia 8%	28,786	1. Germany (54%) 2. France (11%) 3. United States (10%) 4. Austria (4%) 5. Italy (5%)	1:4
Latvia	2,390	North America Western Europe —	Central and Eastern Europe 4%	South and West Asia —	3,730	1. Russia (27%) 2. Germany (25%) 3. United States (11%) 4. Estonia (8%) 5. United Kingdom (5%)	1:2

Source: Mau and Büttner (2010), on the basis of data from the UNESCO Institute for Statistics (2006) for 2004. *This table shows the numbers of incoming and outgoing students in selected EU Member States as well their main regions of origin and main destinations respectively (as percentage of respective numbers). Definition of world regions according to UNESCO Institute of Statistics (2006).

from new to old EU member countries and from non-EU countries to the new Eastern European Member States of the EU. In particular, intra-European East–West migration points to the emergence of a European education market in which many young people from the new Member States spend part of their programme of studies elsewhere in Europe.

Gaining experience of Europe during their studies has a special significance for many students. In addition to professional advancement, students are particularly interested in broadening their social and cultural horizons. Students who have spent time abroad in Europe learn new languages and make new contacts. Surveys of Erasmus students show that many of them consider time abroad important for their career. Erasmus students and students who have completed part of their training abroad also remain internationally and Europe-oriented once they have completed their programme of studies. In their professional lives, those who have participated in the Erasmus programme are twice as likely to have contacts abroad as non-mobile students (Bracht et al, 2006).

The social advantages of going abroad

This expansion of student mobility in Europe has also led to the creation of cross-border student organisations and networks. An example is the association AEGEE (*Association des Etats Généraux des Etudiants de l'Europe*), which involves more than 15,000 students from 40 European countries. This organisation was founded by students with the aim of overcoming Euro-scepticism and encouraging European exchanges. In addition to these student organisations, there are numerous associations and activities in the field of youth and school exchanges. The emergence of the hiking movement in the early 20th century constituted an early form of transnational organisation. Today there are large numbers of similar organisations and opportunities for meeting others. Thus, for example, since its inception in 1963, more than seven million young people have participated in the German–French Youth Exchange.

Student organisations

European town twinning

In Europe an extensive network of town twinning has developed, the goal of which is to develop and promote contacts between the citizens of towns in different countries. Not infrequently, these partnerships are based on the initiative of individual citizens, and they generate a series of social and cultural activities that broaden and strengthen these links. There are some very active town-twinning projects in Europe, with regular reciprocal visits and joint events. The European Council supports the idea of town twinning, because this type of exchange serves to enhance intercultural understanding. There is also the Eurocities network, involving over 130 cities in more than 30 European countries, providing a forum for mutual exchange and learning.

Transnational social networks

Comparatively little information is available on transnational social networks, for example, friendship and family networks, or ways of 'doing Europe' (Immerfall et al, 2010; Mau, 2010). It would be interesting to have data on cross-border networks mainly because this would make it possible to better assess the extent to which horizontal networks are relevant to the lives of Europeans, and whether Europe does indeed constitute the prospective horizon for new forms of cross-border mobility. One could justifiably speak in terms of a European community when intense social relationships existed within Europe. Eurobarometer data show how widespread contact between citizens of the EU actually is (Table 13.4). Participants were asked whether in the previous 12 months they had come into contact with citizens from other EU countries. It appears that on average in the EU-27 about 43% of the respondents gave an affirmative response (45% in the EU-15), 19% reported one or two contacts (20% in the EU-15) and 24% reported multiple contacts (25% in the EU-15). Contacts are most frequent in the Netherlands, Luxembourg, Finland and Germany, and least frequent in Portugal, Spain, Hungary and Poland. The figures for Portugal and Spain are especially surprising, since these countries are such popular destinations for European tourism. On the other hand, the data suggest that cross-border contacts have become commonplace for many Europeans and that we are indeed seeing the emergence of a pan-European experiential space.

However, the process of horizontal Europeanisation is not homogeneous in itself, nor does it include all social groups equally. It creates new forms of inequality between one part of the population that takes part in the process and another part whose lives and social relations remain local or national. Empirically, it appears that it is principally higher-status and well-educated groups that are involved in transnational networks and processes of mobility (Fligstein, 2008). People with higher levels of education also have much more choice concerning their connections abroad, in other words their networks of friends and acquaintances. Many of them belong to the transnational class of experts, with a largely internationalised professional profile. There are differences between the sexes, but especially among younger cohorts these differences are less evident. Differences are also found between rural populations and large urban ones, as well as across generations, with city dwellers and younger people maintaining particularly close transnational contacts (Mau, 2010; Mau and Büttner, 2010).

Table 13.4: Contact with other EU citizens

| | In the last 12 months have you socialised with people from another EU country? (%) | | |
	On several occasions	Once or twice	No
EU-15	25.2	20.3	54.5
Belgium	33.0	14.3	52.7
Denmark	37.9	11.3	50.8
Germany	37.8	20.9	41.3
Ireland	24.1	29.7	46.2
Greece	17.5	13.8	68.7
Spain	11.2	12.7	76.2
France	25.3	13.8	60.8
Italy	9.4	25.3	65.3
Luxembourg	72.6	11.0	16.4
The Netherlands	53.8	19.8	26.4
Austria	24.9	25.5	49.5
Portugal	10.4	12.0	77.6
Finland	27.4	30.8	41.7
Sweden	37.8	17.4	44.7
United Kingdom	25.6	29.0	45.4
Czech Republic	18.9	14.6	66.5
Estonia	31.9	18.2	49.9
Cyprus	40.4	16.4	43.3
Latvia	22.9	17.6	59.5
Lithuania	22.4	15.4	62.2
Hungary	8.2	10.9	80.9
Malta	31.2	16.4	52.4
Poland	18.0	13.9	68.1
Slovenia	22.8	16.4	60.8
Slovakia	23.5	24.5	51.9
EU-25	24.0	19.4	56.7

Source: Eurobarometer 65.1 (2006), own calculations.

13.3 Intra-European migration

NOTE ON METHODOLOGY

The discussion of Europeans' willingness to migrate is based on Eurobarometer data. We present the percentage of those who intend to move to another country within the next five years. For the social-structural composition of intra-European migrant groups, we have used publications of the European Commission (2006) and OECD (2007c), which facilitate a characterisation of employed people with EU citizenship who have settled in an EU-15 country within the last five years.

In addition to short-term mobility and transnational exchange relationships, migration is the central form by means of which different societies come into contact. Since the 1950s, Europe has been the destination for many migratory movements (see Chapter 6). To a considerable degree, these are migrants from former colonies in Asia, Africa and Latin America who have migrated to France, Belgium, Britain, Spain and the Netherlands. Another kind of migration is based on various forms of intra-European migration. Originally, these migrations were closely related to the economic boom of the 1950s and 1970s, during which the demand for labour grew rapidly in Western Europe. Germany, Austria, France and Belgium started to recruit workers in various countries of the Mediterranean region. A larger wave of migration came in the wake of social changes in Eastern Europe in 1989/90: on the one hand, many migrant workers came from Eastern Europe, on the other hand, the hotbeds of conflict in the Balkans brought large contingents of refugees to Western Europe. Lately, there has also been growing labour migration within Eastern Europe, for example from the Ukraine and Belarus to Poland, in response to the demand for labour in certain economic sectors.

Low level of intra-European migration While in terms of migration to Europe there are efforts on the part of individual countries as well as the European Union to limit and regulate immigration, within the European Union in recent decades, barriers to mobility have been steadily reduced. With the exception of the Eastern European countries that joined the EU in 2004 and 2007, where a transitional period applies, EU citizens enjoy the right to freedom of movement (European Commission, 2006; OECD, 2007c). In the first phase of integration, this applied only to workers. Since the beginning of 1993 (implementation of the Maastricht resolutions), all EU citizens have had full freedom of movement and the right to settle. However, though it has increased slowly and steadily, the level of geographical mobility in the old Member States remains relatively low. The increase is due mainly to pro-mobility policies and the rise of non-labour migration, and less to classic labour migration (Recchi, 2009).

Currently about 2.3% of EU citizens live in an EU country other than their home country. However, this population varies from 0.05% in Bulgaria to 6.2% in Belgium or even 36% in Luxembourg. A considerable share of the EU citizens who still live abroad are from Mediterranean countries, and who migrated during the labour recruitments in the 1960s and early 1970s (Rother, 2005), during which intra-European migrations reached their quantitative peak (European Commission, 2006). In Germany, which has the highest absolute proportion of foreign citizens of all European countries (eight million people), around one third of all foreign citizens are intra-European migrants (Recchi et al, 2003). Before the enlargement, countries like Germany, the UK, Spain and France experienced the largest influx of intra-European migrants (European Commission, 2006).

The eastern enlargement was accompanied by a substantial increase in mobility and migration from the new Member States into the EU-15. The number of citizens from the eight countries in Central and Eastern Europe joining the EU in 2004 residing in the old Member States increased from 900,000 before the enlargement to 1.9 million in 2007. The number of people coming from Bulgaria and Romania, both joining the EU only in 2007, increased from 700,000 to 1.9 million. While Germany and Austria were the major destinations before enlargement, Ireland and the UK became target countries (with the greatest influx from Poland) as well as Spain and Italy, both with a substantial increase of people from Romania and Bulgaria. Simulation models predict that under conditions of free and unrestricted movement the number of migrants from the new Member States could increase from 1.9 million in 2007 to 4.4 million in 2020, which corresponds to 5.2% of the population of the sending countries (European Integration Consortium, 2009).

New East–West migration

From the perspective of the push-pull model of classical migration research (see also Chapter 6), one can assume that an unequal distribution of employment, income and opportunities in the member countries of the European Union will lead to major migratory movements. This seems to work as a good explanation of the new East–West movements, but to a lesser extent with regard to other regions. It is interesting, therefore, that despite significant economic differences within Western Europe, for example, cross-border migration remains limited. One possible explanation is that, in comparison with the United States, Europe has a weak 'mobility culture'. A survey conducted in 2005 by Eurobarometer shows that, with regard to cross-border migration and even migration to other regions within their own country, Europeans are quite immobile (Vandenbrande et al, 2006). The European Commission estimates the annual levels of international migration at about 1% of the active labour population. Migration within member countries (measured as migration between the largest regional units) is around the same level (European Commission, 2006). This level of migration is similar to that between different Canadian provinces, where also approximately 1% of the active labour population is geographically mobile. Comparable figures for mobility between the various federal states of the United States stand at 3% (OECD, 2007c).

Lack of 'mobility culture'?

A weak culture of mobility is, however, not the only reason for the low level of cross-border migration in some parts of Europe. For instance, it is still not easy to establish oneself successfully in another labour market, since, despite formal recognition of their qualifications, workers are not always employed and paid in accordance with their qualifications. There are also difficulties caused by differences in the social security systems

Mobility barriers

(especially the lack of transferability of accumulated pension and social security benefits) and taxation systems. These factors play a lesser role in migration within the United States. In addition, cultural factors carry more weight in Europe: for instance, a large proportion of Europeans are still not able to speak another European language (TNS Opinion & Social, 2006). We also know that, through family relationships and feelings of belonging, Europeans often develop a strong attachment to a specific regional context, which serves as a brake on large-scale migration movements.

Willingness to migrate

When one compares Europeans' willingness to migrate, one notices large differences between countries, changes over time and differences with respect to the destination regions (Table 13.5). Although the figures do not allow one to form any conclusions about actual migration movements, they do show the migration potential in individual countries. Asked in 2005 about their intention to move in the next five years, 2.7% of the respondents in the EU-15 said that they were planning to do so. Within this group of countries, Scandinavian, French and Irish respondents showed an above-average intention to migrate, with between 4% and 6% of the respective national populations planning to migrate within Europe. Very limited intentions to migrate are found in Italy, Spain and Portugal (all countries that once made a large contribution to intra-European labour migration), and in economically successful Central European countries (Czech Republic, Hungary).

East–West mobility
    The proportion of the population in the new EU Member States that is willing to migrate is significantly higher than in the core EU states. The most recent Eurobarometer survey showed that more than 5% of respondents from the new Member States are willing to migrate (not shown in table). One can interpret this as evidence for the emergence of a 'new' space of European mobility, within which cross-border migration is becoming a normal experience. In East European member countries, the proportion of those who plan to move to other European countries is even higher than the proportion of those who want to move to another region within their own country. In addition, the proportion of those who emigrate to countries outside the EU is significantly lower than the proportion of those who want to migrate within the European Union. By far the highest level of willingness to migrate is found in the Baltic states, where migration potential lies between 9.5% and 10.6% of the population, the majority of whom prefer migration within the EU (see also Section 6.1). A look at the changes between 2001/02 and 2005 points to a significant increase in the willingness to migrate, within both Western and Eastern Europe. While freedom of movement for the

citizens of the accession states remains limited, one nevertheless finds a much higher and growing willingness to migrate there than in the long-standing Member States. In addition, even before accession, many Eastern Europeans managed to find their way to Western European countries, usually with temporary residence status. However, one can assume that the economic crisis will affect migration flows. For example, the total migrant inflows from the new EU Member States to the UK between July 2008 and July 2009 dropped by 42%. However, the drop was not uniform and migrant inflows from some countries actually increased

Table 13.5: Willingness to migrate

	Country within EU (%)		Country outside EU (%)	
	2001/02	**2005**	**2001/02**	**2005**
EU-15	1.5	2.7	1.4	1.9
Belgium	2.2	3.1	1.1	0.9
Denmark	2.7	5.8	2.7	3.4
Germany	0.3	2.1	0.2	1.2
Ireland	2.6	4.3	1.9	3.8
Greece	0.4	2.9	0.7	1.2
Spain	0.6	1.7	0.6	0.7
France	2.5	4.3	2.0	2.6
Italy	1.7	1.6	1.4	1.1
Luxembourg	5.3	4.0	0.0	0.0
Netherlands	2.8	2.8	2.3	2.2
Austria	1.9	2.2	1.4	0.9
Portugal	0.0	1.5	0.0	2.4
Finland	3.7	4.5	1.4	1.7
Sweden	3.8	4.4	2.7	4.0
United Kingdom	1.8	3.4	2.7	3.5
Bulgaria	–	–	–	–
Czech Republic	1.1	1.6	0.8	0.3
Estonia	1.6	8.3	0.2	1.7
Cyprus	2.2	2.7	1.0	0.0
Latvia	2.0	7.4	0.6	2.1
Lithuania	2.5	8.5	1.1	2.1
Hungary	0.8	2.4	0.4	0.2
Malta	0.2	4.5	0.0	4.5
Poland	1.8	7.2	0.3	1.6
Romania	–	–	–	–
Slovenia	0.9	1.8	0.5	1.8
Slovakia	2.0	3.4	1.4	1.4
EU-25	–	3.2	–	1.8

Source: Eurobarometer 54.1, 64.1; candidate countries, Eurobarometer 2002.1; own calculations; data for EU-27 not available.

depending on the economic conditions in the country of origin and the labour market opportunities in the UK. While the number of people coming from Poland and Slovakia decreased substantially, this was not the case for the countries that experienced the highest rises in unemployment and the greatest drop in GDP, as in the Baltic states (Ivlevs et al, 2009).

Causes and forms of intra-European migration

Migration processes are the result of complex decision-making situations. As a rule, in migration research, where the focus is on individual actors and their motives, economic and social factors in the region of origin and in the target region are seen as paramount. Following on from Lee's push-pull model (1966), economic factors (especially imbalances in labour markets and differences in income) are considered to be the most significant motives for migration (Rist, 1978; Hoffmann-Nowotny, 1981; Stark and Bloom, 1985; Castles, 1986; Feithen, 1986; Stark, 1993; Chiswick, 2008). These ideas are complemented by approaches that focus on the importance of social factors, especially social networks, in the formulation of motives for migration (Portes and Rumbaut, 1990; Bauer and Zimmermann, 1997; Faist, 2000; Palloni et al, 2001; Pries, 2001a, 2004a; Hillmann, 2005; Johnston et al, 2006; Portes and DeWind, 2007); other researchers have pointed out the relevance of cultural motives for migration (King and Ruiz-Gelices, 2003; Scott, 2006; Verwiebe, 2010). There are not many recent empirical studies on the causes of intra-European migration. Using a Eurobarometer survey on geographical mobility within Europe, the European Commission (2006) concludes that work-related and family-related reasons constitute the main bases for migration. Each factor plays a role in approximately 40% of decisions to migrate (Figure 13.3, column 2). On the whole, various family-related and social reasons are mentioned even more frequently than work-related or economic motives for migration. From these findings, however, it is also clear that in many cases there is not just one reason but rather a whole raft of reasons behind a decision to migrate (cf. Scott, 2006; Fourage and Ester, 2007; Lundholm, 2007; Verwiebe, 2010).

Economic, social and cultural reasons to migrate

One of the most comprehensive attempts to examine the dynamics of intra-European migration is the PIONEUR Project, led by Ettore Recchi (Recchi et al, 2003; PIONEUR, 2006; Recchi and Favell, 2009).[1] The PIONEUR study is based on a sample of 5,000 European citizens who lived as non-citizens in the five Member States of France, Germany, the UK, Italy and Spain. This survey also clearly showed that the classic push-pull factors cannot fully explain migration processes between EU countries. About 30% of respondents said that they had migrated to another EU country for family reasons or because of a love interest. For 25%, job opportunities were paramount, for 24% the decision was based

Figure 13.3: Reasons for intra-European migration

	European Commission	PIONEUR Survey	TRANSMOB Survey
Economic and professional reasons	About 40%	25%	15% (just economic and professional reasons)
Social and familial reasons	About 40%	30%	30% (marriage, family reunion, networks)
Cultural reasons and education	Not asked	7% studies	15% (studies, interest in foreign languages/cultures or metropolises)
Other reasons	20% quality of life	24% quality of life	40% mixed reasons (of which 28% economic and other reasons)

Sources: European Commission (2006: 231), PIONEUR (2006), Verwiebe (2010).

on quality of life, for 7%, on study opportunities (PIONEUR, 2006). These results suggest that for migration within Europe, the economic aspect is only one reason among others, and that social and cultural reasons play a relatively large role, as the TRANSMOB study also shows (Verwiebe, 2010). Thus, it seems plausible that there has been an overall change in the reasons for migration compared to the period of intra-European labour migration of the 1960s and 1970s, when economic and work-related motives clearly dominated (Castles, 1986; Krane, 1979).

If one looks at the socio-structural composition of Europeans who have migrated within the EU in the last five years, then the assumption regarding a structural change in intra-European migration becomes even more plausible (Verwiebe and Eder, 2006; Fourage and Ester, 2007; OECD, 2007c). The first thing that the data show is the young age of migrants (Table 13.6). Of the EU citizens of working age who settled in an EU-15 country between 2000 and 2005, between 60% (EU-15) and 78% (accession states) were no older than 34. They are thus significantly younger than the domestic population. In addition, intra-European migrants are more likely to be unmarried and less likely to have children. Accordingly, young people without commitments are the most mobile group in Europe. They tend to migrate to metropolitan centres, especially major cities like London, Paris, Berlin and Brussels (Scott, 2006; Verwiebe, 2008), vibrant urban population centres in Ireland and the UK and the prosperous regions of Sweden, Denmark, France, Holland and Switzerland. In this respect, these urban agglomerations are the most multicultural places in Europe (Favell, 2008).

A look at the educational level of the migration groups proves to be no less interesting. In the case of those with EU-15 citizenship, the level is mostly very high. Forty-four per cent of EU migrants have a university degree, compared with 26% of domestic employees. With Eastern European migrants, intermediate skills predominate, while among those without EU citizenship who have migrated to the EU-15, low- and

Migration of the highly qualified

Table 13.6: Social characteristics of intra-European migrant groups

	EU-15	EU-10	Non EU-25	Natives
Age				
15–24	12	27	19	12
25–34	48	51	46	24
35–64	40	22	35	64
Education				
Low	15	15	36	27
Medium	41	63	40	47
High	44	22	24	26
Occupation				
Highly qualified employees	55	16	20	40
Low qualified employees	24	28	25	26
Qualified workers	12	27	21	25
Unqualified jobs	9	30	35	10
Marital status				
Unmarried	61	53	38	39
Married	39	47	62	61
Household				
Single	25	24	16	17
Couple without children	44	48	40	33
Couple or single with at least one child	31	31	44	51

Source: European Commission (2006: 224); OECD (2007c).

medium-level qualifications dominate. Thus, those who migrate within the core EU states are relatively highly qualified, often freely mobile professionals (Salt and Ford, 1993; Koser and Salt, 1997; Beaverstock, 2005; Recchi and Favell, 2009). A glance at the fields in which they are working shows that they are mainly employed in accordance with their qualifications. Among Eastern Europeans and migrants from outside the EU, this is less often the case; they are rarely employed as high-skilled workers. The dominant forms of employment are those for which qualifications are not required. A comparison of their training with the work they are actually doing suggests that this is due to their professional qualifications not being recognised.

Long-term and short-term migration

When studying migration, the focus lies mostly on long-term migration processes. A migrant is generally defined as someone who permanently relocates to a different country. Within Europe, however, many new forms of migration have emerged that no longer meet this definition. Migration movements are increasingly short term or of a temporary nature, taking the form, for example, of seasonal migration, circular migration or retirement migration. One common factor is that, despite migration, stable contacts are maintained in the country of origin, so that it is not always easy to determine in which country migrants are actually based. These forms of migration are frequently not recorded in official statistics, because migrants often do not notify authorities of their departure. Until the early 1990s, seasonal migration or circular migration was especially typical of migrants from Southern Europe. Today, there are quite a number of regions in Europe with a high level of circular migration, for example, between Luxembourg, France and Germany or between Denmark and Germany (Strüver, 2005; Verwiebe et al, 2010). Particularly noteworthy is the circular migration between Eastern and Western Europe. In the last 10 years, many Eastern Europeans have worked in Western Europe on a seasonal basis as nurses, au pairs, cleaners, craftspersons or farm hands at harvest time (Triandafyllidou, 2006; Public Opinion Research Center, 2007).

This trend was strengthened with the accession of the new EU Member States in May 2004. In Poland, for example, with 38.5 million inhabitants, the largest Member State in Eastern Europe, it is estimated that since May 2004 approximately three million people have worked abroad, most of them without permanently leaving their homeland (Public Opinion Research Center, 2007). Until recently, Polish emigrants tended to move to the US and to Australia. Since EU accession, however, most of them no longer migrate overseas, but rather to Western Europe. The geographical proximity of the Western European labour markets reinforces this trend towards temporary migration, where one is 'only working' in an EU country. Restrictions on free movement for citizens of the new Member States in parts of the EU have also contributed to sojourns remaining mainly temporary.

Another aspect of intra-European migration that has recently gained in significance is the migration of older, middle-class Europeans (Williams et al, 1997; King et al, 1998; Recchi and Favell, 2009). In this group, it is becoming increasingly popular to move to attractive areas in France, Portugal, Spain, Italy and Greece, as well as to the south-west of England or Scotland. The central criterion for migration after retirement is quality of life rather than local income levels or the prices of goods and services. Experiences gained in the course of holiday travel can encourage these forms of retirement migration.

Note

[1] Despite the substantial scope of the project, it proved difficult to produce a detailed picture of the motivations, patterns and consequences of intra-European migration. Because of the size of the group, intra-European migrants constituted a 'hidden population': their respective countries did not systematically gather data on them, and it is difficult to reach them with standardised surveys.

14

Subjective Europeanisation

⌐⊡ DEFINITION

Subjective Europeanisation refers to Europe's growing role in the cognitive, affective and normative perceptions and orientations of people, and the weakening of the fixation on the nation-state. Europe appears as an additional frame of reference, superimposed on the level of the nation-state but without necessarily replacing it. ■

Research into social stratification and societal change deals not only with objective living conditions and the unequal distribution of jobs and resources but also with the attitudes, orientations and mentalities typically associated with specific life circumstances (Geiger, 1972 [1932]; Bourdieu, 1984). In the pertinent studies, people are asked about their conceptions of different aspects of life such as family and partnerships, work and leisure, and basic political attitudes. An entire strand of political sociology is devoted to the question of how the social-structural order is linked with socio-political interest formation. Leading the way in this context was the Norwegian political scientist Stein Rokkan (Rokkan, 1999), who in his historical-comparative work undertook an analysis of the structural divisions in Europe. He was concerned with the question: what are the decisive lines of social differentiation that influence structures of conflict in the political system? Such structures of division correspond to socially and structurally identifiable population groups and their interests and orientations. Politically, these social divisions translate into alliances of interest, which lead to a political and organisational representation of the conflicts by political parties and associations (Lipset and Rokkan, 1967; Zuckermann, 1975; Bartolini and Mair, 1990; Berglund and Ekman, 2010).

Cleavage structures and social movements

Europe itself is an emergent social and political space in which a close connection between social structures and the political system has not yet fully developed. There is no established structure of political parties on the European level, there are no opportunities for political involvement comparable to those offered by national political systems, and there is not a clear social-structural stratification of interests. However, especially in relation to the Europeanisation process, it is particularly important to examine citizens' attitudes, because the institutional development and structuring of EU institutions depends greatly on whether there is a basis of shared ideas and understandings. Even if there is a European heritage in terms of common values and self-understandings (see Section 2.2),

Attitudes and integration of social movements

there is as much diversity as there is unity. If one considers the EU as a whole, it can be assumed that interests and attitudes are not primarily structured in accordance with traditional socio–structural parameters (such as Left–Right), but that nation–state affiliation remains central. Relatedly, there are also differences between groups of countries based on criteria such as the degree of modernisation, economic development, and length of membership or geographic location. This is shown by research on attitudes towards various issues, such as the role of civil rights, concepts of equality, the place of law and religion in public life, the state, the market and democracy, and environmental protection (Halman et al, 2005; Gerhards, 2007, 2010; Pollack, 2008). As far as endeavours to promote integration are concerned, differences in attitudes on this front can have major consequences, because the citizens of Member States can have quite different ideas of how a society should be organised. Thus, the inclusion of additional members raises the question of the extent to which these new members fit the social and cultural self-image of the EU, and whether the result is not a greater discrepancy between the values propagated by the EU and the member countries' own sets of values, thus obstructing integration.

The connection between attitudes and the prospects of integration is tighter still when one looks directly at attitudes towards the European Union. The central question is the extent to which further integration efforts on the part of European elites will be supported by the citizens, and whether these efforts will be compensated for by an emerging sense of belonging. This subjective dimension of Europeanisation refers to the social conditions and requirements of Europeanisation. In the following sections, we present citizens' attitudes towards Europe in three key areas: first, the question of legitimacy and support for Europeanisation; second, European identity; and, third, we examine various aspects of subjective Europeanisation, referring to the new ties between European national communities and their citizens. The guiding assumption is that these attitudes interact with and influence the process of European unification.

14.1 Support for Europeanisation

DEFINITION

In order to secure its own legitimacy and viability, every political system is dependent on political support. According to Easton (1975), one can distinguish two types of political support: specific support is related to satisfaction with the output and performance of those in political office and has a short-term orientation; diffuse support has a long-term orientation and is focused on general aspects of the political system – here, the object is assessed not on the basis of its outcomes, but on the basis of what it represents.

NOTE ON METHODOLOGY

For the discussion of support for Europeanisation, various indicators were selected from Eurobarometer surveys: assessment of EU membership is presented for the years 1995 to 2008, using the EU-wide trend of the percentage of those who consider membership to be a good thing. This indicator is also differentiated by country (2008). The perceived problem-solving abilities of national governments and the EU are presented for 2008.

One of the important questions discussed in social science research on Europe concerns the legitimacy of the European unification process (Abromeit, 1998; Gabel, 1998; Kohler-Koch, 2000; Hooghe, 2003; Medrano, 2003; Marks and Steenbergen, 2004). Behind this lies the apprehension that integration is borne primarily by political elites, who have so far not managed to secure adequate support from the broad masses of the population (Rohrschneider, 2002; Hooghe, 2003; Haller, 2008). One can assume that the need for legitimacy has increased in the course of integration, since the consequences of decisions also weigh more heavily in the balance. From the perspective of democratic theory, it is clear that the increasing importance of majority decision-making at the European level creates problems of legitimacy and acceptance, because there is no symmetry between the governed and those who govern. A European people (demos), in the sense of a community of people bound together by language, culture and history, does not yet exist. Within the Council of Ministers, decisions with significant consequences for the citizens of individual Member States can be made by majorities who are acting without having been legitimised by the voters of the countries in question. Furthermore, 'deepened integration' means that increasingly decisions are being made that result in direct social costs – thus, decisions are no longer simply remote policies, but rather have an immediate effect on many groups. Ultimately, the EU is a complex political entity with many planes of political activity and often opaque decision-making structures (Hix, 2008).

The growing quest for legitimacy

Over a long period, the existence of a 'permissive consensus' was the dominant idea in research on the legitimacy of European integration (Lindberg and Scheingold, 1970; Hurrelmann, 2007). This means that the integration process was supported by EU citizens because they trust their national elites to ensure their interests prevail, and that the EU does not possess a more advanced, more reliable, basis of legitimacy. The elites found themselves confronted with a rather disinterested and uninformed public, and therefore have a relatively free hand in the shaping of Europe. Neo-functionalist theories assumed that, as integration proceeded, EU citizens would also orient themselves more strongly towards Europe (Haas, 1968). Once set in motion, and albeit with a certain time lag,

Permissive consensus?

integration would help create its own acceptance. Citizens would become accustomed to the new level of decision-making and come to appreciate its benefits. In part, the democratisation of European institutions was seen as the key to legitimacy, since it facilitates citizen participation. Sceptics argued, however, that more democracy in Europe would jeopardise the existence of the EU, because the social-structural foundations required for solidarity and a sense of belonging were missing. Citizens were still fixated on their national political communities, so that the introduction of democratic rules would lead to an intensification of conflict and disintegration (Bartolini, 2005). On this view, the EU is thus not (yet) capable of fully developed democratic and participatory structures.

Output versus input legitimacy

A key reason for the 'weak legitimacy' of the EU is seen in the fact that the EU's legitimacy as a whole is too determined by direct benefits (output legitimacy) and less by democratic processes of decision-making (input legitimacy) (Scharpf, 1999). The concept of input legitimacy refers to the normative acceptance of a political system. Output legitimacy, on the other hand, is tied to the potential of the system to solve certain problems, and corresponds to the actual, specific level of support (Easton, 1975). It refers to the recipients' degree of satisfaction with policy outcomes. On the input side, there is a structural deficit of democracy in the EU because the forms of political decision-making and involvement are still underdeveloped. There are only a few distinct indications of a genuinely European identity, capable of underpinning a sense of attachment to European actors and institutions. In the case of output legitimacy, support for the EU rests heavily on utilitarian motives, that is, on the question of whether European integration will bring benefits to its citizens. Output legitimacy entails the risk, however, that the people will turn away from Europe as a political project as soon as it no longer yields the expected returns.

Benefits of membership

We know from a number of empirical studies that the (perceived) benefit derived from the European Union is in fact an important predictor of the degree of support (Anderson and Reichert, 1996; Anderson and Kaltenthaler, 1996). Not just governments, but also the peoples of the Member States make their support for membership and for concrete steps towards integration dependent on expected benefits. However, it is extremely difficult to estimate this accurately, especially when one looks not just at the EU budget, but also at the broader effects of the common market and economic integration. The task becomes even more difficult if one includes non-economic effects, such as the establishment of Europe as a realm of peace. At the individual level, one can assume that there is a discrepancy between the objective effects of EU policy and the individual perception of these effects. Ultimately, subjective perception and interpretation are the decisive factors, which are in turn influenced by a multiplicity of other factors, not least media discourse and general attitudes towards the EU (Mau, 2005).

Evaluation of membership

One indicator of support for the EU is therefore the question of whether membership is seen as good or bad, a question that is regularly raised in the Eurobarometer surveys. The positive assessment of membership (for the respondents' own country) increased throughout the 1980s and reached a peak in 1991. Thereafter, the positive rating fell back (Immerfall et al, 2010). This suggests that the ongoing enlargement of the EU and problems of consensus–building have left their marks on public opinion.

Figure 14.1 shows the change in the evaluation of membership over the period 1996–2008. During this period we see a slight upward trend, broken by a slump in 2003/04, when 10 new countries, mainly from Central and Eastern Europe, joined the EU. After that, one sees the return of a slight upward trend, which stopped in 2008. It can be assumed that the evaluation of membership is directly linked with the perceived benefits of membership. Both fluctuate essentially in tandem, so that we can assume that considerations regarding the benefits of membership do indeed play a major role in the evaluation of the EU in general.

Membership as a good thing?

Figure 14.1: Assessment of EU membership over time

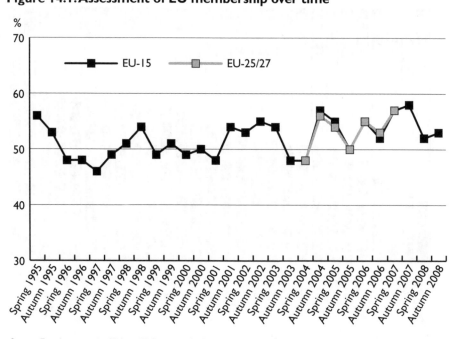

Source: Eurobarometer 45.1 to 70.2; own calculations; survey question: 'Generally speaking, do you think that [OUR COUNTRY]'s membership of the European Union is ...?' The diagram shows the percentage of who agreed that 'membership is a good thing'.

Country
differences

In the general evaluation of membership, one finds significant differences between countries (Figure 14.2). Especially positive attitudes towards membership are encountered in Luxembourg, Ireland and the Netherlands, while people in Latvia, Hungary, the United Kingdom and Austria have a significantly more negative stance. It is not easy to interpret this pattern. On the one hand, there are specific explanations for each country, if one considers tradition, self-image and political factors; on the other hand, the advantages of EU membership seem much more likely to be noticed if a country is, for example, a net recipient of EU funds, the seat of key EU institutions, in a key geographical location or enjoying an economic upswing as a result of EU accession. The Benelux countries have traditionally been open to the idea of a united Europe, while the cohesion country Ireland has been able to make progress in modernisation thanks to EU membership (see Part 2).

By contrast, the British are traditionally sceptical towards Europe, even beyond conventional Left–Right political orientations (Heath et al, 1999): although they are advocates of the common market, they have major reservations about the Europeanisation of politics and bureaucracy. In Italy,

Figure 14.2: EU membership is a good thing

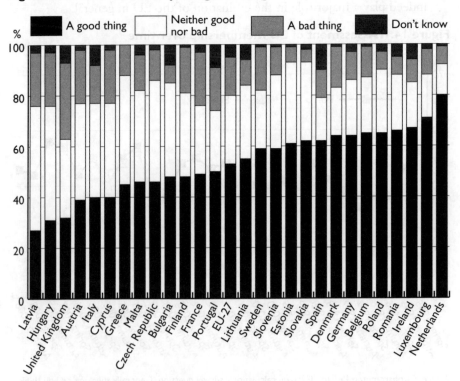

Source: Eurobarometer 70.2 (2008); own calculations; survey question: 'Generally speaking, do you think that [OUR COUNTRY]'s membership in the European Union is ...?'

traditionally a strong supporter of the EU, less than half the population sees membership as a good thing. Presumably this can be explained by the problems of economic adjustment and the employment crisis in Italy, which are often associated with the economic liberalisation initiated by Europe. In some Eastern European countries, one finds strong reservations concerning Europe (Rohrschneider and Whitefield, 2006). The reasons are to be found in the special interests of national autonomy and possible disappointment over the lack of rapid and tangible improvements in living conditions. The country ranking has remained relatively stable over time, although slight convergence processes have been observed. In Eurosceptic countries the assessment has tended to improve, in Europe-friendly countries it has tended to worsen.

Democratic quality and the ability to solve problems

Beyond its beneficial aspects, perception of the democratic quality of the European Union is crucial for the degree of acceptance. Here, the responses given by Europeans yield an ambivalent picture. On the one hand, it is clear that Europeans see considerable room for improvement in the democratic quality of the EU. In a Eurobarometer survey from 2005, 53% of all EU citizens indicated that they believe their voice in the EU does not count. Four out of five Europeans said they had heard about the European Constitution, but 68% indicated that they had very little knowledge of its actual contents (TNS Opinion & Social, 2005). In 2006, only about half of the respondents indicated that they were satisfied with democracy in the EU. It is interesting that in the new Member States there is a higher level of satisfaction with democracy in the EU than there is in the EU-15. In almost all countries, except the Eastern European states and Italy, the level of satisfaction with national democracy is higher than the level of satisfaction with democracy in the EU, although the difference is not especially pronounced (European Commission, 2007a, 2007c). However, if we look at other factors, such as voter turnout for the European Parliament, the picture is less positive. Since the first direct election, voter turnout has declined: in 1979, 60% of voters went to the polls, but by 2009 it was only 43%. Elections for the European Parliament attract far fewer voters than national parliamentary elections (Hix, 2005).

On the other hand, we also see that people have confidence in the problem-solving abilities of the European Union. Obviously, many people are aware that the nation-state is limited in its capacity to deal with many of our present problems. In a Eurobarometer survey from 2008, covering a whole range of policy areas, respondents were asked whether decision-making should take place at the European or national level (Table 14.1). So the question is: which of the two is seen as more competent? It is

Problem-solving capacity

clear that, in a number of areas, the public has more confidence in the EU than in the various national governments. These areas include the fight against terrorism and crime, scientific research, environmental protection, defence and foreign policy, energy policy, support for regions facing economic problems, immigration policy, fighting crime, competition, fighting inflation, the economy and agriculture. Here, a growing awareness of international interdependency and the more global character of these issues may be seen as driving forces behind a growing importance of the supranational level.

Table 14.1: Problem-solving competence of the EU

	National government	European Union	Don't know
Fighting terrorism	18	79	3
Scientific and technological research	24	72	4
Protecting the environment	30	67	3
Defence and foreign affairs	31	64	5
Energy	33	63	4
Support for regions facing economic difficulties	34	62	4
Immigration	37	60	3
Fighting crime	38	59	3
Competition	35	57	8
Fighting inflation	42	54	4
Economy	45	51	4
Agriculture and fishery	45	50	5
Consumer protection	48	48	4
Transports	48	48	4
Fighting unemployment	57	40	3
The educational system	64	33	3
Health	18	33	3
Social welfare	24	32	3
Taxation	30	29	5
Pensions	31	26	4

Source: Eurobarometer 70.2 (2008); own calculations; row percentages; survey question: 'For each of the following areas, do you think that decisions should be made by the [NATIONALITY] Government, or made jointly within the European Union?'

This means that, despite the perceived lack of democracy, the EU is seen as the appropriate political body to turn to for solutions to social, economic and ecological problems. However, in the areas of education, health and social services, taxes and pensions, and the fight against unemployment, most EU citizens believe that decision-making and the power to take action should remain at the national level. It is interesting that, while matters pertaining to science, the economy and risk management are viewed as the EU's domain, the responsibility for welfare is unmistakeably ascribed to the nation-state – the exception being regional policy, a field in which the EU has long played a very active role (see Section 11.3). These preferences are most likely related to the specificity of the policy area in question, perceived deficiencies in performance on the national or European level, and the general acceptance of the EU.

14.2 National and European identity

DEFINITION

The political identity of a community refers to a sense of belonging and common purpose, whether based on common values and objectives, ethnic origin, ideological conviction or historical experience.

NOTE ON METHODOLOGY

The discussion of identities in the EU is based on a question from the Eurobarometer 2007. We show the percentages of respondents who see the EU, national citizenship or both as constitutive of their identity. In a second step, respondents with a European identity are broken down according to different occupational groups.

Identity and integration

For the progress of European integration, utilitarian forms of support depending on cost–benefit calculations on the part of populations and governments are surely not enough. Many authors argue that it is important that people also identify with Europe or the project of European integration in a much broader sense and that the way European identity becomes politicised and contested will be crucial for the deepening of integration (Herrmann et al, 2004; Hooghe and Marks, 2005; Checkel and Katzenstein, 2009). If bonds arise that are not merely of an instrumental nature, but are based rather on a general identification with Europe, then it is easier to garner support for concrete steps towards integration. This is even more the case when one considers that integration is associated not just with benefits, but also with costs. This raises the question of whether, in the process of European integration, the feeling of belonging and of a common identity constitutes a possible resource for ensuring solidarity and loyalty. In particular, if the EU assumes more powers and gains more control in the area of redistribution, it will be necessary to ensure forms of support that are not linked with feeling cognitively and emotionally attached to Europe (Carey, 2002).

National versus European identity

In the research on the EU, there is an ongoing debate about the possibilities of and potential for a European identity (Herrmann et al, 2004; Eder and Spohn, 2005; Eder, 2006). In this debate, significant scepticism has been expressed concerning the existence and resilience of a collective European identity (Lepsius, 2001). This is based mainly on the fact that, over the centuries, nation-states have developed a high degree of normative integration and have built up an exclusive bond with 'their' citizens. Therefore, it is difficult to imagine a European identity that simply supersedes national identity. And the EU can be considered an as yet relatively young object of identification. However, it is questionable whether identification can be conceived as a zero-sum game, in which stronger identification with one level – for example, a region, a nation, or Europe – necessarily means weaker identification with the other levels (Marks and Hooghe, 2003). National identity can exist alongside supranational feelings of belonging and is perfectly compatible with a sense of belonging on other levels. As Citrin and Sides (2004: 175) argue, 'creating support for a stronger European state does not require a European identity that dominates national identity. It is sufficient if a European identity is established alongside one's national identity.'

Do you see yourself as European? We can tap the role of identification with Europe by using data from Eurobarometer, where respondents are regularly asked whether they see themselves exclusively as citizens of their own country, as citizens of their own country and of Europe, or exclusively as Europeans. The cumulative proportion of those who see themselves as both citizens of their own country and European, or exclusively as European, has remained quite stable over the years, at between 50% and 60%, with the majority seeing themselves as citizens of their own country first and as Europeans second (Citrin and Sides, 2004; Nissen, 2004). One third to one half of the respondents indicate, however, that they identify exclusively with their own nationality. If a more rigid criterion is applied, for example, by asking whether one identifies primarily or exclusively with Europe, then the role of European identity is reduced, with only about one in 10 agreeing. For most EU citizens, national identity remains a priority. Here again, we find major differences between countries (Figure 14.3): in the Benelux countries, and in Germany, France and Italy, identification with Europe is significantly greater than it is in Sweden, Finland, Portugal, Greece and the new Member States in Eastern Europe. The feeling of belonging to Europe is particularly weak in the UK and Ireland.

Behind these significant differences lie two main factors: being centrally situated in Europe, and length of EU membership. Obviously, a comparatively long membership tends to promote a sense of European identity. Furthermore, the distribution of identification with the EU is relatively independent of whether the country is a net contributor or net recipient in the EU. In Eastern Europe, one finds a weaker orientation towards Europe because, following the collapse of socialism, the idea of national independence gained in importance (see Drulák, 2001; Rohrschneider and Whitefield, 2006). In Eastern Europe, national sentiment is thus widespread. In particular, the underprivileged classes and the groups of peasants are more strongly oriented towards the nation-state. Their rejection of values or institutions such as democracy and the market economy is particularly evident, as is their Euro-scepticism, so that in this case there is a manifest tension between European and national identity. This means that the conflict between modernisation and traditionalism is superimposed on the relationship with Europe (Heidar, 2003; Berglund and Ekman, 2010).

Figure 14.3: National or European identity

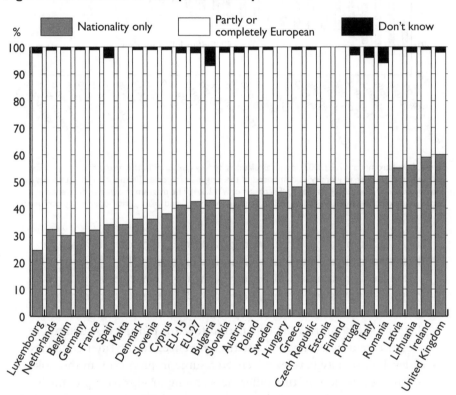

Source: Eurobarometer 67.1 (2007), own calculations; survey question: 'In the near future do you see yourself as ... (1) [Nationality] only; (2) [Nationality] and European; (3) European and[Nationality]; (4) European only; or (5) Don't know?'. The answering category 'partly or completely European' is composed of the original categories '[Nationality] and European', 'European and [Nationality]', as well as 'European only' (2, 3 and 4).

On the question of European identity, there are large differences not only between countries, but also among socio-structural groups. Based on data from the year 2007, Figure 14.4 shows the differences in attitudes to European identity among different occupational groups, in this case between skilled and unskilled workers on the one hand, and, on the other hand, administrative and management professionals, as well as senior academic professions. These are two groups with different degrees of status

Status and identity

Figure 14.4: Occupational status and European identity

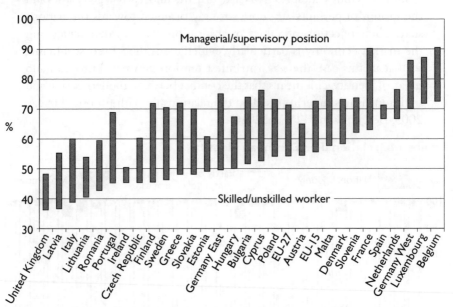

Source: Eurobarometer 67.1 (2007), own calculations; survey question: 'In the near future do you see yourself as...?'. 'European identity' is composed of the original categories '[Nationality] and European', 'European and [Nationality]' as well as 'European only' (2,3,4). The diagram shows the difference in percentage points between 'skilled as well as unskilled workers' and 'managerial/supervisory positions'.

and educational capital. On average, a difference of over 15% separates these two groups on the issue of European identity. The differences are particularly pronounced in countries such as France, Finland, Sweden, Portugal, Cyprus and Poland. Less marked differences between groups are to be found in Ireland and Spain, however, which is an indication that in these countries the orientation towards Europe is structured to a lesser extent by occupational status differences. In the latter countries, all levels of society have experienced a surge in prosperity in the wake of Europeanisation, so that differences among groups have presumably not arisen to such a great degree (Medrano, 2003). In countries with greater differences among groups, affinity with Europe is primarily found among higher status groups. The reason for this is seen in the fact that the latter groups are less adversely affected by the pressures arising from the processes of Europeanisation (such as developing a common market) than groups with low social status, and they also have significantly more opportunities for gaining positive experiences with Europe and Europeans (Section 13.2). The upper and middle ranks of white–collar employees and academic professionals, senior executives in management and administration, and people with higher education are those who are still most likely to be integrated into the transnational space of Europe

(Fligstein, 2008). As Immerfall et al (2010: 349) underscore: 'To a large extent, European integration is an elite project. Little wonder then that European self concepts are comparatively widespread among the educated, owners of businesses, managers and professionals'.

The long-term development of a European identity is often associated with the process of European integration (Risse, 2004). European integration may trigger a higher degree of cross-border connectivity. Strong transnational ties and greater European connectedness, in turn, can be expected to lead to a shift of loyalties and identifications and thus to a strengthening of identification with Europe. However, such a development cannot be expected to occur overnight: the overarching category of 'Europe' has to be filled with concrete content for individuals and be experienced by them socially, for example through offerings in the areas of education, the acquisition of foreign languages and European contact networks. However, there are great differences in the ways in which and degrees to which various social groups are embedded in the process of Europeanisation, and hence their degree of attachment to Europe varies as well. Therefore the crucial question is whether the lower and middle sections of the national populations will also become part of the European undertaking. As Fligstein (2008: 251f) rightly argues:

Long-term development

> If the rest of Europe's citizens do not have the positive feelings generated from systematic interactions or perceptions of shared culture, the EU will remain institutionally where it is. Subsequent rounds of integration will depend on drawing more citizens into finding virtue in increasing their interdependencies on their neighbors.

14.3 Europeans' relationship to each other

NOTE ON METHODOLOGY

The relationship that Europeans have to each other is discussed on the basis of data from the European Values Survey (EVS), which Gerhards (2008) has analysed, and also using data from the European Election Study (2004). Attitudes towards equality between domestic and foreign labour are measured by the percentage of respondents who oppose discrimination against foreigners in the labour market. The degree of transnational trust is measured as the trust of Europeans in other Member State citizens.

In recent research, one finds numerous attempts to examine the relationship between citizens in the countries of the European Union, beyond their attitudes towards Europe and the EU. The central question for us here is also whether signs of Europeanisation can be found in these subjective orientations and perceptions. One can assume, for example, that increasing integration leads to changed perceptions of inequality. Whereas previously national boundaries obstructed the view to the outside world, these barriers to perception should now gradually be dismantled, and a European standard of comparison as well as reference groups in other European countries should increasingly play a role. Besides this aspect, we examine whether there is a fundamental acceptance of equality in status for EU citizens, which is in fact part of the political programme of the EU. Lastly, we present findings on the development of transnational trust between the peoples of Europe.

Cross-national comparisons

Europeanisation and subjective deprivation

There are indications that standards of living, as viewed by the people, are becoming increasingly subjected to cross-national comparisons and that people perceive the quality of life in their own country relative to the EU as a whole (Heidenreich, 2006b). The Eurobarometer poll of 2001 (EB 56.1), for example, shows widely varying percentages of the respective national populations who feel subjectively poor: less than 10% of those in Denmark and Luxemburg perceived themselves as poor, as compared to 41% of Italians, 54% of Greeks and 66% of Portuguese. In Portugal and Greece, more than 90% of respondents were dissatisfied with their financial situation. While it is true that income inequality in countries such as Greece and Portugal is relatively high (see Chapter 9), such a high level of subjective deprivation is nevertheless surprising. One possible explanation is that the respondents are no longer solely using national standards of comparison and national reference groups, but are also situating themselves in relation to their European neighbours (Whelan et al, 2001; Fahey and Smyth, 2004).

Reference groups

In research on inequality, it has long been assumed that the assessment of one's own living conditions occurs mainly in a national context. In a densely settled European space, it is to be expected that Europeans compare themselves and see themselves in relation to each other. From recent research, we know that people have fairly realistic ideas about where they and their country are placed in an international (European) income hierarchy, and that the sense of relative disadvantage has a negative influence on their evaluation of their own situation and satisfaction with their lives (Delhey and Kohler, 2006; Kohler, 2007). Upward comparisons are found to be more relevant than downward comparisons. This means, therefore, that it is particularly the new and poorer Member States that orient themselves on the basis of common European standards. Their citizens expect their own standards of living and levels of economic development to catch up with European standards, rather than to remain permanently behind.

Openness and equality

An important aspect of Europeanisation is the deinstitutionalisation of borders and the removal of barriers to mobility. This change is decisive, since nation-states have been divested of the ability to close off their own markets and welfare systems. This changes the relationship that EU citizens have to each other, because nationality is no longer a relevant criterion for the allocation of social and economic rights. Europeanisation means a transition away from status difference towards equality and mutual recognition (Beck and Grande, 2007). This happens primarily by granting freedom of movement in relation to place of residence, access to employment and the welfare benefits system, and principles of non-discrimination. With this development, a large number of rights formerly bound to nationality are transferred to other EU citizens. When EU citizens are resident in another EU country or have decided to settle there, they have equal rights, with the exception of certain political rights.

From the perspective of social research, the question that necessarily arises is whether the creation of equal status is finding acceptance. Using the example of equal treatment for domestic and foreign workers, Gerhards (2008) has examined whether the EU's propagation of equality is gaining recognition, and how great reservations on the question of expanding the membership area are (Figure 14.5). Using data from the European Values Survey, he is able to show that a majority of respondents reject the notion of equality of all citizens, and still distinguish between citizens of their own country and nationals of other countries. However, responses differ from country to country. In the long-standing member countries, 34% of respondents were in favour of foreigners being granted equal access to the domestic labour market, while in the EU enlargement countries support was at times below 5%. In those countries joining in 2004 the support for non-discrimination was around 12%, and in those joining in 2007 it was around 10%.

Acceptance of status equality among European citizens

With 78% in favour, Sweden is the most 'open' of all. This openness corresponds with their actual policy: together with Ireland and the UK, Sweden was one of the few countries that opened their labour markets to workers from new Member States immediately after the 2004 enlargement. Poland, Lithuania, Malta and Slovakia are at the opposite end of the spectrum, with the lowest percentages of those who agree with the notion of free access to labour markets. While these data show that the enthusiasm for opening national labour markets to foreigners is still extremely weak, revealing a discrepancy between EU policy and the preferences of its citizens, there are nevertheless countries in which the equality norm already has majority support. The marked differences between long-standing and new member countries are an indication that agreement may increase with the duration of membership. We also find status differences within the different countries, with groups with higher educational attainment exhibiting greater openness. Moreover, the younger the respondents, the greater the support for equality of citizens of different nations. In addition, at the country level, one finds a positive correlation with a country's degree of modernisation. However, the higher the unemployment in a given country, the more likely people are to argue for closure (Gerhards, 2008).

Figure 14.5: Attitudes towards equality of native and foreign job-holders

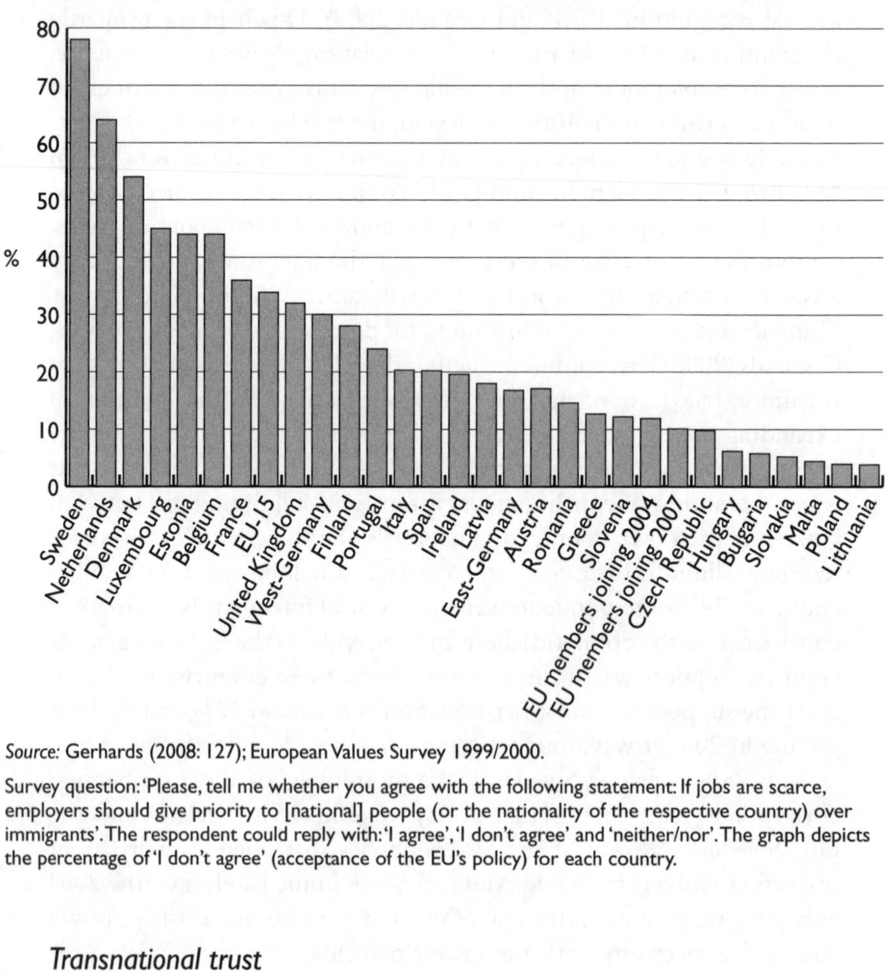

Source: Gerhards (2008: 127); European Values Survey 1999/2000.

Survey question: 'Please, tell me whether you agree with the following statement: If jobs are scarce, employers should give priority to [national] people (or the nationality of the respective country) over immigrants'. The respondent could reply with: 'I agree', 'I don't agree' and 'neither/nor'. The graph depicts the percentage of 'I don't agree' (acceptance of the EU's policy) for each country.

Transnational trust

Trust among Europeans

Another instructive perspective on 'subjective Europeanisation' is afforded by the degree of trust between the peoples of Europe. Delhey (2007) uses the term 'transnational trust' to describe the level of generalised trust in people from other Member States and sees such trust as both the basis for and a possible result of processes of supranational integration. For empirical research, transnational trust is an important indicator for assessing the quality of social relations between nations. Trust is regarded as the 'cement' of a society, because it supports willingness for cooperative action, spurs pro-social behaviour and ensures a positive relationship between partners in interaction. Trust is crucial not just in the context of national or local communities, it is also important in the context of supranational processes of integration. These processes also require positive relationships of trust between the participating nations, in order to take far-reaching steps towards political integration. This is the perspective taken by Deutsch (1966: 17):

> The populations of different territories might easily profess verbal attachment to the same set of values without having a sense of community that leads to political integration. The kind of sense of community that is relevant for integration … turned out to be rather a matter of mutual sympathy and loyalties; of 'we-feeling', trust and mutual consideration; of political identification in terms of self-images and interests; of mutually successful predictions of behaviour and of co-operative action in accordance with it.

Indeed, trust facilitates cooperation. Someone who trusts another person is, despite differences and disparities, willing to cooperate and to work together with that person.

As far as Europe is concerned, one can ask whether the relationship between Europeans is founded on mistrust, or whether the European Union can be understood as a community of trust. We can examine the question of mutual trust with the help of the European Election Study 2004. Respondents were asked to indicate from a list of nations ('the French', 'Belgians', etc) whether they trust the people of the country in question. Table 14.2 shows very clearly the gradations between the different countries. In the EU-25, respondents expressed a particularly high level of trust in Swedes, the Dutch, Danes, Spaniards and Finns. At the lower end of the rankings are countries such as Lithuania, Estonia, Latvia, Slovenia, Slovakia and Cyprus, and for the last three, the percentage of those who express little trust in them is even larger than the percentage of those who express a high level of trust. And a high percentage of respondents did not venture an opinion on people from these countries. On the whole, more trust was expressed in the EU-15 countries than in the accession states, an indication that it takes time to build up trust.

Trust growth and trust gaps

Table 14.2: Trust of Europeans in people from other European nations

Trust in people from:	A lot of trust	Not very much trust	Don't know
Sweden	68.5	15.3	16.2
Netherlands	63.0	19.4	11.7
Denmark	62.7	18.0	19.3
Spain	59.8	23.3	17.0
Finland	59.3	18.9	21.8
Germany	58.3	30.7	11.0
France	58.0	28.3	13.7
Belgium	56.4	21.8	21.8
Luxembourg	55.7	18.4	25.9
Ireland	55.3	22.7	22.0
Austria	54.5	26.4	19.1
Portugal	53.5	24.0	22.6
Italy	51.4	33.3	15.3
Greece	49.4	28.5	22.1
United Kingdom	47.0	38.0	15.0
Czech Republic	45.0	33.0	22.0
Hungary	41.9	33.3	24.7
Poland	41.8	39.6	18.6
Lithuania	36.5	34.2	29.4
Estonia	36.2	32.9	30.9
Latvia	34.9	32.6	32.5
Slovenia	34.6	36.0	29.4
Slovakia	34.5	39.1	26.3
Cyprus	31.6	33.6	35.1

Source: European Election Study 2004; own calculations. Indication as percentage of all respondents; EU-25 (no data for Malta); shown is the average trust of all respondents from the EU-25 states in the particular people/nations; the respective country was excluded from analysis; survey question: 'Now I would like to ask you a question about how much trust you have in people from various countries. Can you please tell me, for each, whether you have a lot of trust of them or not very much trust. If you do not know a country well enough, just say so and I will go on to the next'.

Within the EU-15 group, Portugal, Italy, Greece and the UK inspire lower levels of trust.

A different perspective emerges when one looks at the willingness of individual nations to trust others (not shown in the table). Delhey (2004) reports that in principle Europeans feel closer ties with their own countrymen than with other nations, usually drawing a clear boundary between their own nation and the 'others'. But within Europe there is, overall, a foundation of trust: in most EU countries, the proportion of those who express trust in other European countries is greater than the proportion of those who tend not to. Over time, transnational trust grows, but the gap between national and transnational trust remains fairly stable. Exceptions to the rule are West Germany, Belgium and Luxembourg, where there is not a great difference between the levels of trust in one's own fellow citizens and trust in other Europeans. Significant differences between levels of transnational and national trust are found in France, Italy, Denmark and Greece, but even here there is a general trend towards a higher level of cross-border trust. Generally speaking, the climate of trust among Europeans has improved over time, and trust increases with duration of EU membership. However, enlargements of the EU go hand-in-hand with a drop in the level of trust in the EU as a whole, and longer periods of consolidation and cooperation will presumably be required in order to see an increase in the level of trust in the expanded Union (Delhey, 2007).

The empirical findings clearly show that 'subjective Europeanisation' in the relationship between Europeans is becoming increasingly tangible. When it comes to equality of status and trust, while most Europeans still draw a boundary line between their own nation and other European nations, there are no more deep trenches characterised by distance and hostility. Many Europeans trust their fellow Europeans, and are willing to grant them the same rights. Most of the indicators in this area are rising with time, which suggests that the political process is leading to increasing social bonds among peoples. However, not all the findings are quite so clear. It is therefore not possible to predict whether these processes will lead over the long term to a convergence of European nations, where national differences no longer play a major role, or 'merely' to more substantive relations between nations, where the graduated distinction between one's own countrymen and other EU citizens will remain central. We also found differences between the various status groups. The tendency to embrace Europe is far more pronounced among those with higher socio-economic status, and these privileged groups are especially likely to be the bearers of subjective Europeanisation.

15

Conclusion: rise of a European society?

In this study, we set ourselves the task of describing and analysing European societies, mapping their structure and trajectories of social change. We proceeded in three steps: first, we identified the historical commonalities that bind European societies together. We then adopted a comparative perspective and, on the basis of the leitmotifs of convergence and divergence, we explored the question whether national European societies are becoming increasingly alike. In a further step, we looked into the immediate social-structural effects of Europeanisation and issues of horizontal and subjective Europeanisation. These approaches served to create a conceptual connection between the hitherto unconnected approaches of comparative research on Europe and research into European integration.

In Part 1, the central question concerned the borders of Europe **The structure** and how Europe can be understood as a territorial order. We saw that **of Europe** different factors shaped the spatial consolidation of Europe, its internal structure and its spatial hierarchy. With the emergence of nation–states and the delimitation of their territories and citizenry, a form of horizontal segmentation came into existence. This led to the establishment of separate national societies demarcated from one another – each with its own institutional arrangements, inequality regimes and forms of political regulation. Nevertheless, one can identify social-structural characteristics that are typical of Europe and can be found in many European countries, and which can be traced back to processes of modernisation and industrialisation. In global comparison, Europe today has a well-educated, urbanised, affluent population that subscribes to values such as freedom and self-realisation; it also has typically European forms of the family, employment and consumption, a redistributive welfare state, an institutionalised class compromise, a regulated labour market, a service economy, religious and political tolerance, and well-developed networks of communication and transportation (Therborn, 1995; Beck and Grande, 2007; Outhwaite, 2008; Rumford, 2009; Eigmüller and Mau, 2010; Immerfall and Therborn, 2010).

These commonalities constitute the basis of the aspirations towards **Convergence or** European integration, even though they are by no means a guarantee **divergence?** for the success of integration. In recent discussions about European integration, issues of convergence and harmonisation have been assigned an increasingly important role because it is assumed that greater disparities among – or even a divergent development of – EU Member States would hinder integration efforts. The more varied the social-structural and socio-economic conditions in member countries, the harder it is to reach agreement on further steps towards integration. In Part 2 of the book, we examined more closely the key social characteristics exhibited by European countries, and the extent to which the changes they are undergoing are making them increasingly similar over time. At the level of welfare-state, educational and industrial-relations institutions, established arrangements evince a marked persistence. At the same time, however, we find forms of convergence – for instance, in the profile of social spending (prioritising health care and old-age provision), in higher educational institutions (the Bologna Process) and in the system of industrial relations, where negotiations between employers and employees increasingly occur at the company level. In the area of population and family, one finds relatively stable differences between Southern and Northern Member States. Since the eastward enlargement, however, these differences are being overlaid by additional differences between predominantly Catholic or Orthodox Eastern European countries on the one hand, and predominantly Protestant countries on the other. These are evident in population growth, relationships between couples, life expectancy and fertility rates. What all European states have in common, however, is the trend towards an ageing society, the increasing age at which women have children, the declining importance of marriage and the rising numbers of extra-marital births.

On the migration and immigration front, we observe a reorganisation of established patterns, rather than a stabilisation or simple adaptation of these patterns. On the one hand, in recent years European migration systems have clearly become more differentiated. On the other hand, there has been an increase in intra-European migration from the new Member States into the Union's former core states, which can be regarded as an indicator of European integration. It is also evident that the European labour market has been highly dynamic in recent years. Although differences still exist across countries in terms of labour market participation or unemployment, there is evidence of convergence as well: participation of women in the labour market is increasing (especially in the south of the EU), tertiarisation has gathered momentum, and highly skilled jobs are becoming increasingly important in the occupational structure. In the area of social inequality and quality of life, on the one hand, we continue to see differences, primarily between the core EU states and the Eastern European Member States. In the latter countries, one finds a significantly higher level of social inequality at the household level, more poverty and a lower quality of life (for example, more pollution, increased health risks, poorer living conditions). On the other hand, one also finds tendencies towards equalisation. Thus, gender wage differentials are decreasing in the EU, and educational opportunities for women have improved significantly throughout the EU. Finally, younger women in Europe now have a better education than men.

If one summarises these findings, one can state that significant differences persist among European countries and that, also, in the wake of recent enlargement rounds, the variation between the EU Member States is remarkable (Alber and Gilbert, 2010). However, there are also very important developments in the direction of convergence. Especially in a global perspective, European countries display manifold affinities, for example, in the areas of family structures, labour markets, state–market relations and values. European societies are also well organised and possess a high level of internal integration, which is reflected in the relations between the social structure and political system, in industrial relations and welfare-state arrangements. Europe possesses a 'structured diversity', as Crouch (1999) has described it. This means that in Europe there is a well-ordered and circumscribed diversity of cultural traditions, values, organisational models, institutional architectures and social structures (Müller, 2007). While these are brought into close contact through the political and social process of Europeanisation, they nevertheless remain identifiable segments of a European social structure.

Beyond the question of convergence and divergence, we were interested in the extent to which intense and intricate processes of horizontal exchange are developing among European national societies. Interconnectedness within Europe and across national borders is historically not new, but the process of European integration has definitely created improved possibilities for networking, mobility and exchange. We explained how the European integration process is creating a breach in the system of nation-states and produces both horizontal and vertical connections between different national societies. In our view, there is empirical evidence that people's horizons of life and experience are being 'Europeanised'. Knowledge of Europe and new social experiences are acquired in contexts such as tourism, increasing knowledge of other European countries, education and study abroad, new forms of migration and the emergence of a European labour market, forms of transnational political mobilisation and cross-border consumption. These processes are just getting under way, but with the elimination of national borders, expanded possibilities for freedom of movement and the creation of a European labour market, Europe can be expected to constitute itself more markedly as a social space.

Horizontal Europeanisation

However, we have also shown that integration is not a harmonious process, that it involves new inequalities and dislocations. Especially important in this respect are the processes of market development and liberalisation that, under EU guidance, are influencing and reallocating the life chances of individuals and groups. The increase in regional disparities and the marketisation of living conditions are important trends in the Europeanisation process, which are creating specific groups of winners and losers. Some observers even claim that the ambition of traditional European welfare states to decommodify citizenship and to provide encompassing means of integration is waning and that European countries may become more similar to the United States by adopting more liberal features (Alber and Gilbert, 2010; Münch, 2010). Also, despite the increasing involvement of national populations in the process of Europeanisation, it is evident that Europe is creating more pronounced polarisation between elites and 'ordinary citizens' (Fligstein, 2008; Haller, 2008). As far as attitudes towards different aspects of Europeanisation are concerned, it is likewise apparent that different socio-structural groups position themselves differently. Europe emerges as an important line of conflict within national European societies: as a dispute over openness and closure, over supranational integration versus the isolation of the nation-state. It is a conflict between those who hope for social and economic benefits from Europe and those who continue to direct their expectations towards the nation-state, whether for economic, social or cultural reasons.

In the context of the processes of de-nationalisation, transnationalisation and supranationalisation, we view Europe as an important new level of aggregation that is gaining in autonomy and significance (cf. Müller, 2007). Europe is thus situated between the 'global' level (circumscribed by concepts such as globalisation and global society) and the level of the national society or the nation-state. Europe's social structure now is more than the sum of its parts: it is an emergent, discrete, macro-societal formation. Important preconditions and driving forces of its emergence lie, on the one hand, in its common values, traditions and shared history (see Part 1) and, on the other hand, in the politically initiated integration process, which affects large sectors of society. Core elements in the formation of a European social structure are those we have mentioned: structured diversity, processes of convergence and divergence, and horizontal links between national societies. These three factors are decisive in the formation of a European social structure. They are fundamental to the degree of internal homogeneity, the emergence of a shared social space and the density of social ties among national European societies.

If one takes the Europeanisation of European societies seriously, then researchers will also need to be conceptually innovative – for example, when setting appropriate standards of reference, comparison and measurement (Rainwater, 1992). Nation-states still constitute the main level at which social inequality is studied, and measures of inequality, such as the Gini coefficient, are also applied at the national level. This raises the question, however, whether the measurement of inequality within the European Union should not refer to overall distributions. This would mean, for example, comparing not just the GDP of different countries or regions, but also distributions of personal income within the European

Union, in the sense of an EU–Gini. In the field of poverty measurement, there are some initial proposals towards European reporting on poverty, using European mean income as a basis (Atkinson, 1998; Fahey, 2005). A Europeanised perspective is also required in order to describe social-structural groupings, positions and forms of mobility, or the determinants of inequality. To achieve this, there is a need for more concerted efforts by social scientists in different European countries in order to take account of national specificities on the one hand, and, on the other hand, to facilitate a comprehensive view of Europe as a whole.

Figure 15.1: European society formation

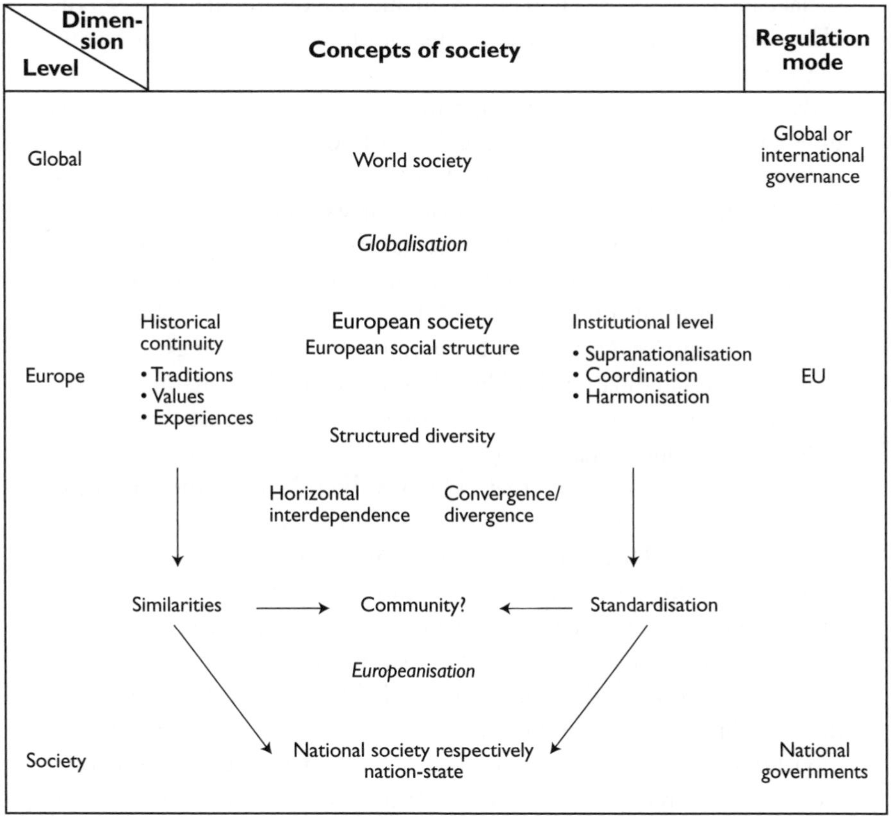

Source: Extension of a figure by Müller (2007: 24).

The overarching question is whether it is actually legitimate to speak in terms of a European society, and, if so, how the latter might be characterised (Delanty and Rumford, 2005; Bach, 2008; Fligstein, 2008; Martinelli, 2008; Eigmüller and Mau, 2010). Is Europe on a development path that resembles that of the nation-state in some way? In the literature, there are sceptical as well as optimistic voices to be heard. The sceptics argue that national identities, self-interest and closure will continue to

A European society?

dominate in Europe, that there is no discernible collective subject that would even remotely justify talk of a European people or a European society. In fact, the difficulties of further integration can be attributed above all to the 'success' of the nation-states, according to the sceptics. The nation-states are seen as possessing a strong capacity to assert themselves and are able to fend off competing claims to the exercise of political functions. In key areas such as foreign policy, social policy and education policy, the nation-state has remained the primary addressee. The inertia of national traditions and institutions is seen as too strong. More than that, a European Union that assumes additional powers is in danger of becoming a detached, technocratic structure lacking a corresponding social base. Thus, sceptics perceive an ineluctable divergence between the elites, who have their sights set on integration, and the broad mainstream of the population.

United States of Europe?   By contrast, optimists argue that in Europe we are witnessing social integration that is following in the wake of political integration, similar to the process that characterised the emergence of nation-states. Neo-functionalist integration theories, for example, have argued that integration in certain political and social areas results in integration in other areas, that there can be spillover effects (Haas, 1968). Nation-states were also not built on a pre-political sense of community, but rather national identity and a sense of belonging developed only as a result of politically initiated nation-building. Political centralisation, the creation of national institutions, democratic participation, national symbols, an independent educational canon, territorial boundaries and integrity – these were all developments that only subsequently led to the formation of national societies, with their own social structures and forms of internal communication. Therefore, the question regarding European society is closely tied to the development of the European institutional system and further steps towards integration. Seen from this perspective, a process of 'Europe-building' analogous to that of 'nation-building' is not to be ruled out. It would involve developments parallel to those that characterised the founding of the United States, such as successive expansions and modalities of accession, the role of internal homogenisation of the market, a common currency and the courts. If the European Union is on the way to becoming a federal state, one can assume that a shift will occur in the long-term orientations and expectations of the citizens, but also in the way the society is organised and structured. Concerning the latter, convergence and greater cohesion would necessarily need to dominate the centrifugal forces of divergence and conflicts. However, as we have demonstrated, the overall picture of the mid-term socio-structural development is far from being clear-cut and growing similarities exist alongside ongoing or even intensifying differences between the European countries (see Part 2).

But one can ask whether the comparison between Europe and its nation-states is at all meaningful. Europe is an entity *sui generis*, which means that it has specific characteristics that are inadequately represented in the comparison with the nation-states. At the same time, Europe is more than the sum of its parts. If we raise the question of European society or of a European social structure, we continue to employ the yardstick of the spatially and socially integrated national society. This implies a certain conception of space, a people, inclusion, identity, belonging and internal communication. But the reality is that Europe will neither attain a degree of integration equivalent to that of national societies, nor will it replace the old national societies. Moreover, Europe is endowed with a number of characteristics that stand in the way of the analogy with national societies.

An important feature of social Europe that deserves to be highlighted is the multi-level structure of political decision-making, social loyalties, allegiances and identities. Whereas the nation-state was in a position to carry out clear acts of inclusion and exclusion, this is not possible in Europe. On the one hand, Europe presents itself as a complementary space of inclusion, as an addition to the existing space of the Member States; on the other hand, the political order is characterised by a distribution of various powers acting at various levels. The political system of the European Union is organised through the allocation and 'nesting' of different levels of political action, namely the European, the national and the subnational levels (Hooghe and Marks, 2001). At the social level, this is reflected in feelings of connectedness and solidarity, and in questions dealing with levels of identification. *[Multi-level structure]*

Another key point is that Europe does not have clear borders, and it is not realistic to expect the EU to develop into a sovereign socio-political union with clearly demarcated political, social and economic boundaries (Beck and Grande, 2007). Rather, because of the special political and social configuration of the European Union, its outer borders will be more diffuse than those of the traditional nation-state: *[Variability and fluidity]*

> The integration process disjoins the hitherto overlapping and coinciding economic, cultural and politico-administrative boundaries of the state, but seems unable to reproduce some new forms of closure and overlapping boundaries at its own level. (Bartolini, 2005: 375)

This is reflected above all in the concentric border structures, brought about by various levels of integration within the EU and specific forms of association with countries outside the European Union. Another particularity of the European Union is its shifting external borders (Vobruba, 2003). The issue of the final borders of Europe is highly contentious and has yet to be resolved, so that the variability of the external borders of Europe will remain an important feature for decades to come (Zielonka, 2002). The EU thus presents itself as a social entity that, alongside all the tendencies towards fortification, is fraying at the edges. Thus, one can assume that, for this social formation, it is not the Westphalian model of a federation – a model predicated on a sharp distinction between inside and outside – that is coming into play. Rather, a neo-medieval structure is developing, which is less marked by concrete borders, centralisation and hierarchical organisation, but rather by overlapping authorities, divided sovereignties and fuzzy boundaries (cf. Wæver, 1997; Zielonka, 2001). In comparison with the borders of nation-states, this means more variability and less unity and homogeneity.

These are all preliminary answers to the question of the formation of European society and its relation to national societies as we know them. With regard to the contours of the Europeanisation of social integration, the next steps towards integration are crucial, because they will bring about a long-term change in the national institutional arrangements. Development of the market, integration through law and politics, expansion, social interconnectedness, community-building, processes of convergence and divergence, horizontal and vertical Europeanisation, and solidarity will all be different facets of these processes. Observing and analysing them in detail is the central task to be taken on in the coming years by social stratification research focused on Europe and Europeanisation. We hope that this book provides some relevant first approaches on this front.

References

Abromeit, H. (1998) *Democracy in Europe. Legitimising Politics in a Non-State Polity*, New York: Berghahn.

Acemoglu, D. (2002) 'Technical Change, Inequality, and the Labor Market', *Journal of Economic Literature*, 40, 1, pp 7–72.

Agnew, J. and Corbridge, S. (1995) *Mastering Space. Hegemony, Territory and International Political Economy*, London: Routledge.

Aguirre, A. and Turner, J. (2007) *American Ethnicity: The Dynamics and Consequences of Discrimination* (4th Edition), New York: McGraw-Hill.

Ahlström, S. et al (2001) 'Gender Differences in Drinking Patterns in Nine European Countries. Descriptive Findings', *Substance Abuse*, 22, 1, pp 69–85.

Aidukaite, J. (2006) 'The Formation of Social Insurance Institutions of the Baltic States in the Post-Socialist Era', *Journal of European Social Policy*, 16, 3, pp 259–70.

Aidukaite, J. (2009) 'The Welfare System of Lithuania', in Schubert, K. et al (eds) *The Handbook of European Welfare Systems*, London: Routledge, pp 294–309.

Alba, R. (2008) 'Why We Still Need a Theory of Mainstream Assimilation', in Kalter, F. (ed) *Migration und Integration. Sonderheft. 48 der KZfSS*, Wiesbaden: VS, pp 37–56.

Alba, R. and Nee, V. (1997) 'Rethinking Assimilation Theory for a New Era of Immigration', *International Migration Review*, 31, 4, pp 826–74.

Alber, J. (1982) *Vom Armenhaus zum Wohlfahrtsstaat. Analysen zur Entwicklung der Sozialversicherung in Westeuropa*, Frankfurt/Main: Campus.

Alber, J. and Gilbert, N. (eds) (2010) *United in Diversity? Comparing Social Models in Europe and America*, Oxford: Oxford University Press.

Alber, J. et al (2008a) 'EU Enlargement and Quality Of Life', in Alber, J. et al (eds) *Handbook of Quality of Life in the Enlarged European Union*, London: Routledge, pp 1–24.

Alber, J. et al (2008b) *Handbook of Quality of Life in the Enlarged European Union*, London: Routledge.

Alderson, A.S. and Nielsen, F. (2002) 'Globalization and the Great U-Turn: Income Inequality Trends in 16 OECD Countries', *American Journal of Sociology*, 107, 5, pp 1244–99.

Aliaga, C. (2006) *How is the Time of Women and Men Distributed in Europe?*, Eurostat, Luxembourg.

Aliaga, C. and Winqvist, K. (2003) *Time Use at Different Stages of Life. Results from 13 European Countries*, Luxembourg: Office for Official Publications of the European Communities.

Allardt, E. (1976) 'Dimensions of Welfare in a Comparative Scandinavian Study', *Acta Sociologica*, 19, 3, pp 227–39.

Allardt, E. (1993) 'Having, Loving, Being. An Alternative to the Swedish Model of Welfare Research', in Nussbaum, M.C. and Sen, A. (eds) *The Quality of Life*, Oxford: Clarendon, pp 88–94.

Allmendinger, J. (1989) *Career Mobility Dynamics. A Comparative Analysis of the United States, Norway, and West Germany*, Berlin: Edition Sigma.

Allmendinger, J. and Hinz, T. (1998) 'Occupational Careers under Different Welfare Regimes: West Germany, Great Britain and Sweden', in Leisering, L. and Walker, R. (eds) *The Dynamics of Modern Society: Poverty, Policy and Welfare*, Bristol: The Policy Press, pp 63–84.

Allmendinger, J. and Hinz, T. (2009) 'Occupational Careers under Different Welfare Regimes: West Germany, Great Britain and Sweden', in Heinz, W. et al (eds) *The Life Course Reader. Individuals and Societies across Time*, Frankfurt/Main: Campus, pp 234–51.

Allmendinger, J. and Leibfried, S. (2003) 'Education and the Welfare State. The Four Worlds of Competence Production', *Journal of European Social Policy*, 13, 1, pp 63–81.

Allmendinger, J. et al (2010) 'Education in Europe and the Lisbon Benchmarks', in Alber, J. and Gilbert, N. (eds) *United in Diversity? Comparing Social Models in Europe and America*, Oxford: Oxford University Press, pp 308–27.

Allum, P. (1995) *State and Society in Western Europe*, Cambridge: Polity.

Alvaredo, F. and Saez, E. (2009) 'Income and wealth concentration in Spain from a historical and fiscal perspective', *Journal of the European Economic Association*, 7, 5, pp 1140–67.

Alvarez, R. (2002) 'Attitudes Toward the European Union. The Role of Social Class, Social Stratification, and Political Orientation', *International Journal of Sociology*, 32, 1, pp 58–76.

Alwin, D.F. et al (2006) 'Modeling the Effects of Time. Integrating Demographic and Developmental Perspectives', in Binstock, R.H. et al (eds) *The Handbook of Aging and the Social Sciences*, London: Academic Press, pp 20–38.

Amit, V. (2002) 'The Moving "Expert". A Study of Mobile Professionals in the Cayman Islands and North America', in Sørensen, N.N. and Olwig, K.F. (eds) *Work and Migration. Life and Livelihoods in a Globalizing World*, London: Routledge, pp 145–60.

Amuedo-Dorantes, C. and Rica, S.D.L. (2007) 'Labour Market Assimilation of Recent Immigrants in Spain', *British Journal of Industrial Relations*, 45, 2, pp 257–84.

Andersen, J.J. (1995) 'Structural Funds and the Social Dimension of EU Policy. Springboard or Stumbling Block', in Leibfried, S. and Pierson, P. (eds) *European Social Policy. Between Fragmentation and Integration*, Washington D.C.: Brookings, pp 123–58.

Anderson, C.J. and Kaltenthaler, K.C. (1996) 'The Dynamics of Public Opinion toward European Integration 1973–93', *European Journal of International Relations*, 2, 2, pp 175–99.

Anderson, C. and Reichert, M.S. (1996) 'Economic Benefits and Support for Membership in the EU. A Cross-National Analysis', *Journal of Public Policy*, 15, 3, pp 231–49.

Anderson, R. et al (2009) *Second European Quality of Life Survey. Overview*, Dublin: European Foundation for the Improvement of Living and Working Conditions.

Andrén, D. and Andrén, T. (2007) *Occupational Gender Composition and Wages in Romania: From Planned Equality to Market Inequality? IZA DP No. 3152*, Bonn: IZA.

Anttila, T. et al (2009) 'Predictors of Time Famine among Finnish Employees. Work, Family, or Leisure?', *Electronic International Journal of Time Use Research*, 6, 1, pp 67–86.

Appelbaum, E. and Schettkat, R. (1994) 'The End of Full Employment? On Economic Development in Industrialized Countries', *Intereconomics*, 29, 3, pp 122–30.

Armstrong, H.W. (1995) 'Convergence among Regions of the European Union, 1950–1990', *Papers in Regional Science*, 74, 1, pp 143–52.

Armstrong, H.W. and Taylor, P. (2000) *Regional Economics and Policy*, Oxford: Blackwell.

Aron, R. (1961) *18 Lectures on Industrial Society*, London: Weidenfeld & Nicolson.

Arrowsmith, J. and Marginson, P. (2006) 'The European Cross-border Dimension to Collective Bargaining in Multinational Companies', *European Journal of Industrial Relations*, 12, 3, pp 245–66.

Arts, W.A. and Gelissen, J. (2002) 'Three Worlds of Welfare Capitalism or More? A State-of-the-Art Report', *Journal of European Social Policy*, 12, 2, pp 137–58.

Arza, C. and Kohli, M. (eds) (2008) *Pension Reform in Europe: Politics, Policies and Outcomes*, London: Routledge.

Åslund, A. (2002) *Building Capitalism. The Transformation of the Former Soviet Bloc*, Cambridge: Cambridge University Press.

Atkinson, A.B. (1998) *Poverty in Europe*, Oxford: Blackwell.

Atkinson, A.B. (2000) 'The Changing Distribution of Income: Evidence and Explanations', *German Economic Review*, 1, 1, pp 3–18.

Atkinson, A.B. (2003) 'Income Inequality in OECD Countries: Data and Explanations', *CESifo Economic Studies*, 49, 4, pp 479–513.

Atkinson, A.B. and Harrison, A.J. (1978) *Distribution of Personal Wealth in Britain*, Cambridge: Cambridge University Press.

Atzmüller, R. and Hermann, C. (2004) *Liberalisierung öffentlicher Dienstleistungen in der EU und Österreich. Auswirkungen auf Beschäftigung, Arbeitsbedingungen und Arbeitsbeziehungen*, Wien: Arbeiterkammer.

Autor, D. H. et al (2006) *The Polarization of the US Labor Market. NBER Working Paper No. 11986*, New York: City University of New York.

Ayres, R. and Barber, T. (2006) *Statistical Analysis of Female Migration and Labour Market Integration in the EU*, Oxford: Oxford Brookes University.

Azmat, G. et al (2006) 'Gender Gaps in Unemployment Rates in OECD Countries', *Journal of Labor Economics*, 24, 1, pp 1–37.

Baars, J. et al (eds) (2006) *Ageing, Globalization, and Inequality. The New Critical Gerontology*, Amityville, NY: Baywood.

Bach, M. (1999) *Die Bürokratisierung Europas. Verwaltungseliten, Experten und politische Legitimation in Europa*, Frankfurt/Main: Campus.

Bach, M. (2000) 'Die Europäisierung der nationalen Gesellschaft? Problemstellungen und Perspektiven einer Soziologie der europäischen Integration', in Bach, M. (ed) *Die Europäisierung nationaler Gesellschaften. KZfSS Sonderheft 40*, Wiesbaden: Westdeutscher Verlag, pp 11–38.

Bach, M. (2008) *Europa ohne Gesellschaft. Politische Soziologie der europäischen Integration*, Wiesbaden: VS Verlag.

Bach, M. et al (eds) (2006) *Europe in Motion. Social Dynamics and Political Institutions in an Enlarging Europe*, Berlin: Edition Sigma.

Bäcker, G. et al (2008) *Sozialpolitik und soziale Lage in Deutschland. Band 1: Grundlagen, Arbeit, Einkommen und Finanzierung*, Wiesbaden: VS.

Bade, K.J. (1987) *Population, Labour and Migration in 19th and 20th Century Germany*, Leamington: Berg.

Bade, K.J. (2003) *Migration in European History*, Oxford: Blackwell.

Bade, K.J. and Oltmer, J. (2011: forthcoming) 'Germany', in Bade, K.J. et al (eds) *The Encyclopaedia of Migration*, Cambridge: Cambridge University Press.

Bade, K. et al (eds) (2011: forthcoming) *The Encyclopaedia of Migration*, Cambridge: Cambridge University Press.

Bahle, T. (2008) 'Family Policy Patterns in the Enlarged EU', in Alber, J. et al (eds) *Handbook of Quality of Life in the Enlarged European Union*, London: Routledge, pp 100–25.

Bahle, T. et al (2010) 'Welfare State', in Immerfall, S. and Therborn, G. (eds) *Handbook of European Societies. Social Transformations in the 21st Century*, Dodrecht: Springer, pp 571–628.

Baldi, S. et al (2007) *Highlights From PISA 2006: Performance of US 15-Year-Old Students in Science and Mathematics Literacy in an International Context. National Center for Education Statistics, Institute of Education Sciences*, Washington, D.C.: US Department of Education.

Baldock, J. (2009) 'Social Policy, Social Welfare, and the Welfare State', in Baldock, J. et al (eds) *Social Policy (3rd Edition)*, Oxford: Oxford University Press, pp 5–30.

Baldock, J. et al (eds) (2009) *Social Policy (3rd Edition)*, Oxford: Oxford University Press.

Baldwin, P. (1990) *The Politics of Social Solidarity: Class Bases of the European Welfare State 1875–1975*, Cambridge: Cambridge University Press.

Baldwin, P. (2010) *The Narcissism of Minor Differences. How Unlike Each Other are America and Europe?*, Oxford: Oxford University Press.

Balibar, É. (ed) (2004) *We, The People of Europe. Reflections on Transnational Citizenship*, Princeton: Princeton University Press.

Ballarino, G. et al (2009) 'Persistent Inequalities? Expansion of Education and Class Inequality in Italy and Spain', *European Sociological Review*, 25, 1, pp 123–38.

Bank of Slovenia (2009) *Annual Report 2008*, Ljubljana: Bank of Slovenia.

Barr, N. (2004) *The Economics of the Welfare State*, Oxford: Oxford University Press.

Barrett, A. et al (2006) 'The Labour Market Characteristics and Labour Market Impacts of Immigrants in Ireland', *Economic and Social Review*, 37, 1, pp 1–26.

Barro, R.J. and Sala-i-Martin, X. (1992) 'Convergence', *Journal of Political Economy*, 100, 2, pp 223–51.

Bartolini, S. (2000) *The Political Mobilization of the European Left 1860–1980. The Class Cleavage*, Cambridge: Cambridge University Press.

Bartolini, S. (2005) *Restructuring Europe: Centre Formation, System Building and Political Structuring between the Nation-state and the European Union*, Oxford: Oxford University Press.

Bartolini, S. and Mair, P. (1990) *Identity, Competition, and Electoral Availability. The Stabilization of European Electorates 1885–1985*, Cambridge: Cambridge University Press.

Bauer, T. and Zimmermann, K.F. (1997) 'Network Migration of Ethnic Germans', *International Migration Review*, 31, 1, pp 143–9.

Baumert, J. and Schümer, G. (2001) 'Familiäre Lebensverhältnisse, Bildungsbeteiligung und Kompetenzerwerb', in Baumert, J. et al (eds) *PISA 2000. Basiskompetenzen von Schülerinnen und Schülern im internationalen Vergleich*, Opladen: Leske + Budrich, pp 323–407.

Baumert, J. et al (eds) (2001) *PISA 2000. Basiskompetenzen von Schülerinnen und Schülern im internationalen Vergleich*, Opladen: Leske + Budrich.

Baumol, W.J. (1967) *Welfare Economics and the Theory of the State*, London: Bell.

Bazant, U. and Schubert, K. (2009) 'European Welfare Systems: Diversity beyond Existing Categories', in Schubert, K. et al (eds) *The Handbook of European Welfare Systems*, London: Routledge, pp 513–34.

Beaverstock, J.V. (2005) 'Transnational Elites in the City. British Highly-Skilled Inter-Company Transferees in New York City's Financial District', *Journal of Ethnic and Migration Studies*, 31, 2, pp 245–68.

Bechmann, G. et al (2007) 'Technology Assessment in a Complex World', *International Journal of Foresight and Innovation Policy*, 3, 1, pp 6–27.

Beck, U. (1992) *Risk Society. Towards a New Modernity*, London: Sage.

Beck, U. (1999) *The World Risk Society*, Oxford: Blackwell.

Beck, U. (2007) 'Beyond Class and Nation: Reframing Social Inequalities in a Globalizing World', *British Journal of Sociology*, 58, 4, pp 679–705.

Beck, U. and Beck-Gernsheim, E. (2004) 'Families in a Runaway World', in Scott, J. et al (eds) *The Blackwell Companion to the Sociology of Families*, Oxford: Blackwell, pp 499–514.

Beck, U. and Grande, E. (2007) *Cosmopolitan Europe*, Cambridge: Polity Press.

Becker, G.S. (1964) *Human Capital. A Theoretical and Empirical Analysis, with Special Reference to Education*, New York: Columbia University Press.

Becker, G.S. (1971) *The Economics of Discrimination*, Chicago, IL: University of Chicago Press.

Becker, G.S. (1981) *A Treatise on the Family*, Cambridge, MA: Harvard University Press.

Becker, R. and Lauterbach, W. (2007) 'Bildung als Privileg – Ursachen, Mechanismen, Prozesse und Wirkungen', in Becker, R. and Lauterbach, W. (eds) *Bildung als Privileg. Erklärungen und Befunde zur Ursachen der Bildungsungleichheit*, Wiesbaden: VS, pp 9–41.

Beckfield, J. (2006) 'European Integration and Income Inequality', *American Journal of Sociology*, 71, pp 964–85.

Beckfield, J. (2009) 'Remapping Inequality in Europe: The Net Effect of Regional Integration on Total Income Inequality in the European Union', *International Journal of Comparative Sociology*, 50, 5, pp 1–24.

Beichelt, T. (2004) *Die Europäische Union nach der Osterweiterung*, Wiesbaden: VS.

Beilock, R. and Dimitrova, D.V. (2003) 'An Exploratory Model of Inter-country Internet Diffusion', *Telecommunications Policy*, 27, 3–4, pp 237–52.

Bell, D. (1973) *The Coming of Post-industrial Society. A Venture in Social Forecasting*, New York: Basic Book.

Bender, S. and Seifert, W. (1998) 'Migrants in the German Labour Market', in Kurthen, H. et al (eds) *Immigration, Citizenship, and the Welfare State in Germany and the United States*, London: Jai, pp 95–117.

Bengtson, V.L. et al (2006a) 'The Lifecourse Perspective on Ageing: Linked Lives, Timing and History', in Johnson, M.L. et al (eds) *The Cambridge Handbook of Age and Ageing*, Cambridge: Cambridge University Press, pp 493–501.

Bengtson, V.L. et al (2006b) 'Self and Identity', in Johnson, M.L. et al (eds) *The Cambridge Handbook of Age and Ageing*, Cambridge: Cambridge University Press, pp 3–20.

Bengtson, V.L. et al (2009a) 'Theory about Age and Aging', in Bengtson, V.L. et al (eds) *Handbook of Theories of Aging (2nd Edition)*, New York: Springer.

Bengtson, V.L. et al (eds) (2009b) *Handbook of Theories of Aging (2nd Edition)*, New York: Springer.

Benjamin, D. et al (2007) *Labour Market Economics (6th Edition)*, Toronto: McGraw-Hill.

Berglund, S. and Ekman, J. (2010) 'Cleavages and Political Transformations', in Immerfall, S. and Therborn, G. (eds) *Handbook of European Societies. Social Transformations in the 21st Century*, Dodrecht: Springer, pp 91–109.

Bermeo, N. (eds) (2001) *Unemployment in the New Europe*, New York: Cambridge University Press.

Bernardes, J. (1997) *Family Studies – An Introduction*, London: Routledge.

Bernardi, F. and Nazio, T. (2005) 'Globalization and the Transition to Adulthood in Italy', in Blossfeld, H.-P. et al (eds) *Globalization, Uncertainty, and Youth in Society*, London: Routledge, pp 359–84.

Bernardi, F. et al (2000) 'Who Exits Unemployment? Institutional Features, Individual Characteristics and Chances of Getting a Job. A Comparison of Britain and Italy', in Gallie, D. and Paugam, S. (eds) *Welfare Regimes and the Experience of Unemployment in Europe*, Oxford: Oxford University Press, pp 218–39.

Bernhardt, A. et al (1995) 'Women's Gain or Men's Losses? A Closer Look at the Shrinking Gender Gap in Earnings', *American Journal of Sociology*, 101, 2, pp 302–28.

Bertagna, F. and Maccari-Clayton, M. (2011: forthcoming) 'Italy', in Bade, K.J. et al (eds) *The Encyclopaedia of Migration*, Cambridge: Cambridge University Press.

Bertaux, D. and Kohli, M. (1984) 'The Life Story Approach. A Continental View', *Annual Review of Sociology*, 10, pp 215–37.

Bertola, G. et al (2007) 'Labor Market Institutions and Demographic Employment Patterns', *Journal of Population Economics*, 20, 4, pp 833–67.

Best, S. (2010) *Leisure Studies. Themes and Perspectives*, London etc.: Sage.

Beyer, J. (2010) 'The Same or Not the Same – On the Variety of Mechanisms of Path Dependence', *International Journal of Social Sciences*, 5, 1, pp 1–11.

Beynon, H. and Nichols , T. (2006) *Patterns of Work in the Post-Fordist Era*, Cheltenham: Edward Elgar.

Biagi, F. and Lucifora, C. (2008) 'Demographic and Education Effects on Unemployment in Europe', *Labour Economics*, 15, 5, pp 1076–101.

Billari, F.C. (2005a) 'Europe and its Fertility: From Low to Lowest Low', *National Institute Economic Review*, 194, 1, pp 56–73.

Billari, F.C. (2005b) 'Partnership, Childbearing, and Parenting. Trends of the 1990s', in Macura, M. et al (eds) *The New Demographic Regime. Population Challenges and Policy Responses*, New York: UNECE, pp 63–94.

Binstock, R.H. et al (eds) (2006) *Handbook of Aging and the Social Sciences*, London: Academic Press.

Bird, C.E. and Rieker, P.P. (2008) *Gender and Health*, Cambridge: Cambridge University Press.

Bireley, R. (2009) 'Early-modern Catholicism as a Response to the Changing World of the Long Sixteenth Century', *Catholic Historical Review*, 95, 2, pp 219–39.

Blanchard, O. (2006) 'European Unemployment. The Evolution of Facts and Ideas', *Economic Policy*, 21, 45, pp 5–59.

Blanden, J. and Gregg, P. (2004) 'Family Income and Educational Attainment: A Review of Approaches and Evidence for Britain', *Oxford Review of Economic Policy*, 20, 2, pp 245–63.

Blank, R.H. and Burau, V. (2007) *Comparative Health Policy*, Houndmills, Basingstoke: Palgrave Macmillan.

Blaszczynski, E.M. (2009) *From Crisis to Recovery: Central Europe's Winners and Losers*, Washingston D.C.: Center for European Policy Analysis.

Blau, F.D. and Kahn, L.M. (2003) 'Understanding International Differences in the Gender Pay Gap', *Journal of Labor Economics*, 21, 1, pp 106–44.

Blau, P.M. and Duncan, O.D. (1967) *The American Occupational Structure*, New York: Plenum.

Blaut, J.M. (1993) *The Colonizer's Model of the World: Geographical Diffusionism and Eurocentric History*, New York: The Guilford Press.

Blossfeld, H.-P. (1986) 'Career Opportunities in the Federal Republic of Germany. A Dynamic Approach to the Study of Life-Course, Cohort, and Period Effects', *European Sociological Review*, 2, 3, pp 208–25.

Blossfeld, H.-P. and Hakim, C. (eds) (1997) *Between Equalization and Marginalization: Women Working Part-Time in Europe and the United States of America*, Oxford: Clarendon.

Blossfeld, H.-P. and Hofmeister, H. (eds) (2006a) *Globalization, Uncertainty and Women's Careers*, Cheltenham: Edward Elgar.

Blossfeld, H.-P. and Hofmeister, H. (2006b) 'Women's Careers in an Era of Uncertainty. Conclusions from a 13-Country International Comparison', in Blossfeld, H.-P. and Hofmeister, H. (eds) *Globalization, Uncertainty, and Women's Careers*, Cheltenham: Edward Elgar, pp 433–50.

Blossfeld, H.-P. and Huinink, J. (2006) 'Life Course Research in the Social Sciences: Topics, Conceptions, Methods, and Problems', *The Journal of Sociology and Social Anthropology*, 9, pp 15–44.

Blossfeld, H.-P. and Mayer, K.U. (1988) 'Labor Market Segmentation in the Federal Republic of Germany: An Empirical Study of Segmentation Theories from a Life Course Perspective', *European Sociological Review*, 4, 2, pp 123–40.

Blossfeld, H.-P. et al (eds) (2005) *Globalization, Uncertainty and Youth in Society*, London: Routledge.

Blossfeld, H.-P. et al (eds) (2006) *Globalization, Uncertainty and Men's Careers*, Cheltenham: Edward Elgar.

Blotevogel, H.H. et al (1993) 'From Itinerant Worker to Immigrant? The Geography of Guestworkers in Germany', in King, R. (ed) *Mass Migration in Europe*, London: Belhaven Press, pp 83–100.

Blume, K. et al (2007) 'At the Lower End of the Table: Determinants of Poverty among Immigrants to Denmark and Sweden', *Journal of Ethnic and Migration Studies*, 33, 3, pp 373–96.

Blyton, P. et al (eds) (2010) *Ways of Living: Work, Community and Lifestyle Choice*, New York: Palgrave Macmillan.

BMAS (2005) *Lebenslagen in Deutschland. Der 2. Armuts- und Reichtumsbericht der Bundesregierung*, Berlin: Bundesministerium für Arbeit und Soziales.

BMAS (2008) *Lebenslagen in Deutschland. Der 3. Armuts- und Reichtumsbericht der Bundesregierung*, Berlin: Bundesministerium für Arbeit und Soziales.

Bobak, M. and Feachem, R.G.A. (1995) 'Air Pollution and Mortality in Central and Eastern Europe. An Estimate of the Impact', *European Journal of Public Health*, 5, 2, pp 82–6.

Bögenhold, D. (2001) 'Social Inequality and the Sociology of Life Style', *Material and Cultural Aspects of Social Stratification*, 60, 4, pp 829–47.

Böhnke, P. and Kohler, U. (2010) 'Well-Being and Inequality', in Immerfall, S. and Therborn, G. (eds) *Handbook of European Societies. Social Transformations in the 21st Century*, Dodrecht: Springer, pp 629–66.

Boje, T. (1996) 'Welfare State Models in Comparative Research: Do the Models Describe the Reality?', in Greve, B. (ed) *Comparative Welfare Systems*, Basingstoke: Macmillan, pp 13–28.

Boje, T.P. et al (eds) (1999) *European Societies. Fusion or Fission?*, London: Routledge.

Bond, J. et al (eds) (1993) *Ageing in Society. An Introduction to Social Gerontology*, London: Sage.

Bonoli, G. (1997) 'Classifying Welfare States. A Two-Dimension Approach', *Journal of Social Policy*, 26, 3, pp 351–72.

Bonoli, G. and Shinkawa, T. (eds) (2005) *Ageing and Pension Reform Around the World. Evidence from Eleven Countries*, Cheltenham: Edward Elgar.

Bornschier, V. et al (2004) 'Political and Economic Logic of Western European Integration. A Study of Convergence Comparing Member and Non-member States, 1980–98', *European Societies*, 6, 1, pp 71–96.

Borzeda, A. (2002) *Do Health Professionals from Candidate Countries Plan to Migrate? The Case of Hungary, Poland, and the Czech Republic*, Paris: Ministry of Social Affairs, Labour and Solidarity.

Bosch, N. et al (2010) 'Is Part-time Employment Here to Stay? Working Hours of Dutch Women over Successive Generations', *Labour*, 24, 1, pp 35–54.

Boudon, R. (1974) *Education, Opportunity and Social Inequality*, New York: John Wiley.

Bourdieu, P. (1984) *Distinction: A Social Critique of the Judgement of Taste*, London: Routledge.

Bourdieu, P. and Passeron, J.-C. (1970) *La reproduction. Eléments pour une théorie du système d'enseignement*, Paris: Minuit.

Bouwen, P. (2002) 'Corporate Lobbying in the European Union. The Logic of Access', *Journal of European Public Policy*, 9, 3, pp 365–90.

Bovagnet, F.-C. (2006a) *How Europeans Go on Holiday*, Luxembourg: Eurostat.

Bovagnet, F.-C. (2006b) *Inbound and Outbound Tourism in the European Union*, Luxembourg: Eurostat.

Bracht, O. et al (2006) *The Professional Value of Erasmus Mobility*, Kassel: International Centre for Higher Education Research, Universität Kassel.

Bradatan, C. and Firebaugh, G. (2007) 'History, Population Policies, and Fertility Decline in Eastern Europe. A Case Study', *Journal of Family History*, 32, 2, pp 179–92.

Bradbury, B. et al (eds) (2001) *The Dynamics of Child Poverty in Industrialised Countries*, Cambridge: Cambridge University Press.

Bradley, H. (1996) *Fractural Identities. Changing Patterns of Inequality*, Cambridge: Polity Press.

Bradshaw, J. (2006) *A Review of the Comparative Evidence on Child Poverty*, York: Joseph Rowntree Foundation/University of York.

Brandolini, A. et al (2004) *Household Wealth Distribution in Italy in the 1990s*, Rome: Bank of Italy.

Brauns, H. et al (1997) *Educational Expansion and Returns to Education. A Comparative Study on Germany, France, the UK, and Hungary. MZES Working Paper No. 23*, Mannheim: MZES.

Braverman, H. (1998 [1974]) *Labor and Monopoly Capital: The Degradation of Work in the Twentieth Century*, New York: Monthly Review Press.

Breen, R. (1997) 'Risk, Recommodification and Stratification', *Sociology*, 31, 3, pp 473–89.

Breen, R. (ed) (2004) *Social Mobility in Europe*, Oxford: Oxford University Press.

Breen, R. and Jonsson, J.O. (2005) 'Inequality of Opportunity in Comparative Perspective. Recent Research on Educational Attainment and Social Mobility', *Annual Review of Sociology*, 31, pp 223–43.

Breen, R. and Luijkx, R. (2004) 'Social Mobility in Europe between 1970 and 2000', in Breen, R. (ed) *Social Mobility in Europe*, Oxford: Oxford University Press, pp 37–75.

Breen, R. and Salazar, L. (2010) 'Has Increased Women's Educational Attainment Led to Greater Earnings Inequality in the United Kingdom? A Multivariate Decomposition Analysis', *European Sociological Review*, 26, 2, pp 143–57.

Breen, R. et al (2009) 'Nonpersistent Inequality in Educational Attainment: Evidence from Eight European Countries', *American Journal of Sociology*, 114, 5, pp 1475–521.

Brettell, C.B. and Hollifield, J.F. (eds) (2008) *Migration Theory: Talking Across Disciplines (2nd Edition)*, London: Routledge.

Brines, J. (1994) 'Economic Dependency, Gender, and the Division of Labor at Home', *American Journal of Sociology*, 100, 3, pp 652–88.

Brinkmann, G. and Hörner, W. (2007) 'Italy', in Hörner, W. et al (eds) *The Education Systems of Europe*, Dordrecht: Springer, pp 394–407.

Brown, C. et al (1982) 'The Effect of Minimum Wages on Employment and Unemployment', *Journal of Economic Literature*, 20, 2, pp 487–528.

Brozo, W.G. et al (2007) 'Engagement in Reading: Lessons Learned From Three PISA Countries', *Journal of Adolescent & Adult Literacy*, 51, 4, pp 304–15.

Brubaker, R. (2001) 'The Return of Assimilation? Changing Perspectives on Immigration and its Sequels in France, Germany, and the United States', *Ethnic and Racial Studies*, 24, 4, pp 531–48.

Brunet, R. (1989) *Les villes europeennes*, Paris: Datar-Reclus.

Brusselmann-Dehairs, C. and Valcke, M. (2007) 'Belgium', in Hörner, W. et al (eds) *The Education Systems of Europe*, Dordrecht: Springer, pp 104–27.

Büchs, M. (2007) *New Governance in European Social Policy. The Open Method of Coordination*, Basingstoke: Palgrave Macmillan.

Budria, S. (2007) *Economic Inequality in Portugal*, Munich: University Library of Munich.

Bukodi, E. and Robert, P. (2006) 'Men's Career Mobility in Hungary during the 1990s', in Blossfeld, H.-P. et al (eds) *Globalization, Uncertainty, and Men's Careers*, Cheltenham: Edward Elgar, pp 203–38.

Burkhauser, R.V. and Couch, K.A. (2010) 'Are the Inequality and Mobility Trends of the United States in European Union's Future?', in Alber, J. and Gilbert, N. (eds) *United in Diversity? Comparing Social Models in Europe and America*, Oxford: Oxford University Press, pp 280–307.

Burkhauser, R.V. and Poupore, J.G. (1997) 'A Cross-National Comparison of Permanent Inequality in the United States and Germany', *The Review of Economics and Statistics*, 79, 1, pp 10–17.

Burnham, J.B. (2003) 'Why Ireland Boomed', *The Independent Review*, 7, 4, pp 537–56.

Bygren, M. et al (2005) 'Elements of Uncertainty in Life Courses. Transitions to Adulthood in Sweden', in Blossfeld, H.-P. et al (eds) *Globalization, Uncertainty, and Youth in Society*, London: Routledge, pp 135–56.

Cabrito, B. (2001) 'Higher Education and Equity in Portugal', *Tertiary Education and Management*, 7, 1, pp 23–39.

Cahuc, P. and Zylberberg, A. (2004) *Labour Economics*, Cambridge: MIT Press.

Caldwell, J.C. (2006) *Demographic Transition Theory*, Dordrecht: Springer.

Caldwell, J.C. and Schindlmayr, T. (2003) 'Explanations of the Fertility Crisis in Modern Societies. A Search for Commonalities', *Population Studies*, 57, pp 241–63.

Campbell, A. et al (1976) *The Quality of American Life*, New York: Russell Sage Foundation.

Card, D. and DiNardo, J.E. (2002) 'Skill-Biased Technological Change and Rising Wage Inequality: Some Problems and Puzzles', *Journal of Labor Economics*, 20, 4, pp 733–83.

Card, D. and Krüger, A.B. (1995) *Myth and Measurement. The New Economics of the Minimum Wage*, New Jersey: Princeton University Press.

Cardoso, A.R. et al (2008) 'Demand for Higher Education Programs: The Impact of the Bologna Process', *CESifo Economic Studies*, 54, 2, pp 229–47.

Cardoso, F. and Cunha, V.G.D. (2005) *Household Wealth in Portugal 1980–2004*, Lisbon: Banco de Portugal.

Carey, S. (2002) 'Undivided Loyalties: Is National Identity an Obstacle to European Integration?', *European Union Politics*, 3, pp 387–413.

Carley, M. et al (2007) *Industrial Relations Developments in Europe 2006*, Luxembourg: Office for Official Publications of the European Communities.

Carlin, P.S. (1999) 'Economics and the Family', in Sussmann, M.B. et al (eds) *Handbook of Marriage and the Family (2nd Edition)*, New York: Plenum Press, pp 525–52.

Carlson, P. (1998) 'Self-Perceived Health in East and West Europe. Another European Health Divide', *Social Science & Medicine*, 46, 10, pp 1355–66.

Carriero, R. et al (2009) 'Do Parents Coordinate Their Work Schedules? A Comparison of Dutch, Flemish, and Italian Dual-Earner Households', *European Sociological Review*, 25, 5, pp 603–17.

Castells, M. (1996) *The Information Age. Economy, Society, and Culture*, Oxford: Blackwell.

Casterline, J.B. (2001) 'The Pace of Fertility Transition. National Patterns in the Second Half of the Twentieth Century', in Bulatao, R.A. and Casterline, J.B. (eds) *Global Fertility Transition*, New York: Population Council, pp 17–52.

Castles, S. (1986) 'The Guest Worker in Western Europe – An Obituary', *International Migration Review*, 20, 4, pp 761–79.

Castles, S. (2004) 'The Factors that Make and Unmake Migration Policies', *International Migration Review*, 38, 3, pp 852–84.

Castles, S. (2006) 'Guestworker in Europe: A Resurrection?', *International Migration Review*, 40, pp 741–66.

Castles, S. and Miller, M.J. (2009) *The Age of Migration (4th Edition)*, New York: Guilford.

Cavelaars, A.E.J.M. et al (2000) 'Educational Differences in Smoking. International Comparison', *British Medical Journal*, 320, 7242, pp 1102–7.

Cavounidis, J. (2006) 'Labour Market Impact of Migration: Employment Structures and the Case of Greece', *International Migration Review*, 40, 3, pp 635–60.

Cazes, S. and Nesporova, A. (eds) (2007) *Flexicurity. A Relevant Approach in Central and Eastern Europe*, Genf: International Labour Office.

Cedefop (2009) *European Journal of Vocational Training No 46. Thematic Issue on Higher Education and VET*, Thessaloniki: Cedefop.

Cerami, A. (2006) *Social Policy in Central and Eastern Europe. The Emergence of a New European Welfare Regime*, Berlin: Lit.

Chadwick, H. and Evans, G.R. (1987) *Atlas of the Christian Church*, London: Macmillian.

Cheal, D. (2008) *Families in Today's World*, London: Routledge.

Checkel, J.C. and Katzenstein, P.J. (eds) (2009) *European Identity*, Cambridge: Cambridge University Press.

Chenu, A. and Lesnard, L. (2006) 'Time Use Surveys. A Review of their Aims, Methods, and Results', *European Journal of Sociology*, 47, 3, pp 335–59.

Chesnais, J.-C. (1992) *The Demographic Transition*, Oxford: Clarendon.

Chiswick, B.R. (2008) 'Are Immigrants Favorably Self-Selected? An Economic Analysis', in Brettell, C.B. and Hollifield, J.F. (eds) *Migration Theory: Talking Across Disciplines (2nd Edition)*, London: Routledge, pp 63–82.

Christaller, W. (1950) *Das Grundgerüst der räumlichen Ordnung Europas. Die Systeme der europäischen zentralen Orte*, Frankfurt/Main: Kramer.

CIA (2009) *The World Factbook*. Available at: www.cia.gov/library/publications/the-world-factbook (accessed 1 January 2010).

Cipolla, C.M. (ed) (1972–76) *The Fontana Economic History*, London: Collins/Fontana.

Citrin, J. and Sides, J. (2004) 'More than Nationals: How Identity Choice Matters in Europe', in Herrmann, R.K. et al (eds) *Transnational Identities. Becoming European in the EU*, Rowman & Littlefield Publishers: Lanham, pp 161–85.

Clark, P. (2009) *European Cities and Towns, 400–2000*, Oxford and New York: Oxford University Press.

Cockerham, W.C. (1999) *Health and Social Change in Russia and Eastern Europe*, London: Routledge.

Cohen, P.N. (2004) 'Inequality and the Family', in Scott, J. et al (eds) *The Blackwell Companion to the Sociology of Families*, Oxford: Blackwell, pp 181–92.

Coleman, D. (2005) 'Population Prospects and Problems in Europe', *Genus*, 31, 3/4, pp 413–64.

Coleman, J. (1990) *Foundations of Social Theory*, Cambridge: Belknap Press.

Collins, R. (1971) 'Functional and Conflict Theories of Educational Stratification', *American Sociological Review*, 36, 6, pp 1002–19.

Coltrane, S. (1998) *Gender and Families*, London: Pine Forge Press.

Coltrane, S. (2000) 'Research on Household Labor. Modeling and Measuring the Social Embeddedness of Routine Family Work', *Journal of Marriage and the Family*, 62, 4, pp 1208–33.

Connell, R. (2009) *Gender in World Perspective*, Bristol: Polity.

Conze, E. and Wienfort, M. (eds) (2004) *Adel und Moderne: Deutschland im europäischen Vergleich im 19. und 20. Jahrhundert*, Köln: Böhlau.

Cornia, G.A. and Paniccia, R. (eds) (2000) *The Mortality Crisis in Transitional Economies*, Oxford: Oxford University Press.

Council of Europe (1994) *Council Directive 94/45/EC*, Brussels: Council of Europe.

Council of Europe (2006) *Recent Demographic Developments in Europe 2005*, Strasbourg: Council of Europe.

Cousins, C. (1999) *Society, Work and Welfare in Europe*, London: Macmillan.

Crompton, R. (2008) *Class and Stratification (3rd Edition)*, Bristol: Polity.

Crossick, G. and Haupt, H.-G. (1995) *The Petite Bourgeoisie in Europe 1780–1914: Enterprise, Family and Independence*, London: Routledge.

Crouch, C. (1993) *Industrial Relations and European State Traditions*, Oxford: Clarendon.

Crouch, C. (1999) *Social Change in Western Europe*, Oxford: Oxford University Press.

Crouch, C. and Streeck, W. (1997) 'The Future of Capitalist Diversity', in Crouch, C. and Streeck, W. (eds) *Political Economy of Modern Capitalism*, London: Sage, pp 1–18.

Cruz-Castro, L. and Sanz-Menendez, L. (2005) 'Politics and Institutions. European Parliamentary Technology Assessment', *Technological Forecasting and Social Change*, 72, 4, pp 429–48.

Czech National Bank (2009) *Annual Report 2008*, Prague: Czech National Bank.

da Costa, N.M.V.N. et al (2009) 'Technological Specialisation Courses in Portugal: Description and Suggested Improvements', *European Journal of Vocational Training. Thematic Issue on Higher Education and VET*, 46, pp 151–73.

Dahrendorf, R. (1959) *Class and Class Conflict in Industrial Society*, Stanford: Stanford University Press.

Dahrendorf, R. (1967) *Society and Democracy in Germany*, New York: Norton & Company.

Dahrendorf, R. (1980) 'Is the Work Society Running Out of Work?', *Omega*, 8, 3, pp 281–5.

Danna, K. and Griffin, R.W. (1999) 'Health and Well-being in the Workplace. A Review and Synthesis of the Literature', *Journal of Management*, 25, 3, pp 357–84.

Daun, H. and Sapatoru, D. (2001) 'Educational Reforms in Eastern Europe. Shifts, Innovation, and Restauration', in Daun, H. (eds) *Educational Restructuring in the Context of Globalization and National Policy*, New York: Routledge, pp 147–80.

Davies, J.B. et al (2008) *The World Distribution of Household Wealth*, Helsinki: UNU-WIDER.

Davies, N. (1996) *Europe: A History*, Oxford: Oxford University Press.

Davis, K. and Moore, W.E. (1945) 'Some Principles of Stratification', *American Sociological Review*, 10, 2, pp 242–9.

De La Fuente Layos, L. (2006) *Air Transport in Europe in 2004*, Luxembourg: Eurostat.

Delanty, G. (1995) *Inventing Europe: Idea, Identity, Reality*, Basingstoke: Macmillan.

Delanty, G. (2009) 'The European Heritage: History, Memory and Time', in Rumford, C. (ed) *The SAGE Handbook of European Studies*, London: Sage, pp 36–51.

Delanty, G. and Rumford, C. (2005) *Rethinking Europe. Social Theory and the Implications of Europeanization*, London/New York: Routledge.

Delhey, J. (2001) 'The Prospects of Catching up for New EU Members. Lessons for the Accession Countries to the European Union from Previous Enlargements', *Social Indicators Research*, 56, 2, pp 205–31.

Delhey, J. (2004) 'Nationales und transnationales Vertrauen in der Europäischen Union', *Leviathan*, 32, 1, pp 15–45.

Delhey, J. (2007) 'Do Enlargements Make the European Union Less Cohesive?', *Journal of Common Market Studies*, 45, 2, pp 253–79.

Delhey, J. and Kohler, U. (2006) 'From Nationally Bounded to Pan-European Inequalities? On the Importance of Foreign Countries as Reference Groups', *European Sociological Review*, 22, 2, pp 125–40.

Delhey, J. et al (2002) 'Quality of Life in a European Perspective. The Euromodule as a New Instrument for Comparative Welfare Research', *Social Indicators Research*, 58, 1, pp 161–75.

Dell'Aringa, C. and Pagani, L. (2007) 'Collective Bargaining and Wage Dispersion in Europe', *British Journal of Industrial Relations*, 45, 1, pp 29–54.

Demos, J. and Boocock, S.S. (eds) (1978) *Turning Points: Historical Sociological Essays on the Family*, Chicago: University of Chicago Press.

de Swaan, A. (1988) *In Care of the State. Health Care, Education and Welfare in Europe and the USA in the Modern Era*, New York: Oxford University Press.

Deutsch, K.W. (1957) *Political Community and the North Atlantic Area: International Organization in the Light of Historical Experience*, Princeton: Princeton University Press.

Deutsch, K.W. (1966) 'Political Community and the North Atlantic Area', in Deutsch K.W. et al (eds) *International Political Communities. An Anthology*, Anchor Books: City Garden, pp 1–91.

Deutsch, K.W. (1968) *The Analysis of International Relations*, Englewood Cliffs: Prentice-Hall.

Dewald, J. (1996) *The European Nobility, 1400–1800*, Cambridge: Cambridge University Press.

Diaz-Serrano, L. (2009) 'Disentangling the Housing Satisfaction Puzzle. Does Homeownership Really Matter?', *Journal of Economic Psychology*, 30, 5, pp 745–55.

Diekmann, A. and Preisendörfer, P. (2003) 'Green and Greenback. The Behavioral Effects of Environmental Attitudes in Low-Cost and High-Cost Situations', *Rationality and Society*, 15, 4, pp 441–72.

Diener, E. (eds) (2009) *Assessing Well-Being. The Collected Works of Ed Diener*, Dordrecht etc.: Springer.

Dietz, R.D. and Haurin, D.R. (2003) 'The Social and Private Micro-Level Consequences of Home Ownership', *Journal of Urban Economics*, 54, 3, pp 401–50.

Diewald, M. et al (2002) 'Back to Labour Markets. Who Got Ahead in Post-Communist Societies after 1989? The Case of East Germany', *European Societies*, 4, 1, pp 27–52.

DiMaggio, P. (1997) 'Culture and Cognition', *Annual Review of Sociology*, 23, pp 263–87.

DiMaggio, P. and Zukin, S. (eds) (1990) *Structures of Capital: The Social Organization of Economic Life*, New York: Cambridge University Press.

DiMaggio, P. et al (2001) 'Social Implications of the Internet', *Annual Review of Sociology*, 27, pp 307–36.

Dinan, D. (2004) *Europe Recast: A History of European Union*, Basingstoke: Palgrave Macmillan.

DiPrete, T.A. (2007) 'What Has Sociology to Contribute to the Study of Inequality Trends? A Historical and Comparative Perspective', *American Behavioral Scientist*, 50, 5, pp 603–18.

DiPrete, T.A. and McManus, P.A. (1996) 'Institutions, Technical Change, and Diverging Life Chances: Earnings Mobility in the United States and Germany', *American Journal of Sociology*, 102, 1, pp 34–79.

DiPrete, T.A. et al (2002) 'Internal Labor Markets and Earnings Trajectories in the Post-Fordist Economy: An Analysis of Recent Trends', *Social Science Research*, 31, 2, pp 175–96.

Dittmann-Kohli, F. (2006) 'Self and Identity', in Johnson, M.L. et al (eds) *The Cambridge Handbook of Age and Ageing*, Cambridge: Cambridge University Press, pp 275–91.

Doeringer, P.M. and Piore, M.J. (1971) *Internal Labour Markets and Manpower Analysis*, Lexington: Heath.

Dolado, J. et al (1996) 'The Economic Impact of Minimum Wages in Europe', *Economic Policy*, 11, 23, pp 317–72.

Domanski, H. (2008) 'Housing Conditions', in Alber, J. et al (eds) *Handbook of Quality of Life in Europe*, London: Routledge, pp 235–53.

Domanski, H. and Alber, J. (2006) 'Paradoxes of Housing in the Enlarged Europe', in Alber, J. and Merkel, W. (eds) *Europas Osterweiterung. Das Ende der Vertiefung? WZB-Jahrbuch 2005*, Berlin: Edition Sigma, pp 85–106.

Donato, K.M. et al (eds) (2006) *A Glass Half Full? Gender in Migration Studies*, Oxford: Blackwell.

Dorling, D. et al (2007) *Poverty, Wealth and Place in Britain, 1968 to 2005*, Bristol: The Policy Press.

Drieskens, S. et al (2010: forthcoming) 'Multiple Risk Behavior. Increasing Socio-Economic Gap over Time?', *European Journal of Public Health*.

Drobnič, S. and Blossfeld, H.-P. (2001) *Careers of Couples in Contemporary Society. From Male Breadwinner to Dual Earner Families*, Oxford: Oxford University Press.

Drobnič, S. and Blossfeld, H.-P. (2004) 'Career Patterns Over the Life Course. Gender, Class, and Linked Lives', *Research in Social Stratification and Mobility*, 21, 2, pp 139–64.

Drobnič S. et al (2010: forthcoming) 'Good Job, Good Life? Working Conditions and Quality of Life in Europe', *Social Indicators Research*.

Drulák, P. (2001) *National and European Identities in the EU Enlargement: Views from Central and Eastern Europe*, Prag: Institute of International Relations.

Duncan, S. (1995) 'Theorizing European Gender Systems', *Journal of European Social Policy*, 5, 4, pp 263–84.

Durkheim, E. (1961 [1925]) *L'Education morale*, Paris: Alcan.

Duro, J.A. (2001) *Regional Income Inequalities in Europe. An Updated Measurement and Some Decomposition Results*, Barcelona: Universitat Autonoma de Barcelona.

Duru-Bellat, M. et al (2008) 'Patterns of Social Inequalities in Access to Higher Education in France and Germany', *International Journal of Comparative Sociology*, 49, 4–5, pp 347–68.

Dustmann, C. (2003) 'Return Migration, Wage Differentials, and the Optimal Migration Duration', *European Economic Review*, 47, 2, pp 353–69.

Dustmann, C. et al (1996) 'Return Migration: The European Experience', *Economic Policy*, 11, 22, pp 213–50.

Eamets, R. and Ukrainski, K. (2000) 'Hidden Unemployment in Estonia. Experience from the Early Years of Transition (1989–1996)', *Post-Communist Economies*, 12, 4, pp 463–84.

Eamets, R. et al (2008) 'Labour Market Developments in the Baltic States', in Gordeev, P.E. (ed) *Demographic Economics Research Perspectives*, New York: Nova Science Publishers, pp 123–41.

Easton, D. (1975) 'A Re-assessment of the Concept of Political Support', *British Journal of Political Sciences*, 5, 4, pp 435–53.

Ebbinghaus, B. (2000a) 'Denmark', in Ebbinghaus, B. and Visser, J. (eds) *Trade Unions in Western Europe since 1945*, London: Palgrave Macmillan, pp 157–99.

Ebbinghaus, B. (2000b) 'Finland', in Ebbinghaus, B. and Visser, J. (eds) *Trade Unions in Western Europe since 1945*, London: Palgrave Macmillan, pp 201–36.

Ebbinghaus, B. (2000c) 'Germany', in Ebbinghaus, B. and Visser, J. (eds) *Trade Unions in Western Europe since 1945*, London: Palgrave Macmillan, pp 279–337.

Ebbinghaus, B. (2009) 'Can Path Dependence Explain Institutional Change? Two Approaches Applied to Welfare State Reform', in Magnusson, L. and Ottosson, J. (eds) *The Evolution of Path Dependence*, Cheltenham: Edward Elgar, pp 191–212.

Ebbinghaus, B. and Kittel, B. (2005) 'European Rigidity vs. American Flexibility? The Institutional Adaptability of Collective Bargaining', *Work and Occupations*, 32, 2, pp 63–195.

Ebbinghaus, B. and Manow, P. (eds) (2001) *Comparing Welfare Capitalism. Social Policy and Political Economy in Europe, Japan and the USA*, London: Routledge.

Ebbinghaus, B. and Visser, J. (1997) 'Der Wandel der Arbeitsbeziehungen im westeuropäischen Vergleich', in Hradil, S. and Immerfall, S. (eds) *Die westeuropäischen Gesellschaften im Vergleich*, Opladen: Leske + Budrich, pp 333–76.

Ebbinghaus, B. and Visser, J. (eds) (2000) *Trade Unions in Western Europe since 1945*, London: Palgrave Macmillan.

Eder, K. (1996) *The Social Construction of Nature. A Sociology of Ecological Enlightenment*, London etc.: Sage.

Eder, K. (2006) 'A Theory of Collective Identity. Making Sense of the Debate on a "European Identity"', *European Journal of Social Theory*, 12, 4, pp 1–21.

Eder, K. and Giesen, B. (eds) (2001) *European Citizenship between National Legacies and Postnational Projects*, Oxford: Oxford University Press.

Eder, K. and Spohn, W. (eds) (2005) *Collective Memory And European Identity: The Effects of Integration and Enlargement*, Aldershot: Ashgate.

Eder, F. et al (2007) 'Austria', in Hörner, W. et al (eds) *The Education Systems of Europe*, Dordrecht: Springer, pp 52–76.

Edwards, P. et al (1998) 'Great Britain: From Partial Collectivism to Neo-liberalism to Where?', in Ferner, A. and Hyman, R. (eds) *Changing Industrial Relations in Europe (2nd Edition)*, Oxford: Blackwell, pp 1–54.

EEA (2009) *Air Pollution by Ozone across Europe during Summer 2008. Overview of Exceedances of EC Ozone Threshold Values for April–September 2008*, Copenhagen: EEA Technical Report.

Eglite, P. (2004) 'Marriage and Families in Latvia', in Robila, M. (ed) *Families in Eastern Europe*, Amsterdam: Elsevier, pp 225–36.

Eigmüller, M. and Mau, S. (eds) (2010) *Gesellschaftstheorie und Europapolitik. Sozialwissenschaftliche Ansätze zur Europaforschung*, Wiesbaden: VS.

Eisenstadt, S.N. (1953) 'Analysis of Patterns of Immigration and Absorption of Immigrants', *Population Studies*, 7, 2, pp 167–80.

Eisenstadt, S.N. (1987) *European Civilization in a Comparative Perspective*, Oslo: Norwegian University Press.

Eisenstadt, S.N. (ed) (2002) *Multiple Modernities*, New Brunswick: Transaction.

Elder, G.H. (2009) 'Perspectives on the Life Course', in Heinz, W. et al (eds) *The Life Course Reader. Individuals and Societies Across Time*, Frankfurt/Main: Campus, pp 91–111.

Engels, F. (1962 [1884]) 'Der Ursprung der Familie, des Privateigentums und des Staats', in Marx, K. and Engels, F. (eds) *Marx-Engels-Werke Bd. 21*, Berlin: Dietz, pp 25–173.

England, P. (1982) 'The Failure of Human Capital Theory to Explain Occupational Sex Segregation', *The Journal of Human Resources*, 17, 3, pp 358–70.

Entorf, H. and Minoiu, N. (2005) 'What a Difference Immigration Policy Makes: A Comparison of PISA Scores in Europe and Traditional Countries of Immigration', *German Economic Review*, 6, 3, pp 355–76.

Entzinger, H. (2000) 'The Dynamics of Integration Policies', in Koopmans, R. and Statham, P. (eds) *Challenging Immigration and Ethnic Relations Politics*, Oxford: Oxford University Press, pp 97–118.

Erikson, E.O. and Fossum, J.E. (2004) 'Europe in Search of Legitimacy: Strategies of Legitimation Assessed', *International Political Science Review*, 25, 4, pp 435–59.

Erikson, R. (1974) 'Welfare as a Planning Goal', *Acta Sociologica*, 17, 3, pp 273–88.

Erikson, R. (1993) 'Descriptions of Inequality. The Swedish Approach to Welfare Research', in Nussbaum, M.C. and Sen, A. (eds) *The Quality of Life*, Oxford: Clarendon, pp 67–87.

Erikson, R. and Goldthorpe, J.H. (1992) *The Constant Flux. A Study of Class Mobility in Industrial Societies*, Oxford: Clarendon.

Esping-Andersen, G. (1990) *The Three Worlds of Welfare Capitalism*, Cambridge: Polity.

Esping-Andersen, G. (1993) 'Mobility Regimes and Class Formation', in Esping-Andersen, G. (ed) *Changing Classes. Stratification and Mobility in Post-industrial Societies*, London: Sage, pp 225–41.

Esping-Andersen, G. (1999) *Social Foundations of Postindustrial Economies*, Oxford: Oxford University Press.

Esping-Andersen, G. (2007) 'Sociological Explanations of Changing Income Distributions', *American Behavioral Scientist*, 50, 5, pp 639–58.

Esping-Andersen, G. et al (2002) *Why We Need a New Welfare State*, Oxford: Oxford University Press.

Espon Project (2004) *Transport Services and Networks. Territorial Trends and Basic Supply of Infrastructure for Territorial Cohesion*, Tours: University of Tours.

Espon Project (2006a) *Espon Atlas. Mapping the Structure of the European Territory*, Bonn: Bundesamt für Bauordnung und Raumwesen.

Espon Project (2006b) *Territory Matters for Competitiveness and Cohesion. Facets of Regional Diversity and Potentials in Europe*, Luxembourg: Ministry of Interior and Spatial Development.

Esser, H. (1982) 'On the Explanation of Contextual Effects on Individual Behavior. The Case of Language Acquisition by Migrant Workers', in Raub, W. (eds) *Theoretical Models and Empirical Analyses. Contributions to the Explanation of Individual Actions and Collective Phenomena*, Utrecht: E.S. Publications, pp 131–65.

Esser, H. (2000) *Soziologie. Spezielle Grundlagen. Band 4: Opportunitäten und Restriktionen*, Frankfurt/Main: Campus.

European Commission (1984) *European Council Decision 85/8/EEC*, Brussels: European Commission.

European Commission (2000) *Eurobarometer. Public Opinion in the European Union. Report No 53*, Brussels: European Commission.

European Commission (2003) *Green Paper on Services of General Interest*, Brussels: European Commission.

European Commission (2004) *A New Partnership for Cohesion Convergence Competitiveness Cooperation Third Report on Economic and Social Cohesion*, Luxembourg: European Commission.

European Commission (2005a) *Cohesion Policy in Support of Growth and Jobs. Community Strategic Guidelines, 2007–2013*, Brussels: European Commission.

European Commission (2005b) *Employment in Europe Report 2005*, Brussels: European Commission.

European Commission (2006) *Employment in Europe Report 2006*, Brussels: European Commission.

European Commission (2007a) *Cohesion Policy 2007–2013 Commentaries and Official Texts*, Luxembourg: European Commission.

European Commission (2007b) *Cultural Statistics*, Luxembourg: Office for Official Publications of the European Communities.

European Commission (2007c) *Eurobarometer 65 Public Opinion in the European Union*, Luxembourg: European Commission.

European Commission (2007d) *Europe's Demographic Future. Facts and Figures on Challenges and Opportunities*, Luxembourg: European Commission.

European Commission (2007e) *Europe in Figures Eurostat Yearbook 2006–07*, Luxembourg: European Commission.

European Commission (2007f) *Growing Regions, Growing Europe. Fourth Report on Social and Economic Cohesion*, Luxembourg: European Commission.

European Commission (2007g) *Joint Report on Social Protection and Social Inclusion*, Luxembourg: European Commission.

European Commission (2008) *Employment in Europe Report 2008*, Brussels: European Commission.

European Integration Consortium (2009) *Labour Mobility Within the EU in the Context of Enlargement and the Functioning of the Transitional Arrangements*, Nuremberg.

Eurostat (2006) *Air Transport in the EU-25*, Luxembourg: Eurostat.

Eurostat (2007a) *Energy, Transport, and Environment Indicators*, Luxembourg: Eurostat.

Eurostat (2007b) *Living Conditions in Europe. Data 2002–2005*, Luxembourg: Eurostat.

Eurostat (2008) *Living Conditions in Europe. Data 2003–2006*, Luxembourg: Eurostat.

Eurostat (2009a) *Europe in Figures Eurostat Yearbook 2009*, Luxembourg: Eurostat.

Eurostat (2009b) *Yearbook 2008*, Luxembourg: Eurostat.

Eurostat (2010a) *Population and social conditions*. Available at: http://eppeurostat.ec.europa.eu/portal/page/portal/statistics/themes (accessed 1 January 2010).

Eurostat (2010b) *Structural Indicators*. Available at: http://eppeurostat.ec.europa. eu/portal/page/portal/statistics/themes (accessed 1 January 2010).

Eurydice (2007) *Key Data on Higher Education in Europe 2007*, Brussels: Eurydice.

Eurydice (2009) *Key Data on Higher Education in Europe 2009*, Brussels: Eurydice.

Evans, M. and Williams, L. (2009) *A Generation of Change, a Lifetime of Difference? Social Policy in Britain since 1979*, Bristol: Policy Press.

Evans, P. (1998) *Why has the Female Unemployment Rate Fallen So Much in Britain?*, London: Bank of England.

Ewald, F. (1986) *L'Etat Providence*, Paris: Bernard Grasset.

Eyal, G. et al (1998) *Making Capitalism without Capitalists. The New Ruling Elites in Eastern Europe*, London: Verso.

Fabbrini, S. (2004) 'The European Union in American Perspective: The Transformation of Territorial Sovereignty in Europe and the United States', in Ansell, C.K. and Palma, G.D. (eds) *Restructuring Territoriality. Europe and the United States Compared*, New York: Cambridge University Press, pp 163–88.

Fahey, T. (2005) *Rich and Poor in the Enlarged EU. An Expanded Approach to Measurement*, Dublin: European Foundation for the Improvement of Living and Working Conditions.

Fahey, T. (2007) 'The Case for an EU-wide Measure of Poverty', *European Sociological Review*, 23, 1, pp 35–47.

Fahey, T. and Smyth, E. (2004) 'Do Subjective Indicators Measure Welfare? Evidence from 33 European Societies', *European Societies*, 6, 1, pp 5–27.

Faist, T. (2000) *The Volume and Dynamics of International Migration and Transnational Social Spaces*, Oxford: Clarendon.

Faist, T. and Ette, A. (eds) (2007) *The Europeanization of National Policies and Politics of Immigration. Between Autonomy and the European Union*, Houndmills: Palgrave Macmillan.

Falkner, G. (1998) *EU Social Policy in the 1990s. Towards a Corporatist Policy Community*, London: Routledge.

Fasani, F. (2009) *Undocumented Migration. Counting the Uncountable. Data and Trends across Europe – Country Report Italy*, Brussels: European Commission.

Fassmann, H. and Münz, R. (eds) (1994) *European Migration in the Late Twentieth Century*, Aldershot: Edward Elgar.

Favell, A. (2005) 'Europe's Identity Problem', *West European Politics*, 28, 5, pp 1109–16.

Favell, A. (2007) 'The Sociology of EU Politics', in Jorgensen, K.E. et al (eds) *Handbook of European Union Politics*, London: Sage, pp 122–8.

Favell, A. (2008) *Eurostars and Eurocities: Free Movement and Mobility in an Integrating Europe*, Oxford: Blackwell.

Favell, A. and Guiraudon, V. (2009) 'The Sociology of the European Union. An Agenda', *European Union Politics*, 10, 4, pp 550–76.

Featherman, D.L. and Hauser, R.M. (1978) *Opportunity and Change*, New York: Academic Press.

Federal Statistical Office (2009) *Statistical Yearbook 2009 for the Federal Republic OF Germany*, Wiesbaden.

Feinstein, C. (1999) 'Structural Change in the Developed Countries during the 20th Century', *Oxford Economic Policy*, 15, 4, pp 35–55.

Feithen, R. (1986) *Determinants of Labour Migration in an Enlarged European Community*, San Domenico: European University Institute.

Feldmann, H. (2005) 'Labour Market Institutions and Labour Market Performance in Transition Countries', *Post-Communist Economies*, 17, 1, pp 47–82.

Feldmann, M. (2006) 'Emerging Varieties of Capitalism in Transition Countries: Industrial Relations and Wage Bargaining in Estonia and Slovenia', *Comparative Political Studies*, 39, 7, pp 829–54.

Fenger, J. (1999) 'Urban Air Quality', *Atmospheric Environment*, 33, 29, pp 4877–900.

Fernández, C. and Ortega, C. (2006) *Labour Market Assimilation of Immigrants in Spain. Employment at the Expense of Bad-Job Matches?*, Barcelona: University of Navarra.

Ferrera, M. (1993) *Modelli di solidarietá*, Bologna: Il Mulino.

Ferrera, M. (1996) 'The "Southern Model" of Welfare in Social Europe', *Journal of European Social Policy*, 6, 1, pp 17–37.

Ferrera, M. (2003) 'European Integration and National Social Citizenship. Changing Boundaries, New Structuring?', *Comparative Political Studies*, 36, 6, pp 611–52.

Ferrera, M. (2005) *The Boundaries of Welfare. European Integration and the New Spatial Politics of Social Solidarity*, Oxford: Oxford University Press.

Findlay, A. et al (2006) 'Ever Reluctant Europeans. The Changing Geographies of UK Students Studying and Working Abroad', *European Urban and Regional Studies*, 13, 4, pp 291–318.

Firebaugh, G. (2003) *The New Geography of Global Income Inequality*, Cambridge: Harvard University Press.

Flaquer, L. (2000) *Family Policy and Welfare State in Southern Europe*, Barcelona: Institut de Ciències Polítiques i Socials.

Fligstein, N. (2008) *Euroclash. The EU, European Identity, and the Future of Europe*, Oxford: Oxford University Press.

Flora, P. (eds) (1986/87) *Growth to Limits. The Western European Welfare States since World War II (5 Bände)*, Berlin: de Gruyter.

Flora, P. (1993) 'Europa als Sozialstaat?', in Schäfers, B. (eds) *Lebensverhältnisse und soziale Konflikte im neuen Europa. Verhandlungen des 26. Deutschen Soziologentages*, Frankfurt/Main: Campus, pp 754–62.

Flora, P. and Alber, J. (1981) 'Modernization, Democratization and the Development of the Welfare States in Western Europe', in Flora, P. and Heidenheimer, A. (eds) *The Development of Welfare States in Europe and America*, London: Transaction, pp 37–80.

Flora, P. and Heidenheimer, A. (eds) (1981) *The Development of Welfare States in Europe and America*, London: Transaction.

Fodor, E. (2002) 'Gender and the Experience of Poverty in Eastern Europe and Russia after 1989', *Communist and Post-Communist Studies*, 35, 4, pp 369–82.

Fodor, E. et al (2002) 'Family Policies and Gender in Hungary, Poland, and Romania', *Communist and Post-Communist Studies*, 35, 4, pp 475–90.

Fossum, J.E. and Schlesinger, P. (eds) (2007) *The European Union and the Public Sphere. A Communicative Space in the Making?*, London: Routledge.

Fourage, D. and Ester, P. (2007) *Factors Determining International and Regional Migration in Europe*, Dublin: European Foundation for the Improvement of Living and Working Conditions.

Fourastié, J. (1949) *Le Grand Espoir du XXe Siècle*, Paris: Presses Universitaires de France.

Franceschi, S. and Naett, C. (1995) 'Trend in Smoking in Europe', *European Journal of Cancer Prevention*, 4, 4, pp 271–84.

Frank, R.H. (2007) *Falling Behind. How Rising Inequality Harms the Middle Class*, Berkeley: University of California Press.

Franzen, A. and Meyer, R. (2010) 'Environmental Attitudes in Cross-National Perspective. A Multilevel Analysis of the ISSP 1993 and 2000', *European Sociological Review*, 26, 2, pp 219-34.

Freeman, R.B. (1996) 'The Minimum Wage as a Redistributive Tool', *Economic Journal*, 106, 436, pp 639–49.

Freeman, R. (2002) 'Is Declining Unionization of the US Good, Bad, or Irrelevant?', in Kelly, J. (eds) *Industrial Relations. Volume II*, London: Routledge, pp 266–90.

Friedrich–Ebert-Stiftung (eds) (2002) *The Roma Population in South Eastern Europe*, Reschitza: Intergraf.

Fritzell, J. and Lundberg, O. (2007) *Health Inequalities and Welfare Resources. Continuity and Change in Sweden*, Bristol: Policy Press.

Fry, J. and Finley, W. (2007) 'The Prevalence and Costs of Obesity in the EU', *Proceedings of the Nutrition Society*, 64, 3, pp 359–62.

Fuchs, S. and Offe, C. (2009) 'Welfare State Formation in the Enlarged European Union: Patterns of Reform in Postcommunist States', in Rumford, C. (ed) *The SAGE Handbook of European Studies*, London: Sage, pp 420–41.

Fuchs, T. and Wößmann, L. (2007) 'What Accounts for International Differences in Student Performance? A Re-examination using PISA Data', *Empirical Economics*, 32, 2–3, pp 433–64.

Gabel, M. (1998) 'Public Support for European Integration: An Empirical Test of Five Theories', *The Journal of Politics*, 60, 2, pp 333–54.

Gabrisch, H. and Hölscher, J. (2007) *The Successes and Failures of Economic Transition. The European Experience*, New York: Palgrave Macmillan.

Gallie, D. and Paugam, S. (2000) 'The Experience of Unemployment in Europe: The Debate', in Gallie, D. and Paugam, S. (eds) *Welfare Regimes and the Experience of Unemployment in Europe*, New York: Oxford University Press, pp 1–22.

Gangl, M. et al (2003) 'Conclusions: Explaining Cross-national Differences in School-to-work Transitions', in Müller, W. and Gangl, M. (eds) *Transitions from Education to Work in Europe. The Integration of Youth into EU Labour Markets*, Oxford: Oxford University Press, pp 277–305.

Garleff, M. (2011: forthcoming) 'Baltic States', in Bade, K.J. et al (eds) *The Encyclopaedia of Migration*, Cambridge: Cambridge University Press.

Geary, D. (1999) 'Working-class Identities in Europe, 1850s–1930s', *Australian Journal of Politics and History*, 45, 1, pp 20–34.

Geary, D. (2004) 'The European Working Classes in the Late Nineteenth and Early Twentieth Centuries', in Kaelble, H. (eds) *The European Way. European Societies during the Nineteenth and Twentieth Centuries*, Oxford: Berghahn, pp 115–37.

Geiger, T. (1969) *On Social Order and Mass Society*, Chicago: University of Chicago Press.

Geiger, T. (1972 [1932]) *Die soziale Schichtung des Deutschen Volkes. Soziographischer Versuch auf statistischer Grundlage*, Darmstadt: Wissenschaftliche Buchgesellschaft.

Geißler, R. (2005) 'Die Metamorphose der Arbeitertochter zum Migrantensohn', in Berger, P.A. and Kahlert, H. (eds) *Institutionalisierte Ungleichheiten*, Weinheim: Juventa, pp 71–100.

Geißler, R. (2006) *Die Sozialstruktur Deutschlands*, Wiesbaden: VS.

Geist, C. (2005) 'The Welfare State and the Home: Regime Differences in the Domestic Division of Labour', *European Sociological Review*, 21, 1, pp 23–41.

Gendron, B. (2009) 'The Vocational Baccalaureate: A Gateway to Higher Education?', *European Journal of Vocational Training. Thematic Issue on Higher Education and VET*, 46, pp 5–27.

Gerhards, J. (2007) *Cultural Overstretch? Differences between Old and New Member States of the EU and Turkey*, London: Routledge.

Gerhards, J. (2008) 'Free to Move? The Acceptance of Free Movement of Labour and Non-discrimination among Citizens of Europe', *European Societies*, 10, 1, pp 121–40.

Gerhards, J. (2010) 'Culture', in Immerfall, S. and Therborn, G. (eds) *Handbook of European Societies. Social Transformations in the 21st Century*, Dordrecht: Springer, pp 157–215.

Gershuny, J. (2000) *Changing Times. Work and Leisure in Postindustrial Society*, Oxford: Oxford University Press.

Gershuny, J. (2004) 'Time, Through the Life Course, in the Family', in Scott, J. et al (eds) *The Blackwell Companion to the Sociology of Families*, Oxford: Blackwell, pp 158–77.

Gershuny, J. and Halpin, B. (1996) 'Time Use, Quality of Life, and Process Benefits', in Offer, A. (ed) *In Pursuit of the Quality of Life*, New York: Oxford University Press, pp 188–210.

Geyer, R.R. (2000) *Exploring European Social Policy*, Cambridge: Polity.

Giddens, A. (1973) *The Class Structure of the Advanced Societies*, London: Hutchinson University Library.

Giddens, A. (1990) *The Consequences of Modernity*, Cambridge and Oxford: Polity Press.

Giddens, A. (2009) *Sociology (6th Edition)*, Cambridge: Polity.

Giddens, A. and Mackenzie, G. (1982) *Social Class and the Division of Labour. Essays in Honour of Ilya Neustadt*, Cambridge: Cambridge University Press.

Giesecke, J. and Groß, M. (2003) 'Temporary Employment. Chance or Risk?', *European Sociological Review*, 19, 2, pp 161–77.

Giesecke, J. and Verwiebe, R. (2009) 'Wages and Labor Market. The Changing Wage Distribution in Germany between 1985 and 2006', *Journal of Applied Social Science Studies*, 129, 2, pp 191–201.

Giskes, K. et al (2005) 'Trends in Smoking Behaviour between 1985 and 2000 in Nine European Countries by Education', *Journal of Epidemiology and Community Health*, 59, 5, pp 395–401.

Glass, C.M. and Kawachi, J. (2005) 'Labor Markets in Transition. Gender, Unemployment, and Labor Force Participation in Poland and Hungary', *Yale Journal of Sociology*, 5, 1, pp 77–121.

Goldring, L. (1997) 'Power and Status in Transnational Social Spaces', in Pries, L. (eds) *Transnationale Migration. Soziale Welt Sonderband 12*, Baden-Baden: Nomos, pp 179–95.

Goldthorpe, J. (1971) 'Theories of Industrial Societies: Reflections on the Recrudenscence of Historicism and the Future of Futurology', *Archives Européenne de Sociologie*, 12, 2, pp 263–88.

Goldthorpe, J.H. (1987) *Social Mobility and Class Structures in Modern Britain*, Oxford: Clarendon.

Goldthorpe, J.H. (1996) 'Class Analysis and the Reorientation of Class Theory. The Case of Persisting Differentials in Educational Attainment', *British Journal of Sociology*, 47, pp 481–505.

Goldthorpe, J.H. (2007) *On Sociology. Volume II. Illustration and Restrospect (2nd Edition)*, Stanford: Stanford University Press.

Golsch, K. (2006) 'Men's Labor Market Mobility in Britain. Globalization, Labor Market Flexibility and Job Security', in Blossfeld, H.-P. et al (eds) *Globalization, Uncertainty, and Men's Careers*, Cheltenham: Edward Elgar, pp 299–327.

Goncalves, M.E. (2006) 'Risk and the Governance of Innovation in Europe. An Introduction', *Technological Forecasting and Social Change*, 73, 1, pp 1–12.

González-Enríquez, C. (2009) *Undocumented Migration. Counting the Uncountable. Data and Trends across Europe – Country Report Spain*, Brussels: European Commission.

Goodin, R.E. et al (2000) 'The Real Worlds of Welfare Capitalism', in Pierson, C. and Castles, F.G. (eds) *The Welfare State Reader*, Oxford: Blackwell, pp 170–89.

Goodin, R.E. et al (2008) *Discretionary Time. A New Measure of Freedom*, Cambridge: Cambridge University Press.

Goos, M. and Manning, A. (2007) 'Lousy and Lovely Jobs: The Rising Polarization of Work in Britain', *The Review of Economics and Statistics*, 89, 1, pp 118–33.

Gordon, J. (2001) 'The Internationalisation of Education. Schools in Europe and the Socrates Programme', *European Journal of Education*, 36, 4, pp 407–19.

Gordon, M.M. (1964) *Assimilation in American Life. The Role of Race, Religion, and National Origin*, New York: Oxford University Press.

Gornitzka, A. (2007) 'The Lisbon Process: A Supranational Policy Perspective', in Maassen, P. and Olsen, J.P. (eds) *University Dynamics and European Integration*, Dordrecht: Springer, pp 155–78.

Gorz, A. (1989) *Critique of Economic Reason*, London: Verso.

Gottschalk, P. and Smeeding, T.M. (1997) 'Cross-National Comparisons of Earnings and Income Inequality', *Journal of Economic Literature*, 35, 2, pp 633–87.

Goul Andersen, J. et al (eds) (2002) *Europe's New State of Welfare. Unemployment, Employment Policies and Citizenship*, Bristol: Policy Press.

Graham, H. (1996) 'Smoking Prevalence among Women in the European Community 1950–1990', *Social Science & Medicine*, 43, 2, pp 243–54.

Grasso, M. and Canova, L. (2008) 'An Assessment of the Quality of Life in the European Union Based on the Social Indicators Approach', *Social Indicators Research*, 87, 1, pp 1–25.

Green, A. et al (1999) *Convergence and Divergence in European Education and Training Systems*, London: Institute of Education, University of London.

Green, F. (2006) *Demanding Work. The Paradox of Job Quality in the Affluent Economy*, Princeton: Princeton University Press.

Greenhalgh, C. and Gregory, M. (2001) 'Structural Change and the Emergence of the New Service Economy', *Oxford Bulletin of Economics and Statistics*, 63, Supplement 1, pp 629–46.

Greenman, E. and Xie, Y. (2008) 'Is Assimilation Theory Dead? The Effect of Assimilation on Adolescent Well-being', *Social Science Research*, 37, pp 109–37.

Green-Pedersen, C. and Klitgaard, M.B. (2009) 'Between Economic Constraints and Popular Entrenchment – The Development of the Danish Welfare 1982 to 2005', in Schubert, K. et al (eds) *The Handbook of European Welfare Systems*, London: Routledge, pp 137–52.

Grip, A.D. et al (1997) 'Atypical Employment in the European Union', *International Labour Review*, 136, 1, pp 49–71.

Grusky, D.B. and Kanbur, R. (2006a) 'Introduction. The Conceptional Foundations of Poverty and Inequality Measurement', in Grusky, D.B. and Kanbur, R. (eds) *Poverty and Inequality*, Stanford: Stanford University Press, pp 1–29.

Grusky, D.B. and Kanbur, R. (eds) (2006b) *Poverty and Inequality*, Stanford: Stanford University Press.

Grzeskowiak, S. et al (2006) 'Housing Well-Being. Developing and Validating a Measure', *Social Indicators Research*, 79, 3, pp 503–41.

Guillén, M.F. and Suárez, S.L. (2005) 'Explaining the Global Digital Divide. Economic, Political and Sociological Drivers of Cross-National Internet Use', *Social Forces*, 84, 2, pp 681–708.

Gupta, N.D. et al (2005) 'Swimming Upstream, Floating Downstream. Comparing Women's Relative Wage Progress in the United States and Denmark', *Industrial and Labor Relations Review*, 59, 2, pp 243–66.

Haas, E.B. (1968) *The Uniting of Europe. Political, Social and Economic Forces 1950–1957*, Stanford: Stanford University Press.

Haavio-Mannila, E. and Rotkirch, A. (2010) 'Sexuality and Family Formation', in Immerfall, S. and Therborn, G. (eds) *Handbook of European Societies. Social Transformations in the 21st Century*, Dordrecht: Springer, pp 465–97.

Habermas, J. and Derrida, J. (2003) 'February 15, or, What Binds Europeans Together: Place for a Common Foreign Policy, Beginning in Core Europe', in Levy, D. et al (eds) *Old Europe, New Europe, Core Europe*, London: Verso, pp 3–13.

Hadjar, A. and Becker, R. (eds) (2009) *Expected and Unexpected Consequences of the Educational Expansion in Europe and USA. Theoretical Approaches and Empirical Findings in Comparative Perspective*, Bern: Haupt.

Hagerty, M.R. et al (2001) 'Quality of Life Indexes for National Policy. Review and Agenda for Research', *Social Indicators Research*, 55, 1, pp 1–96.

Hahn, S. (2011: forthcoming) 'Austria', in Bade, K.J. et al (eds) *The Encyclopaedia of Migration*, Cambridge: Cambridge University Press.

Hajnal, J. (1965) 'European Marriage Patterns in Perspective', in Glass, D.V. and Eversley, D.E.C. (eds) *Population in History*, London: Arnold, pp 101–43.

Haller, M. (1988) 'Grenzen und Variationen gesellschaftlicher Entwicklung in Europa. Eine Herausforderung und Aufgabe für die vergleichende Soziologie', Österreichische Zeitschrift für Soziologie, 13, 4, pp 5–19.

Haller, M. (1997) 'Klassenstruktur und Arbeitslosigkeit. Die Entwicklung zwischen 1960 und 1990', in Hradil, S. and Immerfall, S. (eds) *Die westeuropäischen Gesellschaften im Vergleich*, Opladen: Leske + Budrich, pp 377–431.

Haller, M. (2008) *European Integration as an Elite Process. The Failure of a Dream?*, London/New York: Routledge.

Haller, M. and Höllinger, F. (1995) 'Zentren und Peripherien in Europa. Eine Analyse und Interpretation der Verschiebungen zwischen dem ersten und dritten Viertel des 20. Jahrhunderts', *Historical Social Research*, 20, 2, pp 8–54.

Halman, L. et al (eds) (2005) *Atlas of European Values*, Amsterdam: Brill Academic Publishers.

Hamnett, C. (1999) *Winners and Losers. Home Ownership in Modern Britain*, London: Routledge.

Hamnett, C. (2001) 'Social Segregation and Social Polarization', in Paddison, R. (ed) *Handbook of Urban Studies*, London etc.: Sage, pp 162–76.

Hannerz, U. (1996) *Transnational Connections. Culture, People, Places*, London: Routledge.

Hannigan, J.A. (2006) *Environmental Sociology*, London etc.: Routledge.

Hansen, E.D. (2001) *European Economic History. From Mercantilism to Maastricht and Beyond*, Copenhagen: Copenhagen Business School.

Hardy, J. and Smith, A. (2004) 'Governing Regions, Governing Transformations: Firms, Institutions and Regional Change in Post-Soviet East-Central Europe', in Wood, A. and Valler, D. (eds) *Governing Local and Regional Economies: Institutions, Politics and Economic Development*, Aldershot: Ashgate, pp 147–76.

Hardy, M. (2006) 'Older Workers', in Binstock, R.H. et al (eds) *Handbook of Aging and the Social Sciences*, London: Academic Press, pp 201–18.

Hareven, T. (1982) *Family Time and Industrial Time*, New York: Cambridge University Press.

Harmes, T.O. (1998) 'Institutional Investors and the Reproduction of Neoliberalism', *Review of International Political Economy*, 5, 1, pp 92–121.

Hartmann, M. (2006) *The Sociology of Elites*, London/New York: Routledge.

Hartmann, M. (2010) 'Elites and Power Structure', in Immerfall, S. and Therborn, G. (eds) *Handbook of European Societies, Social Transformations in the 21st Century*, Dordrecht: Springer, pp 291–324.

Harvey, D. (1990) *Condition of Postmodernity*, Oxford: Blackwell.

Häußermann, H. and Siebel, W. (2000) *Soziologie des Wohnens*, Weinheim: Juventa.

Heath, A. et al (1999) 'British National Sentiment', *British Journal of Political Science*, 29, 1, pp 155–75.

Heckman, J.J. and Payner, B.S. (1989) 'Determining the Impact of Federal Anti-discrimination Policy on the Economic Progress of Black Americans', *American Economic Review*, 79, 1, pp 138–76.

Hegedüs, J. and Teller, N. (2005) 'Development of the Housing Allowance Programmes in Hungary in the Context of CEE Transitional Countries', *European Journal of Housing Policy*, 5, 2, pp 187–209.

Heidar, K. (2003) *Parties and Cleavages in the European Political Space*, Oslo: ARENA Working Papers.

Heidenreich, M. (2003) 'Regional Disparities in the Enlarged Europe', *Journal of European Social Policy*, 13, 4, pp 313–33.

Heidenreich, M. (eds) (2006a) *Die Europäisierung sozialer Ungleichheit*, Frankfurt/Main: Campus.

Heidenreich, M. (2006b) 'Die Europäisierung sozialer Ungleichheit zwischen nationaler Solidarität, europäischer Koordinierung und globalem Wettbewerb', in Heidenreich, M. (ed) *Die Europäisierung sozialer Ungleichheit. Zur transnationalen Klassen- und Sozialstrukturanalyse*, Frankfurt/Main: Campus, pp 17–64.

Heidenreich, M. and Wunder, C. (2008) 'Patterns of Regional Inequality in the Enlarged Europe', *European Sociological Review*, 24, 1, pp 19–36.

Heinrich, G. and Hildebrand, V. (2005) 'Returns to Education in the European Union: A Reassessment from Comparative Data', *European Journal of Education*, 40, 1, pp 13–34.

Hendricks, J. and Hatch, L.R. (2006) 'Lifestyle and Aging', in Binstock, R.H. et al (eds) *Handbook of Aging and the Social Sciences*, London: Academic Press, pp 301–19.

Herrmann, R. et al (eds) (2004) *Transnational Identities. Becoming European in the EU*, Lanham: Rowman and Littlefield Publishers.

Hettlage, R. and Müller, H.-P. (eds) (2006) *Die europäische Gesellschaft*, Konstanz: UVK.

Heymann, J. (eds) (2003) *Global Inequalities at Work. Work's Impact on the Health of Individuals, Families, and Societies*, Oxford and New York: Oxford University Press.

Heyns, B. (2005) 'Emerging Inequalities in Central and Eastern Europe', *Annual Review of Sociology*, 31, pp 163–97.

Hillmann, F. (2005) 'Migrants Care Work in Private Households or. The Strength of Bilocal and Transnational Ties as a Last(ing) Resource in Global Migration', in Pfau-Effinger, B. and Geissler, B. (eds) *Care Work in Europe*, London: Macmillan, pp 60–84.

Hillmann, F. (2007) *Migration als räumliche Definitionsmacht? Beiträge zu einer neuen Geographie der Migration in Europa*, Stuttgart: Steiner.

Hillmert, S. (2002) 'Labour Market Integration and Institutions: An Anglo-German Comparison', *Work, Employment & Society*, 19, 4, pp 675–701.

Hills, J. et al (1994) *Beveridge and Social Security*, Oxford: Clarendon Press.

Hix, S. (2005) *The Political System of the European Union, 2nd edn*, Basingstoke: Palgrave Macmillan.

Hix, S. (2008) *What's Wrong with the European Union and How to Fix it*, Cambridge: Polity.

Hochschild, A.R. and Machung, A. (1990) *The Second Shift*, New York: Viking.

Hoffmann, R. (2008) *Socioeconomic Differences in Old Age Mortality*, New York: Springer.

Hoffmann-Nowotny, H.-J. (1981) 'A Sociological Approach Toward a General Theory of Migration', in Kritz, M.M. et al (eds) *Global Trends in Migration: Theory and Research on International Population Movements*, Englewood: Jerome S. Ozer, pp 64–83.

Hohenberg, P.M. and Lees, L.H. (1985) *The Making of Urban Europe 1000–1950*, Cambridge: Harvard University Press.

Hooghe, L. (ed) (1996) *Cohesion Policy and European Integration: Building Multilevel Governance*, Oxford: Oxford University Press.

Hooghe, L. (2003) 'Europe Divided? Elites vs. Public Opinion on European Integration', *European Union Politics*, 4, 3, pp 281–304.

Hooghe, L. and Marks, G. (2001) *Multi-Level Governance and European Integration*, Lanham: Rowman and Littlefield.

Hooghe, L. and Marks, G. (2005) 'Calculation, Community and Cues: Public Opinion on European Integration', *European Union Politics*, 6, 4, pp 419–45.

Höpflinger, F. (1987) *Wandel der Familienbildung in Westeuropa*, Frankfurt/Main: Campus.

Höpflinger, F. and Fux, B. (2007) 'Familien – intereuropäische Beziehungen', in Ecarius, J. (ed) *Handbuch Familie*, Wiesbaden: VS, pp 56–77.

Horak, M. (2001) 'Environmental Policy Reform in the Post-communist Czech Republic. The Case of Air Pollution', *Europe-Asia Studies*, 53, 2, pp 313–27.

Hörner, W. and Döbert, H. (2007) 'Introduction', in Hörner, W. et al (eds) *The Education Systems of Europe*, Dordrecht: Springer, pp 1–11.

Hörner, W. et al (eds) (2007) *The Education Systems of Europe*, Dordrecht: Springer.

Hort, S.E.O. (2009) 'The Swedish Welfare State – A Model in Constant Flux?', in Schubert, K. et al (eds) *The Handbook of European Welfare Systems*, London: Routledge, pp 428–43.

Hout, M. and DiPrete, T. (2006) 'What We Have Learned. RC28's Contributions to Knowledge about Social Stratification', *Research in Stratification and Mobility*, 24, 1, pp 1–20.

Hout, M. et al (2006) 'The Persistence of Classes in Post-Industrial Societies', *International Sociology*, 8, 8, pp 259–77.

Howard, P.N. (2007) 'Testing the Leap-frog Hypothesis: The Impact of Existing Infrastructure and Telecommunications Policy on the Global Digital Divide', *Information, Communication, and Society*, 10, 2, pp 133–57.

Hradil, S. (2006) *Die Sozialstruktur Deutschlands im internationalen Vergleich*, Wiesbaden: VS.

Hradil, S. and Immerfall, S. (1997) 'Modernisierung und Vielfalt in Europa', in Hradil, S. and Immerfall, S. (eds) *Die westeuropäischen Gesellschaften im Vergleich*, Opladen: Leske + Budrich, pp 11–25.

Huberman, M. and Minns, C. (2007) 'The Times They Are Not Changin'. Days and Hours of Work in Old and New Worlds, 1870–2000', *Explorations in Economic History*, 44, 4, pp 538–67.

Hudson, R. (1999) 'The New Economy of the New Europe: Eradicating Divisions or Creating New Forms of Uneven Development?', in Hudson, R. and Williams, A.M. (eds) *Divided Europe. Society and Territory*, London: Sage, pp 29–62.

Huijts, T. et al (2010) 'Education, Educational Heterogamy, and Self-Assessed Health in Europe. A Multilevel Study of Spousal Effects in 29 European Countries', *European Sociological Review*, 26, 3, pp 261–76.

Huinink, J. and Konietzka, D. (2007) *Familiensoziologie. Eine Einführung*, Frankfurt/Main: Campus.

Huinink, J. and Solga, H. (1994) 'Occupational Mobility in the GDR. A Priviledge of the Older Generations', *Zeitschrift für Soziologie*, 23, 3, pp 237–53.

Huisman, M. et al (2005) 'Inequalities in the Prevalence of Smoking in the European Union. Comparing Education and Income', *Preventive Medicine*, 40, 6, pp 756–64.

Hunya, G. (2004) *Manufacturing FDI in New EU Member States. Foreign Penetration and Location Shifts between 1998 and 2002*, Wien: Wiener Institut für Internationale Wirtschaftsvergleiche.

Hurrelmann, A. (2007) 'European Democracy, the "Permissive Consensus", and the Collapse of the EU Constitution', *European Law Journal*, 13, 3, pp 343–59.

Husten, C.G. et al (2000) 'Cigarette Smoking. Trends, Determinants, and Health Effects', in Goldman, M.B. and Hatch, M.C. (eds) *Women and Health*, San Diego: Academic Press, pp 563–77.

Huster, E.-U. (1995) 'Wealth in Germany – the Difficulty of Talking about a Taboo Debate', *Journal of Contemporary Central and Eastern Europe*, 3, 2, pp 46–64.

Hyman, R. (2001) *Understanding European Trade Unionism between Market, Class and Society*, London: Sage.

Iannelli, C. and Raffe, D. (2007) 'Vocational Upper-secondary Education and the Transition from School', *European Sociological Review*, 23, 1, pp 49–63.

IASO/IOTF (2007) *Database on Overweight and Obesity*. Available at: http://www. iotf.org/database/index.asp (accessed 20 August 2008).

Iggers, G.G. et al (2008) *A Global History of Modern Historiography*, Harlow: Person Education Limited.

Imig, D. and Tarrow, S. (2000) 'Political Contention in a Europeanising Polity', *West European Politics*, 23, 4, pp 73–93.

Immerfall, S. (1995) *Einführung in den Europäischen Gesellschaftsvergleich. Ansätze – Problemstellungen – Befunde*, Passau: Rothe.

Immerfall, S. (2006) *Europa – Politisches Einigungswerk und gesellschaftliche Entwicklung. Eine Einführung*, Wiesbaden: VS.

Immerfall, S. and Therborn, G. (eds) (2010) *Handbook of European Societies. Social Transformations in the 21st Century*, Dordrecht: Springer.

Immerfall, S. et al (2010) 'Identity', in Immerfall, S. and Therborn, G. (eds) *Handbook of European Societies. Social Transformations in the 21st Century*, Dordrecht: Springer, pp 325–53.

Inglehart, R. (1990) *Culture Shift in Advanced Industrial Society*, Princeton: Princeton University Press.

Inzelt, A. (2007) 'The Inflow of Highly Skilled Workers into Hungary. A By-product of FDI', *Journal of Technology Transfer*, 33, 4, pp 422–38.

Iversen, T. (2005) *Capitalism, Democracy, and Welfare*, Cambridge: Cambridge University Press.

Iversen, T. and Wren, A. (1998) 'Equality, Employment, and Budgetary Restraint. The Trilemma of the Service Economy', *World Politics*, 50, 4, pp 507–46.

Ivlevs, A. et al (2009) *The Effects of the Economic Downturn on Migration from the New EU Member States to the United Kingdom*, Centre on Migration, Policy and Society, Paper presented at the Annual Conference, Oxford.

Jackson, M. et al (2007) 'Primary and Secondary Effects in Class Differentials in Educational Attainment: The Transition to A-Level Courses in England and Wales', *Acta Sociologica*, 50, 3, pp 211–29.

Jacobs, B. and Ploeg, F.V.D. (2006) 'Guide to Reform of Higher Education: A European Perspective', *Journal of Economic Policy*, 21, 4, pp 535–92.

Jacobs, J.A. (1996) 'Gender Inequality and Higher Education', *Annual Reviews of Sociology*, 22, pp 153–85.

Jacobs, J.A. and Gerson, K. (2004) *The Time Divide. Work, Family, and Gender Inequality*, Cambridge, MA: Harvard University Press.

Jaeger, M.M. (2007) 'Educational Mobility Across Three Generations. The Changing Impact of Parental Social Class, Economic, Cultural, and Social Capital', *European Societies*, 9, pp 527–50.

Jahoda, M. et al (2002 [1933]) *Marienthal. The Sociography of an Unemployed Community*, New Brunswick, NJ: Transaction.

James, P.T. et al (2001) 'The Worldwide Obesity Epidemic', *Obesity Research*, 9, Supplement 4, pp 228–33.

Jamison, A. and Ring, M. (2003) 'Sweden', in Rootes, C. (ed) *Environmental Protest in Western Europe*, Oxford: Oxford University Press, pp 216–33.

Jaumotte, F. (2003) *Female Labour Force Participation. Past Trends and Main Determinants in OECD Countries*, Paris: OECD.

Jenkins, S.P. and Micklewright, J. (eds) (2007) *Inequality and Poverty Re-examined*, Oxford: Oxford University Press.

Joas, H. and Wiegandt, K. (eds) (2008) *The Cultural Values of Europe*, Liverpool: Liverpool University Press.

Joerges, C. and Everson, M. (2000) 'Challenging the Bureaucratic Challenge', in Eriksen, E.O. and Fossum, J.E. (eds) *Democracy in the European Union: Integration Through Deliberation*, London: Routledge, pp 164–88.

Johansson, M. et al (2005) 'Wage Differentials and Gender Discrimination. Changes in Sweden 1981–98', *Acta Sociologica*, 48, 4, pp 341–64.

Johnson, M.L. et al (eds) (2006) *The Cambridge Handbook of Age and Ageing*, Cambridge: Cambridge University Press.

Johnston, R. et al (2006) 'Sustaining and Creating Migration Chains Among Skilled Immigrant Goups', *Journal of Ethnic and Migration Studies*, 32, pp 1227–50.

Jones, N. et al (2009) 'The Influence of Social Capital on Willingness to Pay for the Environment among European Citizens', *European Societies*, 11, 4, pp 511–30.

Jonsson, J.O. (2004) 'Equality at a Halt? Social Mobility in Sweden, 1976–99', in Breen, R. (ed) *Social Mobility in Europe*, Oxford: Oxford University Press, pp 225–50.

Jordan-Bychkov, T.G. and Bychkova Jordan, B. (2003) *The European Culture Area. A Systematic Geography*, Lanham: Rowman and Littlefield.

Julémont, G. (1993) 'The Status of Women and the Position of Children', in Federici, N. et al (eds) *Women's Position and Demographic Change*, Oxford: Clarendon, pp 104–21.

Julian, R. (2004) 'Inequality, Social Differences, and Environmental Resources', in White, R. (ed) *Controversies in Environmental Sociology*, Cambridge etc.: Cambridge University Press, pp 113–31.

Kaczmarczyk, P. (2006) *Highly Skilled Migration from Poland and Other CEE Countries – Myths and Reality. Center for International Relations Warsaw, Reports & Analyses 17/06*, Warsaw: Center for International Relations.

Kaelble, H. (1983) *Soziale Mobilität und Chancengleichheit im 19. und 20. Jahrhundert. Deutschland im internationalen Vergleich*, Göttingen: Vandenhoeck & Ruprecht.

Kaelble, H. (1987) *Auf dem Weg zu einer europäischen Gesellschaft*, München: C.H. Beck.

Kaelble, H. (1989) 'Was Prometheus most Unbound in Europe? The Labour Force in Europe During the late XIXth and XXth Centuries', *Journal of European Economic History*, 18, 1, pp 65–104.

Kaelble, H. (1990) *A Social History of Western Europe, 1880–1980*, Dublin: Gill and MacMillan.

Kaelble, H. (2004a) 'Das europäische Sozialmodell – eine historische Perspektive', in Kaelble, H. and Schmid, G. (eds) *Das europäische Sozialmodell. Auf dem Weg zum transnationalen Sozialstaat. WZB-Jahrbuch 2004*, Berlin: Edition Sigma, pp 31–50.

Kaelble, H. (ed) (2004b) *The European Way. European Societies during the Nineteenth and Twentieth Centuries*, Oxford: Berghahn.

Kaelble, H. (2005) 'Eine europäische Gesellschaft?', in Schuppert, G.F. et al (eds) *Europawissenschaft*, Baden-Baden: Nomos, pp 299–330.

Kaelble, H. (2007) *Sozialgeschichte Europas. 1945 bis zur Gegenwart*, München: C.H. Beck.

Kahn, M. (2003) 'New Evidence on Eastern Europe's Pollution Progress', *Topics in Economic Analysis and Policy*, 3, 1, Article 4.

Kaiser, L.C. (2006) *Female Labor Market Transitions in Europe*, Berlin: DIW.

Kalleberg, A.L. (2000) 'Non-standard Employment Relations: Part-time, Temporary and Contract Work', *Annual Review of Sociology*, 26, pp 341–65.

Kalter, F. and Granato, N. (2002) 'Demographic Change, Educational Expansion, and Structural Assimilation of Immigrants. The Case of Germany', *European Sociological Review*, 18, 2, pp 199–216.

Kangas, O. and Saari, J. (2009) 'The Welfare System of Finland', in Schubert, K. et al (eds) *The Handbook of European Welfare Systems*, London: Routledge, pp 189–206.

Katz, H.C. (2002) 'The Decentralization of Collective Bargaining: A Literature Review and Comparative Analysis', in Kelly, J. (ed) *Industrial Relations. Volume I*, London: Routledge, pp 18–46.

Katz, L.F. and Autor, D.H. (1999) 'Changes in the Wage Structure and Earnings Inequality', in Ashenfelter, O. and Card, D. (eds) *Handbook of Labor Economics*, Amsterdam: Elsevier, pp 1463–555.

Katznelson, I. and Zolberg, A.R. (eds) (1986) *Working-class Formation. Nineteenth-century Patterns in Western Europe and the United States*, Princeton: Princeton University Press.

Kauppi, N. (2005) *Democracy, Social Resources and Political Power in the European Union*, Manchester: Manchester University Press.

Keating, M. (1997) 'The Political Economy of Regionalism', in Keating, M. and Loughlin, J. (eds) *The Political Economy of Regionalism*, London: Sage, pp 17–40.

Keeling, R. (2006) 'The Bologna Process and the Lisbon Research Agenda. The European Commission's Expanding Role in Higher Education Discourse', *European Journal of Education*, 41, 2, pp 203–23.

Kenworthy, L. (2007) 'Inequality and Sociology', *American Behavioral Scientist*, 50, 5, pp 584–602.

Kiernan, K. (2004) 'Changing European Families: Trends and Issues', in Scott, J. et al (eds) *The Blackwell Companion to the Sociology of Families*, Oxford: Blackwell, pp 17–33.

King, R. (2002) 'Towards a New Map of European Migration', *International Journal of Population Geography*, 8, pp 89–106.

King, R. and Ruiz-Gelices, E. (2003) 'International Student Migration and the European Year Abroad', *International Journal of Population Geography*, 9, 3, pp 229–52.

King, R. et al (1998) 'International Retirement Migration in Europe', *International Journal of Population Geography*, 4, 2, pp 91–111.

Kippenberg, H. (ed) (2005) *The Changing Religious Landscape of Europe*, Amsterdam: Het Spinhuis.

Kjeldstadli, K. (2011: forthcoming) 'Scandinavia', in Bade, K.J. et al (eds) *The Encyclopaedia of Migration*, Cambridge: Cambridge University Press.

Kjellberg, A. (2000) 'Sweden', in Ebbinghaus, B. and Visser, J. (eds) *Trade Unions in Western Europe since 1945*, London: Palgrave Macmillan, pp 605–55.

Klanberg, F. (1987) *Armut und ökonomische Ungleichheit in der Bundesrepublik*, Frankfurt/Main: Campus.

Klein, T. (2005) *Sozialstrukturanalyse. Eine Einführung*, Reinbek: Rowohlt.

Kleinman, M., (2002) *A European Welfare State? European Union Social Policy in Context*. New York: Palgrave.

Klevmarken, A.N. (2006) *The Distribution of Wealth in Sweden. Trends and Driving Factors*, Department of Economics, University of Uppsala.

Klingemann, H.-D. et al (eds) (2006) *Democracy and Political Culture in Eastern Europe*, London: Routledge.

Knai, C. et al (2007) 'Obesity in Eastern Europe. An Overview of its Health and Economic Implications', *Economics and Human Biology*, 5, 3, pp 392–408.

Knippenberg, H. (eds) (2005) *The Changing Religious Landscape of Europe*, Amsterdam: Het Spinhuis.

Kocka, J. (1990) '"Bürgertum" and Professions in the 19th Century. Two Alternative Approaches', in Burrage, M. and Torstendahl, R. (eds) *Professions in Theory and History*, London: Sage, pp 62–74.

Kocka, J. (2004) 'The Middle Classes in Europe', in Kaelble, H. (ed) *The European Way. European Societies during the Nineteenth and Twentieth Centuries*, Oxford: Berghahn, pp 15–43.

Kocka, J. (ed) (2010) *Work in a Modern Society. The German Historical Experience in Comparative Perspective*, New York/Oxford: Berghahn Books.

Koehn, P.H. and Rosenau, J.N. (2002) 'Transnational Competence in an Emergent Epoch', *International Studies Perspectives*, 3, 2, pp 105–27.

Kogan, I. (2004) 'Last Hired, First Fired? The Unemployment Dynamics of Male Immigrants in Germany', *European Sociological Review*, 20, 5, pp 445–61.

Kogan, I. and Kalter, F. (2006) 'The Effects of Relative Group Size on Occupational Outcomes: Turks and Ex-Yugoslavs in Austria', *European Sociological Review*, 22, 1, pp 35–48.

Kohl, H. and Platzer, H.-W. (2004) *Industrial Relations in Central and Eastern Europe. Transformation and Integration. A Comparision of the Eight New EU Member States*, Brussels: ETUI.

Kohl, H. and Platzer, H.-W. (2007) 'The Role of the State in Central and Eastern European Industrial Relations. The Case of Minimum Wages', *Industrial Relations Journal*, 38, 6, pp 614–35.

Kohl, J. and Wendt, C. (2004) 'Satisfaction with Health Care Systems. A Comparison of EU Countries', in Glatzer, W. et al (eds) *Challenges for Quality of Life in the Contemporary World. Advances in Quality-of-Life Studies, Theory, and Research*, Dordrecht: Kluwer, pp 311–31.

Kohler, H.-P. et al (2002) 'The Emergence of Lowest-Low Fertility in Europe during the 1990s', *Population and Development Review*, 28, 4, pp 641–80.

Kohler, U. (2007) 'Containers, Europeanisation and Individualisation. Empirical Implications of General Descriptions of Society', in Scherer, S. et al (eds) *From Origin to Destination. Trends and Mechanisms in Social Stratification Research*, Frankfurt/Main: Campus, pp 293–319.

Kohler-Koch, B. (2000) 'Regieren in der Europäischen Union. Auf der Suche nach demokratischer Legitimität', *Aus Politik und Zeitgeschichte*, B 6, pp 30–8.

Kohli, M. (1986) 'The World We Forgot: A Historical Review of the Life Course', in Marshall, V. W. (ed) *Later Life: The Social Psychology of Aging*, London: Sage, pp 271–303.

Kohli, M. (1987) 'Retirement and the Moral Economy: A Historical Interpretation of the German Case', *Journal of Aging Studies*, 1, 2, pp 125–44.

Kohli, M. (2006a) 'Aging and Justice', in Binstock, R.H. et al (eds) *Handbook of Aging and the Social Sciences*, London: Academic Press, pp 457–78.

Kohli, M. (2006b) 'Generational Changes and Generational Equity', in Binstock, R.H. et al (eds) *The Cambridge Handbook of Age and Ageing*, Cambridge: Cambridge University Press, pp 518–26.

Kohli, M. et al (2009) 'The Social Connectedness of Older Europeans: Patterns, Dynamics and Contexts', *Journal of European Social Policy*, 19, 4, pp 327–40.

Konietzka, D. (2003) 'Vocational Training and the Transition to the First Job in Germany. New Risks at Labor Market Entry?', in Bills, D.B. (ed) *The Sociology of Job Training*, Amsterdam: Elsevier, pp 161–95.

Konrad, G. and Szelényi, I. (1974) *Intellectuals on the Road to Class Power*, New York: Harcourt Brace Jovanovich.

Korpi, W. (1983) *The Democratic Class Struggle*, London: Routledge and Kegan Paul.

Korpi, W. (2003) 'Welfare-state Regress in Western Europe. Politics, Institutions, Globalization, and Europeanization', *Annual Review of Sociology*, 29, pp 589–609.

Korupp, S.E. and Szydlik, M. (2005) 'Causes and Trends of the Digital Divide', *European Sociological Review*, 21, 4, pp 409–22.

Koser, K. and Salt, J. (1997) 'The Geography of Highly Skilled International Migration', *International Journal of Population Geography*, 3, 4, pp 285–303.

Kovac, D. et al (2009) 'Occupational Gender Segregation in Slovenia: Sustainable Economy Perspective', *International Journal of Sustainable Economy*, 1, 4, pp 335–51.

Kraaykamp, G. et al (2009) 'Working Status and Leisure. An Analysis of the Trade-off between Solitary and Social Time', *Time and Society*, 18, 2–3, pp 264–83.

Kracauer, S. (1998 [1930]) *The Saleried Masses. Duty and Destruction in Weimer Germany*, London/New York: Verso.

Krane, R.E. (ed) (1979) *International Labor Migration in Europe*, New York: Praeger.

Kriegel, A. and Becker, J.-J. (1964) *Le guerre et le mouvement ouvrier francais*, Paris: Armand Colin.

Krieger, H. (2008) 'Migration and Mobility Culture', in Alber, J. et al (eds) *Handbook of Quality of Life in the Enlarged European Union*, London: Routledge, pp 355–84.

Kriesi, H. et al (2008) *West European Politics in the Age of Globalization*, Cambridge: Cambridge University Press.

Kristen, C. (2008) 'Primary School Choice and Ethnic School Segregation in German Elementary Schools', *European Sociological Review*, 24, 4, pp 495–510.

Kristen, C. and Granato, N. (2007) 'The Educational Attainment of the Second Generation in Germany. Social Origins and Ethnic Inequality', *Ethnicities*, 7, 3, pp 343–66.

Kruger, D.J. and Nesse, R.M. (2007) 'Economic Transition, Male Competition, and Sex Differences in Mortality Rates', *Evolutionary Psychology*, 5, 2, pp 411–27.

Krumme, H. (2004) 'Fortwährende Remigration. Das transnationale Pendeln türkischer Arbeitsmigrantinnen und Arbeitsmigranten im Ruhestand', *Zeitschrift für Soziologie*, 33, 2, pp 138–53.

Kuhlmann, S. and Edler, J. (2003) 'Scenarios of Technology and Innovation Policies in Europe: Investigating Future Governance', *Technological Forecasting and Social Change*, 70, 7, pp 619–37.

Kurz, K. (2004) 'Labour Market Position, Intergenerational Transfers, and Home Ownership. A Longitudinal Analysis for West German Birth Cohorts', *European Sociological Review*, 20, 2, pp 141–59.

Kurz, K. and Blossfeld, H.-P. (eds) (2004) *Home Ownership and Social Inequality in Comparative Perspective*, Stanford: Stanford University Press.

Kurz, K. et al (2005) 'Case Study Germany. Global Competition, Uncertainty and the Transition to Adulthood', in Blossfeld, H.-P. et al (eds) *Globalization, Uncertainty, and Youth in Society*, London: Routledge, pp 47–78.

Kurz, K. et al (2006) 'Increasing Instability in Employment Careers of West German Men? A Comparison of the Birth Cohorts 1940, 1955 and 1964', in Blossfeld, H.-P. et al (eds) *Globalization, Uncertainty, and Men's Careers*, Cheltenham: Edward Elgar, pp 75–113.

Kuznets, S. (1955) 'Economic Growth and Income Inequality', *The American Economic Review*, 45, 1, pp 1–28.

Lahusen, C. (2005) 'Kommerzielle Beratungsfirmen in der Europäischen Union', in Reising, R. and Kohler-Koch, B. (eds) *Interessenpolitik in Europa*, Baden-Baden: Nomos, pp 251–80.

Lampert, T. (2010) 'Smoking, Physical Inactivity, and Obesity. Associations with Social Status', *Deutsches Ärzteblatt International*, 107, 1–2, pp 1–7.

Land, K.C. and Yang, Y. (2006) 'Morbidity, Disability, and Mortality', in Binstock, R.H. et al (eds) *Handbook of Aging and the Social Sciences*, London: Academic Press, pp 41–58.

Landes, D.S. (1969) *The Unbound Prometheus. Technological Change and Industrial Development from 1750 to the Present*, Cambridge: Cambridge University Press.

Lane, J.-E. and Ersson, S. (1987) *Politics and Society in Western Europe*, London: Sage.

Lang, T. and Rayner, G. (2005) 'Obesity. A Growing Issue for European Policy?', *Journal of European Social Policy*, 15, 4, pp 301–27.

Laslett, P. (1988) 'The European Family and Early Industrialization', in Baechler, J. (ed) *Europe and the Rise of Capitalism*, Oxford: Blackwell, pp 234–42.

Lattes, G.B. (2005) 'Ideas of Europe', in Lattes, G.B. and Recchi, E. (eds) *Comparing European Societies: Towards a Sociology of the EU*, Bologna: Monduzzi Editore, pp 33–65.

Lauerová, J.S. and Terrell, K. (2002) *Explaining Gender Differences in Unemployment with Micro Data on Flows in Post-Communist Economies*, Ann Arbor: William Davidson Institute.

Layard, R. et al (2005) *Unemployment. Macroeconomic Performance and the Labour Market*, Oxford: Oxford University Press.

Layte, R. and Whelan, C.T. (2004) 'Class Formation and Trends in Social Fluidity in the Republic of Ireland 1973–94', in Breen, R. (ed) *Social Mobility in Europe*, Oxford: Oxford University Press, pp 175–93.

Layte, R. and Whelan, C.T. (2009) 'Explaining Social Class Inequalities in Smoking. The Role of Education, Self-Efficacy, and Deprivation', *European Sociological Review*, 25, 4, pp 399–410.

Lee, C.-S. et al (2007) 'Income Inequality, Global Economy and the State', *Social Forces*, 86, 1, pp 77–111.

Lee, E.S. (1966) 'A Theory of Migration', *Demography*, 3, 1, pp 47–57.

Lee, Y.-S. and Waite, L.J. (2005) 'Husbands' and Wives' Time Spent on Housework. A Comparison of Measures', *Journal of Marriage and Family*, 67, 2, pp 328–36.

Lees, A. and Hollen Lees, L. (2008) *Cities and the Making of Modern Europe*, Cambridge: Cambridge University Press.

Lefèbvre, M. (2007) *The Redistributive Effects of Pension Systems in Europe. A Survey of Evidence*, Luxembourg: LIS.

Lefrere, P. (2007) 'Competing Higher Education Futures in a Globalising World', *European Journal of Education*, 42, 2, pp 201–12.

Le Galès, P. (2002) *European Cities, Social Conflicts and Governance*, Oxford: Oxford University Press.

Leibfried, S. (1996) 'Wohlfahrtsstaatliche Perspektiven der Europäischen Union: Auf dem Wege zu positiver Souveränitätsverflechtung?', in Jachtenfuchs, M. and Kohler-Koch, B. (eds) *Europäische Integration*, Opladen: Leske + Budrich, pp 455–77.

Leibfried, S. and Mau, S. (2008) 'Introduction', in Leibfried, S. and Mau, S. (eds) *Welfare States: Construction, Deconstruction, Reconstruction*, Cheltenham: Edward Elgar, pp 1–54.

Leibfried, S. and Pierson, P. (eds) (1995) *European Social Policy: Between Fragmentation and Integration*, Washington D.C.: Brookings.

Leibfried, S. et al (1995) *Zeit der Armut. Lebensläufe im Sozialstaat*, Frankfurt/Main: Suhrkamp.

Leisering, L. and Leibfried, S. (1999) *Time and Poverty in Western Welfare States*, Oxford: Oxford University Press.

Lenski, G. (1966) *Power and Privilege. A Theory of Social Stratification*, New York: McGraw-Hill.

Leonardi, R. (1995) *Convergence, Cohesion and Integration in the European Union*, New York: St. Martin's Press.

Leonardi, R. (2005) *The Cohesion Policy of the European Union. The Building of Europe*, London: Palgrave.

Leonardi, R. (2006) 'Cohesion in the European Union', *Regional Studies*, 40, 2, pp 155–66.

Lepsius, M.R. (1979) 'Soziale Ungleichheit und Klassenstrukturen in der Bundesrepublik Deutschland', in Wehler, H.-U. (ed) *Klassen in der europäischen Sozialgeschichte*, Göttingen: Vandenhoeck & Ruprecht, pp 166–209.

Lepsius, M.R. (2001) 'The European Union. Economic and Political Integration and Cultural Plurality', in Eder, K. and Giesen, B. (eds) *European Citizenship between National Legacies and Postnational Projects*, Oxford: Oxford University Press, pp 205–21.

Lesnard, L. (2008) 'Off-scheduling within Dual-earner Couples. An Unequal and Negative Externality for Family Time', *American Journal of Sociology*, 114, 2, pp 447–90.

Levels, M. and Dronkers, J. (2008) 'Educational Performance of Native and Immigrant Children from Various Countries of Origin', *Ethnic and Racial Studies*, 31, 8, pp 1404–25.

Levels, M. et al (2008) 'Immigrant Children's Educational Achievement in Western Countries: Origin, Destination, and Community Effects on Mathematical Performance', *American Sociological Review*, 73, 5, pp 835–53.

Levitt, P. et al (2003) 'International Perspectives on Transnational Migration', *International Migration Review*, 37, 3, pp 565–75.

Lewis, J. (1992) 'Gender and the Development of Welfare Regimes', *Journal of European Social Policy*, 2, 3, pp 159–73.

Lindberg, L.N. and Scheingold, S.A. (1970) *Europe's Would-be Polity: Patterns of Change in the European Community*, Englewood Cliffs: Prentice-Hall.

Lipset, S.M. (1996) *American Exceptionalism. A Double-edged Sword*, New York: Norton.

Lipset, S.M. and Bendix, R. (1959) *Social Mobility in Industrial Society*, Berkeley: University of California Press.

Lipset, S.M. and Rokkan, S. (1967) 'Cleavage Structures, Party Systems, and Voter Alignments', in Lipset, S.M. and Rokkan, S. (eds) *Party Systems and Voter Alignments: Cross-national Perspectives*, New York: The Free Press, pp 1–64.

Ljungvall, Å. and Gerdtham, U.-G. (2010) 'More Equal but Heavier. A Longitudinal Analysis of Income-related Obesity Inequalities in an Adult Swedish Cohort', *Social Science & Medicine*, 70, 2, pp 221–31.

Lockwood, D. (1958) *The Blackcoated Worker. A Study in Class Consciousness*, London: Unwin Uniersits Books.

Lörz, M. and Schindler, S. (2009) 'Educational Expansion and Effects on the Transition to Higher Education: Has the Effect of Social Background Characteristics Declined or Just Moved to the Next Stage?', in Hadjar, A. and Becker, R. (eds) *Expected and Unexpected Consequences of the Educational Expansion in Europe and USA. Theoretical Approaches and Empirical Findings in Comparative Perspective*, Bern: Haupt, pp 97–110.

Lucassen, J. and Lucassen, L. (2011: forthcoming) 'The Netherlands', in Bade, K.J. et al (eds) *The Encyclopaedia of Migration*, Cambridge: Cambridge University Press.

Luhmann, N. (1989) *Ecological Communication*, Chicago, IL: University of Chicago Press.

Luijkx, R. et al (2006) 'The Impact of Globalization on Job and Career Mobility of Dutch Men. Life-history Data from the Mid-1950s to the Year 2000', in Blossfeld, H.-P. et al (eds) *Globalization, Uncertainty, and Men's Careers*, Cheltenham: Edward Elgar, pp 75–143.

Lundholm, E. (2007) *New Motives for Migration*, Umea: Umea University.

Lunn, K. (2011: forthcoming) 'Great Britain', in Bade, K.J. et al (eds) *The Encyclopaedia of Migration*, Cambridge: Cambridge University Press.

Lutz, B. (1990) *Le mirage de la croissance marchande: essai de réinterprétation du développement du capitalisme industriel dans l'Europe du XXe siècle*, Paris: Ed. de la Maison des Sciences de l'Homme.

Lutz, W. et al (eds) (2006) *The New Generations of Europeans. Demography and Families in the Enlarged European Union*, London: Earthscan.

Lux, M. (2003) 'Efficiency and Effectiveness of Housing Policies in the Central and Eastern Europe Countries', *European Journal of Housing Policy*, 3, 3, pp 243–65.

Luy, M. (2003) 'Causes of Male Excess Mortality: Insights from Cloistered Populations', *Population and Development Review*, 29, 4, pp 647–76.

Maas, W. (2007) *Creating European Citizens*, Lanham: Rowman and Littlefield.

Mabry, J.B. et al (2004) 'Generations, the Life Course, and Family Change', in Scott, J. et al (eds) *The Blackwell Companion to the Sociology of Families*, Oxford: Blackwell, pp 87–108.

Mach, B.M. (2004) 'Intergenerational Mobility in Poland: 1972–88–94', in Breen, R. (ed) *Social Mobility in Europe*, Oxford: Oxford University Press, pp 175–93.

Machin, S. (2008) 'An Appraisal of Economic Research on Changes in Wage Inequality', *LABOUR*, 22, Special Issue, pp 7–26.

Maddison, A. (2001) *The World Economy. A Millennial Perspective*, Paris: OECD.

Magnusson, C. (2009) 'Gender, Occupational Prestige, and Wages: A Test of Devaluation Theory', *European Sociological Review*, 25, 1, pp 87–101.

Mailand, M. and Due, J. (2004) 'Social Dialogue in Central and Eastern Europe: Present State and Future Development', *European Journal of Industrial Relations*, 10, 2, pp 179–97.

Majone, G. (1996) *Regulating Europe*, London: Routledge, Chapman and Hall.

Malmberg, B. et al (2010) *Global Population Ageing and Migration in Europe*, London: Routledge.

Malthus, T.R. (1999 [1798]) *An Essay on the Principle of Population*, Oxford: Oxford University Press.

Mandel, H. and Semyonov, M. (2006) 'A Welfare State Paradox. State Interventions and Women's Employment Opportunities in 22 Countries', *American Journal of Sociology*, 111, 6, pp 1910–49.

Manning, P. (2004) 'Diversity and Change in Pre-accession Central and Eastern Europe since 1989', *Journal of European Social Policy*, 14, 3, pp 211–32.

Marks, G.N. (2005) 'Accounting for Immigrant–Non-immigrant Differences in Reading and Mathematics in Twenty Countries', *Ethnic and Racial Studies*, 28, 5, pp 925–46.

Marks, G. and Hooghe, L. (2003) *National Identity and Support for European Integration*, Berlin: WZB.

Marks, G. and McAdam, D. (1999) 'On the Relationship of Political Opportunities to the Form of Collective Action. The Case of the European Union', in Della Porta, D. et al (eds) *Social Movements in a Globalizing World*, London: Macmillan, pp 97–111.

Marks, G. and Steenbergen, M. (eds) (2004) *European Integration and Political Conflict*, Cambridge: Cambridge University Press.

Marks, G. et al (1996) *Governance in the European Union*, London: Sage.

Marmot, M. and Wilkinson, R.G. (eds) (2006) *Social Determinants of Health*, Oxford and New York: Oxford University Press.

Marshall, T.H. (1950) *Citizenship and Social Class, and other Essays*, Cambridge: Cambridge University Press.

Martin, P. (2003) 'Public Policies and Economic Geography', in Funck, B. and Pizatti, L. (eds) *European Integration, Regional Policy, and Growth*, Washington: World Bank, pp 19–32.

Martin, S. and Lowell, L.B. (2002) 'US Immigration Policy. Admission of High Skilled Workers', *Georgetown Immigration Law Journal*, 16, 3, pp 619–36.

Martinelli, A. (ed) (2008) *Transatlantic Divide. Comparing American and European Society*, Oxford: Oxford University Press.

Martines, L. (1988) *Power and Imagination: City-states in Renaissance Italy*, Baltimore: Johns Hopkins University Press.

Marx, K. (1963 [1852]) *The Eighteenth Brumaire of Louis Bonaparte*, New York: International Publishers.

Marx, K. (1964 [1850]) *Class Struggles in France 1848–1850*, New York: International Publishers.

Marx, K. (1992 [1867]) *Capital: Volume 1: A Critique of Political Economy*, New York: Penguin Classics.

Marx, K. and Engels, F. (1952 [1848]) *Manifesto of the Communist Party*, Chicago: Encyclopedia Britannica.

Mason, A. (2005) 'Economic Demography', in Poston, D.L. and Micklin, M. (eds) *Handbook of Population*, New York: Springer, pp 549–75.

Massey, D.S. and Denton, N.A. (1993) *American Apartheid. Segregation and the Making of the Underclass*, Cambridge: Harvard University Press.

Masson, J.-R. (2009) 'Vocational Education and Training and Higher Education in the Transition Countries', *European Journal of Vocational Training. Thematic Issue on Higher Education and VET*, 46, pp 89–113.

Mattingly, M. and Bianchi, S. (2003) 'Gender Differences in the Quantity and Quality of Free Time. The US Experience', *Social Forces*, 81, 3, pp 999–1030.

Mau, S. (2003) *The Moral Economy of Welfare States. Britain and Germany Compared*, London: Routledge.

Mau, S. (2005) 'Europe from the Bottom. Assessing Personal Gains and Losses and its Effects on EU-support', *Journal of Public Policy*, 25, 3, pp 289–311.

Mau, S. (2010) *Social Transnationalism. Lifeworlds beyond the Nation State*, London/New York: Routledge.

Mau, S. and Büttner, S. (2010) 'Transnationality', in Immerfall, S. and Therborn, G. (eds) *Handbook of European Societies. Social Transformations in the 21st Century*, Dodrecht: Springer, pp 537–69.

Mau, S. and Veghte, B. (eds) (2007) *Social Justice, Legitimacy, and the Welfare State*, London: Ashgate.

Mayer, K.U. (2000) 'Promises Fulfilled? A Review of 20 Years of Life Course Research', *Archives Européennes de Sociologie*, XLI 2, pp 259–82.

Mayer, K.U. (2001) 'The Paradox of Global Social Change and National Path Dependencies. Life Course Patterns in Advanced Societies', in Woodward, A. and Kohli, M. (eds) *Inclusions and Exclusions in European Societies*, London: Routledge, pp 89–110.

Mayer, K.U. (2009) 'New Directions in Life Course Research', *Annual Review of Sociology*, 35, pp 413–33.

Mayer, K.U. and Tuma, N.B. (eds) (1990) *Event History Analysis in Life Course Research*, Madison, WI: University of Wisconsin Press.

Mayer, K.U. et al (2009) 'The Process and Impacts of Educational Expansion: Findings from the German Life Course Study', in Hadjar, A. and Becker, R. (eds) *Expected and Unexpected Consequences of the Educational Expansion in Europe and USA. Theoretical Approaches and Empirical Findings in Comparative Perspective*, Bern: Haupt, pp 27–48.

McArdle, S. et al (2007) 'Employability during Unemployment. Adaptability, Career Identity, and Human and Social Capital', *Journal of Vocational Behavior*, 71, 2, pp 247–64.

McCashin, A. and O'Shea, J. (2009) 'The Irish Welfare System', in Schubert, K. et al (eds) *The Handbook of European Welfare Systems*, London: Routledge, pp 260–76.

McDill, E.L. and Coleman, J.S. (1965) 'Family and Peer Influences in College Plans of High School Students', *Sociology of Education*, 38, pp 112–26.

McDowell, I. (2006) *Measuring Health. A Guide to Rating Scales and Questionnaires*, Oxford and New York: Oxford University Press.

McGinnity, F. and Hillmert, S. (2004) 'Persistent Class Inequality? Comparing Class-specific Unemployment in British and German Life Courses', *European Societies*, 6, 3, pp 383–408.

McGovern, P. et al (2007) *Market, Class, and Employment*, Oxford and New York: Oxford University Press.

McIlroy, J. (2009) 'A Brief History of British Trade Unions and Neoliberalism in the Age of New Labour', in Daniels, G. and McIlroy, J. (eds) *Trade Unions in a Neoliberal World*, London: Routledge, pp 21–62.

McLaughlin, C. (2009) 'The Productivity-enhancing Impacts of the Minimum Wage: Lessons from Denmark and New Zealand', *British Journal of Industrial Relations*, 47, 2, pp 327–48.

McManus, P. (1999) 'Market, State, and the Quality of New Self-employment Jobs among Men in the US and Western Germany', *Social Forces*, 78, 3, pp 865–905.

Meardi, G. (2007) 'More Voice after More Exit? Unstable Industrial Relations in Central Eastern Europe', *Industrial Relations Journal*, 38, pp 503–23.

Meardi, G. (2009) 'A Suspended Status: The Puzzle of Polish Workers in the West Midlands', in Fassmann, H. et al (eds) *Migration and Mobility in Europe: Trends, Patterns and Control*, Aldershot: Edward Elgar, pp 102–22.

Medrano, J.D. (2003) *Framing Europe: Attitudes to European Integration in Germany, Spain and the United Kingdom*, Princeton: Princeton University Press.

Medrano, J.D. (2008) *Europeanization and the Emergence of a European Society, Working Paper No. 12*, Barcelona: Institut Barcelona d'Estudis Internacionals (IBEI).

Meehan, E. (1993) *Citizenship and the European Community*, London: Sage.

Mehmet, Ö. et al (2007) 'Labor Mobility and Labor Market Convergence in Cyprus', *Turkish Studies*, 8, 1, pp 43–69.

Menz, G. (2005) *Varieties of Capitalism and Europeanization: National Response Strategies to the Single European Market*, Oxford: Oxford University Press.

Merriman, J. (2004) *A History of Modern Europe, From the Renaissance to the Present*, New York: W.W. Norton and Company.

Meslé, F. (2004) 'Mortality in Central and Eastern Europe. Long-term Trends and Recent Upturns', *Demographic Research*, 2 (Special Collection), pp 45–70.

Metcalf, D. (2007) *Why Has the British National Minimum Wage Had Little or No Impact on Employment?*, London: LSE.

Meurs, D. et al (2008) 'Discrimination Despite Integration: Immigrants and the Second Generation in Education and the Labour Market in France', in Bonifazi, C. et al (eds) *International Migration in Europe. New Trends and New Methods of Analysis*, Amsterdam: Amsterdam University Press, pp 247–69.

Meyers, E. (2002) 'The Causes of Convergence in Western Immigration Control', *Review of International Studies*, 28, 1, pp 123–41.

Michalos, A.C. (2004) 'Social Indicators Research and Health-related Quality of Life Research', *Social Indicators Research*, 65, 1, pp 27–72.

Michalos, A.C. et al (2000) 'Health and the Quality of Life', *Social Indicators Research*, 51, 3, pp 245–86.

Michalowitz, I. (2007) *Lobbying in der EU*, Wien: Facultas.

Michelson, W. (2005) *Time Use. Expanding Explanation in the Social Sciences*, Boulder, CO: Paradigm.

Mikkelsen, F. (2005) 'Working-class Formation in Europe and Forms of Integration: History and Theory', *Labor History*, 46, 3, pp 277–306.

Miles, S. (2000) *Youth Lifestyles in a Changing World*, Philadelphia: Open University Press.

Mills, M. et al (2005) 'Becoming an Adult in Uncertain Times. A 14-Country Comparison of the Losers of Globalization', in Blossfeld, H.-P. et al (eds) *Globalization, Uncertainty, and Youth in Society*, London: Routledge, pp 438–58.

Mincer, J. (1974) *Schooling, Experience, and Earnings*, New York: Columbia University Press.

Mirowsky, J. and Ross, C.E. (2003) *Education, Social Status, and Health*, New York: de Gruyter.

Moch, L.P. (2011: forthcoming) 'France', in Bade, K.J. et al (eds) *The Encyclopaedia of Migration*, Cambridge: Cambridge University Press.

Moen, P. and Spencer, D. (2006) 'Converging Divergences in Age, Gender, Health, and Well-Being: Strategic Selection in the Third Age', in Binstock, R.H. et al (eds) *Handbook of Aging and the Social Sciences*, London: Academic Press, pp 127–44.

Moore, R. (2004) *Education and Society: Issues and Explanations in the Sociology of Education*, Cambridge: Polity Press.

Moravcsik, A. (1998) *The Choice for Europe: Social Purpose and State Power from Messina to Maastricht*, Ithaca, NY: Cornell University Press.

Morgan, S.L. et al (eds) (2006) *Mobility and Inequality*, Stanford: Stanford University Press.

Mouw, T. and Kalleberg, A.L. (2007) *Occupations and the Structure of Wage Inequality in the United States, 1980–2000s*, Chapel Hill: University of North Carolina.

Mulder, C.H. and Smits, J. (1999) 'First-time Home-ownership of Couples. The Effect of Inter-generational Transmission', *European Sociological Review*, 15, 3, pp 323–37.

Müller, H.P. (2007) 'Auf dem Weg in eine europäische Gesellschaft. Begriffsproblematik und theoretische Perspektiven', *Berliner Journal für Soziologie*, 17, 1, pp 7–31.

Müller, W. (2001) 'Education and Labour Market Outcomes: Commonality or Divergence?', in Haller, M. (ed) *The Making of the European Union: Contributions of the Social Sciences*, Heidelberg: Springer, pp 287–308.

Müller, W. (2005) 'Education and Youth Integration into European Labour Markets', *International Journal of Comparative Sociology*, 46, 5–6, pp 461–85.

Müller, W. and Kogan, I. (2010) 'Education', in Immerfall, S. and Therborn, G. (eds) *Handbook of European Societies. Social Transformations in the 21st Century*, Dodrecht: Springer, pp 217–90.

Müller, W. and Pollack, R. (2004) 'Social Mobility in West Germany: The Long Arms of History Discovered', in Breen, R. (ed) *Social Mobility in Europe*, Oxford: Oxford University Press, pp 77–113.

Müller, W. et al (1997) 'Bildung in Europa', in Hradil, S. and Immerfall, S. (eds) *Die westeuropäischen Gesellschaften im Vergleich*, Opladen: Leske + Budrich, pp 177–246.

Müller-Rommel, F. (2002) 'The Lifespan and the Political Performance of Green Parties in Western Europe', *Environmental Politics*, 11, 1, pp 1–16.

Münch, R. (2010) *European Governmentality*, London/New York: Routledge.

Münch, R. and Büttner, S. (2006) 'Die europäische Teilung der Arbeit. Was können wir von Emile Durkheim lernen?', in Heidenreich, M. (ed) *Die Europäisierung sozialer Ungleichheit. Zur transnationalen Klassen- und Sozialstrukturanalyse*, Frankfurt/Main: Campus, pp 65–107.

Murray, C.L. and Lopez, A.D. (1997) 'Alternative Projections of Mortality and Disability by Cause 1990–2020: Global Burden of Disease Study', *The Lancet*, 349, 9064, pp 1498–1504.

Natali, D. (2009) 'The Italian Welfare State (Still) in Transition: The Progressive Recalibration of Social Programmes and Greater Flexibility of Labour Market Policies', in Schubert, K. et al (eds) *The Handbook of European Welfare Systems*, London: Routledge, pp 277–93.

National Statistical Institute of Bulgaria (2008) *Population*. Available at: http://www.nsi.bg/Census/Ethnos.htm (accessed 5 December 2008).

Naumann, R. and Stoleroff, A. (2000) 'Portugal', in Ebbinghaus, B. and Visser, J. (eds) *Trade Unions in Western Europe since 1945*, London: Palgrave Macmillan, pp 545–72.

Neave, G. and Maassen, P. (2007) 'The Bologna Process: An Intergovernmental Policy Perspective', in Maassen, P. and Olsen, J.P. (eds) *University Dynamics and European Integration*, Dordrecht: Springer, pp 135–53.

Neumann, L. (2002) 'Does Decentralized Collective Bargaining Have an Impact on the Labour Market in Hungary?', *European Journal of Industrial Relations*, 8, 1, pp 11–31.

Newman, K.S. (1999) *Falling from Grace: Downward Mobility in Age of Affluence*, Berkeley: University of California Press.

Neyer, J. (2005) 'Die Krise der EU und die Stärke einer deliberativen Integrationstheorie', *Zeitschrift für Internationale Beziehungen*, 12, 2, pp 377–82.

Niess, F. (2001) *Die europäische Idee – aus dem Geist des Widerstands*, Frankfurt/Main: Suhrkamp.

Nissen, S. (2004) 'Europäische Identität und die Zukunft Europas', *Aus Politik und Zeitgeschichte*, B 38, pp 21–9.

Noguera, C.S. (2006) 'Hard Choices: Can Spanish Women Reconcile Job and Family?', in Blossfeld, H.-P. and Hofmeister, H. (eds) *Globalization, Uncertainty, and Women's Careers*, Cheltenham: Edward Elgar, pp 376–401.

Noguera, C.S. et al (2005) 'The Spanish Case. The Effects of the Globalization Process on the Transition to Adulthood', in Blossfeld, H.-P. et al (eds) *Globalization, Uncertainty, and Youth in Society*, London: Routledge, pp 385–414.

Nolan, B. and Whelan, C.T. (1996) *Resources, Deprivation, and Poverty*, Oxford: Clarendon.

Nolan, B. and Whelan, C.T. (2007) 'On the Multidimensionality of Poverty and Social Exclusion', in Jenkins, S.P. and Micklewright, J. (eds) *Inequality and Poverty Re-examined*, Oxford: Oxford University Press, pp 146–65.

Noll, H.-H. (2002) 'Towards a European System of Social Indicators. Theoretical Framework and System Architecture', *Social Indicators Research*, 58, 1, pp 47–87.

Noll, H.-H. (2004) 'Social Indicators and Quality of Life Research. Background, Achievements, and Current Trends', in Genov, N. (ed) *Advances in Sociological Knowledge over Half a Century*, Wiesbaden: VS, pp 151–81.

Nollmann, G. (2002) 'Die Einführung des Euro. Vom Edelmetall zum reinen Beziehungsgeld', *Kölner Zeitschrift für Soziologie und Sozialpsychologie*, 54, 2, pp 226–45.

Norris, M. (2008) 'Institutional Drivers of Housing Inequalities in the Enlarged EU', in Alber, J. et al (eds) *Handbook of Quality of Life in the Enlarged European Union*, London: Routledge, pp 254–75.

Norris, M. and Redmond, D. (eds) (2005) *Housing Contemporary Ireland. Policy, Society, and Shelter*, Dublin: Institute of Public Administration.

Norris, M. and Shiels, P. (2007) 'Housing Inequalities in an Enlarged European Union. Patterns, Drivers, Implications', *Journal of European Social Policy*, 17, 1, pp 65–76.

North, D. (1990) *Institutions, Institutional Change and Economic Performance*, Cambridge: Cambridge University Press.

Notten, N. et al (2009) 'Digital Divide across Borders. A Cross-national Study of Adolescents' Use of Digital Technologies', *European Sociological Review*, 25, 5, pp 551–60.

Nóvoa, A. and Lawn, M. (eds) (2008) *Fabricating Europe: The Formation of an Education Space*, Cambridge: Cambridge University Press.

Nowak-Lewandowska, R. (2006) 'Emigro, ergo sum. Die Emigration der Polen und ihre Folgen', *Osteuropa*, 56, 11–12, pp 167–78.

Nyborn, T. (2007) 'A Rule-governed Community of Scholars: The Humboldt Vision in the History of the European University', in Maassen, P. and Olsen, J.P. (eds) *University Dynamics and European Integration*, Dordrecht: Springer, pp 55–79.

O'Boyle, E. (1999) 'Towards an Improved Definition of Poverty', *Review of Social Economy*, 57, 3, pp 281–301.

O'Boyle, L. (1966) 'The Middle Class in Western Europe 1815–1848', *American Historical Review*, 71, 3, pp 826–45.

OECD (1998) *Employment Outlook 1998*, Paris: OECD.

OECD (2001) *Knowledge and Skills for Life. First Results from the OECD Programme for International Student Assessment (PISA) 2000*, Paris: OECD.

OECD (2002) *OECD Economic Surveys 2001–2002. Denmark*, Vienna: OECD.

OECD (2003) *The Pisa 2003 Assessment Framework*, Paris: OECD.

OECD (2004) *Employment Outlook*, Paris: OECD.

OECD (2005a) *Housing Finance Markets in Transition Economies*, Paris: OECD.

OECD (2005b) *OECD Economic Survey. France*, Paris: OECD.

OECD (2005c) *OECD Economic Survey. Italy*, Paris: OECD.

OECD (2006a) *Information Technology Outlook 2006*, Paris: OECD.

OECD (2006b) *OECD Economic Survey. Czech Republic*, Paris: OECD.

OECD (2006c) *OECD Economic Survey. Germany*, Paris: OECD.

OECD (2006d) *OECD Economic Survey. Poland*, Paris: OECD.

OECD (2006e) *OECD Economic Surveys. Ireland*, Paris: OECD.

OECD (2006f) *OECD Economic Surveys. Portugal*, Paris: OECD.

OECD (2006g) *Society at a Glance*, Paris: OECD.

OECD (2007a) *Education at a Glance*, Paris: OECD.

OECD (2007b) *International Migration Outlook*, Paris: OECD.

OECD (2007c) *OECD Economic Survey. European Union*, Paris: OECD.

OECD (2007d) *OECD Economic Survey. Hungary*, Paris: OECD.

OECD (2007e) *OECD Economic Survey. Slovak Republic*, Paris: OECD.

OECD (2007f) *OECD Economic Surveys. Euro Area*, Paris: OECD.

OECD (2007g) *PISA 2006. Science Competencies for Tomorrow's World. Volume 1: Analysis*, Paris: OECD.

OECD (2008a) *OECD Economic Survey. Germany*, Paris: OECD.

OECD (2008b) *OECD Economic Surveys. Spain*, Paris: OECD.

OECD (2009a) *Economic Outlook No. 86 – December 2009 – Annual Projections for OECD Countries*. Available at: http://stats.oecd.org (accessed 3 March 2010).

OECD (2009b) *Education at a Glance*, Paris: OECD.

OECD (2009c) *Equally Prepared for Life? How 15-Year-Old Boys and Girls Perform in School Programme*, Paris: OECD.

OECD (2009d) *International Migration Outlook*, Paris: OECD.

OECD (2009e) *International Migration Outlook. SOPEMI 2009. Special Focus: Managing Labour Migration Beyond the Crisis*, Paris: OECD.

OECD (2009f) *International Migration Statistics*, Paris: OECD.

OECD (2009g) *Labor Force Statistics 1988–2008*, Paris: OECD.

OECD (2009h) *OECD Economic Survey. France*, Paris: OECD.

OECD (2009i) *OECD Economic Survey. Italy*, Paris: OECD.

OECD (2009j) *OECD Economic Surveys. Ireland*, Paris: OECD.

OECD (2009k) *Pensions at a Glance*, Paris: OECD.

OECD (2009l) *Society at a Glance*, Paris: OECD.

Offe, C. (1985) 'The Future of the Labour Market', in Keane, J. (ed) *Disorganized Capitalism*, Oxford: Polity, pp 52–79.

Offe, C. (2003) 'The European Model of "Social" Capitalism: Can it Survive European Integration?', *Journal of Political Philosophy*, 11, 4, pp 437–69.

Offe, C. and Fuchs, S. (2007) *Welfare State Formation in the Enlarged European Union. Patterns of Reform in the Post-Communist New Member States*, Berlin: WZB.

Oinonen, E. (2008) *Families in Converging Europe. A Comparison of Forms, Structures and Ideals*, New York: Palgrave Macmillan.

Olsen, K.M. and Dahl, S.-Å. (2007) 'Health Differences between European Countries', *Social Science & Medicine*, 64, 8, pp 1665–78.

Oorschot, W.V. (2009) 'The Dutch Welfare System – From Collective Solidarity Towards Individual Responsibility', in Schubert, K. et al (eds) *The Handbook of European Welfare Systems*, London: Routledge, pp 363–77.

Opaschowski, H.W. (2006) *Tourismusanalyse 2005*, Hamburg: BAT Freizeit Forschungsinstitut.

O'Rourke, K.H. and Sinnott, R. (2006) 'The Determinants of Individual Attitudes towards Immigration', *European Journal of Political Economy*, 22, 4, pp 838–61.

Ostner, I. and Knijn, T. (2002) 'Commodification and De-commodification', in Hobson, B. et al (eds) *Contested Concepts in Gender and Social Politics*, Cheltenham: Edward Elgar, pp 141–169.

Ostner, I. and Lewis, J. (1995) 'Gender and the Evolution of European Social Policy', in Pierson, P. and Leibfried, S. (eds) *European Social Policy. Between Fragmentation and Integration*, Washington D.C.: The Brookings Institution, pp 159–93.

Oswald, A.J. and Wu, S. (2010) 'Objective Confirmation of Subjective Measures of Human Well-being. Evidence from the USA', *Science*, 327, 5965, pp 576–9.

Otterbach, S. and Sousa-Poza, A. (2010) 'How Accurate are German Work-time Data? A Comparison of Time-diary Reports and Stylized Estimates', *Social Indicators Research*, 97, 3, pp 325–39.

Ours, J.C.V. and Veenman, J. (2003) 'The Educational Attainment of Second-generation Immigrants in The Netherlands', *Journal of Population Economics*, 16, 4, pp 739–53.

Outhwaite, W. (2008) *European Society*, Cambridge: Polity.

Özcan, V. and Seifert, W. (2000) 'Self-employment of Immigrants in Germany: Exclusion or Path to Integration?', *Soziale Welt*, 51, 3, pp 289–302.

Paastela, J. (2002) 'Finland', *Environmental Politics*, 11, 1, pp 17–38.

Pager, D. and Shepherd, H. (2008) 'The Sociology of Discrimination: Racial Discrimination in Employment, Housing, Credit, and Consumer Markets', *Annual Review of Sociology*, 34, pp 181–209.

Palloni, A. et al (2001) 'Social Capital and International Migration', *American Journal of Sociology*, 106, 5, pp 1262–98.

Pampel, F.C. (2001) 'Cigarette Diffusion and Sex Differences in Smoking', *Journal of Health and Social Behavior*, 42, 4, pp 388–404.

Papatheodorou, C. (2009) 'Inequalities and Deficiencies in Social Protection: The Welfare System of Greece', in Schubert, K. et al (eds) *The Handbook of European Welfare Systems*, London: Routledge, pp 225–43.

Park, R.E. (1936) 'Human Ecology', *American Journal of Sociology*, 42, 1, pp 1–15.

Parsons, T. (1952) *The Social System*, London: Tavistock.

Parsons, T. (1964a) 'Das Verwandtschaftssystem in den Vereinigten Staaten', in Parsons, T. (ed) *Soziologische Texte*, Neuwied: Luchterhand, pp 84–108.

Parsons, T. (1964b) 'Evolutionary Universals in Society', *American Sociological Review*, 29, 3, pp 339–57.

Parsons, T. and Bales, R.F. (1956) *Family Socialization and Interaction Process*, London: Routledge.

Peixoto, J. (2001) 'The International Mobility of Highly Skilled Workers in Transnational Corporations', *International Migration Review*, 35, 4, pp 1030–53.

Pereirinha, J.A. et al (2009) 'The Portuguese Welfare System: From a Corporative Regime to a European Welfare State', in Schubert, K. et al (eds) *The Handbook of European Welfare Systems*, London: Routledge, pp 398–414.

Perrucci, R. and Perrucci, C.C. (eds) (2007) *The Transformation of Work in the New Economy*, Oxford: Oxford University Press.

Petersen, T. and Morgan, L.A. (1995) 'Separate and Unequal: Occupation-establishment Sex Segregation and the Gender Wage Gap', *American Journal of Sociology*, 101, 2, pp 329–65.

Pettinger, L. et al (eds) (2006) *A New Sociology of Work?*, Oxford: Wiley.

Pettit, B. and Hook, J. (2005) 'The Structure of Women's Employment in Comparative Perspective', *Social Forces*, 84, 2, pp 779–801.

Piazolo, D. (2002) 'Entwicklungsunterschiede innerhalb einer erweiterten EU', *Aus Politik und Zeitgeschichte*, B 1–2, pp 11–22.

Pickles, J. (2008) 'State, Society and Hybrid Post-socialist Economies', in Pickles, J. (ed) *State and Society in Post-Socialist Economies*, New York: Palgrave Macmillan, pp 253–62.

Pickvance, C. (2009) 'Housing and Housing Policy', in Baldock, J. et al (eds) *Social Policy (3rd Edition)*, Oxford: Oxford University Press, pp 509–40.

Pietschmann, H. (2011: forthcoming) 'Spain and Portugal', in Bade, K.J. et al (eds) *The Encyclopaedia of Migration*, Cambridge: Cambridge University Press.

Pilbeam, P.M. (1990) *The Middle Classes in Europe 1789–1914. France, Germany, Italy and Russia*, London: Macmillan.

PIONEUR (2006) *Pioneers of European Integration 'From Below'. Mobility and the Emergence of European Identity among National and Foreign Citizens in the EU. Key Findings.* Available at: http://www.obets.ua.es/pioneur/difusion/PioneurExecutiveSummary.pdf (accessed 20 August 2008).

Pisati, M. and Schizzerotto, A. (2004) 'The Italian Mobility Regime: 1985–97', in Breen, R. (ed) *Social Mobility in Europe*, Oxford: Oxford University Press, pp 149–74.

Pisati, M. and Schizzerotto, A. (2006) 'Mid-career Women in Contemporary Italy. Economic and Institutional Changes', in Blossfeld, H.-P. and Hofmeister, H. (eds) *Globalization, Uncertainty, and Women's Careers*, Cheltenham: Edward Elgar, pp 352–75.

Plantenga, J. and Remery, C. (2006) *The Gender Pay Gap. Origins and Policy Responses. A Comparative Review of Thirty European Countries*, Utrecht: Utrecht School of Economics.

Pollack, D. (2008) 'Religious Change in Europe: Theoretical Considerations and Empirical Findings', *Social Compass*, 55, pp 168–86.

Popova, S. et al (2007) 'Comparing Alcohol Consumption in Central and Eastern Europe to Other European Countries', *Alcohol and Alcoholism*, 42, 5, pp 465–73.

Portes, A. (2003) 'Conclusion: Theoretical Convergencies and Empirical Evidence in the Study of Immigrant Transnationalism', *International Migration Review*, 37, 3, pp 874–92.

Portes, A. and DeWind, J. (eds) (2007) *Rethinking Migration: New Theoretical and Empirical Perspectives*, New York City: Berghan Books.

Portes, A. and Rumbaut, R.G. (1990) *Immigrant America: A Portrait*, Berkeley: University of California Press.

Portes, A. et al (2005) 'Segmented Assimilation on the Ground: The New Second Generation in Early Adulthood', *Ethnic and Racial Studies*, 28, 6, pp 1000–40.

Präg, P. et al (2010: forthcoming) 'Quality of Work and Quality of Life of Service Sector Workers. Cross-National Variations in Eight European Countries', in Bäck-Wiklund, M. et al (eds) *Quality of Work and Life. Theory, Practice, and Policy*, Houndmills, Basingstoke: Palgrave Macmillan.

Praszalowicz, D. (2011: forthcoming) 'Poland', in Bade, K.J. et al (eds) *The Encyclopaedia of Migration*, Cambridge: Cambridge University Press.

Pridham, G. (1994) 'National Environmental Policy-making in the European Framework. Spain, Greece, and Italy in Comparison', in Baker, S. et al (eds) *Protecting the Periphery. Environmental Policy in Peripheral Regions of the European Union*, Portland: Frank Cass, pp 80–101.

Pries, L. (2001a) *Internationale Migration*, Bielefeld: Transcript.

Pries, L. (2001b) *New Transnational Social Spaces*, London: Routledge.

Pries, L. (2004a) 'Determining the Causes and Durability of Transnational Labour Migration between Mexico and the United States: Some Empirical Findings', *International Migration*, 42, 2, pp 3–39.

Pries, L. (2004b) 'Transnationalism and Migration. New Challenges for the Social Sciences and Education', in Luchtenberg, S. (ed) *Migration, Education and Change*, London: Routledge, pp 15–39.

Pritchard, R. (2004) 'Humboldtian Values in a Changing World: Staff and Students in a Changing World', *Oxford Review of Education*, 30, 4, pp 509–28.

Promberger, M. et al (2008) 'Beschäftigungsfähigkeit, Arbeitsvermögen und Arbeitslosigkeit', *WSI-Mitteilungen*, 61, 2, pp 70–6.

Public Opinion Research Center (2007) *Poles Working Abroad*, Warsaw: CBOS.

Ragacs, C. (2002) 'Warum Mindestlöhne die Beschäftigung nicht reduzieren müssen: neoklassische Ansätze im Überblick', *Wirtschaft und Gesellschaft*, 28, 1, pp 59–84.

Rainwater, L. (1992) 'Changing Inequality Structure in Europe: The Challenge to Social Science', in Dierkes, M. and Bievert, B. (eds) *European Social Science in Transition: Assessment and Outlook*, Frankfurt/Main: Campus, pp 391–415.

Rajevska, F. (2009) 'The Welfare System in Latvia after Renewing Independence', in Schubert, K. et al (eds) *The Handbook of European Welfare Systems*, London: Routledge, pp 328–43.

Rapley, M. (2003) *Quality of Life Research. A Critical Introduction*, Thousand Oaks, CA: Sage.

Räsänen, P. (2006) 'Information Society for All? Structural Characteristics of Internet Use in 15 European Countries', *European Societies*, 8, 1, pp 59–81.

Raza, W.G. and Wedl, V. (2003) 'Auswirkungen der Liberalisierung öffentlicher Dienstleistungserbringung', *Wirtschaft und Gesellschaft*, 29, 3, pp 415–44.

Razum, O. et al (2005) 'Health, Wealth or Family Ties? Why Turkish Work Migrants Return from Germany', *Journal of Ethnic and Migration Studies*, 31, 4, pp 719–39.

Recchi, E. (2009) 'Cross-state Mobility in the EU. Trends, Puzzles, Consequences', *European Societies*, 10, 2, pp 197–224.

Recchi, E. and Favell, A. (eds) (2009) *Pioneers of European Integration: Citizenship and Mobility in the EU*, Cheltenham: Edward Elgar.

Recchi, E. et al (2003) *Intra-EU Migration: A Socio-demographic Overview*, Florence: PIONEUR Project.

Redclift, M.R. and Woodgate, G. (eds) (2010) *The International Handbook of Environmental Sociology*, Cheltenham: Edward Elgar.

Reher, D. (2007) 'Towards Long-term Population Decline. A Discussion of Relevant Issues', *European Journal of Population*, 23, 2, pp 189–207.

Rehm, J. et al (2006) 'Volume of Alcohol Consumption, Patterns of Drinking and Burden of Disease in the European Region 2002', *Addiction*, 101, 8, pp 1086–95.

Reimer, D. and Pollak, R. (2009) 'Educational Expansion and its Consequences for Vertical and Horizontal Inequalities in Access to Higher Education in West Germany', *European Sociological Review*, 25, Advance Access published 11 June, pp 1–16.

Reinalda, B. and Kulesza, E. (2005) *The Bologna Process: Harmonizing Europe's Higher Education*, Opladen: Barbara Budrich.

Remond, R. (1999) *Religion and Society in Modern Europe*, Oxford: Blackwell.

Richter, M. and Lampert, T. (2008) 'Socioeconomic Differences in Adolescent Smoking', *Archives of Public Health*, 66, 2, pp 69–87.

Ridgeway, C. (1997) 'Interaction and the Conservation of Gender Inequality: Considering Employment', *American Sociological Review*, 62, 2, pp 218–35.

Rieger, E. (1995) 'Protective Shelter or Straitjacket: An Institutional Analysis of the Common Agricultural Policy of the European Community', in Leibfried, S. and Pierson, P. (eds) *European Social Policy: Between Fragmentation and Integration*, Washington D.C.: Brookings, pp 194–230.

Riley, N.E. (2005) 'Demography of Gender', in Poston, D.L. and Micklin, M. (eds) *Handbook of Population*, New York: Springer, pp 109–41.

Riphahn, R.T. (2003) 'Cohort Effects in the Educational Attainment of Second Generation Immigrants in Germany: An Analysis of Census Data', *Journal of Population Economics*, 16, 4, pp 711–37.

Risse, T. (2004) 'European Institutions and Identity Change: What Have We Learnt?', in Herrmann, R.K. et al (eds) *Transnational Identities. Becoming European in the EU*, Lanham: Rowman and Littlefield Publishers, pp 247–71.

Rist, R.C. (1978) *Guestworker in Germany*, New York: Praeger.

Ritter, G.A. and Tenfelde, K. (1992) *Arbeiter im deutschen Kaiserreich*, Bonn: Dietz.

Robert, P. and Bukodi, E. (2004) 'Changes in Intergenerational Mobility in Hungary: 1973–2000', in Breen, R. (ed) *Social Mobility in Europe*, Oxford: Oxford University Press, pp 287–314.

Robine, J.-M. et al (2003) 'Creating a Coherent Set of Indicators to Monitor Health across Europe. The Euro-REVES 2 Project', *European Journal of Public Health*, 13, Supplement 1, pp 6–14.

Roche, W.K. (2000) 'Ireland', in Ebbinghaus, B. and Visser, J. (eds) *Trade Unions in Western Europe since 1945*, London: Palgrave Macmillan, pp 339–70.

Rodriguez-Pose, A. (1998) *The Dynamics of Regional Growth in Europe. Social and Political Factors*, Oxford: Clarendon Press.

Rodríguez-Pose, A. (2002) *The European Union. Economy, Society and Polity*, Oxford: Oxford University Press.

Rogers, E.M. and Shoemaker, F.F. (1971) *Communication of Innovations. A Cross-cultural Approach*, New York: Free Press.

Rogerson, R. (2008) 'Structural Transformation and the Deterioration of European Labor Market Outcomes', *Journal of Political Economy*, 116, 2, pp 235–59.

Rohrschneider, R. (2002) 'The Democracy Deficit and Mass Support for an EU-wide Government', *American Journal of Political Science*, 46, pp 463–75.

Rohrschneider, R. and Whitefield, S. (eds) (2006) *Public Opinion, Party Competition and the European Union in Eastern Europe*, London: Palgrave Macmillan.

Rokkan, S. (1974) 'Dimensions of State Formation and Nation Building', in Tilly, C. (ed) *The Formation of National States in Western Europe*, Princeton: Princeton University Press, pp 562–600.

Rokkan, S. (1999) *State Formation, Nation-building and Mass Politics in Europe. The Theory of Stein Rokkan based on his Collected Works, Selected and Rearranged by Peter Flora, Stein Kuhnle and Derek Urwin*, Oxford: Oxford University Press.

Romanian National Institute of Statistics (2008) *Regional Statistics*. Available at: http://www.insse.ro/cms/rw/pages/index.ro.do (accessed 5 December 2008).

Rootes, C. (ed) (2003) *Environmental Protest in Western Europe*, Oxford: Oxford University Press.

Rosa, H. and Scheuerman, W.E. (eds) (2009) *High-speed Society. Social Acceleration, Power, and Modernity*, University Park, PA: Pennsylvania State University Press.

Rosholm, M. et al (2006) 'The Times They are A-Changin'. Declining Immigrant Employment Opportunities in Scandinavia', *International Migration Review*, 40, 2, pp 318–47.

Rothenbacher, F. (2002) *The European Population 1850–1945*, London: Palgrave Macmillan.

Rothenbacher, F. (2005) *The European Population since 1945*, London: Palgrave Macmillan.

Rother, N. (2005) 'Wer zieht innerhalb der EU wohin und warum? Das Pioneur-Projekt', *ZUMA-Nachrichten*, 56, pp 94–7.

Rucht, D. and Roose, J. (2003) 'Germany', in Rootes, C. (ed) *Environmental Protest in Western Europe*, Oxford: Oxford University Press, pp 80–108.

Rudolph, H. and Hillmann, F. (1998) 'The Invisible Hand Needs Visible Heads: Managers, Experts, and Professionals from Western Countries in Poland', in Koser, K. and Lutz, H. (eds) *The New Migration in Europe: Social Constructions and Social Realities*, London: MacMillan, pp 60–89.

Rüegg, W. (1996) 'Foreword', in Ridder-Symoens, H.D. (ed) *A History of the University in Europe (Volume 1): Universities in the Middle Ages*, Cambridge: Cambridge University Press, pp xix–xxviii.

Rumford, C. (2002) *The European Union. A Political Sociology*, Oxford: Blackwell.

Rumford, C. (2008) *Cosmopolitan Spaces. Europe, Globalization, Theory*, London/ New York: Routledge.

Rumford, C. (ed) (2009) *The SAGE Handbook of European studies*, London: SAGE.

Sachße, C. and Tennstedt, F. (1982) 'Krankenversicherung und Wohnungsfrage', in Asmus, G. (eds) *Hinterhof, Keller und Mansarde. Einblicke in Berliner Wohnungselend 1901–1920*, Reinbek: Rowohlt, pp 271–97.

Saar, E. et al (2008) 'Transition from Educational System to Labour Market in the European Union. A Comparison between New and Old Members', *International Journal of Comparative Sociology*, 49, 1, pp 31–59.

Sabel, C.F. and Zeitlin, J. (1985) 'Historical Alternatives to Mass Production', *Past and Present*, 108, 1, pp 133–76.

Sainsbury, D. (eds) (1999) *Gender and Welfare State Regimes*, Oxford: Oxford University Press.

Sala-i-Martin, X. (1996) 'The Classical Approach to Convergence Analysis', *Economic Journal*, 106, July, pp 1019–36.

Salt, J. (1992) 'Migration Processes amongst the Highly Skilled in Europe', *International Migration Review*, 26, 2, pp 484–505.

Salt, J. and Findlay, A.M. (1989) 'International Migration of Highly-Skilled Manpower', in Appleyard, R.T. (ed) *The Impact of International Migration on Developing Countries*, Paris: OECD, pp 159–80.

Salt, J. and Ford, R. (1993) 'Skilled International Migration in Europe. The Shape of Things to Come?', in King, R. (ed) *Mass Migration in Europe*, London: Belhaven Press, pp 293–309.

Sampson, R.J. et al (2002) 'Assessing "Neighborhood Effects". Social Processes and New Directions in Research', *Annual Review of Sociology*, 28, pp 443–78.

Samuelson, P.A. and Nordhaus, W.D. (2005) *Economics (18th Edition)*, New York: McGraw-Hill.

Sánchez-Barricarte, J. and Fernández-Carro, R. (2007) 'Patterns in the Delay and Recovery of Fertility in Europe', *European Journal of Population*, 23, 1, pp 145–70.

Sanders, C. et al (1998) 'Reporting on Quality of Life in Randomised Controlled Trials. Bibliographic Study', *British Medical Journal*, 317, 7167, pp 1191–4.

Sardon, J.-P. (2004) 'Recent Demographic Trends in the Developed Countries', *Population (English Edition)*, 59, 2, pp 263–314.

Sayer, L.C. (2010) 'Trends in Housework', in Treas, J. and Drobnič, S. (eds) *Dividing the Domestic. Men, Women, and Household Work in Cross-national Perspective*, Stanford, CA: Stanford University Press, pp 19–40.

Schaefer, R.T. (2007) *Sociology (10th Edition)*, Boston: McGraw-Hill.

Schaefer, R.T. (2008) *Sociology Matters (3rd Edition)*, Boston: McGraw-Hill.

Schäfer, M. et al (2004) 'Bringing Together the Concepts of Quality of Life and Sustainability', in Glatzer, W. et al (eds) *Challenges for Quality of Life in the Contemporary World. Advances in Quality-of-life Studies, Theory, and Research*, Dordrecht: Kluwer, pp 33–43.

Scharpf, F.W. (1986) 'Structures of Postindustrial Society or Does Mass Unemployment Disappear in the Service and Information Economy?', in Appelbaum, E. and Schettkat, R. (eds) *Labor Market Adjustments to Structural Change and Technological Progress*, New York: Praeger, pp 17–35.

Scharpf, F.W. (1999) *Governing in Europe. Effective and Democratic?*, Oxford: Oxford University Press.

Scharpf, F.W. and Schmidt, V. (eds) (2000) *Welfare and Work in the Open Economy*, Oxford: Oxford University Press.

Schätzl, L. (1993) *Wirtschaftsgeographie der Europäischen Gemeinschaft*, Paderborn: Schöningh.

Schimmelfennig, F. and Sedelmeier, U. (eds) (2005) *The Politics of European Union Enlargement. Theoretical approaches*, London/New York: Routledge.

Schludi, M. (2005) *The Reform of Bismarckian Pension Systems: A Comparison of Pension Politics in Austria, France, Germany, Italy and Sweden*, Amsterdam: Amsterdam University Press.

Schmidt, S.K. (2001) 'Die Einflussmöglichkeiten der Europäischen Kommission auf die europäische Politik', *Politische Vierteljahresschrift*, 42, 1, pp 173–92.

Schmitt, H. and Thomassen, J. (eds) (1999) *Political Representation and Legitimacy in the European Union*, Oxford: Oxford University Press.

Schnepf, S.V. (2007) 'Immigrants' Educational Disadvantage: An Examination Across ten Countries and Three Surveys', *Journal of Population Economics*, 20, 3, pp 527–45.

Schofer, E. and Meyer, J.W. (2005) 'The Worldwide Expansion of Higher Education in the Twentieth Century', *American Sociological Review*, 70, 6, pp 898–920.

Schulten, T. and Watt, A. (2007) *European Minimum Wage Policy. A Concrete Project for a Social Europe*, Brussels: ETUI-REHS.

Scott, S. (2006) 'The Social Morphology of Skilled Migration: The Case of the British Middle Class in Paris', *Journal of Ethnic and Migration Studies*, 32, 7, pp 1105–29.

Sen, A. (1985) *Commodities and Capabilities*, Amsterdam: North-Holland.

Sen, A. (1993) 'Capability and Well-being', in Nussbaum, M.C. and Sen, A. (eds) *The Quality of Life*, Oxford: Clarendon, pp 30–53.

Sennett, R. (2006) *The Culture of the New Capitalism*, New Haven, CT: Yale University Press.

Settersten, R.A. (2006) 'Aging and the Life Course', in Binstock, R.H. et al (eds) *Handbook of Aging and the Social Sciences*, London: Academic Press, pp 3–19.

Shavit, Y. and Müller, W. (eds) (1997) *From School to Work. A Comparative Study of Qualifications and Occupational Destinations*, Oxford: Clarendon.

Shavit, Y. and Müller, W. (2000) 'Vocational Secondary Education. Where Diversion and Where Safety Net?', *European Societies*, 2, 1, pp 29–50.

Shaw, M. (2004) 'Housing and Public Health', *Annual Review of Public Health*, 25, pp 397–418.

Shelton, B.A. and John, D. (1996) 'The Division of Household Labor', *Annual Review of Sociology*, 22, pp 299–322.

Siegrist, J. and Marmot, M. (eds) (2006) *Social Inequalities in Health. New Evidence and Policy Implications*, Oxford: Oxford University Press.

Sierminska, E. et al (2006) *Comparing Wealth Distribution across Rich Countries. First Results from Luxembourg Wealth Study*, Luxembourg: Luxembourg Income Study Project.

Sirgy, M.J. et al (2006) 'The Quality-of-life (QOL) Research Movement. Past, Present, and Future', *Social Indicators Research*, 76, 3, pp 343–466.

Smith, A.D. (1991) *National Identity*, Harmondsworth: Penguin.

Smyth, W.C. (2011: forthcoming) 'Ireland and Northern Ireland', in Bade, K.J. et al (eds) *The Encyclopaedia of Migration*, Cambridge: Cambridge University Press.

Sobal, J. and Stunkard, A.J. (1989) 'Socioeconomic Status and Obesity. A Review of the Literature', *Psychological Bulletin*, 105, 2, pp 260–75.

Solga, H. (1995) *Auf dem Weg in die klassenlose Gesellschaft? Klassenlagen und Mobilität zwischen den Generationen in der DDR*, Berlin: Akademie.

Solga, H. (2002) 'Stigmatization by Negative Selection: Explaining Less-educated People's Decreasing Employment Opportunities', *European Sociological Review*, 18, 2, pp 159–78.

Sombart, W. (1976 [1906]) *Why is There No Socialism in the United States?*, New York: M.E. Sharpe.

Sørensen, A.B. (1983) 'Process of Allocation to Open and Closed Positions in Social Structure', *Zeitschrift für Soziologie*, 12, pp 203–24.

Sørensen, A.B. (2000) 'Toward a Sounder Basis for Class Analysis', *American Journal of Sociology*, 105, 6, pp 1523–58.

Sorokin, P.A. (1927) *Social Mobility*, New York: Harper and Row.

Soskice, D. (1999) 'Divergent Production Regimes: Coordinated and Uncoordinated Market Economies in the 1980s and 1990s', in Kitschelt, H. et al (eds) *Continuity and Change in Contemporary Capitalism*, Cambridge: Cambridge University Press, pp 101–34.

Sperber, J. (2009) *Europe 1850–1914 Progress, Participation and Apprehension*, Harlow: Pearson Education Limited.

Stanat, P. and Christensen, G. (2006) *Where Immigrant Students Succeed: A Comparative Review of Performance and Engagement in PISA 2003*, Paris: OECD.

Standing, G. (1997) 'Globalization, Labour Flexibility and Insecurity: The Era of Market Regulation', *European Journal of Industrial Relations*, 3, 1, pp 7–37.

Stark, D. and Bruszt, L. (1998) *Postsocialist Pathways. Transforming Politics and Property in East Central Europe*, Cambridge: Cambridge University Press.

Stark, O. (1984) 'Discontinuity and the Theory of International Migration', *Kyklos*, 37, 2, pp 206–22.

Stark, O. (1993) *The Migration of Labor*, Cambridge: Blackwell.

Stark, O. and Bloom, D.E. (1985) 'The New Economics of Labor Migration', *American Economic Review*, 75, 2, pp 173–8.

Statistical Office of the Slovak Republic (2008) *Demography*. Available at: http://portal.statistics.sk (accessed 5 December 2008).

Statistical Service of Cyprus (2009) *Demographic Report 2008*, Nicosia: Statistical Service of Cyprus.

Statistics Netherlands (2009) *Press release PB09-079*. Available at: www.cbs.nl (accessed 12 December 2009).

Statistics Sweden (2010) *Wealth Statistics*. Available at: www.scb.se/Pages/Product____83227.aspx (accessed 1 January 2010).

Steidl, A. et al (eds) (2009) *European Mobility. Internal, International, and Transatlantic Moves in the 19th and Early 20th Centuries*, Göttingen: V & R.

Stevens, A. and Stevens, H. (2001) *Brussels Bureaucrats? The Administration of the European Union*, London: Palgrave Macmillan.

Stjernø, S. (2004) *Solidarity in Europe. The History of an Idea*, Cambridge: Cambridge University Press.

Stone Sweet, A. et al (eds) (2001) *The Institutionalization of Europe*, Oxford: Oxford University Press.

Strang, H. (1970) *Erscheinungsformen der Sozialhilfebedürftigkeit. Beitrag zur Geschichte, Theorie und empirischen Analyse der Armut*, Stuttgart: Enke.

Streeck, W. (2005) 'The Sociology of Labor Markets and Trade Unions', in Smelser, N.J. and Swedberg, R. (eds) *The Handbook of Economic Sociology (2nd Edition)*, Princeton: Princeton University Press, pp 254–83.

Streeck, W. and Trampusch, C. (2005) 'Economic Reform and the Political Economy of the German Welfare State', *German Politics*, 14, 2, pp 174–95.

Strelow, H. (2006) *Passenger Transport in the European Union*, Luxembourg: Eurostat.

Strüver, A. (2005) 'Spheres of Transnationalism within the European Union. On Open Doors, Thresholds, and Drawbridges along the Dutch–German Border', *Journal of Ethnic and Migration Studies*, 31, 2, pp 323–43.

Sullivan, O. and Katz-Gerro, T. (2007) 'The Omnivore Thesis Revisited. Voracious Cultural Consumers', *European Sociological Review*, 23, 2, pp 123–37.

Swanson, D. and Siegel, J.S. (eds) (2004) *The Methods and Materials of Demography*, San Diego: Academic Press.

Sylos-Labini, P. (1975) *Saggio sulle classi sociali*, Bari: Laterza.

Szmigin, I. and Carrigan, M. (2001) 'Learning to Love the Older Consumer', *Journal of Consumer Beaviour*, 1, 1, pp 22–34.

Szydlik, M. (2007) 'Familie und Sozialstruktur', in Ecarius, J. (ed) *Handbuch Familie*, Wiesbaden: VS, pp 78–93.

Taft, R. (1953) 'The Shared Frame of Reference Concept Applied to the Assimilation of Immigrants', *Human Relations*, 6, 1, pp 45–55.

Tang, H. (2005) *Winners and Losers of EU Integration: Policy Issues for Central and Eastern Europe*, Washington D.C.: World Bank Publications.

Tausz, K. (2009) 'From State Socialism to a Hybrid Welfare State: Hungary', in Schubert, K. et al (eds) *The Handbook of European Welfare Systems*, London: Routledge, pp 244–59.

Taylor-Gooby, P. (ed) (2004) *Making a European Welfare State? Convergences and Conflicts over European Social Policy*, Malden: Blackwell.

Telhaug, A.O. et al (2004) 'From Collectivism to Individualism? Education as Nation Building in a Scandinavian Perspective', *Scandinavian Journal of Educational Research*, 48, 2, pp 141–58.

Therborn, G. (1995) *European Modernity and Beyond. The Trajectory of European Societies 1945–2000*, London: Sage.

Therborn, G. (2004) *Between Sex and Power: Family in the World 1900–2000*, London: Routledge.

The World Bank (2009) *World Development Indicators 2009*, Washington, D.C.: International Bank for Reconstruction and Development.

Thompson, J.A.F. (1998) *The Western Church in the Middle Ages*, London: Arnold Publishing.

Threllfall, M. (2003) 'European Social Integration: Harmonization, Convergence and Single Social Areas', *Journal of European Social Policy*, 13, 2, pp 121–39.

Thurow, L.C. (1975) *Generating Inequality*, New York: Basic Books.

Titmuss, R.M. (1958) *Essays on the Welfare State*, London: Allen and Unwin.

Titmuss, R.M. (1974) *Social Policy*, London: Allen and Unwin.

TNS Opinion & Social (2005) *Eurobarometer 63. Die öffentliche Meinung in der Europäischen Union. Vollständiger Bericht*, Brussels: European Commission.

TNS Opinion & Social (2006) *Europeans and Their Languages. Analytical Report Special Eurobarometer 243/EB 64.3*, Brussels: European Commission.

Tocqueville, A.D. (2000 [1835/40]) *Democracy in America*, New York: Perennial Classics.

Tomaskovic-Devey, D. and Skaggs, S. (2002) 'Sex Segregation, Labor Process Organization, and Gender Earnings Inequality', *American Journal of Sociology*, 108, 1, pp 102–28.

Tomka, B. (2004) *Welfare State in East and West. Hungarian Social Security in International Comparison 1918–1990*, Berlin: Akademie Verlag.

Tomlinson, J. (2007) *The Culture of Speed. The Coming of Immediacy*, London etc.: Sage.

Toniolo, G. (1998) 'Europe's Golden Age, 1950–1973: Speculations from a Long-run Perspective', *The Economic History Review*, 51, 2, pp 252–67.

Townsend, P. (1979) *Poverty in the United Kingdom: A Survey of Household Resources and Standards of Living*, Harmondsworth: Penguin Books.

Townsend, P. (1985) 'A Sociological Approach to the Measurement of Poverty', *Oxford Economic Papers*, 37, 4, pp 659–68.

Traxler, F. (2003a) 'Bargaining, State Regulation and the Trajectories of Industrial Relations', *European Journal of Industrial Relations*, 9, 2, pp 141–61.

Traxler, F. (2003b) 'Coordinated Bargaining. A Stocktaking of its Preconditions, Practices, and Performance', *Industrial Relations Journal*, 34, 3, pp 194–209.

Traxler, F. and Brandl, B. (2009) 'Towards Europeanization of Wage Policy: Germany and the Nordic Countries', *European Union Politics*, 10, 2, pp 177–201.

Treas, J. and Drobnič, S. (eds) (2010) *Dividing the Domestic. Men, Women, and Household Work in Cross-national Perspective*, Stanford, CA: Stanford University Press.

Trepper, T.S. and Rouse, L.P. (2002) *Marital and Sexual Lifestyles in the United States: Attitudes, Behaviors, and Relationships in Social Context*, London: Routledge.

Triandafyllidou, A. (2006) *Contemporary Polish Migration in Europe*, Lewiston: Mellen.

Trumm, A. and Ainsaar, M. (2009) 'The Welfare System of Estonia: Past, Present and Future', in Schubert, K. et al (eds) *The Handbook of European Welfare Systems*, London: Routledge, pp 153–70.

Turner, B.S. (2004) 'Religion, Romantic Love, and the Family', in Scott, J. et al (eds) *The Blackwell Companion to the Sociology of Families*, Oxford: Blackwell, pp 289–305.

Turner, M.A. and Ross, S.L. (2005) 'How Racial Discrimination Affects the Search for Housing', in Souza Briggs, X.D. (ed) *The Geography of Opportunity: Race and Housing Choice in Metropolitan America*, Washington D.C.: Brookings Institute Press, pp 81–100.

Uhlenberg, P. (2005) 'Demography of Aging', in Poston, D.L. and Micklin, M. (eds) *Handbook of Population*, New York: Springer, pp 143–67.

Ule, M. (2004) 'Changes in Family Life Courses in Slovenia', in Robila, M. (ed) *Families in Eastern Europe*, Amsterdam: Elsevier, pp 87–101.

UNDATA (2008) *UN Statistical Database*. Available at: http://data.un.org/ (accessed 7 May 2008).

UNESCO (2006) *Global Education Digest 2006. Comparing Education Statistics across the World*, Montreal: UNESCO Institute for Statistics.

UNESCO (2009) *Global Education Digest 2009*, Montreal: UNESCO Institute for Statistics.

UNWTO (2006) *Tourism Highlights. 2006 Edition*. Available at: http://www.unwto.org/facts/eng/highlights.htm (accessed 20 October 2006).

Upchurch, M. (2007) 'After Unification: Trade Unions and Industrial Relations in Eastern Germany', *Industrial Relations Journal*, 26, 4, pp 280–92.

Vallet, L.-A. (2004) 'Change in Intergenerational Class Mobility in France from the 1970s to the 1990s and its Explanation', in Breen, R. (ed) *Social Mobility in Europe*, Oxford: Oxford University Press, pp 115–47.

Valverde, J.R. and Vila, M.R. (2003) 'Internal Migration and Inequalities. The Influence of Migrant Origin on Educational Attainment in Spain', *European Sociological Review*, 19, 3, pp 299–317.

van de Kaa, D.J. (1987) 'Europe's Second Demographic Transition', *Population Bulletin*, 42, 1, pp 3–57.

Vandenbrande, T. et al (2006) *Mobility in Europe*, Luxembourg: Office for Official Publications of the European Communities.

van der Lippe, T. (2007) 'Dutch Workers and Time Pressure. Household and Workplace Characteristics', *Work, Employment, and Society*, 21, 4, pp 693–711.

van der Lippe, T. and Peters, P. (2007) 'Finding Time', in van der Lippe, T. and Peters, P. (eds) *Competing Claims in Work and Family Life*, Cheltenham: Edward Elgar, pp 1–17.

van der Lippe, T. and van Dijk, L. (2002) 'Comparative Research on Women's Employment', *Annual Review of Sociology*, 28, 1, pp 221–41.

van der Meer, M. (2000) 'Spain', in Ebbinghaus, B. and Visser, J. (eds) *Trade Unions in Western Europe since 1945*, London: Palgrave Macmillan, pp 573–603.

Van der Meer, P.H. (2008) 'Is the Gender Wage Gap Declining in the Netherlands?', *Applied Economics*, 40, pp 149–60.

Veenhoven, R. (2000) 'The Four Qualities of Life. Ordering Concepts and Measures of the Good Life', *Journal of Happiness Studies*, 1, 1, pp 1–39.

Venn, D. (2009) *Legislation, Collective Bargaining and Enforcement: Updating the OECD Employment Protection Indicators. OECD Social, Employment and Migration Working Papers*, Paris: OECD.

Verbakel, E. and DiPrete, T. (2008) 'Non-working Time, Income Inequality, and Quality of Life Comparisons. The Case of the US vs. the Netherlands', *Social Forces*, 87, 2, pp 679–712.

Verwiebe, R. (2004) *Transnationale Mobilität innerhalb Europas*, Berlin: Edition Sigma.

Verwiebe, R. (2008) 'Migration to Germany. Is a Middle Class Emerging among Intra-European Migrants?', *Migration Letters*, 6, 1, pp 1–19.

Verwiebe, R. (2010) 'Why Do Europeans Migrate to Berlin? Social-structural Differences for Italian, British, French and Polish Nationals in the Period between 1980 and 2002', *International Migration*, 48, 3, pp 273–93.

Verwiebe, R. and Eder, K. (2006) 'The Integration of Transnationally Mobile Europeans in the German Labour Market', *European Societies*, 8, 1, pp 141–67.

Verwiebe, R. et al (2010: forthcoming) 'Skilled German Migrants and their Motives for Migration within Europe', *Journal of Integrational Migration and Integration*, 11, 3.

Villota, P.D. and Vázquez, S. (2009) 'The Welfare State in Spain: Unfinished Business', in Schubert, K. et al (eds) *The Handbook of European Welfare Systems*, London: Routledge, pp 171–88.

Vis, B. et al (2008) 'The Politics of Welfare State Reform in the Netherlands: Explaining a Never-ending Puzzle', *Acta Politica*, 43, 2–3, pp 333–56.

Visser, J. (2000a) 'France', in Ebbinghaus, B. and Visser, J. (eds) *Trade Unions in Western Europe since 1945*, London: Palgrave Macmillan, pp 237–77.

Visser, J. (2000b) 'Italy', in Ebbinghaus, B. and Visser, J. (eds) *Trade Unions in Western Europe since 1945*, London: Palgrave Macmillan, pp 371–428.

Visser, J. (2002) 'The First Part-time Economy in the World. A Model to be Followed?', *Journal of European Social Policy*, 12, 1, pp 23–42.

Visser, J. (2005) 'Beneath the Surface of Stability: New and Old Modes of Governance in European Industrial Relations', *European Journal of Industrial Relations*, 11, 3, pp 287–306.

Visser, J. (2006) 'Union Membership Statistics in 24 Countries', *Monthly Labor Review*, 129, 1, pp 38–49.

Visser, J. (2009) *ICTWSS: Database on Institutional Characteristics of Trade Unions, Wage Setting, State Intervention and Social Pacts in 34 countries between 1960 and 2007.* Available at: http://www.uva-aias.net/ (accessed 3 February 2010).

Vlad, C.-M. (2004) 'Labor Market Participation for Women in Romania', *Studia Universitatis Babes-Bolyai: Sociologia*, 49, 1, pp 109–18.

Vleuten, E.V.D. and Kaijser, A. (eds) (2006) *Networking Europe. Transnational Infrastructures and the Shaping of Europe, 1850–2000*, Sagamore Beach, MA: Science History Publications.

Vobruba, G. (2003) 'The Enlargement Crisis of the European Union. Limits of the Dialectics of Integration and Expansion', *Journal of European Social Policy*, 13, 1, pp 35–62.

Vobruba, G. (2005) *Die Dynamik Europas*, Wiesbaden: VS.

Völker, B. and Flap, H. (1999) 'Getting Ahead in the GDR: Social Capital and Status Attainment under Communism', *Acta Sociologica*, 42, 1, pp 17–34.

Wæver, O. (1997) 'Imperial Metaphors: Emerging European Analogies to Pre-nation State Imperial Systems', in Tunander, O. et al (eds) *Geopolitics in Post-wall Europe*, London: Sage, pp 59–93.

Wagner, M. and Weiß, B. (2006) 'On the Variation of Divorce Risks in Europe. Findings from a Meta-analysis of European Longitudinal Studies', *European Sociological Review*, 22, 5, pp 483–500.

Wagner, P. (2008a) 'Does Europe Have a Cultural Identity?', in Joas, H. and Wiegandt, K. (eds) *The Cultural Values of Europe*, Liverpool: Liverpool University Press, pp 357–68.

Wagner, P. (2008b) *Modernity as Experience and Interpretation. A New Sociology of Modernity*, Cambridge: Polity Press.

Walker, A. and Maltby, T. (1997) *Ageing Europe*, Buckingham: Open University Press.

Wall, R. and Robin, J. (eds) (1983) *Family Forms in Historic Europe*, Cambridge: Cambridge University Press.

Wallace, C. and Vincent, K. (2009) 'Recent Migration from the New European Borderlands', in Fassmann, H. et al (eds) *Migration and Mobility in Europe: Trends, Patterns and Control*, Aldershot: Edward Elgar, pp 144–60.

Wallace, H. and Wallace, W. (eds) (2000) *Policy-Making in the European Union*, Oxford: Oxford University Press (4th edn).

Wallerstein, I. (1974) *The Modern World-system, Volume I: Capitalist Agriculture and the Origins of the European World-economy in the Sixteenth Century*, New York/London: Academic Press.

Wallerstein, I. (1980) *The Modern World-system, Volume II: Mercantilism and the Consolidation of the European World-economy, 1600–1750*, New York/London: Academic Press.

Wallerstein, I. (1989) *The Modern World-system, Vol. III: The Second Great Expansion of the Capitalist World-economy 1730–1840s*, San Diego: Academic Press.

Walwei, U. (1999) 'Die Europäisierung der nationalen Arbeitsmärkte', in Döring, D. and Metzger, E. (eds) *Sozialstaat in der Globalisierung*, Frankfurt/Main: Suhrkamp, pp 168–91.

Wardle, J. et al (2002) 'Sex Differences in the Association of Socioeconomic Status with Obesity', *American Journal of Public Health*, 92, 8, pp 1299–304.

Watson, D. and Webb, R. (2009) 'Do Europeans View their Homes as Castles? Home Ownership and Poverty Perception throughout Europe', *Urban Studies*, 46, 9, pp 1787–805.

Weber, M. (1934) *Die protestantische Ethik und der Geist des Kapitalismus*, Tübingen: Mohr.

Weber, M. (1978 [1922]) *Economy and Society: An Outline of Interpretive Sociology*, Berkeley: University of California Press.

Wedderburn, D. (ed) (1974) *Poverty, Inequality and Class Structures*, Cambridge: Cambridge University Press.

Weeden, K.A. et al (2007) 'Social Class and Earnings Inequality', *American Behavioral Scientist*, 50, 5, pp 702–36.

Weiler, J.H.H. et al (1995) 'European Democracy and its Critique', *West European Politics*, 18, 3, pp 4–39.

Wendt, C. et al (2010) 'How Do Europeans Perceive Their Healthcare System? Patterns of Satisfaction and Preference for State Involvement in the Field of Healthcare', *European Sociological Review*, 26, 2, pp 177–92.

West, C. and Zimmerman, D.C. (1987) 'Doing Gender', *Gender and Society*, 1, 2, pp 125–51.

Western, B. et al (2008) 'Inequality among American Families with Children, 1975 to 2005', *American Sociological Review*, 73, pp 903–20.

Whelan, C.T. and Maitre, B. (2008) 'Poverty, Deprivation and Economic Vulnerability in the Enlarged EU', in Alber, J. et al (eds) *Handbook of Quality of Life in the Enlarged European Union*, London: Routledge, pp 201–17.

Whelan, C.T. et al (2001) 'Income, Deprivation, and Economic Strain. An Analysis of the European Community Household Panel', *European Sociological Review*, 17, 4, pp 357–72.

White, R. (ed) (2004) *Controversies in Environmental Sociology*, Cambridge etc.: Cambridge University Press.

WHO (1986) *Ottawa Charter for Health Promotion*. Available at: http://www.euro. who.int/ (accessed 24 December 2009).

WHO (2007) *European Health for All Database*. Available at: www.euro.who.int/ hfadb (accessed 23 December 2009).

Wiener, A. (1998) *European Citizenship Practice. Building Institutions of a Non-state*, Boulder: Westview.

Wientzek, O. and Meyer, H. (2009) 'The Slovak Welfare System: Neo-liberal Nightmare or Welfare Pioneer of Middle-eastern Europe?', in Schubert, K. et al (eds) *The Handbook of European Welfare Systems*, London: Routledge, pp 462–77.

Wilensky, H.L. (1975) *The Welfare State and Equality. Structural and Ideological Roots of Public Expenditure*, Berkeley: University of California Press.

Williams, A. et al (1997) 'A Place in the Sun. International Retirement Migration from Northern to Southern Europe', *European Urban and Regional Studies*, 4, 2, pp 115–34.

Wilthagen, T. and Tros, F. (2004) 'The Concept of "Flexicurity": A New Approach to Regulating Employment and Labour Markets', *Transfer*, 2, 4, pp 166–86.

Witte, J. (2006) *Change of Degrees and Degrees of Change. Comparing Adaptions of European Higher Education Systems in the context of the Bologna Process*, Twente: University of Twente.

Wolff, E.N. (1996) 'International Comparisons of Wealth Inequality', *Review of Income and Wealth*, 42, 4, pp 433–51.

Wolff, E.N. (ed) (2006) *International Perspectives on Household Wealth*, Northampton: Edward Elgar.

Wright, E.O. (1985) *Classes*, London: Verso.

Wright, E.O. (1997) *Class Counts*, Cambridge: Cambridge University Press.

Zaidi, A. et al (2006) *Pension Policy in EU25 and its Possible Impact on Elderly Poverty*, London: Centre for Analysis of Social Exclusion.

Zaidi, A. (2006) *Poverty of Elderly People in EU25*, Vienna: European Centre fpr Social Welfare Policy and Research.

Zambarloukou, S. (2007) 'Is There a South European Pattern of Post-industrial Employment?', *South European Society and Politics*, 12, 4, pp 425–42.

Zapf, W. (1984) 'Individuelle Wohlfahrt. Lebensbedingungen und wahrgenommene Lebensqualität', in Glatzer, W. and Zapf, W. (eds) *Lebensqualität in der Bundesrepublik*, Frankfurt a. M. and New York: Campus, pp 13–26.

Zapf, W. (1986) 'Development, Structure, and Prospects of the German Social State', in Rose, R. and Shiratori, R. (eds) *The Welfare State: East and West*, New York: Oxford University Press, pp 126–55.

Zeitlhofer, H. (2011: forthcoming) 'Czech Republic and Slovak Republic', in Bade, K.J. et al (eds) *The Encyclopaedia of Migration*, Cambridge: Cambridge University Press.

Zielonka, J. (2001) 'How New Enlarged Borders will Reshape the European Union', *Journal of Common Market Studies*, 39, 3, pp 507–36.

Zielonka, J. (ed) (2002) *Europe Unbound. Enlarging and Reshaping the Boundaries of the European Union*, London: Routledge.

Zielonka, J. (2006) *Europe as Empire. The Nature of the Enlarged European Union*, Oxford: Oxford University Press.

Zuboff, S. (1989) *In the Age of the Smart Machine: The Future of Work and Power*, New York: Basic Books.

Zuckermann, A.S. (1975) 'Political Cleavages. A Conceptual and Theoretical Analysis', *British Journal of Political Sciences*, 5, pp 231–58.

Index

Page references for notes are followed by n